THE COMPLETE BOOK OF

BASEBALL

THE NEW YORK TIMES SCRAPBOOK
ENCYCLOPEDIA OF SPORTS HISTORY

FOOTBALL
BASEBALL
BASKETBALL
TRACK AND FIELD
GOLF
TENNIS
BOXING
SOCCER/PROFESSIONAL HOCKEY
WINTER SPORTS
OUTDOOR SPORTS
INDOOR SPORTS
WATER SPORTS
HORSE RACING/AUTO RACING

THE COMPLETE BOOK OF
BASEBALL

EDITED BY
GENE BROWN

INTRODUCTION BY
FRANK LITSKY

ARNO PRESS
A NEW YORK TIMES COMPANY
NEW YORK/1980

THE BOBBS-MERRILL COMPANY, INC.
INDIANAPOLIS · NEW YORK

Library of Congress Cataloging in Publication Data

Main entry under title:

The Complete book of baseball.

(The New York times scrapbook encyclopedia of sports history.)

Issued also under the title: Baseball.
Collection of articles reprinted from the New York times.

Bibliography: p.

Includes index.

SUMMARY: Traces the history of baseball as presented in articles in the "New York Times."
1. Baseball   [1. Baseball]   I. Brown, Gene.   II. New York Times.   III. Series.

GV863.A1B326   1979   796.357   79-92320
ISBN 0-405-12686-7 (Arno)
ISBN 0-672-52635-2 (Bobbs Merrill)

Manufactured in the United States of America

Appendix © 1979, *The Encyclopedia Americana.*

The editors express special thanks to The Associated Press, United Press International, and Reuters for permission to include a number of dispatches originally distributed by those news services.

Project Editors: Arleen Keylin and Christine Bent
Editorial Assistant: Jonathan Cohen

Photographs on the following pages courtesy of UPI: X, 3, 5, 18, 27, 39, 47, 58, 70, 83, 96, 98, 118, 131, 150, 176, 177, 190, 191, 192, 193.

CONTENTS

CONTENTS

Baseball has been regarded as America's national pastime since 1876, when the major leagues began. It is played by children using home-made equipment on sandlots; it is played in highly structured competition by youngsters in Little League, Babe Ruth League, American Legion, etc.; by students in high school and in college; and by professionals in major and minor leagues.

Baseball is highly popular in most nations of North and South America and the Caribbean. There are professional leagues in Japan, strong youth teams in Taiwan and a few semiprofessional and amateur teams in Italy and the Netherlands.

Except for domed arenas in Houston and Seattle, baseball is played outdoors in stadiums that vary in size but meet certain requirements. Games generally last 2 to 2½ hours, but unlike football, basketball, ice hockey and soccer, time is not relevant. There is a fine balance between offense and defense, and slight changes in rules or equipment can mean broad changes in the balance.

All evidence points to two English games—cricket and rounders—as the predecessors of baseball. Cricket was introduced to the United States about 1751. In each game, a thrown ball is struck with a bat, batters run bases and a batter is retired if his batted ball is caught before it hits the ground.

A game called Town Ball was played in Pennsylvania in 1831 and a variation called the New York Game was played in 1842. These were patterned after rounders. At first, the bases were set in a square. By 1842, they formed a diamond.

In 1845, the Knickerbocker Baseball Club of New York was formed, the first team ever. In the winter of 1845-46, a committee headed by Alexander Cartwright, a draftsman-surveyor, wrote standard rules. They included foul balls, strikeouts, three outs to an inning, 90 feet between bases, batting order and the balk, all part of the rules today.

In 1846, the New York Nine (there were now nine players to a team) challenged Knickerbocker to a game. In Hoboken, N.J., across the Hudson River from New York City, they laid out a baseball field on an old cricket ground in Elysian Fields. They met on June 19, 1846, in the first known baseball game. The New York Nine won, 23-1, in four innings.

The rules called for the pitching mound to be 46 feet from home plate. It accidentally was set 45 feet away. It remained at that distance until 1881, when it was moved back to 50 feet. In 1893, the distance was changed to 60 feet. Because of a surveyor's error, the mound was placed 60 feet 6 inches from the plate, and present rules make that the official distance.

The New York Nine was not heard from again, and Knickerbocker players played practice games with teammates from 1846 to 1851. In 1857, the rules were changed to make a game last nine innings instead of 21 runs.

In 1858, 25 clubs from New York City and nearby New Jersey cities organized the National Association of Baseball Players and took control of the game from Knickerbocker. The sport spread, and in 1865, after the Civil War had ended, 91 clubs attended the association's convention. All were amateur, and more were from the Midwest than the East. However, spectators seemed more interested in betting on the games than in the games themselves. Many teams paid players illegally.

In 1869, the Cincinnati Red Stockings, an amateur club, became professional. All players were paid a salary, of between $600 and $1,400 for an eight-month season. In their first season, they won 64 games, lost none and tied one. They attracted 200,000 spectators and made a profit. Professional baseball was here to stay.

The amateur organization crumbled. Many clubs left it, and nine—five from the East and four from the Midwest—formed the National Association of Professional Baseball Players. The franchise fee was $10. In subsequent years, clubs were added and subtracted. Gambling on games again became important, and public confidence and interest in the sport diminished.

In 1876, a rival league, the National League of Professional Baseball Clubs, was founded. The National Association died and the new National League took its best players. This is the same National League that exists today, and this was the start of modern baseball.

The National League soon had company. The American Association was founded in 1882 and succeeded because it offered Sunday baseball, sold beer in its parks and charged 25 cents for admission instead of 50 cents. In 1884, the Union Association was formed, raided the other leagues for talent, played one year with insufficient capital and folded.

Next came the Players (or Brotherhood) League, formed by players who feared they would not be paid their promised salaries. This league played in 1890 only, but it attracted more spectators than the National League or the American Association. This episode hurt the American Association financially, and it disbanded after the 1891 season when its money ran out. Four of its clubs were taken into the National League, which played in 1892 with 12 clubs. The National was the only remaining major league.

Ban Johnson, a sports writer, wanted to start a second major league. He became head of the Western League, a minor league, and in 1900 he disbanded it, formed the American League with mostly Western League cities and asked the National League to recognize the American as a major league.

The National League ignored Johnson, but the American League played in 1900 with clubs in Buffalo and seven Midwest cities. Johnson wanted to add Eastern cities in 1901 and asked the National League to meet with him. The National League agreed and asked him to wait outside a conference room until it was ready to talk with him. While Johnson waited, the National League executives sneaked out a side door.

An angry Johnson promptly gave an American League franchise to Boston, which already had a National League club. He gave franchises to Connie Mack in Philadelphia and Wilbert Robinson and John McGraw in Baltimore. American League clubs tried to woo National League players by offering them more money.

In 1903, realizing that the American League would be successful, the National League proposed one 12-team major league. The American League declined. The National League, swallowing its pride, then agreed to recognize two separate major leagues with territorial rights. And it agreed to a World Series each fall between the champions of the two leagues.

In the first World Series, played in 1903, the Boston Americans defeated the Pittsburgh Nationals, 5 games to 3. There was no World Series in 1904 because McGraw, now managing the New York Giants in the National League, said he would not "demean" his club by allowing it to play a club from the other league. National League club owners chastised McGraw, and the World Series resumed permanently in 1905.

The only other major league to play since then was the Federal League in 1914 and 1915. It raided the other leagues for players and spent much of its time in court defending its tactics.

The integrity of baseball was shaken in 1920 when eight players on the Chicago White Sox were accused of having accepted bribes from gamblers to lose the 1919 World Series to the Cincinnati Nationals. The players included Shoeless Joe Jackson, one of the leading hitters in history, and Eddie Cicotte, an outstanding pitcher.

The club owners decided to attempt to regain public confidence by naming a commissioner with sweeping powers to keep the game clean. They chose Kenesaw Mountain Landis, a United States District Court judge who had presided over much of the Federal League litigation. His integrity and fearlessness were unquestioned, partly because he had once fined the Standard Oil Company $29 million.

The eight Chicago players were acquitted in court, but Landis banned them from baseball for life. Landis was commissioner from 1920 until his death in 1944, and his actions helped rebuild public respect for the game.

More baseball history was written in 1920 when the Boston Red Sox sold Babe Ruth, a young pitcher-turned-outfielder, to the New York Yankees. The price was $125,000, the highest in baseball history to that time.

Coincidentally, the company that made American League baseballs accidentally started manufacturing a livelier ball in 1920. In substituting Australian yarn for American yarn, the ball could be wound tighter and thus become harder. And that meant it could be hit farther.

Ruth hit 54 home runs in 1920, by far a major-league record for one season. He hit 59 in 1921, 60 in 1927. His 60 home runs remained the major-league record until Roger Maris of the Yankees hit 61 in 1961. Ruth's 714 lifetime home runs were the most in major-league history until Henry Aaron of the Atlanta Braves surpassed it in 1974. Ruth became the most famous of all baseball players.

Baseball's popularity also increased with the introduction of night games in 1935. Major-league clubs now play most of their weekday games at night, and minor-league clubs seldom play except at night.

Of all American sports, baseball has the greatest volume of statistics, some reaching back to the beginnings of the major leagues. Ironically, the widest gap in baseball's history concerns its founding.

In 1939, the major leagues celebrated the 100th anniversary of the invention of baseball by Abner Doubleday in Cooperstown, N.Y. The Baseball Hall of Fame was opened in Cooperstown that year. The United States Government issued a commemorative stamp honoring the founding of the game.

The only problem was that the Abner Doubleday story was apparently fiction. It was the creation of Abraham G. Mills, for two years (1883-84) the president of the National League. Mills became involved because of a disagreement between Albert G. Spalding, a former pitcher and manager who published the "Baseball Guide," and Henry Chadwick, editor of the guide.

Chadwick had played cricket and rounders in his native England. In 1903, he wrote that the rounders he played in England in 1833 was the same game as the

Town Ball introduced into Pennsylvania in 1831. Town Ball grew into baseball.

Spalding disagreed with Chadwick's contention, though he did not have a better answer. Spalding and Chadwick agreed to have a seven-man commission try to determine the origins of baseball.

Mills, the commission chairman, seemed to be the only commission member interested in the project. In 1907, he issued a personal report that said the first known diagram of a baseball diamond with players was drawn in 1839 by Abner Doubleday, a student in Cooperstown, N.Y. He said Doubleday devised this alignment so that players would not crash (there were 11 to a side then) and could not be put out by hitting them with a thrown ball.

Mills said Spalding had furnished some of his information, but Spalding denied this. Spalding and Chadwick, baseball's foremost experts, had never heard of Doubleday except that he had been a Civil War general. Research showed that in 1839 Doubleday was a West Point cadet, and for three years before West Point he had been a surveyor, not a baseball player. Mills, a close friend of Doubleday for the last 30 years of Doubleday's life, presumably would have known this.

There was no evidence, aside from Mills's report, that linked Doubleday with baseball. But Spalding dutifully published the Mills report in 1910, and major-league leaders resurrected it in the 1930's.

Baseball interest was dwindling in the Depression years, and officials sought a way to rekindle interest. When someone remembered the Mills report, baseball had found its answer. It accepted the Doubleday story as fact and set a baseball centennial celebration for 1939.

From 1903 to 1953, major-league baseball was confined to the East and Midwest. For years, there were eight clubs in the National League and eight in the American, and five cities (New York, Boston, Philadelphia, Chicago and St. Louis) had two teams each.

In 1953, the Boston Braves moved to Milwaukee, setting off a widespread migration. In 1954, the St. Louis Browns became the Baltimore Orioles. In 1958, the major leagues moved to the Pacific Coast when the Brooklyn Dodgers moved to Los Angeles and the New York Giants to San Francisco. Since then, relocation and expansion have brought the total major league teams to 26, representing 24 cities. Two teams are now based in Canada.

For most of its history, organized baseball allowed only white players. Blacks and Latin-Americans played only in the Negro Leagues or on touring clubs.

In 1946, the Brooklyn Dodgers signed Jackie Robinson to a minor-league contract, making him the first black player in modern minor-league history. In 1947, when Robinson joined the Dodgers, he became the first black in modern major-league history. Other clubs quickly signed black players, and now about one-third of major-league players are black. In 1974, Frank Robinson of the Cleveland Indians became the major leagues' first black manager.

The most significant baseball development of the 1970's was player freedom. Baseball operated with a reserve clause in every player's contract. This clause bound the player to his team until the team sold, traded or released him. In 1970, Curt Flood, a $90,000-a-year outfielder, sued baseball because he did not want to report to the club to which he had been traded. He contended that the reserve clause in the standard baseball contract violated federal antitrust laws and was thus unconstitutional. In 1972, the Supreme Court of the United States upheld the reserve clause, but the reserve system was crumbling.

In 1975, Peter M. Seitz, an arbitrator, ruled that two pitchers who had played the 1975 season without having signed contracts had thus become free agents and were no longer bound to their teams. In 1976, the club owners, fearing chaos, agreed with their players on a compromise plan that allowed players to become free agents after six years.

Many outstanding players became free agents and the subject of bidding wars that resulted in multi-million-dollar, multi-year contracts. For example, 37-year-old Pete Rose of the Cincinnati Reds became a free agent after the 1978 season and signed with the Philadelphia Phillies for $800,000 a year for four years.

The best players negotiated large salaries even when they chose to remain with their teams rather than become free agents. One example was Dave Parker of the Pittsburgh Pirates, the National League batting champion in 1977 and 1978. After the 1978 season, he signed a new contract with the Pirates for more than $1 million a year for five years.

Attendance at baseball games has grown steadily. In 1973, major-league attendance reached 30 million. In 1978, attendance for the 26 major-league teams (14 in the American League, 12 in the National) passed 40 million. In 1978, the Los Angeles Dodgers, playing in a stadium with 56,000 seats, averaged 41,000 attendance for their 81 home games.

Baseball is deeply woven into the fabric of American life. The game's heroes have always been larger than life—Babe Ruth, Ty Cobb, Honus Wagner, Walter Johnson and Christy Mathewson in the earliest years; Joe DiMaggio, Ted Williams, Bob Feller, Yogi Berra and Dizzy Dean in a later period; Willie Mays, Mickey Mantle, Henry Aaron and Tom Seaver in recent years. Their statistics, their exploits, and the memory of their flaming days is very much a part of this country.

— Frank Litsky

CHAPTER 1

THE MODERN GAME TAKES FORM

Babe Ruth has just hit his 23rd home run of the 1921 season. This one traveled about 475 feet.

THE NATIONAL GAME

Close of the First Decade of Ball-Playing

Brief Review of the Past Season—The Play of Professionals and Amateurs—The Championship Question.

There is no outdoor sport in which all classes of our people can so fully participate, or one which has so few objectionable surroundings, as the national game of baseball; and no season in the brief history of the game has more conclusively shown the fact of its great popularity with our people than the season which has just closed. Baseball started on its voyage of life in 1860, for its existence prior to that year may be said to have amounted only to a series of trial trips, as it were, preparatory for its great trip around the civilized world. In 1860, what we now term "amateur" playing was then in its glory. In that year the Excelsior Club of Brooklyn—ranking second to none in social standing at any time—then occupied the highest position in the country as the leading exemplars of the beauties of the game; and during that year the Excelsior Club did more to establish baseball on a permanent and reputable footing than had before been attempted by any other organization, the veteran Knickerbocker Club of this City—the social equals of the Excelsiors—having been more limited in their sphere of operations. The advent of CREIGHTON—the ball-player *par excellence* of the period—during that memorable year, with the accompanying brilliant career of the Excelsior nine, would have been promptly followed by the strenuous efforts of rival organizations during ensuing seasons but for the inauguration of the great rebellion in 1861, which, of course, materially interfered with the progress of baseball; indeed, in effect it put it back several years, and it was not until 1864 that the game began to recover its lost ground. In that year, however, the great struggle for the honors of the championship was commenced, all prior contests for the title having been merely nominal battles for something which had only a questionable existence; for up to 1864 the circle of the baseball arena did not extend far beyond the place of its christening, if not of its birth, viz.: New York. In 1864, the system of professional ball-playing began to openly manifest itself, for though previously in existence to some extent, it had not been prominently brought into public notice. With

his new system came the real struggle for the championship title. Since then professional baseball playing has been officially recognized as a legitimate occupation; and no doubt the distinction of classes which now exists will prevail as long as the game is known. Unfortunately, certain evils have followed in the train of professional ball-playing, which, if not checked in their progress, will ultimately so damage the reputation of the fraternity as to materially interfere with the future welfare of the game.

A REVIEW OF THE SEASON

The brilliant success of the noted Red Stocking nine of the Cincinnati Club in 1869 was the incentive to the establishment of rival nines not only in New York, Philadelphia and other leading cities, but especially in Chicago, where the most strenuous exertions were made to organize a nine which should grasp the palm of superiority from the victorious Cincinnati Club. In the East, too, the desire to regain the laurels of 1869, which had been so creditably won from the older clubs by the comparatively new nine of the Western club, led to more than ordinary efforts to strengthen the nines of the Eastern organizations so as to recover their lost prestige.

The appended statistics are from the scores of games in which these professional clubs have played with each other:

Clubs	Games lost.	Games won	Average
Cincinnati, "Red Stockings"	6	14	14
Chicago, "White Stockings"	7	13.2	14
Athletic, "Blue Stockings"	3	15.16	16
Union, "Haymakers"	10	14.16	7
Forest City, Cleveland	10	11.13	4
Forest City, Rockford	10	13.0	6
Minni, "Green Stockings"	10	11.19	13
Atlantic, "Old Champions"	15	11.10	7

The estimate of the fewest games lost is the fairest test of skill, and in this respect the two Western clubs take the lead. In the averages of runs made by opponents, on which an estimate of fielding is generally made, shows that the opposing nines on the Cincinnati Club have made the smallest average, the Athletics being second and the Chicago third.

THE CHAMPIONSHIP

At present the Mutual Club hold the nominal title of the champion club of the United States; but, in reality, there is no champion club this season, and consequently, all the more interest will be imparted to the campaign of 1871, in which season the questions involved in championship disputes will be permanently disposed of. The Chicago Club claim the championship, but on what grounds we do not exactly see.

There is no doubt that professional baseball playing is an established institution, but in order for it to be permanent some changes are

necessary in its management, for the general impression from the past season in regard to the conduct of professional clubs, has been that it has been characterized by too much of the hippodrome principle, and that professionals have played too much into the hands of regular gamblers. Be this as it may, there is no questioning the fact that at present some professional players and their clubs are in bad odor with the public. In regard to amateur organizations the success of the Star Club, of Brooklyn; the Harvards, of Boston; the Experts and Intrepids, of Philadelphia; the Pastimes, of Baltimore, and the Amateurs, of Chicago, not to number a dozen other first-class amateur clubs, shows pretty conclusively that the amateur interest is still strong in the land.

The brilliant success, pecuniary and otherwise, attendant upon the Red Stocking nine in 1869 has had the effect of innoculating a number of capitalists with quite a fever for organizing professional nines. This year Chicago, Cleveland, Fort Wayne and Riverside added professional men to the list of existing organizations of that class, and now there is a prospect of an addition to the list from Boston, Indianapolis and Brooklyn. To offset this increase of professionalism, we have to record the disbandment of the noted Cincinnati "Red Stocking" nine, and the return of the Club to the old amateur basis. The fact is, the fraternity of Cincinnati, and especially the class who have had to put their hands deep in their pockets in order to insure the success of the professional experiment, have begun to realize the fact that the credit and renown attached to the success of the professional nine of the Club does not inure to the credit of the Club as a Western organization, from the fact that the players who have won the laurels are experts who belong to the East. Not fancying this style of things any longer, they now propose to organize a nine on the footing of employing only amateur talent and home players at that. In this the Club do wisely, for despite the victories obtained by the three professional nines of Cincinnati, Chicago and Cleveland, this season, the career of the Rockford nine, in reality, is the most creditable of all the Western organizations, inasmuch as their success has been obtained at the hands of bona fide Western players. This example the Cincinnati Club propose to follow in 1871, in which year they will endeavor to bear off the palm of supremacy in the amateur arena, as they did in 1869 in the professional circle.

THE CONVENTION

The year of baseball for 1871 will close with the annual Convention of the National Association, which takes place at the Grand Central Hotel on Wednesday next at 11 A.M. At this meeting delegates from all the States containing baseball associations will gather, the principal business being a revision of the laws of the game.

November 27, 1870

BASEBALL

A MEETING OF THE MANAGERS OF THE PROFESSIONAL NINES—THE PHILADELPHIA CLUB EXCLUDED FROM THE CHAMPIONSHIP CONTESTS—NEW RULES.

A meeting of the managers of all the professional baseball organizations in the country, excepting the Philadelphia Club, was held at the Grand Central Hotel on Wednesday, Feb. 2, at 2 o'clock. The first action was the passage of a resolution preventing two clubs from any one city entering for the championship. As the Athletics were represented at the meeting, and took part in its action, the Philadelphias were, as a consequence, shut out from entering their nine for the whip pennant. The next action was the passage of a resolution preventing any two clubs from playing in a city in which neither of them belongs. This was done for the purpose

of "heading off" two or three clubs and preventing their going to Philadelphia during the Exhibition and playing a series of games. This will be a sore disappointment to those clubs, and will doubtless result in the disbanding of more than one of them before the season is half over. The amending of the rules was taken up, and several important changes were made. Among others, a rule allowing the base-runner to run on a foul fly catch, after he has touched his base, the same as on a fair fly-catch, was adopted. Another of the new rules allows a base-runner to return to his base after a foul ball has been hit, without running the risk of being put out, and still another virtually allows the batsman who refuses to strike at it, warn the striker, but shall not be allowed to call a strike until still another fair ball has been pitched.

The following clubs entered for the championship: Athletic, Mutual, New-Haven, Hartford, Boston, Chicago, St.Louis, Louisville, and Cincinnati. The association

will be known as the National League of Professional Baseball Clubs, and has nothing whatever to do with the old National Association. The officers are M.G. Buckley, of the Hartford Club, President, and N.E. Young, of Washington, Secretary. The League will be governed by a board of five Directors. Those chosen for the current year are from the Hartford, Louisville, Boston, Mutual, and St.Louis Clubs. This board will sit annually as a Board of Appeals to decide all disputed points and their decisions will be final. A most wholesome regulation of this League is one to the effect that when a player has been suspended he must wait until the end of the season, or until December, when the Directors meet before his appeal can be heard. Thus, if a player is expelled from a club, he cannot join another nine and continue in the field, as under the old system. The League will hold its next meeting in March of next year.

February 7, 1876

Christie Mathewson, the old-time New York Giants pitching great.

A NEW BASEBALL LEAGUE.

Organization of Eight Clubs Was Formed in Chicago Yesterday— New York Is Represented.

CHICAGO, Sept. 17.—A new baseball league, whose circuit will include cities in both the National and Western Leagues and which will be known as the American Association of Baseball Clubs, was formed here today at a meeting of baseball men and lovers of the National game.

The circuit, as decided on today, will include the following cities: St. Louis, Milwaukee, Detroit, and Chicago in the West, and Baltimore, New York, Philadelphia, and Washington in the East.

Those present at the meeting were the following: Chris Von Der Ahe, George Shafer, and Al Spinks, representing St. Louis, and a reputed agent of a brewing company of that city, which is supposed to be intered in the new league: H.D. Quinn, formerly of the American Association Club, and Alderman Havenor, representing Milwaukee; A.C. Anson and his son-in-law, W.H. Clough, representing Chicago; Assemblyman Beckley, representing New York; Frank Hough, sporting editor of The Philadelphia Enquirer,representing Philadelphia; M. Scanlan, representing Washington.The names of the representative of Detroit and Baltimore were not given out.

Tom Loftus of the Grand Rapids team of the Western League was in consultation with the new league representatives during the day, but was not present at the meeting. "Ted" Sullivan, the veteran baseball manager, was also present at the meeting.

A.C. Anson was offered the Presidency of the new league, but he refused to accept, and H.D. Quinn of Milwaukee was elected Temporary President. Other temporary officers were elected as follows: Vice President—M.D.Scanlan; Treasurer—George Shaefer; Secretary—frank Hough; Directors—Chris Von Der Ahe, M.D. Scanlan, Frank Beckley, and C.S. Havenor.

The platform of the new league was announced as follows: "Honest competition, no syndicate baseball, no reserve rule, to respect all contracts, and popular prices."

The surprise of the conference was the avowal of the promoters to invade Western League territory. All of the gentlemen present disclaimed any intention of going to war with the minor league, but they strongly intimated that it was war to the finish with the National organization.

By abolishing the reserve ule the new league thinks it will get a hold on the best baseball talent in the country, and by catering to the public with lower prices, is certain to get the masses. The promoters also argue that the evils engendered by forcing syndicate ball upon the public are too patent to be overlooked.

September 18, 1899

BALTIMORE IN THE LEAGUE.

American Baseball League Now Complete with Eight Clubs.

BALTIMORE, Nov. 13.—After a series of conferences among the promoters of the American Baseball League and a number of local capitalists and sports, it was decided today that Baltimore will be included in the eight-club circuit of the new association. McGraw and Robinson of last season's St. Louis team, it was announced, own the Baltimore franchise, and say they will go ahead at once to secure grounds and players for the coming season. The circuit as planned at present is as follows: Philadelphia, Baltimore, Washington, and Buffalo in the East, and Cleveland, Detroit, Chicago, and Milwaukee in the West.

President "Ban" Johnson of the American League, Charley Comiskey of Chicago, and Charles Somers of Cleveland, with the others who had been in Baltimore since Monday afternoon, left tonight for Chicago. Before leaving President Johnson said that a meeting of the American League will be held in Chicago on Nov. 20. The details of the new circuit will be arranged at that time and other matters necessary of adjustment will be considered. Among the more important of these will be a new agreement with the National League.

November 14, 1900

NATIONAL BASEBALL AGREEMENT

~~~~~~~

Minor League Organizations Will Discuss Provisions of Proposed Uniformity of Rules To-day—Professional Interests in the Game Throughout the Country to be Protected.

~~~~~~~

An important meeting of minor baseball representatives will take place today at the Victoria Hotel, Broadway and Twenty-seventh Street, at which the new National agreement, adopted by the National League and American League delegates at Buffalo, last week, will be discussed in detail. This meeting has been called by President P.T. Powers of the National Association of Minor Baseball Leagues, an organization which embraces all the professional baseball associations in this country, with the exception of the two big leagues.

Ever since the baseball war between the major organizations was amicably settled by the signing of the Cincinnati peace pact last January, most of the those who have interests in baseball clubs throughout the United States and part of Canada have been urging the adoption of a new National agreement for the protection of every person, club owners as well as players, connected with the game. President Johnson of the American League was opposed to the arranging of a measure of such importance as a National agreement until the clubs in the National as well as the American League could be certain that there would be no friction in the workings of the peace agreement.

The case of George Davis and the New York National League Club, which was allowed to play Davis on its team for a short time, while the Chicago American League Club, to which he was assigned at the Cincinnati conference, strenuously objected, having been adjusted at a meeting of the National League club owners, left the way clear for the American League President to take definite action on the National measure.

The Presidents of the major leagues, with two representatives from each organization, were in conference recently in Buffalo, and the outcome of the conference was the adoption of

a lengthy document embracing, seemingly, every point of importance for the absolute government of professional baseball. One of its articles created a National commission for the purpose of enforcing the terms and provisions of the agreement. The members of this body were named as August Herrmann of Cincinnati, Chairman; President Johnson of the American League; and President Pulliam of the National League.

The most important objects of the new agreement are as follows:

(1) Perpetuation of baseball as the National pastime of America by surrounding it with such safeguards as will warrant absolute public confidence in its integrity and methods, and by maintaining a high standard of skill and sportsmanship in its players.

(2 Protection of the property rights of those engaged in baseball as a business without sacrificing the spirit of competition in the conduct of the clubs.

(3) Promotion of the welfare of ball players as a class by developing and perfecting them in their profession, and enabling them to secure adequate compensation for expertness.

(4) Adoption of a uniform code of rules for playing baseball.

The agreement is to be indissoluble except by the unanimous vote of the parties to it. Each party to the agreement retains the right to conduct its affairs and govern its players according to its constitution and by-laws, but there shall be no conflict between such constitution and by-laws and the objects and terms of the agreement. Should the measure be adopted by the National Association of Minor Leagues, these minor organizations will have absolute control of their own affairs.

Under the terms of the agreement the major Leagues shall adopt all rules governing the game of baseball. Neither major League circuit shall be changed without the consent of a majority of the clubs of each major League, and the circuit of each League is to consist of the following cities:

National League—Boston, New York, Brooklyn, Philadelphia, Pittsburg, Chicago, St. Louis, and Cincinnati. American League—Boston, New York, Philadelphia, Washington, Cleveland, Detroit, Chicago, and St. Louis.

Contracts with players must be respected under the penalties specified. The right and title of a major league club to its players shall be absolute, and can only be terminated by release or failure to reserve under the terms of the agreement by the club to which a player has been under contract.

The practice of "farming" is prohibited. All right or claim of a major league club to a player shall cease when such player becomes a member of a minor league club, and no arrangement between the clubs for the loan or return of a player shall be binding between the parties to it or recognized by other clubs.

The right of a minor league club to its players shall be absolute, except that from Aug. 15 to Oct. 15 of each year major leagues shall have the privilege of selecting players from National association clubs for the following season upon payment of $750 for each player so selected from clubs in Class A leagues; $500 for each player so selected from clubs in Class B leagues; $300 for each player so selected from clubs in Class C leagues, and $200 for each player so selected from clubs of a lower class.

A major league club may at any time purchase the release of a player from a minor league club, to take effect forthwith or at a specified date, provided such purchase is recorded with the Secretary of the commission for promulgation within five days of the date of the transaction.

Many of the articles in the agreement are designed to protect the interests of the players, one of which gives a player suspended for a period of longer than ten days the right to appeal to the commission. The leagues are strictly enjoined to enforce the provision in the constitution against open betting on baseball grounds, and club officials are obliged to cause the arrest and prosecution of those who may engage in such practice.

No game or a series of games are to be played for a stake between clubs of any league according to the agreement, and neither clubs nor players shall accept or agree to accept a sum of money or present of great value as an inducement or reward for winning or trying to win a game.

Articles of the agreement which do not find favor with the minor league representatives are the drafting clause and the method of paying for players drafted. Under the terms of the agreement the major leagues have two months in which to draft players, while the old rule gave them only one month.

At the meeting this afternoon there will be present representatives of the Eastern League, New York State League, Southern League, American Association, Central League, Connecticut League, and New England League. President Powers says that there is a good deal of work to be done, but he expects that the labors of the delegates will be concluded late this evening.

August 30, 1903

Lou Gehrig (L), Babe Ruth (R) and Christy Walsh at Yankee Stadium in September 1927. This photograph of Ruth was taken only days before Ruth went on to make baseball history by hitting his sixtieth home run in a single season.

McGinnity Pitched Two Winning Games for New York Against Philadelphia.

Pitching two winning games of baseball on the same afternoon is an unusual feat, but "Joe" McGinnity of the New York National League Club has accomplished it three times this season. A few weeks ago he won both games of a double-header on the Boston grounds, and duplicated the trick against the Brooklyn team on the Polo Grounds six days later. Yesterday afternoon he again scored a double win, the Philadelphia players being the victims. The actual time of both contests was three hours and three minutes, and at the end McGinnity showed no sign of fatigue—in fact, he seemed fresh enough to tackle the visitors for a third contest if that were necessary.

Gloomy weather kept many of the local "rooters" from the grounds during the afternoon, but there were over 3,000 of the more enthusiastic patrons on hand. They went away well pleased with the excellent exhibitions which the local team gave during both games. In the earlier contest neither side made a misplay, and this was remarkable considering the wretched condition of the field from the recent heavy rains.

McGinnity began by giving Thomas a base on balls, and Gleason's sacrifice sent the runner to second. Wolverton caught Wolverton's fly, and Titus was hit with a pitched ball, but Barry hit to McGann, who tossed the ball to McGinnity as the latter ran to first base. Frazer failed to locate the plate, and Browne walked to first; Bresnahan drove the ball safely between short and third, and both men advanced a base each on McGann's neat sacrifice. Mertes was fielded out at first base, but Browne scored on the play, and Babb foul flied to Wolverton. In the second inning the first two of the visiting side were disposed of quickly on a fly and an out at first base, and the third, Zimmer, struck out. In New York's half of this inning Lauder drove a liner over short and Dunn was hit with a pitched ball. Warner bunted safely, filling the bases. Then McGinnity singled, scoring Lauder. Browne did the same for Dunn with a single to left. Bresnahan struck out and Thomas caught McGann's fly, but Warner scored on the return of the ball, and Mertes sent one straight into Hulswitt's hands, retiring the side. After this both pitchers were very effective, and there was no further scoring until the Philadelphians went in for their ninth turn at bat. Titus doubled to centre and Barry struck out, as did Douglass. Hulswitt's drive to left field got past Mertes, who fell in his attempt to stop it, and Titus scored the only tally made for Philadelphia, as Zimmer ended the game, being thrown out, Lauder to McGann.

Thomas got a base on balls for a starter in the second game, but neither side scored until the third inning, when Titus, with a line drive past Bresnahan for two bases, scored Gleason and Wolverton. These were the only runs the visitors got in this game, and the home team tallied once in the following inning, and took the lead in the fifth with two more. They scored again in the sixth, and swamped the visitors by tallying five times in the seventh. During the fourth inning Hulswitt objected very vigorously to a decision made by Umpire Hurst, who called Bresnahan safe in a steal to second. While the argument was going on Bresnahan stole to third, and scored on Duggleby's wild throw. Hulswitt was put out of the game and ordered off the field, his position being played by Hallman during the remainder of the game. The scores:

NEW YORK.						PHILADELPHIA.					
	R	1B	PO	A	E		R	1B	PO	A	E
Browne, rf.	1	1	1	0	0	Thomas, cf.	0	1	1	0	0
Bresnahan, cf	0	1	6	0	0	Gleason, 2b	0	1	3	1	0
McGann, 1b.	0	0	9	1	0	Wolv'rton, 3b	0	1	1	1	0
Mertes, lf.	0	2	2	1	0	Titus, rf	1	1	0	0	0
Babb, ss.	0	2	2	3	0	Barry, lf	0	0	2	0	0
Lauder, 3b.	1	0	3	0	0	Douglass, 1b	0	0	11	0	0
Dunn, 2b.	1	1	1	3	0	Hulswitt, ss.	0	1	1	3	0
Werner, c.	1	1	4	0	0	Zimmer, c.	0	0	3	2	0
McGinnity, p.	0	1	2	1	0	Frazer, p.	0	0	2	6	0
Totals.	4	9	27	12	0	Totals.	1	5	24	12	0

New York . . . . 1 3 0 0 0 0 0 0 x—4
Philadelphia . . . . 0 0 0 0 0 0 0 0 1—1

Earned runs—New York, 2; Philadelphia, 1. Two-base hits—Titus, Hulswitt. Left on bases—New York, 10; Philadelphia, 7. Sacrifice hits—Bresnahan, McGann, Lauder, Gleason. Stolen bases—Bresnahan. Double plays—Mertes, Babb, and McGann. First base on balls—Off McGinnity, 3; off Frazer, 4. Hit by pitched ball—By McGinnity, 1; by Frazer, 1. Struck out—by McGinnity, 4; by Frazer, 4. Time—1:30. Umpire—Messrs. Hurst and Moran.

SECOND GAME.

NEW YORK.						PHILADELPHIA.					
	R	1B	PO	A	E		R	1B	PO	A	E
Browne, rf.	0	1	1	0	0	Thomas, cf.	0	0	1	0	0
Bres'h'n, cf.	3	4	1	0	0	Gleason, 2b.	1	0	3	1	0
McGann, 1b.	0	0	8	0	0	Wolv'ton, 3b	1	2	3	2	0
Mertes, lf.	0	0	3	0	0	Titus, rf	1	3	0	0	0
Babb, ss.	0	0	3	3	0	Barry, lf	0	0	1	0	0
Lauder, 3b.	1	2	0	0	0	Douglass, 1b.	0	0	8	1	1
Dunn, 2b.	1	0	0	3	1	Hulswitt, ss.	0	0	2	1	2
Warner, c.	2	1	11	1	0	Hallman, ss.	0	0	0	1	1
McGinnity, p	3	0	3	0	0	Dooin, c.	0	0	2	2	0
						Duggleby, p.	0	2	1	2	1
Total	9	11	27	10	1	Total	2	6	24	12	6

New York . . . . 0 0 0 1 2 1 5 0 .—9
Philadelphia . . . . 0 0 2 0 0 0 0 0 0—2

Left on bases—New York, 5; Philadelphia, 6. Two-base hits—Bresnahan, 2; Titus. Sacrifice hits—McGann, Dunn, Douglass. Stolen bases—Bresnahan, McGann. Double plays—Duggleby and Gleason. First base on balls—Off McGinnity, 1; off Duggleby, 4. First base on errors—New York, 4; Philadelphia, 1. Struck out—By McGinnity, 9. Wild pitch—Duggleby. Time—One hour and thirty-three minutes. Umpires—Messrs. Moran and Hurst. Attendance—3,496.

September 1, 1903

BOSTON'S CHAMPION TEAM.

Pittsburg Unable to Score in the Deciding Game of the Championship Baseball Series.

BOSTON, Oct. 13.—The Boston Americans shut out the Pittsburg Nationals to-day and won the world's baseball championship, to the almost frenzied delight of 7,000 enthusiasts. While the attendance at all the previous games of the series has been larger than to-day, the demonstration which followed Dineen's striking out of "Hans" Wagner in the ninth equaled any college football game.

Phillippi, who was such an enigma to the Bostons in the first few games, essayed to pitch for the visitors for the sixth time. He was not only batted hard, but he saw his rival, Dineen, carry off the honors by holding the Nationals down to four scattered hits, which, backed by perfect fielding, prevented a single Pittsburg man getting further than third base. Dineen struck out seven men, and his support by Criger contributed materially to the success of the game. The latter's bluff throw to second in the fourth inning, followed by a quick snap of the ball to Collins, catching Leach off the bag, was the best piece of work in the game.

Other features were mainly contributed by the visitors, and Boston's score would undoubtedly have been larger but for the great running catches of Beaumont and Clarke, Wagner's work at short, and Leach's at third base. For the home team, Parent's hauling down of a liner from Clarke's bat roused the greatest enthusiasm. The score:

BOSTON.						PITTSBURG.					
	R	1B	PO	A	E		R	1B	PO	A	E
D'herty, lf.	0	0	3	0	0	B'mont, cf.	0	0	5	0	0
Collins, 3b.	0	1	0	2	0	Clarke, lf.	0	1	3	0	0
Stahl, cf.	0	0	2	0	0	Leach, 3b.	0	0	3	3	0
Freeman, rf.	1	1	2	0	0	Wagner, ss.	0	1	3	0	1
Parent, ss.	1	0	1	1	0	Br'nsf'd, 1b.	0	0	7	1	1
Lach'ce, 1b.	1	1	11	0	0	Ritchey, 2b.	0	2	1	0	0
Ferris, 2b.	0	2	0	3	0	Sebring, rf.	0	1	1	1	0
Criger, c.	0	2	8	3	0	Phelps, c.	0	0	3	3	0
Dineen, p.	0	1	0	3	0	Phillippi, p.	0	1	0	2	0
Total	3	8	27	12	0	Total	0	4	24	8	3

Boston . . . . 0 0 0 2 0 1 0 0 .—3
Pittsburg . . . . 0 0 0 0 0 0 0 0 0—0

Earned runs—Boston, 2. Three-base hits—Freeman, Lachance, and Sebring. Sacrifice hits—Lachance. Stolen base—Wagner. Double plays—Criger and Lachance. First base on balls—Off Dineen, 2. Struck out—By Dineen, 7; by Phillippi, 2. Time of game—One hour and thirty-five minutes. Umpires—Messrs. O'Day and Connolly. Attendance—7,455.

October 14, 1903

GIANTS CHAMPIONS, THE SCORE, 2-0

Two neatly dressed, ruddy faced, athletic looking young men, grinning broadly; one a giant in contrast to the squatiness of the other, walked along the veranda of the clubhouse at the Polo Grounds about 5 o'clock yesterday afternoon. Below them was a sea of 10,000 faces, wildly emitting a thunderous eruption of enthusiasm. The two young men looked down upon the reverberating ocean of humanity for a moment, and then walked to a point directly in front of the plaza, where they were in view of all. The ten thousand throats bellowed forth a tribute that would have almost drowned a broadside of twelve-inch guns.

The two smiling athletes stopped, one of them drew forth a long sheet of yellow paper rolled under his arm. As the crowd pushed and fought and cheered he unwrapped an impromptu banner and let it flutter on the breeze. The multitude pressed forward like a wave to read this inscription:

> THE GIANTS,
> WORLD'S CHAMPIONS, 1905.

Geological records show that Vesuvius disturbs the earth and that seismic demonstrations are felt by the greater number. But if that doctrine had been promulgated in the vicinity of the Polo Grounds yesterday, as Christie Mathewson and Roger Bresnahan of the New York Baseball Club unfurled their victorious banner, it would have been minimized. For, as volcanoes assert themselves upon the earth's surface surely must that deafening, reverberating roar have lifted Manhattan's soil from its base.

The Giants, the most intelligent, the quickest, strongest, and grittiest combination of baseball players that have ever represented this city in any league, demonstrated beyond opportunity for quibble or claim their paramount superiority over anything extant in diamond life of to-day by winning the fourth and deciding game of the world's championship series by the score of 2 to 0.

The victory meant an honor which has not hitherto fallen to the lot of New York through any other team, and by the victory of yesterday the Giants may hold up their heads in the athletic world as being the one collection of peerless ball tossers.

The crowd, in the neighborhood of 27,000 people, saw the battle, and a battle it was, to cheer the baseball heart and satisfy the innermost cravings of the rooter's mind. It was a fight of slow stages, but at no time during the contest were the Giants in danger, and at all times were they masters. It settled the question so often propounded whether the National or the American League offers the better brand of baseball. The championship decree of yesterday, to be accepted as final, lays at rest all doubt and demonstrates the transcendent superiority of the National brand and the indisputable invulnerability of the Giants.

And be it recorded right here that New York possesses the pitching marvel of the century, Christie Mathewson, the giant slabman, who made the world's championship possible for New York, may be legitimately designated as the premier pitching wonder of all baseball records. The diamond has known its Clarkson, its Keefe, and its Caruthers. Their records radiate. But to Mathewson belongs the palm, for his almost superhuman accomplishment during the series which closed yesterday will stand as a mark for all pitchers of the future.

Mathewson's Great Record.

Figures show best just what Mathewson accomplished. In the three victories over which he presided he twirled twenty-seven innings. During that series he allowed not a single run; not an Athletic even reached third base. He was touched for only a total of fifteen hits, and by men who are reckoned as the American League's strongest batters; he allowed only one pass to first, hit only a single batsman, and struck out sixteen men. The record is a classic. Baseball New York appreciates this work. That fact was amply demonstrated yesterday, when it gave Mathewson a marvelous vocal panegyric and placed upon his modest brow a bellowed wreath that evoked only a half-suppressed smile and bow.

The game yesterday was one of giants—clean, fast, and decisive. Both teams were keyed to the point of desperation, for to the Giants it meant rosy conquest and to the Athletics a saving clause which would offer them yet a chance to redeem themselves. But the Giants were not to be repulsed. They went at the ball in the first inning with a we-never-can-lose expression of dogged determination, and there was not a minute during play in which that spirit didn't manifest itself. Philadelphia tried its best, but, strive as hard as it did, it was only a shadow reflecting the masterful Mathewson's will. He bestrode the field like a mighty Colossus, and the Athletics peeped about the diamond like pigmies who struggled gallantly for their lives, but in vain.

Bender, the much feared brave from the Carlisle reservation, sought to repeat his scalping bee of Tuesday, but the Spartan McGraw laconically expressed the situation when at the beginning of the game he remarked good-naturedly to the Athletics' pitcher:

"It will be off the warpath for you to-day, Chief." The stolid, phlegmatic copper-colored man only smiled grimly.

"It's uncertain," he replied, "but I did it once, and I'm going to do my best to do it again."

Analyzed to the statistical point the twirling feature of the game shows little advantage to either side, but when weighed in parts Mathewson had by far the advantage. Five hits were all that the Giants could register off Bender, while the Athletics rang up for a total of six against Mathewson. Mathewson fanned only three to Bender's five, but the Indian gave three passes. Mathewson proved a surprise to his admirers by poorly fielding his position. He made two errors, but they luckily resulted in nothing harmful in the net result.

Giants Get $1,141 Each.

The Giants were well rewarded for their hard work in defeating the Athletics, for by the week's labor each man to-day has a check in his wallet for $1,141.41. That is the share of each of the eighteen Giants for the series. The figures given out officially yesterday show the receipts of the first four games, from which the players derive their profit, to have been $50,730.50. The share for which the two teams struggled amounted to $27,394. Seventy-five per cent. of that amount was divided among the Giants. The remainder went in equal shares to the Athletics.

The crowd which saw yesterday's game was immense, exceeding by a small margin that of Tuesday. All the stands were filled, while men and women stood in a line ten deep back of the ropes from the right to the left field bleachers. Men hung on the fence and sat on the grandstand roof, and some peered at the game through glasses from distant poles and housetops. The crowd was there to cheer its idols, and every move was followed by a roar.

The New York management had a band on the field to enliven things until play began, and it was kept busy as the players walked to the field and started practice. As McGraw appeared on the diamond, coming from the clubhouse, he was met with a volley of applause and was obliged to lift his hat in response.

"Clinch it to-day, Mac," yelled the crowd. "Nothing but the championship will suit us now."

"That's what you'll get," he responded smilingly.

While McGraw was walking across the field the Athletics appeared from the clubhouse with Bender in the lead.

"Back to the tepee for yours," hooted a rooter. "Giants grab heap much wampum," yelled another, giving an imitation Indian yell. Bender looked at his foes in stolid silence, but smiled widely as the running fire of comments continued. James J. Corbett, with an eye for all public opportunities, walked into the field with the Giants and helped the players to warm up. He was subjected to a good deal of bantering. Just before play was called Corbett and Bresnahan posed with an Irish flag between them and were snapped by a photographer. Mathewson was the last to arrive on the scene and got a magnificent reception. He was applauded for a full minute and the crowd yelled for him to doff his cap. Instead of doing so, however, he walked over to McGinnity, the conqueror of yesterday, and ostentatiously removed Joe's headgear. McGinnity returned the compliment.

"Shake 'em up, Matty. Go after 'em," screamed the bleachers. Mathewson waved his arm as though he would do his utmost. As McGraw went to the plate to bat out in practice the band began to play:

We'll all get stone blind,
Johnnie go fill up the bowl

The crowd cheered, and a half dozen men went through the grandstand offering to bet 100 to 75 that the Giants would win the game. There were no takers.

Couldn't Rattle Bender.

Time and again Bender was yelled at, for the crowd wanted to rattle him, but its noise might as well have been directed at a steamboat, for he was impassive

* * * * *

The score:

PHILADELPHIA.	R	1B	PO	A	E	NEW YORK.	R	1B	PO	A	E
Hartsel, lf.	0	2	4	1	0	Bresn'h'n, c.	0	2	5	2	0
Lord, cf.	0	0	3	0	0	Browne, rf.	0	1	0	0	0
Davis, 1b.	0	1	10	0	0	Donlin, cf.	0	0	1	0	0
L. Cross, 3b.	0	0	1	1	0	M'Gann, 1b.	0	0	12	1	0
Seybold, rf.	0	1	0	0	0	Mertes, lf.	1	1	1	0	0
Murphy, 2b.	0	0	0	0	0	Dahlen, ss.	0	0	3	4	0
M. Cross, ss.	0	1	1	5	0	Devlin, 3b.	0	0	1	4	0
Powers, c.	0	1	5	1	0	Gilbert, 2b.	0	1	3	6	0
Bender, p.	0	0	0	5	0	M'th'son, p.	1	0	1	3	1
Total	0	6	24	13	0	Total	2	5	27	20	1

Philadelphia	0	0	0	0	0	0	0	0	0	—0
New York	0	0	0	0	1	0	0	1	..	—2

First base on errors—Philadelphia, 1. Bases on balls—Off Bender, 3. Struck out—By Mathewson, 4; by Bender, 4. Left on bases—New York, 4; Philadelphia, 6. Two-base hits—Powers, Bresnahan. Sacrifice hits—Devlin, Mathewson. Double plays—Dahlen, Gilbert, and McGann; Hartsel, M. Cross, and L. Cross. Umpires—Messrs. Sheridan and O'Day. Time of game—One hour and twenty-eight minutes. Attendance—24,187.

and cool at all stages. In one inning he gave two bases on balls in succession and the crowd jumped to its feet in glee. Bender was thunderously informed that at that particular stage he was booked for the soap factory, but stuck grimly to his task. At another time two bunts were made in succession. Again the crowd rose in its might and expressed itself as of the opinion that the chief would surely go to the happy hunting grounds, but he refused to die and stood gamely and quietly to the end.

Danny McGann was again a target for the Bender brand of curves, and added to his strike-out performance of Tuesday, when he slashed the air in a way that was distressing. The first time up yesterday McGann, with his strike-out record fresh in the minds of the fans, was cautioned to be wary and smash the ball to the earth's ends.

"Look out, Danny, the Heap-Much-Kill-'em-Giants man'll get you. Lace it out of the lot."

McGann's face bespoke ill for the future of the ball, but, much to the chagrin of the rooters, he was called out on strikes. As McGann walked toward the home bench the crowd raised a hiss of protest at Sheridan. McGraw, Dahlen, Bresnahan, and Clark had heart-to-heart talks with the indicator, but they were shooed away.

As the game proceeded the crowd saw that it was to be a magnificent pitching struggle, and both twirlers were cheered. After the fourth, when Bender had acquitted himself by retiring the Giants in one, two, three order, he was heartily applauded.

"You're the real thing: kangaroo out of the American and come to us next season," howled one fan. Bender lifted his cap in acknowledgment.

Philadelphia had men on bases in the first, second, third, fifth, and sixth innings, but couldn't get one past the second sack. In the fifth inning they came close to pushing a man to third, but Mathewson, evidently intent upon keeping his record intact, interfered. Powers had made a two-base hit to left. Bender, the next man up, lined one to Mathewson. There were two out, and by the ordinary rules of baseball the batter should have been retired. Powers started off for third, however, and Mathewson, seeing him approaching the bag, took the insult to heart. He threw quickly to Devlin, who touched the runner before he could put his spikes upon the bag.

New York made its runs in the fifth and eighth. In the fifth inning Mertes got a pass and Dahlen followed suit by passing four bad ones. With two on bases the crowd, keen for an opportunity to root, stood up and roared for Devlin to drive in a run.

"Show 'em the way to the clubhouse, Arthur," shouted Clark, who stood upon the coaching line. Devlin, however, had his orders and bunted. He sacrificed the runners to third and second, respectively and as the men chased down the line the crowd nearly yelled itself hoarse.

Besieged by the Rooters.

"Come on, Gilbert, you can do it!" roared the stands. Then came a volley of taunts to Bender, who viewed the situation with absolute imperturbability and wound up his pitching arm for New York's second baseman. But Gilbert was equal to the occasion, for he caught one of Bender's twists on the end of his bat and sent the sphere to deep left. Hartzel got under the base and caught it, but Mertes on third raced home with the first tally of the game. Then the crowd went wild and cheered everything and everybody.

In the eighth the Giants rolled up another. After Gilbert had flied to Lord, Mathewson went to the bat amid a storm of yells. He passed four bad ones, and walked. Bresnahan put an extra coat of dust upon his hands as he stalked to the plate and carefully inspected the business end of his bat. The crowd yelled for him to "Swat it off the earth!"

"Put it in a balloon, Roger, and send it away for good!" screamed the fans. Roger did the next best thing by driving the ball on a straight line to the left field bleachers. Ordinarily it would have counted for a home run, but under the ground rules he was allowed only two bases. Even Matty was enamored of the coup, for as he trotted around to third he paused, under the ground rule allowance, and clapped his hands with satisfaction. Browne, the next up, did his best to imitate Bresnahan, and swung viciously at one of Bender's curves. It went like a shot straight for the Indian. Bender grabbed at the leather, and it struck his right hand, caroming off to Murphy, who retired Browne. Matty, however, jumped across the rubber and registered a second tally.

The Giants also came within an ace of

scoring in the sixth. Mathewson went out to Lord on a high fly, to be followed by Bresnahan who bunted safely along the third-base line. The crowd wanted blood in this round, and told as much to Browne, who followed.

"Once more, boys," yelled McGraw, who was standing on the coaching line.

"Let's get at the Indian here and fix 'em."

Browne was equal to the occasion and put one exactly where Roger had sent it. Donlin walked to the plate with the air of a man capable of great things.

"I'm sorry, old Pitch-Em-Heap," he remarked to Bender jokingly, "but here's where you go back to the reservation."

"Is that so?" answered Bender sarcastically. "Your conclusion, Mr. Donlin, is right in this immediate vicinity." Donlin went out to Lord, and McGann, who followed, cut off three slices of air, and walked away a heart-broken man.

October 15, 1905

NO HITS FOR YANKEES OFF VETERAN YOUNG

Veteran Boston Pitcher's Remarkable Performance in Hilltop Game.

MAKES THREE HITS HIMSELF

Did you hear about what old Young did up at the American League Park yesterday? He didn't exactly beggar description, but he came mighty nigh it. He beggared the Elberfeld aggregation so far as runs were concerned, and he made hitless Yankees out of the whole outfit, and he smashed out singles thisaway and thataway, and he scored people that he liked, and he scored people that we don't know whether he cares much about or not, and he was the jolly old plot of the piece, and there wasn't an inning that you could lose track of him.

Even aside from his pitching proclivities, this gay old blade was the life of the party. He galloped around the bases like he was out for the Swift Stakes, and an observant clocker whose occupation at the track is o'er now that they're insisting that somebody pay some attention to the law, gave it out honest and official when he said to the stand generally:

"They must have gave that old skate the electric battery; watch um sail past them bags—why, he's fast as a ghost, I tell you."

The score, which is an entirely immaterial consideration, was 8. That's all, just 8. There were several reasons for this. To wit:

Pitcher Manning.
Pitcher Newton.
Pitcher Lake.

If the gentle reader will imagine quotation marks before and after the word pitcher in each of the foregoing instances he won't go wrong. Manning was so wild his reformation was despaired of after an inning and a half. He started out by assaulting Thoney so that Thoney had to be out of the game after the first inning. Sullivan flied to Keeler, and, after the pain-crazed Thoney had got himself out between bases and sought the restful bench, Manning passes McConnell, Gessler, and Laporte one dozen bad balls in succession, which we beg to submit is going some. Unglaub's hit scores McConnell.

There's another run for Boston in the second inning, consequent upon the senile Mr. Young's hit to centre, and hits by Cravath—who succeeded Thoney—and Sullivan and a long fly to Stahl by McConnell. Newton is pitching the last part of the second inning, the entire third, and the first half of the fourth—pitching and tossing, more like a boat than a gent on the American League payroll.

And Boston goes right on, getting in runs whether it needs them or not, and now and then there is a long, low ominous growl, and it sure is the voice of the slugger, and we hear him exclaim, "Let's score a few more just to sew up the game."

The good old man Young had his eye and his hand on the ball yesterday. In the third inning he pounded one over to right and faraway, and on this substantial encouragement Unglaub and Wagner scored. And again, by one of those curious quick repetitions of history that sometimes happen on the ball field. Uncle Cy does exactly the same thing in the ninth. That is, his slam is to left, in this instance, but he scores the same two men, Unglaub and Wagner.

Lake finished the session for the Yanks, and had the bad taste to question some of Silk O'Loughlin's decisions. Not only the bad taste but the bad judgment. Nothing in this for you at all. Jose, amigo. Besides, it's too hot. Silk looks around at the Yankee bench to see if there are any more pitchers available. No more. Oh, very well, pitch the game out, you fiery Lake.

W. W. AULICK.

With malice toward Young—

BOSTON	R	H	P	O	A	E		NEW YORK	R	H	P	O	A	E
Thoney, lf.	0	0	0	0	0			Niles, 2b.	0	0	3	6	0
Cravath, lf.	0	1	4	0	0			Keeler, rf.	0	0	2	1	1
Sullivan, cf.	1	1	1	0	0			Morty, 1b.	0	0	10	1	1
McC'nell, 2b.	2	2	2	4	0			H'phill, cf.	0	0	0	0	0
Gessler, rf.	0	1	2	0	0			Ball, ss.	0	0	3	3	0
Laporte, 3b.	0	2	2	2	0			Stahl, lf.	0	0	2	1	0
Ungl'b, 1b.	2	2	13	0	0			Conroy, 3b.	0	0	1	0	
Wagner, ss.	2	1	0	3	0			Blair, c.	0	0	7	2	0
Criger, c.	0	0	3	2	0			Manning, p.	0	0	0	2	0
Young, p.	1	3	0	1	0			Newton, p.	0	0	0	1	1
								Lake, p.	0	0	9	0	
Total	8	13	27	12	0			Total	0	0	27	18	3

Boston .... 1 1 2 1 0 1 0 0 2—8
New York .... 0 0 0 0 0 0 0 0 0—0

Hits—Off Manning, 3 in one and two-thirds innings; off Newton, 8 in two-thirds of an inning; off Lake, 7 in five and two-thirds innings. Sacrifice hits—McConnell, (2.) Criger, (2.) Stolen base—McConnell. Double play—Stahl and Blair. Left on bases—Boston, 11. First base on balls—Off Manning, 3; off Newton, 1; off Lake, 1; off Young, 1. First base on errors—Boston, 2. Hit by pitcher—By Manning, 1; by Newton, 1. Struck out—By Manning, 1; by Newton, 1; by Lake, 4; by Young, 2. Time of game—Two hours. Umpire—Mr. O'Loughlin.

YOUNG'S FAMOUS CAREER.

Most Remarkable Pitcher in Point of Excellent Service in Baseball.

The performance of Denton T. (Cy) Young yesterday at the American League Park in shutting out the Yankees without a hit stamps him as the most remarkable pitcher in the history of major league baseball. Not only is he the oldest pitcher in National or American League ranks, but he is the only player in the history of the National pastime who has shut out an opposing team without a hit on three different occasions. In addition, he shares with John M. Ward the unique distinction of pitching a no-hit game with no player reaching first base. Ward performed the feat for Providence against Buffalo in 1880, while Young established his record on May 15, 1904, against the Philadelphia Athletics while pitching for Boston. Yesterday only one New York player reached first base—Niles, on a base on balls.

"Cy" Young pitched his first no-hit game for Cleveland against Cincinnati in 1897. This was in the National League. His next shut-out game was against the Philadelphia Athletics in 1904, and his third yesterday.

In addition to his remarkable record for no-hit games Young holds the record for effective pitching in the major league, pitching fifty-four innings without a run in 1904.

The last shut-out game in the American League was on Sept. 27, 1905, when Dineen did the trick for Boston against Chicago. In the National League, Pfeffer for Boston against Cincinnati, and Maddox for Pittsburg against Brooklyn performed the "shut-out" feat last year.

Young was born at Gilmore, Ohio, March 29, 1867, stands 6 feet in height, and weighs 210 pounds. Canton, Ohio, was where "Cy" made his first appearance, and the Cleveland Club took him in charge that year, 1890, making eighteen years' active pitching in the major league. He remained with Cleveland until that club was transferred to St. Louis, where he remained one year and then went to Boston the first year of the American League. Young is the most remarkable ball player the game has yet produced when good work for a long period is considered.

July 1, 1908

PITCHER JOHNSON AGAIN DOWNS YANKS

Washingtonian Prevents New Yorks Scoring in Three Straight Games.

AMERICAN LEAGUE.

Scores of Yesterday's Games.
MORNING GAMES.
Detroit, 4; St. Louis, 3.
Boston, 6; Philadelphia, 1.
Cleveland, 6; Chicago, 0.

AFTERNOON GAMES.
Washington, 4; New York, 0.
Washington, 9; New York, 3.
Boston, 3; Philadelphia, 2.
Cleveland, 5; Chicago, 2.
Detroit, 9; St. Louis, 3.

Where They Play To-day.
New York at Philadelphia.
Boston at Washington.
St. Louis at Cleveland.
Chicago at Detroit.

Standing of the Clubs.

	W.	L.	P.C.		W.	L.	P.C.
Detroit	72	51	.585	Phila'phia	61	63	.492
Chicago	71	55	.564	Boston	61	65	.484
St. Louis	70	55	.567	Washington	54	67	.446
Cleveland	69	58	.543	New York	40	85	.320

We are grievously disappointed in this man Johnson of Washington. He and his team had four games to play with the champion (sic) Yankees. Johnson pitched

the first game and shut us out. Johnson pitched the second game and shut us out. Johnson pitched the third game, and shut us out. Did Johnson pitch the fourth game and shut us out? He did not. Oh, you quitter!

Most pitchers would have gone on and taken a chance after this demonstration of comparative strength. But did Johnson? No, Sir. He weakened. He passed up the fourth game, refusing to sit in as slabsman, and another Washingtonian, named Youse, according to Umpire Evans, and spelled Hughes, according to the card, pitched the final of yesterday's doubleheader, and beat the local wonders even worse than is customary. Oh, rare Pitcher Johnson! Why did you not preserve your record intact? Oh, thou of little faith!

Johnson won the first game of the holiday by a score of 4 to shut-out, and 10,000 souls chanted his service. Washington's runs came this way: Third inning—Johnson is hit by a pitched ball and walked. Chesbro's a good-natured person ordinarily, but something's got to be done to keep this Johnson from continuous performance. Pickering is safe on Laporte's fumble, though later he is out trying to make third. Ganley is safe on Conroy's fumble, and two score when Unglaub doubles. Then, in the seventh, Street doubles and scores on Johnson's single to centre. Whose single? Oh, you know. And Delehanty's single scores Johnson. (Can't help it if the composing room does run out of upper case "J's".)

We could write a sensational tale about any second-story chapter, but one inning, the sixth, will suffice. Hogg had started in to pitch, but they didn't root very much for Hogg and he died after five innings and four runs had been recorded. Then along comes the dilatory Doyle, and the groan that went up from the would-be early home-goers was deeper than the disgust over the ninth inning from Philadelphia.

When Mr. Doyle sets out to pitch he takes the heel of his shoe and scrapes determinedly at the inoffensive earth, like a plow making a furrow, or a dime-novel reading boy after a Capt. Kidd treasure in the backyard. Then he stares condemningly at the batter for thirty seconds and forms his arms into a maltese cross. And after he has fixed his little cap straight he is ready to pitch. Not all of the vicissitudes of that sixth inning spoiled his schedule. To be brutally photographic, here it is, or was—Hughes made first on Hemphill's muff. Pickering was safe on Conroy's bad throw. Ganley flied out. Unglaub singled to left, scoring Hughes. Delehanty walked. Clymer doubled,

scoring Pickering and Unglaub. Freeman went out on a squeeze play and Delehanty scored, and, if you will believe it, while Doyle was pawing up the earth and fixing his little cap and arranging his arm, Clymer stole home, right out in public, and we don't believe Doyle knows it yet. Count those runs up and see if they don't make five.

After that Mr. Billiard obliged, and the Washingtons didn't score any more. The Yanks went exactly thirty-three innings in the series with the Senators before they counted, and the three runs they got toward the finish seemed only a part of the great big joke of getaway day. And the funniest part of the afternoon was a managerial envoy coming around and confiding the importantly true tidings that Cree and Warhop of Williamsport and Quinn of Richmond are joiners to-morrow and that it'll be all off with the other fellows from now on. Amen.

W. W. AULICK.

The last sad writes—

WASHINGTON.	AB	R	H	PO	A		NEW YORK.	AB	R	H	PO	A
Picker'g, cf.	4	0	0	1	1		Conroy, 3b.	4	0	0	2	2
Ganley, lf.	5	1	0	3	0		McIlv'n, rf.	4	0	1	0	0
Unglaub, 3b.	5	0	4	1	3		Laporte, 2b.	4	0	1	3	
Deleh'ty, 2b.	5	0	2	3	4		H'phill, cf.	4	0	0	2	0
Clymer, rf.	4	0	0	1	0		Mor'ty, 1b.	2	0	0	10	1
Freem'n, 1b.	3	0	0	12	0		O'Rourke, lf	3	0	0	4	0
McBride, ss.	4	0	1	1	3		Ball, ss.	3	0	1	3	0
Street, c.	4	1	1	5	0		Kleinow, c.	3	0	0	5	3
Johnson, p.	2	1	0	2			Chesbro, p.	3	0	0	0	2
Total ...	36	4	9	27	14		Total ...	30	0	2	27	11

Errors—Freeman, Conroy, Laporte, Ball, (2,) Kleinow.

Washington ....0 0 2 0 0 0 2 0 0—4
New York ....0 0 0 0 0 0 0 0 0—0

Two-base hits—Unglaub, Street. Three-base hit—Delehanty. Sacrifice hit—Johnson. Stolen

bases—Ganley, Ball. Left on bases—Washington, 9; New York, 3. First base on balls—Off Chesbro, 2. Hit by pitcher—By Chesbro, 1; by Johnson, 1. Struck out—By Chesbro, 4; by Johnson 5. Time of game—One hour and forty minutes. Umpire—Mr. Evans.

SECOND GAME.

WASHINGTON:	AB	R	H	PO	A		NEW YORK.	AB	R	H	PO	A
Picker'g, cf.	5	2	0	0	1		Conroy, 3b.	4	0	1	6	0
Ganley, lf.	5	1	0	3			McIlv'n, rf.	3	0	0	1	0
Unglaub, 3b.	5	3	8	1	1		Laporte, 2b.	4	0	3	2	5
Deleh'ty, 2b.	4	1	2	3			H'phill, cf.	3	1	1	3	0
Clymer, rf.	5	1	2	0	1		O'Rourke, lf	3	1	1	1	0
Freem'n, 1b.	1	0	1	7	0		Mor'ty, 1b.	4	0	0	7	1
McBride, ss.	3	0	1	2	5		Ball, ss.	4	0	1	1	6
Street, c.	3	0	0	6	2		Kleinow, c.	1	0	0	2	1
Warner, c.	1	0	1	4	0		Blair, c.	2	1	2	2	1
Hughes, p.	4	1	0	0	0		Hogg, p.	1	0	0	0	2
							Doyle, p.	0	0	0	0	1
Total ...	36	9	11	26	12		Billiard, p.	2	0	1	1	1
							Total ...	31	3	9	27	15

*Conroy out; hit by batted ball.
Errors—Ganley, Conroy, McIlveen, Laporte, Hemphill, Ball.

Washington ....1 0 0 0 3 5 0 0—9
New York ....0 0 0 0 0 0 2 0 1—3

Two-base hits—Unglaub, Laporte. Home run—Blair. Hits—Off Hogg, 6 in 5 innings; off Doyle, 2 in 1 inning; off Billiard, 3 in 3 innings. Sacrifice hits—Pickering, Freeman, (2,) McBride, Hughes, McIlveen. Stolen bases—Clymer, O'Rourke. Left on bases—Washington, 11; New York, 5. First base on balls—Off Hughes, 6; off Hogg, 3; off Doyle, 2; off Billiard, 1. First base on errors—Washington, 5. Struck out—By Hughes, 7; by Hogg, 1; by Billiard, 2. Time of game—One hour and fifty-five minutes. Umpire—Mr. Evans.

BLUNDER COSTS GIANTS VICTORY

Merkle Rushes Off Base Line Before Winning Run Is Scored, and Is Declared Out.

CONFUSION ON BALL FIELD

Chance Asserts That McCormick's Run Does Not Count— Crowd Breaks Up Game.

UMPIRE DECLARES IT A TIE

Singular Occurrence on Polo Grounds Reported to President Pulliam, Who Will Decide Case.

Censurable stupidity on the part of player Merkle in yesterday's game at the Polo Grounds between the Giants and Chicagos placed the New York team's chances of winning the pennant in jeopardy. His unusual conduct in the final inning of a great game perhaps deprived New York of a victory that would have been unquestionable had he not committed a breach in baseball play that resulted in Umpire O'Day declaring the game a tie.

With the score tied in the ninth inning at 1 to 1 and the New York's having a runner, McCormick, on third base waiting

Fred Merkle

for an opportunity to score and Merkle on first base looking for a similar chance. Bridwell hit into centre field. It was a fair hit ball and would have been sufficient to win the game had Merkle gone on his way down the base path while McCormick was scoring the winning run. But instead of Merkle going to second had to make sure that McCormick had touched home with the run necessary to a victory. Merkle ran toward the clubhouse, evidently thinking that his share in the game was ended when Bridwell hit the ball into safe territory.

Manager Chance of the Chicago Club quickly grasped the situation and directed that the ball be thrown to second base, which would force out Merkle, who had not reached that corner.

Manager Chance, who plays first base for the Chicago club, ran to second base and the ball was thrown there, but immediately Pitcher McGinnity interfered in the play and a scramble of players ensued, in which, it is said, McGinnity obtained the ball and threw it into the crowd before Manager Chance could complete a force play on Merkle, who was far away from the base line. Merkle said that he had touched second base, and the Chicago players were equally positive that he had not done so.

Manager Chance then appealed to Umpire O'Day, who was head umpire of the game, for a decision in the matter. The crowd, thinking that the Giants had won the game, swarmed upon the playing field in such a confusion that none of the "fans" seemed able to grasp the situation, and finally their attitude toward Umpire O'Day became so offensive that the guards ran into the crowd and protected the umpire, while arguments were being heard pro and con on the point in question by Manager Chance and McGraw and the umpire.

Umpire O'Day finally decided that the run did not count, and that inasmuch as the spectators had gained such large numbers on the field that the game could not be resumed. O'Day declared the game a tie. Although both Umpires O'Day and Emslie, it is claimed, say that they did not see the play at second base. Umpire O'Day's action in declaring that McCormick's run did not count was based upon the presumption or fact that a force play was made on Merkle at second base. The rule covering such a point is as follows:

One run shall be scored every time a base runner, after having legally touched the first three bases, shall legally touch the home base before three men are put out, provided, however, that if he reach home on or during a play in which the third man be forced out or be put out before reaching first base a run shall not count. A force-out can be made only when a base runner legally loses the right to the base he occupies and is thereby obliged to advance as the result of a fair hit ball not caught on the fly.

The singular ending of the game aroused intense interest throughout the city, and everywhere it was the chief topic of discussion. Early in the evening a report was widely circulated that President Pulliam had decided the game was a tie and must be played again. When this rumor reached Mr. Pulliam he authorized the following statement:

"I made no decision in the matter at all and I will not do so until the matter is presented to me in proper form. The statement on the "ticker" that I had decided the game a tie is entirely unauthorized."

But according to Umpire O'Day the game is a tie and will remain so until either the National League or the National Commission decides the matter. Last night Umpire O'Day made an official report of the dispute to President Pulliam. Manager Chance declared that the game was a tie, and the management of the Giants has recorded the game as a 2 to 1 victory.

The result of this game may prove to be the deciding factor in the championship race, and inasmuch as it is a serious matter to be dealt with President Pulliam may ask the league to act upon the question or go still further and place it in the hands of the National Commission—the supreme court of baseball.

In any event there will be no double-header this afternoon, and it may be several days before the problem will be decided. The official reporter of the league in New York credits the Giants with a victory, but, of course, this is subject to any action President Pulliam or the league may take in the matter.

President Murphy of the Chicago Club last night entered formal claim to yesterday's Chicago-New York game in behalf of Chicago. President Murphy bases his claim on the ground that Merkle of the New York team, who was at first when the ball was hit safely to centre by Bridwell in the ninth inning, had failed to continue to second when his team mate scored the winning run from third. President Murphy entered his claim in a letter to President Harry C. Pulliam of the National League, wherein Mr. Murphy cites in support of his contention the decision rendered in the game at Pittsburg, Sept. 4. between Pittsburg and Chicago. in which precisely the same contingency, he asserts, arose. The Chicago club protested the game, but the protest was not allowed, because the single umpire who officiated declared that he had not seen the play In yesterday's game the omission of Merkle to continue to second. Mr. Murphy declares, was noted by Umpire O'Day.

CLASSY AND THRILLING BALL.

Third Battle of Leading Teams Produces Sensational Sport.

Well, anyway, it was a classy baseball game from the time in the first inning when Roger Bresnahan makes an entrance, accompanied by a dresser, who does him and undoes him in his natty mattress and knee pads, till the end of the ninth, when Bridwell singles safely to centre, bringing in what looks like the winning run.

And, from a spectacular point of view, that mix-up at the finish was just the appropriate sensation to a bang-up, all-a-quiver game. They all know they have seen a mighty snappy game of ball; that New York has brought over one more run than the enemy, whether the run counts or not; that McGinnity in holding on to the ball after the ninth-inning run, has done so with the idea that it belongs to the home team, and that good Master O'Day has said, as he exits: " I didn't see the play on second—the run doesn't count."

Up to the climactic ninth it was the toss of a coin who would win. For here is our best-beloved Mathewson pitching as only champions pitch, striking out the power and the glory of the Cubs, numbering among his slain Schulte in the first, Pfeister in the third, Steinfeldt in the fourth, Pfeister in the fifth. Hayden and Schulte in the sixth, Hayden in the eighth, and Evers and Schulte in the ninth—these last in one-two order. Proper pitching, and for this and other things we embrace him.

But then, Pfeister is pitching good ball, too. Not so good as the Matty article for this isn't to be expected, or desired, even. Pfeister doesn't strike anybody out, and Pfeister gives an occasional base on balls, and once he hits a batter, but aside from these irregularities Pfeister must be accounted in the king row of Wednesday matinée pitchers. The gentleman who feels the weight of the delivery, and thereafter takes his base, is the plodsome McCormick. It is in the second inning, and Pfeister whirls up a curve that doesn't break right—In fact, it breaks directly in McCormick's tummy, and Pfeister is forced to figure that the joke's on him. After the heroic Dr. Creamer has emptied half a hydrant on the prostrate McCormick the latter walks wanly to first, but he has to wait to walk home till the ninth inning.

Meantime, the game has progressed swiftly, remarkable for excellent plays by a number of us on either side, and remarkable also for the in-and-out work of Evers at second for Chicago.

It is in the fifth that the Cubs, or one of them, find the solitary run that represents the day's work. Hofman has been thrown out at first by Bridwell, and then the admirable Tinker takes his bat in his hand and faces Matty with determination writ large on his expressive features. Mr. Tinker drives the ball away out to right centre for what would be a two-bagger if you or I had made it, gentle reader—and this is no disparagement of the Tinker, for he is well seeming in our sight. As the ball approaches Master Donlin this good man attempts to field it with his foot. It's a home run all right, when you get down to scoring, but if this Donlin boy was our boy we'd have sent him to bed without his supper, and ye mind that, Mike.

We found the stick all right in the sixth, and tied the score. Herzog—and, by the way, he led the batting list yesterday in the absence of Tenney; that is, the playing absence, for Fred was among those present in the stand—Herzog, that is, boldly to Steinfeldt, and it's a hit all right, but the throw that Steinfeldt makes to first is particularly distressing, and Herzy goes on to second. Bresnahan yields up a sacrifice bunt. Donlin hits over second base. Herzog scores, and 18,-000 people go out of their minds.

It is at this stage of the game that reputable prophets speak confidently of ten innings, mayhap eleven, or so many thereof as may be pulled off before play becomes night. But darkness never stops this Wednesday game at the Polo Grounds. It goes the limit without interference by the dimming skies. We fancy ourselves mightily in the ninth. after

Devlin has made a clean single to centre. To be sure, Seymour has just gone out at first on a throw by Evers, but we have a chance. Devlin is on first, and the start is splendid. But here is McCormick, with a drive over to Evers, who throws out Devlin at second, and we're not very far advanced—and two are down and out. Merkle, who failed us the day before in an emergency is at bat, and we pray of him that he mend his ways. If he will only single we will ignore any errors he may make in the rest of his natural life.

On this condition, Merkle singles. McCormick advances to third, and everybody in the inclosure slaps everybody else and nobody minds. Perfect ladies are screaming like a batch of Coney barkers on the Mardi Gras occasion, and the elderly banker behind us is beating our hat to a pulp with his gold handled cane. And nobody minds. Aided by these indications of the popular sentiment, Master Bridwell hits safely to centre, McCormick trots home, the reporter boys prepare to make an asterisk under the box score of the game with the line—" Two out when winning run was scored "—the merry villagers flock on the field to worship the hollow where the Mathewson feet have pressed, and all of a sudden there is a doings around second base. McGinnity, walking off the field with the ball, as is the custom of some member of the winning team, is held up by Tinker and Evers, who insist that the run does not count, as Merkle has not touched second. And then begins the argument which will keep us in talk for the rest of the season, and then some. Certainly the Cubs have furnished us sport.

W. W. AULICK.

Bewildering biography of a grizzly—

September 24, 1908

Cleveland

Wins Remarkable Game

CLEVELAND, Oct. 2.—Cleveland defeated Chicago to-day in the most remarkable game of the year in the big leagues by the score of 1 to 0. Joss, pitching for Cleveland, not only shut Chicago out without a hit, but he did not allow one of his opponents to reach first base, although the visitors used three pinch hitters in the ninth inning. Joss was aided by some remarkable support from Manager Lajoie, who made several phenomenal pick-ups. On the other hand, Walsh, the Chicago man, pitched a sensational game, striking out fifteen men in eight innings. He struck out Goode four times and Lajoie and Clarke twice each, and these three are Cleveland's best batters. Cleveland was able to bat but four balls past the infield, and only five of the locals reached first base. Cleveland scored its only run in the third. Birmingham led off with a single. Walsh caught him napping off first, but Isbell's throw to second hit the runner in the head, and he went to third. He

when Walsh and Schreck became crossed in their signals, and a ball went to the grand stand. With Joss at bat in the eighth, Schreck had a finger broken, which will keep him out of the game for the rest of the season. Score:

October 3, 1908

THE CUBS WIN THE PENNANT

Hit Mathewson for Four Runs in Third Inning of Decisive Game and Beat the Giants.

GIANTS SCORE TWO RUNS

"Three-Fingered" Brown, Chicago's Star Twirler, Has Home Team at His Mercy.

40,000 SEE GREAT CONTEST

Probably as Many More Shut Out Wall Street Left Outside—One Would-Be Spectator Killed by a Fall.

A rather bulky person, with a persistent and annoying habit of twisting his arms and legs into cabalistic designs and then shooting a ball with terrific speed and snakelike twist toward a man sixty feet away took the National League championship pennant away from the Giants at the Polo Grounds yesterday and gave it to the Chicago team in a deciding game the like of which, for spectacular setting, had never been witnessed in the history of baseball.

This pitcher, who wrung the hearts of near a hundred thousand New York fans, was referred to with an approach to familiarity, as "Three Fingered" Brown. Against him was placed the idol of New York baseball lovers, Mathewson, called sometimes "Matty," and again "Big Six," originator of the "fade away." And if it was grievous to the vast multitude who rose and yelled greetings to this "fade away" inventor, to see "Three Fingered" fan out the faithful and tried Giants it was more than grievous to behold Matty himself fade gradually until he disappeared from the box and the gangling, left-handed Wiltse taking his place to lead the forlorn hope.

The close race for the pennant carried the deciding game of yesterday beyond the length of the season because of the decision making a tie of a game which would have been won from the Chicago team by the New Yorks but for the error of judgment of First Baseman Merkle, who destroyed a run by failing to run to second base on another player's safe hit. New Yorkers felt that their team were entitled to the pennant and had won it, but they were game enough to view with keen sporting spirit the contest which resulted yesterday and confident enough to believe that they would win up to the minute the last out was made.

There is no record of a sporting event that stirred New York as did the game of yesterday. No crowd so big ever was moved to a field of contest as was moved yesterday. Perhaps never in the history of a great city, since the days of Rome. and its arena contests, has a people been pitched to such a key of excitement as was New York "fandom" yesterday.

The break of day found men and boys waiting at the gates of the Polo Grounds to secure admission hours afterward. The early morning started the flow of humanity northward through the main avenues of travel which the tight little island affords.

At 10 o'clock there were 2,000 people gathered at the gates, and in another half an hour more than 5,000, with trains beginning to bulk with human freight and streets blacken

with hurrying men, women, and children.

Thousands piled upon thousands in a fearful tangle in the howwlo below Coogan's Bluff, and the rusty structure of the elevated railroad tracks. The police were swept aside like corks before a torrent, and the horses of the mounted men were pushed and jammed against the high walls surrounding the grounds.

At 12:45 o'clock, more than two hours before the appointed time for the start of the game, the last inch of standing and sitting room in the grounds had been filled, and between 35,000 and 40,000 people were in view of the field where the battle was fought out. Thousands of people congested in he aisles of the grandstand and flocking into spaces around the bleachers, suddenly burst through the bonds that kept them from the field, and a great rush was made across the grounds for places on the sward beyond the whitewash lines of the diamond.

Outside the grounds as many more would-be spectators fought or begged for admission. An hour of desperate effort, which was futile, turned he wits of hundreds to planning methods of forcing an entrance. The great 15-foot fence back of the grandstand, topped with two strands of barbed wire, was scaled by scores of men and boys. These showed an agility that was remarkable, and a daring in jumping within the grounds that one might look for, perhaps, in life convicts endeavoring to break jail. The fence at the north end of the field was also hurdled, and several hundred people got in there without paying.

So greatly was the capacity of the grounds taxed that finally the high-pitched roof of the grandstand was reached by hundreds. Toward the sky the crowd seemed to pile, and over the highest fringe of fans reared the 155th Street viaduct and Coogan's Bluff, higher yet and dense with men, women, and children.

Man Killed Trying to See Game

The elevated trains dumped thousands at the 155th Street station after it was impossible for them to get anywhere near the grounds. These flocked upon the tracks, seeking points of vantage, daring even the third rail. One man was killed by falling from the structure, which was the only fatality of the day. His vacant place was quickly filled.

When the crowd on the elevated structure got beyond control of the railroad employes a special detachment of police was sent to dislodge it. Those who had clambered to the tops of trains were quickly disposed of by having the trains moved away from the neighborhood, carrying the fans, wildly gesticulating and screaming protests.

With the first wild outbursts of applause inside the grounds as the spectators greeted their favorite players when they came on the field the mobs outside made even more desperate attempts to get within view of the field. Black specks could be seen climbing the thin edge of a giant sign reared high above the roof of the elevated station, and within a few

minutes the top of the sign was black lined with men and boys, many of whom would have gone to certain death had the frail structure toppled. Even on the tops of signal posts of the elevated structure some of them as high as a hundred feet from the ground—said a man for each post.

Starting with only 150 policemen, under Inspector Thompson, the department did not show up well in the face of the crushing demand on it, and it was a wonder that many people were not crushed to death or trampled under foot. The universal good nature of the great throng made more to do with averting a catastrophe than did the police with clubs and horses. Reinforcements were sent for, and throughout the afternoon men were rushed to the grounds from almost every precinct in the city. Chief inspector Cortwright and Gen. Bingham both reported for duty to prepare for the outrush of the multitude at the end of the game and its orderly dispersal.

Conservative estimates put the number of persons who either witnessed the game or tried to witness it at 80,000. Other estimates went as high as 100,000 and this latter estimate may have been a good one, for there was no keeping tabs on the hundreds and thousands who rode to the grounds and turned around and rode right back without trying to reach the gates.

40,000 See Game Begun

At last 3 o'clock came. The weather was ideal for the contest. The sunshone brightly, and the shadows of the fielders were cast black and sharp cut upon the rich, velvety spread of greensward. The multitude in grandstand and on bleachers rose for one big, comforting stretch before the passing of the first ball over the plate. Then an umpire tossed a disk of white toward the pitcher's box. The ball sent up a little puff of clay dust, and Matty, the idol, baywreathed in the hearts of the thousands of New Yorkers who love the game he has played so well for them, picked up the ball and hunched himself.

One long, deafening roar from 40,000 throats went up to cheer him on to victors, and the game was on.

Sheckard picked up a bat and, rubbing his shoes into the clay, made a firm foothold for himself. He drew back the stick, and it was easy to see that it was easy to see and understand that in Sheckard's mind and heart and soul had sprung the determination to hit that ball so hard it would never again see the field. But Matty, who was as limber and strong and clear of head as ever in his life, or will be again, sent the ball whizzing into Bresnahan's hands, and air. Sheckard smote it not.

Whiff! Whiff! Whiff! went Mr. Sheckard's bat, and as he retired from further endeavor the multitude arose again and proclaimed Matty their little idol of baseball worship with wild screams of "The Fade Away! Matty! You're giving us the pennant!"

Evers and Schulte followed and suffered a like fate, the "fade away" ball with its sudden drop toward the shanks of each batsman fooling them. The Chicagos were retired, and as Matty walked in from the box the people went crazy with excitement. The din was ear-splitting, horns and megaphones punctuating the wild cries of exultant fans, while at regular intervals the tooting of a trumpeter split the

Then as the Chicago team went to the field the trumpeter played "Taps" over it as a last rite for the militant dead and the crowd understood and laughed a great, big, hearty laugh of delight.

The enthusiasm over the early and fatal work of the "fade" was as nothing to the enthusiasm which followed when the Giants began by sending men to the bases. Tenney got to first by being hit by a pitched ball and Herzog sent him to second by waiting for four bad ones from Pfeister. Bresnahan struck out and Herzog was run down between first and second. But there was Mike Donlin at the bat, and if there was a human being who held a tight hold on the hearts of the fans, next to Matty, it was that same Mike.

And Mike found the ball and sent it red hot, along the first base line past Chance for a two-bagger, bringing in Tenney with the first run. The multitude was seeing the game through

Champions of the Past.

Year.	Champions.	Won.	Lost.	P.C.
1876.	Chicago	52	14	.788
1877.	Boston	31	17	.646
1878.	Boston	41	19	.707
1879.	Providence	55	23	.705
1880.	Chicago	67	17	.798
1881.	Chicago	55	29	.655
1882.	Chicago	63	35	.643
1883.	Boston	63	35	.643
1884.	Providence	84	28	.750
1885.	Chicago	87	25	.779
1886.	Chicago	90	34	.725
1887.	Detroit	79	45	.637
1888.	New York	84	47	.641
1889.	New York	83	43	.659
1890.	Brooklyn	86	43	.667
1891.	Boston	87	51	.630
1892.	Boston	102	48	.680
1893.	Boston	86	44	.662
1894.	Baltimore	89	39	.695
1895.	Baltimore	87	43	.669
1896.	Baltimore	90	39	.698
1897.	Boston	93	39	.705
1898.	Boston	102	47	.685
1899.	Brooklyn	101	47	.682
1900.	Brooklyn	82	54	.603
1901.	Pittsburg	90	49	.647
1902.	Pittsburg	103	36	.745
1903.	Pittsburg	91	49	.650
1904.	New York	106	47	.693
1905.	New York	105	48	.686
1906.	Chicago	116	36	.763
1907.	Chicago	107	45	.704
1908.	Chicago	99	55	.643

rose-colored spectacles now, and in its mind's eye the pennant was already done up in camphor, to float next season over New York's home grounds.

But Capt. Chance gave pause, and after pondering somewhat waved a gloved paw in the air, and "Three Fingered" Brown got in the game and Mr. Pfeister disappeared. In short order the tide turned. The way "Three Fingered" contorted his bulky person and shot the ball over the plate during the subsequent innings was awful. There was a quick subsidence of exultation. There were half-hearted toots of defiance and shrill cries from hopeful small boys, and a woman or two piped words of cheer, but the Titanic yawps of the leather-lunged 40,000 faithful had ceased.

Tinker's Slashing Three-bagger

The third inning almost brought sobs from the crowd. One Tinker of the busy Chicago crew got next to Matty's celebrated "fadeaway," and with a sharp crack the ball shot toward the sky. Smaller and smaller grew that ball, and faster and faster it sailed high above Cy Seymour's head, and all the while Mr. Tinker's stout legs were twinkling as he shot around the bases like a drab streak. When the multitude regained consciousness they beheld Mr. Tinker sitting placidly on third base.

Then Kling reached down and found and annihilated another "fade," bringing in the industrious Mr. Tinker. Thereupon "Three-Fingered" Brown took the bat and sacrificed Kling to second. Matty evidently began to see things in a blur, for he gave the next man his base on balls and let Schulte drive out a cracking hit, which brought in Kling. Evers, who meanwhile had got to first on balls, moved around to third on the hit and scored, with Schulte, when Chance drove out a hot double to right field.

Matty, from being the bay-wreathed pet of a sport-loving people had now become just a somewhat perplexed and hard-working baseball pitcher. The inning ended with the Chicago team having four runs to the Giants' one.

There had been at first some inclination on the part of the Chicago team to be disagreeable and "kick." Hofman was ordered out of the game for barking and snapping at Umpire Johnstone, but thereafter the game settled down to hard, grinding work. The plays were swift and clean, and the work of the Chicago team frequently showed head of that of the home team.

Hopes Dashed in the Seventh

Until the seventh inning things looked good and black for the Giants, and then came the one big chance to win the game and the pennant. "Three-fingered" Brown had been burning holes in the air over the plate with such success that he began to take things a bit easier. He would stop occasionally, pick up a bit of sand, and finger it in a nonchalant manner, as if to convey the idea to the 40,000 and their ball players that it was just a simple problem for him.

But the seventh inning saw the Giants open up with fine promise and the heart came back to the crowd. Devlin singled to centre and the old yell with trimmings broke forth. McCormick followed with another clean hit, and "Three-fingered" got rattled and gave Bridwell his base on balls. Capt. Chance went to his pitcher of bulk and varied convolutions and addressed him earnestly for a few minutes. The bases were filled, and Matty was due to take the bat. But McGraw decided to replace him with Doyle, who stepped to the plate to see what he could do.

"If you knock a home run you'll be made the Governor of this State!" yelled an excited fan through a megaphone.

Instead Mr. Doyle produced nothing more than a pop foul of such insignificant nature that Kling had only to hold out his hands and let the ball drop into them. So disappointed was the crowd that a shower of empty bottles, cushions, and bundles of paper was sent toward Kling as he caught Doyle out.

Tenney by a sacrifice brought in Devlin and the score was two for the Giants against four for the "Cubs." It never changed. The big chance had been and was lost. The "Three-fingered" one was once more steady on his pins, while Matty was replaced at the start of the eighth by Wiltse.

There was no hope for the Giants after that promising but unproductive seventh, and the last half of the ninth brought a quick finish to a great game. The first three men up went out in order, and with the last play the mighty throng of fans poured forth across the field and started for home to fight all over again a wordy baseball contest. The game had been cleanly fought and was lost because New York's opponents were better ball players and "Three-fingered" Brown had once again sent down to defeat Matty, the pride of Manhattan and inventor of the "fade away."

* * * * *

The score:

CHICAGO.	AB	R	H	PO	A	NEW YORK.	AB	R	H	PO	A
Sheck'd, lf.	4	0	0	4	0	Tenney, 1b..	2	1	1	9	0
Evers, 2b..	3	1	1	0	3	Herzog, 2b.	3	0	0	1	2
Schulte, rf..	4	1	1	4	0	Bres'h'n, c.	4	0	1	10	2
Chance, 1b.	4	0	3	13	0	Donlin, rf..	4	0	1	0	0
St'nf'dt, 3b.	4	0	1	0	3	Seym'r, cf.	3	0	0	2	0
Hofm'n, cf..	0	0	0	0	0	Devlin, 3b..	4	1	1	2	0
Howard, cf.	4	0	0	1	0	McC'm'k, lf.	4	0	1	8	1
Tinker, ss..	4	1	1	1	4	B'dwell, ss.	3	0	0	0	1
Kling, c...	3	1	1	4	1	M'th'son, p.	2	0	0	0	3
Pfeister, p..	0	0	0	0	0	*Doyle	1	0	0	0	0
Brown, p...	2	0	0	0	1	Wiltse, p..	0	0	0	0	0
Total...	32	4	8	27	12	Total...	30	2	5	27	9

Error—Tenney.
*Batted for Mathewson in seventh inning.

Chicago	0	0	4	0	0	0	0	0	0	—4
New York	1	0	0	0	0	0	1	0	0	—2

Two-base hits—Donlin, Schulte, Chance, Evers. Three-base hit—Tinker. Hits—Off Pfeister, 1 in two-thirds of an inning; off Brown, 4 in eight and one-third innings; off Mathewson, 7 in seven innings; off Wiltse, 1 in two innings. Sacrifice hits—Tenney, Brown. Double plays—Kling and Chance, McCormick and Bresnahan. Left on bases—Chicago, 3; New York, 6. First base on balls—Off Pfeister, 2; off Brown, 1; off Mathewson, 1. First base on error—Chicago. Hit by pitcher—By Pfeister, 1. Struck out—By Mathewson, 7; by Wiltse, 2; by Pfeister, 1; by Brown, 1. Time of game—One hour and forty minutes. Umpires—Messrs. Johnstone and Klem.

October 9, 1908

Ball Makes Triple Play Unassisted.

CLEVELAND, Ohio, July 19.—Cleveland and Boston broke even to-day in the first double-header of the year here, Cleveland winning the first, 6 to 1, and Boston the second, 3 to 2. Ball's playing was a decided feature. He made an unassisted triple play in the second inning, and when he came to bat in the same inning he hit for a home run to deep centre. He had six more put outs than either the first baseman or the catcher. Scores:

FIRST GAME.

CLEVELAND.	AB	R	H	PO	A	BOSTON.	AB	R	H	PO	A
Flick, rf...	4	2	1	0	[illegible]	Niles, lf...	4	0	1	1	[illegible]
Stovall, 1b.	[illegible]	0	1	6	2	Lord, 2b...	4	0	0	1	0
Easterly, c.	4	1	1	6	[illegible]	Speaker, cf	[illegible]	0	0	1	1
H'hman, lf.	3	1	2	1	[illegible]	Gessler, rf..	4	0	1	0	2
Perring, 2b.	[illegible]	0	0	3	3	Wagner, ss.	4	0	1	2	5
Bir'ham, cf.	4	0	2	2	0	Stahl, 1b...	4	1	3	9	0
Bradley, 3b.	4	1	1	0	0	McCon'l, 2b.	2	0	0	4	4
Ball, ss....	4	1	2	[illegible]	2	Donohue, c.	[illegible]	0	1	5	2
Young, p...	3	0	0	0	2	Chech, p...	1	0	0	0	0
						Collins, p..	2	0	1	1	2
Total...	[illegible]	6	10	27	[illegible]	*Welter ...	1	0	0	0	0
						†Gardner ..	1	0	0	0	0
						Total...	[illegible]	1	6	24	16

*Batted for Donohue in ninth inning.
†Batted for Collins in ninth inning.
Errors—Stovall, Ball, Gessler, (2,) Stahl.

Cleveland	1	1	2	0	0	0	0	2	.	—6
Boston	0	0	0	0	0	0	1	0	0	—1

Two-base hit—Ball. Home run—Ball. Sacrifice hits—Perring, McConnell. Sacrifice fly—Hinchman. Stolen bases—Hinchman, McConnell. Double play—Collins and Stahl. Triple play—Ball, (unassisted.) Hits—Off Chech, 6 in three innings; off Collins, 4 in five innings. First base on balls—Off Young, 1; off Chech, 1. Hit by pitched balls—By Young, 1, (Speaker;) by Chech, 1, (Flick.) Struck out—By Young, 2; by Chech, 1; by Collins, 2. Passed ball—Donohue. First base on errors—Cleveland, 3; Boston, 1. Left on bases—Cleveland, 5; Boston, 8. Time of game—One hour and forty-one minutes. Umpires—Messrs. Kerin and Sheridan.

July 20, 1909

Cleveland and St. Louis Divide Double Header, Closing the Season.

ST. LOUIS, Mo., Oct. 9.—Cleveland and St. Louis divided a double-header today, the locals winning the first 5 to 4, and the visitors taking the second 3 to 0. Lajoie got eight hits in eight times at bat. Today's games closed the local season. Scores:

FIRST GAME

ST. LOUIS	AB	R	H	PO	A	CLEVELAND	AB	R	H	PO	A
Tru'd'e 2b..	5	0	0	1	3	Bronkie, 3b	3	1	1	1	1
Cor'den, 3b.	5	2	3	1	1	Graney, lf..	4	1	1	4	0
Stone, lf..	5	0	2	1	0	Jackson, cf.	4	1	2	1	0
Griggs, 1b..	5	1	0	13	1	Lajoie, 2b..	4	1	4	4	1
Wallace, ss..	3	0	1	3	6	East'ly, rf..	4	0	0	1	0
North'n, cf..	4	0	0	2	0	Stovall, 1b.	4	0	2	7	0
H'rtzell, rf..	3	2	1	1	0	Smith, c...	4	0	0	4	1
Stephens, c	3	0	2	4	4	P'k'p'h, ss..	4	0	0	2	6
Nelson, p..	3	0	1	1	6	Brand'g, p..	4	0	0	0	1
Total...	36	5	10	27	21	Total...	35	4	10	24	10

None out when winning run was scored.

Errors—Truesdale, Wallace, Bronkie.

St. Louis	1	1	1	0	0	1	0	0	1	—5
Cleveland	3	1	0	0	0	0	0	0	0	—4

SECOND GAME

CLEVELAND	AB	R	H	PO	A	ST. LOUIS	AB	R	H	PO	A
Bir'h'm, 3b.	4	1	2	1	5	Tr'dale, 2b.	4	0	0	2	0
Graney, lf...	5	2	0	1	0	Cor'den, 3b	4	0	2	3	1
Jackson, cf..	4	0	2	1	0	Stone, lf.....	4	0	1	0	0
Lajoie, 2b....	4	0	4	0	4	Griggs, 1b..	4	0	0	10	0
East'ly, rf...	4	0	0	2	0	Wallace, ss.	3	0	1	1	4
Hn'h'st, 1b..	3	0	1	18	0	North'n, cf.	3	0	0	2	0
McGuire, c..	3	0	0	2	1	H'rtzell, rf..	3	0	1	2	0
P'k'p'h, ss...	4	0	1	2	4	O'Con'er, c.	0	0	0	1	0
Falk'b'g, p..	3	0	0	0	5	Malloy, p....	3	0	0	0	5
						Killifer, c....	3	0	0	6	2
Total...	34	3	10	27	19	Total...	31	0	5	27	12

Eroors—Truesdale, Corriden, Malloy, Graney, (2).

Cleveland	1	0	2	0	0	0	0	0	0	—3
St. Louis	0	0	0	0	0	0	0	0	0	—0

Two-base hits—Jackson, Corriden, Griggs, Graney, Stephens. Three-base hits—Lajoie, Griggs. Sacrifice hit—Stephens. Stolen bases—Bronkie, Stovall, Griggs. Wild pitch—Blanding. Bases on balls—Off Nelson, 1; off Blanding, 4. struck out—By Nelson, 4; by Blanding, 4. Left on bases—St. Louis, 12; Cleveland, 5. Time of game—One hour and forty-two minutes. Umpire—Mr. Evans.

Two-base hits—Birmingham, Corriden. Sacrifice hit—Lajoie. Double plays—Malloy, Truesdale, and Griggs; Lajoie, Peckinpaugh, and Hohnhorst. Passed balls—McGuire, Killifer. Stolen base—Stone. Hit by pitched ball—By Malloy (McGUIRE.(Wild pitch—Malloy. Bases on balls—Off Malloy, 4. Struck out—By Malloy, 6; by Falkenberg, 1. Left on bases—St. Louis, 4; Cleveland, 10. Time of game—One hour and sixteen minutes. Umpire—Mr. Evans.

October 10, 1910

Lajole Leads Cobb In Batting.

CLEVELAND, Ohio, Oct. 9.—By making eight hits in eight times at bat in St. Louis to-day, Napoleon Lajoie of the Cleveland team pulled ahead of Tyrus Cobb of Detroit in the race for the batting championship of the American League. According to the unofficial figures, Lajoie's average now is 386.8 and Cobb's 383.4.

October 10, 1910

COBB'S GREAT RECORD

Detroit Player Leads in Hitting, Run-Getting, and Base-Running.

The official batting averages of the American League were announced last night by President Ban Johnson, and they differ only slightly from unofficial averages of the players already announced. Ty Cobb, the Detroit slugger, of course tops the list with an average of .420, which is only two points short of equaling the league record of .422 made by Lajoie when he was a member of the Philadelphia club in 1901. Second to Cobb is Joe Jackson of Cleveland, who has an average of .408. Birdie Cree is the highest Yankee in the list, and ranks ninth among the batsmen, with an average of .348.

The world's champion Athletics have seven men in the select .300 class, Collins leading with .365. The others are Lapp, .353; "Home Run" Baker, .334; Murphy, .329; McInnes, .321; Coombs, .319, and Lord, .310. Baker, the hero of the World's Series, leads the home-run hitters with a total of nine circuit smashes, while Cobb is close behind him with eight. Jackson of Cleveland had seven home runs, and Ping Bodie of the White Sox, who came into the league heralded as a sensation, had four home runs all season, one of which was made on the Hilltop last Summer.

The Athletics lead the league in club batting, with an average of .299, with Detroit second with .291. The Yankees ranked fifth in team batting, with an average of .270.

Cobb of Detroit also led the league in run-getting, scoring 147 times, and also made the largest number of hits, 248. Of these, 47 were two-base hits and 24 were three-base drives. Cobb is the leader in stolen bases, with a total of 83, and Milan of Washington is second, with 58. Cree of the Yankees is third, with 48 stolen bases.

Other members of the New York team in the .300 class of batters are Chase, .315; Brockett, .308; Wolter, .304, and Dolan, .204.

November 6, 1911

MARQUARD DRIVEN FROM BOX BY CUBS

Giants' Great Pitcher Defeated After Winning Nineteen Successive Games.

THE SCORE:

```
Chicago ...0 2 0 2 0 2 0 1 .—7
New York ...0 0 1 0 1 0 0 0 0—2
```

CHICAGO.

	AB.	R.	H.	PO.	A.	E.
Sheckard, lf	4	0	0	1	0	0
Shulte, rf	4	0	1	1	0	0
Tinker, ss	4	0	0	3	2	0
Zimmerman, 3b	3	1	1	0	3	0
Leach, cf	3	2	1	3	0	0
Saier, 1b	4	3	3	7	1	0
Evers, 2b	2	0	2	1	4	0
Archer, c	3	1	1	11	2	0
Lavender, p	4	0	1	0	2	0
Total	31	7	10	27	13	0

NEW YORK.

	AB.	R.	H.	PO	A.	E.
Snodgrass, lf	2	1	1	0	0	0
Becker, cf	4	1	1	2	1	0
Merkle, 1b	4	0	1	11	0	0
Murray, rf	3	0	0	1	0	0
Herzog, 3b	3	0	0	7	1	0
Meyers, c	3	0	0	1	0	0
Wilson, c	1	0	0	2	0	0
Fletcher, ss	3	0	0	3	3	1
Groh, 2b	3	0	0	3	1	0
Marquard, p	2	0	0	0	0	0
*Devore	1	0	0	1	0	0
Tesreau, p	1	0	0	0	0	0
	30	2	5	24	11	3

*Batted for Marquard in the seventh inning.

Two-base hit—Saier. Three-base hit—Evers. Hits—Off Marquard, 8 in 6 in-

nings; off Tesreau, 2 in 2 innings. Sacrifice hits—Evers, 2. Sacrifice fly—Archer. Double play—Groh to Merkle. Left on bases—Chicago, 6; New York, 5. First base on balls—Off Lavender, 2; off Marquard, 3. Hit by pitcher—By Lavender, (Fletcher, Snodgrass.) Struck out—By Marquard, 5; by Lavender, 7; by Tesreau, 1. Wild pitch—Marquard. Time of game —Two hours and five minutes. Umpires—Messrs. Klem and Bush.

Special to The New York Times.

CHICAGO, Ill., July 8.—Rube Marquard's winning streak was smashed by the Cubs this afternoon, after the great southpaw had annexed nineteen successive victories. The score was 7 to 2, and the Chicago win was due to the timely hitting of the locals, together with their knack of taking advantage of every slip of the visitors.

Rube pitched better ball than the score indicates, although the Cubs scored six of their tallies during the six innings that he was on the mound. The Giants had an off day in the field, booting the pellet around four times, and in addition pulling a "bonehead" play which paved the way for the first Cub counter.

While the home boys were touching up the offerings of the eleven-thousand-dollar pitcher, the New Yorkers were having considerable difficulty in locating the slants served by Jimmy Lavender, who before the Giants had scored their first run had pitched thirty-six consecutive innings of shutout ball. Lavender yielded only five hits, but had trouble finding the pan in the early frames. But he steadied down every time a couple of Giants were on the runways, being assisted by some wonderful support. The Cubs played errorless ball, and in the pinches came through with the marvelous efforts which were needed to check the visitors.

In the third inning Schulte cut down Merkle at the plate with a perfect throw when Fred tried to count on Murray's long single. Archer and Tinker broke up an attempted double steal by Becker and Merkle in the fifth inning by clever headwork and accurate throwing which nipped Merkle at the plate again.

The Cubs were the first to score, getting two runs in the second inning, when Zimmerman and Leach singled at the start.

DETROIT PLAYERS FINED

Each One of Cobb's Sympathizers Must Pay $100 for Striking.

Special to The New York Times.

PHILADELPHIA, Penn., May 21.—All that superfluous language and the forty-eight hour vacation taken by the eighteen members of the Detroit team who endeavored to pursuade fandom that they and not Ban Johnson were running the American League will cost each of them $100 in cash. This is the punishment meeted out to the "strikers" today by President Johnson and the eight owners of the American League Clubs or their representatives. The "strikers" will have to pay $50 each for every day they were loyal to Ty Cobb. Cobb still is under suspension for his attack upon Claude Lucker, the New York fan, whom he attacked in the grand stand, during the game last Wednesday, between the Tigers and the Yankees.

Mr. Johnson left this afternoon for New York to gather evidence of the attack. Before going he intimated that he would be lenient with Cobb. President Navin of the Detroit team, will be unable to keep his promise to the eighteen strikers that the club will pay all fines. When the fines were imposed it was expressly declared that they must be paid by the individual players and not by the club. Navin said he felt no uneasiness over this ruling as he knew the players were with him and that they would stand by him to the end.

Another action, the direct outcome of the baseball strike, was a change in the rules by which the individual clubs hereafter will be held responsible for the action of the fans attending the games. The clubs must take some action to prevent the abuse of players by fans, but it is left to the clubs as to the best method to bring about this result. It is likely that the majority of the clubs will hire special officers who will be stationed in the stands and bleachers during the game and who will have the authority to eject any noisy or abusive fan. Warning posters will be displayed at all American League Parks calling upon the spectators at games to be orderly.

Cobb, who was under suspension at the inauguration of the strike, will not have to pay a fine just yet, but he may be given a little extra fine for appearing on the field in uniform while he was under suspension. "Wild Bill" Donovan, who is ill, also escapes a fine, as does Manager Jennings.

May 22, 1912

Baler then hit to Greh, who would have started an easy double play by tossing to Fletcher, but Hank tried to touch Leach as he ran past him and then hurl to Merkle. Tommy upset the dope by turning back toward first, and the move surprised Groh so much that he clung to the ball until too late to get Zimmerman, who had moved around from second on the play. This stupid move on the part of Groh filled the sacks, with none out, but Marquard promptly fanned the three following batters, although a wild pitch while the third man was at the bat allowed another run to cross.

Lavender walked the first man up in the first two frames, and in the second inning also hit a man after one was down, but in both instances pitched himself out of danger. He started the third by hitting Snodgrass. Becker came through with a single, sending Fred to third. Merkle then hit a hard grounder through the box, which Lavender knocked down after a hard try, and succeeded in running down Snodgrass. This play was a life-saver, as Murray came through with a hit to right, and Becker scored.

The Cubs' two runs in the fourth were made without a hit. A pass, two errors, and two sacrifices were all that was necessary.

Devore batted for Marquard in the seventh, and the crowd yelled in glee at the announcement, for it meant that the Cubs had driven the southpaw from the slab.

Josh fanned, but Snodgrass, Becker, and Merkle singled in succession, the first named counting. At this juncture the Becker-Merkle attempted double steal was queered, and Schulte made a good catch off Murray's bat.

The Giants failed to hit safely in any round except in the ones in which they counted. In the last four innings Lavender retired the side in order and fanned five.

The Cubs got their final runs off Marquard in the sixth on Saler's single, Evers's triple, and Lavender's Texas Leaguer, which Snodgrass kicked against the bleachers and then threw over Meyers's head.

Tesreau succeeded Marquard in the seventh and Wilson displaced Meyers, but the Cubs nicked this new battery for their seventh run on Saler's double, a sacrifice, and a single.

July 9, 1912

SOX CHAMPIONS ON MUFFED FLY

Snodgrass Drops Easy Ball, Costing Teammates $29,514, Boston Winning, 3-2.

GIANTS EXPLODE IN TENTH

Bostonians, Angry at Sox Management, Start Boycott, Keeping Crowd Down to 17,000.

LUCK WITH SOX—FULLERTON

Boston Outguessed and Outgeneraled, He Declares—McGraw Blames Nobody—$490,833 Receipts.

Special to The New York Times.

BOSTON, Mass., Oct. 16.—Write in the pages of world's series baseball history the name of Snodgrass. Write it large and black. Not as a hero; truly not. Put him rather with Merkle, who was in such a hurry that he gave away a National League championship. Snodgrass was in such a hurry that he gave away a world championship. It was because of Snodgrass's generous muff of an easy fly in the tenth inning that the decisive game in the world's series went to the Boston Red Sox this afternoon by a score of 3 to 2, instead of to the New York Giants by a score of 2 to 1.

It is the tenth inning of the eighth game of the series. The score of games is 3 to 3, and the score of this contest is 1 to 1. Mathewson, the veteran, has given the lie to his own announcement that he could never again pitch in such a contest by holding the Red Sox enemy at bay for nine innings in decisive fashion. One run has been made off him, but that has been through the fortunate hit of a youngster who has never faced him before. The regular members of the Boston team have been helpless in the face of his speed and his elusive fadeaway. They have been outfought, outgeneraled, outspeeded, and their only hope is that Wood, who has gone in fresh only two innings before, will hold out until the veteran shall give way to the strain.

Murray Breaks the Tie.

And who is this that comes to the bat for the Giants? 'Tis "Red" Murray—once the hitless. And what does he do? He pierces the mark of one of the smokiest of Wood's shoots and puts the ball far over the head of Speaker into the left field stands. It is a home run hit, but ground rules limit it to two bases. Yet what is the difference? Merkle also sees through the smoke, and the ball which Wood has sent so speedily toward him is returned so fast that Wood can hardly see it as it goes toward centre field. So Murray is in with the run that unties the score, and it only remains for Mathewson to hold himself for one more inning and New York has a world championship and the Giant players the lion's share of the big purse hung up for the players, a difference of $29,514.

Is Mathewson apprehensive as he walks to the box? He is not. All the confidence that was his when the blood of youth ran strong in his supple muscles is his now. Even though the mountainous Engle faces him—this Engle who brought in the two runs of the Red Sox on Monday—he shows not a quiver, and he is right. All that Engle can do with the elusive drop served up is to hoist it high between centre and right fields. Snodgrass and Murray are both within reach of it, with time to spare. Snodgrass yells, "I've got it," and sets himself to take it with ease, as he has taken hundreds of the sort. Murray stops, waiting for the play that will enable him to line the ball joyfully to the infield just to show that his formidable right wing is still in working order.

When the Fly Ball Falls.

While the ball is soaring its leisurely way let us pause for a moment to think what hangs upon that fly.

It is not the 2,000 Giant rooters who are gayly waving their blue and white flags and yelling exultantly over the certain downfall of the foe. It is not the 15,000 Boston fans who have groaned and sat silent, as though at a funeral. A President is forgetting the bitter assaults that have been made upon him. A former President is being eased of his pain by his interest in it. A campaign which may mean a change in the whole structure of the Nation's Government has been put into the background. What happens will be flashed by telegraph the length and breadth of the land, and thereby carried over and under the sea, and millions will be uplifted or downcast.

And now the ball settles. It is full and fair in the pouch of the padded glove of Snodgrass. But he is too eager to toss it to Murray and it dribbles to the ground. Before Snodgrass can hurl the ball to second Engle is perching there.

Mathewson stands in the box, stunned for a moment, then swings his gloved hand in a gesture that is eloquent of his wrath. He has lost none of his courage and determination, but it can be seen as he faces Hooper that there is just a bit of uncertainty in his bearing. Proof comes that he has lost some of his cunning, for Hooper hits the ball so hard that Snodgrass has to sprint and reach to pull down his liner. For Yerkes he cannot put them over at all, and two Red Sox are on the bases.

Three Giants Let It Drop.

And now that something which upsets a ball team—which McGraw has called an explosion—becomes evident. Speaker pops up a high foul near first base, and Merkle, Meyers, and Mathewson converge on it with none collected enough to say which shall take it, and it drops among them. The three who have made the mess walk to the box arguing, Mathewson saying things which he emphasizes with angry gestures.

Now the Boston throng calls for the blood of the veteran—and gets it.

His control is gone, and Speaker, saved by a blunder, hammers the ball hard to right field, and Engle is over the plate. Lewis stands still while four bad ones pass him, and then Gardner steps up and puts all his weight against the ball, and it goes far out to Devor, too far for him to stop Yerkes with the winning run, even though his throw comes true as a bullet.

Too bad! Too bad! The world championship belongs in New York and Boston is perfectly aware of it. Here as well as there admiration is ungrudging for a team that could come from behind, win two decisive victories on its gameness, and deserve two in a third, and sympathy is widespread for a gallant pitcher and his gallant mates, who were cheated of their triumph by a bit of bravado. After the game the Red Sox rooters gave hearty cheers "for the best player on the Giants' team—Snodgrass."

Most of all the sympathy is due to Mathewson. Three times he has given prodigally of his waning vigor to bring the world championship to New York, and three times he has deserved victory, but has had it denied because his team has failed to play its real game behind him. What it meant to him to pitch the game to-day he only knows.

As he sat in the corridor of his hotel this morning it could be seen that he had little left to give. The skin was drawn tightly over the bone on his jaw and chin, and in his hollowed cheeks the furrows that have been graven by hard campaigns of recent years were startling in their depth. As he warmed up his gauntness was evident, and the Boston fans gloated over the thought that he could not long stand the rush of their sluggers.

Yet up to that disastrous tenth he was "Big Six" at his best. His fast ball shot with a thud into the glove of Meyers, his drop shot down in front of the batters and his fadeaway had the best of them, breaking their backs. Now and again he seemed in trouble, and the Boton rooters yelled that he was going, but no sign of a crack appeared, and only eight safe hits were made off him in the ten periods.

THE OFFICIAL SCORE

BOSTON.	AB.	R.	H.	TB.	SO.	BB.	SH.	SB.	LB.	TC.	PO.	A.	E.
Hooper, rf.	5	0	0	0	0	0	0	0	0	3	3	0	0
Yerkes, 2b	4	1	1	1	1	1	0	0	0	3	0	3	0
Speaker, cf.	4	0	2	2	1	1	0	0	2	3	2	0	1
Lewis, lf.	4	0	0	0	1	1	0	0	2	1	1	0	0
Gardner, 3b	3	0	1	2	0	1	1	0	0	7	1	4	2
Stahl, 1b	4	1	2	3	1	0	0	0	2	16	15	0	1
Wagner, ss.	3	0	1	1	0	1	0	0	2	9	3	5	1
Cady, c.	4	0	0	0	0	0	0	0	0	8	5	3	0
Bedient, p.	2	0	0	0	0	0	0	0	0	1	0	1	0
Wood, p.	0	0	0	0	0	0	0	0	0	2	0	2	0
*Henriksen	1	0	1	2	0	0	0	0	1	0	0	0	0
†Engle	1	1	0	0	0	0	0	0	0	0	0	0	0
Total	35	3	8	11	4	5	1	0	9	53	30	18	5

NEW YORK.	AB.	R.	H.	TB.	SO.	BB.	SH.	SB.	LB.	TC.	PO.	A.	E.
Devore, rf.	3	1	1	1	0	2	0	1	2	5	3	1	0
Doyle, 2b	5	0	0	0	0	0	0	0	0	7	1	5	1
Snodgrass, cf.	4	0	1	1	0	1	0	0	2	5	4	1	1
Murray, lf.	5	1	2	4	0	0	0	0	1	3	3	0	0
Merkle, 1b	5	0	1	1	1	0	0	0	1	10	10	0	0
Herzog, 3b	5	0	2	3	1	0	0	0	2	3	2	1	0
Meyers, c.	3	0	0	0	0	1	1	0	2	5	4	1	0
Fletcher, ss.	3	0	1	1	1	0	0	0	1	5	2	3	0
Shafer, ss.	0	0	0	0	0	0	0	0	0	0	0	0	0
Mathewson	4	0	1	1	1	0	0	0	0	3	0	3	0
‡McCormick	1	0	0	0	0	0	0	0	0	0	0	0	0
Total	38	2	9	12	4	4	1	1	11	46	§29	15	2

Boston	0	0	0	0	0	0	1	0	0	2—3
New York	0	0	1	0	0	0	0	0	0	1—2

Two-base hits—Gardner, Stahl, Henriksen, Murray, (2,) Herzog. First base on errors—Boston, 1; New York, 1. Struck out—By Bedient, 2; by Wood, 2; by Mathewson, 4. Bases on balls—Off Bedient, 3; off Wood, 1; off Mathewson, 5. Hits—Off Bedient, 6 in 7 innings, (at bat, 26;)* off Wood, 3 in 3 innings, (at bat, 12.) Sacrifice fly—Gardner. Left on bases—Boston, 9; New York, 11.

Umpire in chief, Mr. O'Loughlin; umpire on bases, Mr. Rigler; left field umpire, Mr. Klem; right field umpire, Mr. Evans.

Time of game—Two hours and thirty-seven minutes.

It was in the first inning that he showed what he meant to do. Yerges, second up, fanned on a fadeaway. Speaker got to second on an error by Dovie, but Lew's went out on three pitched balls. With two on bases in the second and one out, he made Carly pop up, and Trident went a grounder to Doyle. In the third he sent the Red Sox to the field with three pitched balls.

So he went along to the seventh, holding the game as he wished, and it was only in this round that two hits were bunched on him. That luck had some part here cannot be denied. Stahl got on with a pop up, which first eluded the rush of Murray, Snodgrass, and Doyle. Wagner walked, but it seemed as though nothing would come of it when "Big Six" with two out had fooleld Henriksen, who was batting for Bedient, twice on strikes and had started a fadeaway over the plate. Henriksen had never faced him before and was not at all familiar with the fadeaway, but his bat happened to connect with the ball as he made a wide swing, and the sphere shot over third base for a double, bringing in Stahl. The ball was rapidly curving over the foul line, and six inches more of this deflection would have made the hit vain.

In the eighth and ninth the Sox hit him hard, but could not place the ball out of reach of the Giant fielders. In the fatal tenth the whole Boston side should have been put out on flies and none should have reached first base.

Yet credit must not be denied to young Bedient. When he went to the box Gardner, Stahl, and Cady were as solicitous for his welfare as though he were an only child with the croup. After each ball in the early innings, Gardner walked in and told him pleasant things and soothed him, and on frequent occasions the others added their attentions. It was made evident before the game had gone very far, however, that others on the Red Sox team were in far greater need of an anchor than he.

Whatever nervousness he might have had at first, it was not long before both his feet were firmly planted on the ground and he refused to let them be lifted. He was dangerously wild at times, but in the pinches he was as cool as the east wind that wafted its chilling way across the field. At first he was exceedingly deliberate in his work, but as the game went on he took things calmly and pitched almost as fast as Mathewson. His departure from the box after the seventh inning was a matter of batting strategy, not of necessity.

The one run scored against him in the third inning had in it elements of luck and misfortune. He let Devore walk to first, but a double play would have been possible had not Gardner, too intent for watching him, fumbled Foyle's swift grounder. Murray's drive to left centre which scored Devore was just missed by Speaker, his fingers touching the ball. In the fourth Bedient showed his class. With Herzog on third and only one out he forced Fletcher, who had made a safe hit the first time up, and Mathewson to send up high flies.

Wood, who went to the box in the eighth, gave promise at first showing the form of the first two games he won in the ninth. However, the Giants showed that they could find his smoke ball, and in the tenth they made it plainly evident that he could not last long. Murray's drive was one of the hardest hits of the series, and Merkle's fairly sizzled. Meyers sent one of the same sort to the Box, and it was simply good fortune that Wood's bare hand found itselt in the way. He gave plain indication of distress and was legally out of the game. Engle having batted for him in the last half of the tenth. Collins was warming up to take his place when the Giants exploded.

At the bat, in the field and in the baserunning the Giants excelled. They got nine hits off Bedient and Wood to eight off Mathewson, in the error column they showed up two to five and in the baserunning they were fast, while the Sox at times were slow and blundering.

In the error-making Garnder was the worst offender. He made a bad mess of a slow tap by Meyers in the second, the ball being right in his hand. He was equally bad on an attempted double steal in the same inning when he muffed a perfect throw by Wagner to cut down the Indian. he contributed another on Doyle's drive in the third when he missed the double play.

After that he settled down and was in the game whenever opportunity offered. Wagner also was an offender, dropping a fine throw by Cady to head off a steal by Snodgrass. Stahl contributed the fifth Red Sox bungle in the seventh, when he badly misjudged a high foul and let it get away from him.

On the Giants' side Doyle erred in the first inning, when he muffed a perfect throw by Dovore to catch Speaker, who was trying to stretch a long single. The other was made by Snodgrass. Nothing more need be said. He will miss the $1,283 it cost him.

Mixed in with the errors were some fine plays. The best of all was the catch of Hooper of a high drive from Doyle's bat, which was going for a home run into the bleachers back, of right field. He picked it out of the air with a jump and almost fell over the low fence.

Fletcher made a startling play in the second. On a hard hit by Stahl with Wagner on first, Doyle threw wildly to the shortstop on the bag. Fletcher dived forward and retrieved the ball, jamming his foot on the bag just before Gardner rushed into it. On the base paths the worst exhibition was that of Yerkes. He was on third when Speaker started a steal from first. Meyers whipped the ball to Mathewson, and he shot it to Herzog, and Yerkes was nipped by feet.

A peculiar piece of hard-luck for the Giants resulted from a protest that had been made by Manager McGraw. In Saturday's game Lewis scored one of the Red Sox runs because of a triple he drove into a blind alley off the left field to bleachers. McGraw insisted that thereafter such a hit should be good for only two bases, and the rule was made. Herzog, in the fourth with nobody out, drove a vicious ball into this same alley, and was waved back to second after easily getting to the third sack. He did not get home, as he probably would have except for McGraw's protest. With his run scored the series would have been won by the Giants in the ninth, for there would have been no fatal tenth inning.

The setting for the most stirring finish of a world championship in the history of baseball was not calculated to be inspiring. Little would one have thought that such an event was taking place in one of the best baseball cities in the country. There was an atmosphere of dreariness about the affair. The ramshackle structures of the Boston field, the rusty grass interspersed with dry patches did not look good to one who had been used to the glories of the Brush Stadium. The sun shone brightly, but the east wind was chilly.

The Royal Rooters were not there. Offended by the neglect to recognize their unwavering loyalty by providing seats for them the day before they boycotted the game and their influence was shown by the fact that thousands of others did the same thing.

Then, too, there was a general feeling among the Boston roofers that the series had been lost by the routs of Monday and Tuesday. One could scarcely find one this morning who believed that the Red Sox could stop the rush of the Giants. Mixed with this was some worse feeling. There had been many rumors afloat of trouble among the Red Sox. It was said that Wood on the train coming from

New York on Monday had accused O'Brien of deliberately giving his game to the Giants, and that they had engaged in a fight which accounted for the inability of Wood to win his third victory. According to a local newspaper report charges were widely made among fans that the management of the Boston's had deliberately sent O'Brien in to be slaughtered for the purpose of swelling their income from the series. At all such things the persons responsible for baseball here scoffed, but they had their effect in keeping down the attendance.

Of the 17,000 odd who were present, however, many were loyal to the team and were quite willing to show it when the occasion arose. The management of the club helped them to make noise by distributing thousands of rattles, which, when beaten together or on the backs of seats, set up a chorus like that of giant crickets. At times this noise was weird in the extreme.

When the game was over there was no Royal Rooters' band to lead a zigzag procession and no delirious outburst. Hundreds of fans, however, made a rush on the Boston bench, where they cooped the players in almost suffocating confinement and insisted on cheering them again and again, not even forgetting Snodgrass of the Giants.

Here the only really violent incident of the hard-fought series occurred. After

the game was finished Manager McGraw ran over to the Red Sox bench to shake hands with Manager Stahl and congratulate him on his victory and sportsmanship. A Boston fan, rushing from behind, ran into him and almost tipped him into the bench pit. McGraw turned and in saving himself half pushed, half struck the man. There was a bit of excitement for a moment, but good feeling was running too high for anything serious to happen, and the Giants' manager was able to pay his courtesies and escape.

Boston has shown no great jubilation to-night over the victory. What it wanted was proof of the superiority of the Red Sox, not a championship handed to them as a gift. Fans admit that the Sox were played to a standstill and that no large honor accrues to them. Beyond the cheering at the grounds there has been no demonstration in the city.

Mayor Fitzgerald, however, is determined that the team shall have some recognition. After the game he went to the clubhouse and congratulated Manager Stahl and President McAleer and suggested that a big dinner be given to the team. This was declined because the men were anxious to get away and take up other affairs. There will be instead a parade to-morrow morning from the ball park to Faneuil Hall and addresses there at noon.

October 17, 1912

Federal Ball League Formed

INDIANAPOLIS, Ind., March 8. — John T. Powers of Chicago was elected President of the Federal League of Baseball Clubs here late this afternoon. The organization was incorporated under the laws of Indiana earlier in the day. Other officers are: M.R. Bramley, Cleveland, Vice President; James A. Ross, Indianapolis, Secretary, and John A. George, Indianapolis, Treasurer. The Board of

Managers is composed of: William T. McCullough, Pittsburgh; Michael Kinney, St. Louis; Charles X. Zimmerman, Cleveland; John A. Spinney, Cincinnati; James A. Ross, John A. George, and John S. Powell, Indianapolis, and Charles L. Sherlock, Chicago. Each club will be required to post a forfeit of $5,000 before the opening of the season, which is scheduled to take place between May 10 and May 15. It was announced that the Indianapolis club would be incorporated Tuesday with a capital of $100,000.

March 9, 1913

JOHNSON'S GREAT PITCHING RECORD

Figures Prove Latest Performance the Best in Recent Years.

A sigh of regret echoed the length and breadth of the baseball world on Thursday last when word was flashed that Walter Johnson's second notable effort of the season to hang up a world's record of consecutive pitching victories had been broken just at a time when it seemed that the king of pitchers was destined to achieve success. Bill Carrigan's hit, that barely went over the Washington infield, brought to a close one of the greatest pitching performances of baseball history, at the same time showing Johnson greater in defeat than in victory. But Walter Johnson needs no records of consecutive victories to establish beyond doubt his title as the greatest pitcher of modern days, undoubtedly the greatest game has produced.

Last year Johnson hung up a record of sixteen consecutive wins, a mark also made last year by Joe Wood, and now standing as the best performance since the American League branched out as a major league organization. In the National League Rube Marquard's 1912 performance of nineteen straight stands as the mark for aspiring moundsmen to shoot

at. But neither the memorable run of the New York southpaw nor the performances of Wood and Johnson a year ago show any such figures as were compiled by Johnson in his recent run of victories. He fell two games short of his 1912 mark, but in achievement he far excelled his previous run.

That the best pitched game of ball shown in either major league this season was the one which could not carry Johnson along on his winning streak is an example of the irony of fate in toying with ball tossers. No such pitching performance as Johnson showed last Thursday was shown by the Senatorial marvel while he was compiling his run of victories, yet he went down to defeat with it, and his chance of establishing a new mark for consecutive wins is gone, for the present year at least. Johnson will undoubtedly close the year with the best pitching record, counted by games won and lost, in either league, and he will carry the distinction of two successive runs of victories—eleven the first time and fourteen the second—which in themselves constitute a record in later day baseball. But the time is too short for Johnson or any other pitcher to hang up a new mark during 1913.

Every run of victories has its share of luck for the player or team most interested, and there is no denying that Johnson did not escape. Against Cleveland on Aug. 8 the Naps had Washington 3 to 2 when the Senators went to bat in the ninth inning. Johnson was taken out of the game when it came his turn to bat, and Alva Williams was sent in as a pinch hitter. Williams delivered the hit and Germany Schaefer was put in as runner for Williams, ultimately scoring the run which tied up the game. It was won in the same inning when Moeller followed Williams over the plate.

But luck was the exception, and not the rule, while the Washington speed marvel was adding up one victory after another. Hard luck, or misfortune, was

a bit more prominent than the so-called luck of baseball. In two months of play, over which Johnson's great winning streak extended, his two finest efforts in pitching went for nothing. On July 25 he pitched eleven and one-third innings of a game that went fifteen innings against St. Louis, holding the Browns to a single run, and striking out sixteen batsmen in that time. He went into the game with Washington one run behind, and even this high-class performance was not sufficient to bring him a victory. The game was called with the teams deadlocked, 8 to 8. On Aug. 28, when Johnson turned in the best pitching performance of the year, allowing three hits and fanning ten men in eleven innings, he suffered a shutout and saw his winning streak broken.

A close analysis of the figures shows just how wonderful Johnson was in that winning streak. On June 25 Walter was knocked out of the box by the Athletics in four innings, during which time a double, three singles, and a home run by Frank Baker put the coming champions on the road to an easy victory. Two days later Johnson came back at the same team, the hardest hitting club in either league, held them to three hits, and scored a shutout victory, 2 to 0. That was the start of his long run which culminated on Thursday last in the eleven-inning defeat by the Red Sox. Between these two defeats there was one pitching classic after another.

In some of the games Johnson did not have to go the full route, being taken out when the game was safely packed away by the Senators. Including his tie game against St. Louis and his defeat by Boston last Thursday, as both are part of Johnson's wonderful work since he began his now-broken winning streak, the Washington star figured in 127 1-3 innings, just a shade more than fourteen nine-inning games. In that time Johnson allowed only eighteen runs, an average of less than 1 1-3 runs to each nine-inning game. He was reached for eighty-two hits, an average of less than six hits per game, and as Johnson is a heady pitcher, who does not go after strike-outs unless pressed, the hit record of his opponents is more to be marveled at than would ordinarily be the case.

Johnson gave sixteen bases on balls in fourteen full games, showing that the wonderful speed is not the only asset of his great success. He struck out seventy-eight batsmen, less than six to each game.

The record is all the more remarkable in view of the fact that the batting ability of Johnson's own team, which really plays a prominent part in every pitcher's winning or losing, is not of high ranking. Every team in the National League and four of the eight teams in the American League rank above the Senators in batting strength, only the Browns, Yankees and White Sox being lower in team batting than Griffith's team. This was a handicap that Johnson had to battle against in game after game, requiring pitching that was next to the shutout brand. He had to go fifteen innings to beat Ray Collins, 1 to 0, on July 3, and in eight of the sixteen games tabulated below the Senators scored two runs or less while Johnson was in the box. In some of these games Johnson did not work the full nine innings, but was called upon to work with the score close. Six of the four-

teen games which Johnson won were decided by a single run over the regulation nine-inning period or longer, and another was a 1 to 1 tie for nine innings, with Washington getting four runs in the tenth.

On Aug. 2 Johnson celebrated his sixth anniversary as a major leaguer, and each succeeding year sees him add more glory to himself and his team. Three years ago the baseball world suspected that Johnson carried more natural ability than any other pitcher in the game. To-day every baseball fan is certain that the Washington speed marvel stands first among the pitchers. Such pitching as he has shown during the present season, considered from the standpoint of effectiveness alone, and with no consideration of consecutive victories, far excels the work of any other pitcher of recent years. The dim past may carry some records that in black figures look better than what Johnson has done this season, but few present-day fans will believe that the pitching equal of the Washington star ever graced the diamond.

Following are the pitching records of Johnson since he began his winning streak on June 27, including his eleven-inning defeat at Boston during the last

week. The scores given are not the full scores of games in every instance, simply showing the number of runs scored by Washington while Johnson occupied the box. The other columns, in order, show the runs scored off Johnson, the number of innings he pitched, with the bases on balls and strike-outs in each game. The figures:

Washington.

Date. Runs.	Runs.	Innings.	Hits.	Strike-outs. BB.	
June 27—2 Phila.	0	1	4	1	6
June 30—1 Boston	1	4	1	2	4
July 3—1 Boston	0	15	15	1	4
July 9—7 Detroit	0	6	2	1	1
July 13—5 Cleveland	4	9	10	0	6
July 17—2 St. Louis	0	1	1	0	0
July 18—5 St. Louis	1	4	0	0	3
July 21—2 Chicago	1	9	4	2	5
July 25—2 St. Louis	1	11½	7	3	16
Aug. 2—3 Detroit	2	9	9	1	4
Aug. 6—6 Detroit	0	4	1	0	3
Aug. 8—4 Cleveland	3	9	7	3	5
Aug. 15—5 Detroit	2	7	6	1	0
Aug. 19—5 Cleveland	1	10	7	1	5
Aug. 24—2 Cleveland	1	9	6	0	6
Aug. 28—0 Boston	1	11	3	0	10
56	18	127½	82	16	78

August 31, 1913

BASEBALL SALARIES REACH TOP MARK

Federal League's Promise of $75,000 to Cobb for 5 Years' Play Is Banner Offer.

The high-water mark in the frenzied finance of baseball was reached with the Federal League's big offer to "Ty" Cobb of $15,000 a year for five years. Cobb last year was the highest salaried outfielder in the game, receiving $12,000 from Detroit. He has assured President Navin of the Tigers that he will sign a contract for next year, stating in a recent communication that he was satisfied with the terms of last year's contract.

Cobb has always been a bone of contention on the Detroit team, and on more than one occasion has sulked and had to be humored before he would consent to come back into the fold. As he is in baseball for the money, as he has stated often before, it would not be surprising if Cobb used the Federal League offer as a means to obtain more money from the Tigers. But it isn't supposed that he will take the Federal's offer seriously.

The recent activity of the outlaw league in threatening to invade the territory of the major league clubs has given an artificial impetus to the sal-

aries of baseball players. Experienced baseball men say that the high salaries which are now being offered are absurd, in contrast to the profits made in baseball, and that when the reaction comes the result will be the loss of a great deal of money by club owners. The only baseball clubs which really make money from season to season are those which are in the first three positions in the pennant race. A losing team does not draw crowds in its home city or on the road.

During the past few years club owners have been trying to outdo each other in paying abnormal prices for baseball players. Since the days when Boston gave $10,000 to Chicago for catcher Mike Kelly, the price of players has soared until it now reaches a stage when Cobb is promised $75,000 for five years' service on the diamond. During the Brotherhood trouble and during the American League raid, the value of baseball players jumped considerably, and the price has been going up ever since. At the time of the Brotherhood war, the National League had a monthly salary limit of $2,000 a month. There is no salary limit in the major leagues now, and in the International League, the leading minor organization, the salary limit is $6,000, $4,000 more than the salary limit of the National League in 1888.

Club owners nowadays have become so reckless that they take a gambler's chance in purchasing players. Sometimes the player is worth what is paid for him, but oftentimes he fails to come up to the value that is placed upon him. In the case of "Rube" Marquard, for whom New York paid $11,000, the pitcher was carried by the

club for a few seasons before he showed any real merit. In the case of "Lefty" Russell, for whom Connie Mack paid $12,000, the pitcher failed to measure up to major league calibre and was shipped back to the minors. Larry Chappelle, for whom the White Sox paid $18,000, has not yet shown anything like that value.

Joe Tinker is the latest example of the uncertainty of baseball deals. Tinker was sold by Cincinnati to Brooklyn for $25,000, the largest amount ever involved in the purchase of a single player. Tinker refused to abide by the transaction and jumped to the Federal League, whereby the Brooklyn Club is running a chance of losing $15,000 on the transaction. At best the deal will probably involve much litigation and trouble before final settlement of the Tinker matter is made. Tinker's reported arrangement with the Federal League is another example of the frenzied condition of baseball finance. He has been promised $30,000 for three years, and $15,000 of this is already supposed to be in a Chicago bank in Tinker's name, and that he is now drawing the interest on this deposit. Otto Knabe is also supposed to have received $7,000 of his three years' guarantee. Minor Brown also says that he has received part of his St. Louis Federal League salary in advance. If this state of affairs is true, it is contrary to the business principles of baseball, and the leveler heads of the game predict that it is sure to result in a financial smash.

Last year, Cobb refused to sign a contract unless Detroit gave him $15,000 a year salary. President Navin replied to Cobb's demands by showing him that, although he was one of the

greatest drawing cards of the game, the amount of money taken in by the Detroit Club would not warrant paying any one man such a large amount. So Cobb finally consented to take $12,000. There are several players who receive almost as much as that. Mathewson of the Giants and Wagner of the Pirates have been $10,000 men for several seasons, and they have been worth it. Walter Johnson is said to receive $10,000 from Washington.

Last year, when Detroit was having trouble signing Cobb, Clarke Griffith of Washington startled the baseball world by saying that the Washington Club would be willing to buy Cobb from Detroit for $100,000. This offer, however, was not taken seriously by any one, but Griffith pointed out that Cobb would bring back much of this money in the advertising the club would receive. Connie Mack says that Eddie Collins is worth $100,000 to the Athletics. Pittsburgh paid $22,500 for Pitcher Marty O'Toole, but the Pirate twirler has not shown that he was worth the price as a player. Pittsburgh, however, did not lose much by the investment, because O'Toole has been a big attraction everywhere Pittsburgh plays. There is no sport in the world which gets the publicity that baseball receives, and clubowners are quick to see this, and know that any deal which involves a large amount of money will get countrywide attention. This is the principle on which the Federal League has been working, and they have made known only the deals which involve large purchase prices or large salaries. They say nothing of their attempts to sign players to make up the rank and file of the eight clubs.

January 18, 1914

Ty Cobb Versus Walter Johnson

Walter Johnson has faced Cobb in the capacity of pitcher just 133 times, and of that many times at bat the champion batsman of the American League has been sent back to the bench 100 times hitless, the gentleman from Georgia falling to swat the ball in his usual consistent and blithesome manner when facing the consistent Mr. Johnson. Now Walter Johnson has the honor of being about the only hurler to hold the fiery Cobb, the champion batsman of the Tigers and the world, in subjugation. In the 133 times that Cobb faced the Washington start he made 31 base hits, 9 runs; just 6 of the hits were better than singles, consisting of three doubles and three triples. These figures give Cobb a batting average for the eight seasons he has maintained a calling acquaintance with Mr. Johnson of 233.

May 30, 1915

Ty Cobb was one of the greatest hitters of all time. His base stealing record stood until Maury Wills broke it in the 1960's.

(United Press International)

Detroit Beats Cleveland

DETROIT, Oct. 3.—Detroit, playing its last game of the season, defeated Cleveland 6 to 5, and established an American League record. The Tigers won 100 games this year, something no club in the league, which finished in second place, had previously accomplished. Cobb also set a base stealing record. His theft of second base in the second inning gave him an unofficial total of ninety-seven stolen sacks. The Tigers won the game in the eighth when Burns scored on Dubuc's sacrifice fly. Score:

DETROIT.	AB	R	H	PO	A	CLEVELAND.	AB	R	H	PO	A
Bush, ss	5	2	2	2	4	Wille, lf	4	1	2	2	0
Vitt, 3b	4	0	1	2	2	Ch'an, ss	4	1	2	2	7
Cobb, cf	3	0	2	1	0	Roth, cf	5	0	1	1	0
Veach, lf	4	0	0	0	0	Smith, rf	5	1	1	2	0
C'ford, rf	4	0	0	1	0	Kirke, 1b	5	0	2	14	0
Burns, 1b	4	2	3	12	0	H'bare, 3b	4	1	0	1	2
Young, 2b	4	0	1	2	4	T'rner, 2b	4	0	0	0	2
McKee, c	4	1	3	7	1	O'Neil, c	4	2	2	2	3
'leskie, p	2	1	1	0	5	Klepfer, p	3	0	1	0	2
†Moriarty	1	0	0	0	0	*W'gans	1	0	0	0	0
James, p	0	0	0	0	2	Jones, p	0	0	0	0	2
Dubuc, p	0	0	0	0	0						
Total	35	6	13	27	17	Total	38	5	12	24	18

*Batted for Klepfer in the eighth inning.
†Batted for Coveleskie in the sixth inning.
Errors—Roth, Smith, Kirke, Veach.

Detroit .... 1 3 1 0 0 0 0 1 0—6
Cleveland .... 0 0 0 1 2 1 0 1 0—5

Three-base hit—Smith. Stolen bases—Bush, Cobb, O'Neil. Earned runs—Cleveland, 4; Detroit, 2. Sacrifice fly—Dubuc. Double plays—Turner, Chapman and Kirke; Cobb, Bush and McKee. Left on bases—Cleveland, 9; Detroit, 7. Bases on balls—Off Klepfer, 1; off Coveleskie, 1. First base on errors—Detroit, 1. Hits—Off Coveleskie, 10 in 6 innings; off Hames, 2 in 2 innings; off Dubuc, 0 in 1 inning; off Klepfer, 11 in 7 innings; off Jones, 2 in 1 inning. Struck out—By Klepfer, 2; by Coveleskie, 4; by James, 1. Umpires—Messrs. Wallace and Evans. Time of game—One hour and forty-five minutes.

October 4, 1915

LONG BASEBALL WAR IS SETTLED

Federal League Passes Out of Existence—Contract Jumpers Reinstated.

BEST PLAYERS TO BE SOLD

Major Leagues Agree to Reimburse Ward Interests in Brooklyn—New Owners for Cubs and Browns.

CINCINNATI, Dec. 22.—The most disastrous war that the baseball game has ever experienced came to a close here tonight when a treaty of peace between the Federal League and both parties to the national baseball agreement, known as Organized Baseball, was signed. The war has lasted about two years.

Two major league clubs will change hands as the result of the bringing about of peace and two new faces will be seen among major league club owners in the future. Charles H. Weeghman, who has been President of the Chicago Federal League Club, will purchase the controlling interest in the Chicago National League team from Charles P. Taft of Cincinnati. Philip Ball and his associates, who were connected with the St. Louis Federal League team, gain control of the St. Louis American League Club from Robert Hedges, John E. Bruce, and others, who have long been connected with major league circles.

Contract Jumpers Reinstated.

The agreement gives immunity to all men who have jumped their contracts from both the major and minor leagues of Organized Baseball, as well as all other Federal League players. All of them have been reinstated or made eligible to Organized Baseball.

That there will be a wild scramble for some of the best Federal League players was clearly indicated by a provision in the treaty that the Federal League, as a league, and which, in so far as actual baseball playing is concerned, ceases to exist, will assume all of the contracts of Federal League players.

In this connection rumors flew thick and fast here tonight regarding the future status of a number of Federal League players. One of these, despite the lack of confirmation, was that Benny Kauff of the Brooklyn Federal League team would be seen next season in a Giant uniform.

Semi-officially it became known that several former Federal players will be seen in the New York American League club.

The agreement does not go into the distribution of any players, and it was announced that the bars have been thrown down, and that inasmuch as all are eligible, those who are for sale will probably go to the highest bidder.

The Federal League clubs in Chicago and St. Louis are excepted, inasmuch as Weeghman and Ball will be permitted to keep what players they desire of the Federal League clubs in these cities.

Major Leagues to Pay Wards $400,000.

The announcement concerning the reimbursement of the Ward interests in the Brooklyn Federal League Club was short. It was:

"The Ward interests will be reimbursed, both major leagues assuming this responsibility."

There was no announcement of any figures in respect to this, but it is unofficially, though authoritatively, stated it will be $400,000, payable at the rate of $20,000 a year.

These five principal conditions took little time of the meeting, which extended over two days. The chief stumbling block in the way of a quick decision to have peace was the International League. Two propositions were concerned. One was that the Buffalo Federal League club wanted to be consolidated with the Buffalo International League club, but the International League would not agree to this.

Dunn Claims Baltimore Territory.

The other was relative to the Baltimore Federal League Park. Jack Dunn of the Richmond, Va., team has for some time, according to President E. G. Barrow of the International League, been considered as having the legitimate right to an International League franchise in Baltimore when peace was declared. Dunn appeared here today and demanded this right, and, it was reported, made an offer for the Federal League grounds. The Federal League made a counter proposition, but the difference in the two figures was so wide that no agreement was reached.

However, in order not to delay the signing of the treaty of peace, it was mutually agreed by all of the conferees at today's session that a committee be appointed with full power to act in settling both of these questions relative to the International League.

Following the appointing of this committee the conferees made quick work of the remainder of the business, and shortly before 6 o'clock tonight they announced that all of the provisions of the treaty of peace had been agreed to; that the lawyers were then drawing up the document and putting it into legal form and that it would be signed as soon as this was completed.

Those who signed the agreement were August Herrmann, Chairman of the National Commission; President John K. Tener of the National League, President B. B. Johnson of the American League, President James A. Gilmore of the Federal League, President Charles Weeghman of the Chicago Federal League Club, Harry N. Sinclair of the Newark Federal League Club, Secretary J. H. Farrell of the National Association, President Edward G. Barrow

of the International League, and President Thomas Chivington of the American Association.

Anti-Trust Suit to be Withdrawn.

When asked what disposition would be made of the suit of the Federal League against organized baseball charging violation of the anti-trust law, now pending before Judge Landis in Chicago, President Tener of the National League, acting as spokesman, said: "The suit will be withdrawn."

Mr. Weeghman, who will become the new owner of the Chicago Cubs, intended to leave tonight for Texas to make the final transfer, as Mr. Taft is on a hunting trip there. He changed his mind at the last moment, however, and will see Mr. Taft on Jan. 4 on his return to this city.

The meeting of the committee to take up the International League question will be held here in conjunction with the annual meeting of the National Commission on Jan. 3 next.

It was announced late tonight that all suits pertaining to baseball pending in any court would be withdrawn in the next day or two.

When asked tonight as to the future status of Roger Bresnahan, Charles H. Weeghman, who will purchase the Cubs, said:

"I don't know what disposition will be made of Bresnahan. Tinker, of course, will be our manager, and that

> ### Five Principal Conditions In Baseball Peace Terms
>
> Chicago Nationals and St. Louis Americans to be sold to Federal League club owners.
>
> Reinstatement of all players who have jumped their contracts.
>
> Federal League players, excepting those of Chicago and St. Louis clubs, to be sold to highest bidders.
>
> Federal League club owners to assume all contracts of their players.
>
> National and American Leagues to reimburse Ward interests.

is as far as I have taken up the question of players."

The National Commission issued a statement tonight praising the attitude that was taken during the entire negotiations by President Gilmore of the Federal League.

"He has played the game with the cards on the table, and has been fair in every respect," said the statement.

Philip Ball, who gains control of the St. Louis Americans, stated tonight that Fielder Jones would be the new manager of the team. Inasmuch as Branch Rickey's contract as manager of the St. Louis Americans expired last season, nothing definite was officially announced about him, but rumors had it he would retire from the league.

A majority of those who attended the meeting here departed for their homes tonight, following the adjournment of the conference.

December 23, 1915

INDIANS WEAR NUMBERS

Players Carry Them on Sleeves for First Time in Baseball History.

CLEVELAND, Ohio, June 26.—Cleveland American League players wore numbers on the sleeves of their uniforms in today's game with Chicago for the first time in the history of baseball so far as is known. The numbers corresponded to similar numbers set opposite the players' names on the score cards, so that all fans in the stands might easily identify the members of the home club.

June 27, 1916

BRAVES END FLARE OF GIANTS' METEOR

McGraw's Men Win First Game, the Twenty-sixth Straight, and Then Fall.

BOSTON BATS ARE VICIOUS

Multitude of 38,000 Sadly Watches Visitors Pile Up Five Runs in Seventh and Win 8 to 3.

The Giants lost a game, not an unusual happening in the routine of baseball, but it filled with grief 38,000 spectators at the Polo Grounds yesterday. From every quarter of the big city hero worshippers flocked to the baseball park firm in the belief that the machine built up by John McGraw would remain invincible. The belief grew to conviction after the first game of the doubleheader with Boston, in which the Braves were shut out and the twenty-sixth straight victory perched on the home team's banner by the score of 4 to 0. Then came a shock great as the fall of Troy, when the heavy hitters from the Hub came back in the second with a terrific bombardment which buried the Giants under an avalanche of eight runs, to three collected by the home contingent.

It was hard for the immense crowd to realize that an end had come to the remarkable winning streak, which has gained more renown for the local team than would be achieved by the winning of a brace of pennants. Every club in the National League had been met and conquered in the forced march of the Giants on an almost hopeless chase for the coveted pennant before the disaster came with crushing force. All major league straight victory marks had fallen by the wayside, and the only record left to shoot at was that of the Corsican team of twenty-seven victories, made in the four-club Texas League in 1902.

Another victory would have tied that, and under vastly more trying conditions than those that prevailed away down in Texas. But the breaks that have been with the New Yorkers in this unparalleled run went against them, and the chance to finish the season with the string unbroken faded away under the influence of the lusty bats of the boisterous Braves.

It took the best efforts of George Tyler, one of the most formidable left handed pitchers in the National League, to subdue the bold warriors who make Coogan's Bluff their stamping ground. Yet, capable as was his work on the mound, it is doubtful whether he would have succeeded where so many others had failed if it had not been for the almost superhuman efforts of the diminutive Maranville, probably the most alert shortstop in captivity.

Maranville Nips Off Runs

This energetic little parcel of humanity jumped all around the edge of the diamond with the celerity of a grasshopper and on nearly every leap he was instrumental in cutting off runs and nipping desperate rallies in the bud. Formidable as were the numerals arrayed against them, they were by no means overwhelming when matched against the sturdy batters who face Tyler. But whenever the vigorous stickwork threatened runs in any liberal quantity little Maranville pounced on the ball and by a marvelous catch per lightning fielding rendered the efforts futile.

Even before the scoreboard was disfigured by anyhostile runs the sinister influence of the active shortstop made itself felt. A well-planned double steal in the second inning, when two were out, was shut off when he cut the throw to catch McCarty racing to second, but kept in position to nail Holke by a well-directed heave as he made his dash for the plate. Again, in the fourth he ran almost to left field to catch a fly by Fletcher that would have brought one run in and left only one out. His crowning achievements came in the fifth, when the Giants had Tyler up in the 3rd, and, though they tallied twice and tied the score at that time, there is no knowing how many more runs would have crossed the plate but for one of the smartest double plays seen this season, in which Maranville was the chief factor.

Slim Sieles was the pitcher sacrificed in the game which terminated the record run. Three others followed in the forlorn hope of redeeming the situation, and Feareau was almost as badly treated by the Braves, who were making runs while the making was good. The slender lad might well have been called Had Sallee as he left the mound in the fatal seventh. When three runs had been scored with none out, so crestfallen did he appear with the consciousness that he had failed to sustain the winning streak. In intenuation it may be recalled that he has been ill nearly all the time the Giants have been compiling their long list of victories. He was scarcely keyed up to the same pitch as the other twirlers, and gave way under the terrific onslaught of the fighting braves. An error by Fletcher also helped in his defeat, as the Braves (first conceived the idea that they at last had a chance to perform the almost impossible after his bad throw had given Maranville a life in the fourth, with two runs resulting.

Braves Ruthless with Bats.

It was in the seventh that the real whaling commenced, however, the hitting being of a character seldom seen in these days of pitching effectiveness. Sufficient to say that the cluster of ball tallies which put the seal on the leagues of the Giants included two home runs most remarkable of all being the first that they were made in succession. That inning is the real story of the collapse of McGraw's mighty organization, and it was the pesky Kouetchy, who twice during the series has robbed the Giant pitchers of a no-hit game, that began the attack.

FIRST GAME.

NEW YORK. (N.)	Ab	R	H	Po	A		BOSTON. (N.)	Ab	R	H	Po	A
Burns,lf	4	1	1	2	0		Snodgr's,cf	4	0	0	3	2
Herzog,2b	4	1	2	3	5		Mar'ville,ss	3	0	0	0	27
Roberts'n,rf	3	0	0	1	0		Fitzp'k,rf	3	0	0	1	0
Zim'man,3b	3	0	0	0	5		Konetc'y, 1b	3	0	1	19	0
Fletcher,ss	4	1	2	0	5		Smith,3b	3	0	0	2	2
Kauff,cf	3	1	2	1	0		Magee,lf	3	0	0	3	1
Holke,1b	2	0	1	15	0		Egan,2b	3	0	0	0	0
McC'arty,c	3	0	1	3	0		Gowdy,c	2	0	0	3	0
Benton,p	3	0	0	0	2		Rudolph,p	2	0	0	0	3
							aBlackburn	1	0	0	0	0
Total...	29	4	9	27	17		Total...	27	0	1	24	19

a-Batted for Rudolph in ninth inning.

Boston ....0 0 0 0 0 0 0 0 0—0
New York ....0 0 0 0 0 0 2 2 .—4

Errors—Smith, Zimmerman.
Three-base hits—Burns, Fletcher. Stolen bases—Kauff, (2); Holke. Sacrifice hit—Robertson. Sacrifice fly—Zimmerman. Double plays—Fletcher, Herzog, and Holke; Benton, Herzog, and Holke. Left on bases—New York, 4; Boston, 1. First base on errors—New York, 1; Boston, 1. Bases on balls—Off Benton, 1; off Rudolph, 1. Earned runs—Off Rudolph, 2. Struck out—By Benton, 5; by Rudolph, 2. Time of game—One hour and twenty-seven minutes. Umpires—Messrs. Rigler and Byron.

SECOND GAME.

BOSTON. (N.)	Ab	R	H	Po	A		NEW YORK. (N.)	Ab	R	H	Po	A
Snodg's,cf	3	0	2	1	0		Burns,lf	5	0	1	2	0
Chappelle,rf	2	0	2	0	0		Herzog,2b	4	0	0	3	4
F'patrick,rf	3	0	0	1	0		R'tson,rf	4	0	1	1	0
Collins,cf	2	0	0	1	0		Zim'man,3b	4	0	0	0	1
Konetchy,1b	4	2	2	8	2		Fletcher,ss	4	0	2	1	2
J. Smith,3b	5	1	1	2	1		Kauff,cf	4	0	0	1	1
Magee,lf	3	1	2	0	0		Holke,1b	4	1	1	11	1
Egan,2b	4	1	2	1	1		McC'arty,c	3	2	3	5	2
Blackburn,c	4	2	1	8	2		Sallee,p	2	0	0	0	1
Tyler,p	3	0	1	1	3		Tesreau,p	2	0	0	0	0
							Anderson,p	0	0	0	0	0
							aLobert	1	0	0	0	0
Total...	35	8	13	27	11		G. Smith,p	0	0	0	1	0
							bKocher	1	0	0	0	0
							Total...	36	3	8	27	14

a-Batted for Anderson in seventh inning.
b-Batted for G. Smith in ninth inning.
Errors—J. Smith, Egan, Tyler, Fletcher, (2).

Boston ....0 0 0 2 0 0 5 0 1—8
New York ....0 0 0 0 0 2 1 0 0—3

Two-base hits—Konetchy, Robertson, Fletcher, McCarty. Three-base hit—McCarty. Home runs—J. Smith, Magee. Sacrifice hits—Maranville, (2); Tyler. Double plays—Sallee, Herzog, and Holke; Maranville and Konetchy; Holke, Fletcher, and Holke. Left on bases—Boston, 4; New York, 7. First base on errors—New York, 2; Boston, 2. Bases on balls—Off G. Smith, 1; off Tyler, 1. Hits and earned runs—Off Sallee, 7 hits and 3 runs in six innings, none out in seventh; off Tesreau, 4 hits and 2 runs, (only four men faced him;) off Anderson, no hits and no runs in one inning; off G. Smith, 2 hits and no runs in two innings; off Tyler, no runs. Struck out—By Sallee, 3; by G. Smith, 1; by Tyler, 6. Wild pitches—Tyler, 1; Tesreau, 1. Passed ball—Blackburn. Time of game—Two hours and eighteen minutes. Umpires—Messrs. Byron and Rigler.

He fired the ambition of the visiting batsmen by singling to centre and was followed to the plate by Smith. This same Smith was the perpetrator of the first home run, and it was committed with malice aforethought. He fouled about half a dozen times, one of these going so nearly safe and into the crowd that the mighty throng was seized with cold shivers. The premonition of danger was fulfilled a few seconds later when he caught the ball squarely and it zailed far over Burns's head to find a resting place among the occupants of the left field bleachers. Needless to say Konetchy and the instigator of the home run strolled home at their leisure. Had McGraw realized that the visitors had solved Sallee's slants the defeat might have been less decisive, but it is scarcely in the book for one home run to follow another. Magee, the next up, it is true, used to have a reputation as a home run hitter, and Smith had revived the feeling. His eye was on the spot where Smith's pellet lay buried and the very first ball that the unfortunate Salle served had a mighty smash, for an even longer journey than the one that had preceded it. The curfew bell rang loudly for Sallee then, and Tesreau came in to take his share of the furious attack.

Tesreau Falls to Stem Tide.

Egan singled to left, and when Blackborn bunted he managed to reach first safely, as the bag was not covered. This put Egan on second and Tesreau speeded up the progress of both runners with a wild pitch. Tyler's little tap enabled Egan to score and Chapple entering the game to bat for Snodgrass, banged one to left so that Blackburn could keep up the procession of runs.

That ended Big Jeffs short but eventful career, two more runs having come in with no casualties to the batters. Anderson was more successful, as Maranville sacrificed, Collins, batting for Fitzpatrick, fanned, and the pitcher threw out Konetchy, who came up for his second turn at the feast.

October 1, 1916

BABE RUTH LED HIS LEAGUE.

Red Sox Twirler Gave Fewest Earned Runs in American Circuit.

Babe Ruth of the Boston Red Sox led the American League pitchers last season, according to the official averages, which were made public by President Ban Johnson yesterday. The pitchers are rated on the same basis as in the National League twirlers, not on the games won and lost, but on the number of earned runs per game. Ruth allowed only 1.75 runs per game and he took part in forty-four games. Eddie Cicotte of Chicago was second, allowing 1.78 runs per game. Walter Johnson of Washington was third. He allowed 1.89 runs per game.

Davenport of St. Louis was the hardest worked pitcher, taking part in fifty-nine games. Reb Russell of Chicago was next, with fifty-six, and Bob Shawkey of the Yankees pitched in fifty-three games. Walter Johnson, however, pitched the greatest number of innings, 371. He also led the league in strikeouts, with 228 to his credit. Myers of the Athletics was the most liberal of the twirlers, and gave 168 bases on balls. Joe Bush of the Athletics was the wildest, with fifteen wild heaves. Dauss of Detroit did the most damage to his opponents by hitting sixteen players.

Nick Cullop led the Yankee pitchers, permitting 2.05 earned runs per game. He stood ninth among the league pitchers. Shawkey was eleventh, and he took part in more games than any other of Donovan's boxmen. Mogridge was rated twelfth in the list.

December 10, 1916

NO HITS, NO RUNS FOR NINE INNINGS

Reds Nose Out Cubs in Tenth by 1 to 0 When Kopf and Jim Thorpe Get Singles.

CHICAGO, May 2.—Probably a world's record was established here today in a ten-inning game between Cincinnati and Chicago. Neither club registered a hit or run in nine full innings. Cincinnati won in the tenth, 1 to 0.

For the nine innings Vaughn, assisted by remarkable defense by the Chicago in field, did not permit a Cincinnati player to reach second base, and in doing this feat only slightly surpassed his pitching opponent. Toney, who allowed only one Chicago runner to reach second. Vaughn struck out ten Cincinnati batsmen while three were being fanned by Toney.

The game was won in the tenth inning after one out. Kopf singled, advanced in third when Williams dropped Chase's fly, and scored when Therper hit a slow bounder in Vaughn.

The Cincinnati outfielders several times saved the game for Toney, Cheto one outer occasion backing into the left field for Merkle's fly.

The score:

CINCINNATI (N.)	Ab	R	H	Pe	A		CHICAGO (N)	Ab	R	H	Pe	A
Grob,1b	1	0	0	2	2		Zelder,ss		4	0	0	1	0
Goetz,1b	1	0	0	2	1		Wolfton,rf	1	1	0	0	0	0
Kolf,ss	4	1	1	1	1		Doyle, 2b		1	0	0	5	4
Neale, cf	4	0	0	1	0		Merkle, 1b	4	0	0	K	7	1
Chase, 1b	4	0	0	12	0		Williams, cf		2	0	0	7	1
Thorpe, rf	4	0	1	1	0		Mastin, lf		3	0	0	0	0
Shean, 2b	3	0	0	3	2		Wilson, o		3	0	0	14	1
Cheto, lf	3	0	0	5	0		Deal, 3b		3	0	0	1	0
Hubney	3	0	0	3	0		Vaughn,p		3	0	0	0	3
Toney, p	3	0	0	0	1								
Total	30	1	2	30	10		Total		30	0	0	30	0

Errors—Zehler, Williams.

Cincinnati...............000 000 000 1—1
Chicago...............00 000 000 0—0

Stolen bases. Chase. Double plays—Doyle, Markle, and Zelder, Vaughn, Doyle, and Merale. Left on base—Chicago 2: Cincinnati 1. First base on errors—Cincinnati. 2 Bases on balls off Toney, 2. Vaughn , 2 Base runs—Off Vaughn, none in 18 to Ling. Toney, Lone in 10. Streck and Vaughn. . Toney. 3. Time 1 hour, 30 minutes. Dimplimnes—forth and Eigler.

May 3, 1917

SHORE JOINS RANKS OF NO-HIT PITCHERS

Red Sox Whitewash Senators Twice — Ruth Strikes Umpire Owens.

BOSTON, June 23.—A no-hit, no-run, no-man-reached-first base pitching performance by Ernest Shore, Boston twirler; an assault upon Umpire Owens

---

by Babe Ruth, another Boston pitcher, in which the umpire was struck behind the ear, and the defeat of Walter Johnson by Dutch Leonard, were incidents of the world champions' double victory over Washington today. The scores were 4 to 0 and 5 to 0.

Shore's entry into the select list of pitchers who have shown perfect performances was made possible by Ruth's banishment from the first game. Ruth had pitched only to Ray Morgan, and Umpire Owens had given the latter his base on balls. Ruth argued the decision, the umpire ordered him off the field, and the Boston pitcher then struck at Owens. Other players intervened, and Ruth left the field.

Shore was called in with Morgan on first base, but a moment later the latter was thrown out attempting to steal second. Thereafter the Boston pitcher and his fielders turned back every Washington batsman. Ayers, who pitched for Washington, was hit hard.

In the second game Leonard held Washington to four hits, while the world champions cracked out hits in bunches off Johnson and, with errors, won easily. The scores:

FIRST GAME.

BOSTON, (A.)	Ab	R	H	Po	A		WASHINGTON, (A.)	Ab	R	H	Po	A
Hooper,rf	4	0	1	0	0		Morgan,2b	2	0	0	4	2
Barry,2b	4	0	0	2	1		Foster,3b	3	0	0	1	3
Hoblitzell,1b	4	0	0	12	2		Leonard,3b	0	0	0	0	1
Gardner,3b	4	1	1	2	1		Milan,cf	3	0	0	3	0
Lewis,lf	4	0	3	2	0		Rice,rf	3	0	0	3	0
Walker,cf	3	1	1	4	0		Gharrity,1b	3	0	0	0	0
Scott,s	3	0	0	0	5		Judge,1b	3	0	0	11	1
Thomas,c	3	0	0	0	0		Jamieson,lf	3	0	0	0	0
Agnew,c	3	1	3	2	1		Shanks,ss	3	0	0	1	0
Ruth,p	0	0	0	0	0		Henry,c	3	0	0	2	8
Shore,p	2	1	0	2	6		Ayres,p	2	0	0	2	8
							aMenosky	1	0	0	0	0
Total	31	4	9	27	16		Total	26	0	0	24	17

a Batted for Ayres in ninth.
Errors—Foster, (2.) Rice.

Boston..............010 000 30.—4
Washington..............000 000 000—0

Two-base hits—Walker, Agnew. Sacrifice hits—Walker, Shore, Scott. Double plays—Ayres, Foster, and Judge; Ayres and Judge. Left on bases—Boston, 6. First base on errors—Boston, 8. Base on balls—Off Ruth, 1. Hits and earned runs—Off Ruth, no hits, no runs in no inning, (none out in first;) Shore, none and none in 9; Ayres, 9 and 2 in 8. Struck out—By Shore, 2. Time—1 hour 40 minutes. Umpires—Owen, McCormick, and Dineen.

SECOND GAME.

BOSTON, (A.)	Ab	R	H	Po	A		X SECOND BOX. WASHINGTON, (A.)	Ab	R	H	Po	A
Hooper,rf	3	0	0	1	1		Morgan,2b	5	0	1	1	5
Barry,2b	3	1	2	1	3		J.Leonard,3b	2	0	0	1	0
Hoblitzell,1b	3	1	0	11	1		Milan,cf	3	0	2	4	0
Gardner,3b	3	0	1	2	3		Rice,rf	4	0	1	3	0
Lewis,lf	4	1	1	3	0		Gharrity,1b	4	0	0	8	0
Walker,cf	3	0	0	1	0		Shanks,ss	3	0	0	1	4
Scott,ss	4	1	2	0	2		Ainsmith,c	4	0	0	6	1
Thomas,c	4	1	3	7	0		Johnson,p	3	0	0	0	1
H.Leonard,p	3	0	0	1	2		aHenry	0	0	0	0	0
							Jamieson,lf	3	0	0	0	0
Total	31	5	9	27	12		Total	31	0	4	24	11

a Batted for Jamieson in ninth.
Errors—Milan, Shanks.

Boston..............002 000 21..—5
Washington..............000 000 000—0

Two-base hit—Scott. Sacrifice hit—Walker. Double plays—Shanks, Morgan, and Gharrity. Left on bases—Boston, 7; Washington, 10. First base on errors—Boston, 1. Bases on balls—Off Johnson, 2; Leonard, 6. Earned runs—Off Johnson, 4 runs in 8 innings. Leonard, 0 in 9. Hit by pitcher—By Johnson, (Barry, Hoblitzell.) Struck out—By Leonard, 7; Johnson, 5. Wild pitch—Leonard. Time—1 hour 58 minutes. Umpires — McCormick, Dineen, and Owens.

June 24, 1917

ALEXANDER BREAKS PITCHERS' RECORDS

Has Hurled in Greatest Number of Few-Hit and No-Run Games Since 1893.

During the season just ended, Grover Cleveland Alexander, the great pitcher of the Phillies, equaled the phenomenal record which up to that time was held only by Christy Mathewson, the former Giant idol, in winning thirty games for three successive years. Alex the Great is the only twirler baseball has produced who has been able to equal this mark.

A year ago Alexander showed that he ranked with the greatest in the game when he established a newer record by winning sixteen of his 1916 victories by the shut-out route. This is one of the truly wonderful feats of major league pitching. Alexander has completed his seventh year as a major league twirler, and he is not through yet by any means. Before he lays aside his uniform it will not be surprising if he is hailed as Alexander the Greatest, instead of just the Great.

Old Cy Young, Ed Walsh, and Bill Dineen displayed great work in the box year after year, but none of the game's great pitchers have been able to win thirty victories three years in succession but Matty and Alexander. Toward the end of the season it was doubtful whether Alex would equal Matty's record, as the Quakers' winning streak was snapped and their pennant chances spoiled in the last Giant series in New York.

Then everybody was asking. "Will Alex equal Matty's great record?" During the final series with the Giants in Philadelphia Alexander had won 29 games and lost 13. The day before the season closed Alex pitched against the Giants and won his thirtieth victory. In 1915, with a pennant-winning club behind him, Alexander won 31 games and lost 10, and in 1916 he won 33 games and lost 12.

"Not only is Alexander great because of his pitching work," says Pat Moran, leader of the Phillies, "but he's an invaluable member of the team because of his splendid character. He is the easiest star pitcher to handle I have ever known. He is willing to work out of turn, no matter what the weather, no matter if he is feeling fit or not. He is always ready for the call of duty. He is a model athlete and one of the cleanest, manliest fellows I have ever known."

November 5, 1917

BASEBALL SEASON WILL CLOSE SEPT. 1

National League Votes Against Continuing Pastime with Men Not in Draft.

There will be no major league baseball after Sept. 1, the date set by Secretary of War Baker for the ball players within the draft age to get into essential work. This was decided yesterday at a special meeting of the National League in this city. Some of the club owners were in favor of continuing play after that date with clubs made up of players under and above the draft age, but the majority ruled that major league baseball of this inferior type would injure the game more than it would help it.

The National League was to have met here today, but when August Herrmann, Chairman of the National Commission, called a meeting of that body at Cleveland for today he also called a meeting of the National League club owners. President Tener, a member of the National Commission, has refused to meet with the commission because of the American League's refusal to abide by the decision of that body in the Scott-Perry case. Most of the National League club owners were ready to abandon today's meeting of the National League and attend the joint meeting of the two leagues in Cleveland.

With the leagues and the club owners at loggerheads, the baseball season is very likely to end in a bad muddle, and the whole structure of the national pastime may have to be reconstructed after the war.

There was not a full representation of the National League at the meeting here, but a majority of the clubs were represented. After the league had passed a resolution deciding that no championship games would be played after Labor Day, Barney Dreyfuss was appointed a committee of one to attend the meeting with the American League in Cleveland. He is vested with full power to act in regard to any readjustment of the schedule.

There is sure to be a clash between the leagues over the world's series. The American League—that is, President B. B. Johnson—wants to end the season on Aug. 20 and play the series before Sept. 1, the time set by Secretary Baker. Chairman August Herrmann of the National Commission believes that the clubs should play right up to Sept. 1 before awarding the pennant, and then play the world's series. He takes this attitude on the assumption that the players on the two winning clubs will have another time extension until the big series is finished. It is not known that Mr. Herrmann has any grounds for believing that Provost General Crowder will grant this extra time to the world's series contestants.

The National League club owners are strongly opposed to closing the leagues by Aug. 20 because they want all the clubs to play out their schedules up to Sept. 2 and get the benefit of the receipts up to that date. It is believed that Dreyfuss at Cleveland will strongly oppose any attempt of the American League to start the world's series on Aug. 20. It is not unlikely that, if the American League insists on starting the series on Aug. 20, some arrangement may be made whereby all the clubs will share in the world's series money. Under a new arrangement, adopted last Winter, the first four clubs in each league will share in the receipts, but it may be necessary to declare every club owner in on the division in order to keep peace in the baseball family.

August 3, 1918

FREAK PITCHING IS DOOMED IN MAJORS

American League Comes Out for Reform in Deliveries— National Favors Plan.

CHICAGO, Oct. 30.—President Ban Johnson of the American League tonight requested August Herrmann, Chairman of the National Commission, and John A. Heydler, President of the National League, to call a joint meeting of the Rules Committee of the two Leagues to take action in regard to the abolition of the "spitball," the "shineball," and other freak pitching deliveries. President Johnson said these deliveries should be legislated out of the major leagues. He also has several suggestions to make on the scoring rules.

This action by the President of the American League, who will be backed up by his club owners, foreshadows the end of the spitball, a delivery which has been used with marked success by many major league boxmen during the past twenty years. At various times in the last few seasons reports have spread that the major leagues would take action against the delivery, but not until now has any official action been directed at this and other of the so-called freak deliveries.

That the National League will prove a willing ally in Johnson's effort to curb the practice of using foreign substances on the ball or in any way changing the surface condition of the sphere goes withing saying. President John Heydler has been against such pitching for some time. Barney Dreyfuss, owner of the Pittsburgh club, has been a strong opponent of freak pitching for some time, and only a few weeks ago he announced that he will bring the matter to the attention of the National League at its coming meeting in December. Other club owners are known to hold similar views.

Ban May Be Delayed.

If the majors vote to place a ban on the spitball they will not be original in their action, as the American Association went on record a year ago against the use of the delivery. During the past season umpires in the big minor league of the Middle West were instructed to see that the pitchers made no attempt to put saliva on the ball, and as a result numerous spitball pitchers, ineffective with this delivery curbed, were sent to other leagues.

Just what procedure the major leagues will follow in putting an end to the use of the spitball is problematical. It is expected that the ban will not become effective immediately after its passage. Such a move would drive from the majors several boxmen who rely almost entirely on the delivery, either in actual use or as a threat, to retain their places in the big leagues. The argument has been advanced that these pitchers would have time to perfect themselves in another style of delivery, and it would not be surprising if the rule makers should decide to make the ban effective one or two seasons after passage.

A rule forbidding the pitcher to raise the ball above his shoulder before delivering it to the batsman or to wet his fingers with saliva should put an end to the spitball. The other deliveries can be stopped by enforcing a rule that neither the pitcher nor any other player shall rub the ball against any part of his uniform or roughen the outside surface of the ball. These are the methods employed in doctoring the ball for the deliveries other than the spitter. By giving umpires broad powers in enforcing these rules and adding a fine for violation the freak deliveries would soon go.

Stricklett the Pioneer.

The spitball discovery has been variously claimed, but it is generally agreed that Elmer Stricklett, a pitcher who flourished about twenty years ago, developed the delivery until it attracted wide attention. Old timers contend that they got peculiar breaks in pitching by wetting the ball, but none specialized in this peculiar delivery up to the time of Stricklett. Jack Chesbro and Ed. Walsh, outstanding stars of the pitching ranks between the seasons of 1901 and 1910, were perhaps the most successful of the spitballers. Many boxmen have used the delivery in recent years, but none attained the success of either Chesbro or Walsh. In recent seasons every major league club has carried a pitcher or two who depended upon the spitball for success.

The shine ball and other freak deliveries have been of more recent origin. Russell Ford started a craze with the emery ball which finally resulted in the delivery being legislated out of the game. Eddie Cicotte and Hod Eller are supposed to be shine ball experts, but the methods used in doctoring this particular ball never has been clearly explained.

Many prominent pitchers of both the National and American League will be affected by a rule that would bar the use of the so-called freak deliveries.

October 31, 1919

YANKS BUY BABE RUTH FOR $125,000

Highest Purchase Price in Baseball History Paid for Game's Greatest Slugger.

Babe Ruth of the Boston Red Sox, baseball's super-slugger, was purchased by the Yankees yesterday for the largest cash sum ever paid for a player. The New York Club paid Harry Frazee of Boston $125,000 for the sensational batsman who last season caused such a furore in the national game by batting out twenty-nine home runs, a new record in long-distance clouting.

Colonel Ruppert, President of the Yanks, said that he had taken over Ruth's Boston contract, which has two years more to run. This contract calls for a salary of $10,000 a year. Ruth recently announced that he would refuse to play for $10,000 next season, although the Boston Club has received no request for a raise in salary.

Manager Miller Huggins is now in Los Angeles negotiating with Ruth. It is believed that the Yankee manager will offer him a new contract which will be satisfactory to the Colossus of the bat.

President Ruppert said yesterday that Ruth would probably play right field for the Yankees. He played in left field for the Red Sox last season, and had the highest fielding average among the outfielders, making only two errors during the season. While he is on the Pacific Coast Manager Huggins will also endeavor to sign Duffy Lewis, who will be one of Ruth's companions in the outfield at the Polo Grounds next season.

Home Run Record in Danger.

The acquisition of Ruth strengthens the Yankee club in its weakest department. With the added hitting power of Ruth, Bob Shawkey, one of the Yankee pitchers, said yesterday the New York club should be a pennant winner next season. For several seasons the Yankees have been experimenting with outfielders, but never have been able to land a consistent hitter. The short right field wall at the Polo Grounds should prove an easy target for Ruth next season and, playing seventy-seven games at home, it would not be surprising if Ruth surpassed his home-run record of twenty-nine home runs next Summer.

Ruth was such a sensation last season that he supplanted the great Ty Cobb as baseball's greatest attraction, and in obtaining the services of Ruth for next season the New York club made a ten-strike which will be received with the greatest enthusiasm by Manhattan baseball fans.

Ruth's crowning batting accomplishment came at the Polo Grounds last Fall when he hammered one of the longest hits ever seen in Harlem over the right field grandstand for his twenty-eighth home run, smashing the home record of twenty-seven, made by Ed Williamson way back in 1884. The more modern home-run record, up to last season, had been held by Buck Freeman, who made twenty-five home runs when a member of the Washington club in 1899. The next best home-run hitter of modern times is Gavvy Cravath, now manager of the Phillies, who made twenty-four home runs a few seasons ago.

Ruth's home-run drives were distributed all over the circuit, and he is the one player known to the game who hit a home run on every park on the circuit in the same season.

Specializes in Long Hits.

Ruth's batting feats last season will stand for many years to come, unless he betters the record himself with the aid of the short right field under Coogan's Bluff. The record he made last season was a masterpiece of slugging. He went up to the bat 432 times in 130 games and produced 159 hits. Of these hits 75 were for extra bases. Not only did he make 29 home runs, but he also made 34 two-baggers and 12 three-baggers. Ruth's batting average for extra base hits was .657, a mark which probably will not be approached for many years to come.

Ruth scored the greatest number of runs in the American League last season, crossing the plate 103 times. Cobb scored only 97 runs last year. Ruth was so dangerous that the American League pitchers were generous with their passes and the superlative hitter walked 101 times, many of these passes being intentional. Ruth also struck out more than any other batsman in the league, fanning 58 times. He also made three sacrifice hits and he stole seven bases.

Ruth is a native of Baltimore and is 26 years old, just in his prime as a baseball player. He was discovered by Jack Dunn, owner of the Baltimore Club, while playing with the baseball team of Mount St. Joseph's, a school which Ruth attended in that city, in 1913. In 1914 Ruth played with the Baltimore team and up to that time little attention had been paid to his batting. It was as a pitcher that he attracted attention in Baltimore. Boston bought Ruth along with Ernie Shore and some other players in 1914. The price paid for Ruth was said to have been $2,700.

Babe Ruth

Holds World's Series Record

Ruth was a big success in the major league from the start. In 1916, when the Red Sox won the pennant, he led the American League pitchers in effectiveness and in the world's series of 1916 and 1918, Ruth hung up a new world's series pitching record for shut out innings. He pitched twenty-eight consecutive scoreless innings, which beat the record of twenty-seven scoreless innings made in world's series games by Christy Mathewson of the Giants.

For the past few seasons Ruth's ambition has been to play regularly. While he was doing only pitching duty with Boston he was a sensational pinch hitter and when he played regularly in the outfield last season he blossomed forth as the most sensational batsman the game has ever known. He was also a great success as a fielder and last season he made only two errors and had 230 putouts. He also had twenty-six assists, more than any outfielder in the American League. This was because of his phenomenal throwing arm. His fielding average last season was .992. Ruth didn't do much pitching last season. He pitched thirteen games and won eight and lost five.

Manager Huggins is expected back in New York at the end of next week with Ruth's contract in his inside pocket. It is believed that the New York Club will not try to hold Ruth to the Boston contract which he has decided is unsatisfactory.

The new contract which the Yankees have offered Ruth is said to be almost double the Boston figure of $10,000 a year. While he is out on the coast interviewing Ruth, Huggins is also getting into line, not only Duffy Lewis, but also Bob Meusel, the sensational young slugger of the Pacific Coast League, who is regarded by baseball scouts as the minor league find of the year.

The Perfect Hitter.

Ruth's principle of batting is much the same as the principle of the golfer. He comes back slowly, keeps his eye on the ball and follows through. His very position at the bat is intimidating to the pitcher. He places his feet in perfect position. He simply cannot step away from the pitch if he wants to. He can step only one way—in. The weight of Ruth's body when he bats is on his left leg. The forward leg is bent slightly at the knee. As he stands facing the pitcher more of his hips and back are seen by the pitcher than his chest or side. When he starts to swing his back is half turned toward the pitcher. He goes as far back as he can reach, never for an instant taking his eye off the ball as it leaves the pitcher's hand.

The greatest power in his terrific swing comes when the bat is directly in front of his body, just half way in the swing. He hits the ball with terrific impact and there is no player in the game whose swing is such a masterpiece of batting technique.

January 6, 1920

Largest Sums on Record for Purchase of Ball Players

Babe Ruth, Boston to Yankees	$125,000
Tris Speaker, Boston to Cleveland	*50,000
Eddie Collins, Athletics to Chicago	50,000
Carl Mays, Boston to Yankees	*40,000
Art Nehf, Boston to Giants	*40,000
Frank Baker, Athletics to Yankees	37,500
Joe Jackson, Cleveland to Chicago	*31,500
Benny Kauff, Feds to Giants	30,000
Lee Magee, Feds to Yankees	22,500
Strunk, Schang, and Bush, Athletics to Boston	*60,000
Alexander and Killefer, Phillies to Chicago	*55,000
*And players.	

LONG TIE IN HUB SETS NEW RECORD

BOSTON, May 1.—The Robins and the Braves celebrated May Day in this ordinarily peaceful city by staging a prolonged, heart-breaking struggle for twenty-six innings at Braves Field and bombing to bits all major league records for duration of hostilities. When darkness drew its mantle over the scene, forbidding further battling, both teams were still on their feet, interlocked in a death clutch and each praying for just one more inning in which to get in the knockout blow.

As far as results in the chase for the pennant go the game was without effect, for the final score was 1 to 1. In the matter of thrills, however, the oldest living man can remember nothing like it, nor can he find anything in his granddad's diary worthy of comparison. Heart disease was the mildest complaint that grasped the spectators as they watched inning after inning slip away and the row of ciphers on the scoreboard began to slide over the fence and reach out into the Fenway. Nervous prostration threatened to engulf the stands as the twentieth inning passed away in the scoreless routine and the word was passed from the knowing fans to those of inferior baseball erudition that the National League record was twenty-two innings, the Robins having beaten the Pirates by 6 to 5 in a game of that length played in Brooklyn on August 22, 1917.

The twenty-second inning passed in the history-making clash, and then the twenty-third, with a total result of four more ciphers on the scoreboard and a new National League record for duration. The less hardy of the fans began to show signs of the strain by moving restlessly in their seats and babbling about perpetual motion and eternity.

But the warriors down there on the field had no thoughts of records and no eyes for the fans, whose very presence they seemed to have forgotten. With a gameness that makes pebbles seem like chewing gum by comparison, they bent apparently unflagging energies on that one great object—to "beat these guys."

Rooting for a New Record.

Now the old-timers in the stands began to whisper to each other with tense faces that the big-league record was twenty-four innings, established in an American League game in the Hub on Sept. 1, 1906, on which occasion the Athletics downed the Red Sox by a tally of 4 to 1. The Robins and the Braves didn't care. They didn't even know it. They simply worried along in their sublime ignorance and tied this record, then smashed it, and by way of emphasis, tacked on a twenty-sixth session.

At this stage of the proceedings Umpire McCormick yawned twice and observed that it was nearly bedtime. He didn't seem particularly thrilled by what was going on. To him and his brother arbiter, Hart, it was merely an infernally long day's work. McCormick remembered that he had an apointment pretty soon with a succulent beefsteak. He wondered if it wasn't getting dark. He held out one hand as a test and decided that in the gloaming it resembled a Virginia ham. He knew it wasn't a Virginia ham and became convinced that it was too dark to play ball. Thereupon he called the game to the satisfaciton of himself and Mr. Hart and the chagrin of everybody else concerend.

Some Great Fielding Bits.

The fielding on both sides was brilliant in the crises. Olson saved Brooklyn in the ninth, when, with the bases filled and one out, he stoped Pick's grounder, tagged Powell on the base line and then threw out the batter.

In the seventeenth inning one of the most remarkable double plays ever seen in Boston retired Brooklyn. The bases were filled and one was out when Elliott grounded to Osshger. Wheat was forced at the plate, but Gowdy's throw to Kolke was low and was fumbled. Konstchy tried to score from second and Gowdy received Holke's throw to one

side and threw himself blindly across the plate to meet Konetchy's spikes with bare flat.

Joe Osschgev and Leon Caders were the real outstanding heroes among a score of heroes in the monumental affray of this afternoon. The two twirlers went the entire distances, pitching each practically the equivalent of three full games in this one contest, and inirable dictu, instead of showing any sign of weakening under the prolonged strain, each of them appeared to grow stronger. In the final six innings neither artist allowed even the shadow of a safe bingle.

The Braves twirler had rather the better of the dual in some respects. Fewer hits were made from his delivery than from that of Cadore. Ossehger practically twirled three three-hit games in a row, while Cadore pitched three five-hit games in the afternoon's warfare. In only one inning, the seventeenth, did Ossehger allow two safe blows and Cadore let the local batters group him only in the sixth and ninth.

At the receiving end of the batteries, O'Neill gave way to Gowdy for the braves before hostilities were concluded, and Eliott took Krueger's place behind the bat for Brooklyn.

Sparks Without Fireworks.

There was no indication in the early stages of the combat that anything startling was brewing. The Robins got one less single in the first, second and fourth innings, and the Braves got lone hits in the

second, third and fourth, but without terrible results in the score column.

In the fifth Robbie's men got thier valuable tally. Krueger was walked by Oschger, who offended in this way very seldom this afternoon. Krueger went down tos eond while Osschger was fielding Cadore's litte pat and getting his man at first. Ivy Olson played a most important role at this juncture by slashing a line driver over Maranville's head for a single, on which Krueger completed his journey and weighed in at the home plate. Olson went to second on a wild pitch but was left there as Osschger tightened up and fanned Neis and Johnston lined to Mann in left field.

The Braves tied up the score in the succeeding inning, jamming over the final run of a game which was destined to go on for twenty scoreless innings thereafter, tying the existing record in this respect.

In the sixth session Cadore fielded Mann's bounder and threw him out at first. Cruise came along with a mighty drive to the scoreboard which netted three bases. Holks popped up- a short fly to left which Wheat ran in and caught. Boeckel delivered the goods in the form of a single to centre upon which Cruise tallied. When Maranville followed with a double to centre it looked a bit dubious for Mr. Cadore and his pals. Boeckel was caught at the plate, however, in the effort to score on the rabbit's blow, hood, Cedore and Krueger participating in the putout.

After this session, save for the Braves flash in the ninth and the Robins' effort in the seventeenth, the two twirlers were entire masters of the situation.

The score:

BROOKLYN (N.)						BOSTON (N.)					
	Ab	R	H	Po	A		Ab	R	H	Po	A
Olson	10	0	1	6	9	Powell,cf	7	0	1	8	0
Neis,rf	10	0	1	9	0	Pick,2b	11	0	0	5	10
Johnston,3b	10	0	2	8	1	Mann,lf	10	0	2	6	0
Wheat,lf	9	0	2	3	0	Cruise,rf	9	1	1	4	0
Myers,cf	2	0	1	2	0	Holke,1b	10	0	2	32	1
Hood,cf	6	0	1	3	1	Boeckel,3b	11	0	3	1	7
Konetch'y,1b	9	0	1	30	1	Maran'le,ss	10	0	3	1	9
Ward,ss	10	0	0	5	3	O'Neil,c	2	0	0	4	3
Krueger,c	2	1	0	4	3	aChristen'y	1	0	1	0	0
Elliott,c	7	0	0	1	2	Gowdy,c	8	0	1	6	1
Cadore,p	10	0	0	1	13	Oeschger,p	8	0	1	1	0

Total....85 1 9 78 54   Total....85 1 15 78 42
a Batted for O'Neil in ninth inning.
Errors—Pick (2), Olson, Krueger.

Brooklyn.........0 0 0 0 0 0 1 0 0 0 0 0 0—1
Boston..........0 0 0 0 0 0 0 1 0 0 0 0 0 0—1
Called darkness.
Two-base hits—Maranville, Oeschger. Three-base hit—Cruise. Stolen bases—Myers. Sacrifice hits—Hood, Oeschger, Powell, O'Neil, Holke, Cruise. Double plays—Olson and Konetchy. Bases on balls—Off Cadore 5, Oeschger 3. Struck out—By Cadore 8, Oeschger 4. Wild pitch—Oeschger. Umpires—Messrs. McCormack and Hart.

May 2, 1920

Major League Baseballs Not Changed One Iota, Says Shibe

PHILADELPHIA, June 5.—The big increase in home runs this season is not due to any change in the ball, according to Thomas Shibe, a member of the firm that manufactures all the baseballs used in the major leagues, and Vice President of the Philadelphia American League Club.

"The baseball used this year," said Mr. Shibe, " is the same as used last year and several seasons before that. The specifications this year called for the same yarn, the same cork centre, the same size and weight of rubber and the same horsehide. It has not been changed one iota and no effort has been made to turn out a livelier ball."

Mr. Shibe said his theory was that the abolition of all freak deliveries was the cause of the hard hitting. "With all freak deliveries dead," he said, " and the spitter almost dead, the batsmen are able to hit the ball more solidly."

June 6, 1920

KLEM IS ATTACKED BY PITCHER LUQUE

Red Twirler Accuses Umpire of Abusive Language—Cards Win Twice, 5-0 and 4-3.

CINCINNATI, June 26.—St. Louis went to second place in the National League race today by winning both games of a double header from the champions, 5 to 0 and 4 to 3. Both teams played perfect ball in the field, but the hitting of the visitors was much more effective than that of the Reds. Ruether was pounded hard in the first game, while Haines pitched almost perfectly, allowing only three hits. In the second game, long drives by the Cardinals gave them the win.

In the eighth inning of the second game, Pitcher Luque of the Reds attacked Umpire Klem and dealt him sev-

eral hard blows about the head. The assault took place while Luque was in the box with no one on base, and the pitcher claims that it was due to vicious language used by the official. Luque and Catcher Allen of the Reds both made affidavit that Klem had used such language.

If the claims are proved, the club will bring charges against Klem. Luque was put out of the game and Eller finished it. Previous to this incident, a shower of pop bottles had fallen around Klem, when he called Fournier safe at the plate in the sixth inning. Wingo was put out of the game at this time for abusive language.

The scores:

FIRST GAME.

ST. LOUIS (N.)						CINCINNATI (N.)					
	Ab	R	H	Po	A		Ab	R	H	Po	A
Janvrin,lf	4	1	1	4	0	Rath, 2b	4	0	0	2	2
Schultz,rf	4	0	1	3	0	Groh, 3b	4	0	1	2	2
Stock, 3b	5	2	3	0	1	Roush, lb	3	0	0	1	1
Hornsby, 2b	4	0	0	1	3	Duncan, lf	3	0	0	1	0
Fournier, lb	4	1	2	10	1	Kopf, ss	3	0	1	1	0
McHenry,rf	4	1	1	2	0	Neale, rf	3	0	0	3	0
Lavan, ss	3	0	1	3	6	See, cs	2	0	0	5	0
Dilhoefer, c	4	0	2	4	1	Wingo, c	3	0	0	2	2
Haines, p	3	0	0	0	3	Ruether, p	3	0	1	0	1

Total.... 35 5 11 27 15   Total.... 28 0 3 27 8

St. Louis..............2 0 0 0 0 0 0 3 0—5
Cincinnati ....0 0 0 0 0 0 0 0 0—0

SECOND GAME.

ST. LOUIS (N.)						CINCINNATI (N.)					
	Ab	R	H	Po	A		Ab	R	H	Po	A
Shotten, lf	3	1	0	2	0	Rath, 2b	3	0	1	1	4
Heathcote, cf	3	0	1	0	0	Groh, 3b	3	0	0	0	2
Stock, 3b	4	0	2	0	1	Roush, lb	3	0	0	13	1
Hornsby, 2b	4	0	1	4	0	Duncan, lf	4	0	2	0	0
Fournier, lb	4	1	1	13	0	Kopf, ss	4	1	1	3	4
Schultz, rf	3	1	1	3	0	Neale, rf	4	0	1	0	0
Lavan, ss	4	0	1	2	7	See, cf	3	0	1	1	0
Clemons, c	4	1	1	3	2	aCrane, 1	1	0	0	0	0
Doak, p	3	0	1	0	2	Wingo, c	2	0	0	4	4
Sherdel, p	1	0	0	0	2	Allen, c	1	1	0	3	0
						Laque, p	2	0	0	2	3
						Eller, p	1	0	0	0	1

Total.... 33 4 9 27 18   Total.... 29 3 6 27 19

Two-base hits—Kopf. Janvrin, Stock, McHenry. Three-base hits—Fournier, Dilhoefer, Sacrifice hits—Sehultz, Haines. Left on bases—St. Louis, 7: Cincinnati, 3. Base on balls—Off Ruether 2, Haines 1. Hit by pitcher—By Haines 1. Struck out—By Ruether 1. Haines 1. Umoires—Klem and Emslie.

June 27, 1920

RAY CHAPMAN DIES; MAYS EXONERATED

Widow Takes Body of Ball Player, Killed by Pitched Ball Back to Cleveland.

HUNDREDS WEEP AT BIER

Pitcher Who Threw Ball Unnerved by Accident—Other Teams Would Bar Him.

MIDNIGHT OPERATION FAILS

Player's Brain Crushed by Force of Blow—District Attorney Says Accident Was Unavoidable.

The body of Ray Chapman, the Cleveland shortstop, who died early yesterday in St. Lawrence Hospital after being hit in the head by a pitched ball thrown by Carl Mays at the Polo Grounds Monday afternoon was taken to his home in Cleveland last night. A group of baseball fans stood with bared heads at the Grand Central Terminal as the body was taken through the gates to the train. The ball player's widow, who went with the body, was accompanied by her brother, Daniel Daly of Cleveland; Miss Jane McMahon, a friend; Tris Speaker, manager of the ball club, and Joe Wood, one of the players.

Chapman's death has cast a tragic spell over the baseball fans of the city, and everywhere the accident was the topic of conversation. Chapman was a true sportsman, a skillful player, and one of the most popular men in the major leagues. And this was to have been his last season in professional baseball.

Carl Mays, the New York pitcher, who threw the ball which felled Chapman on Monday, voluntarily went before assistant District Attorney Joyce and was exonerated of all blame.

The game which was to have been played between Cleveland and New York was put over until Thursday and the players of both clubs joined in mourning.

Cleveland Suppreses Bitterness.

Although there is some bitterness against Mays among some of the Cleveland players, Manager Tris Speaker of the Cleveland Club, in a telephone conversation with Colonel T. L. Huston, part owner of the New York Club, said he and his clubmates would do everything in their power to suppress this feeling.

"It is the duty of all of us," said Speaker," of all the players, not only for the good of the game, but also out of respect to the poor fellow who was killed, to suppress all bitter feeling. We will do all in our power to avoid aggravating the unfortunate impression in any way."

Chapman died at 4:40 o'clock yesterday morning following an operation performed by Dr. T.M. Merrigan, surgical director of the institution. He was unconscious after he arrived at the hospital.

The operation began at 12:29 o'clock and was completed at 1:44. The blow had caused a depressed fracture in Chapman's head three and a half inches long. Dr. Merrigan removed a piece of skull about an inch and a half square and found the brain had been so severely jarred that blood clots had formed. The shock of the blow had lacerated the brain not only on the left side of the head where the ball struck but alos on the right side where the shock of the blow had forced the brain against the skull. Dr. Merrigan said.

Teammates Wait in Hospital.

For a time following the operation Chapman breathed easier and his pulse improved. His teammates who had been waiting anxiously in the hospital were relieved. They went back to their hotel with the hope that the dawn would bring encouraging news. They were notified, instead, of Chapman's death.

This news spread rapidly. Among Chapman's clubmates and among their rivals for the American League pennant alike it caused universal grief. With all the players Chapman was popular. To many of them he had confided his hopes and plans. If Cleveland got into the World's Series this season he would retire from baseball and enter busines in Cleveland. He wanted to be with the wife whom he had married only a year ago, and to whom he gave his last conscious thoughts. As the injured ball player was being taken from the clubhouse at the ball park on his way to the hospital he tried to speak to Percy Smallwood, trainer of the Cleveland Club. Before the game the player had paced in the trainer's custody his diamond ring, a gift from his wife. Several times the stricken man tried to say "Ring". But he could not speak. He pointed to his finger. Smallwood then understood and gave him his wife's gift.

Mrs. Chapman had been notified of the accident shortly after it occured and before it was believed to be so serious.

Wife Is Told of Death.

In response to this message Mrs. Chapman arrived here at 10 A.M. to be at her husband's bedside. She was met at the train by Father Connors, a Philadelphia friend of the ballplayer, who had come to New York immediately on hearing of the accident. Father Conners accompanied Mrs. Chapman to a hotel. There he told her of her husband'sdeath. She fainted.

Chapman's body was removed in the afternoon to the undertaking establishment of James F. McGowan, 153d Street and Amsterdam Avenue. There it was viewed by hundreds of baseball fans, many of whom had gone to the Polo Grounds expecting to see a game. The players of both the New York and Cleveland team also viewed the body there. Several completely lost control of their emotions, and at one time there was not a dry eye among the scores of men who thronged the room about the bier.

Mays is greatly shocked over the accident. He said he had tried to be unusually careful this season to avoid just such an accident. Mays said that Chile Fewster was his close friend, and when the Yankee player was seriously injured in the same way last Spring, the horror of the accident made a deep impression on him. Mays believed that one of the reasons for his failure to pitch succesfully earlier in the season was due to the fact that he pitched the ball too far away from the batsman because he was wary of repeating the Fewster accident.

Thought Ball Hit Bat.

Mays said he threw a high, fast ball at a time when Chapman was crouched over the plate. He thought the ball hit the handle of Chapman's bat, for he fielded the ball and tossed it to first base. It wasn't until after that when he saw Umpire Connelly calling to the stands for a physician, that he realized he had hit Chapman in the head.

"Chapman was one of the gamest players and one of the hardest men to pitch to in the league," said Mays. "I always dreaded pitching to him because of his crouching position at the bat."

The pitcher first learned of Chapman's death through a telephone message from a newspaper. He immediately communicated with the District Attorney's office, and visited Assistant District Attorney Joyce of the Homicide Bureau at 1 o'clock.

"It is the most regrettable incident of my baseball career," he said, "and I would give anything if I could undo what has happened. Chapman was a game, splendid fellow," After hearing Mays's version of the accident, the Assistant District Attorney exonerated Mays from all blame, and as far as the office is concerned the case is closed.

Manager Tris Speaker stayed in his room at his hotel and received no callers.

Manager Miller Huggins of the Yankees believes Chapman's left foot may have caught in the ground in some manner which prevented him from stepping out of the ball's way. Manager Huggins explained that batsmen usually had one foot loose and free at just such moments and Chapman had got

out of the way of the same kind of pitched balls before. The fact that he did not move his feet made Manager Huggins believe his spikes might have caught when he tried to duck.

Ray Caldwell, one of the Cleveland pitchers, and a former member of the Yankees said that, as it looked to him from the Cleveland bench, Chapman ducked his head right into the path of the ball. He said that if he had stood up straight and not attempted to duck, the ball probably would have hit him on the shoulder.

The fatality is expected to have a depressing effect on the Cleveland and New York players. It is feared that it may impair Mays's effectiveness as a pitcher, although he said it would do him no good to brood over something which seemed unavoidable. The Cleveland players are so badly affected by the loss of one of their star players that their chances of winning this year's pennant have received a severe setback. Manager Speaker has no seasoned player to put in the vacant position, and grief among the players over Chapman's death is sure to offset their playing for some time to come.

Flags Ordered at Half-Mast

When Colonel Huston of the New York Club was asked about the reported action of the Boston and Detroit players to have Mays barred from organized baseball, he said the New York Club viewed the fatality purely as an accident, and he did not care to express an opinion on any action, which the players mentioned might anticipate. If these players, however, do send a petition to the league asking for the removal of Mays, the New York Club will then take action.

President Reydler of the National League yesterday ordered all flags at National League parks at half-mast for a week. Similar action is expected by President Johns of the American League.

Raymond Chapman was born in McHenry. Ky., Jan 15, 1891. He had been a member of the Cleveland American League team since Aug. 20, 1912, and was considered one of the best shortstops in the game.

Chapman played his first professional baseball in 1900 with Mount Vernon, Ill. In 1910 he went to Springfield, Ill., and from there to Davenport, Iowa, in the Three I League.

Cleveland first obtained Chapman from Davenport in 1911 and sold him to Toledo in the American Association on option. He was recalled to Cleveland in 1912 and had played in more than 1,000 games in an Indian uniform.

Chapman was one of the fastest men in baseball. On Sept. 27, 1917, Tim Murnane Day at Boston, he won a loving cup for the fastest time in circling the bases, doing it in fourteen seconds.

In 1917 he broke all major league sacrifice hit records with a total of sixty-seven and also led the American League in sacrifices in the following two years.

August 18, 1920

EIGHT WHITE SOX PLAYERS ARE INDICTED ON CHARGE OF FIXING 1919 WORLD SERIES; CICOTTE GOT $10,000 AND JACKSON $5,000

COMISKEY SUSPENDS THEM

Special to The New York Times

CHICAGO, Sept. 28.—Seven star players of the Chicago White Sox and one former player were indicted late this afternoon, charged with complicity in a conspiracy with gamblers to "fix" the 1919 world's series. The indictments were based on evidence obtained for the Cook County Grand Jury by Charles A Comiskey, owner of the White Sox, and after

confessions by two of the players told how the world's championship was thrown to Cincinnati and how they had received money or were "double-crossed" by the gamblers.

The eight players indicted are:
EDDIE CICOTTE, star pitcher.
"SHOELESS JOE" JACKSON, left fielder and heavy hitter.
OSCAR "HAP" FELSCH, centre fielder.
CHARLES "SWEDE" RISBERG, short-stop.
GEORGE "BUCK" WEAVER, third baseman.

ARNOLD GANDIL, former first baseman.
CLAUDE WILLIAMS, pitcher.
FRED McMULLIN, utility player.

The specific charge against the eight players is "conspiracy to commit an illegal act," which is punishable by five years' imprisonment or a fine up to $10,000, but this charge may be changed when the full indictments are drawn by the Grand Jury.

No sooner had the news of the indictments become public than Comiskey suspended the seven players, wrecking the team he had given years to build up and almost certainly forfeiting his chances to beat out Cleveland for the American League pennant.

Would Run Them Out of Baseball

His letter notifying the players of their suspension follows:

Chicago, Sept. 26

To Charles Risberg, Fred McMullin, Joe Jackson, Oscar Felsch, George Weaver, C.P. Williams and Eddie Cicotte:

You and each of you are hereby notified of your indefinite suspension as a member of the Chicago American League Baseball Club.

Your suspension is brought about by information which has just come to me directly involving you and each of you in the baseball scandal resulting from the world's series of 1919.

If you are innocent of any wrongdoing you and each of you will be reinstated; if you are guilty you will be retired from organized baseball for the rest of your lives if ican accomplish it.

Until there is a finality to this investigation it is due to the public that Itake this action, even though it costs Chicago the pennant.

CHICAGO AMERICAN BASEBALL CLUB.

By CHARLES A COMISKEY

Officials of the Grand Jury lifted the curtain on the proceedings and declared that Cicotte and Jackson made open confessions, Cicotte admitting receiving $10,000 and throwing two games, and Jackson admitting receiving $5,000 of $20,000 promised him by the gamblers and telling of his efforts to defeat his own team.

Cicotte Breaks Down and Weeps

Cicotte's confession came after he and Alfred S. Austrian, counsel for the White Sox management, had conferred with Judge Charles A. McDonald in the latter's chambers.

Toward the end of this conference they were joined by Assistant State Attorney Hartley Replogle. Afew moments later he and Cicotte proceeded to the Grand Jury room.

There the great baseball pitcher broke down and wept.

"My God! think of my children," he cried. Cicotte has two small children.

"I never did anything I regretted so much in my life," he continued. "I would give anything in the world if Icould undo my acts in the last world's series. I've played a crooked game and Ihave lost, and Iam here to tell the whole truth.

"I've lived a thousand years in the last year."

Describing how two games were thrown to Cincinnati, Cicotte, according to court officials, said:

"In the first game at Cincinnati Iwas knocked out of the box. I wasn't putting a thing on the ball. You could have read the trade mark on it when I lobbed the ball up to the plate.

"In the fourth game, played at Chicago, which I also lost, I deliberately intercepted a throw from the outfield to the plate which might have cut off a run. I muffed the ball on purpose.

"At another time in the same game I purposely made a wild throw. All the runs scored against me were due to my own deliberate errors. I did not try to win."

Cicotte, it was learned late tonight confessed first to Comiskey, "He went to the latter's office early in the morning."

"I don't know what you'll think of me," he said, "but Igot to tell you how I double-crossed you. Mr. Comiskey, I did double-cross you. I'm a crook, and I got $10,000 for being a crook."

"Don't tell it to me," replied Comiskey," tell it to the Judge."

Cicotte told it to the Judge in tears and shame, slowly, haltingly, hanging his head, now and then pausing to wipe his streaming eyes.

"Risberg and Gandil and McMullin were at me for a week before the world's series started," he said. "They wanted me to go crooked. I didn't know—Ineeded the money. I had the wife and the kids. The wife and kids

don't know this. I don't know what they'll think.

Says He Needed It to Pay Mortgage

"I bought a farm. There was a $4,000 mortgage on it. There isn't any mortgage on it now. I paid it off with the crooked money.

"The eight of us (the eight under indictment) got together in my room three or four days before the games started. Gandil was the master of ceremonies. We talked about throwing the games. Decided we could get away with it. We agreed to do it.

"I was thinking of the wife and kids and how I needed the money. I guess I'm through with baseball. I wasn't wise enough, like Chick, to have the cash in advance. I didn't want any checks. I didnt want any promise, as I wanted the money in bills. I wanted it before I pitched a ball.

"We all talked quite a while about it, I and the seven others. Yes, all of us decided to do our best to throw the games to Cincinnati.

"When Gandil and McMullin took us all, one by one, away from the others, and we talked 'turkey,' they asked me my price. I told them $10,000. And I told them that $10,000 was to be paid in advance.

" 'Cash in advance,' I said. 'Cash in advance, and nothing else.'

"It was Gandil I was talking to. He wanted to give me some money at the time, the rest after the games were played and lost. But it didn't go with me.

" ' I said cash.' I reminded him. 'Cash in advance, and not C.O.D. If you can't trust me. I can't trust you. Pay or I play ball.'

Well, the arguments went on for days—the arguments for 'some now and some later.' But I stood pat. I wanted the $10,000 and got it. "And how I wih that I didn't'.

"The day before I went to Cincinnati I put it up to them squarely for the last time, that there would be nothing doing unlesₒ I had the money.

"That night I found the money under my pillow. There was $10,000, I counted it. I don't know who put it there but it was there. It was my price. I had sold out 'Commy', I had sold out the other boys, sold them for $10,000 to pay off a mortgage on a farm, and for the wife and kids.

"If I had reasoned what that meant to me, the taking of that dirty crooked money-the hours of mental torture, the days and nights of living with an unclean mind; the weeks and months of going along with six of the seven crooked players and holding a guilty secret, and of going along with the boys who had stayed straight and clean and honest— boys who had nothing to trouble them—say it was hell.

"I got the $10,000 cash in advance, that's all."

Jackson Only "Tapped" Ball

Cicotte after his testimony was taken from the courtroom by a back door, and shortly afterward Austrian appeared with Joe Jackson. There was another conference in the chambers of Judge McDonald and a meeting with Assistant State Attorney Replogle, and then Jackson ran the gantlet of newspaper cameramen to the Grand Jury room.

Jackson hung his head and covered his face with his hands. Replogle tried to kerₒ th cameramen away. They refused and there was a volley of flashes. Jackson cursed newspapermen, gamblers and basebaₗ aₙd fled to the security of the jury room.

His story, it was learned, was a confirmation of Cicotte's. It was the story of a low "feeling out" of the cupidity of players by Gandil, McMullin and Risberg.

Joe Jackson, in his confession, said he went into the deal through the influence of Gandil and Risberg. He was promised $20,000 and got $5,000, which was handed to him in Cincinnati by "Lefty" Williams. When he threatened to talk about it, Williams, Gandil and Risberg said, "You poor simp, go ahead and squawk. Where do you get off if you do? We'll all say you're a liar, and every honest baseball player in the world will say you're a liar.You're out of luck. Some of the boys were promised a lot more than you, and got a lot less."

"And that's why I went down and told Judge McDonald and told the Grand Jury what I knew about the frame-up," said Jackson tonight. And I'm giving you a tip. A

lot of these sporting writers who have been roasting me have been talking about the third game of the World's Series being square. Let me tell you something. The eight of us did our best to kick it and little Dick Kerr won the game by his pitching. And because he won it these gamblers 'double-crossed' us for 'double-crossing' them.

"They've hung it on me. They ruined me when I went to the shipyards. But I don't care what happens now. I guess I'm through with baseball. I wasn't wise enough, like Chick, to beat them to it. But some of them will sweat before the show is over.

"Who gave me the money." Lefty Williams slipped it to me the night before I left for Cincinnati and told me I'd get the other $15,000 after I delivered the goods. I took Lefty's word for it. Now Risberg threatens to bump me off if I squak. That's why I had all the bailiffs with me when I left the Grand Jury room this afternoon.

"I'm not under arrest yet and I've got the idea that after what I told them old Joe Jackson isn't going to jail. But I'm not going to get far from my protectors until this blows' over. Swede is a hard guy."

Jackson testified, according to the officials, that throughout the series he either struck out or hit easy balls when hits would mean runs. Jackson also testified, it is said, that Claude Williams received $10,000.

Jackson Comes Out Smiling

Jackson was before the Grand Jury nearly two hours, and he came out walking erect and smiling.

"I got a big load off my chest," he told a friend who accosted him. I'm feeling better."

"Don't ask Joe any questions," Replogle cautioned the newspaper men.

"He's gone through beautifully and we don't want him bothered."

Joe intimated he was "willing to tell the world now, if they'll let me."

The crowd outside the Criminal Court buildings cheered and jeered as he rode off in the custody of bailiffs.

Cicotte is also in the custody of officers from the State Attorney's office.

"We are taking no chances on anything," was the only explanation Mr. Replogle offered of this.

Mrs. Henrietta Kelley, owner of an apartment house on Grand Boulevard, with whom many of the players and their families lived, gave testimony in the morning which Mr. Replogle declared was "extremely important."

Mrs. Kelley herself denied that she had given any important evidence.

President Heydler Testifies

President Heydler of the National League also was a witness. No hint of the nature of his testimony could be obtained from the prosecutors. Mr. Replogle dismissed questioners with his stock statement, "It is of great importance."

Mr. Austrian, attorney for the White Sox, said:

"Mr. Comiskey and myself, as his counsel, have been working on this for a year. We have spent a great deal of Mr. Comiskey's money to ferret it out. It is because of our investigation the lid has been blown off this scandal."

"Mr. Heydler is also testifying," he said: "Mr. McGraw will appear also—of their own volition, of course."

The significance of Heydler's testimony appeared when it was announced that two National League players would be summoned by the Grand Jury, Olsen, shortstop, of Brooklyn, and Rawlings, second baseman, of Philadelphia. Each is said to have won $2,000 on the first two games of the 1919 world's series.

The announcement of the calling of these players was followed by the intimation from the State Attorney's office that the investigation would soon reach far beyond Bill Maharg, former pugilist; Bill Burns, a retired ball player now interested in the oil industry of Texas, and Abe Attell who so far have been named in the investigation as connected with 'the gamblers' end.

The Grand Jury recessed for the day with the conclusion of Jackson's testimony, but there was promise of more fireworks tomorrow.

(United Press International)

Ed Cicotte, Chicago White Sox pitcher, whose career was brought to an abrupt end by the "Black Sox" scandal of 1919.

(United Press International)

Judge Kenesaw Mountain Landis, just after he was named First Commissioner of Baseball in 1920.

"It'll be hotter, and there'll be more of it," Mr. Repiogle promised. He declined to say whether immunity had been promised Jackson and Cicotte or whether it would be promised any others.

Two witnesses, Dr. Raymond B. Prettyman, a friend of Buck Weaver and John J. McGraw, manager of the New York Giants, who appeared to testify today, were told they could not be heard until tomorrow.

Claude "Lefty" Williams, the man who handed Joe Jackson $5,000 will be the central figure in the baseball investigation tomorrow.

Williams will be asked who handed him the money. He also may be asked as to his career in the Coast League, and he may be asked as to his knowledge of a scandal regarding fixed games after Salt Lake City entered the league.

Williams was questioned tonight as to his part in the conspiracy, but was non-committal.

Mr. Comiskey tonight made the following statement:

"The consideration which the Grand Jury gave to this case should be greatly appreciated by the general public. Charles A. McDonald, Chief Justice, and the foreman of the Grand Jury, Harry Brigham, and his associates, who so diligently strived to save and make America's great game the clean sport which it is, are to be commended in no uncertain terms by all sport followers, in spite of what happened today.

"Thank God it did happen. Forty-four years of baseball endeavor have convinced me more than ever that it is a wonderful game and a game worth keeping clean.

"I would rather close my ball park than send nine men on the field with one of them holding a dishonest thought toward clean baseball-the game which John McGraw and I went around the world with to show to the people on the other side.

"We are far from through yet. We have the nucleus of another championship team with the remainder of the old world's championship team."

He named the veterans, Eddie and John Collins, Ray Schalk, Urban Faber, Dick Kerr, Eddie Murphy, Nemo Leibold and Amos Strunk and declared that, with the addition of Hodge, Falk, Jordan and McClellan. "I guess we can go along and win the championship yet."

Buck Weaver, when seen just after receiving notice of his suspension, declared he never received any of the money said to have been distributed and denied all knowledge of the deal to throw games in the world's series.

He said his own record, in the series of 1919, in which he batted .333 and made only four errors out of thirty chances, ought to exonerate him.

"Any man who bats .333 is bound to make trouble for the other team in a ball game," he said. "The best team cannot win a world's championship without getting the breaks."

How Chicago Lost Championship

CHICAGO, Sept. 28 (Associated Press). —Last year's world series records show that in the first inning of the first game Cicotte started by hitting Rath, the first Cincinnati batter, in the back. Daubert followed with a single over second base that sent Rath to third, and he scored when Groh flied to Jackson, Rath beating Jackson's throw to the plate.

Chicago tied this run in the next inning, Kopf putting Jackson on second with a wild throw. Feisch sacrificed him to third and Gandil dropped a little fly safely in centre, scoring Jackson.

The end of Cicotte's pitching and the runs that ultimately won the game were scored by Cincinnati in the fourth inning. All the damage was done with two out. With Kopf on first, Neale and Wingo singled and Reuther, the hard-hitting Cincinnati pitcher, drove a three-base hit to the centre field bleachers. Rath doubled and Daubert singled, the combination resulting in five runs.

Wilkinson took Cicotte's place after Daubert's single and Groh flied to Feisch. The final score of this game was 9 to 1.

The fourth game, played at Chicago, was won by the Reds by a score of 2 to 0, Ring pitching for Cincinnati, holding the American League champions to three hits. Both Cincinnati runs were made in the fifth inning, when two of Cincinnati's hits were bunched with a wild throw to first by Cicotte and a bad throw to the plate by Jackson, which the pitcher intercepted and muffed. The play of this inning was sent over the Associated Press as follows:

"Rousch was out, Schalk to Gandil, the ball rolling half way to the pitcher's box. Duncan was safe when Cicotte threw his drive wide to first, the ball going to the stand and Duncan reaching second. Kopf singled to left and Duncan stopped at third, but scored when Jackson threw wild to the plate. Kopf reached second.—Correction: The official scorer gives Cicotte the error for muffling Jackson's throw. Neale sent one over Jackson's head and Kopf scored. Neale reached second. It was a two-base hit. Wingo, out, Ed. Collins to Gandil, Neale going to third. Ring drove a vicious grounder that Ed Collins got and threw him out at first. Two runs. Two hits. Two errors.

The rest of the game was played sharply and, so far as the records show cleanly. Cicotte pitched through the nine innings.

Cicotte's next appearance in the series was in the sixth game, when Cincinnati had four victories to its credit against one defeat, Richard Kerr, the diminutive left-handed pitcher, having shut out the National League champions in the third game. The veteran twirler, who today confessed the big gambling deal, went through nine innings and held his opponents to seven hits. Chicago won the game 4 to 1, hitting Sallee hard in the first five innings. Jackson and Feisch each got two hits and between them drove in all of Chicago's runs.

Billy Manarg, Philadelphia prize fighter, who last night, in Philadelphia, issued a statement connecting Cicotte with the gambling deal and charging Abe Attell, former fighter, headed the gambling clique asserted that the Sox were "double-crossed" by Attell and never received $100,000 which had been promised them. It was late in the series before they found this out, Maharg asserted, as Attell kept postponing the day of settlement, saying he needed the money to bet.

Besides the two defeats registered against Cicotte in the series, three others were chalked up against Claude Williams. The latter, a "side arm" left-hander, was wild in the second and fifth games, which went to the Reds 4 to 2 and 5 to 9. In the eighth and last game of the series he was found for four solid hits in the first inning, and that game and the title of world champions went to Cincinnati, 10 to 5. Williams's lack of control was generally recorded as the cause of his defeats, the record

of the second game saying:

"While Cincinnati obtained only four hits, these came at opportune times when they had been preceded by bases on balls off Williams."

The fifth game of the series was a shut out triumph for Hod Eller, the big "shine ball" expert of the Cincinnati pitching staff. Only three hits were two successive innings. All told, Eller had nine strikeouts that day.

Four of Cincinnati's five runs were grouped in the sixth inning. Eller doubled, Rath scored him with a single and moved to second on Daubert's "bunt perfectly laid," as the report of the game said. Williams walked. Groh. Rousch drove a three-base hit to Feisch's territory, scoring two runners and himself tallied after Duncan flied to Jackson.

Both Cicotte and Jackson were closeted with the Grand Jury for a considerable time today, and later court officials reported that they told their stories in substantial detail. As they left the room they were taken in custody by detectives of the State's Attorney's office. Their detention was not in the nature of an arrest, and it was announced that they would be released later.

Cicotte, who earlier in the day had vehemently denied any part in the alleged plot, as described by Maharg at Philadelphia yesterday, admitted on the stand, officials of the courts said that the Philadelphian's story was substantially correct.

The court officials also quoted Cicotte as saying that the players had believed that "Chick" Gandil who, he said, was interested in the dealings with the gamblers had "double-crossed" them, and that Maharg's story was the first intimation they had had that Attell had "held out" on the $100,000 which had been promised them.

The investigation by the Grand Jury will continue until all phases of baseball gambling have been bared, it was said by officials. The investigation started two weeks ago following reports that a game played here Aug. 31 by the Cubs and the Philadelphia Nationals was "fixed" and the inquiry into last year's world series came up only as an incident to the other inquiry

Assistant State's Attorney Hartley Repiogle, in charge of the case, said tonight that indictments to be drawn up tomorrow on today's true bills may contain several counts. The true bills themselves specified but one alleged offense, "conspiracy to commit an illegal act." The penalty provided upon conviction on this count would be one to five years in the penitentiary, and a fine of not more than $10,000.

"This is just the beginning" Mr. Repiogle said tonight. "We will have more indictments within a few days and before we get through we will have purged organized baseball of everything that is crooked and dishonest.

"We are going after the gamblers now. There will be indictments within a few days against men in Philadelphia, Indianapolis, St. Louis, Des Moines, Pittsburgh, Cincinnati and other cities. More baseball players also will be indicted. We've got the goods on these men and we are going the limit."

Harry Grabiner, Secretary of the White Sox, announced that the club would play out the schedule to the end if it had to "employ Chinamen" to fill the vacancies in the team.

September 29, 1920

SMITH THE HERO AS INDIANS WIN FROM ROBINS, 8-1

Special to The New York Times.

CLEVELAND, Oct. 10.—The unromantic name of Smith is on everybody's

lips in Cleveland tonight, for Elmer Smith, the right fielder of Speaker's Indians, accomplished something in the fifth world's series clash this afternoon that is the life ambition of every big league ball player. Elmer crashed a home run over the right field fence with the bases full in the first inning and sent the Indians on their merry way to a 8 to 1 victory over Brooklyn. Fate tried to conceal this lucky boy by naming him Smith, but with that tremendous slap Elmer shoved his commonplace

identity up alongside the famous Smiths of history, which include Captain John, the Smith Brothers, and the Village Smithy.

This home-run punch which shoved over four runs in a cluster is the first of its kind that has ever been made in a world's series game. Cleveland now has won three games to Brooklyn's two, and an overjoyed city this evening has about come to the conclusion that the championship streamer will float over the proud fifth city of the U.S.A.

While the delirous crowd of more than 35,000 was still rejoicing over Smith's stumptous smash. Bill Wambegans broke into the celebration to steal some of Smithy's thunder by accomplishing the first unassisted triple play that was ever whisked a world's series populace up to the heights of happiness.

The crowd was already husky-voiced and nerve-wrecked with wild excitement when Wamby started to make baseball history. It seemed as if everything that must happen to make Cleveland's joy had happened.

Along in the fifth inning, when Bagby, with a commonwing lead behind him, was taking it easy, Kilduff and Otto Miller both made singles and were perched on second and first. Clarence Mitchell, who had long since succeeded the badly wrecked Burleigh Grimes on the pitching mound, was at bat, and for the first time during the afternoon it looked as if the slipping Robins were going to accomplish something.

Uncle Robbie had evidently wigwagged a sign from the bench for a hit and run play, which means that the runners were expected to gallop just as soon as Mitchell swung his bat.

Mitchell connected solidly and jammed a tearing liner over second base. Wamby was quite a distance from second, but he leaped over toward the cushion and with a mighty jump speared the ball with one hand. Kilduff was on his way to third base and Miller was almost within reach of second.

Wamby's noodle began to operate faster than it ever did before. He hopped over to second and touched the bag, retiring Kilduff, who was far down the alley toward third base. Then Wamby turned and saw Otto Miller standing there like a wooden Indian. Otto was evidently so surprised that he was glued to the ground, and Wamby just waltzed over and touched him for the third out.

The crowd forgot it was hoarse of voice and close to nervous exhaustion and gave Wamby just as great a reception as it had given Elmer Smith.

Those two-record-breaking feats were not all that happened in today's game to make Cleveland feel proud of its baseball club and itself. Not by a long shot! Along in the fourth inning when Grimes was still trying to pitch, Jim Bagby, the Indians' big, slow, lazy boxman, became suddenly inspired and with two fellow Indians on the bases he soaked a home run into the new bleachers which protrude far out into right centrefield.

No World's Series pitcher has ever received such a humiliating cudgeling as Grimes did this afternoon, for the simple reason that no other pitcher has ever been kept in the box so long after he had started to slip. Uncle Robbie kept him on the mound for three and two-third innings and in that time he was badly plastered for nine hits, including two home runs and a triple.

With half a dozen able-bodied pitchers basking in the warm sun, Grimes was kept in the game until he was so badly battered that the game became a joke. Instead of being enormously wealthy in pitchers as Robbie was supposed to be, he became a pauper as far as pitching talent is concerned. When the Indians had the score 7 to 0 Grimes limped out of the game and Clarence Mitchell, who had been faithfully warming up ever since he hit Cleveland, went out to the box and one more run was the best that the Indians could do off him.

That first inning is one which will ever linger in baseball memory. The Sunday crowd jammed every inch of the park and was even more enthusiastic than the throng at the opening game here. Strong-lunged young men went through the grandstands with megaphones and implored the fans to give the Indians their vocal and moral encouragement as they had at the opening game. "We want to make it four straight," they yelled, "and fly the world's championship silk from our flagpole."

The memory of Grimes's great pitching still lingered in the minds of the spectators, but the Cleveland Club on its own meadow is a far different kind of ball club from that which the residents of Flatbush saw last week. The Indians were on their toes and ran back and forth to their positions in the field like a college baseball nine.

The roar of the faithful followers was like a tonic and Speaker's men reveled in the wonderful reception they received. The thing that was uppermost

Official Score of Fifth World's Series Game

CLEVELAND (A. L.)

	AB.	R.	H.	TB.	2B.	3B.	HR.	BB.	SO.	SH.	SB.	PO.	A.	E.
Jamieson, lf......	4	1	2	1	0	0	0	0	0	0	0	2	1	0
Graney, lf......	1	0	0	0	0	0	0	0	1	0	0	0	0	0
Wambsgans, 2b..	5	1	1	1	0	0	0	0	0	0	0	7	2	0
Speaker, cf.......	3	2	1	1	0	0	0	1	0	0	0	1	0	0
E. Smith, rf......	4	1	3	8	0	1	1	0	0	0	0	0	0	0
Gardner, 3b......	4	0	1	1	0	0	0	0	0	0	0	2	2	1
W. Johnston, 1b..	3	1	2	2	0	0	0	0	0	1	0	9	1	0
Sewell, ss........	3	0	0	0	0	0	0	1	0	0	0	2	4	0
O'Neill, c........	2	1	0	0	0	0	0	2	0	0	0	3	1	1
Thomas, c........	0	0	0	0	0	0	0	0	0	0	0	1	0	0
Bagby, p........	4	1	2	5	0	0	1	0	0	0	0	0	2	0
Total	33	8	12	19	0	1	2	4	1	1	0	27	13	2

BROOKLYN (N. L.)

	AB.	R.	H.	TB.	2B.	3B.	HR.	BB.	SO.	SH.	SB.	PO.	A.	E.
Olson, ss........	4	0	2	2	0	0	0	0	0	0	0	3	5	0
Sheehan, 3b......	3	0	1	1	0	0	0	0	0	1	0	1	1	1
Griffith, rf......	4	0	0	0	0	0	0	0	1	0	0	0	0	0
Wheat, lf........	4	1	2	2	0	0	0	0	1	0	0	3	0	0
Myers, cf........	4	0	2	2	0	0	0	0	0	0	0	0	0	0
Konetchy, 1b....	4	0	2	4	0	1	0	0	1	0	0	9	2	0
Kilduff, 2b......	4	0	1	1	0	0	0	0	0	0	0	5	6	0
Miller, c........	2	0	2	2	0	0	0	0	0	0	0	0	1	0
Krueger, c.......	2	0	1	1	0	0	0	0	0	0	0	2	1	0
Grimes, p.......	1	0	0	0	0	0	0	0	0	0	0	0	1	0
Mitchell, p.......	2	0	0	0	0	0	0	0	0	0	0	1	0	0
Total	34	1	13	15	0	1	0	0	3	1	0	24	17	1

SCORE BY INNINGS.

Cleveland	4	0	0	3	1	0	0	0	..—8
Brooklyn	0	0	0	0	0	0	0	0	1—1

Triple play—Wambsgans, unassisted. Double plays—Olson, Kilduff and Konetchy; Jamieson and O'Neill; Gardner, Wambsgans and W. Johnston; W. Johnston, Sewell and W. Johnston. Left on bases—Brooklyn, 7; Cleveland, 6. Bases on balls—Off Grimes, 1; Mitchell, 3. Struck out—By Bagby, 3; Mitchell, 1. Hitts—Off Grimes, 9 in 3 1-3 innings; Mitchell, 3 in 4 2-3. Wild pitch—Bagby. Passed ball—Miller. Losing pitcher—Grimes. Umpires—Klem (N. L.), at plate; Connolly (A. L.), first base; O'Day (N. L.), second base; Dinneen (A. L.), third base. Time of game—One hour and forty-nine minutes.

in their minds was to show the home folks that they appreciated the loyalty. The best way they could show it was to win and they showed 'em. It didn't matter that it was a one-sided ball game and that the Brooklyn Club, minus good pitching, looked woefully weak and with the absence of the injured Jimmy Johnston at third base was inclined to be panicky. The only thing that mattered was that Cleveland was winning the ball game and the more runs the Indians could make the more fun there was in it for the Cleveland fans.

Jamieson was the first Indian to face Burleigh Grimes in the opening inning. He pounded a roller down through Koney which was too warm for the Dodger first baseman to handle. Wamby poked another single off Grimes and Jamieson went to second. The crowd chanted a flattering chorus of cheers to Speaker when he came to the bat. The wee bit of a tap which bounded off Tris's bat dropped in the infield and Grimes ran over to pick up the Indian manager's bunt and throw him out at first. Grimes slipped as he was about to pick up the ball and he was reclining on his back when he made a useless throw to first. It was a hit, and the bases were loaded with no one out.

The National Boiler Works laboring overtime never made the racket that was now taking place in the ball park. The noise waves flowed up in gushes and echoed all over the city of Cleveland, finally rumbling far out on Lake Erie.

Elmer Smith is at the bat. You'll find Smiths here, there and everywhere, so there was nothing about the name to arouse enthusiasm. Elmer took a fond look at the high screen on top of the right field fence and Grimes began to pitch to him. The three Indians on the bases jumped up and down on their toes impatiently.

Elmer took two healthy swings at the ball and missed, and the next one was wide and he let it waft by.

Grimes looked around the bases and saw that he was entirely surrounded by Indians. He was ambushed by the Redskins. He felt that danger lurked in this Smith boy at the bat.

When Grimes hurled the next ball over, Smith took a mighty blow at the ball and it rose like a bird, went so far up in the air that it looked like a quinine pill.

Jamieson, Wamby and Speaker all took one good look at that rapidly rising ball, then they bent their heads, dug their spikes into the dirt and started to run. Grimes was knocked dizzy. As he looked about him he could see nothing but Indians chasing themselves around in a circle.

Smith, who just a few seconds before was just plain Elmer Smith, had become Home Run Smith before he had trotted as far as second base. When he had reached third, he was Hero Smith, and by the time he had crossed the plate he was a candidate for a bronze statue in City Square along with General Moses Cleveland, who founded this town, and Tom L. Johnson, who decorates the park just opposite old Geenral Mose.

Manager Speaker, still a young man, yet gray and bald from baseball worries, was waiting at the plate when Smith touched the platter. Around Smith's neck went Tris's arm and he was the first to pat him on the back. Grimes stood out in the pitcher's box stupefied. The other Brooklyn players walked about in a daze and waited for the noise riot to subside.

Grimes was still pitching when the game was resumed. The Cleveland players wondered just what had to be done to a Brooklyn pitcher before he is taken out of the game. However, Grimes became a little better, and the side was retired after Burleigh had been aided by a double play.

Big Ed Konetchy walloped a triple to left centre field in the Brooklyn second, with one gone, but when Kilduff hoisted a fly to Jamieson and Koney tried to score after the catch Jamieson chucked him out at the plate with a perfect throw.

This was the first of a series of three double plays which, with Wamby's matchless triple killing, furnished a defense for Bagby's loose pitching that would have prevented any pitcher from losing, no matter how badly he was flinging. The Dodgers got ten hits off Bagby in eight innings and couldn't put over a single run. Peerless defensive work saved him.

Brooklyn's most wasteful inning was the third, when Miller singled and Grimes hit into a double play. Olson and Sheehan, who was playing by special dispensation at third in place of the injured Jimmy Johnston, both singled. Griffith hoisted a foul to Gardner, ending the inning. There were three smacking singles without a runner getting beyond second base.

Smith got a tremendous cheer when he came to the bat in the third inning. There were two down at the time, and he jarred a terrific triple to left centre. The smash went to seed because Kilduff tossed Gardner out at first for the final out of the inning.

The next citizen to be hailed as a hero is lazy James Bagby. No pitcher was ever before pounded for thirteen hits in a world's series and emerge a hero. Jim Bagby, big Sergeant Jim, did it. He pitched what was really a bad game of ball, but when it was over he was proud of it.

Doc Johnston opened the fourth inning when he bounded a hit off Grimes's leg. Yes, Grimes is still pitching for Brooklyn. Clarence Mitchell is warming up out in left field. He warmed up all day yesterday and started warming up early today.

Anyway, Doc got his hit off Grimes's leg. He went to second on a passed ball and to third as Sheehan was retiring Sewell at first. Grimes walked O'Neill purposely to get Bagby, and that is just where Jim, the barge, has the laugh on Grimes. Bagby slammed a long drive to right centre which dropped just inside the fence that is built around the new centre field bleachers. Johnston and O'Neill both romped home ahead of Jim amid scenes of wild, barbarous disorder.

Grimes Still on Mound.

When the riot was quelled, Grimes was still pitching for Brooklyn. Does this fellow Grimes stand so strongly with Uncle Robbie that he is never taken out of a game, no time, no place, no how?

Jamieson spanked a roller down to first base, and although three Brooklyn fielders, Grimes, Koney and Kilduff, tried to retire the runner at first, Jamieson was too swift and got a hit for himself out of the confusion.

It suddenly dawned upon Manager Robinson that the Indians were hitting Grimes, so he took him out and Mitchell went to the box.

Sheehan was naturally nervous in his first big game, and in the fifth, when Speaker hit a roller to him, Sheehan threw the ball right over Konetchy's head, and Speaker went to second. "Home Run" Smith got a single and Speaker went to third. Gardner cracked a single to centre and Speaker crossed the plate with the Indians' last run.

Brooklyn's run came in the ninth inning when many of the jubilant Cleveland spectators were hurrying toward the gates. They were already shouting Cleveland victory to the world and the scoring of the lone tally commanded absolutely no attention at all.

Bagby fanned Griffith as a starter, and then, as he listlessly chucked the ball over, Wheat singled to right. Jim was still listless when he threw the ball at Myers, who slapped a single to centre which sent Wheat to second. Konetchy hit a mean hopper down through Doc Johnston, the ball bounding out into the field as Wheat scampered home and saved the Dodgers from a shutout.

Brooklyn's stock has taken an awful drop.

October 11, 1920

BASEBALL PEACE DECLARED; LANDIS NAMED DICTATOR

Chicago Jurist Is Appointed a One-Man Court of Last Resort for Major Leagues.

CLUB OWNERS COMPROMISE

Adjust Points of Difference in Three-Hour Conference—Expect Minors to Concur.

LANDIS RETAINS OLD POST

Stays on Bench While Accepting $42,500 Salary in New Position—A Seven-Year Arrangement.

Special to The New York Times.

CHICAGO, Nov. 12.—With Judge Kenesaw Mountain Landis of the United States District Court as arbitrator, a one-man court of last resort, peace will obtain in professional baseball for at least seven years, while the eminent jurist will also continue to strike terror into the hearts of criminals by retaining his position as a Federal Judge.

Sixteen club owners of the National and American Leagues reached this happy solution of their difficulties after a three-hour conference at the Congress Hotel today. They then adjourned, to wait upon Judge Landis in a body and present their proposition to him. After only a few minutes' talk with the major league magnates, the Judge accepted the highest responsibility that can be conferred by the promoters of the national sport, and in his acceptance made it plain that he was undertaking the task as a public trust, having in mind the millions of fans of all ages who are interested in baseball.

By this action the former three-man National Commission was permanently discarded, and the supreme authority over baseball was centralized in the hands of one man. Up to date this statement applies only to the major leagues, but it is expected the minors will join with the big fellows in submitting all their future disputes, which they cannot decide within their own ranks, to the decision of Judge Landis. The committee of six named at the Kansas City meeting of the minor leagues to confer with a committee of three each from the National and American Leagues will function only in the matter of drafting a new agreement and a set of rules to govern future relations. That committee has no voice in the selection of the proposed Board of Control, which has now been concentrated into a membership of one man, the unanimous choice of sixteen club owners.

Expect Minors to Concur.

If the minors fail to approve the action of the majors they will be permitted to handle their own affairs in any way they may choose, but it is not expected they will fail to concur.

The joint committee now will have only to prepare the rules and regulations of their combined business affairs. The interpretation and enforcement of these rules and regulations will be vested in a one-man commission.

In their conference with Judge Landis the major leaguers quickly sensed the fact that he was unwilling to leave his position on the bench despite his great interest in the game which he had characterized several years ago as a national institution. The club owners had made their financial argument so strong that they thought it would be unanswerable, but Judge Landis made it plain that his hesitancy was due solely to his great reluctance to quit the bench. They then suggested the plan which was accepted whereby the jurist could continue to interpret the criminal laws of the land and at the same time keep crooks out of baseball.

The Salary Arrangement.

When this point was reached Judge Landis proposed that the salary offered him by the baseball magnates be reduced by the amount of his salary as District Court Justice, so that instead of receiving $50,000 a year as the Supreme Court of baseball, he would get $42,500.

In accepting the responsibility Judge Landis gave out a formal statement, in which he emphasized his reasons in the following words:

"The opportunities for real service to baseball are limitless. It is a matter to which I have devoted nearly forty years on the question of policy. All I have to say is this: The only thing in anybody's mind now, is to make baseball what the millions of fans throughout the United States want it to be."

This climax to nearly a month of "crucial" days is believed to mark the beginning of a new era in professional baseball. For the first time in the history of the sport, its promoters have sought and obtained a supreme ruler who has not had, and never expects to have, any interest in the pastime other than that which is born in every red-blooded American. They have selected in Judge Landis a man in whom the men of all branches of sport, as well as business, have such great confidence that if one of his important decisions were ever questioned by a club owner, player or fan, the questioner would be in bad favor with the public and the burden of proof would rest with him. Hitherto, when a club owner has emitted a yell about a verdict of the National Commission, he has been sure of the sympathy of at least the fans of his own town. Now he will not get even that.

Resolutions Adopted.

The formality of reaching this settlement of their differences occupied the magnates several hours, during which they aired their varying views without the aid of league Presidents or other intermediaries. The magnates selected as their Chairman President Baker of the Philadelphia Nationals, who was obliged to leave to catch a train for the East before the conclusion was reached. His successor in the Chair was President Veick of the Chicago Cubs. After reaching an understanding informally, the meeting became formal enough to pass the following resolutions:

That the Chairman of the Board of Control shall be elected by a majority vote of the clubs composing the American and National Leagues.

"That his successor be elected in the same manner and that this shall be incorporated in the new national agreement.

"That upon all questions of an interleague nature or in any matter coming up at a joint meeting of the two major leagues, the roll be called and, after voting by clubs of each league, if there be a division, then the American League shall cast one vote and the National League one vote. Should these two votes be at variance, then the Commissioner shall cast the deciding vote and there shall be no appeal therefrom.

"Further, that the Commissioner shall preside at all joint meetings."

A Compromise Measure.

The foregoing means that the club owners reached a compromise on the chief point of difference which has kept them apart for weeks. That was the controversy over the right to vote by clubs or by leagues. The National League contention that, in the selection of a governing body, the majority vote of the sixteen clubs should decide, was conceded by the American League. In all other matters it was conceded by the National League that interleague disputes should be decided by a vote of the leagues, each having an equal voice, but that, if no agreement could be reached in this way, the commission should have the right to decide without appeal.

In disposing of the question of associate members of the commission to act with Judge Landis, no final action was taken at this meeting, but it was provided that the President of the American League should appear before the commissioner as a special pleader in cases involving the American League and that the President of the National League should be empowered to act in a similar capacity in cases involving the veteran circuit. And it was further understood that these men should appear only in cases in which their respective leagues of clubs were concerned.

It was also stipulated that, if the minor leagues decide to operate with the majors in the new arrangement, they shall appoint a special pleader to appear before the commission in all cases in which a minor league or a minor club-owner may be involved.

Lasker Plan Approved.

President Herrmann of the Cincinnati Club introduced a resolution which was seconded by President Dunn of the Cleveland Club indorsing the Lasker plan without specifically mentioning its author.

Details of the new agreement for the control and perpetuation of baseball will be worked out by a draft committee to be composed of twelve members equally divided between the majors and minors. The minors already have named their six. The National League had nominated a committee of four consisting of Herrmann, Ebbets, Dreyfuss and Ruppert, but this will be reduced to three and it is likely that President Heydler of the National League will be included on it. Likewise it is believed the committee of three to be appointed by the American League will include President Johnson of that circuit and Clark Griffith of the Washington Club, who is generally credited with having been the most efficacious factor in bringing about peace between the warring factions.

Statement of Owners.

CHICAGO, Nov. 12.—The following statement was issued by the sixteen club owners after today's meeting:

"At the joint meeting of the sixteen club owners of the major leagues held at the Congress Hotel today, Judge Kenesaw Mountain Landis was unanimously elected as the head of organized baseball for a term of seven years. The clubs of the American and National Leagues were represented by club owners and club Presidents. All of the differences existing between members of the American and National Leagues were adjusted in such a manner that the decision was agreeable to all.

"The following men were in the meeting room:

"American League—Cleveland, James C. Dunn; Chicago, Charles A. Comiskey, Harry Grabiner; Boston, Harry Frazee; New York, Jacob Ruppert; Philadelphia, Theodore Shibe, Connie Mack; St. Louis, Phil D. C. Ball, Robert Quinn; Detroit, Frank C. Navin; Washington, Clark Griffith.

"National League—Boston, George W. Grant; Brooklyn, Charles H. Ebbets; Chicago, William L. Veeck, A. D. Lasker; Cincinnati, Garry Herrmann; New York, Charles Stoneham, John McGraw; Philadelphia, William F. Baker, Charles Roch; St. Louis, Sam Breadon; Pittsburgh, Barney Dreyfuss."

The following resolution was introduced by Garry Herrmann of the Cincinnati Club and seconded by James C. Dunn of the Cleveland Club and unanimously adopted:

"Resolved, That the meeting endorse the principles of ethical control of baseball proposed in the plan submitted to all professional league clubs by four major league club owners in October last, and instruct the Drafting Committee that the spirit contained therein be embodied in the new national agreement.

"That the unreviewable control of all ethical matters be invested in the Chairman of the Control Board."

"A Peace That Will Last."

"We've made a real peace—one that will last," was the comment of President Veeck of the Chicago National League Club as the meeting broke up. "The full details of the reorganization have not been settled, of course, but we expect to issue a formal statement soon telling all about it. It's enough to say now that the war is over and every one of us is mighty glad of it."

Chicago will be headquarters for the baseball commissioners, and offices will be opened here immediately.

If second and third members are chosen for the commission, it is virtually certain, according to the club owners, that Judge Charles A. MacDonald of Chicago will be one of them, although no vote was taken today. Judge MacDonald indirectly brought on the baseball war, for he started the baseball scandal investigation which brought about the proposals for reorganization of control of baseball.

Judge Landis was hearing a case in which $15,000 bribery in connection with an income tax was charged when the committee of magnates filed into the courtroom, hats in their hands. The Judge sharply banged his gavel and ordered them to make less noise. When informed of their mission he had them escorted to his chambers, where they were kept in waiting for forty-five minutes before the Judge would listen to the offer which increased his annual salary from $7,500 a year to $50,000.

While the magnates waited the Judge conducted the bribery trial in his usual vigorous fashion and gave vent to some scathing remarks about the men who falsify their income tax returns. Waiting on the Judge were Charles Comiskey, President of the Chicago American League club; William Veeck, President of the Chicago Nationals; Jacob Ruppert of the New York Americans, Clark Griffith of Washington, Charles Ebbets of Brooklyn, Garry Herrmann of Cincinnati, Barney Dreyfus of Pittsburgh and John Breadon of the St. Louis Nationals. Later they were joined by Connie Mack of the Philadelphia Americans, Robert Quinn and James Dunn of Cleveland.

Why Judge Landis Accepted.

After the meeting Judge Landis took Clark Griffith, a personal friend, over to a window.

"Grif," he said, "I'm going to tell you just why I took this job. See those kids down there on the street? See that airplane propeller on the wall? Well, that explains my acceptance.

"You see that propeller was on the plane in which my son, Major Reed Landis, flew while overseas. Reed and I went to one of the world's series games at Brooklyn. Outside the gate was a bunch of little kids playing around. Reed turned to me and said: 'Dad, wouldn't it be a shame to have the game of these little kids broken up? Wouldn't it be awful to take baseball away from them?' Well, while you gentlemen were talking to me, I looked up at this propeller and thought of Reed. Then I thought of his remark in Brooklyn. Grif, we've got to keep baseball on a high standard for the sake of the youngsters—that's why I took the job, because I want to help."

Johnson Says He's Satisfied.

President B. B. Johnson of the American League, leader of the opponents of the Lasker plan, received his first information concerning the meeting from The Associated Press and expressed pleasure at the action taken.

"I am for Judge Landis and I think these club owners have acted wisely," he said. "Baseball will be placed on the highest possible standard now, and there will be no more fights. I am well satisfied with everything that took place today."

President John Heydler of the National League made the following statement to The Associated Press:

"I am very happy over this solution of the baseball problem. It is an upward step for baseball, and forever eliminates politics from the national game. One of the chief worries of a League President is to vote fairly in the National Commission, and I am glad to be relieved of that responsibility."

HAD HARDING'S GOOD WISHES.

Lasker Says President-Elect Hoped for Peace in Baseball.

CHICAGO, Nov. 12.—A. D. Lasker, originator of the Lasker plan of baseball control, tonight let it become known that he had given up a trip to the South with President-elect Harding to attend today's baseball meeting and that Senator Harding had requested him to remain at the meeting here rather than join him in the trip.

"Senator Harding called me by telephone a few days ago to ask me to join him, but when I told him of the meeting scheduled for today, he said to me by all means to stay here. He said he was very much interested in baseball and hoped everything would be settled peacefully."

November 13, 1920

LANDIS A NATIONAL FIGURE.

Has Sat in Many Famous Cases—A Close Student of Baseball.

CHICAGO, Nov. 12.—Judge Landis is a national figure for the important cases he has passed upon, and his wit and sarcasm—sometimes humorous and sometimes caustic—which he directs at prisoners and counsel from his bench have made him famous.

Baseball has always been one of his hobbies. In the little town of Logansport, Ind., where he was reared, the Judge played on amateur and semi-professional teams. His brilliant playing brought him many offers to turn professional, but he always declined, saying he played merely for love of the game.

In 1914 Judge Landis presided in the legal battle which resulted from the greatest baseball war in history—the fight of the Federal League against the National and American Leagues. The Judge never rendered a decision in this case, however, for it was settled out of court while he was still forming his official opinion. While studying the case the Judge spent many hours looking into baseball history, examining the national agreement and other documents giving information concerning baseball. This knowledge acquired during this period made him a legal authority on the administration of the game's affairs.

Judge Landis attends many major league games here every year and seldom misses a world's series. At the annual ball classic, he generally may be found in a box back of third base, his old, black slouch hat pulled down over his eyes and a long black cape falling from his shoulders. He never talks during a game, but studies every play closely and enjoys analysing the strategy used by the opposing players. One of his hobbies at a game is to try to guess the next play.

Judge Landis was born in Millville, Ohio, Nov. 20, 1866, and was named for Kenesaw Mountain, near Atlanta, Ga., where his father was wounded in the civil war. He first became nationally prominent when he fined the Standard Oil Company $29,240,000, after forcing John D. Rockefeller to come here to testify. His decision was reversed by the Appellate Court, however.

During the World War Judge Landis presided at the famous I W W trial, sentencing Big Bill Haywood, Secretary-Treasurer of the organization, and ninety-two other members to prison. Shortly afterward an explosion in the Federal building killed several persons, but the Judge was uninjured. He also sentenced Congressman Victor Berger to prison for alleged obstruction of the nation's war preparations.

Judge Landis drew Congressional attention shortly after the war. He found that most of the lawyers appearing before him were not wearing wrist watches had not been in the service.

"Have all these wrist-watch lawyers file a statement what branch of the service they were in," he ordered his clerk.

Senator Thomas of Colorado in an address in the Senate said Judge Landis should be impeached for his order. The Judge's only comment was: "Doesn't it beat the devil what some Senators will do to pass the time away?"

November 13, 1920

HOME RUN EPIDEMIC HITS MAJOR LEAGUES

Spring Slugging Puts Records in Danger — Yanks Lead American, Phils National.

An epidemic of home run hitting has broken out in both major leagues and if the average maintained to date continues through the season some new records in circuit drives will be established. In the 1920 campaign the American League set up the remarkable total of 370 circuit drives, while clubs of the other major organization hit a total of 261. Both figures were so far beyond the normal totals for home runs that they occasioned considerable comment. The 1920 figures, however, seem destined for decisive eclipse in the campaign now under way.

A livelier ball is the only answer that fits the case. It is true that the restrictions which were imposed upon pitchers, starting with the opening of the 1920 pennant races and still in force, have made hitting easier, but even this does not explain the great advance in home run hitting. The fact that many players who seldom hit for the circuit have branched out as long distance sluggers is not explained satisfactorily by changes in pitching rules. They are no stronger physically than before, yet their drives are carrying far beyond the former limits.

The firm which manufactures the baseballs used in the two leagues makes the statement that it is following exactly the same procedure as in the years when the hitting did not attract as much attention. The same amount of cork and wool is used in each ball, but the manufacturers admit that they are getting a better grade of Australian wool. This may be the answer. At any rate the ball is livelier than in the past and home runs are blooming where they never bloomed before.

Home-run hitting in the National League has increased this year to a greater extent than in the American League. With about one-fifth of the playing scheduled completed, the clubs of the Heydler circuit have batted more than one-third of their 1920 total in circuit drives. The Brooklyn team already has made 14 homers, as against 28 during the pennant-winning campaign last year. The Cardinals are within one homer of reaching one-half of their 1920 total, having 15 to date, as against 32 last season.

Pirates and Giants High.

The Pirates and Giants are closing in on the mark which will equal half of their grist in 1920. Pittsburgh made 16 last year and has 6 to date, while the Giants got 46 a year ago and now have 17. At their present clip, the Phillies should reach the century mark, the Braves should double their last year's total and the Reds should collect several more than in 1920. The Cubs alone in the National League are falling behind their pace of last season.

In the American League six of the eight clubs have been hitting homers at a rate which should carry them beyond their 1920 marks. The White Sox have taken a big slump, but this can be answered by the passing of Jackson and Felsch, their leading long-distance hitters. The Mackmen have not been getting home runs as frequently as during the preceding season, but the six other clubs are doing much better. Even the Yankees, who set a record far above the best previous mark, are likely to improve on their 1920 total of 115.

Taking the individual records, the improvement in figures also is quite marked. Ty Cobb hit twice for the circuit last season and he has made five homers this Spring. Wrightstone of the Phillies, with six to date, has doubled his 1920 total; Max Carey has three now, as against one all last season; Earl Smith of the Giants can show four, as against a solitary homer in 1920, while Sam Rice and Jacques Fournier already have equaled their last year's totals. Babe Ruth, the Meusel brothers and Cy Williams are hitting homers more frequently than last year, and George Kelly needs only three more to reach his 1920 total. These players are mentioned because all have three or more to date. Many players on this year's home-run list did not make one all last year.

As might be expected, the Yankees are showing the way in hitting for the circuit. The Hugmen have hit 25 homers to date, of which number Ruth has poled 12. Babe has equaled the Cleveland total, and has more to his credit than any of the six other American League clubs. Four National League teams also have failed to hit as many circuit drives as Ruth alone has made.

Phillies Lead National.

In the National League the Phillies are showing the way with 21, and the Giants are second with 17. The Cardinals with 15 and the Robins with 14 also have done better than any American League club, with the exception of the Yankees. The White Sox trail all other clubs, having only four to their credit.

Three players in the American League and four in the National have hit five or more home runs to date. Ruth is in front with twelve, and Kelly is next in line with eight. Wrightstone and Emil Meusel of the Phillies have six apiece, while Ty Cobb, Bob Meusel and Jacques Fournier have five each. Players who have hit four homers are Earl Smith of the Giants, Cy Williams of the Phillies, Austin McHenry of the Cardinals, Elmer Smith of Cleveland and Harry Heilman of Detroit. In the appended list are forty-eight National and thirty-nine American Leaguers who have made one or more home runs this season. Following is the complete list of home runs made in the major leagues to date:

AMERICAN LEAGUE.

New York 25—Ruth 12, Meusel 5, Pipp 2, Roth 2, Schang 2, Ward, Peckinpaugh.
Cleveland 12—Smith 4, Speaker 2, Gardner 2, Uhle, O'Neill, Sewell, Stephenson.
Detroit 11—Cobb 5, Heilman 4, Veach 2.
St. Louis 11—Sisler 3, Williams 3, Tobin 2, Severeid, Wetzel, Gerber.
Washington 9—Rice 3, Shanks 3, Gharrity 2, Judge.
Philadelphia 8—Dugan 2, Perkins 2, C. Walker 2, Dykes, Griffin.
Boston 5—Pratt 2, Menosky, Jones, Ruel.
Chicago 4—Falk 2, Hooper, Mostil.
Total—85.

NATIONAL LEAGUE.

Philadelphia 21—Meusel 6, Wrightstone 6, Williams 4, Meadows 2, Bruggy, R. Miller, Lebourveau.
New York 17—Kelly 8, Smith 4, Walker 2, Young, Burns, Snyder.
St. Louis 15—Fournier 5, McHenry 4, Schultz 2, Hornsby 2, Mann, Shotton.
Brooklyn 14—Wheat 3, Griffith 3, Neis 3, Konetchy 2, Johnston, Krueger, Miller.
Boston 9—Cruise 2, Powell 2, Fillingim, McQuillan, Nicholson, Southworth, O'Neil.
Chicago 6—Terry, Sullivan, Twombley, Grimes, Flack, O'Farrell.
Pittsburgh 6—Carey 3, Tierney 2, Whitted.
Cincinnati—Hargrace, Duncan, See, Fonseca, Wingo, Bressler.
Total—94.

May 24, 1921

FANS MAY KEEP BASEBALLS.

Pittsburgh Official Rules That Police Are Not to Interfere.

PITTSBURGH, July 9.—Fans who attend games at the National baseball park here may keep balls knocked into the stands without fear of being molested by policemen, according to an order issued yesterday by Robert J. Alderdice, Director of Public Safety. Director Alderdice made the ruling following threatened damage suits against policemen who placed three fans under arrest for refusing to throw balls back onto the diamond.

Policemen placed in the park are there to preserve order and to protect the public, the director said. Hereafter, any action taken against fans for refusing to give up balls must be taken by park employes, Mr. Alderdice said.

July 10, 1921

BASEBALL LEADERS WON'T LET WHITE SOX RETURN TO THE GAME

Judge Landis, Ban Johnson and Comiskey Not Moved by Jury Verdict.

HOLD CROOKEDNESS SHOWN

And the Decision in Court Was Only Technical Under State Law.

Special to The New York Times.

CHICAGO, Aug. 3.—The rulers of organized baseball promptly declared today that the acquitted White Sox players would not be reinstated despite the verdict of the jury last night.

Charles A. Comiskey, the White Sox owner; Judge Landis, who is official arbitrator, and Ban Johnson, President of the American League, issued separate statements, each of which contributed its bit toward destroying any hopes the players may have had for reinstatement.

"Cicotte confessed to me that he had been 'crooked,'" said Mr. Comiskey, "and implicated seven other players. Until they all are able to explain this to my satisfaction none of them will play with the Sox."

Judge Landis gave out this statement:

"Regardless of the verdict of juries, no player that throws a ball game; no player that undertakes or promises to throw a ball game; no player that sits in a conference with a bunch of crooked players and gamblers where the ways and means of throwing games are planned and discussed and does not promptly tell his club about it, will ever play professional baseball.

"Of course, I don't know that any of these men will apply for reinstatement, but if they do, the above are at least a few of the rules that will be enforced. Just keep in mind that, regardless of the verdict of juries, baseball is entirely competent to protect itself against crooks, both inside and outside the game."

President Johnson said:

"The trial of the indicted players and gamblers which closed yesterday uncovered the greatest crime it was possible to commit in baseball. The fact that the men were freed by a Cook County jury does not alter the conditions one iota or minimize the magnitude of such offenses."

"The energetic prosecution of the State clearly indicates that crimes of this character will not be permitted to go unchallenged."

Speculation as to whether there will be any further prosecution of the indicted players was definitely disposed of by the State's Attorney, Robert E. Crowe.

"As far as I am concerned the case is closed," said Mr. Crowe. "There are several other indictments against the men, but the one under which they were tried contained virtually all the charges. We shall quash the remaining indictments."

Despite the statements of Judge Landis, Comiskey and Johnson, not all of the "Black Sox" have abandoned hope for reinstatement.

"I am entirely innocent and the jury has proved that," said Risberg. "I leave my future in the hands of organized baseball."

"I never had anything to do with the so-called conspiracy," said Happy Felsch. "The jury has cleared my name."

"If it had not been for those two liars, Bill Burns and Billy Maharg, I would not have been mixed up in this," said "Chick" Gandil. "Anyway, it's all over now."

Eddie Cicotte refused to discuss the case.

"I talked once on this, never again," he said. "All I want is to get back to Detroit."

Joe Jackson, former outfielder, said he was through with baseball. He and Claude Williams are said to have prospered with a Chicago poolroom, and it is not thought likely either will make much effort to get back on the diamond.

It is said that "Buck" Weaver will probably bring suit to recover payments that stopped when he was suspended.

There were rumors of suits on "injuries to reputations," but attorneys for the defense did not confirm these.

"My clients, so far as I have been informed, will not seek any redress," said Benedict Short, who defended Cicotte, Williams and Jackson. "The jury has cleared them, and I believe they will be content to let it go at that."

Thomas D. Nash and Michael J. Ahern, attorneys for Weaver, Felsch and Risberg, also seemed inclined to "let well enough alone," so far as damage suits were concerned. But Mr. Ahern said that Weaver had a legitimate claim in connection with his contract.

Mr. Comiskey was undisturbed by reports concerning civil action.

"We are prepared for any of these men who want to 'go to law' with us," said the Old Roman. "They have all been paid every nickel they had coming."

August 4, 1921

Johnson Passes Cy Young's Total of 2,290 Strike-Outs

A major league record which had endured for years was broken yesterday, and Walter Johnson now takes a place in baseball's Hall of Fame where Cy Young had held forth. In a stretch of twenty-two seasons of pitching in the majors, Cy registered a total of 2,290 strikeouts. Johnson, now in his seventeenth consecutive year with the Washington club, has been steadily approaching this mark, and he needed only three to equal Young's record when he went into the box yesterday morning at Philadelphia against the Mackmen. At the Polo Grounds last week Johnson retired seven Yankees on strikes, thereby running his total up to 2,287. Six Mackmen fell before Walter's speed yesterday morning, so the Washington Siege Gun now has to his credit three more strike-outs than Young recorded over a considerably longer period. It is probable, too, that Johnson will see many more batsmen carry their bats back to the bench before he passes out of major league baseball.

September 6, 1921

ROBERTSON PITCHES PERFECT BALL GAME

Only 27 Tigers Face White Sox Rookie, Who Allows Neither a Hit Nor a Run.

FIVE OTHERS TURNED TRICK

Bradley, Richmond, Ward, Young and Joss Performed Stunt—Chicago Beats Detroit by 2-0.

Special to The New York Times.

DETROIT, April 30.—Charley Robertson, a rookie pitcher with the Chicago White Sox, carved a niche in sport's hall of fame for himself here this afternoon when he twirled a perfect game against the Detroit Tigers. He pitched a no-hit and no-run game and not a Detroit player reached first base, but twenty-seven men facing him. This is not the first time that the feat has been performed in major league baseball, but it is the first time since Addie Joss, then pitching for Cleveland, performed the stunt in a game against the White Sox on Oct. 2, 1908. The White Sox today won by a score of 2 to 0.

Robertson was obtained from the Minneapolis Club of the American Association and today's was the second victory of the year that he has turned in for Kid Gleason's clan. Last year he had a pitching average of .531 while with the Millers.

In turning in the feat Robertson was accorded fine support by his teammates. He fanned six batters as a part of his share in the afternoon's work. McClellan and Collins were particularly brilliant afield. They retired six Tigers at first base and Collins also retired four others on flies. Only six balls were driven into the outfield and these were corralled by Hooper and Mostil.

Pillette, who pitched for the Tigers, was effective in all but the second inning, when the White Sox scored their two runs. He allowed the Chicagoans but seven hits. These, however, proved ample.

In the long history of major league baseball since 1875 but five other perfectly pitched games in which no batter reached first base safely have been turned in.

The first of these was pitched by G. W. Bradley of St. Louis against Hartford in the old National League on July 15, 1876. On June 12, 1880, J. L. Richmond, pitching for Worcester, turned the trick against Cleveland in the National League, and in the same year on June 17 John M. Ward, later manager of the Giants, while pitching for Providence, defeated the Buffalo National League Club in like fashion.

Then followed a stretch of twenty-four years before another hurler was able to duplicate these performances. It was the pitcher of pitchers, Denton T. (Cy.) Young who performed the feat. He was pitching for the Boston Red Sox of the American League against the Philadelphia Athletics, and the game was played on May 5, 1904.

Thus but two other pitchers besides Charles Robertson have been able to contribute such an excellent piece of work to baseball history under modern rules—Joss and Young. When Bradley, Richmond and Ward succeeded in pitching perfect games the old rules were in force.

The score of the White Sox-Tigers game follows:

CHICAGO (A.)	Ab	R	H	Po	A	DETROIT (A.)	Ab	R	H	Po	A
Mulligan,ss	4	0	1	0	0	Blue,1b	3	0	0	11	3
McClellan,3b	3	0	1	1	3	Cutshaw,2b	3	0	0	2	3
Collins,2b	3	0	1	4	3	Cobb,cf	3	0	0	1	0
Hooper,rf	3	1	0	3	0	Veach,lf	3	0	0	2	0
Mostil,lf	4	1	1	3	0	Heilmann,rf	3	0	0	1	0
Strunk,cf	3	0	0	0	0	Jones,3b	3	0	0	1	5
Sheely,1b	4	0	2	9	0	Rigney,ss	2	0	0	2	1
Schalk,c	4	0	1	7	1	Manion,c	3	0	0	7	1
Robertson,p	4	0	0	0	1	Pillette,p	2	0	0	0	3
						aClark	1	0	0	0	0
Total.....	32	2	7	27	8	bBassler	1	0	0	0	0
						Total....	27	0	0	27	16

a Batted for Rigney in ninth.
b Batted for Pillette in ninth.
Error—Blue.

Chicago ....0 2 0 0 0 0 0 0 0—2
Detroit ....0 0 0 0 0 0 0 0 0—0

Two-base hits—Mulligan, Sheely. Sacrifices—McClellan, Collins, Strunk. Left on bases—Chicago 8, Detroit 0. Bases on balls—Off Pillette 2. Struck out—By Pillette 5, Robertson 6. Umpires—Nallin and Evans. Time of game—1:56.

May 1, 1922

HORNSBY RETAINS BATTING LAURELS

Finishes Season With .401, the Highest National League Mark Since 1899.

CHICAGO, Oct. 1.—Rogers Hornsby of the St. Louis Cardinals today batted himself into the Hall of Fame, among feat since 1899 when Ed Delehanty of the Philadelphia club won the batting honors with an average of .408. Hornsby's mark for the season is .401. This is the third consecutive year the St. Louis star has won the batting championship of the senior major league.

Hornsby's name will be recorded alongside of those of R. Barnes, Chicago, who hit .403 in 1876; Cap A. C. Anson, Chicago, .407 in 1879, and who in 1877 made a mark of .421; J. Stenzel, Pittsburgh, .409 in 1893; Hughey Duffy, Boston, .438 in 1894; Jess Burkett, Cleveland, who won the championship in 1895 and 1896 with marks of .423 and .410; Willie Keeler, Brooklyn, .432 in 1897, and Ed Delehanty, the last of the .400 hitters until the present day.

Hornsby's average was .397 last season. The year previous he topped the league with .370. On his first appearance at the plate he smashed one of Kaufmann's offerings for a single. The crowd cheered and applauded the new champion. He repeated his performance on his next trip to the plate. Silence fell over the crowd when he smashed out his third drive. It was a hot grounder to Kelleher, who made a great stop. Kelleher recovered and set himself for the throw but the peg was wild, and the officials scored it an error. The throw if perfect would have beaten the St. Louis star by a step. On his fourth time up Fred Fussell, a southpaw, was on the mound, and Hornsby cracked a single to right, his third hit of the day. On his last appearance at the plate he flied to Hollocher in deep short.

October 2, 1922

American League Batting Title Is Won by Sisler; Cobb Second

Johnson Overrules Official Scorer Here to Give Detroit Manager His Third Mark of .400 or Better—St. Louis Takes First Honors in Club Averages.

The leading batter of the year in the American League, according to the official records released for publication today, was George H. Sisler, star first baseman of the St. Louis Browns, who hung up the remarkable average of .419, the second successive year in which this player has reached the .400 mark.

However, the greatest surprise in the records was contained in the average credited to Ty Cobb of Detroit, whose mark has been changed by Ban Johnson from its original .398 to .401, thereby entitling the veteran to join Jesse Burkett in the very select circle which can boast of three .400 marks or better in its big-league career. The records reveal for the first time that President Johnson officially overrode the decision of the scorer in New York on one play and changed an official error into an official hit.

In the game with the Yanks here on May 15 Cobb hit a grounder to Scott, who fumbled and was credited with an error by the official scorer. The unofficial box score gave Cobb a single, and it was this one play which made the difference between .398 and .401. At the end of the season, while reviewing the records to see if Cobb had been unjustly deprived of a .400 average, Johnson came upon this discrepancy, and now he has ruled in favor of the Detroit manager.

Every team had its home run hero, Kenneth R. Williams of the Browns being the leader with 39, 20 less than the mark set by Ruth in 1921. C. W. Walker of Philadelphia was second with 37, while Babe Ruth in 110 games cracked out 35 circuit smashes. Several other "fly ball hitters" made home-run records that would have won them much attention in former years.

The advance guard of a new army of extra-base sluggers appeared, and it was largely through the efforts of these new men that the greatly improved pitching made so little impress on the season averages. No less than sixteen men in their first or second year are found among the .300 hitters.

St. Louis ousted Detroit from its favorite position as batting leader. The Browns' record is .313, as compared with .316 for the Tigers in 1921, while Boston, low club this season with .263, is 11 points below the Athletics' mark of .274 last year.

There was a slight increase in the use of the sacrifice to advance runners, 1,582, as compared with 1,551 last year, but there were 12 fewer bases stolen, the figures being 681, against 693. Cleveland worked opposing hurlers for 554 bases on balls, Detroit had 530, the champion New York team 497, Chicago 482 and St. Louis 473 passes.

December 4, 1922

ROBINS BEATEN, 17-3; BOTTOMLEY IS STAR

Cards' Infielder Sets Record, Driving In 12 Runs on 6 Hits in Row, 2 of Them Homers.

LOSERS USE FIVE HURLERS

Ehrhardt, Hollingsworth, Decatur, Wilson and Roberts Fail— Sherdel Is Winner.

James Bottomley of the St. Louis Cardinals did some real batting at Ebbets Field yesterday afternoon that was entirely unappreciated by a crowd of about 8,000 spectators who had assembled for the sole purpose of seeing the Robins win a ball game and not Mr. Bottomley crack records by knocking baseballs all out of shape. As may be expected, this lack of appreciation toward Mr. Bottomley was due to the fact that the Robins did not win.

Instead, they took a terrific drubbing by a count of 17 to 3, and at a late hour last night accountants still were brushing up a few details in the official box score. It is safe to say no Brooklynite will ever look at the job when it's done, for the matter is one to be forgotten as swiftly as possible. With the Reds splitting a pair of games with the Giants, the opportunity was at hand for the Robins to edge half a game closer to the top. Instead, the day saw them advance half a game to the rear, and now they are one and a half games away from the top.

It was a terrific offensive that struck the Robins in which Bottomley easily was the leading offender. All this young man did was to drive out six consecutive hits, which included two homers in succession, a double and three singles for a total of thirteen bases. More destructive than this, however, was the fact that he batted in twelve runs for the Cardinals, smashing all known records for this sort of thing in a single game. The best previous mark was eleven set by Wilbert Robinson, who sat as an unwilling onlooker to the deed yesterday. Robbie performed his feat away back in 1892 for the Baltimore Orioles in a game against, incidentally, the St. Louis National League club. Bottomley's work also effaced the modern mark of eight kept since 1907, in which six players are listed as joint holders, including George Kelly, who made the mark this year, and Travis Jackson, who did it a year ago.

Five Robin Hurlers Battered.

In addition to this, Bottomley crossed the plate with still another run, so that, in all, he accounted directly or indirectly for thirteen of the Cardinals' seventeen runs. Five Robin pitchers fell in this amazing exhibition of effective swatting, and Bottomley smacked them all, which is probably another record.

Rube Ehrhardt was the first to fall, going out after four hits he had scored four runs before a man had been retired. This, incidentally, finished his little winning streak which he painstakingly had built up to five. The Rube was followed, in order of appearance, by Hollingsworth, Decatur, Wilson and Roberts. Bottomley made his two homers off Decatur, one in the fourth with the bases full and the other in the sixth with one on.

The spectators had barely settled back in their seats before the Cards' scoring began. Ehrhardt drew the distinction of starting the thing himself by walking Blades, the first man to face him. Douthit then got an infield hit to short and Hornsby beat out a bunt, filling the bases. Bottomley here inserted his first blow of the afternoon, a single, scoring Blades and Douthit, and Hornsby and Bottomley counted when Hafey tripled.

That finished Ehrhardt, and Hollingsworth came in to see what he could do about it. He retired the next three batters. But two walks and a double by the troublesome Mr. Bottomley accounted for another tally in the second.

Bottomley Clears Bags.

The fourth, however, was the real heartbreaker for the Robins, for up to then they still appeared to have a fighting chance, having picked up a run in the second on a pass to Fournier and hits by Brown and De Berry. Sherdel started the Cards' drive in this frame with a double. Blades walked and Decatur relieved Hollingsworth. Douthit sacrificed Blades and Sherdel to second and third, respectively, whereupon Decatur passed Hornsby, filling the bases. The unsuspecting Decatur did not know that Bottomley, next up, had selected this day for a record. The St. Louis first baseman hit the ball over the right field fence, clearing the bases.

In the sixth Douthit walked and Bottomley again lifted the ball over the right field fence. A single by Hafey, a triple by Gonzales and Cooney's single accounted for two more runs.

In the seventh, with Wilson pitching and men on second and third, Bottomley singled, scoring both. Bottomley took a rest in the eighth while the Cards scored a run on Sherdel's single and Mueller's triple, but he came back for a final shot in the ninth, with Roberts pitching. Hornsby tripled and Bottomley sent him home with his sixth straight hit of the day, a single. He had no chance at Wilbert Robinson's consecutive mark of seven hits, set in 1892, as he did not come a seventh time to bat.

As for the Robins, they were helpless before Lefty Sherdel. After their run in the second, they didn't get another until the eighth, when hits by Taylor and High and an out scored a tally. Rehm, working the ninth inning, presented the Robins with another tally by issuing three passes and adding a wild pitch to boot.

The score:

ST. LOUIS (N.)	Ab	R	H	Po	A		BROOKLYN (N.)	Ab	R	H	Po	A
Mueller, rf	3	3	2	4	0		High, 2b	4	0	2	4	0
Douthit, cf	3	3	1	2	0		Mitchell, ss	4	0	1	1	4
Hornsby, 2b	2	3	0	1	0		Wheat, lf	4	0	0	3	0
Blades, 2b	3	2	0	0	0		Fournier, 1b	2	1	0	5	1
Bottomley, 1b	6	3	6	5	0		Loftus, 1b	2	0	1	3	0
Smith, rf	1	1	0	0	0		Brown, cf	3	1	1	3	0
Hafey, cf	6	1	2	3	1		Stock, 3b	3	1	1	1	3
Gonzales, c	4	1	1	2	0		De Berry, c	3	0	1	4	0
Clemons, c	2	0	1	0	0		Ehrhardt, p	0	0	0	0	0
Toporcer, 3b	1	0	0	0	0		Hollingsworth, p	1	0	0	0	0
Cooney, 3b	3	0	6	4			Decatur, p	0	0	0	1	1
Thevenow, ss	4	2	1	0	1		aJohnston	1	0	1	0	0
Sherdel, p	4	2	3	0	0		Wilson, p	1	0	0	0	0
Rehm, p	0	0	0	0	0		bTaylor	1	1	1	0	0
							Roberts, p	0	0	0	0	1
Total	42	17	18	27	7		cHargreaves	1	0	0	0	0
							Total	31	3	9	27	9

Errors—St. Louis 6, Brooklyn 1 (Fournier).

a Batted for Decatur in sixth.
b Batted for Wilson in eighth.
c Batted for Roberts in ninth.

St. Louis .... 4 1 0 4 0 4 2 1 1—17
Brooklyn .... 0 1 0 0 0 0 0 1 1— 3

Two-base hits—Bottomley, Sherdel. Three-base hits—Mueller, Hornsby, Hafey, Gonzales. Home runs—Bottomley (2). Stolen bases—Douthit, Cooney. Sacrifices—Douthit (2), Hornsby. Double plays—Thevenow and Hornsby; Thevenow, Hornsby and Bottomley; Mueller (unassisted). Left on bases—St. Louis 7, Brooklyn 6. Bases on balls—Off Ehrhardt 1, Hollingsworth 3, Decatur 2, Sherdel 2, Rehm 3. Struck out—By Hollingsworth 2, Wilson 1, Sherdel 1. Hits—Off Ehrhardt 4 in 0 innings (none out in first), Hollingsworth 2 in 2 (none out in fourth), Decatur 5 in 2, Wilson 4 in 2, Roberts 2 in 1, Sherdel 8 in 8, Rehm 1 in 1. Wild pitches —Decatur 1, Rehm 1. Passed ball—Clemons. Winning pitcher—Sherdel. Losing pitcher—Ehrhardt. Umpires—Klem and Wilson.

Time of game—1:55.

September 17, 1924

TWO NEW RECORDS MADE BY HORNSBY

St. Louis Star Leads League in Batting Fifth Year in Row With Mark of .42351.

ST. LOUIS, Sept. 29.—Rogers Hornsby, Cardinal second baseman, today took a place beside the greatest hitters in baseball history. In the season just closed Hornsby established two new records, one in batting average and the other in leading his league for the fifth consecutive season.

Hornsby finished with 227 hits in 142 games, making a season average of .42351, 4 points above George Sisler's mark of two years ago. Sisler had an approximate .420 average which tied Tyrus Cobb's record set in 1911, the high mark of modern baseball.

The previous consecutive year batting record was held by Honus Wagner, who led his league four successive years.

Hornsby failed in his effort to lead the league in runs scored. He tallied only once in the double-header yesterday and thus raised his total to 121, which ties Frankie Frisch of the New York Giants.

Between games yesterday the Cardinal slugger was presented with a silver bat and ball, known as the Dick Richards trophy, for leading his team in batting.

September 30, 1924

COBB TIES RECORD WITH 3 HOME RUNS

Leads Tigers to 14-8 Victory Over Browns, Also Getting 2 Singles and a Double.

BREAKS TOTAL BASE MARK

ST. LOUIS, May 5.—Tying the modern major league record, the veteran Ty Cobb, playing manager of the Detroit Tigers, poled out three home runs in today's game against the St. Louis

Browns, which the Tigers won by a score of 14 to 8. In all Cobb made six hits, getting two singles and a double in addition to his three circuit drives.

Cobb made the first of his homers in the first inning off Bush. Van Gilder was the victim of his second in the second inning, while the third drive was made off Gaston in the eighth.

George Sisler, manager of the Browns, hit safely in his twentieth consecutive game.

Cobb in smashing out six hits collected a total of sixteen bases, a new world's record for modern major league baseball. The previous record for modern baseball was held by Eddie Gharity, Washington catcher, who ran his total of bases for one game to thirteen, in June, 1919.

The old record, made before the advent of the American League, was held jointly by Bobby Lowe of the Boston Nationals, who in 1894 collected four homers and a single, and Ed Delehanty of the Philadelphia Nationals duplicated the stunt in 1896. Each of these players had a total of seventeen bases.

The only other major league players who have made three home runs in a single game in the twentieth century are George Kelly of the Giants, Ken Williams of the Brown, Cy Williams of the Phillies and Walter Henline of the Phillies.

The score:

DETROIT (A.)	Ab	R	H	Po	A
Blue,1b	5	3	2	8	1
O'Rourke,2b	5	3	3	4	2
Cobb,cf	6	4	6	5	0
Heilmann,rf	3	1	2	1	0
Manush,lf	4	2	1	2	1
Rigney,ss	2	0	0	0	2
Tavener,ss	1	0	0	3	3
Jones,3b	4	1	1	1	3
Woodall,c	2	0	2	0	0
Leonard,p	3	0	1	0	0
Holloway,p	0	0	0	0	0
Wells,p	2	0	1	1	1
aWingo	0	0	0	0	0
Total	37	14	17	27	13

ST. LOUIS (A.)	Ab	R	H	Po	A
Robe'son,3b	4	1	1	2	2
Bennett,rf	6	1	1	3	0
Sisler,1b	5	1	2	11	1
Williams,lf	3	2	4	2	0
McManus,2b	3	1	0	0	1
Jacobson,cf	4	2	2	1	0
Gerber,ss	5	0	3	4	5
Dixon,c	1	0	0	2	1
Rego,c	1	0	0	1	2
Bush,p	0	0	0	1	1
VanGilder,p	1	0	0	0	2
Giard,.p	0	0	0	0	2
Stauffer,p	0	0	0	0	0
Gaston,p	1	0	1	0	0
Springer,p	0	0	0	0	1
bEvans	1	0	0	0	0
cRice	0	0	0	0	0
dTobin	1	0	0	0	0
eSevereld	1	0	0	0	0
Total	39	8	14	27	16

Errors—Detroit 1 (Cobb); St. Louis 1 (McManus).

a Batted for Rigney in sixth.
b Batted for Giard in fourth.
c Batted for Dixon in fifth.
d Batted for Stauffer in fifth.
e Batted for Springer in ninth.

Detroit .... 3 5 1 1 0 1 0 2 1—14
St. Louis .... 4 0 0 0 4 0 0 0 0— 8

Two-base hits—O'Rourke (3), Robertson, Blue, Cobb, Heilmann, Wells, Jones, Gerber. Three-base hit—Blue. Home runs—Cobb (3), Jacobson, Manush. Stolen base—Gerber. Sacrifices—Heilmann, Manush, McManus, O'Rourke. Double plays—Bush, Gerber and Sisler; Robertson, Rego and Sisler. Left on bases—Detroit 9, St. Louis 12. Bases on balls—Off Leonard 2, Holloway 1, Wells 4, Bush 2, Vangilder 1, Gaston 3, Stauffer 1, Giard 1, Springer 2. Struck out—By Leonard 1, Wells 1, Bush 1, Stauffer 1. Hits—Off Leonard 10 in 4 1-3 innings, Vangilder 4 in 2-3, Holloway 0 in 0, Giard 1 in 1 2-3, Wells 4 in 4 2-3, Stauffer 0 in 1, Bush 5 in 1 2-3, Gaston 6 in 3, Springer 1 in 1. Wild pitch—Holloway. Winning pitcher—Leonard. Losing pitcher, Bush. Umpires—Evans and Hildebrand and Rowland. Time of game—2:44.

May 6, 1925

---

13 RUNS IN EIGHTH WIN FOR ATHLETICS

Mackmen Stage Most Spectacular Rally Ever Seen in Philadelphia to Beat Indians, 17-15.

UMPIRE OWENS IS INJURED

Taken to Hospital After Collision With Player—Hauser Retires for the Season.

Special to The New York Times.

PHILADELPHIA, June 15.—When the eighth inning dawned on the Athletics in their game with the Cleveland Indians here today it also dawned on the Mackmen that they were eleven runs behind the Indians and that if they were to win the game they would have to do some hard and fast hitting. They determined to take the game then and there and they did. They scored thirteen runs in the eighth and beat their rivals, 17 to 15.

The rally was by far the greatest ever seen in this city and has few equals in the annals of baseball. Once the Ath-

letics got started it seemed that they never would stop and before it was over the Indians also were very much of the same opinion.

This is how, in the eighth inning, the Athletics scored their thirteen runs: Galloway walked. Glass flied to Lee and Bishop walked. Dykes lined the ball to the scoreboard for three bases scoring Galloway and Bishop. Lamar then singled over second scoring Dykes. Speaker yanked W. Miller and Speece went into pitch, but Simmons bounced a hit over Knode's head and Lamar went to third. Welch singled to right, scoring Lamar and putting Simmons on third. Berry singled to left and scored Simmons and that finished Speece.

Yowell went to the hill. Poole walked, filling the bases. Galloway singled to left centre, scoring Welch and Berry and putting Poole on third. Hale went to bat for Glass and Uhle, the Cleveland ace, came in from the bullpen to replace Yowell. Hale drove a single that hopped over J. Sewell's head, scoring Poole and putting Galloway on third. Hale stole second. Bishop singled over second, scoring Galloway and Hale. Dykes forced Bishop, J. Sewell to Spurgeon.

French ran for Dykes. Lamar walked. Simmons hammered the ball on to the roof of the left field grandstand for a home run that scored Dykes, Lamar and himself and gave the Athletics a two-run lead. Welch then flied to Lee.

In the second inning of the game, Spurgeon of Cleveland crashed into Umpire Owens at the plate and the latter was so painfully hurt that he had to be taken to the hospital. There, however, it was reported that he had suffered only a sprain in his back and would be able to report for duty within a day or so.

Connie Mack announced today that Joe Hauser, veteran first baseman, would be retired for the rest of the season. He was hurt in a pre-season game and has not been in the best of condition since. It also was announced that Ed Andrews, a pitcher, had been released.

PHILADELPHIA (A)	Ab	R	H	Po	A
Bishop,2b	4	1	2	1	2
Dykes,3b	6	2	2	1	2
aFrench	0	1	0	0	0
Lamar,lf	3	4	2	1	0
Simmons,cf	6	2	3	7	0
E.Miller,rf	2	0	0	0	0
Welch,rf	3	1	1	0	0
Perkins,c	2	0	0	6	1
Berry,c	2	1	2	2	0
Cochrane,c	0	0	0	0	0
Poole,1b	4	3	2	6	0
Rommel,p	3	2	2	1	0
Baum'g'er,p	0	0	0	0	0
bFox	0	0	0	0	0
Heimach,p	0	0	0	0	0
Stokes,p	0	0	0	0	2
Glass,p	1	0	0	0	0
Hale,3b	1	1	1	0	0
Walberg,p	0	0	0	0	0
Total	40	17	19	27	8

CLEVELAND (A.)	Ab	R	H	Po	A
Jamieson,lf	6	2	5	2	0
McNulty,rf	1	0	0	1	0
Lee,rf	4	1	2	5	0
Speaker,cf	6	1	2	5	0
J.Sewell,ss	6	1	4	2	7
Myatt,c	6	3	2	2	0
Spurgeon,2b	6	2	2	2	2
Luzrke,3b	6	1	4	2	7
Knode,1b	5	0	4	6	1
cL.Sewell	1	0	0	0	0
J.Miller,p	5	0	1	0	2
Speece,p	0	0	0	0	2
Yowell,p	0	0	0	0	0
Uhle,p	0	0	0	0	0
Total	50	15	24	24	10

Errors—Philadelphia 2 (Berry, Galloway); Cleveland 0.
a Ran for Dykes in eighth.
b Batted for Baumgartner in second.
c Batted for Knode in ninth.

Philadelphia .... 0 1 1 0 0 1 1 13 .—17
Cleveland .... 0 4 2 2 4 2 1 0 0—15

Two-base hits—Lee, Poole, Dykes, Jamieson, Speaker, Lamar. Three-base hits—Lee, Poole, Dykes. Home runs—J. Sewell, Myatt, Simmons. Stolen bases—Jamieson (2), Spurgeon, Myatt, Luzrke, Hale. Sacrifices—Glass, Myatt, Luzrke. Double plays—Sewell and Knode; Sewell, Spurgeon and Knode. Left on bases—Cleveland 11, Philadelphia 9. Bases on balls—Off J. Miller 6, Yowell 1, Uhle 1, Rommel 1, Stokes 1. Struck out—By W. Miller 2, Baumgartner 1, Stokes 3, Glass 1, Walberg 2. Hits—Off J. Miller 12 in 7 1-3 innings, Speece 2 in 0 (pitched to three batters), Yowell 1 in 0 (pitched to two batters), Rommel 5 in 1, Uhle 3 in 2-3, Baumgartner 2 in 2-3, Heimach 6 in 1 1-3, Stokes 3 in 1 2-3, Glass 7 in 3, Walberg 1 in 1. Hit by pitcher—By J. Miller (Welch). Wild pitches—Rommel, Stokes. Winning pitcher—Glass. Losing pitcher—Uhle. Umpires—Owens, Dineen and Rowland. Time of game—3:00.

June 16, 1925

MAGNATES APPROVE THE 'RABBIT BALL'

National League Owners Decide Against Changes, but Suggest Help to Pitchers.

TEST SHOWS NO ALTERATION

Prof. Fales of Columbia Finds Sphere Same as in 1914—Cut for World Series Players.

The "rabbit ball" wil not be caged. The so-called lively sphere, which has been responsible for the home run epidemic, according to many followers of the game, will remain the official horsehide in the National League. This action was taken yesterday at the regular midsummer meeting of the club owners of the National League, held in the offices of John A. Heydler, President of the league, 8 West Fortieth Street. During the four-hour discussion, which started at 11 o'clock yesterday morning, two reports were read on the "rabbit ball," one by Professor Harold A. Fales of the chemistry division at Columbia University, and the other by Julian A. Curtis, President of the A. G. Spalding Company which supplies baseballs for the National League.

It was the testimony of Professor Fales which had much to do with the decision made by the magnates. The professor experimented with balls used in 1914, 1923 and 1925 and after making many tests concluded that to all intents and purposes, there is only a slight difference in the spheres in use during the last eleven years. It was apparent, the professor reported, that the recent rules restricting the pitcher, the larger number of new balls put into play in each game and the smoother, tighter surface of the ball and the closer "undercut" stitching of the seam, all have conspired in favor of freer and longer hitting.

So convincing was Professor Fales's report that the magnates authorized President Heydler to confer with Ban Johnson, President of the American League, as to the advisability of the umpire bringing a bag of resin to each game and placing it behind the pitcher's box for the pitcher's use in drying his perspiring hands and enabling him to get a better grip on the ball, which now is being done in the Southern Association. The magnates also seemed agreed when the meeting adjourned that the tighter, thinner and all but seamless cover had more to do with the freer hitting and home runs than has any difference in the make and manufacture or the materials placed in the ball.

The summary of Professor Fales's report follows:

"The 1925 ball is larger in size, weighs more, and gives the pitcher much less control in that the seam of the ball is much smoother and the thread of same almost completely countersunk so as to be flush with the leather of the seam. The elasticity of the ball for small heights of fall, namely 13.5 feet, is practically the same."

Just to show the increased use of new balls, it was announced that a few years ago twelve dozen balls were used on an average weekly at the Polo Grounds and that now the total is ninety dozen a week.

Mr. Curtis, in his talk to the magnates, said:

"Gentlemen, I give you my word of honor that there has been absolutely no change in the manufacture of the ball in recent years. Since 1919 we have used a little better material in the way of wool yarn, otherwise the ball is exactly the same. It is the same weight, the same size and has the same resiliency."

Mr. Curtis said his belief that the increase in home runs was due to the fact that the players nowadays are taking a toe hold and swinging and not choking their bats as they did in the old days in an effort to place their hits. The fame and fortune acquired by Babe Ruth as a home-run hitter had a lot to do with starting the epidemic, Mr. Curtis said.

It also was said that no action was taken on the suggestion of Barney Dreyfuss of the Pittsburgh club to limit the drives over short fences and into short left and right field stands to two base hits instead of allowing them to go as home runs. It was said that the size of the ball parks did not enter into the discussion.

The league unanimously ratified the advisory council's amendment to the world series rules which provides for including fourth-place teams as participants in the players' share of the world series receipts. Such distribution calls for a reduction of the players' share from 75 to 70 per cent of the players' pool. The new rule would give the players finishing second and third exactly the same proportion as they have received heretofore, the 5 per cent taken from the world series teams going to the fourth place teams. Figures from the last five world series showed that under the new plan of distribution a single winning player's share would be reduced approximately $350, and the losing player's share would be reduced approximately $250.

Resolutions of regret were passed on the deaths of four prominent baseball men. They were Charles H. Ebbets, President of the Brooklyn club; Edward McKeever, Vice President of the Brooklyn club; Sam Crane, baseball writer, and John Montgomery Ward.

Those attending the meeting, in addition to President Heydler, were: Charles A. Stoneham, President of the New York club; Wilbert Robinson, President of the Brooklyn club; Judge Emil Fuchs, President of the Boston club; Barney Dreyfuss, President of the Pittsburgh club; L. C. Widrig of the Cincinnati club; Sam Breadon, President of the St. Louis club, and William A. Veeck of the Chicago club. William A. Baker of the Philadelphia club was unable to attend.

July 16, 1925

SPORT NEWS SERVICE ARRANGED BY WRC

PLAY-BY-PLAY descriptions of all games to be played out of town by the Washington American League champions will be broadcast this season by WRC.

The out-of-town season will begin April 21 when the Senators make their début at Greater Shibe Park, Philadelphia, against the Mackmen. Beginning with the Philadelphia series, WRC will be on the air continuously during every game played on both the Eastern and Western trips. Plans for broadcasting the opening games of the season in Washington, April 13, are under consideration.

In addition to the play-by-play descriptions of games played by the Washington team, bulletins from other major league games will be announced between innings throughout the season.

Complete scores in all leagues will be announced every evening by WRC. The latter information will be included in a sports résumé that will contain late news from all the sporting world, including golf, tennis, rowing and the important turf races of the season.

April 4, 1926

JOHNSON TRIUMPHS IN 15 INNINGS, 1-0

Washington Veteran Shuts Out Athletics to Start His 19th Season.

VICE PRESIDENT ATTENDS

Dawes Among 25,000 Who Brave Chilly Weather—S. Harris Scores Lone Run.

WASHINGTON, April 13 (Æ).—Washington and Philadelphia opened the baseball season in gala style here today, battling fifteen innings before the champion Senators won, 1 to 0. The game was a brilliant duel between pitching veterans, Walter Johnson for the Senators, beginning his twentieth season, and Ed Rommel for the Athletics.

More than 25,000 fans braved the chilly weather and saw Vice President Dawes toss out the first ball. A floral piece was presented to Manager Bucky Harris, and Johnson received a loving cup.

Manager Harris crossed the plate with the winning run after he had singled, Goslin doubled and Joe Harris singled. Twice the Senators had filled the bags with two out only to fall before Rommel's pitching. The Senators went hitless during the first four innings.

Twelve of the Athletics went down by the strike-out route, Johnson's curves and fast ones appearing as effective as ever. Rommel struck out one man and walked five, while Johnson passed three.

The veteran Peckinpaugh sat on the bench and watched his substitute, Buddy Myer, play at short. The youngster handled four chances and muffed one.

The box score:

WASHINGTON (A)	ab.	r.	h.	po.	a.	e.		PHILADELPHIA (A)	ab.	r.	h.	po.	a.	e.
Rice, cf...	7	0	2	4	0	0		Bishop, 2b..	5	0	1	5	5	0
S. Harris, 2b.	5	1	1	3	5	0		Lamar, lf..	6	0	2	3	0	0
Goslin, lf...	5	0	1	5	0	0		French, rf..	5	0	1	3	0	0
J. Harris, rf..	7	0	2	5	0	0		Simmons, cf.	6	0	1	2	0	0
Judge, 1b...	5	0	2	14	1	0		Hauser, 1b...	4	0	0	23	0	0
Bluege, 3b...	5	0	1	1	2	0		Cochrane, c..	6	0	2	9	0	0
Myer, ss....	5	0	1	2	1	1		Dykes, 3b...	6	0	1	2	1	0
Ruel, c....	4	0	0	11	0	0		Galloway, ss.	5	0	2	3	4	0
Sewerid, c...	1	0	1	0	0	0		Rommel, p...	6	0	0	1	1	0
Johnson, p...	5	0	0	0	3	0								
aTobin	1	0	0	0	0	0		Total....	49	0	6	43	23	0

Total....49 1 9 45 12 1

*One out when winning run was scored.
aBatted for Ruel in twelfth.

Washington .....0 0 0 0 0 0 0 0 0 0 0 0 0 0 1—1
Philadelphia ....0 0 0 0 0 0 0 0 0 0 0 0 0 0 0—0

Two-base hits—French, Goslin. Stolen base —Rice. Sacrifices—Judge, French (2), Goslin, Galloway. Double play—S. Harris, Meyer and Judge. Left on bases—Philadelphia 10, Washington 13. Bases on balls—Off Rommel 5, Johnson 3. Struck out—By Rommel 1, Johnson 12. Hit by pitcher—By Rommel 1 (Myer). Umpires—Connolly, Nallin and Geisel.

Time of game—2:33.

April 14, 1926

RUTH HITS 3 HOMERS AND YANKS WIN, 10-5; SERIES EVEN AGAIN

By JAMES R. HARRISON.

Special to The New York Times.

ST. LOUIS, Oct. 6.—Contrary to reports, the king is not dead. Long live the king, for today he hit three home runs and smashed six world's series records as completely as his fellow-Yankees smashed the Cardinals, to tie the world's series at two victories apiece.

After all, there is only one Ruth. He is alone and unique. Tonight he is securely perched on the throne again, and the crown does not rest uneasy on this royal head. For to his record of fifty-nine homers in one season he added today the achievement of three home runs in one world's series game.

Behind his bulky, swaggering figure, the Yankees marched to an over-whelming victory, 10 to 5. When they were going down for the third and almost the last time, Ruth tossed them the rope of three homers. He took personal charge of the world's series and made the game his greatest single triumph. He led the charge of a faltering battalion and turned the tide of battle so much that tonight most of the neutral critics were conceding the championship to the Yankees.

Yanks Find Batting Eye.

Hearing the old familiar ring of Ruth's big bat, the Yankees came out of their coma, made ten runs and fourteen hits and bore the Cardinals to earth with a rugged, slashing attack.

Besides setting world's series records that may stand for all time, George Herman Ruth hit a baseball where only two other men had hit it—into the centrefield bleachers of Sportsmans Park. It is 430 feet to the bleacher fence. The wall is about twenty feet high. Back of it stretches a deep bank of seats, and almost squarely in the middle of this bank Ruth crashed the third homer that made all the history.

It was not one of his longest drives but it was by all odds his best, for

it automatically wiped four marks off the record book. It was, as noted above, the first time anybody had hit that many homers in a series game. It made Ruth's number of homers for all series games seven, beating by one the former record of "Goose" Goslin. It made his total bases in one game twelve, three more than Harry Hopper in 1915. His extra bases on long hits amounted to nine. Again three better than any other man had ever done.

Besides those four marks, which were shattered by the one heroic blow, Ruth broke two more. He scored four runs, the most which any player has scored in a world's series game, beating a record of three set by Mike Donlin in 1905, which has been equalled often. Ruth also raised his own record of eighteen extra bases achieved in world series games to a grand total of twenty-seven.

Ruth's first contribution to the gayety of more than 40,000 fans today came in the first inning, when Flint Rhem, the first of five Cardinal pitchers, decided that a fast ball, adroitly served, would fool the king. Ruth swung under the ball and raised it high in the air. The pellet floated out to right field, hugging the foul line and blown by the wind toward foul territory.

Over the Fence It Goes.

At the last moment, with the ball veering closer and closer to the chalk line of extinction, it disappeared over the stand and fell to the broad avenue below—not two feet from the foul line.

In the third, when Ruth came up next, young Mr. Rhem had changed his mind and decided that a fellow who could hit speed that far might be slightly deceived by a pitch of slower pace. So he tossed up a dew-drop slow ball between the waist and shoulder and on the inside corner. Ruth must have been expecting it, for he leaned back, swung from the floor and, with perfect timing, drove a long, high and hard poke over the bleacher roof in deep right-centre.

In both cases he swung at the first ball. Two pitches and two home runs. Two pitches and the game was practically over, with the Yanks inspired and rejuvenated and crowding to the plate to hit with old-time vim.

Two pitches and, who knows, the series was practically over. With his star left-hander, Pennock, thoroughly rested and ready to pitch tomorrow, Miller Huggins has the upper hand once more, with the Yanks finally awake and out of their batting slump.

After the third inning, the Cardinal pitchers treated Mr. Ruth with great aloofness and attempted no familiarities but one. That one was disastrous. In the sixth inning, Herman Bell, a young right-hander, was pitching. Combs opened with a single too deep for Thevenow to handle. Koenig fanned and Bell was so pleased with this conquest that he attempted conclusions with Ruth, which was equivalent to tampering with a stick of dynamite.

When the count was finally three and two Mr. Bell did a foolish thing. He drew back his arm and cut loose with a fast ball straight through the middle. When Ruth is hitting as he was today, there is not a pitcher in the world who can afford this gamble. Even a schoolboy pitcher knows better than that.

Ruth waded into the fast ball and put all his shoulders and back behind the 52-ounce bat that has brought more ruin than any other in baseball. He caught the ball as flush as an expert marksman. It was a terrific blow and there was no doubt where it was going.

Doulhit ran back as far as he could, and having no scaling irons or ladder, stood by helplessly while the ball shot over the wall and landed in the laps of the St. Louis rooters. It was still going with unabated speed when it arrived. It struck with force and bounced up, and then there came the finest ovation that St. Louis has ever given a visiting athlete.

Babe Gets Ovations.

Three home runs in one world's series game. Only seven men in modern baseball

Ruth and Hornsby Before Tuesday's Game in St. Louis.

Times Wide World Photos

have hit three in any ordinary game. Even the hardened partisans of St. Louis had to admit the grandeur of the feat. In Boston or New York or several other cities they would have torn the grandstand down and given Babe the pieces, but for St. Louis it was a gigantic tribute that poured out from more than 40,000 threats.

The folks in the grandstand were inclined to be a bit conservative. A few sunders committed the less-majestic of booing the king, but out in the bleachers it was all tumult and uproar. The boys in the sun seats in left, where Ruth was stationed, got to their feet as if one man. They waved papers and programs and Cardinal banners and tossed a few ancient straw hats out on the field.

There have been few more gallant figures than Ruth leading the charge of the Yanks today. It had been a dark hour for the New York gladiators. Before the game, it was reported. Ban Johnson, President of the American League, went to the yankee dressing room to give the players the sort of talk that a football coach delivers to his men before the big game. There was a general conviction that the Cards were the better team and wold win, an opinion that was not changed until the slumbering menace in Babe Ruth's bat awoke and made a new team of the Yanks.

There have been few figures as gallant as

Ruth as he strode from the bench to receive the thrice-repeated homage of an enemy crowd-his portly frame swaggering ever so slightly, his face alight with the fire of determination.

If the Babe was going down, he would go down fighting. There was only one man who could jar the Yanks out of their depressing slump. It is still a one-man team and the happy fortune today was that the one man found his batting eye and blazed the trail for his dejected colleagues.

A Lively Ball Game.

With the greatest home-run hitter of them all hitting three homers, it was, naturally enough, a lively occasion. The game was long and one-sided, but it was a good one—a great game, indeed, with attacks and counterattacks, a seesawing score. Twenty-eight hits on both sides and sensation following sensation, even to the almost disastrous collision of two Cardinal outfieldrs.

The paid attendance was 38,825, more than 1,000 above yesterday's first St. Louis game. This number of people paid $168,190 at the gate, bringing the total receipts of the series up to $730,001, a new record.

The previous record for receipts in four games was $723,104, made in 1926. The record for players' share, also made in that year, was $368,783.

With the playing of the fourth game, the players ceased to share in the receipts. However, the players' pool totaled $372, 300, a world's series record, surpassing by more than $4,000 the record set in 1923. Of this total the world's series players will share in only 70 per cent., as the remaining 30 per cent, goes to the second, third and fourth place teams in the pennant races of the two leagues.

On this basis the world's series players will divide 260.610. Each club has twenty-five eligible players, which means that each player for the winning team will receive about 6,254 and each player for the losing team will get 4,168. Both these sums are records in world's series.

The series is sure to go back to New York, and that means a Saturday game at the Stadium, with the two club owners cutting heavily into the net proceeds. With Pennock at hand, refreshed by a four-day rest, and the New York war clubs again playing the music of the solid wallop, the Yanks are favorites here to win, when last night they were poor second-money choices.

It was, until today, a lifeless world's series. Three games had been played, and in none of them was there a great play or a thrilling rally, or hardly an event that the baseball field had not seen dozens of times before.

The Series Awakes.

But today the series awoke and put on its best show. And there was sparkling fielding and the heavy ring of busy bats and enough mistakes to keep the fans on edge from start to finish.

The Cardinals opened brusquely on Waite Hoyt, but fell behind until the fourth. Then four hits and three runs put them one to the good, and raised the grave suspicion that Mr. Hoyt would take an early trip to the clubhouse. But to gain those three runs in the fourth Hornsby had to take out Rhem. Arthur Reinhart, his left-handed successor, threw the game away in the fifth by setting another world's series record, and giving five bases on balls. Four, as a matter of fact, were charged to Reinhart and the fifth to Herman Bell. With only one hit, the Yanks scored four runs, and in the sixth Ruth struck another home run blow and the game was over.

With all this friendly assistance Hoyt was able to stagger through, although he did not pitch a good game. He struck out eight, but was so much in trouble that Urban Shocker pitched almost a complete game in the bull pen, where he was joined later by Shawkey and Pennock, as the Cardinals made their constant threats.

Once Rhem had passed out, Hornsby was at sea and called on four more pitchers in vain. Reinhart, Bell, a young southpaw named William Hallahan and the right-hander, Vic Keen, strayed forth from the bench at odd moments, with Keen showing in the ninth the only flash of ability.

There was one other record tied during the sunny afternoon. Between and among them the five Cardinal pitchers issued ten bases on balls.

In the fourth the exultant fans were frightened speechless as Chick Hafey and Taylor Deuthit, two of the outfield guard, crashed together in pursuit of a fly and were knocked groggy. Lazzeri was on first base with one out, when Joe Dugan looped as fly to left centre. Douthit rushed over from centre and Hafey dashed in from left. Eyes glued on the ball, they saw nothing else in the world. Players of more experience would have avoided the crash. Either of them could have caught the ball, but as Douthit touched it he bumped into Hafey, and the ball flew to the ground. Both players were stretched out apparently unconscious.

They were so badly dazed that neither could get up and chase the ball. Bell rushed out from third and retrieved it, but by that time Lazzeri was almost at the plate.

Doctor Rushes Out.

Douthit, as he rushed in, rammed his elbow against Hafey's chest and stomach, and the left fielder was the worse hurt of the two. He went down on his side and lay still. Players of both teams ran out. On their heels came the St. Louis trainer and the club doctor. For a moment it looked like a stretcher case, with the Cardinals out two good ball players, but smelling salts, a dash of cold water and frenzied towel-swinging did the trick and brought them both back to normal.

Douthit did one of the gamest things of the series only a minute later. With Dugan on second, Severeid sliced a pretty single to dead centre. Although only sixty seconds before he had been reclining on his back, Douthit sprinted in and tore loose a wonderful throw which nailed Joe fast at the plate.

It was one of four great throws today. In the second Lazzeri hit against the left field bleachers, but was out at third on Thevenow's fine relay of the ball from Douthit. In the fourth Douthit tried to score from second on a single, but was cut down by Ruth's marvelous line fling straight into Severaid's glove.

Again in the sixth, Meusel singled to right and tried a smart manoeuvre by rounding first base slowly and then suddenly putting on a burst of speed, hoping that Southworth would be taken in by the trick. Billy, however, was wide awake. He erased the big city slicker at second with a throw true and straight.

There was still another interval where the medical talents of the club trainer were needed to resuscitate an athlete. In the fourth, Bob Meusel suddenly stopped the game and walked into the diamond to complain of a dizzy spell and failing eyesight. The fans were not surprised to hear it, for they believed that by that time the Cardinals had knocked all the Yanks dizzy. Expert first-aid ministrations by Trainer Woods restored Robert, and there were no more complaints during the afternoon.

Rhem, in the first inning, struck out Combs and Koening, but after this gay beginning, he teased the celebrated fast ball to Mr. Ruth who stewed it away on the outside of the park. Meusel walked and Gehrig singled to right. The Cards and trouble getting hold of the ball and Meusel, smartly, kept on running from first to the plate. That he didn't make it was no fault of the strategy, for a better slide would have landed him safe and sound.

For the Cardinals, Deuthit outran a tap to deep short, and Southworth sent him to third with a single through second. Hornsby emulated Ruth to some degree by dashing a rugged hit to right, scoring Douhit and moving Southworth to second.

Official Score of Fourth Game of World's Series

NEW YORK YANKEES.

	AB.	R.	H.	TB.	2B.	3B.	HR.	BB.	SO.	SH.	SB.	PO.	A.	E.
Combs, cf	5	2	2	3	1	0	0	1	1	0	0	4	0	0
Koenig, ss	6	1	1	2	1	0	0	0	3	0	0	1	3	1
Ruth, lf	3	4	3	12	0	0	3	2	0	0	0	1	1	0
Meusel, rf	2	1	1	1	0	0	0	3	0	0	0	1	0	0
Gehrig, 1b	3	0	2	3	1	0	0	1	1	1	0	8	0	0
Lazzeri, 2b	3	1	1	2	1	0	0	1	0	1	0	1	3	0
Dugan, 3b	4	0	1	2	1	0	0	1	0	0	0	1	2	0
Severeid, c	4	1	3	3	0	0	0	1	0	0	0	10	0	0
Hoyt, p	4	0	0	0	0	0	0	0	1	1	0	0	0	0
Total	34	10	14	28	5	0	3	10	6	3	0	27	9	1

ST. LOUIS CARDINALS.

	AB.	R.	H.	TB.	2B.	3B.	HR.	BB.	SO.	SH.	SB.	PO.	A.	E.
Douthit, cf	5	1	2	3	1	0	0	0	0	0	0	2	2	0
Southworth, rf	5	0	3	3	0	0	0	0	0	0	0	1	2	0
Hornsby, 2b	5	1	2	2	0	0	0	0	2	0	1	3	4	0
Bottomley, 1b	4	0	1	1	0	0	0	1	0	0	0	6	1	0
L. Bell, 3b	4	0	1	1	0	0	0	0	0	1	0	3	0	0
Hafey, lf	5	1	1	1	0	0	0	0	2	0	0	0	0	0
O'Farrell, c	4	1	2	2	0	0	0	0	0	0	0	8	1	0
Thevenow, ss	4	1	2	3	1	0	0	0	1	0	0	3	2	0
Rhem, p	1	0	0	0	0	0	0	0	1	0	0	0	1	0
aToporcer	0	0	0	0	0	0	0	0	0	1	0	0	0	0
Reinhart, p	0	0	0	0	0	0	0	0	0	0	0	0	0	0
H. Bell, p	0	0	0	0	0	0	0	0	0	0	0	0	0	0
bFlowers	1	0	0	0	0	0	0	0	1	0	0	0	0	0
Hallahan, p	0	0	0	0	0	0	0	0	0	0	0	1	0	0
Holm	1	0	0	0	0	0	0	0	1	0	0	0	0	0
Keen, p	0	0	0	0	0	0	0	0	0	0	0	0	1	0
Total	39	5	14	16	2	0	0	1	8	2	1	27	14	0

a Batted for Rhem in the fourth.
b Batted for H. Bell in the sixth.
c Batted for Hallahan in the eighth.

SCORE BY INNINGS.

New York	1	0	1	1	4	2	1	0	0	10
St. Louis	1	0	0	3	0	0	0	0	1	5

Left on bases—New York 10, St. Louis 10. Bases on balls—Off Rhem 2, Reinhart 4, H. Bell 1, Hallahan 3, Hoyt 1. Struck out—By Rhem 4, H. Bell 1, Hallahan 1, Hoyt 8. Hits—Off Rhem 7 in 4 innings, Reinhart 1 in none (pitched to five men in fifth inning), H. Bell 4 in 2, Hallahan 2 in 2, Keen none in 1. Balk—H. Bell. Losing pitcher—Reinhart. Umpires—Klem (N. L.) at plate, Dinneen (A. L.) at first base, O'Day (N. L.) at second base, Hildebrand (A. L.) at third base. Time of game—2:39.

Cardinals Hitting Fiercely.

The Cardinal hitting was fierce, and Hornsby wisely ordered Bottomley to keep the attack going instead of bunting. Bottomley, however flied to Ruth and Lester Bell did likewise to Combs. Hoyt got out of a very bad hole by fanning Hafey.

Lazzeri's two bagger to left opened the second. Tony thought the ball was going into the stand, and loafed down to first. So was a second late in arriving at third, where Bell did a nice job of touching. Followed Severeid's single, on which Lazzeri could have scored. It was one of three or more runs tossed away by the opulent Yanks.

The second Ruthian product enlivened the third inning. The score was now: Ruth 2, St. Louis 1. The Yanks showed more signs of life in the fourth, when Lazzeri walked and scored during the Hafey-Douthit head-on collision, which also allowed Dugan to reach second. On Severeid's single Joe was tagged out at home, Joe's speed being less than his earnest intentions.

The fourth was almost the end for Waite Hoyt. Up to this time he had done excellent work. Although his curve was nothing to boast about, he had nice control and an effective change of pace, working the corners with low fast balls that were called strikes but were hard to hit.

Koenig charged out to left to make a rattling good catch of L. Bell's fly. Hafey singled and then the Yankee shortstop made up for his good work by fumbling O'Farrell's grounder, an error which nearly cost the game, giving the Cards three unearned runs.

It was a bad break of luck for Hoyt. Thevenow whipped a two-bagger an inch inside first base and Hafey scored while O'Farrell paused at second. Hornsby had no confidence in Rhem and yanked him for Pinch Hitter Toporcer. It was a move that Rogers lived to regret, for Rhem certainly would have done better than the miscellaneous collection of talent which followed him.

Toporcer didn't deliver much at that, though his sacrifice fly to Combs scored O'Farrell with the tying run. Combs's throw was fast, but badly aimed.

Douthit's Two-Baggar

Here, Douthit sent a rollicking two-bagger out to the bleacher wall in right centre and put his team a run ahead, while the local enthusiasts went crazy with joy. Sportsman's Park was a madhouse for two or three minutes, and the purple-faced rosters went into another spasm when Southworth singled to left. Douthit went for home and Ruth stopped him dead. The vocal storm subsided somewhat.

Back came the Yanks in the fifth to have the game presented to them on a silver platter. Reinhart, a stalwart left-hander with a tricky service like Sherdel, was nervous and wild. Altogether he gave the most pathetic spectacle of many a world's series. He walked Combs without getting over even one strike, and the Yanks got a break when Koening popped a flukey double down the right-field line, the ball leading in the one exact spot where no fielder could reach it.

Normsby slipped when he picked up the ball, and Combs was fast enough to score. With Ruth at bat, Reinhart went on an ascension and neglected to take his parachute with him.

True, he favored Mr. Ruth with a strike, but the other four were balls. Another walk to Meusel filled up the bases and Reinhart went from bad to worse by chucking two bad ones to Gehrig.

Here was the point where Kernsby should have acted. He had Herman Bell warmed up, and it was no secret that Reinhart was now in the clouds. The left-hander steadied a little, but when the count was two and two he walked Gehrig, forcing Koening in and sending New York ahead.

Bell took up the assignment with the bases still full and no one out, and no one thinking of getting out. Lazzeri's fly to Southworth scored Ruth, while Meusel occupied third after the catch. Dugan's grounder spouted up in the air and during his subsequent demise at the hands of O'Farrell, Meusel raced home with the fourth run.

In the sixth came Combs's single and the third of the Ruth home-run series. The score was now 9 to 4. The Cards in their half of the inning made attempts at reprisals. O'Farrell and Thevenow singled, but Flowers, a hitter for H. Bell fanned. Douthit and Southworth were powerless.

A single by Severeid, Hoyt's sacrifice, and Combs's two-bagger inside

third put the Yanks into double figures in the seventh. Protected by his big lead, Hoyt went along in able style now. When O'Farrell led off with a single in the eighth, there was a flutter in the New York bull pen. but it was all a mistake. Hoyt struck out Thevenow and also Holm, who batted for Hallahan. Douthit flied to centre.

Wee Willie Sherdel will come back for the Cards tomorrow and the Cards need that victory very much, for it will be their last home game. Tomorrow night the procession wends back to New York.

October 7, 1926

BOY REGAINS HEALTH AS RUTH HITS HOMERS

John D. Sylvester, Son of National City Bank Executive, Now on Road to Recovery.

Special to The New York Times.
ESSEX FALLS, N. J., Oct. 7.—John Dale Sylvester, 11 years old, to whom physicians allotted thirty minutes of life when he was stricken with blood poisoning last week, was pronounced well on the road to recovery this

afternoon, after he had contentedly listened to the radio returns of the Yankees' defeat of the Cardinals. His father, Horace Sylvester Jr., Vice President of the National City Bank, and the physicians are convinced that John owes his life to messages of encouragement which the boy received Wednesday from Babe Ruth and other world series players. They had learned of his plight and of his request for autographed baseballs from his father.

The physicians say that the boy's return to health began when he learned the news of Ruth's three homers in the fourth game of the series. His fever began to abate at once, and the favorable course was hastened today after he had listened to the radio returns, clutching the autographed baseballs which he received by air mail on

Wednesday night.

John's intense interest in the world series and in home runs especially, were explained to his family today when his chums told of the boy's ability on the sand lots. He had modestly refrained from mentioning the fact that he has a reputation as a home run hitter and a skillful third baseman.

His recovery had reached the point tonight where he was already making plans for a return to the diamond, and he promised one caller that he would soon bring his team to a neighboring town for a game.

The boy's father sent letters to the managers of both teams today thanking them for their assistance in helping his boy to recover.

October 8, 1926

GIANTS GET HORNSBY; TRADE BIG SURPRISE

Record Baseball Deal Sends Frisch and Ring to Cardinals for Famous Batsman.

ST. LOUIS REFUSES TERMS

Demand by Manager of World's Champions of $150,000 for Three Years Brings Break.

By JAMES R. HARRISON.

In the biggest deal of modern baseball history, Rogers Hornsby, greatest batsman of the game, and manager of the world's champion St. Louis Cardinals, was traded to the Giants last night for Frank Frisch and Pitcher Jimmy Ring.

The transaction, completed over the long-distance telephone between St. Louis and New York at 7:30 last night, involves players valued at more than half a million dollars and brings to this city the second of the two outstanding figures of the sport—Babe Ruth, king of the long distance hitters, and Hornsby, six-time batting champion of the National League.

Although President Charles A. Stoneham of the Giants declared that no money was paid to the Cardinals, baseball men were unanimous in insisting that the New York club must have handed over at least $100,000, in addition to its star second baseman and a veteran pitcher who is almost at the end of his career.

Hornsby, it was pointed out, is worth much more than $300,000 at present baseball prices. Several years ago John McGraw, manager of the Giants, offered $250,000 and five players for

him. Not long afterward the Brooklyn club raised this figure to a straight $275,000.

Value Increased Steadily.

Since that time Hornsby's value has increased greatly. He went on to win his sixth successive hitting championship of the league, was universally recognized as the finest right-handed batter of them all and climaxed his career last season by leading the Cardinals to the first pennant ever won by a modern St. Louis team and later to the world's championship.

At the very peak of his career, when his money value was close to the $350,000 mark, Hornsby is traded for Frank Frisch, who might bring $250,000 in the open market, and for a pitcher of slight value.

There is a difference here of about $100,000 that baseball experts wanted explained to them last night. They considered it unbelievable that President Breadon of the Cardinals would have traded the popular hero of St. Louis for Frisch and Ring alone.

On the other hand, the Giants would gladly turn over Frisch and Ring and $100,000, for in Hornsby they have the long-sought metropolitan rival for Babe Ruth. That they would pay Hornsby $50,000 a year for three years was likewise taken for granted; his box office value in the biggest baseball city is tremendous.

Moreover, Hornsby now looms up as the next manager of the Giants, to take the reins when John McGraw finally decides to lay them down, as he has threatened to do for the past year.

It was President Breadon of the Cardinals who suggested this trade involving $600,000 worth of ball players. Breadon and Hornsby had a conference in St. Louis yesterday on salary matters; they disagreed hopelessly, and Breadon then did the next best thing by offering him to the Giants.

Deal Closed in Few Minutes.

Shortly after the meeting with Hornsby, Breadon called President Stoneham of the Giants on the phone. According to Stoneham, the St. Louis club owner broached the trade of Hornsby for Frisch and Ring. It was immediately accepted; a few minutes of telephone conversation and the big deal was put through.

President Stoneham denied that the trade had been previously arranged.

"In an off-hand way," he said, "we had talked with Breadon about trad-

Complete Record of Hornsby Since Entering Organized Ball

Year.	Club.	G.	AB.	R.	H.	SB.	P.C.
1914—	(a)Dallas	..	..	..	..	..	...
1914—	(b)Hugo	..	..	..	..	..	...
1914—	Dennison	113	393	47	91	19	.232
1915—	(c)Dennison	119	429	75	119	24	.277
1915—	St. Louis	18	57	5	14	..	.246
1916—	St. Louis	139	495	63	155	17	.313
1917—	St. Louis	145	523	36	171	17	.327
1918—	St. Louis	115	416	51	117	8	.281
1919—	St. Louis	138	512	68	163	17	.318
1920—	(d)St. Louis	149	589	96	218	12	.370
1921—	St. Louis	154	592	131	235	13	.397
1922—	St. Louis	154	623	141	250	17	.401
1923—	St. Louis	107	424	89	163	3	.384
1924—	(e)St. Louis	143	536	121	227	5	.424
1925—	(f)St. Louis	138	504	133	203	5	.403
1926—	St. Louis	134	528	96	167	3	.316

World's Series Record.

		G.	AB.	R.	H.	SB.	P.C.
1926—	St. Louis	7	28	2	7	1	.250

Complete Major League Totals.

Years.	Games.	A.B.	R.	Hits.	SB.	P.C.
12	1,534	5,790	1,080	2,083	117	.359

a On trial, released April 29.
b Released July 2—Hugo to Dennison.
c Sold Aug. 20 to St. Louis, reported sales price $500.
d Started six-year National League batting championship string.
e Set modern major league batting mark of .425.
f Appointed St. Louis manager June 1, 1925. Won National League Most Valuable Player Award.

ing Hornsby, but the negotiations did not get very far. We were not very hopeful, and when Breadon called us tonight I was as much surprised as any one."

According to another story, however, Breadon had agreed that if he could not make Hornsby accept a one-year contract at $50,000 a year, he would trade his manager and star batsman to the Giants after yesterday's conference. President Stoneham, this account said, was writing here for the long-distance call.

John McGraw, who pulled the strings of this momentous trade, was mysteriously in the background last night and it could not be learned whether or not he was present when the telephone bell rang.

The rival second basemen greeted the news with a marked lack of enthusiasm. Hornsby was quoted in St. Louis as saying that "it doesn't look

right that I should be traded from a club that I just managed to a world's championship."

At his home in this city Frisch, the Fordham Flash, born and brought up in New York, seemed stunned by the tidings.

"It's pretty hot out there, but I suppose I'll play," he said in a listless tone.

Among other things, this is the first time in baseball history that a manager has been traded within a year of his having won the world's championship. From that angle alone the trade was enough to set the baseball tongues wagging.

McGraw's Ambition Gratified.

The acquisition of Hornsby gratifies an ambition long cherished by John McGraw. For many years he has cast a covetous eye at the man whom McGraw himself called "the greatest right-handed hitter of all time." Fabulous offers were in vain. The Cardinals would have traded Hornsby for Frisch and other players several years ago, but McGraw declared that he would not give up Frisch for Hornsby under any circumstances.

The next move came last week at the meetings of the major leagues, when the split between Hornsby and Breadon loomed up as very serious. It was known that McGraw again was talking trade with the Cardinals; the trail became so hot that he canceled a reservation on the Twentieth Century Limited to travel with Breadon to Chicago on another train.

It was in a compartment on this train, the story goes, that the deal was completed which was announced last night—conditional, of course, on Breadon's failing to sign Hornsby to a one-year contract instead of the three-year agreement that Rogers demanded.

Two years ago Hornsby signed a three-year contract at $30,000 a season. When he was made manager in the middle of the 1925 season, his contract as a player went on and Rogers received nothing extra for being manager. However, as soon as the Cardinals had won the world's series, Hornsby announced that he wanted his present contract torn up and a new document drawn up calling for $150,000 for three years.

The dispute between Breadon and Hornsby involved only the question of one year or three. President Breadon considered the latter risk too great.

One of his arguments was that

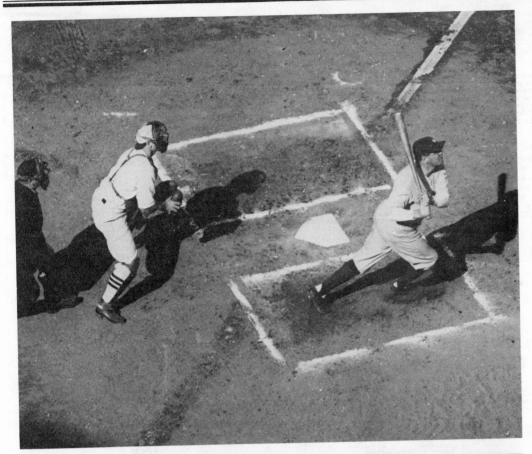

Babe Ruth hits the first of his three home runs in the fourth game of the 1926 World Series.

Rogers Hornsby, St. Louis Cardinals slugger, hit .424 in 1924, the highest season's average in major league history.

Hornsby as a player had been for below his usual level this year. Rogers batted only .316 almost 100 points under his customary figure; both his batting and fielding suffered from the strain of piloting a team through the thick of a pennant battle.

Breadon and his popular manager also had sharp disagreements on other matters. Hornsby insisted on the complete retirement from the club of Vice President Branch Rickey, Rogers's predecessor as manager. Although Hornsby owned 15 per cent. of the club, Breadon stuck to Rickey, his chief adviser.

McGraw-Frisch Also Split.

There was also a rupture between McGraw and Frisch, who suddenly left the team last August in St. Louis and came home. Frisch was angered by

McGraw's biting remarks and by the manager's intention to switch him to third base.

The trouble was smoothed over, but Frisch, after being ill for some time, was fined $500 when he returned to uniform. It was a foregone conclusion then that this season would be his last as a Giant.

Not since the sale of Ruth to the Yankees in 1920 has there been a baseball trade which might be compared with the trading of a world's championship manager and possibly the flashiest second baseman of any day.

Last year was Hornsby's eleventh full season with the Cardinals. He played minor league ball at Dallas and Dennison, Texas, in 1914 and was sold to St. Louis on Aug. 20, 1915, for the munificent sum of $500. For five years

alternating among shortstop, third base and second, he finally drifted to the latter position.

At the same time his tremendous hitting began to attract attention. His first big year was 1920, when he batted .370. After reaching .397 the next year, he went over the .400 mark in 1922, 1924 and 1925.

His .424 in 1924 established a new modern major league batting mark. In 1922 he hit forty-two homers, still the National League record. His batting feats eclipsed even those of Delehanty and Honus Wagner. Last year he was voted the most valuable player in his league.

Frisch, a baseball and football star at Fordham, joined the Giants in 1919 after the Yanks had bid unsuccessfully for him. He became a full-fledged reg-

ular in 1921, hit .341 that year and .345 in 1923, his greatest season.

Frisch was probably the best of all world's series players and holds a record in having hit .300 or better in four series. His spectacular fielding and dazzling speed made him a popular favorite, but he was below form in both 1925 and 1926, hitting only .314 last season.

Ring was a star for the Reds in the world's series of 1919. In 1921 he was traded to the Phillies and last Winter to the Giants for Dean, Bentley and cash. He pitched only five full games for McGraw and had a record of 11 won and ten lost.

December 21, 1926

NEUN'S TRIPLE PLAY CHECKS INDIAN RALLY

Feat, Second in Two Days, Comes in Ninth to Clinch Detroit Victory, 1 to 0.

DETROIT, May 31 (AP).—The breaks of a tight game favored Johnny Neun, Detroit first baseman, in the game with the Indians here today and he executed one of the rarest of baseball plays—an unassisted triple play.

His lightning action also won the game for the Tigers, 1 to 0, by retiring the three Cleveland runners in the ninth inning who threatened to tally after the Indians had been held scoreless for eight innings.

Myatt batted for Buckeye in the Cleveland half of the ninth and drew the second pass issued by Collins. Jamieson bunted toward first and beat it out, putting Myatt on second. Summa lined to Neun, who took the ball standing still, ran over and tagged

Jamieson between first and second and continued to second base, landing there before Myatt could return.

The box score:

CLEVELAND (A.)	ab.	r.	h.	po.	a.	e.		DETROIT (A.)	ab.	r.	h.	po.	a.	e.
Jamieson, lf.	3	0	1	1	0	0		Warner, 3b.	4	1	1	1	1	0
Summa, rf.	4	0	1	1	0	0		Gehringer, 2b.	3	0	0	1	3	0
Fonseca, 2b.	3	0	0	3	5	0		Manush, cf.	2	0	1	1	0	0
Burns, 1b.	3	0	0	10	0	0		Fothergill, lf.	3	0	1	2	0	0
J. Sewell, ss.	3	0	0	3	2	0		Heilmann, rf.	3	0	0	0	0	0
L. Sewell, c.	3	0	1	0	3	1		Neun, 1b.	3	0	1	13	0	0
Neis, cf.	3	0	1	3	0	0		Tavener, ss.	3	0	1	3	2	1
Hodapp, 3b.	3	0	0	2	3	0		Wendall, c.	2	0	0	2	1	0
Buckeye, p.	2	0	0	0	2	0		Collins, p.	2	0	1	0	9	0
aMyatt	0	0	0	0	0	0								
Total	27	0	4	24	15	1		Total	25	1	6	27	17	0

aBatted for Buckeye in ninth.

Cleveland ....0 0 0 0 0 0 0 0 0—0
Detroit ....1 0 0 0 0 0 0 0 x—1

Three-base hit—L. Sewell. Double play—Hodapp, Fonseca and Burns; J. Sewell, Fonseca and Burns; Buckeye, Fonseca and Burns; Collins, Gehringer and Neun. Triple play—Neun (unassisted). Left on bases—Cleveland 2, Detroit 3. Bases on balls—Off Buckeye 3, Collins 2. Struck out—By Collins 1. Umpires—Evans, Hildebrand and McGowan. Time of game—1:34.

June 1, 1927

RUTH CRASHES 60TH TO SET NEW RECORD

Babe Makes It a Real Field Day by Accounting for All Runs in 4-2 Victory

1921 MARK OF 59 BEATEN

Fans Go Wild as Ruth Pounds Ball Into Stands With One On, Breaking 2-2 Tie

CONNECTS LAST TIME UP

Babe Ruth scaled the hitherto unattained heights yesterday. Home run 60, a terrific smash off the southpaw pitching of Zachary, nestled in the Babe's favorite spot in the right field bleachers, and before the roar had ceased it was found that this drive not only had made

home run record history but also was the winning margin in a 4 to 2 victory over the Senators. This also was the Yanks' 109th triumph of the season. Their last league game of the year will be played today.

When the Babe stepped to the plate in that momentous eighth inning the score was deadlocked. Koenig was on third base, the result of a triple, one man was out and all was tense. It was the Babe's fourth trip to the plate during the afternoon, a base on balls and two singles resulting on his other visits plateward.

The first Zachary offering was a fast one, which sailed over for a called strike. The next was high. The Babe took a vicious swing at the third pitched ball and the bat connected with a crash that was audible in all parts of the stand. It was not necessary to follow the course of the ball. The boys in the bleachers indicated the route of the record homer. It dropped about half way to the top. No. 60 was some homer, a fitting wallop to top the Babe's record of 58 in 1921.

While the crowd cheered and the Yankee players roared their greetings the Babe made his triumphant, almost regal tour of the paths. He jogged around slowly, touched each bag firmly and carefully and when he imbedded his spikes in the rubber disk to record officially Homer 60 hats were tossed into the air, papers were torn up and tossed liberally and the spirit of celebration permeated the place.

The Babe's stroll out to his position was the signal for a handkerchief salute in which all the bleacherites, to the last man, participated. Jovial Babe entered into the carnival spirit and punctuated his Ringly strides with a succession of snappy military salutes.

Ruth 4, Senators 2

Ruth's homer was a fitting climax to a game which will go down as the Babe's personal triumph. The Yanks scored four runs, the Babe personally crossing the plate three times and bringing in Koenig for the fourth. So this is one time where it would be fair, although not original, to record Yankee victory 109 as Ruth 4, Senators 2.

There was not much else to the game. The 10,000 persons who came to the Stadium were there for no other purpose than to see the Babe make home run history. After each of Babe's visits to the plate the expectant crowd would relax and wait for his next effort. They saw him open with a base on balls, follow with two singles and then clout the epoch-making circuit smash.

The only _unhappy individual within the Stadium was Zachary. He realized he was going down in the records as the historical home run victim, in other words the goat. Zachary was one of the most interested spectators of the home run fight. He tossed his glove to the ground, muttered to himself, turned to his mates for consolation and got everything but that. There is no denying that Zachary was putting everything he had on the ball. No pitcher likes to have recorded after his name the fact that he was Ruth's victim on his sixtieth homer.

The ball that the Babe drove, according to word from official sources, was a pitch that was fast, low and on the inside. The Babe puffed away from the plate, then stepped into the ball, and wham! According to Umpire Bill Dinneen at the plate and Catcher Muddy Ruel the ball traveled on a line and landed a foot inside fair territory about half way to the top of the bleachers. But when the ball reached the bleacher barrier it was about ten feet fair and curving rapidly to the right.

Fan Rushes to Babe With Ball

The ball which became Homer 60 was caught by Joe Forner of 1937 First Avenue, Manhatta. He is about 40 years old and has been following baseball for thirty-five, according to his own admission. He was far from modest and as soon as the game was over rushed to the dressing room to let the Babe know who had the ball.

For three innings both sides were blanked. The Senators broke through in the fourth for two runs.

The Yanks came back with one run in their half of the fourth. Ruth opened with a long single to right and moved to third on Gehrig's single to centre. Gehrig took second on the throw to third. Meusel drove deep to Goslin, Ruth scoring and Gehrig taking third after the catch.

With two out in the sixth Ruth singled to right. Gehrig's hit was so fast that it went right through Gillis for a single, Ruth holding second. The Babe tied the score on Meusel's single to centre. Lazzeri was an easy third out.

The box score:

WASHINGTON (A.)	ab	r	h	po	a	e
Rice, rf	3	0	1	2	0	0
Harris, 2b	3	0	0	3	4	0
Genzel, cf	4	0	1	1	0	0
Gostin, lf	4	1	1	5	0	0
Judge, 1b	4	0	0	5	0	0
Ruel, c	2	1	1	2	0	0
Riuege, 3b	3	0	1	1	4	0
Gillis, ss	4	0	0	2	1	0
Zachary, p	2	0	0	0	1	0
aJohnson	1	0	0	0	0	0
Total	30	2	5	24	10	0

NEW YORK (A.)	ab	r	h	po	a	e
Combs, cf	4	0	0	3	0	0
Koenig, ss	4	1	1	3	5	0
Ruth, rf	3	3	3	4	0	0
Gehrig, 1b	4	0	2	10	0	1
Meusel, lf	4	0	1	3	0	0
Lazzeri, 2b	3	0	0	2	2	0
Dugan, 3b	3	0	1	1	1	0
Benguogh, c	8	0	1	1	2	0
Piperas, p	2	0	0	0	2	0
Pennock, p	1	0	0	0	1	0
Total	30	4	0	25	13	1

a Batted for Zachary in nineth.

Washington	0 0 0 2 0 0 0 0 0	-2
New York	0 0 0 1 0 1 0 2	-4

Two-base hit — Rice, Tree-base hit — Koenig. Home run — Ruth. Stolen bases — Ruel. Bluerge, Rice. Sacrifices — Meusert. Double plays — Harris and Bruege. Gillis, Harris and Judge. Left on bases — New York 4, Washington 7. Bases on balls — Off Pipgras 4, Pennock, 1, Zachary 1. Struck out — By Zachary 1. Hits — Off Pipgras 4 in 6 innings. Pennock 1 in 3. Hit by pitcher — By Pipgras (Rice). Winning pitcher — Pennock. Umpires — Dinneen, Connolly and Owens. Time of game — 1:38.

October 1, 1927

ALEXANDER EQUALS MATHEWSON'S FEAT

Beats Robins for Cards, 5-2, Tying League Record of 372 Games Won.

EXHIBITS PERFECT CONTROL

By ROSCOE McGOWEN.

Special to The New York Times.

ST. LOUIS, Aug. 1.—By beating the Robins today, 5 to 2, Grover Cleveland Alexander, veteran righthander of the Cardinals, equaled a record held by Christy Mathewson

in the National League.

Alexander pitched himself into his 372d winning box score of the many years he has been a headliner in the National League. The veteran pitched a typical Alexander game, his greatest asset, control, being in evidence from start to finish. No bases on balls, no wild pitches or hit batters marred his performance. Alexander has been in the National League since 1911.

A first inning assault on Johnny Morrison gave Alex a four-run lead to work on and Jim Bottomley's twenty-third home run of the season added the fifth run in the eighth.

Del Bissonette bounced a home run off the right field pavilion roof in the fifth to give the Robins their first run and Bressler's double in the seventh followed by an infield out and Jake Flowers's sacrifice fly to Douthit made up the Brooklyn total.

Air-tight support kept him out of trouble several times, notably in each of the first three innings when three double plays, in all of which Frankie Frisch figured prominently. cleared the bases and stopped the Robins.

The fast time of the game was particularly fitting, as the contest was delayed in getting underway by the ceremonial greetings accorded to the Robin fliers, Jackson and O'Brine, who briefly occupied a special box near the Cardinal dugout.

Morrison was not threatened much after the first inning. In the fourth and sixth innings, Herman singled and Hendrick followed with a double, but the first time Herman was held at third and the next time thrown, out at the plate on a fast relay, Roettger, Bottomley and Wilson.

Bissonette hit a long triple almost against the centre field wall in the ninth after two were out, but Frisch went far into right to nab Flowers's pop fly to end the game.

BROOKLYN (N).	ab	r	h	po	a	e
Frederick, cf	4	0	1	5	0	0
Moore, ss	1	0	0	0	0	0
Banrroft, ss	3	0	0	0	4	0
Herman, rf	4	0	2	3	0	0
Hendrick, 3b	4	0	3	0	1	0
Bressler, lf	4	1	3	3	0	0
Bissonette, 1b	4	1	2	7	0	0
Flowers, 2b	3	0	0	5	3	0
Henline, c	3	0	2	1	1	0
Morrison, p	3	0	0	0	0	0
Total	33	2	11	24	8	0

ST. LOUIS (N).	ab	r	h	po.	a	e
Douthit, cf	4	0	1	4	1	0
High, 3b	2	1	0	1	0	0
Frisch, 2b	4	0	0	3	5	0
Bottomley, 1b	4	2	2	11	1	0
Orsatti, lf	4	2	2	1	0	0
Roettger, rf	4	1	3	0	0	0
Gelbert, ss	4	0	1	1	3	0
Wilson, c	5	0	1	0	1	0
Alexander, p	3	0	0	0	1	0
Total	31	5	9	27	11	0

Brooklyn	0 0 0 0 1 0 1 0 0	-2
St. Louis	4 0 0 0 0 0 0 1	-5

Runs batted in—Roettger 2. Gelbert 2, Bissonette 1. Flowers 1. Bottomley 1. Two-base hits—Bottomley, Roettger, Hendrick 2, Douthit, Wilson, Bressler. Three-base Hit—Bissonette. Home runs—Bissonette, Bottomley. Sacrifices—High, Flowers. Stolen base—Gelbert. Double plays—Frisch, Gelbert and Bottomley; Gelbert, Frisch and Bottomley; Frisch and Bottomley. Bases on Ball—Off Morrison 2. Left on bases—St. Louis 5, Brooklyn 5. Umpires—Rigler, Jorda and Hart. Time of game—1:26.

August 2, 1929

ATHLETICS' 10 RUNS IN 7TH DEFEAT CUBS IN 4TH SERIES GAME

Trailing, 8-0, Mackmen Unleash Attack That Beats McCarthy's Men, 10-8, Before 30,000.

---

15 MEN BAT IN ONE INNING

Four Pitchers, Root, Nehf, Blake and Malone, Used Before Athletics Are Retired.

DYKES'S DOUBLE DECIDES

By JOHN DREBINGER.

Special to The New York Times.

PHILADELPHIA, Pa., Oct. 12.—Somebody dropped a toy hammer on a stick of dynamite today and touched off an explosion that shook to its heels a

continent that Christopher Columbus had discovered 437 years ago to the day.

It happened in the seventh inning of the fourth game of the world's series at a time when more than 30,000 spectators sat in the packed stands of Shibe Park steeped in despair. For all one knows, they may have been the same 30,000 who jammed those game stands the day before, for the number of paid admissions, 29,991, was exactly the same.

The receipts, $140,815, also were the same, making the total for the four games $718,679 and the total paid attendance 160,709. But the feelings of the crowd—all but those of the 500 loyal rooters of Chicago—were infinitely worse.

For the Athletics, beaten in the third game yesterday, were trailing, 8 to 0, and if there is anything at all that can appear certain in this most curious of all possible worlds it was that the Cubs would win this game and square the series at two all.

Chicago Rooters Stunned.

Then started the seventh and it brought in its wake a typhoon, tornado and hurricane, a rush of blood to the head of the spectators and the complete collapse of the 500 loyal rooters from Chicago as a surging Mack attack swept on and flattened all before it to roll up a total of ten runs for the inning.

And so to the Athletics went the fourth game of the series by a score of 10 to 8, and the hopes of the shattered Cub forces tonight are hanging on

Underwood and Underwood.

Jimmy Dykes.

something slightly thinner than a thread. For the Athletics are now leading in this world's series by a margin of three victories to one, and they need only one more game to conclude the struggle and win for themselves the lion's share of the spoils.

Never in all world series history was there such an inning. Records, large and

small, collapsed in whole-sale lots, while a crowd, held speechless for hours, howled itself into a perfect delirium and smashed a few more records.

Boot Appeared Out for Revenge.

For six innings the bulky, stolid Charlie Boot, whom the fates had treated rather unkindly in the first game in Chicago, appeared riding on his way to a merited revenge. Over the period he had held the mightiest of Mack sluggers in a grip of iron, allowing only three scattered hits and mowing them down as though they were men of straw.

And while Charlie was doing this the Cubs, atlast thoroughly aroused, cuffed, and battered four of Connie Mack's prized hurlers to all sectors of the field. They hammered Jack Quinn, who brought his forty-odd years and his famed spitball into the fray with high hopes only to carry both cut badly shattered. They pulverized Rube Walberg and smashed Ed Rommel.

Charlie Grimm hit a homer, Rogers Hornsby hit a single and a triple. Kiki Cuyler hit three singles in a row, and the 500 loyal rooters from Chicago split their 500 throats. The Philadelphians tried hard to ignore them, but it is difficult to ignore 500 loyal rooters from Chicago.

It was warm and sunny, but the great crowd sulked and sat in silence as Al Simmons stepped to the plate to open the Athletic half of the seventh. Two and three-fifths seconds later the storm broke.

Simmons Collects Homer.

Simmons crashed a home-run on top of the roof of the left-field pavilion. It was Al's second circuit clout of the series and the crowd gave him a liberal hand, though the applause was still lacking in enthusiasm.

"Well," they said, "that at least saves us from a shutout."

But the rumbling continued and increased in volume. Jimmy Foxx singled to right. Bing Miller singled to centre and Jimmy Dykes singled to left. The Dykes' hit scored Foxx and when Joe Boley singled to centre Miller raced over the plate.

There was a momentary pause as the veteran George Burns, coming up in the rôle of pinch hitter, popped to Shortstop English but when Max Bishop laced a single to centre, Dykes counted, the Athletics had four runs over and the Cub lead had been cut squarely in half.

By now the crowd had set up a terrifying din. The Cubs began to squirm uneasily and there was much activity on the Chicago bench as Manager Joe McCarthy waved frantically to four or five pitchers warming up furiously in the bull pen. Root was taken out of the box and Arthur Nehf, veteran lefthander, took his place.

There were two on the bases and only one out as George William Haas, called mule for short, stepped to the plate. A moment later there was a roar that almost shook the famed Liberty Bell off its pedestal six miles away.

Haas hit a long high fly to deep centre. The squat Hack Wilson, Cub centrefielder, wheeled about and ran at top speed, his short, stubby legs leaving nothing but a blur as they carried him over the ground. He got under the ball in time to make the catch, but as it came down it crossed the glaring sun. Hack lost sight of it. The ball almost struck him as it landed at his feet, and as it rolled away Boley and Bishop scampered wildly over the plate and Haas, too, completed the circuit for a home run.

The hit had scored three runs and the Athletics were now only one run behind. A sinking feeling must have gripped the Cubs, and as for the five hundred loyal rooters from Chicago, they had passed out long ago. But the assault was not ended yet. Its fury seemed to gain momentum with each succeeding minute.

Cochrane walked and Manager McCarthy unceremoniously yanked Nehf, a world's series hero of another day, and called on Sheriff Blake to stem the surging Mack attack. He stemmed it like a man sticking his head in an electric fan.

Simmons up for 2d Time.

Simmons, up for the second time, singled to left. Foxx singled to centre for his second hit of the inning and Cochrane crossed the plate.

That tied the score at 8-all and the turmoil in the stands was now quite indescribable. A great gathering of staid Philadelphians had suddenly gone completely out of their minds.

McCarthy, fairly beside himself, waved again to his rapidly fading forces in the Chicago bull pen and called on Pat Malone to succeed Blake.

Pat's first effort resulted in Miller getting a crack in the ribs with the ball, and that filled the bases. Then came the concluding stroke.

Dykes, who, it will be remembered, had singled the first time up in this inning, sent a low, hard liner screaming to the left corner of the playing field. Riggs Stephenson, Cub left fielder, chased it desperately, got both hands on the ball, but failed to hold it and, as it bounded away for a two-base hit, Simmons and Foxx scored the two runs that finally put the Mackmen in front.

That was all. It was enough. Malone struck out Boley. He also fanned Burns, who was still in the game as a pinch-hitter, and the crowd fell back in its seats exhausted. No attempts were made to revive the 500 Chicagoans.

All Sorts of Records Toppled.

All sorts of records had been broken as the game collapsed on top of the heads of the stunned Cubs. By scoring ten tallies the Athletics surpassed by two the record for most runs scored in a single inning by a team in a world series game, which was set by the Giants against the Yankees on Oct. 7, 1921.

In that same game and inning the Giants had totaled eight runs, which stood as the record until today, when the Athletics pummeled the four luckless Chicago pitchers for ten in that one tumultuous round.

Again, in that same inning eight years ago, the late Ross Young hit safely twice to stand as the only player ever to perform this feat in world series play. Today Simmons, Foxx and Dykes equaled that achievement.

And there was still another record equaled, for after this tempestuous hitting orgy had put the Athletics two runs ahead Connie Mack still had an ace in the hole with which to protect that margin. He trotted out Lefty Grove to pitch the eighth and ninth innings.

Grove Retires Bewildered Cubs.

Lefty Bob, his smoke ball fairly burning down the trail, retired the bewildered Cubs in order in both innings, fanning four of them. And when he fanned the fourth it brought the Cubs' total of strike-outs for the game up to eight and for the series, forty-four.

This enabled the Cubs to tie the rather unenviable record set by the Giants in the series of 1911 in six games and tied by the Yankees in eight games in 1921. The Cubs, it will be noted, have equaled that mark in four.

Up to the moment that that cataclysm descended upon their unsuspecting heads, the Cubs had appeared almost certain winners of this game. Mack had chosen old John Quinn as his pitcher, and though old John skirted safely through the first three innings he plunged into difficulties in the fourth.

Cuyler singled in this round and raced all the way to third when Right Fielder Miller allowed the ball to get away from him. Stephenson's pop fly held the fleet Kiki glued to third, but Grimm walloped the ball over the right-field barrier for a homer and the Cubs were two runs in front.

Quinn's Downfall Comes in Sixth.

Quinn regained his composure in the fifth, but his years and also the Cubs got to him in the sixth and he went down in a heap. Hornsby, who previously had struck out for the seventh time in the series, slashed a single to centre. Wilson and Cuyler also singled, the latter's hit scoring the Rajah. Came another single by Stephenson to drive in Wilson and old John was carted tenderly off the playing field.

Rube Walberg, left-handed ace of the Mack staff, replaced him and added to the confusion. He fielded a tap by Grimm and hurled it wildly past first. It was scored as a hit for Grimm, an error for Walberg and accounted for two more runs, as both Cuyler and Stephenson tallied on the misplay, while Grimm pulled up at third. A moment later Grimm came in with the fifth Chicago run for the round on a sacrifice fly by Zach Taylor to Haas in centre.

Although Walberg succeeded in ending the inning well enough by fanning the next two batters, Mack chose to withdraw him, and when the Cubs came up for the seventh they found the right-handed Ed Rommel opposing them.

Hornsby Triples in Seventh.

This did not seem to displease them at all. With one out, Hornsby tripled to left centre and, after Wilson had walked, Cuyler banged a single to right to score the Rajah. It was Kiki's third straight hit and the entire Cub machine was now clicking perfectly.

Root, in the meantime, was pitching superby and never did he appear greater than in the fifth when Miller beat out an infield hit and Wilson, in some inexplicable manner, muffed a pop fly that fell squarely in his hands in centre.

But a piece of Mack strategy went wrong here and helped the Cubs. Maybe it was the now alert Cub team which caught the sign. In any event Miller and Dykes dashed for second and third as Root wound up to pitch to Boley. It was a hit-and-run play, but there was no hit, as Root pitched wide of the plate and as catcher Taylor whipped the ball to third Miller was thrown out at the post by yards.

Then Wilson redeemed himself by making a spectacular catch of a mighty wallop to right centre by Boley and another Mack rally had been effectually blocked.

In the sixth Root effaced the leaders of the Mack batting order in less time than it takes to tell it. The Cub machine was now moving along magnificently and in all its glistening splendor. Twenty minutes later it lay strewn all over the field, a jangled mass of junk.

Whether McCarthy will be able to patch the broken pieces together is a matter that all Philadelphia is convinced cannot be done. To win the series the Cubs must take three in a row. One more game, the fifth, will be played here on Monday, there being no game tomorrow, and if the Cubs do manage to win that one the series will have to move back to Chicago for completion. But Philadelphia is confident Chicago will not see its Cubs in action again this year.

Official Box Score of the Fourth World's Series Game

CHICAGO CUBS.

	AB.	R.	H.	TB.	2B.	3B.	HR.	BB.	SO.	SH.	SB.	PO.	A.	E.
McMillan, 3b	4	0	0	0	0	0	0	1	2	0	0	1	3	0
English, ss	4	0	0	0	0	0	0	1	1	0	0	2	1	0
Hornsby, 2b	5	2	2	4	0	1	0	0	1	0	0	1	1	0
Wilson, c	3	1	2	2	0	0	0	1	0	0	0	3	0	1
Cuyler, rf	4	2	3	3	0	0	0	0	1	0	0	0	0	1
Stephenson, lf	4	1	1	1	0	0	0	0	0	0	0	2	1	0
Grimm, 1b	4	2	2	5	0	0	1	0	0	0	0	7	0	0
Taylor, c	3	0	0	0	0	0	0	0	1	1	0	8	1	0
Root, p	3	0	0	0	0	0	0	0	1	0	0	0	0	0
Nehf, p	0	0	0	0	0	0	0	0	0	0	0	0	0	0
Blake, p	0	0	0	0	0	0	0	0	0	0	0	0	0	0
Malone, p	0	0	0	0	0	0	0	0	0	0	0	0	0	0
aHartnett	1	0	0	0	0	0	0	0	1	0	0	0	0	0
Carlson, p	0	0	0	0	0	0	0	0	0	0	0	0	1	0
Total	35	8	10	15	0	1	1	3	8	1	0	24	8	2

PHILADELPHIA ATHLETICS.

	AB.	R.	H.	TB.	2B.	3B.	HR.	BB.	SO.	SH.	SB.	PO.	A.	E.
Bishop, 2b	5	1	2	2	0	0	0	0	0	0	0	2	3	0
Haas, cf	4	1	1	4	0	0	1	0	0	1	0	2	0	0
Cochrane, c	4	1	2	3	1	0	0	1	0	0	0	9	0	0
Simmons, lf	5	2	2	5	0	0	1	0	2	0	0	0	0	0
Foxx, 1b	4	2	2	2	0	0	0	0	0	0	0	10	0	0
Miller, rf	3	1	2	2	0	0	0	0	0	0	0	3	0	1
Dykes, 3b	4	1	3	4	1	0	0	0	0	0	0	0	2	0
Boley, ss	3	1	1	1	0	0	0	0	1	1	0	1	5	0
Quinn, p	2	0	0	0	0	0	0	0	2	0	0	0	0	0
Walberg, p	0	0	0	0	0	0	0	0	0	0	0	0	0	1
Rommel, p	0	0	0	0	0	0	0	0	0	0	0	0	0	0
bBurns	2	0	0	0	0	0	0	0	1	0	0	0	0	0
Grove, p	0	0	0	0	0	0	0	0	0	0	0	0	0	0
Total	36	10	15	23	2	0	2	1	6	2	0	27	10	2

a Batted for Malone in the eighth.

b Batted for Rommel in the seventh.

SCORE BY INNINGS.

Chicago	0	0	0	2	0	5	1	0	0	—8
Philadelphia	0	0	0	0	0	0	10	0	x	—10

Runs batted in—Cuyler 2, Stephenson 1, Grimm 2, Taylor 1, Bishop 1, Haas 3, Simmons 1, Foxx 1, Dykes 3, Boley 1.

Left on bases—Chicago 4, Philadelphia 6. Bases on balls—Off Quinn 2, Rommel 1, Nehf 1. Struck out—By Quinn 2, Walberg 2, Grove 4, Root 3, Malone 2, Carlson 1. Earned runs—Off Quinn 5, Rommel 1, Root 6, Nehf 2, Blake 2. Hits—Off Quinn, 7 in 5 innings (none out in sixth); Walberg, 1 in 1; Rommel, 2 in 1; Grove, 0 in 2; Root, 9 in 6 1-3; Nehf, 1 in 0 (pitched to two batters); Blake, 2 in 0 (pitched to two batters); Malone, 1 in 2-3; Carlson, 2 in 1. Double plays—Dykes, Bishop and Foxx. Hit by pitcher—By Malone (Miller). Winning pitcher—Rommel. Losing pitcher—Blake. Umpires—Van Graflan (A. L.) at plate, Klem (N. L.) at first base. Dinneen (A. L.) at second base, Moran (N. L.) at third base. Time of game—2:12.

Terry Topped National League In Batting With Average of .401

New York Star Tied Record for Most Hits With 254, Official Figures Show—Hack Wilson's 56 Homers New Mark—Giants' .319 Average Set Modern Record.

Bill Terry, crack first baseman of the New York Giants, captured the National League batting championship for the 1930 season with a mark of .401, according to the official averages released today.

Terry also made the most safe hits, 254, tying the National League record, made by Lefty O'Doul, new Brooklyn outfielder, while playing with Philadelphia in 1929. Terry also collected the most one-base hits, 177.

The runner-up to Terry for the hitting crown was Babe Herman, slugging outfielder of the Brooklyn Robins, who finished with an average of .393. Chuck Klein, young Philadelphia outfielder, was third on the list with .386.

Terry's achievement brought the batting championship to the local club for the first time since 1915, when Larry Doyle finished first in the National League with the comparatively low mark of .320.

Klein was credited with 158 runs, the highest number, and drove out the most two-base hits, 59, creating new records in both these departments, and also gained the most bases on his hits with a total of 445.

The former record for runs scored was 156, made by Rogers Hornsby while playing with Chicago in 1929. Edward J. Delehanty, Philadelphia outfielder, set the former two-base-hit record of 56 way back in 1899.

Adam Comorosky of Pittsburgh pounded out the most triples, 23, while Hack Wilson, in clouting 56 home runs, set a league record. Klein set the previous record with 43 in 1929. Kiki Cuyler of Chicago led in stolen bases for the third season in a row, totaling 37.

A total of seventy-one players batted .300 or better, and six men took part in every game played by their respective clubs, including Klein and Tommy Thevenow, Philadelphia; Cuyler and Woody English, Chicago; Terry, New York, and Taylor Douthit, St. Louis.

Club batting honors were captured by the Giants with the mark of .319, a new modern record. The former mark, .309, was made by Pittsburgh in 1928 and tied by Philadelphia in 1929.

December 26, 1930

WILSON, CUBS' STAR, LED THE SLUGGERS

His Average of .723 Was Best in the National League, Official Figures Show.

DROVE IN THE MOST RUNS

Total of 190 Created New Record— Klein of Phillies Hit for Most Total Bases, 445.

Hack Wilson, powerful hitter of the Chicago Cubs, was the National League's leading slugger for the season of 1930, the official averages announced yesterday show. His percentage of .723 was the best compiled during the year. In addition, he had the largest total of runs batted in, 190, establishing a new record. He broke his own mark of 159, made in 1929.

Wilson drew the most bases on balls, 105, and also struck out more often than any other player. He was called out on strikes 84 times.

Chuck Klein of the Phillies not only gained the most total bases on his hits, 445, but also shattered Wilson's old record of runs batted in, the young outfielder driving 170 tallies across the plate.

The Cubs had the best club slugging percentage, .481, the most bases on balls, 588, the most strike-outs, 635, and the most hit batsmen, 37. The St. Louis Cardinals set a new record in runs batted in, driving across 942, which surpassed the mark of 933 made by the Cubs in 1929.

December 30, 1930

GROVE IS BEATEN AFTER 16 IN A ROW

Coffman of Browns Victor in Duel, 1-0—Athletics Suffer First Shut-Out of Year.

LOSERS HELD TO 3 HITS

Hoyt Pitches Brilliantly in Nightcap to Blank St. Louis, 10-0, With Four Safeties.

ST. LOUIS, Aug. 23 (AP).—Robert Moses Grove will have to be content with being a joint holder of the American League record for consecutive pitching victories for the present at least, instead of owning the record outright.

Already a joint holder of the record of sixteen straight games, established in 1912 by Smoky Joe Wood of the Boston Red Sox and equaled the same year by Walter Johnson of the Washington Senators, Grove attempted to better it today at the expense of the St. Louis Browns, but ran up against a three-hit pitching performance by Dick Coffman, who shut out the Athletics, 1 to 0, in the first game of a double-header. The Athletics won the nightcap, 10 to 0, behind Waite Hoyt's airtight hurling.

Grove, as usual, was good today, but Coffman was a little better. The Browns touched the southpaw fireball artist for seven hits, compared to the three allowed by Coffman. Grove fanned six, two more than Coffman. The only base on balls was issued by Coffman. Grove made a wild pitch.

The Browns put over the only run in the third inning on a single by Schulte and a double, which Moore misjudged, by Melillo after two were out.

Grove's record for the season now is twenty-five triumphs, against only three defeats.

Hoyt limited the Browns to four hits in the second game, while the Athletics were pounding Stewart, Stiles and Kimsey for seventeen. Coffman, in blanking the Mackmen, became the first American League pitcher of the year to accomplish the feat.

The box scores:

FIRST GAME.

PHILADELPHIA (A).	ab.	r.	h.	po.	a.	e.	ST. LOUIS (A).	ab.	r.	h.	po.	a.	e.
Bishop, 2b.	4	0	0	3	1	0	Schulte, cf.	4	1	3	2	0	0
Cramer, cf.	4	0	0	2	0	0	Melillo, 2b.	4	0	2	1	4	0
Cochrane, c.	4	0	1	8	0	0	Goslin, lf.	4	0	0	2	0	0
Moore, lf.	3	0	1	0	0	0	Kress, 3b.	3	0	0	2	2	0
Foxx, 1b.	4	0	1	6	1	0	Bettencourt, rf.	3	0	1	1	0	0
Miller, rf.	2	0	0	2	0	0	Burns, 1b.	3	0	0	11	3	0
McNair, 3b.	3	0	0	0	2	0	Bengough, c.	3	0	1	4	0	0
Williams, ss.	3	0	0	1	2	0	Levey, ss.	3	0	0	1	2	0
Grove, p.	3	0	1	1	0	0	Coffman, p.	2	0	0	3	2	0
Total	30	0	3	24	5	0	Total	30	1	7	27	13	0

Philadelphia .... 0 0 0 0 0 0 0 0 0—0
St. Louis .... 0 0 1 0 0 0 0 0 .—1

Run batted in—Melillo. Sacrifices—Moore, Coffman. Left on bases—Philadelphia 5, St. Louis 5. Base on balls—Off Coffman 1. Struck out—By Grove 6, Coffman 4. Wild pitch—Grove. Umpires—Van Graflan, Guthrie and Dinneen. Time of game—1.25.

SECOND GAME.

PHILADELPHIA (A).	ab.	r.	h.	po.	a.	e.	ST. LOUIS (A).	ab.	r.	h.	po.	a.	e.
Bishop, 2b.	4	1	1	4	4	0	Schulte, cf.	3	0	1	5	0	0
Cramer, cf.	5	1	3	5	0	0	Melillo, 2b.	4	0	0	1	1	0
Heving, c.	1	1	1	2	0	0	Goslin, lf.	3	0	1	3	0	0
Moore, lf.	5	0	0	3	0	0	Kress, 3b.	4	0	1	2	0	0
Foxx, 1b.	5	1	1	12	0	0	Bettencourt, rf.	4	0	0	2	0	0
Miller, rf.	5	2	3	1	0	0	Burns, 1b.	3	0	0	3	0	0
Dykes, 3b.	4	1	3	0	2	0	Ferrell, c.	3	0	0	1	3	0
Williams, ss.	5	2	2	1	3	0	Levey, ss.	3	0	0	1	1	0
Hoyt, p.	5	1	3	0	2	0	Stewart, p.	2	0	1	0	0	0
							Stiles, p.	1	0	0	0	0	0
Total	44	10	17	27	10	0	Kimsey, p.	1	0	0	0	0	0
							aGrimes	1	0	0	0	0	0
							Total	30	0	4	27	4	0

aBatted for Stiles in eighth.

Philadelphia .... 0 0 0 0 2 1 4 0 3—10
St. Louis .... 0 0 0 0 0 0 0 0 0—0

Runs batted in—Hoyt 3, Cramer, Dykes 4, Heving 2, Miller. Two-base hits—Schulte, Hoyt, Goslin, Williams, Miller 2, Heving. Double play—Williams, Bishop and Foxx. Left on bases—Philadelphia 9, St. Louis 5. Bases on balls—Off Hoyt 2, Stewart 3. Struck out—By Hoyt 2, Stewart 5, Stiles 3, Kimsey 2. Hits—Off Stewart 9 in 6 innings (none out in seventh), Stiles 3 in 2, Kimsey 5 in 1. Losing pitcher—Stewart. Umpires—Guthrie, Dinneen and Van Graflan. Time of game—2.00.

August 24, 1931

Gehrig Ties All-Time Record With Four Straight Home Runs

EQUALS TWO MARKS IN 20 TO 13 VICTORY

Lou Ties Record of Four Circuit Drives in One Game as the Athletics Are Beaten.

DUPLICATES LOWE'S FEAT

He Connects in First Four Times at Bat and Nearly Makes Fifth in Ninth.

RUTH PRODUCES HIS 15TH

By WILLIAM E. BRANDT.
Special to THE NEW YORK TIMES.

PHILADELPHIA, June 3.—Henry Louis Gehrig's name today took rank in baseball's archives along with Bobby Lowe and Ed Delehanty, the only other sluggers who, in more than half a century of recorded diamond battles, ever hit four home runs in one major league game.

Largely because of Gehrig's quartet of tremendous smashes the Yankees outstripped the Athletics in a run-making marathon, winning, 20 to 13, after twice losing the lead because of determined rallies by the American League champions.

Homers by Combs, Lazzeri and Ruth, the latter the Babe's fifteenth of the season, enabled the Yankees to tie the all-time record of seven homers by one club in one game, performed three times before 1900, by Detroit, New York and Pittsburgh, of the old National League and once in modern times, by the Athletics on June 3, 1921.

Yankees Set Team Mark.

The Yanks, with their twenty-three hits, also set a new modern club-batting record for total bases, with fifty, which eclipsed the previous modern major league mark of forty-six and the American League's best total of forty-four. This achievement

fell short by only five bases of the all-time record, set by Cincinnati in 1923. Both clubs' total of seventy-seven bases also set an American League mark.

Gehrig in his first four times at bat hammered the ball outside the playing area. In the first and fifth innings he sailed balls into the stands in left centre. In the fourth and seventh he fired over the right-field wall.

Saltzgaver was on base when Lou connected in the first inning, but the other three came with the bases empty. His fifth-inning homer, which made him the first man in baseball history ever to hit three homers in one game for the fourth time, came after Combs and Ruth had reached Earnshaw for drives over the right-field wall.

Lazzeri Clears Bases.

Lazzeri's drive into the left-field stands in the ninth, the last Yankee homer, came with the bases filled In Philadelphia's half of the ninth Jimmy Foxx, the major league leader, sent his nineteenth homer of the year shooting into the left-field stands.

Cochrane had driven the ball over the right-field wall in the first inning, but the collective homer total, nine, fell one short of the major league record for both teams in a game.

The outcome of the game evened the series, two to two, but the crowd of 5,000 seemed to concentrate on encouraging Gehrig to hit a fifth homer and thus surpass a brilliant record in

baseball's books.

Lou had two chances. He grounded out in the eighth, but in the ninth he pointed a terrific drive which Simmons captured only a few steps from the furthest corner of the park. A little variance to either side of its actual line of flight would have sent the ball over the fence or into the stands.

As it was, Lou's four homers tied the all-time record of Lowe in hitting for the circuit in four successive times at bat in 1894. Only three of Delehanty's were in successive times at bat. Both Lowe and Delehanty had a single in the same game with their four homers, so that Gehrig fell one short of tying their record for total bases.

Gehrig's four made his season's total eleven, six of which have been hit against Philadelphia, four off Earnshaw and two off Mahaffey.

The defeat of the Mackmen, coupled with the Indians' double victory, dropped the Athletics to fifth place, Cleveland supplanting them in fourth.

Lazzeri's homer with the bases filled was his fifth hit of the game. He and Gehrig each drove in six runs.

The box score:

NEW YORK (A.)	ab.	r.	h.	po.	a.	e.
Combs, cf.	5	2	3	3	0	0
Saltzger, 2b.	4	1	1	3	2	0
Ruth, lf.	4	2	2	3	0	1
Hoag, lf.	0	1	0	1	0	0
Gehrig, 1b.	6	4	4	7	0	1
Chapman, rf.	5	3	2	4	0	0
Dickey, c.	4	2	2	5	0	0
Lazzeri, 2b.	6	3	5	0	1	0
Crosetti, ss.	6	1	1	3	4	2
Allen, p.	2	0	0	1	0	1
Rhodes, p.	1	0	1	0	0	0
Brown, p.	1	0	0	0	1	0
Gomez, p.	1	1	1	0	0	0
Total	46	20	23	27	9	5

PHILADELPHIA (A.)	ab.	r.	h.	po.	a.	e.
Bishop, 2b.	4	2	2	3	2	0
Cramer, cf.	5	1	1	1	0	0
aShettger	1	0	0	0	0	0
Miller, lf.	6	0	0	0	0	0
Cochrane, c.	5	1	1	3	2	0
bWilliams	1	0	0	0	0	0
Foxx, 1b.	3	3	2	6	0	0
Coleman, rf.	6	2	2	1	0	0
McNair, ss.	5	1	3	1	2	0
Dykes, 3b.	4	1	1	1	0	0
Earnshaw, p.	2	0	0	0	2	1
cFoss	1	0	1	0	0	0
Mahaffey, p.	0	0	0	0	0	0
Walberg, p.	0	0	0	0	0	0
Krause, p.	0	0	0	0	0	0
dMadjeski	1	0	0	0	0	0
Rommel, p.	0	0	0	0	1	0
Total	42	13	13	27	11	1

aBatted for Cramer in eighth.
bBatted for Cochrane in ninth.
cBatted for Earnshaw in fifth.
dBatted for Krause in eighth.

New York .... 2 1 0 2 2 2 3 6—20
Philadelphia .... 3 0 0 6 0 2 0 2 1—13

Runs batted in—Gehrig 6, Combs, Ruth, Corsetti 2, Saltzgaver, Lazzeri 6, Chapman, Dickey, Cochrane 2, Cramer 3, Coleman 2, Foxx, McNair 2. Two-base hits—Lazzeri, McNair, Ruth, Coleman. Three-base hits—Bishop, Cramer, Chapman, Lazzeri, Foxx. Home runs—Gehrig 4, Cochrane, Combs, Ruth, Lazzeri, Foxx. Stolen base—Lazzeri. Sacrifices—Bishop, Saltzgaver. Double plays—Cochrane and McNair; Bishop and Foxx; Coleman and Cochrane. Left on bases—New York 9, Philadelphia 11. Bases on balls—Off Allen 5, Rhodes 2, Brown 2, Earnshaw 2, Walberg 1, Rommel 3. Struck out—By Allen 1, Gomez 1, Earnshaw 3, Walberg 2. Hits—Off Allen 7 in 3 2-3 innings, Rhodes 1 in 1 1-3, Brown 3 in 2, Gomez 2 in 2, Earnshaw 9 in 5, Mahaffey 6 in 1 (none out in seventh), Walberg 2 in 1, Krause 4 in 1, Rommel 2 in 1. Wild pitch—Rhodes. Winning pitcher—Brown. Losing pitcher—Mahaffey. Umpires—Geisel, McGowan and Van Graflan. Time of game—2:55.

Lou Gehrig

June 4, 1932

FOXX HITS NO. 58, BUT MACKMEN BOW

Senators Win, 2-1, Despite His Perfect Day at Bat—Take Season's Series, 12-10.

WASHINGTON, Sept. 25 (P).—Jimmy Foxx blasted his fifty-eighth home run of the season in a perfect day at bat, but the Senators defeated the Athletics by 2 to 1 today in clos-

ing their 1932 rivalry.

Foxx made a homer and two singles in three times at bat.

General Alvin Crowder of the Senators took the league lead in games won, chalking up his twenty-sixth of the year and fifteenth straight. Except for Foxx, only two Athletics got as far as second and none to third off his delivery.

The victory gave the third-place Washington team a lead of two games over the Mackmen for the season, the Senators winning 12 and losing 10 to their second-place opponents.

Cain, the Philadelphia pitcher, got into trouble right off the start, but a double play, McNair to Foxx, saved him and resulted in the Senators being held to one run on four singles in the first inning.

The box score:

PHILADELPHIA (A.)	ab.	r.	h.	po.	a.	e.
Williams, 2b.	1	0	1	1	1	0
Haas, rf.	4	0	0	2	0	0
Madjeski, c.	4	0	0	6	1	0
Simmons, lf.	4	0	1	4	0	0
Foxx, 1b.	3	1	3	6	0	0
McNair, ss.	4	0	2	2	2	1
Miller, rf.	4	0	0	1	0	0
Madge, 3b.	3	0	0	2	0	0
Dykes, 3b.	3	0	0	2	1	0
Cain, p.	3	0	1	0	1	0
Total	33	1	6	24	6	1

WASHINGTON (A.)	ab.	r.	h.	po.	a.	e.
Rice, lf.	3	1	1	0	0	0
Kerr, 2b.	3	0	0	2	6	0
Reynolds, rf.	4	1	1	0	0	0
Cronin, ss.	4	0	2	4	1	1
Kuhel, 1b.	3	0	1	10	0	0
West, cf.	4	0	1	4	0	0
Bluege, 3b.	3	0	0	2	0	0
Spencer, c.	3	0	1	2	0	0
Crowder, p.	3	0	0	0	5	0
Total	29	2	7	27	12	1

Philadelphia .... 0 0 0 0 0 0 0 0 1—1
Washington .... 1 0 0 0 0 0 0 1 .—2

Runs batted in—Kuhel, Cronin, Foxx. Two-base hits—Cronin. Home run—Foxx. Sacrifice—Kerr. Double plays—McNair and Foxx; Cronin, Kerr and Kuhel; Madjeski and Williams. Left on bases—Philadelphia 6, Washington 6. Bases on balls—Off Cain 2, Crowder 1. Struck out—By Cain 4, Crowder 1. Umpires—McGowan, Van Graflan and Nallin. Time of game—1:42.

September 26, 1932

YANKEES BEAT CUBS FOR 3D IN ROW, 7-5, AS 51,000 LOOK ON

Ruth and Gehrig, Each With 2 Homers, Set Pace as New York Nears Series Title.

BABE'S FIRST TALLIES 3

His Second Brings Wild Acclaim —Hartnett and Cuyler Also Deliver Circuit Drives.

PENNOCK STARS ON MOUND

Veteran Relieves Pipgras in Ninth and Halts Chicago Rally—Governor Roosevelt in Crowd.

By JOHN DREBINGER.

CHICAGO, Oct. 1.—Four home runs, two by the master hitter of them all, Babe Ruth, and the other pair by his almost equally proficient colleague, Columbia Lou Gehrig, advanced the New York Yankees to within one game of their third World's Series sweep today.

The American League champions once again overpowered the Cubs to win their third straight game of the current classic which, for the first time, went on display in this city.

Those four blows made the final score 7 to 5. They crushed not only the National League standard-bearers, but a gathering of 51,000 which jammed Wrigley Field to the limits of its capacity and packed two wooden temporary bleachers outside the park. Included in the gathering was Governor Roosevelt of New York, the Democratic Presidential candidate.

It was by far the most turbulent and bitterly fought engagement of the series thus far. The Cubs, inspired by a show of civic enthusiasm, battled fiercely and courageously.

They even struck back with a couple of lusty homers on their own account, one by Kiki Cuyler, the other by Gabby Hartnett.

Wallop Retires Pipgras.

Hartnett's wallop came in the ninth inning and brought about the retirement of George Pipgras, the first Yankee pitcher to appear in the series who had also taken part in the clean-sweep triumphs of 1927 and 1928.

But this move merely provided a setting that added still further to the glamour of the Yankee triumph. For it brought on the scene one of the greatest world's series pitchers of all time, the talented Herbie Pennock, who started pitching in these classics

back in 1914. In that long interval he had recorded five personal triumphs without a single defeat. Consequently he did not mean to let this game slip from his fingers even though credit for the victory still would remain with Pipgras.

In short, the famous Squire of Kennett Square sharply halted the belated Cub rally, fairly smothering the desperate bid of the Chicagoans with consummate ease and skill. With a Cub lurking on the base paths poised to dart for the plate, Pennock fanned a pinch-hitter and retired the next two on soft, infield taps, one of which he fielded himself. The other was snared by Gehrig for the final put-out.

Chance to Add to Record.

Thus, with three victories tucked away against no defeats, the Yankees, now skillfully piloted by Joe McCarthy, who bossed these same Cubs only two years ago, have advanced to a point where they need only one more game to clinch the world's championship. In addition they have a chance to add still further to their remarkable world's series record. They have now competed in eleven straight series encounters without suffering a single reversal.

Both the game and all its trimmings provided a much livelier spectacle than either of the two previous encounters. In sharp contrast to the rather matter-of-fact manner in which New York had accepted the first two battles, the crowd today was as keyed up as the players, if not more so.

It was a warm day, clear and sunny, though rather windy. There was a gay, holiday spirit in the air that never forsook the gathering, for Chicago puts a great deal more fervor in its baseball than does New York. It seemed as though the fans of this mid-Western metropolis simply would not believe how severely and decisively their champions had been manhandled by the mighty Yankees in the first two games in the East.

Ruth's Drive Awes Throng.

They roared their approval of every good play made by the Cubs. They playfully tossed bright yellow lemons at Babe Ruth and booed him thoroughly as the great man carried on a pantomime act while standing at the plate.

Then they sat back, awed and spellbound, as the Babe, casting aside his buffoonery, smashed one of the longest home runs ever seen at Wrigley Field.

It was an amazing demonstration by baseball's outstanding figures, who a few weeks ago was ill and confined to his bed. It confounded the crowd, which in paid attendance numbered 49,986 and which had contributed $211,912 in receipts.

The Cubs took the field with their hopes resting upon the stout right arm of Charlie Root, but Charlie was unequal to the task. He failed to survive five rounds, retiring immediately after Ruth and Gehrig had blasted their second two homers. These came in succession in the fifth like a flash of lightning and a clap of thunder.

Both were held fairly well in restraint in the latter rounds by Pat Malone and the left-handed Jakie May. But aside from providing the crowd with a chance to give vent to

boos, the earlier damage these two had inflicted proved far sufficient to carry the day.

Ruth and Gehrig simply dominated the scene from start to finish, and they began their performance early. When the two marched to the plate during the batting rehearsal they at once thrilled the crowd by uncorking a series of tremendous drives into the temporary wooden bleachers.

Almost Clears Bleachers.

The Babe's very first practice shot almost cleared the top of the wooden structure, and he followed it with several more prodigious drives. Gehrig produced some more, and each time the ball soared into those densely packed stands the crowd gasped. The spectacle certainly could not have been very heartening to the Cubs.

And when the battle proper began, both kept right on firing. The Babe's two homers were his first of the current series, but they sent his all-time world's series record for home runs to fifteen. For Gehrig, his two gave him a total of three for the series and an all-time record of seven.

Fittingly enough, the Babe was the first to touch off the explosion and his opening smash sent the Yanks away to a three-run lead in the very first inning. In fact, the crowd had scarcely recovered its composure after a tumultuous reception it had accorded a tumultuous reception when it was forced to suffer its first annoyance.

There was a sharp wind blowing across the playing field toward the right-field bleachers that threatened to raise havoc with the players, and it did very shortly.

Jurges Makes Wild Throw.

Eager and tense, the crowd watched Root pitch to Earle Combs, the first Yankee batter. It at once roared approbation as Combs sent a drive squarely into the hands of

Box Score of Third Game of World's Series.

CHICAGO CUBS.

	ab.	r.	h.	tb.	2b.	3b.	hr.	bb.	so.	sh.	sb.	po.	a.	e.
Herman, 2b	4	1	0	0	0	0	0	1	0	0	0	1	2	1
English, 3b	4	0	0	0	0	0	0	1	0	0	0	0	3	0
Cuyler, rf	4	1	3	7	1	0	1	0	0	0	0	1	0	0
Stephenson, lf	4	0	1	1	0	0	0	0	0	0	0	1	0	0
J. Moore, cf	3	1	0	0	0	0	0	1	0	0	0	3	0	0
Grimm, 1b	4	0	1	2	1	0	0	0	0	0	0	8	0	0
Hartnett, c	4	1	1	4	0	0	1	0	0	0	0	10	1	1
Jurges, ss	4	1	3	4	1	0	0	0	0	0	0	1	3	2
Root, p	2	0	0	0	0	0	0	0	1	0	0	1	0	0
Malone, p	0	0	0	0	0	0	0	0	0	0	0	0	0	0
May, p	0	0	0	0	0	0	0	0	0	0	0	0	0	0
Tinning, p	0	0	0	0	0	0	0	0	0	0	0	0	0	0
aGudat	1	0	0	0	0	0	0	0	0	0	0	0	0	0
bKoenig	0	0	0	0	0	0	0	0	0	0	0	0	0	0
cHemsley	1	0	0	0	0	0	0	0	0	1	0	0	0	0
Total	35	5	9	18	3	0	2	3	2	0	1	27	9	4

NEW YORK YANKEES.

	ab.	r.	h.	tb.	2b.	3b.	hr.	bb.	so.	sh.	sb.	po.	a.	e.
Combs, cf	5	1	0	0	0	0	0	0	2	0	0	1	0	0
Sewell, 3b	2	1	0	0	0	0	0	2	0	0	0	2	2	0
Ruth, lf	4	2	2	8	0	0	2	1	1	0	0	2	0	0
Gehrig, 1b	5	2	2	8	0	0	2	0	0	0	0	13	1	0
Lazzeri, 2b	4	1	0	0	0	0	0	1	1	0	0	3	4	1
Dickey, c	4	0	1	1	0	0	0	1	0	0	0	2	1	0
Chapman, rf	4	0	2	3	1	0	0	1	1	0	0	0	0	0
Crosetti, ss	4	0	1	1	0	0	0	1	0	0	0	4	4	0
Pipgras, p	5	0	0	0	0	0	0	0	5	0	0	0	0	0
Pennock, p	0	0	0	0	0	0	0	0	0	0	0	0	1	0
Total	37	7	8	21	1	0	4	7	10	0	0	27	13	1

a Batted for Malone in seventh.
b Batted for Tinning in ninth.
c Batted for Koenig in ninth.

SCORE BY INNINGS.

New York .... 3 0 1 0 2 0 0 0 1—7
Chicago .... 1 0 2 1 0 0 0 0 1—5

Runs batted in—New York: Ruth 4, Gehrig 2, Chapman 1. Chicago: Cuyler 2, Grimm 1, Hartnett 1.

Left on bases—New York 11, Chicago 6. Double plays—Sewell, Lazzeri and Gehrig; Herman, Jurges and Grimm. Hits—Off Root 6 in 4 1-3 innings, Malone 1 in 2 2-3, May 1 in 1 1-3, Tinning 0 in 2-3, Pipgras 9 in 8 (none out in ninth), Pennock 0 in 1. Struck out—By Root 4, Malone 4, May 1, Tinning 1, Pipgras 1, Pennock 1. Bases on balls—Off Root 3, Malone 4, Pipgras 3. Hit by pitcher—By May (Sewell). Winning pitcher—Pipgras. Losing pitcher—Root. Umpires—Van Graflan (A. L.) at the plate; Magerkurth (N. L.) at first base; Dinneen (A. L.) at second base; Klem (N. L.) at third base. Time of game—2:11.

young Billy Jurges who was again playing shortstop for the Cubs in place of the injured Mark Koenig.

But the next moment the throng voiced its dismay as Jurges unfurled a throw that sailed high over Manager Charlie Grimm's head at first and into the Yankee dugout.

Root was plainly flustered as Combs, under the prevailing ground rule, was allowed to advance to second base. Root strove to steady himself, but he passed Joey Sewell and faced Ruth. Cheers and jeers mingled as the great Yankee batter made his first official appearance at the plate in Chicago's portion of the setting.

Root pitched cautiously, fearful of what would happen if he allowed the Babe to shoot one high in the air with that brisk breeze behind it. His first two offerings went wide of the plate. Then he put one over, and away the ball went. It was a lofty shot that soared on and on until it dropped deep in the temporary stands. Thus, the Cubs, who had planned to fight so desperately for this game, already were three runs to the bad.

Cubs Fight Courageously.

But desperately they fought, nevertheless, and in the lower half of the same inning they gave their cohorts the chance to do some wholehearted cheering by getting one of these tallies back.

The wind, which had annoyed Root so much, also seemed to trouble Pipgras. He passed Herman, whereupon the crowd set up a roar as though the series already had been won. Woody English was retired on a fly to Ruth, who was performing in left field today in order to avoid the glare of the sun.

But Kiki Cuyler, who might have been the hero of this struggle had Ruth and Gehrig been playing elsewhere, lifted a two-bagger over Ben Chapman's head in right against the wire screening in front of the bleachers, and Herman scored amid tumultuous cheering.

But two innings later Gehrig, after an uneventful first inning, stepped into the picture. Leaning heavily into Root's pitch, he sent another mighty shot soaring into the right-field bleachers. That made the score 4 to 1.

At this point, however, the Cubs staged their most gallant fight of the day. With one out in the lower half of the third, Cuyler again produced a jubilant uproar by shooting a homer into the right-field stands, and this at once inspired his comrades to redouble their efforts against Pipgras. Stephenson slashed a single to right, and though he was forced by Johnny Moore Manager Grimm lined a drive to right that Chapman did not play any too well. The ball shot past the Alabama arrow for a two-bagger and Moore scored all the way from first.

That left the Cubs only one run in arrears, and in the fourth they drew even amid the most violent vocal demonstration of the afternoon. Jurges, eager to make amends for his earlier miscue, slapped a low liner to left, and the crowd howled with glee as Ruth failed in a heroic attempt to make a shoe-string catch of the ball. Jurges gained two bases on the hit.

Ruth Doffs His Cap.

Good naturedly, the Babe doffed his cap in acknowledgment to the adverse plaudits of the fans and the play went on. Tony Lazzeri made a spectacular catch of Herman's high, twisting pop-fly back of second base. But the next moment Tony booted English's grounder and Jurges raced over the plate with the tally that tied the score at 4-all.

But it seems decidedly unhealthy for any one to taunt the great man Ruth too much and very soon the crowd was to learn its lesson. A single lemon rolled out to the plate as Ruth came up in the fifth and in no mistaken motions the Babe notified the crowd that the nature of his retaliation would be a wallop right out the confines of the park.

Root pitched two balls and two

strikes, while Ruth signaled with his fingers after each pitch to let the spectators know exactly how the situation stood. Then the mightiest blow of all fell.

It was a tremendous smash that bore straight down the centre of the field in an enormous arc, came down alongside the flagpole and disappeared behind the corner formed by the scoreboard and the end of the right-field bleachers.

It was Ruth's fifteenth home run in world's series competition and easily one of his most gorgeous. The crowd, suddenly unmindful of everything save that it had just witnessed an epic feat, hailed the Babe with a salvo of applause.

Root, badly shaken, now faced Gehrig and his feelings well can be imagined. The crowd was still too much excited over the Ruth incident to realize what was happening when Columbia Lou lifted an enormous fly high in the air. As it sailed on the wings of the lake breeze the ball just cleared the high flagpole and dropped in the temporary stand.

Grimm, the player-manager of the Cubs, called time. Consolingly he invited Root to retire to the less turbulent confines of the clubhouse and ordered Pat Malone to the mound.

Pat filled the bases with three passes but he escaped the inning without further trouble. From then on the game, like its two predecessors, passed on to its very obvious conclusion with the exception of a final flurry in the ninth.

May Takes Up Mound Duties.

Two very fine plays by Grimm and Moore rescued Malone from possible trouble in the sixth. He also went well through the seventh despite a second misplay by Jurges and a single by Crosetti, then he faded out for a pinch-hitter. Jakie May, lone lefthander of the Chicago pitching staff, came to the mound to pitch the eighth.

Jakie got by that inning exceedingly well, closing out by inducing Ruth to slap into a double play. But in the ninth Jakie found that trouble can be found at either end of the Yankee batting order.

The lake breeze had now developed into a young gale and it seemed as though the Yanks strategically had decided upon capitalizing on it to the full. Gehrig, Lazzeri and Chapman successively touched off three skyrocket infield flies that in their descent veered in all directions.

Woody English caught the first one right in the centre of the diamond after bumping into three of his comrades. But Gabby Hartnett, the ambitious Cub catcher, insisted on going after the second one and dropped it.

Then Herman muffed Dickey's and the Yankees had two aboard, one of which scored immediately on Chapman's double to left, a low drive for which the Cubs seemingly were totally unprepared. That blow removed May, and Bud Tinning, an apprentice right-hander, collected the last two outs that finally checked the Yanks.

Hartnett's Drive Stirs Crowd.

The score was now 7 to 4, and, as Pipgras had done some really fine pitching from the fifth through the eighth, the crowd appeared definitely wilted. But it seems to be a simple matter to revive a Chicago crowd, and when Hartnett, first Cub up in the ninth, walloped a homer over the left-field wall into the temporary bleachers there was again a mighty roar.

The applause doubled in volume when Jurges whistled a single into left, and Manager McCarthy decided to withdraw Pipgras, for he had still another trump card up his sleeve. It was Herbie Pennock, and the veteran southpaw's finishing strokes to the combat produced another masterpiece.

Hemsley, batting for Tinning, struck out on three tantalizing slow balls. Herman topped one into the dirt in front of the plate which Pennock himself fielded, and Gehrig smothered English's grounder. That also smothered the Cubs.

Johnny Allen is scheduled to pitch tomorrow for the Yankees. His opponent will be Guy Bush. The weather forecast is fair and warmer.

October 2, 1932

ALL-STAR TEAMS TO PLAY.

Pick of Leagues to Meet in World's Fair Feature.

CHICAGO, May 18 (P).—The baseball fans' dream—a game between the pick of American and National League talent—will be sponsored July 6 by The Chicago Tribune as a World's Fair feature. It became possible through the cooperation of the sixteen club owners.

The fans of the country will select the teams by vote to help settle arguments over the relative merits of the players in the two leagues for the first time in the history of the game.

The newspaper will underwrite the expense of staging the game. The profits will be turned over to the Association of Professional Baseball Players of America, baseball's charity organization.

May 19, 1933

GIANTS WIN TWICE, 1ST IN 18 INNINGS

Beat Cards in Both Contests by 1-0 to Extend League Lead to 5½ Games.

HUBBELL IRON-MAN HERO

By JOHN DREBINGER.

Pitching of a superman variety that dazzled a crowd of 50,000 and

bewildered the Cardinals gave the Giants two throbbing victories at the Polo Grounds yesterday over a stretch of six hours.

Carl Hubbell, master lefthander of Bill Terry's amazing hurling corps, blazed the trail by firing away for eighteen scoreless innings to win the opening game from the Cards, 1 to 0. A single by Hughie Critz broke up this four-hour struggle in the last half of the eighteenth.

Then the broad-shouldered Roy Parmelee strode to the mound and through semi-darkness and finally a drizzling rain, blanked the St. Louisans in a nine-inning nightcap, 1 to 0. A homer in the fourth inning by Johnny Vergez decided this battle.

The two triumphs gave the Giants the series with the Cards, three out of five, and enabled them to conclude their home stand against the West with a record of eleven victories against five defeats. It also lengthened their margin over the second-place Cardinals to five and a half games.

The opener was a titanic pitching duel in which Hubbell gave one of the most astounding exhibitions of endurance and mound skill seen in many years as he survived the combined efforts of the elongated Tex Carleton and the veteran Jess Haines.

Carleton, who stepped the first sixteen innings for the Cards, gave no mean performance himself. As he had beaten the Giants in the opening game of the series on Thursday, it was not his turn to pitch. Yet he requested that he start, despite only two days of rest, and for sixteen rounds kept the straining Terrymen away from the plate.

But it was Hubbell who commanded the centre of the stage.

The tall, somber left-hander rose to his greatest heights, surpassing even his brilliant no-hit classic of 1928. He pitched perfect ball in twelve of the eighteen innings yesterday, with not a man reaching first base.

Fans Twelve of Cards.

He allowed six hits, never more than one to an inning. Two of the blows were doubles, the others were infield singles. He fanned twelve and gave no bases on balls. As The Giants played errorless ball behind him, only the hitters reached first base.

Five of the hitters advanced as far as second and only one reached third. It was an exhibition that held the packed arena spellbound throughout the four hours.

Carleton, allowing eight hits in his sixteen innings, was only slightly less brilliant. He issued seven

"Columbia" Lou Gehrig, the slugging mate of Babe Ruth, is shown here in action in 1938.

New York Giant's pitcher Carl Hubbell struck out Ruth, Gehrig, Foxx, Simmons, Cronin and Gomez consecutively in the 1933 All-Star game.

passes, four of them intentional, but really was only crowded twice.

The first Giant threat did not appear until the eleventh, when O'Doul walked and took second on Terry's sacrifice. Ott was passed intentionally, but Vergez also drew four wide ones and the bases were filled with only one out.

Threat Fails to Materialize.

Carleton, however, refused to break ground any further. Moore hit into a forced play at the plate and Mancuso ended the threat by also grounding out.

With two out in the fifteenth, Terry drove a tremendous triple to left centre. But Carleton again purposely passed Ott and retired Verges on a foul.

With Carleton retiring for a pinch-hitter in the seventeenth, the 39-year-old Haines took up the pitching in the lower half for the Cards and safely skirted by that round, though the Giants got two on base.

But in the eighteenth the veteran ran into difficulty. Moore walked, Mancuso sacrificed, and Jackson, batting for Ryan, was purposely passed. Hubbell forced Jackson, but Moore landed on third and a moment later was over the plate when Critz rifled a single to right centre.

Dean Hurls After Day's Rest.

So desperate was Manager Street after this reversal that he called on his other star right-hander, Dizzy Dean, to start the second game, despite the fact that the Dizzy one had blanked the Giants on Friday and therefore had only a single day's rest.

He drew Parmelee for his opponent and in the gloaming the two embarked on another scoreless battle which was interrupted in the fourth when Verges shot his homer into the upper left tier.

That margin Parmelee preserved right through to the end, which was reached in almost total darkness, with Parmelee allowing only four hits and striking out thirteen, tying the season's record.

The box scores:

FIRST GAME.

ST. LOUIS (N.)

	ab.	r.	h.	po.	a.	e.
Martin, 3b	7	0	0	3	6	0
Frisch, 2b	7	0	0	7	5	0
Orsatti, cf	7	0	1	0	0	0
Collins, 1b	7	0	2	15	5	0
Medwick, lf	7	0	1	7	0	0
Allen, rf	6	0	0	4	0	0
Wilson, c	6	0	2	11	1	0
Durocher, ss	3	0	0	3	4	1
aHornsby	1	0	0	0	0	0
Slade, ss	1	0	0	1	2	0
Carleton, p	4	0	0	2	3	0
bO'Farrell	1	0	0	0	0	0
Haines, p	0	0	0	0	2	0
Total	57	0	6	*33	28	1

NEW YORK (N.)

	ab.	r.	h.	po.	a.	e.
Critz, 2b	9	0	3	4	12	0
O'Doul, lf	4	0	1	0	0	0
cJames	0	0	0	0	0	0
Davis, cf	2	0	0	2	0	0
Terry, 1b	6	0	2	26	1	0
Ott, rf	6	0	0	2	0	0
Vergez, 3b	5	0	0	3	1	0
Moore, cf.lf	7	1	0	3	0	0
Mancuso, c	7	0	1	13	1	0
Ryan, ss	6	0	2	0	5	0
dJackson	0	0	0	0	0	0
Hubbell, p	7	0	1	1	7	0
Total	59	1	10	54	27	0

*Two out when winning run scored.
aBatted for Durocher in eleventh.
bBatted for Carleton in seventeenth.
cRan for O'Doul in eleventh.
dBatted for Ryan in eighteenth.

St. Louis	000	000	000	000	000	000	—0
New York	000	000	000	000	000	001	—1

Run batted in—Critz.

Two-base hits—Orsatti, Collins. Three-base hit—Terry. Sacrifices—Carleton, Hubbell, Terry, Davis, Mancuso, Slade. Double play—Ryan, Critz and Terry. Left on bases—New York 19, St. Louis 5. Bases on balls—Off Carleton 7, Haines 3. Struck out—By Hubbell 12, Carleton 7, Haines 1. Hits—Off Carleton 8 in 16 innings, Haines 2 in 1 2-3. Losing pitcher—Haines. Umpires—Klem, Pfirman and Barr. Time of game—4:03.

SECOND GAME.

ST. LOUIS (N).

	ab.	r.	h.	po.	a.	e.
Martin, 3b	4	0	0	0	1	0
Frisch, 2b	4	0	1	4	3	0
Orsatti, cf	4	0	1	4	0	0
Collins, 1b	3	0	0	7	0	0
Medwick, lf	3	0	0	1	0	0
Watkins, rf	3	0	0	1	0	0
O'Farrell, c	2	0	0	5	0	0
aCrawford	1	0	1	0	0	0
Wilson, c	0	0	0	1	0	0
Durocher, ss	2	0	0	0	2	0
bCrabtree	1	0	0	0	0	0
Slade, ss	0	0	0	1	0	0
Dean, p	2	0	0	0	2	0
cHornsby	1	0	1	0	0	0
dAllen	0	0	0	0	0	0
Total	30	0	4	24	8	0

NEW YORK (N).

	ab.	r.	h.	po.	a.	e.
Critz, 2b	4	0	1	2	2	0
O'Doul, lf	3	0	0	0	0	0
Terry, 1b	4	0	0	4	0	0
Ott, rf	4	0	1	1	0	0
Vergez, 3b	3	1	1	1	2	1
Moore, cf	3	0	0	0	0	0
Mancuso, c	3	0	1	15	2	0
Ryan, ss	0	0	0	1	0	0
Jackson, ss	2	0	1	3	0	0
Parmelee, p	3	0	0	0	0	0
Total	29	1	5	27	6	1

aBatted for O'Farrell in eighth.
bBatted for Durocher in eighth.
cBatted for Dean in ninth.
dRan for Hornsby in ninth.

St. Louis	000	000	000	—0
New York	000	100	00.	—1

Run batted in—Vergez.

Two-base hit—Mancuso. Home run—Verges. Left on bases—New York 6, St. Louis 3. Bases on balls—Off Dean 2. Struck out—By Parmelee 13, Dean 6. Umpires—Pfirman, Barr and Klem. Time of game—1:25.

July 3, 1933

AMERICAN LEAGUE BEATS RIVALS, 4-2

49,000 See Ruth's Homer Yield Two Runs as Nationals Are Toppled.

LONG HIT COMES IN THIRD

Frisch Also Gets Circuit Smash —Gomez, Crowder, Grove Baffle Losers.

By JOHN DREBINGER.
Special to THE NEW YORK TIMES.

CHICAGO, July 6.—The National League is still trying to catch up with Babe Ruth, but apparently with no more success than in recent world's series conflicts.

Today, in the presence of a capacity throng of 49,000 in Comiskey Park, the great man of baseball fittingly whaled a home run into the right-field pavilion that gave the American League's all-star cast the necessary margin to bring down the pick of the National League in the "game of the century."

That smash, propelled off Willie Hallahan, star left-handed pitcher of the Cardinals, and with a runner on base, gave the team piloted by the venerable Connie Mack the victory by a score of 4 to 2. There was nothing the equally sagacious John J. McGraw could do about it.

McGraw, coming out of retirement for this singular event, the first of its kind in the history of the two major leagues, threw practically all his available manpower into the fray.

Stage Mild Uprising.

But there seemed to be no way whatever of effacing the effect of that Ruthian wallop, even though the National Leaguers later staged a mild uprising of their own with Frankie Frisch, the erstwhile Fordham flash, banging a homer into the stands.

Mack and McGraw, matching wits for the first time since their last world series clash in 1913, each sent three hurlers to the mound, but to Mack went the honors because the greater power was to be found in the mighty bludgeons of the American Leaguers.

Mack's selections were Vernon Gomez, ace left-hander of the Yankees; Alvin Crowder, star right-hander of the Senators, and finally his own master southpaw, Lefty Bob Grove. Each went three innings, and only off Crowder were the National League forces able to make any headway. They scored both their tallies off the Washington flinger.

Hallahan, Lon Warneke, brilliant right-hander of the Cubs, and Carl Hubbell, foremost left-hander of the National League, did the pitching for McGraw. Though the battle plan had been that this trio, too, should work three rounds apiece, the plan bogged down when Hallahan sagged in the third.

It was in this round that Ruth belted his homer. Before the round had ended the tall Warneke had to be rushed to Hallahan's assistance. It seems that when the Babe smacks one, the whole park rocks and few survive.

Hallahan Not Effective.

Hallahan, who unfortunately had pitched a full nine-inning game for the Cardinals only the day before yesterday, was obviously not quite himself as he squared off with Gomez. The latter, incidentally, also had had only a single day's rest after pitching a trying game against the Senators on the Fourth, but the willowy Yankee left-hander apparently is made of a little sterner stuff.

Hallahan's troubles began in the second when, with one out, he passed Dykes and Cronin. He seemed out of his difficulties when he retired Rick Ferrell and had only Gomez to face, but the gallant Castillian, known for his eccentricities, here did a very odd thing.

Admittedly one of the weakest hitters in all baseball, in this "game of the century" with the greatest clouters assembled, he struck the first damaging blow. He rifled a single to centre and

Box Score of Chicago Game

NATIONAL LEAGUE.

	AB	R	H	TB	2b	3b	hr	bb	so	sh	sb	po	a	e
Martin, St. L., 3b	4	0	0	0	0	0	0	0	1	0	0	0	3	0
Frisch, St. L., 2b	4	1	2	5	0	0	1	0	0	0	0	5	3	0
Klein, Phila., rf	4	0	1	1	0	0	0	0	0	0	0	3	0	0
P. Waner, Pitt., rf	0	0	0	0	0	0	0	0	0	0	0	0	0	0
Hafey, Cincin., lf	4	0	1	1	0	0	0	0	0	0	0	0	0	0
Terry, N. Y., 1b	4	0	2	2	0	0	0	0	0	0	0	7	2	0
Berger, Boston, cf	4	0	0	0	0	0	0	0	0	0	0	4	0	0
Bartell, Phila., ss	2	0	0	0	0	0	0	0	1	0	0	0	3	0
a Traynor, Pitt	1	0	1	2	1	0	0	0	0	0	0	0	0	0
Hubbell, N. Y., p	0	0	0	0	0	0	0	0	0	0	0	0	0	0
b Cuccinello, Bklyn	1	0	0	0	0	0	0	0	1	0	0	0	0	0
J. Wilson St. L., c	1	0	0	0	0	0	0	0	0	0	0	2	0	0
c O'Doul, N. Y	1	0	0	0	0	0	0	0	0	0	0	0	0	0
Hartnett, Chi., c	1	0	0	0	0	0	0	0	1	0	0	2	0	0
Hallahan, St. L., p	1	0	0	0	0	0	0	0	0	0	0	1	0	0
Warneke, Chi., p	1	1	1	3	0	1	0	0	0	0	0	0	0	0
English, Chi., ss	1	0	0	0	0	0	0	0	0	0	0	0	0	0
Total	34	2	8	14	1	1	1	0	4	0	0	24	11	0

AMERICAN LEAGUE.

	AB	R	H	TB	2b	3b	hr	bb	so	sh	sb	po	a	e
Chapman, N. Y., lf., rf.	5	0	1	1	0	0	0	0	1	0	0	1	0	0
Gehringer, Detr., 2b	3	1	0	0	0	0	0	2	0	0	1	1	3	0
Ruth, N. Y., rf	4	1	2	5	0	0	1	0	2	0	0	1	0	0
West, St. L., cf	0	0	0	0	0	0	0	0	0	0	0	0	0	0
Gehrig, N. Y., lb	2	0	0	0	0	0	0	2	1	0	0	12	0	1
Simmons, Chi., cf., lf.	4	0	1	1	0	0	0	0	0	0	0	4	0	0
Dykes, Chi., 3b	3	1	2	2	0	0	0	1	0	0	0	2	4	0
Cronin, Wash., ss	3	1	1	1	0	0	0	1	0	0	0	2	4	0
R. Ferrell, Boston, c	3	0	0	0	0	0	0	0	0	1	0	4	0	0
Gomez, N. Y., p	1	0	1	1	0	0	0	0	0	0	0	0	0	0
Crowder, Wash., p	1	0	0	0	0	0	0	0	0	0	0	0	0	0
d Averill, Cleve	1	0	1	1	0	0	0	0	0	0	0	0	0	0
Grove, Phila., p	1	0	0	0	0	0	0	0	0	0	0	0	0	0
Total	31	4	9	12	0	0	1	6	4	1	1	27	11	1

a Batted for Bartell in seventh. b Batted for Hubbell in ninth. c Batted for Wilson in sixth. d Batted for Crowder in sixth.

SCORE BY INNINGS.

National League	0	0	0	0	0	2	0	0	0—2
American League	0	1	2	0	0	1	0	0	..—4

Runs batted in—American League: Ruth 2, Gomez, Averill. National League: Martin, Frisch.

Left on bases—American League 10, National League 5. Double plays—Bartell, Frisch and Terry; Dykes and Gehrig. Hits—Off Hallahan 2 in 2 (none out in third), Warneke 6 in 4, Hubbell 1 in 2, Gomez 2 in 3, Crowder 3 in 3, Grove 3 in 3. Struck out—By Hallahan 1, Warneke 2, Hubbell 1, Gomez 1, Grove 3. Bases on balls—Off Hallahan 5, Hubbell 1. Winning pitcher, Gomez; losing pitcher, Hallahan. Umpires—Dinneen (A. L.) at the plate, Klem (N. L.) at first, McGowan (A. L.) at second, Rigler (N. L.) at third, for the first four and one-half innings; Klem (N. L.) at the plate, McGowan (A. L.) at first, Rigler (N. L.) at second, Dinneen (A. L.) at third, for remainder of game. Time of game—2:05.

Dykes tallied.

In the third, Hallahan's misfortunes engulfed him in less than a jiffy. He passed Gehringer and tried to whip one past Ruth. But the Babe drove it on a low line, just inside the right field foul pole and into the lower pavilion. The crowd, sweltering in the heat of a broiling sun, roared in acclamation.

Warneke Goes to Rescue.

Hallahan then pitched four more wide ones to Lou Gehrig, who also was waving his bat menacingly, and the tall, angular Warneke came rushing on the scene. He checked the American Leaguers for a time, but in the sixth dropped a run himself when Cronin singled, Ferrell sacrificed and Earl Averill, batting for Crowder, also singled.

Only for a brief moment did Gomez appear in trouble. That was at the start of the second when Chick Hafey and Bill Terry opened fire with a pair of one-base wallops. But Berger slapped into a double play and Bartell struck out. Gomez then swept through the third without allowing a man to reach first.

Crowder did equally well through the fourth and fifth, but in the sixth Warneke did a surprising thing. He banged a long hit down the right field foul line which the aging Ruth did not play any too well. Before the ball was retrieved, Warneke had converted the smash into a triple.

Pepper Martin's out sent the Chicago pitcher hustling over the plate with the Heydler circuit's first run and a moment later Frisch slashed a drive into the lower right pavilion for the circuit.

Crowder Halts Attack.

Though Chuck Klein followed with a single, Crowder clamped down the lid and the high spot of the National League's attack had passed.

With the seventh, baseball's two greatest southpaws, Grove and Hubbell, took the mound. Both blanked the opposition, though the McGraw legions did threaten Grove twice. Terry opened the seventh with his second single of the day and Pie Traynor, pinch-hitting for Bartell, doubled to right centre, between Simmons and Ruth. But Grove fanned Gabby Hartnett, retired Woody English on a fly and the back of that rally was broken.

In the eighth Frisch, flashing as of yore, drove a single to right. There was a cry of keen expectancy from the National League support-ers in the crowd as Hafey sent a soaring fly heading in the direction of the right-field pavilion. But the Babe caught this one just as he was about to back into the wall, and the last National League threat faded.

Three Mack Stars Idle.

With the exception of Hal Schumacher, who was held in reserve in case Hubbell ran into difficulties, McGraw used all his available players. But the finish saw Mack with still a lot of punch up his sleeve which he never had to use. Jimmy Foxx, Tony Lazzeri and Bill Dickey did not get into the fray at all.

The official attendance was 49,200, which was not a record for Comiskey Park, but on this occasion no standing room was permitted, by order of Commissioner Landis. The receipts totaled $51,000, which will be turned over to the National Association of Professional Baseball Players, which takes care of retired ball players in need.

During the early preliminaries the great crowd could not have found itself more occupied had a nine-ringed circus been in progress.

Never before had baseball put on a show with all its greatest luminaries on the stage at the same time.

But the greatest ovation of all seemed to go to Hubbell as the Giant left-hander started tuning up his mighty arm that pitched eighteen scoreless innings last Sunday.

There was some disappointment when these two aces did not start the game, especially as the two starting hurlers, Hallahan and Gomez, both had pitched in regular league assignments on Tuesday.

Ruth, of course, was the chief magnet of the autograph seekers. But there was plenty of attention bestowed upon the other great performers such as Terry, Klein, Foxx, Simmons and Cronin.

One of the warmest receptions of the day was tendered to Lefty Grove when the crowd's attention was called to the fact that the famous Mack southpaw was warming up in the bull pen.

July 7, 1933

Dean Fans 17 and Wilson Gets 18 Putouts For Two New Records as Cards Win Twice

Times Wide World Photo.
Dizzy Dean, Cardinals.

By The Associated Press.

ST. LOUIS, July 30.—Two modern baseball records fell today before the brilliant pitching of Jerome (Dizzy) Dean and the stellar catching of Jimmy Wilson of the St. Louis Cardinals. The Cards took both ends of a double-header from the Chicago Cubs, 8 to 2 and 6 to 5.

Dean struck out seventeen men and Wilson made eighteen putouts in the first game for new modern records.

The Cardinals, by their double victory, regained third place in the National League by one point, shoving the Cubs to fourth.

While other pitchers nearly half a century ago struck out more batters in a nine-inning game, Dean set a record for modern baseball. Wilson's eighteen putouts had not been equalled in almost a similar length of time.

The previous modern record of sixteen strikeouts was held jointly by Frank Hahn, Christy Matheson, Rube Waddell and Nap Rucker. Wilson's figure of eighteen put-outs beats the modern National League record (since 1900) of seventeen set by Hank De Berry of the Dodgers on June 17, 1928. The all-time record is held by Vincent Nava of Providence, who had nineteen in a game played June 7, 1884. The American League record is sixteen, held jointly by Spencer of the Browns, Lapp of the Athletics and Ruel of the Yankees.

Hahn of the Reds made his record against Boston on May 22, 1901. It was equalled by Mathewson of the Giants, pitching against St. Louis on Oct. 3, 1904; by Waddell for the Browns against the Athletics, July 29, 1908, and by Rucker for the Dodgers against St. Louis, July 24, 1909.

The all-time record of nineteen was made in 1884 by Sweeney of Providence and tied the same year by Dailey of Chicago.

The box scores:

FIRST GAME.

CHICAGO (N).	ab.	r.	h.	po.	a.	e.		ST. LOUIS (N).	ab.	r.	h.	po.	a.	e.
Koenig, 3b.	4	1	1	1	1	0		Martin, 3b.	5	0	1	1	3	1
W.Herm'n,2b	4	0	2	4	4	1		Watkins, rf.	4	0	1	2	0	0
Cuyler, lf.	3	0	0	1	0	0		Frisch, 2b.	4	0	0	0	2	0
F.Herman,rf	4	0	0	3	0	0		Cr'wford,1b.	3	1	0	6	0	0
Demaree, cf.	4	1	1	2	0	0		Medwick, lf.	4	2	4	0	0	0
Campbell, c.	3	0	1	3	1	0		Orsatti, cf.	2	1	2	0	0	0
Hendrick,1b	4	0	0	8	0	0		Wilson, c.	3	1	1	18	0	0
Jurges, ss.	4	0	1	2	4	0		Durocher, ss	4	2	1	1	1	0
Bush, p.	2	0	0	0	3	0		Dean, p.	4	1	3	0	1	0
Grimes, p.	1	0	0	0	1	0								
aMosolf	1	0	0	0	0	0								
Total	34	2	6	24	14	2		Total	33	8	13	27	7	1

aBatted for Grimes in ninth.

Chicago ....100 100 000—2
St. Louis ....100 005 02—8

Runs batted in—W. Herman, Campbell, Frisch, Orsatti 2, Wilson, Durocher, Dean 2.

Two-base hits—Koenig, Watkins, W. Herman, Dean 2, Campbell, Orsatti, Durocher, Demaree. Stolen base—Martin. Sacrifices—Orsatti 2. Double plays—Jurges and Hendrick; Jurges, W. Herman and Hendrick. Left on bases—Chicago 7, St. Louis 5. Bases on balls—Off Bush 1, Dean 1, Grimes 1. Struck out—By Bush 2, Dean 17, Grimes 1. Hits—Off Bush 10 in 5 1-3 innings, Grimes 3 in 2 2-3. Hit by pitcher—By Dean (Campbell). Wild pitch—Grimes. Losing pitcher—Bush. Umpires—McGrew and Magerkurth. Time of game—1:47.

SECOND GAME.

CHICAGO (N).	ab.	r.	h.	po.	a.	e.		ST. LOUIS (N).	ab.	r.	h.	po.	a.	e.
English, 3b.	4	1	0	0	1	0		Martin, 3b.	3	2	2	0	0	0
W. Her'n,2b	4	0	1	3	1	0		Watkins, rf.	3	0	1	4	0	0
Cuyler, lf.	2	2	1	5	0	0		Frisch, 2b.	3	0	0	1	4	0
F. Herman rf	4	0	1	5	1	0		Crawford, 1b.	3	1	1	8	0	0
Demaree, cf.	3	2	2	0	0	0		Medwick, lf.	4	1	1	1	0	0
Hartnett, c.	4	0	1	3	0	0		Orsatti, cf.	3	1	0	5	0	1
Hendrick, 1b.	4	0	1	7	0	1		O'Farrell, c.	4	0	1	7	1	1
Jurges, ss.	3	0	1	3	3	1		Durocher, ss	4	0	1	1	2	9
Tinning, p.	2	0	0	0	1	3		Hallahan, p.	0	0	0	0	0	0
Henshaw, p.	0	0	0	0	0	0		Johnson, p.	1	0	0	0	0	0
Root, p	1	0	0	0	0	0		Haines, p.	1	0	1	0	1	0
aMosolf	1	0	0	0	0	0		Vance, p.	0	0	0	0	0	0
bCampbell	1	0	0	0	0	0		cAllen	1	0	0	0	0	0
Total	33	5	7	24	7	4		Total	30	6	8	27	7	2

aBatted for Jurges in ninth.
bBatted for Root in ninth.
cBatted for Johnson in fourth.

Chicago ....300 002 000—5
St. Louis ....381 011 00.—6

Runs batted in—Demaree 2, Hartnett, Medwick 3, Crawford, Watkins, Haines.

Two-base hits—Durocher, Watkins, Haines, Hendrick. Three-base hit—Martin. Home runs—Demaree, Medwick. Stolen bases—English, Cuyler. Sacrifices—Frisch, Cuyler. Left on bases—Chicago 5, St. Louis 5. Bases on balls—Off Tinning 3, Henshaw 1, Hallahan 2, Haines 1. Struck out—By Root 1, Hallahan 1, Johnson 1, Haines 4. Hits—Off Tinning 5 in 4 innings (none out in fifth), Henshaw 1 in 1 1-3, Johnson 2 in 3 1-3, Haines 5 in 4 (none out in ninth), Vance 0 in 1. Winning pitcher—Haines. Losing pitcher—Henshaw. Umpires—Magerkurth and McGrew. Time of game—2:05.

July 31, 1933

50,000 See American League Triumph

AMERICAN LEAGUE VICTOR AGAIN, 9-7

By JOHN DREBINGER.

Packing thrill upon thrill, the foremost professional ball players of the nation battled for two and three-quarter hours at the Polo Grounds yesterday in the 1934 edition of the ball game of the century, with the forces of the American League demonstrating for the second successive year that at this newly devised form of interleague competition they still hold the edge.

For, by uncorking a devastating six-run rally in the fifth inning, the all-stars of the American League carried the day over Memphis Bill Terry and his carefully chosen National League cast by a score of 9 to 7.

A capacity crowd of 50,000 witnessed the struggle. It was a gathering that occupied every seat in the historic arena, jammed the aisles and roared itself purple.

$52,982 to Players' Fund.

About 15,000 more roared, too, when the gates were locked fifteen minutes before game time, shutting all out who had not already purchased reserved seat tickets. The paid attendance totaled 48,363 and the receipts donated to the players' charity fund were $52,982, net.

It was a crowd, too, which at the outset seemed undecided with which side it was to align itself. The National Leaguers were the home team and they were being bossed by Bill Terry. The American circuit had Joe Cronin, boy pilot of the Senators, at the head, and this sort of gave it a renewed setting of last Fall's world's series.

On the other hand, the American Leaguers also had Babe Ruth and Lou Gehrig and no New Yorker could very well be expected to root against either of these two. Whereupon the crowd simply compromised and bellowed unreservedly for whichever side was showing to advantage for the moment.

In rather sharp contrast with the all-star game in Chicago last year, this conflict developed into a titanic struggle of hitters, during which great names in the pitching industry were rudely jostled about.

Contrast With 1933 Game.

In the 1933 conflict a homer by Babe Ruth won the struggle for the American League, 4 to 2, but while the great Bambino, appearing in only five innings yesterday, was held in more or less restraint, others did some thunderous walloping. Frankie Frisch and Joe Medwick hit homers for the National Leaguers, while Earl Averill banged three runs across with a triple and a double in two successive innings.

Of the eight pitchers to step to the mound, three for the American League and five for the National, only two survived with their prestige intact. One, as can readily be imagined, was the invincible Carl Hubbell, who gave a masterful exhibition of his left-handed talents during his assignment for the first three innings.

The other was Mel Harder, trim right-hander of the Cleveland Indians, who checked a National League rally in the fifth after the Americans had swept to the fore, and hurled scoreless baseball for the remainder of the distance.

Gomez Touched for Four Runs.

Vernon Gomez, ace left-hander of the American circuit, who opposed Hubbell for the first three rounds, fell for four runs during his tenure of office on the wings of the homers hit by the two Cardinals, Frisch and Medwick.

His right-handed Yankee colleague, the burly Charlie Ruffing, was routed summarily from the mound in the fifth, while for the National Leaguers, Lon Warneke of the Cubs and Van Lingle Mungo of the Dodgers came down with a grand crash in the fourth and fifth as the forces of the junior circuit amassed a total of eight runs.

In the minutes before the game there was a respectful silence as a memorial tablet to the late John J. McGraw was unveiled in front of the centre-field clubhouse, and a full-throated, hearty cheer went up as the popular Hubbell received a plaque from the Baseball Writers Association for his services last year as the outstanding player of the campaign.

Excitement Starts at Once.

This done, the spectators warmed quickly to the battle at hand. Nor was there much delay in providing them with plenty of provocation for exercising their vocal accomplishments. Charlie Gehringer, leading off the American League batting order, greeted Hubbell with a single to centre and when Wally Berger momentarily fumbled the ball the fleet Tiger swept down to second. Came a pass to Heinie Manush and there was some uneasiness on the National bench.

Hubbell looked around to his infield, apparently awaiting the familiar Giant huddle. However, for this occasion the lean southpaw was not flanked by Blondy Ryan or Hughie Critz. True, he had his manager, Terry, on one side of him, and behind him, at short, was Travis Jackson, his ailing eye sufficiently improved to permit him to play at the last moment. But at second base was Frisch and at third Pie Traynor of the Pirates, both aliens to him during the regular campaign.

So Hubbell merely bore down to his work with renewed vigor and at this point turned on some of the most magnificent flinging seen in years as he mowed down the best of the American League's batting strength.

Ruth was called out on strikes, the Babe looking decidedly puzzled as a screw ball just clipped the outside corner for the third one. Then Gehrig struck out with a grand flourish, and not even the fact that Gehringer and Manush executed a double steal right under Gabby Hartnett's nose as Lou fished for the third one perturbed the long, lean left-hander.

Amid a deafening uproar Hubbell completed the string by fanning Jimmy Foxx, who at the last moment had been inserted in the American League line-up as the third baseman in place of Frank Higgins.

Scarcely had the furor of this master stroke subsided than the crowd was thrown into an another uproar as Frisch, first up for the Nationals, caught one of Gomez's speed balls and lined it into the densely packed upper right tier. Unmindful of this, Gomez retired the next three, and then all eyes again focused on Hubbell.

And once again the famous southpaw held the crowd and American Leaguers spellbound alike as he continued his sweep down the batting order. He fanned the great Al Simmons and also Cronin, making it five in a row. Bill Dickey, the Yankee catcher, clipped him for a single to left, but Gomez was also swept aside on strikes to make it six strike-outs for the first two innings.

Ovation for Hubbell.

For the third, Gehringer flied to Cuyler in right, Manush grounded out, Ruth drew a pass, Gehrig flied out, and as Hubbell marched to the centre-field clubhouse, his afternoon's assignment completed, he was accorded a tremendous ovation from all sides of the packed arena.

Less fortunate was Gomez, who almost got by with nothing worse than the Frisch homer in the first when trouble overtook him with two out in the third. Frisch walked, Traynor singled and Medwick larruped the ball into the upper left tier to give the National League a 4-0 margin.

With the retirement of Hubbell, however, things suddenly took a turn for the worse for the Terry forces. The tall, angular Warneke came on, and the American Leaguers at once bristled with action.

The Cub righthander retired Foxx on a grounder to start the fourth, but Simmons doubled to left and counted on a single by Cronin. Dickey fanned, then Averill, coming into the battle as pinch hitter for Gomez, hit a tremendous triple which dropped just in front of the bleachers in right centre, and Cronin tallied.

Then came the fifth, in which the fortunes of the National Leaguers toppled like a house of cards. Warneke passed both Ruth and Gehrig, and Terry, after a brief conference with Catcher Hartnett, waved Warneke out and called on Mungo, the ace of Casey Stengel's pitching staff in Brooklyn.

There was no checking the American Leaguers now. Foxx hammered a single to centre and Ruth scored. Jackson made a marvelous stop of Simmons's sharp grounder toward left, but when his hurried toss to second went wide, Simmons received credit for a hit and Gehrig counted, tying the score.

Runs now began to pour over the plate in a torrent. There was a slight pause as Cronin fouled out, but Dickey walked, filling the bases, and Averill, who had remained in the game as the centre fielder, now doubled down the right field foul line, scoring two more.

Gehringer was intentionally passed to fill the bases, again in the hope of enticing Ruffing, now the American League pitcher, to slap into a double play. Ruffing, instead, slapped a single into left and the fifth and sixth runs hustled across the plate.

With Ruth and Gehrig the next hitters, Mungo's troubles loomed almost endless, but at this point the Dodger regained his poise, and ended the inning by retiring the Babe on a grounder and fanning Lou.

National Leaguers Rally.

That seemed to settle the issue quite definitely, but the National League still had a wealth of material on the bench and in this same inning, the fifth, Terry unloaded it. It resulted in a three-run rally that routed Ruffing and was checked just one run short of a tie.

Pepper Martin, the Cardinal thunderbolt, batted for Mungo and walked. Then followed three successive singles by Frisch, Traynor and Chuck Klein, the latter entering the game here as Medwick's successor in the National League outfield.

Two runs had come in during this outburst and Ruffing was asked to withdraw in favor of Harder. The

Box Score of the Game

AMERICAN LEAGUE.

	ab.	r.	h.	tb.	2b.	3b.	hr.	bb.	so.	sh.	sb.	po.	a.	e.
Gehringer, Det., 2b...	3	0	2	2	0	0	0	3	0	0	1	2	1	0
Manush, Wash., lf....	2	0	0	0	0	0	0	1	0	0	1	0	0	0
Ruffing, N. Y., p.....	1	0	1	1	0	0	0	0	0	0	0	0	0	0
Harder, Cleve., p.....	2	0	0	0	0	0	0	0	1	0	0	1	0	0
Ruth, N. Y., rf.......	2	1	0	0	0	0	0	2	1	0	0	0	0	0
Chapman, N. Y., rf...	2	0	1	3	0	1	0	0	0	0	0	0	1	0
Gehrig, N. Y., 1b....	4	1	0	0	0	0	0	1	3	0	0	11	1	1
Foxx, Phila., 3b......	5	1	2	3	1	0	0	0	2	0	0	1	2	0
Simmons, Chi., cf, lf..	5	3	3	5	2	0	0	0	1	0	0	3	0	0
Cronin, Wash., ss....	5	1	2	3	1	0	0	0	1	0	0	2	8	0
Dickey, N. Y., c.....	2	1	1	1	0	0	0	2	1	0	0	4	0	0
Cochrane, Det., c....	1	0	0	0	0	0	0	0	0	0	0	1	1	0
Gomez, N. Y., p......	1	0	0	0	0	0	0	0	1	0	0	0	0	0
Averill, Cleve., cf....	4	1	2	5	1	1	0	0	1	0	0	1	0	0
West, St. L., cf......	0	0	0	0	0	0	0	0	0	0	0	1	0	0
Total...............	39	9	14	23	5	2	0	9	12	0	2	27	14	1

NATIONAL LEAGUE.

	ab.	r.	h.	tb.	2b.	3b.	hr.	bb.	so.	sh.	sb.	po.	a.	e.
Frisch, St. L., 2b.....	3	3	2	5	0	0	1	1	0	0	0	0	1	0
aHerman, Chi., 2b....	2	0	1	2	1	0	0	0	0	0	0	0	1	0
Traynor, Pitt., 3b....	5	2	2	2	0	0	0	0	0	0	1	1	0	0
Medwick, St. L., lf...	2	1	1	4	0	0	1	0	1	0	0	0	0	0
Klein, Chi., lf........	3	0	1	1	0	0	0	0	0	0	0	1	0	0
Cuyler, Chi., rf......	2	0	0	0	0	0	0	0	0	0	0	2	0	0
Ott, N. Y., rf........	2	0	0	0	0	0	0	0	0	0	1	0	1	0
Berger, Bos., cf......	2	0	0	0	0	0	0	0	1	0	0	0	0	1
P. Waner, Pitt., cf...	2	0	0	0	0	0	0	0	1	0	0	1	0	0
Terry, N. Y., 1b.....	3	0	1	1	0	0	0	1	0	0	0	4	0	0
Jackson, N. Y., ss....	2	0	0	0	0	0	0	0	1	0	0	0	1	0
Vaughan, Pitt., ss....	2	0	0	0	0	0	0	0	0	0	0	4	0	0
Hartnett, Chi., c.....	2	0	0	0	0	0	0	0	0	0	0	9	0	0
Lopez, Brook., c......	2	0	0	0	0	0	0	0	1	0	0	5	1	0
Hubbell, N. Y., p.....	0	0	0	0	0	0	0	0	0	0	0	0	0	0
Warneke, Chi., p.....	0	0	0	0	0	0	0	0	0	0	0	0	0	0
Mungo, Brook., p....	0	0	0	0	0	0	0	0	0	0	0	0	0	0
bMartin, St. L.......	0	1	0	0	0	0	0	1	0	0	0	0	0	0
J. Dean, St. L., p....	1	0	0	0	0	0	0	0	0	0	0	0	0	0
Frankhouse, Bos., p..	1	0	0	0	0	0	0	0	0	0	0	0	0	0
Total...............	36	7	8	15	1	0	2	3	5	0	2	27	5	1

a Batted for Hubbell in third, but was permitted to replace Frisch in the seventh. b Batted for Mungo in the fifth.

SCORE BY INNINGS.

American League......	0	0	0	2	6	1	0	0	0—9
National League.......	1	0	3	0	3	0	0	0	0—7

Runs batted in—American League: Averill 3, Cronin 2, Ruffing 2, Foxx, Simmons. National League: Medwick 3, Frisch, Traynor, Klein.

Left on bases—American League 12, National League 5. Double play—Lopez and Vaughan. Hits—Off Gomez 3 in 3 innings, Ruffing 4 in 1 (none out in fifth), Harder 1 in 5, Hubbell 2 in 3, Warneke 3 in 1 (none out in fifth), Mungo 4 in 1, Dean 5 in 3, Frankhouse 0 in 1. Struck out—By Gomez 3, Harder 2, Hubbell 6, Warneke 1, Mungo 1, Dean 4. Bases on balls—Off Gomez 1, Ruffing 1, Harder 1, Hubbell 2, Warneke 3, Mungo 2, Dean 1, Frankhouse 1. Winning pitcher—Harder. Losing pitcher—Mungo. Umpires—Pfirman (N. L.) at the plate, Owens (A. L.) at first, Stark (N. L.) at second and Moriarty (A. L.) at third, for the first four and one-half innings; Owens (A. L.) at the plate, Stark (N. L.) at first, Moriarty (A. L.) at second and Pfirman (N. L.) at third, for remainder of game. Time of game—2:44.

shift brought an abrupt halt to the National charge. For though a third tally was carried in by Traynor on a double steal with Frisch while Paul Waner was striking out, it proved the last marker for the Terry cast.

In the remaining four innings, with Terry hurling all his available man-power into the fray, the National Leaguers obtained just one single off the elusive Cleveland right-hander. That was a double by Billy Herman, Cub second baseman, in the ninth. The sturdy Mel Ott, up twice in the closing stages of the battle, went hitless, as also did Arky Vaughan, who replaced Jackson in the fifth.

One More for the Americans.

As for the American Leaguers, they merely tightened their grip by jamming one more run across off Dizzy Dean in the sixth as this tall and eccentric Cardinal right-hander started on his three innings of labor. A high fly by Simmons in short right which Frisch dropped after a sturdy chase went for a double and a run resulted almost immediately when Cronin pulled a robust two-bagger to left.

The American Leaguers might

even have made more, only for the fact that Cronin got himself trapped off second base while Averill was striking out, thereby ending the inning.

Fred Frankhouse, star righthander of the Braves, went through a commendable ninth for the National League and did his very best to start a rally in the lower half. With no more pinch-hitters available, Terry had to permit Frankhouse to bat for himself in this inning and Fred almost started something with a bunt in front of the plate. But Mickey Cochrane, who had replaced Dickey as the

American League catcher, pounced on the ball and caught the Boston pitcher by a step at first.

As a result, the bases were still empty when Billy Herman followed with his double and neither Traynor nor Klein could improve on the situation. Whereupon the crowd filed out well satisfied that it had seen all the baseball that could possibly be crowded into a single afternoon.

July 11, 1934

RUTH HITS 700TH AS YANKS SCORE, 4-2

Reaches Goal of His Career With Mighty Homer in the Third Against Tigers.

GEHRIG, ILL, FORCED OUT

Consecutive-Game Streak May End—Dickey's Two-Bagger Decides the Contest.

By JAMES P. DAWSON.
Special to THE NEW YORK TIMES.

DETROIT, July 13.—The incomparable Babe Ruth reached his goal today with his 700th home run, a wallop that helped in sending the Yankees back into the lead in the American League pennant race.

It came in the third inning, a drive of about 480 feet high over the right-field wall. Earle Combs was on first when Ruth drove the ball out of the lot, fashioning two runs off Tom Bridges, the Detroit pitcher.

It seemed the blow would carry victory for Charley (Red) Ruffing, who was locked in an intense pitching duel with Bridges as 21,000 looked on.

In the end, however, it was a two-base drive off the bat of reliable Bill Dickey in the eighth inning which brought the triumph by a count of 4 to 2 and restored to the Yankees their slender lead over the Tigers in first place.

Wallop Sends Two Home.

Dickey's hit, one of two for the backstop, chased Ruth and Ben Chapman home with the runs that put the game on the Yankees' side of the ledger.

Tonight the Yanks are happy, and Ruth is the happiest of all. They humbled the ace right-hander of the Tigers' hurling staff with a nine-hit attack and can look forward less apprehensively now to the remaining two games in this crucial series.

Ruffing, hamered to shelter in his last two championship starts and in his all-star game effort as well, selected the right time to return to his winning ways. He gave the Tigers six scant hits.

A pass and a double, with a high fly, brought the first Tiger run in the third, and the only other score came in the eighth, when Ruffing le the Tigers cluster a single and a triple.

Gehrig's Status in Doubt.

Lou Gehrig, playing in his 1,426th consecutive championship game, was involuntarily withdrawn in the second inning, suffering from an attack of lumbago which may very well bring an end to his unique record. Whether he will play tomorrow was undetermined tonight.

With one out in the third, Combs singled Then, after Saltzgaver had fanned, Ruth, with the count three and two, blasted his fourteenth homer of the season.

That was all the Yankee scoring until the eighth, when, with one out, Ruth drew a pass and took second on Rolfe's single. Rolfe was caught off first, then Chapman walked. Dickey here slashed a double to centre.

Manager McCarthy sent Red Rolfe to short and shifted Saltzgaver to first and Crosetti to third.

The box score:

NEW YORK (A.)	ab.	r.	h.	po.	a.	e.	DETROIT (A.)	ab.	r.	h.	po.	a.	e.
Combs, cf.	5	1	1	4	0	0	Fox, rf	5	0	0	4	1	0
Saltz'r,3b,1b	4	0	0	7	1	0	White, cf	2	1	0	2	0	0
Ruth, lf	3	2	1	1	0	0	Goslin, lf	4	0	1	1	0	0
Byrd, lf	0	0	0	0	0	0	Ge'inger, 2b	4	0	1	1	1	0
Gehrig, 1b	1	0	1	1	0	0	Rogell, ss	4	1	1	2	4	0
Rolfe, ss	2	0	1	1	2	0	Gr'nberg, 1b	4	0	2	8	0	0
Chapman, rf	3	1	1	0	0	0	Cochrane, c	3	0	1	3	2	0
Dickey, c	4	0	2	5	0	0	Owen, 3b	3	0	0	1	0	0
Cro'tti,ss,3b	3	0	1	2	3	0	Bridges, p	3	0	0	0	2	0
Heffner, 2b	4	0	1	6	0	0	aWalker	1	0	0	0	0	0
Ruffing, p	4	0	0	0	0	0							
Total	33	4	9	27	6	0	Total	33	2	6	27	10	0

aBatted for Bridges in ninth.

New York .... 0 0 2 0 0 0 0 2 0—4
Detroit .... 0 0 1 0 0 0 0 1 0—2

Runs batted in—Ruth 2, Gehringer, Dickey 2, Greenberg.

Two-base hits—Greenberg, Goslin, Dickey. Three-base hit—Greenberg. Home run—Ruth. Stolen bases—White, Chapman, Cochrane. Double play—Fox and Gehringer. Left on bases—Detroit 8, New York 8. Bases on balls—Off Bridges 4, Ruffing 4. Struck out—By Bridges 8, Ruffing 3. Wild pitches—Bridges 2. Umpires—Donnelly, McGowan and Owens. Time of game—2:12.

July 14, 1934

BABE RUTH.

Times Wide World Photo.

Ruth's Record of 700 Home Runs Likely To Stand for All Time in Major Leagues

Special to THE NEW YORK TIMES.

DETROIT, July 13.—A record that promises to endure for all time was attained on Navin Field today when Babe Ruth smashed his seven-hundredth home run in a lifetime career. It promises to live, first, because few players of history have enjoyed the longevity on the diamond of the immortal Bambino, and, second, because only two other players in the history of baseball have hit more than 300 home runs.

In his twenty-first year of play, and what is expected to be his farewell season, Ruth rounded out the record he had set for himself before retiring.

He has another mark he is shooting at and which he should attain before the end of the current campaign. He wants to go out with 2,000 bases on balls to his credit, a reflection of the respect rival pitchers have for him. He is only a few short of the mark.

Lou Gehrig and Rogers Hornsby are the only players who have exceeded 300 home runs in their careers. Gehrig boasts 314 and Hornsby 301. The improbability of a parallel to the Ruth mark is appreciated with the knowledge that Gehrig will have to survive ten more years of play, and then average about forty home runs a year, to equal it.

Today a youth was happy and richer by $20. Even before he circled the bases, Ruth was shouting to mates on the field: "I want that ball! I want that ball!" Emissaries were sent scurrying after the youth who recovered the ball after it cleared the fence, and it was restored to Ruth in the Yankee dugout, in exchange for $20.

Ruth paid $20 for his five-hundredth home-run ball, hit in Cleveland, and a similar amount for the home-run ball that touched the 600 mark three years ago. This one was hit in St. Louis.

Ruth had his greatest home-run year in 1927, when he created the modern season's record of 60. He hit 59 in 1921, and 54 in both 1920 and 1928. In 1930 he smashed 49.

Following is a table of the home runs hit by Ruth in championship games and world's series contests:

CHAMPIONSHIP GAMES.

Year.	Team.	Homers.	Year.	Team.	Homers.
1914	Red Sox	0	1926	Yankees	47
1915	Red Sox	4	1927	Yankees	60
1916	Red Sox	3	1928	Yankees	54
1917	Red Sox	2	1929	Yankees	46
1918	Red Sox	11	1930	Yankees	49
1919	Red Sox	29	1931	Yankees	46
1920	Yankees	54	1932	Yankees	41
1921	Yankees	59	1933	Yankees	34
*1922	Yankees	35	1934	Yankees	14
1923	Yankees	41			
1924	Yankees	46		Total	700
†1925	Yankees	25			

*Out until May 20, suspended for barnstorming after 1921 world's series.
†Out until June with illness after collapsing during training trip.

WORLD'S SERIES GAMES.

Yr.	Against.	Homers.	Yr.	Against.	Homers.
1915	Phillies	0	1926	Cardinals	4
1916	Dodgers	0	1927	Pirates	2
1918	Cubs	0	1928	Cardinals	3
1921	Giants	1	1932	Cubs	2
1922	Giants	0			
1923	Giants	3		Total	15

July 14, 1934

PAUL DEAN, CARDS, HURLS NO-HIT GAME

Stops Dodgers, 3-0, After His Brother, Dizzy, Pitches 3-Hit Shutout, 13-0.

GIVES ONE BASE ON BALLS

Just Misses Perfect Performance—18,000 Thrilled by Baseball Drama.

By ROSCOE McGOWEN.

Those highly publicized Dean brothers lived up to every advance notice as they hurled the Cardinals to a double victory over the Dodgers at Ebbets Field yesterday. The elder brother, Dizzy, allowed three safeties, the first coming in the eighth inning, as the Cards took the opener, 13 to 0.

But good as Dizzy was, he went into eclipse behind the extraordinary feat of his youthful brother, who gave 18,000 fans the thrill that comes once in a baseball lifetime by hurling a no-hit game. The Cards made seven safe blows off Ray Benge to win, 3 to 0.

Paul's work was just one point short of perfection. He issued one pass, drawn by Len Koenecke in the first inning after two were out, but thereafter the Stengel athletes just marched to the plate and right back again with monotonous regularity.

Advance in the Race.

By taking two games while the Giants were winning one from the Braves, the Cardinals advanced to within three games of the league-leading New Yorkers.

The tension among the players on the Cardinal bench and among the fans could almost be felt as Paul went to the mound in the ninth. Thousands of fans rose to their feet and leaned forward to watch every move on the field, while two or three Cardinals in the dug-out could be seen holding their fingers crossed.

Stengel gave Paul no break as the youngster was knocking on the door of baseball's hall of fame. Casey sent Jimmy Bucher, a dangerous southpaw hitter, to bat for Al Lopez, and that youth cut viciously at the first pitch. But Paul slipped both the second and third strikes across the outside corner of the plate, and cheers cascaded from the stands.

Then Johnny McCarthy, another portside swinger, was sent in to bat for Benge. He connected hard with the ball and for a split second the fans held their breath. But the ball went high in the air and nestled into Frankie Frisch's glove for the second out.

Durocher Pounces on Ball.

Now only Ralph Boyle stood between Paul and his goal, and Buzz came closest to spoiling everything. He drove a slashing grounder toward short that sizzled into Durocher's glove on the short hop and Leo couldn't hold it. But he pounced on the ball like a cat and by a lightning throw just beat Boyle to first to end the game.

As Umpire Sears waved high to signify the put-out, thousands of fans swarmed onto the field and engulfed the young pitcher. But his brother Dizzy and several park policemen were there first and managed to clear a way for him off the field through the Brooklyn dugout.

Aside from Boyle's last-inning smash, there were only two other occasions when the Dodgers came close to hitting Paul safely. In the first inning Lonnie Frey sliced a drive toward left centre and Joe Medwick ran over fast to snare the ball.

In the seventh it was Sam Leslie who hit the ball hard, driving it close to the barrier in left centre, but again Medwick saved the day by racing over and making a gloved-hand catch.

Paul fanned six men, three of them in the last two innings, and thirteen other Dodgers were retired on balls not hit out of the infield.

A Great Day for Deans.

It was the greatest day the Dean brothers ever experienced, a day in which one all-time record was smashed and two amazing predictions by Dizzy were fulfilled.

In winning his twenty-seventh game Dizzy broke a mark established by Cy Young in 1899 as a Cardinal hurler to win the most games in a season. Cy won 26 and lost 15 that season. Dizzy has lost only seven.

When Paul won the nightcap it marked his eighteenth victory, and thus made good Dizzy's boast in the Spring that "Paul and I will win forty-five games for the Cardinals this year."

The dizziest prophecy of all which was made good was voiced in the Cardinals' hotel yesterday morning, when the elder Dean told a St.

Times Wide World Photo.

PAUL AND DIZZY DEAN.

Louis writer that "Zachary and Benge will be pitching against one-hit Dean and no-hit Dean today." Dizzy fell down only on his own assignment by allowing three hits instead of one.

Field Day at Bat.

As for the run-scoring, which was almost lost sight of in the drama of Paul's performance, the Cardinals had a field day at bat in the opener against Tom Zachary, Lefty Clark,

Owen Carroll and Walter Beck.

They amassed seventeen hits, six of them for extra bases, including Jim Collins's thirty-fourth homer of the year, made off Carroll in the fourth. They counted twice in the first and five times in the third, when Zachary was driven to cover. Three more in the fourth, two in the sixth and one in the seventh were made off Carroll. One hit and no runs were counted off Beck in the ninth.

Collins, who drove in six runs in the first encounter, batted in two of the three scored in the nightcap. The other was sent home by Pepper Martin and it was Paul Dean who carried it across.

Paul scored in the sixth for the first run of the contest, paving the way by driving a two-bagger to deep left centre for the second hit off Benge.

Medwick doubled in the seventh and scored on Collins's single, and in the ninth banged a three-bagger to the exit gate. He tallied the final run as Collins grounded sharply to Jordan.

Fine Support for Benge.

Some fine support was accorded Benge, Cuccinello making a remarkable leaping catch of Frisch's line drive in the first inning and Jordan coming up with a sparkling play on Rothrock's grounder in the fourth.

The Brooklyn management announced that Catcher Walter Millies, purchased from Dayton, will report today, as Ray Berres is out with a lame arm.

The box scores:

FIRST GAME.

ST. LOUIS (N.).	ab.	r.	h.	po.	a.	e.
Martin, 3b	4	1	1	1	1	0
Whiteh'd, 2b	1	0	0	0	0	0
Rothrock, rf	4	3	2	2	0	0
Frisch, 2b	4	2	3	0	3	0
Crawford, 3b	0	0	0	0	0	1
Medwick, lf	4	2	2	1	0	0
Collins, 1b	5	3	4	8	1	0
V. Davis, c	3	1	1	7	0	0
Fullis, cf	5	0	1	4	0	0
Durocher, ss	5	0	1	3	1	1
J. Dean, p	5	1	2	1	2	0
Total	40	13	17	27	8	2

BROOKLYN (N.).	ab.	r.	h.	po.	a.	e.
Boyle, rf	4	0	1	3	0	0
Frey, ss	3	0	0	2	4	1
Koenecke, cf	4	0	0	3	0	0
Leslie, 1b	3	0	1	5	1	0
Cuc'nello, 2b	3	0	0	3	1	0
Bucher, 2b	1	0	0	0	0	0
Frederick, lf	4	0	0	1	0	0
Stripp, 3b	4	0	1	0	2	0
Lopez, c	3	0	0	11	0	0
Zachary, p	0	0	0	0	0	1
Clark, p	0	0	0	0	0	0
Carroll, p	1	0	0	0	1	0
aMcCarthy	1	0	0	0	0	0
Beck, p	0	0	0	0	1	0
bTremark	1	0	0	0	0	0
Total	33	0	3	27	10	2

aBatted for Carroll in eighth.
bBatted for Beck in ninth.

St. Louis	2 0 5	3 0 2	1 0 0	—13
Brooklyn	0 0 0	0 0 0	0 0 0	— 0

Runs batted in—Collins 6, Frisch 2, Davis 2, Medwick, Fullis, Durocher.

Two-base hits—Rothrock, Collins 2, Davis. Three-base hit—Martin. Home run—Collins. Stolen base—Frisch. Sacrifice—Rothrock. Double plays—Frey, Cuccinello and Leslie; Frey and Leslie. Left on bases—St. Louis 6, Brooklyn 9. Bases on balls—Off Zachary 2, Carroll 3, J. Dean 4. Struck out—By Zachary 2, Clark 1, Carroll 4, Beck 1, J. Dean 7. Hits—Off Zachary 5 in 2 1-3 innings, Clark 2 in 2-3, Carroll 9 in 5, Beck 1 in 1. Wild pitch—Clark. Losing pitcher—Zachary. Umpires—Bigler, Klem and Sears. Time of game—1:54.

SECOND GAME.

ST. LOUIS (N.)	ab.	r.	h.	po.	a.	e.
Martin, 3b	4	0	1	0	1	0
Rothrock, rf	4	0	0	1	0	0
Frisch, 2b	4	0	0	1	3	0
Medwick, lf	4	2	2	0	0	0
Collins, 1b	4	0	1	9	1	0
DeLancey, c	4	0	1	7	0	0
Orsatti, cf	3	0	0	1	0	0
Durocher, ss	3	0	0	1	3	0
P. Dean, p	3	1	2	1	2	0
Total	33	3	7	27	10	0

BROOKLYN (N.)	ab.	r.	h.	po.	a.	e.
Boyle, rf	4	0	0	2	0	0
Frey, ss	3	0	0	4	3	0
Koenecke, cf	3	0	0	1	1	0
Leslie, 1b	3	0	0	10	1	0
Cuccin'lo, 3b	3	0	0	3	0	0
Frederick, lf	3	0	0	2	0	0
Jordan, 2b	3	0	0	1	6	1
Lopez, c	2	0	0	3	1	0
aBucher	1	0	0	0	0	0
Benge, p	3	0	0	1	1	0
bMcCarthy	1	0	0	0	0	0
Total	27	0	0	27	13	1

aBatted for Lopez in ninth.
bBatted for Benge in ninth.

St. Louis	0 0 0	0 0 1	1 0 1	—3
Brooklyn	0 0 0	0 0 0	0 0 0	—0

Runs batted in—Martin, Collins 2.

Two-base hits—P. Dean, Martin, Medwick. Three-base hit—Medwick. Left on bases—St. Louis), Brooklyn 1. Base on balls—Off P. Dean 1. Struck out—By Benge 1, P. Dean 6. Umpires—Klem, Sears and Bigler. Time of game—1:[illegible].

September 22, 1934

Cards Rout Reds and Win Pennant As Giants Are Beaten by Dodgers

National League Race Comes to Dramatic Close With St. Louis Two Games in Front—Brooklyn Triumphs by 8-5 in Tenth —World Series to Start Wednesday in Detroit.

By JOHN DREBINGER.

The Giants' dream of continued world domination in baseball crumbled almost simultaneously on two fronts yesterday as the curtain rang down on one of the most dramatic finishes in the history of the National League.

Out in St. Louis the Cardinals, who had begun the final day of the race one game ahead, pressed relentlessly on toward their goal as they walloped the last-place Cincinnati Reds for the fourth successive day, with one of their invincible Deans again on the firing line.

But a few seconds before this had come about the National League pennant already had been clinched for them by a vengeful band of Dodgers bent on making Bill Terry regret to the last his ill-fated taunt of last Winter when he asked whether Brooklyn was still in the league.

For in the presence of a gathering of more than 45,000, that almost packed the Polo Grounds to capacity, the Dodgers, after getting bowled over for four runs in the first inning, came back to bag their second and final triumph with a withering three-run blast that brought down the Giants in the tenth inning, 8 to 5.

As a result, the National League pennant goes to the Cardinals, who for the fifth time in the last nine campaigns will carry the banner of the Heydler circuit in the World Series, which opens in Detroit on Wednesday.

As for the Giants nothing now remains for them but the bitter reflection of having been made the victims of one of the most astonishing break-downs in major league baseball.

Two years in a row now Terry's players have confounded critics and public alike. Expected to finish no better than the second division in 1933, they amazed the baseball world by not only winning the National League pennant but the world championship as well.

This year they swept to the fore on June 8, and when by Sept. 7 they were still far in front by a margin of seven full games, it looked an absolute certainty that Terry would again flash home in front.

But then came the break-down, a long, painful affair, which finished in semi-darkness yesterday as the Giants wound up the season two games in back of the Cardinals after losing their fifth straight game. Ironically enough, that happened to be their longest losing streak of the year.

Strangely, too, did this game epitomize with striking likeness the fortunes of the Giants this year. Terry threw into the fray all he had.

He tossed in Freddy Fitzsimmons, Hal Schumacher, and finally Carl Hubbell, once the flower of his pitching staff, but though Fitz went off to an imposing start and further aided his cause with a home run in the fourth, there was no fending off those merciless Dodgers.

In the eighth they routed Fitz and drew abreast. In the tenth they chased Schumacher. They finished off against the arm-weary Hubbell as the stunned Giant sympathizers sat silently in the stands, utterly unable to believe their eyes while a jubilant Brooklyn horde, which had helped swell the paid attendance to 44,055, bellowed its delight.

Fans Storm the Park.

Taking full advantage of a situation which they had never conjectured in their fondest dreams, the Brooklyn fans literally stormed the park. Weeks ago they had visioned nothing more entertaining for the last day of the season than to drop around and spend a pleasant afternoon chiding the remnants of another sixth-place ball club.

But here were their Dodgers—their Dodgers, of all people—occupying a spot with the eyes of the entire baseball world upon them. Rain had cheated the fans on Saturday, when many of them remained away in the full belief no game could possibly be played.

But once the skies cleared at noon yesterday they stampeded across the river in battalions and literally knocked each other down in the wild scramble to get through the turnstiles.

Once inside, they turned on a terrific din, augmented by whistles, horns and bells, thus providing another unprecedented setting for a situation which already had set a record quite unparalleled in all baseball. For this probably marked the first time where a team making a last stand for a pennant came on its home field with as many jeers as cheers ringing in its ears.

Giants Appear Relaxed.

The Giants tore into the battle in a vengeful mood and appeared to be more relaxed than at any other time during the last harrowing month.

Having been relieved of the pressure of keeping themselves on top, nerves which had been kept taut almost to the breaking point finally had loosened up and the Terrymen played with the carefree abandon of a team which no longer had anything to lose but everything to gain.

It was with this spirit that they routed Ray Benge in the first inning and built up a four-run lead for the stoutish Fitzsimmons.

A two-bagger off Joe Moore's bat that hooked just inside the right-field foul line started the Giants on this opening drive. Critz followed with a bunt toward first and when Leslie skidded coming in for the ball, winding up by sitting down, it went for a hit.

That moved Moore around to third and when Terry outgalloped an infield hit to Frey Jo-Jo skipped home with the first run. There was a pause here, as Ott, still in the throes of a fearful batting slump, forced Terry at second and Jackson struck out. But at this point Benge suddenly took an unexpected turn for the worse.

Run is Forced Across.

He walked Watkins, filling the bases, and then passed Mancuso, forcing in the second tally. The Dodgers let out a terrific blast on Umpire Stark's decision on the fourth ball and for a time it looked as though Catcher Lopez, the volatile Spaniard, and Dolly would settle the pennant right then and there at the plate, with or without masks.

When order was finally restored Blondy Ryan sliced a single into right and as Ott and Watkins dashed home the Giants had four for the round, while the Brooklyn contingent sat in a smoldering rage. That last blow also finished Benge and Emil Leonard came on, thereby making it a struggle between two talented exponents of the knuckle-ball mode of pitching.

Leonard checked the r[illegible]ly, but the situation at this point looked pretty bad for Brooklyn. However, the Dodgers have long made a specialty of picking themselves up from a knocked-down position, so that it was no great surprise to anybody when Cuccinello up and tripled over Watkins's head in centre in the second inning and rode home on a single by Taylor.

Two innings later the Dodgers tore into Fitzsimmons, with two former Giant recruits doing the damage. Len Koenecke, for whom the late John McGraw once paid $75,000 in players, only to be dismissed with a wave of the hand by Terry when the latter became manager, cracked a double to left. Behind this shot Sambo Leslie singled to right.

Three-Run Lead Restored.

Fitz, however, wiped out this tally almost at once by belting Leonard for a homer, the ball smacking with a dull thud against the front of the upper balcony. That restored the three-run lead and kept the Flatbush flock quiet until the sixth, when they broke out afresh.

Boyle opened this round by bouncing a single off Fitz's glove, and when Ryan, after fielding the ball, tagged a wild throw to the end of it, Boyle grabbed an extra base. That just put him in the proper position to score as Frey tore off a hit to right.

The Dodgers even threatened to do more damage, for after Koenecke and Leslie had slapped into force plays at second Cuccinello banked a single to centre, sending Leslie to second. At this ticklish point Fitz unfurled a wild pitch that put the runners on second and third. But with a chance to tie the score, Taylor this time grounded out to Critz.

But this delectable dish the Dodgers were merely saving for the eighth, when they routed Fitz and counted twice to draw even. Boyle started this outrage against the Giants' feelings with a single, and after Frey had grounded out, Koenecke laced his second double to left, driving Boyle over the plate and Fitz to the clubhouse.

Fitz, however, had the satisfaction of knowing that he was leaving the game with his homer still giving the Giants a one-run margin.

There was a touch of super dramatics at this point as Hal Schumacher, coming up from the bullpen, started taking his last warm-up pitchers preparatory to relieving Fitz. With the Giants huddled around their pitcher, a sudden roar went up from the crowd. It was a full-throated Brooklyn roar for at that moment the scoreboard revealed a fat "3" for the Cardinals in the fourth giving St. Louis a 5-0 lead over the Reds. One could almost feel the sinking feeling the Giants must have been experiencing at this trying point.

A moment later the tying Dodger run swirled across the plate. Leslie grounded to Tyan and Koenecke was run down between second and third. But Leslie grabbed second while this was going on and when Schumacher uncorked a wild pitch that rolled

toward the Brooklyn dug-out Sambo never stopped running until he had hit the plate while the dazed Giants scrambled madly for the ball. That deadlocked the score.

There was a brief giant flurry in the last of the eighth when, with one out, Frey fumbled Jackson's grounder and Watkins singled to centre.

But as Manager Terry called on Lefty O'Doul to bat for Mancuso, Manager Stengel supplanted Leonard with the ancient but still crafty Tom Zachary and Terry felt it necessary to make another switch. He sent Harry Danning up to bat in place of O'Doul, but it all came to naught. For Danning ended the inning by slamming into a double play.

With darkness settling down on the field, things now moved hurriedly on to the climax. Johnny Babich, recruit pitcher from the Coast, replaced Zachary in the ninth after Schumacher, palpably worn and tired,

staggered through a scoreless round.

In the tenth came the final collapse. Leslie opened fire with a single and when Cucinello tore off a double to left for his third hit of the day Schumacher went out and the once matchless Hubbell came on the scene.

Hubbell fanned Babich, then purposely passed Stripp to fill the bases. But it was all in vain, Lopez hit a sharp grounder at Ryan, who fumbled the ball and Leslie scored, leaving the bases still full. Came a long fly by Chapman that drove in Cuccinello and when Boyle weighted in behind this with his third single of the day the Dodgers were three up.

To finish the giants in this condition was but the work of a couple of minutes for the youthful Babich, the only interruption coming when Umpire stark got cracked in the Adam's apple by a foul tip.

The box score:

BROOKLYN (N.)							NEW YORK (N.)						
	ab	r	h	po	a	e		ab	r	h	po	a	e
Boyle,rf	4	2	3	4	0	0	Moore,lf	1	1	1	1	0	0
Frey,lf	5	0	1	3	5	1	Critz,rf	5	1	1	1	5	0
Koenecke,cf	5	1	2	0	0	0	Terry,1b	4	0	1	4	1	0
Leslie,1b	5	1	2	2	2	0	Off,rf	0	1	0	0	0	0
McCaffy,1b	0	1	0	2	0	3	Locker,rb	4	0	0	5	0	0
Cornelia,1b	1	2	5	1	4	0	Watkins,cf	3	1	1	2	0	0
Taylor, lf.	5	0	4	0	0	0	Mancuso,c	2	0	1	0	0	0
Babich,p.	1	0	0	0	2	0	O'Dolle	0	0	0	0	0	4
Stripp,3b	4	1	0	0	2	0	Danning,c	1	0	0	3	0	0
Lopez,c	5	0	0	4	0	0	Ryan, ss	4	0	1	5	4	2
Benge,p.	0	0	0	0	0	0	Fitz'm'ns,p	3	1	1	2	0	0
Leonard,p.	3	0	2	0	2	0	S'm'cher,p	1	0	0	2	0	
Zachary,p	0	0	0	0	0	0	Hubbell,p	0	0	0	0	0	0
Chapmen,lf	1	0	0	0	0	0							
Total	42	8	12	3			Total	37	5	7	30	17	2
		0	17	1									

a Batted for Mancuso in the seventh

| Brooklyn | 0 | 1 | 0 | 1 | 0 | 1 | 0 | 2 | 0 | 3 – 8 |
| New York | 0 | 1 | 0 | 1 | 0 | 0 | 0 | 0 | 0 – 5 |

Runs batted in– Terry, Mancuso, Ryan 2, Taylor, Leslie, Fitzsimmons, Frey, Koenecke, Chapman, Boyle.

Two base hits–Moore, Koenecke 2, Cuccinello. Three-base hit–Cuccinello. Homr run – Fitzsimmon. Stolen base – Boyle Double plays– Critz, Ryan and Terry, Frey, Cuccinello and Leslie. Left on bases– New York 5, Brooklyn 8 Bases on balls – Off Benge 1, Fitzsimmons 4, Leonard 1, Schumacher 1, Habich 5, Hubbell 1, HIts – Off, Benge 4 in 2. Danning, Leonard 3 in 6.2-3. Zachary 6 in 2:5, Babich 0 in 2. Fitzsimmons 9 in 7 1-7. Schumacher, 2 in 1-2-3 (none out in tenth). Hubbell 1 in 1. Wild pitches– Fitzsimmons. Schumacher. Winning pitcher– Babich, Losing pitcher – Schumacher Umpires– Stark, Magerkurth and Pfirman. Time of game - 5.37.

CARDS WIN SERIES, BEAT DETROIT, 11-0; TIGER FANS RIOT

DEAN EASILY THE VICTOR

Six Pitchers Used by the Losers Against Dizzy in Deciding Contest.

7 RUNS SCORED IN THIRD

Frisch's Double With Bases Filled Starts Drive—13 Men Bat in Inning.

WILD SCENES MARK GAME

Landis Banishes Medwick After Aroused Fans Shower Missiles on Player.

By JOHN DREBINGER

Special to THE NEW YORK TIMES.

DETROIT, Oct. 9.—Amid the most riotous scenes in the history of modern world series play. Frankie Frisch's ripsnorting band of Cardinals today brought an amazing and crushing finish to the seven-game struggle for the world's baseball championship.

The interventio of Commissioner K.M. Landis was made necessary before the Cardinals, who already had achieved unprecedented deeds this year by coming from nowhere to win a pennant in the final leap to the tape, won the crown.

With their inimitable Dizzy Dean back on the firing line once more to give a final display of his matchless pitching skill, the National League champions fairly annihilated the Tigers, led by thier wounded but doughty Mickey Cochrane. The score of the seventh and deciding game was 11 to 0.

Smash Clears the Bases.

Figuratively and literally this most astonishing ball club of modern times tore the game apart. In a whirlwind sweep they blasted seven runs across the plate in the third inning, the first three riding home on a base-clearing two-bagger by the indomitable Frisch himself. They routed Elden Auker, Schoolboy Rowe only a short time ago the pride of all Detroit, and two other pitchers.

For a finish, one of their cast, Jersey Joe Medwick, touched off the spark that sent part of the crowd into a raging demonstration that interrupted the game for twenty minutes and for a time threatened to terminate the battle without further play. Commissioner Landis then took a hand and quelled the disturbance by ordering the Cardinal outfielder from the field.

The uproar got its inception during the upper half of the sixth inning. Medwick bounced a triple off the right-field bleachers and finished his dash around the bases with a slide into third base while the disconsolate gathering looked sullenly on.

Lashes Kick at Owen.

Just what provoked Medwick could not be seen as he crashed into the bag in a cloud of dust, with Marvin Owen, the Tiger third baseman, standing over him. Suddenly the St. Louis player was seen to lift his left foot and strike out with his spikes toward Owen's chest.

Medwick missed his mark, but the flare-up was sufficient to arouse the hostile feeling between the rival teams that had been brewing for several days and players of both sides rushed to the spot. However, the four umpires quickly stepped in between the irate players. When Umpire Bill Klem, dean of the National League staff and the arbiter at that base, decided to take no action, the uproar subsided with only a few minutes delay.

It looked like the end of the disturbance, but it proved only to be the beginning.

With the end of the Cardinal inning, Medwick started out for left field and was greeted by rounds of boos from the 17,000 fans packed solidly in the huge wooden bleachers that had been constructed especially for the series.

Retreats Toward Infield.

Pop bottles, oranges, apples and anything else that came ready to hand were hurled out on the field and the Cardinal player beat a retreat toward the infield while the umpires called time. Attendants rushed out to clear away the debris and Medwick returned to his post. The din now increased two-fold, more bottles and fruit were showered on the field, and once more the umpires had to call time.

Four times the performance was repeated and each time the anger of the fans, rather than showing any abatement, increased in its intensity. In vain an announcer bellowed through the amplifiers imploring the fans to desist and allow the game to continue. But these Detroit fans were boiling mad and doubtless would have continued the demonstration until the end of time. Finally, after one more attempt to resume play ended in another deluge of refuse on the playing field, Commissioner Landis rose in his box, a short distance from the Cardinal bench, and waved the umpires to come to him. He ordered Umpire Klem, the two players,

Owen and Medwick, and the rival managers, Frisch and Cochrane, to come before him, and there out in full view he held an open court.

Frisch Tries to Protest.

The hearing lasted not more than a minute and the upshot of it was that Landis ordered Medwick to remove himself quickly and quietly from the field. The fiery Frisch attempted to protest, but Landis, with an angry gesture, motioned the St. Louis leader to get out on the field and resume play without further delay.

Chick Fullis, utility outfielder, took Medwick's place in left and the crowd, very much appeased by this turn of events, actually cheered this unassuming St. Louis player as he came trotting out.

Later Commissioner Landis, in explaining his action, stated he primarily ordered Medwick off the field as the only means of continuing the game in the face of the crowd's hostile demonstration.

"Before the series," said baseball's czar, "the umpires are instructed not to put any player off the field unless the provocation is very extreme. I saw as well as everybody what Medwick did, but when Umpire Klem took no action and the players quieted down I hoped the matter was ended.

"But when it became apparent that the demonstration of the crowd would never terminate I decided to take action. I did not call Medwick and Owen in any attempt to patch up the difference between the players.

No Further Action Planned.

"I asked Owen whether he knew of any excuse why Medwick should have made such an attack on him. He said he did not, and with that I ordered Medwick off the field. I do not intend to take any further action."

A few minutes later, after play was resumed, Medwick left the Cardinal bench and crossed over to the Tiger dugout as his only means of exit. There was more jeering, but five policemen rushed out from the boxes in order to discourage any further demonstration on the part of the crowd. This did not prevent the overwrought fans from tossing a final cushion down from the upper tier, the pillow just missing the departing St. Louis player.

The uproar, of course, quite overshadowed all else that happened on the field, even taking the play away from the marvelous Dizzy Dean, who was out to revenge himself in convincing fashion for the beating he had taken in the fifth game in St. Louis last Sunday.

Although he had only one day of rest, the elder Dean was in marvelous form as he shut out the Tigers in six hits to round out the fourth and final victory of the celebrated Dean family. Paul, his 20-year-old brother, had won the third and sixth games of the series. He himself had won the first game, but had suffered a subsequent setback.

Displays Complete Mastery

Now Dizzy was back to display his complete mastery with the only shutout of the entire series. With his brother he had pitched the Cardinals into a pennant when the entire nation deemed the feat impossible. Together the pair had brought to St. Louis its third world's championship since 1926.

Among other things, Dizzy brought to a dramatic close the sixth million-dollar series since interleague warfare began under present rules in 1905.

The paid attendance was 40,902 and the receipts were $138,063, bringing the total for the seven games up to $1,031,341. This was less than $200,000 short of the record gate which the Cardinals and Yankees set in 1926 when their seven games drew $1,207,864.

The total attendance for the series just ended was 281,510, the highest since 1926 when the Cards and Yanks set the record of 328,051.

The conclusion of the struggle marked the third time that the Cardinals had engaged in a million-dollar series. It was also their third appearance in a seven-game tussle. Curiously enough, the Cards were returned the victors in all three.

Try to Rally Around Leader

Against the sort of pitching the elder and greater Dean turned on the Tigers simply had nothing to offer. They strove valiantly, however, to rally around their leader, the stout-hearted Cochrane. Despite the fact that he had spent the night in a hospital nursing a spike wound in his left leg received yesterday Mickey insisted on playing behind the bat.

When in that torrid third inning the Tiger pitchers crumbled before the fury of that aroused St. Louis host the entire bottom fell out of the game. In all, Cochrane, who pluckily stuck in the battle until the end of he eighth inning, tossed six hurlers into the fray.

All the Detroit pitchers who had appeared previously in the series passed in review. But there was no restraining this remarkable St. Louis team. Shortly after Labor Day these same Cardinals had trailed the New York Giants by eight games in the National League pennant race, only to rout last year's world champions out of the picture on the final two days. They thus gained the right to give the National circuit its second successive world series triumph over the American League.

The crowd, which had been rather tardy in arriving, was still coming through the gates and climbing over one another in the reserved sections of the upper and lower tiers of the grand stand as the rival forces squared off grimly for the important business at hand.

There was something of an embarrassing moment just before the game began when a delegation of loyal and well-meaning Detroit fans rolled a huge floral horseshoe out toward the plate. But its sponsors sadly underestimated the inherent superstitious characteristics of ball players.

Neither Cochrane nor any other member of the Tiger team could be induced to come out of the Detroit dugout and accept the gift. So, after a deal of futile coaxing, the delegation hauled its offering away in silence.

The crowd, however, did not have to wait long for its first chance to cheer. The opening blast came when Auker, after pitching three straight balls to Martin, fanned the overanxious Pepper on his next three deliveries.

This was followed by a touch of uneasiness as Jack Rothrock rammed a double into deep left centre, but the confidence of the gathering returned when Auker, apparently getting a better grip on himself, retired Frisch on a pop fly to Rogell and Medwick on a foul to Owen.

There was even more cheering in the second as the Cards, though they clipped Auker for two more hits, wound up the inning without a run or a man left on base. After Collins singled, De Lancey wiped him off the bases by grounding into a double play, snappily executed by Owen, Gehringer and Greenberg. Orsatti, after sending a hit into right, finished himself by getting thrown out on an attempted steal.

Crowd Cheers Defensively.

However, there was a rather ominous feeling to all this and the cheering itself, while whole-hearted enough, was entirely of a defensive nature. It seemed as though the crowd, expecting only the Cards to do something on the offensive, was delighted over the success with which their Tigers were holding the invaders in restraint.

The Tigers themselves had been able to make no headway whatsoever against Dean in those first two innings, only one of their cast reaching first base. He got on only because Collins dropped a low throw by Durocher after Leo had made quite a dashing pick-up of Rogell's awkward bounder in the infield.

Then, in the teeth of a lively gale that swept from the northeast over the right-field wall and made it a bit chilly even though the sun shone brightly in a clear sky, the first explosion came.

It came without warning, as most explosions do, with Durocher opening the third inning by lifting a high fly to White in centre. Nothing still threatened as Dizzy strode to the plate.

Dean lifted a high foul behind the plate and right there, had the usually alert Cochrane been himself, a lot of subsequent disaster might have been avoided. The ball dropped just inside the front row of boxes. Cochrane, had he made a try for it, doubtless could easily have caught it. But he never even looked around to see where the ball was going and allowed it to drop harmlessly for a strike.

The next moment the singular Dean person shot a double to left. Martin outsprinted an infield hit to Greenberg, who delayed too long making up his mind what to do with the ball, Dean going to third. A moment later Martin stole second. Then the charge was on.

Auker, pitching as cautiously as he could, passed Rothrock, filling the bases, and Frisch came up. He ran the count to two and two. He fouled a long shot off to the right, another to the left. Then he hammered a double down the right-field foul line, and as the ball glanced off Fox's glove all the three Cardinals on the bases crossed the plate.

Rowe Replaces Auker.

Frisch's blow finished Auker, and Rowe was called to the mound in an attempt to check the onrushing Cardinals, but didn't stay there long. Schoolboy pitched to three batters and then his day's work was done. He got Medwick on a grounder, but then Collins's sharp single to left chased Frisch across the plate. De Lancey connected for a long two-bagger to right, Collins was in with the fifth run, and Rowe was out.

Elon Hogsett was Cochrane's next selection and the left-hander, too, had a short stay in the box. Orsatti, the first man to face him, walked. Durocher, making his second appearance at the plate during the inning, hit a single to right, and again the bases were filled. Dean scratched a hit along the third-base line and De Lancey came in, leaving the bags still filled.

Martin drew a walk on four straight balls, forcing Orsatti over the plate for the seventh St. Louis run. Now Tommy Bridges, victor over Dizzy Dean in last Sunday's game, relieved Hogsett and managed to bring the inning to a close, Rothrock grounding to Gehringer to force Martin at second for the third out. Thirteen Cardinals came to bat in the inning.

Bridges stopped the scoring until the sixth, although he was clipped for a single by Collins in the fourth.

Martin opened the sixth with a drive to left and raced to second when Goslin handled the ball poorly. Pepper was held at second while Goslin gathered in Rothrock's fly. Frisch then flied to centre, bringing Medwick up and Jersey Joe walloped the triple which brought on his entanglement with Owen after he slid into the base. Martin scored while trouble threatened at third.

Lashes Single to Centre.

After the immediate flare-up had subsided Collins lashed a single to centre, where White fumbled the ball. Medwick came home with the second run of the inning and the ninth of the battle.

Not even the twenty-minute uproar that preceded Medwick's final retirement from the game under orders from Landis interrupted the trend of the engagement. Dizzy, wearing a bright Cardinal windbreaker, stood around the infield while the demonstration was going on in full blast, utterly unmindful of what was going on. Now and then he took a brief warm-up with his catcher.

When play was finally resumed for the last of the sixth the wonder pitcher of the day returned to his task of mowing down the Tigers. Now and then somebody poked him for a hit.

Apparently Dizzy was bent on making this a shutout regardless of how enormous the Cards made the score. Whenever the Tigers threatened Dizzy merely turned on the heat and poured his blazing

Box Score of the Seventh Game

ST. LOUIS CARDINALS.

	ab.	r.	h.	tb.	2b.	3b.	hr.	bb.	so.	sh.	sb.	po.	a.	e.
Martin, 3b	5	3	2	2	0	0	0	1	1	0	2	0	1	0
Rothrock, rf	5	1	2	4	2	0	0	1	1	0	0	4	0	0
Frisch, 2b	5	1	1	2	1	0	0	0	0	0	0	3	6	0
Medwick, lf	4	1	1	3	0	1	0	0	0	0	0	1	0	0
Fullis, lf	1	0	1	1	0	0	0	0	0	0	0	1	0	0
Collins, 1b	5	1	4	4	0	0	0	0	0	0	0	7	1	1
De Lancey, c	5	1	1	2	1	0	0	0	1	0	0	5	0	0
Orsatti, cf	3	1	1	1	0	0	0	2	0	0	0	2	0	0
Durocher, ss	5	1	2	4	0	1	0	0	0	0	0	3	4	0
J. Dean, p	5	1	2	3	1	0	0	0	1	0	0	1	0	0
Total	43	11	17	26	5	2	0	4	4	0	2	27	12	1

DETROIT TIGERS.

	ab.	r.	h.	tb.	2b.	3b.	hr.	bb.	so.	sh.	sb.	po.	a.	e.
White, cf	4	0	0	0	0	0	0	0	1	0	0	3	0	1
Cochrane, c	4	0	0	0	0	0	0	0	0	0	0	2	2	0
Hayworth, c	0	0	0	0	0	0	0	0	0	0	0	1	0	0
Gehringer, 2b	4	0	2	2	0	0	0	0	0	0	0	3	5	1
Goslin, lf	4	0	0	0	0	0	0	0	0	0	0	4	0	1
Rogell, ss	4	0	1	1	0	0	0	0	0	0	0	3	2	0
Greenberg, 1b	4	0	1	1	0	0	0	0	3	0	0	7	0	0
Owen, 3b	4	0	0	0	0	0	0	0	0	0	0	1	2	0
Fox, rf	3	0	2	4	2	0	0	0	0	0	0	3	0	0
Auker, p	0	0	0	0	0	0	0	0	0	0	0	0	0	0
Rowe, p	0	0	0	0	0	0	0	0	0	0	0	0	0	0
Hogsett, p	0	0	0	0	0	0	0	0	0	0	0	0	0	0
Bridges, p	2	0	0	0	0	0	0	0	1	0	0	0	0	0
Marberry, p	0	0	0	0	0	0	0	0	0	0	0	0	0	0
Crowder, p	0	0	0	0	0	0	0	0	0	0	0	0	0	0
aG. Walker	1	0	0	0	0	0	0	0	0	0	0	0	0	0
Total	34	0	6	8	2	0	0	0	5	0	0	27	11	3

aBatted for Marberry in eighth.

SCORE BY INNINGS.

St. Louis	0	0	7	0	0	2	2	0	0—11
Detroit	0	0	0	0	0	0	0	0	0— 0

Runs batted in—St. Louis: Frisch 3, Collins 2, De Lancey, J. Dean, Martin, Medwick, Rothrock.

Left on bases—St. Louis 9, Detroit 7. Struck out—By J. Dean 5, Auker 1, Bridges 2, Crowder 1. Bases on balls—Off Auker 1, Hogsett 2, Marberry 1. Double play—Owen, Gehringer and Greenberg. Hits—Off Auker 6 in 2 1/3 innings, Rowe 2 in 1/3, Hogsett 2 in 0 (none out in third), Bridges 6 in 4 1/3, Marberry 1 in 1, Crowder 0 in 1. Losing pitcher—Auker. Umpires—Geisel (A. L.) at the plate, Reardon (N. L.) at first base, Owens (A. L.) at second base, Klem (N. L.) at third base. Time of game—2:19.

fast ball and sharp-breaking curve right down the middle.

One could scarcely imagine that this man in the final week of the National League pennant race had pitched his team to victory in three successive starts, that he was making his third appearance in this series and with only forty-eight hours intervening since his last game.

Jokes Through It All.

It was superhuman. Three days ago he had entered a game as a pinch-runner and had received a belt on the head with a thrown ball that might have slain most any other man. But nothing perturbs Dizzy, except when he is in a fit of anger. Then he may tear up uniforms and do all sorts of things. But nothing disturbed his equanimity today. He smiled and joked through it all.

In the seventh the Cards scored two more, probably just for the sheer fun of the thing. Certainly they never needed the runs.

Leo Durocher tripled to the exact spot where he had hit his two-bagger yesterday, the hit which preceded Paul Dean's game-winning blow. Gehringer fumbled Martin's grounder and Leo counted. Martin stole his second base of the day. Then came a long double to left centre by Rothrock and the Wild Horse of the Osage thundered over the plate.

In vain Cochrane tossed in pinch hitters. Fred Marberry pitched the eighth and fell for a hit, but escaped without a score against him. Alvin Crowder, who had started that ill-fated first game when the Tiger infield exploded five errors all around him, pitched the ninth. Perhaps he might have been Cochrane's best bet today. At least, such is the opinion of the vast army of second-guessers.

But what would it have mattered? Crowder at his best could only have obtained a scoreless tie, even though he did retire three Cards in a row in the ninth.

The Tigers had only two scoring chances in the entire battle. They had runners on second and third with only one out in the fifth. They also had runners on first and second with one out in the ninth. Whereupon Dizzy fanned Greenberg for the third time, turning around even before the third strike reached the plate, and Owen ended the battle with a grounder to Durocher.

And so Detroit, faithful to its Tigers to the last, is still seeking its first world's championship. It won three pennants in a row in the days of Ty Cobb and the immortal Hughie Jennings from 1907 to 1909, but lost all three world series clashes. It waited twenty-five years for another chance.

But an amazing ball club, with two of the most remarkable pitchers baseball ever was to see grow up in one family, blocked the path.

Less than a month ago these Cardinals did not appear to have one chance in a thousand of reaching their present goal. But they edged Bill Terry and his Giants right off the baseball map and today they crushed the Tigers.

October 10, 1934

REDS' NIGHT GAME DRAWS 25,000 FANS

Many Notables See Contest, First Under Lights in History of Major Leagues.

By The Associated Press.

CINCINNATI, May 24.—Night baseball came up from the minors for its first big league tryout tonight, and 25,000 fans and the Cincinnati Reds liked the innovation. Some of the affection of the Reds for the nocturnal pastime was because they defeated the faltering Phillies, 2 to 1.

The official paid attendance was announced at 20,422, the third largest crowd of the season.

The flood light inaugural, with President Roosevelt switching on the lights from Washington, was staged before a host of baseball notables, including Ford Frick, president of the National League, and Prexy Will Harridge of the American.

The contest was errorless, despite the fact it was the first under lights for practically all the players. The hurlers, Paul Derringer for the Reds and Bowman for the Phils, performed in great style, the former allowing six hits and the visitor only four.

Wilson Gives Approval.

Manager Jimmy Wilson of the Phils said the lights had nothing to do with the low hit total.

"Both pitchers just had all their stuff working, that's all. You can see that ball coming up to the plate just as well under those lights as you can in daytime."

Jimmy, however, let it be known that he "thinks night baseball is all right, if the fans want it, but I'd rather play in the daytime."

Picture plays were prevalent throughout the game. Myers went far back into left field for Todd's fly in the seventh, Byrd crashed into the centre field wall in the sixth but held on to Camilli's drive, while Camilli snatched several throws out of the dirt from the Phil infield at first.

Myers Comes Home.

Two long flies were dropped by Philadelphia outfielders, but both were scored as hits. The first led to the Red score in the opening frame, Myers pulling up at second as Watkins let the ball get away when he fell against the left-field wall. Myers came home as Riggs and Goodman grounded out.

Singles by Sullivan and Pool, and Campbell's infield out produced the winning Red marker in the fourth. The Phils got their lone tally in the fifth when Todd singled, took third on Haslin's drive to centre, and counted on Bowman's roller to Myers.

The box score:

PHILADELPHIA (N).	ab.r.h.po.a.e.	CINCINNATI (N).	ab.r.h.po.a.e.
Chiozza, 2b.	4 0 0 1 3 0	Myers, ss..	3 1 1 2 3 0
Allen, cf..	4 0 1 0 0 0	Riggs, 3b..	4 0 0 0 3 0
Moore, rf..	4 0 1 0 0 0	Goodman, rf.	3 0 0 3 0 0
Camilli, 1b.	4 0 1 15 0 0	Sullivan, 1b.	3 1 2 8 1 0
Vergez, 3b..	4 0 1 0 4 0	Pool, lf..	3 0 1 0 0 0
Todd, c..	3 1 1 3 0 0	Campbell, c.	8 0 0 5 0 0
Watkins lf.	3 0 0 5 0 0	Byrd, cf..	3 0 0 4 0 0
Haslin, ss..	3 0 1 0 5 0	Kamp'is, 2b.	3 0 0 4 3 0
Bowman, p..	2 0 0 0 2 0	Derringer, p.	3 0 0 1 2 0
aWilson	1 0 0 0 0		
Birin, p..	0 0 0 0 0 0	Total..	28 2 4 27 12 0
Total..	32 1 6 24 14 0		

aBatted for Bowman in eighth.

Philadelphia .... 0 0 0 0 1 0 0 0 0—1
Cincinnati .... 1 0 0 1 0 0 0 0.—2

Runs batted in—Bowman, Goodman, Campbell. Two-base hit—Myers. Stolen bases—Vergez, Bowman, Myers. Double play—Riggs, Kampouris and Sullivan. Left on bases—Philadelphia 4, Cincinnati 3. Bases on balls—Off Bowman 1. Struck out—By Bowman 1, Birin 1, Derringer 3. Hits—Off Bowman 4 in 7 innings, Birin 0 in 1. Losing pitcher—Bowman. Umpires—Klem, Sears and Pinelli. Time of game—1:55.

May 25, 1935

ESTIMATED YAWKEY HAS SPENT $3,500,000

Huge Sum Expended for Red Sox and Players in Search of Pennant Winner.

CHICAGO, Dec. 10 (AP).—Baseball men today figured that Tom Yawkey had spent more than $3,500,000 since 1932 when he purchased the Boston Red Sox. Reputedly a multi-millionaire, most of his wealth inherited from his foster father, Yawkey, unofficial but reliable records show, spent huge sums as follows:

$1,000,000 for purchase of Red Sox.

$1,500,000 to rebuild Fenway Park.

$125,000 for Lefty Grove from the Athletics.

$250,000 for Manager Joe Cronin from Washington.

$35,000 for Lyn Lary from New York.

$25,000 for Julius Solters from Baltimore.

$60,000 for Bill Werber and George Pipgras from Yankees.

$55,000 for Rick Ferrell and Lloyd Brown from St. Louis.

$25,000 for Carl Reynolds from St. Louis.

$25,000 for Wes Ferrell from Cleveland.

$350,000 for Jimmy Foxx, John Marcum, Roger Cramer and Eric McNair from Philadelphia (Foxx and Marcum sale announced. Cramer and McNair reported as made, but will not be announced until January).

$100,000 for miscellaneous, but important, deals.

And yet, his great dream of a pennant for Boston has not been realized.

December 11, 1935

Ty Cobb Achieves Highest Niche In Modern Baseball Hall of Fame

Georgian Gets 222 Votes, 4 Short of Perfect Score and 7 More Than Ruth and Wagner—Mathewson and Johnson Only Others With Enough Ballots to Be Named in Nation-Wide Poll.

By The Associated Press.

CHICAGO, Feb. 2.—Tyrus Raymond Cobb, fiery genius of the diamond for twenty-four years, will be the No. 1 immortal in baseball's permanent hall of fame.

The famous Georgian, who shattered virtually all records known to baseball during his glorious era, won the distinction as the immortal of immortals today by outscoring even such diamond greats as Babe Ruth, Honus Wagner and Christy Mathewson in the nation-wide poll to determine which ten players of the modern age should be represented in the game's memorial hall at Cooperstown, N. Y.

Margin of Seven Ballots.

Only Cobb, Ruth, Wagner, Mathewson and Walter Johnson, probably the speed ball king of them all, received the required majority to win places in the hall of fame, but Cobb had a margin of seven votes over his closest rivals, Ruth and Wagner.

Of 226 ballots cast by players and writers, the Georgia Peach received 222, or four less than a unanimous vote. Ruth and Wagner received 215 each. Mathewson was fourth with 205 and Johnson fifth with 189. Seventy-five per cent of the total votes, or 169, were needed.

Napoleon Lajoie, Tris Speaker, Cy Young, Rogers Hornsby and Mickey Cochrane ran in that order for the other five positions left for the moderns, players who starred from 1900 and on, but as none received 75 per cent of the total vote their cases will be submitted to the Cooperstown committee in charge of the memorial to be erected in time for baseball's centennial in 1939. Their names will be submitted in another poll next year with five or seven places open.

Young Honored in Two Polls.

Their votes were: Lajoie 146, Speaker 133, Young (who also received 32½ votes for the pre-1900 hall of fame) 111, Hornsby 105, and Cochrane 80.

The committee in charge of the vote tabulation, headed by Henry Edwards, secretary of the Baseball Writers Association, figured the struggle for ballots among the moderns would be a two-man battle between Cobb and Ruth. When the first 100 votes were counted, both Cobb and the home run king were

Times Wide World Photo.
TY COBB.

unanimous.

Ruth was the first to fall out, losing a vote from a writer who had watched him hang up some of his greatest records. The committee was amazed. Vote counting stopped momentarily for a discussion on how any one could leave the great Ruth off the list of immortals.

The same happened when Cobb missed his first vote. Too, there was some surprise when the usual vote of Cobb, Ruth and Speaker was broken up with a series of ballots for other outfielders.

Sisler Ranked Eleventh.

George Sisler, whose great career with the St. Louis Browns was halted by impairment of vision, ranked eleventh, with 77 votes.

Fifty-one stars, past and present, were named, but few of the present ones received much support, for the reason that the voters figured they would get their chances later, as one or two will be added to the list of immortals each year.

Dizzy Dean, Charley Gehringer and Charles (Gabby) Hartnett, rated as three of the greatest stars of the game today, received only 1 vote apiece. There were many surprises of famous stars receiving only a handful of votes.

The others received votes as follows:

Eddie Collins, 60; Jimmy Collins (former Boston third baseman), 58; Grover Cleveland Alexander, 55; Lou Gehrig, 51; Roger Bresnahan, 47; Willie Keeler (he also received 33 in the old-timer poll), 40; Rube Waddell, 33; Jimmy Foxx, 21; Ed Walsh, 20; Ed Delehanty (also a leader in the old-timer poll), 17; Harold (Pie) Traynor, 16; Frank Frisch, 14; Robert Moses Grove, 12; Hal Chase, 11; Ross Young, 10; Bill Terry, 9; Johnny Kling, 8; Lew Criger, 7.

Johnny Evers, 6; Mordecai Brown, 6; Frank Chance, 5; Ray Schalk, John McGraw and Al Simmons, 4 each; Chief Bender, Eddie Roush and Joe Jackson, 2 each, and 1 vote each to the following: Rube Marquard, William Bradley, Nap Rucker, Jake Daubert, Sam Crawford, Connie Mack, Norm Elberfeld, Frank (Home Run) Baker, Fred Clarke, Dazzy Vance.

February 3, 1936

CHAPTER 2

BASEBALL AT ITS PEAK

Bobby Thomson is about to touch the plate after hitting the home run that brought the New York Giants the pennant in the dramatic ninth inning of the final 1951 playoff game. It you look closely on the right, you can see that among his delighted teammates—with his number partially obscured—is a young rookie who had only recently joined the club: Willie Mays.

Lazzeri Smashes Four Batting Records

YANKS OVERWHELM ATHLETICS, 25 TO 2

Lazzeri Sets American League Record by Driving In Eleven of the Runs.

CONNECTS FOR 3 HOMERS

Two Come With Bases Filled, New Mark for the Majors— Also Hits a Triple.

By JAMES P. DAWSON
Special to THE NEW YORK TIMES.

PHILADELPHIA, May 24.—Tony Lazzeri hammered his way to baseball fame today with an exhibition of batting unparalleled in American League history as he set the pace in the Yankees' crushing 25-2 victory over the Athletics at Shibe Park.

The 32-year-old veteran of the New York infield blasted three home runs, two of them with the bases loaded, two of them in successive times at bat. He missed a fourth by a matter of inches and had to be content with a triple. With his three-bagger in the eighth with two on Lazzeri erased the American League record for runs batted in by a player in a single game. His homers with the bases filled came in the second and fifth. His third started the seventh.

Tony's hitting today gave him the distinction of driving in eleven runs. The best previous mark was that of Jimmy Foxx, who drove home nine in Cleveland with a double, a triple and a home run in 1933. The National League record is twelve, set by Jim Bottomley in 1924.

Ruth Next in Line

Lazzeri's two homers with the bases filled in a single game created a new major league record. Babe Ruth comes closest to this distinction. He hit homers with the bases loaded in two consecutive games, accomplishing the feat twice, once in 1927 and again in 1929.

Lazzeri also set another major league mark with six homers in three consecutive games. He walloped three in yesterday's doubleheader and three today. In addition, he smashed seven in four consecutive games, still another major league record.

The McCarthymen collected nineteen hits today for forty-six total bases, on six homers, three triples, as many doubles and seven singles. Their total of runs scored was three short of the modern record made by the Cardinals in 1929.

Frankie Crosetti hit two homers in successive times at bat with no one on and Joe DiMaggio also smashed one. In addition, Joe had a double and a single.

Fifty-two Runs in Three Games

In the three games of the series the Yanks have clouted thirteen homers, Lazzeri showing the way with his six, five of them in two games. The squad has hit for a total of 107 bases, made 52 runs, 40 in two games, and collected 49 hits. Adding to the general confusion today were sixteen passes issued by five Athletic hurlers, two short of the all-time mark for a team in a single game.

The New Yorkers established a new major league standard for most homers by one club in two consecutive games. They hit five in yesterday's nightcap and six today for a total of eleven. The Pirates set the old record of ten in 1925. The previous American League mark of nine was made by the Yankees in 1930.

Lazzeri Almost Mobbed

Lazzeri was almost mobbed when his triple gave him a new American League mark for runs batted in and at the conclusion of the game he had to fight his way through a cluster of autograph seekers, without police aid by the way, after 8,000 wildly enthusiastic fans suppressed the disappointment of being unable to see him in a chance to improve on his mark.

Monte Pearson coasted to his sixth victory of the season under protection of the McCarthymen's amazing hitting outburst that blistered the offerings of five Philadelphia hurlers—George Turbeville, Bill Dietrich, Malton Bullock, Herman Fink and Woodie Upchurch.

Mack Not on Hand

Connie Mack wasn't around to see this annihilation of his club. He was in Bridgeport, attending memorial services for the late Mike Flanagan, an old friend who died recently.

A trick of construction robbed Dickey of a home run in the fifth when his tremendous drive bobbled atop the fence over the scoreboard and dropped inside instead of outside the park. Bill had to be content with a triple.

Lazzeri's homers brought him several odd marks. His first four-master today gave him the distinction of three homers in four trips to the plate, for he hit two in his last three times up in yesterday's nightcap. In his last eight times up he drove five homers and a triple and fanned twice.

The box score:

NEW YORK (A.)	ab.	r.	h.	po.	a.	e.
Crosetti, ss.	6	2	2	3	5	0
Rolfe, 3b.	4	2	0	3	2	0
DiMag'o, lf.	7	2	3	2	0	0
Gehrig, 1b.	4	3	2	7	0	0
Dickey, c.	5	3	2	3	0	1
Chapman, cf.	2	4	2	2	0	0
Selkirk, rf.	5	3	1	2	0	0
Lazzeri, 2b.	5	4	4	2	1	0
Pearson, p.	5	2	3	0	1	0
Jorgens, c.	1	0	0	0	1	0
Saltz'r, 1b.	1	0	0	3	0	0
Total	**45**	**25**	**19**	**27**	**9**	**2**

PHILADELPHIA (A.)	ab.	r.	h.	po.	a.	e.
Finney, 1b.	3	1	2	5	0	0
Dean, 1b.	1	0	1	0	0	0
Warstler, 2b.	2	1	1	3	3	0
Peters, ss.	1	0	1	0	1	0
Moses, cf.	4	0	0	4	0	0
Puccin'i, rf.	3	0	1	1	0	0
Higgins, 3b.	4	0	1	3	1	0
Johnson, lf.	2	0	0	1	0	0
Moliho, 1f.	2	0	0	1	0	0
New'e, ss-2b.	4	0	0	1	4	0
Berry, c.	4	0	0	6	0	0
Turbev'e, p.	0	0	0	0	0	0
Dietrich, p.	1	0	1	0	0	0
aNiemiec	1	0	0	0	0	0
Bullock, p.	0	0	0	0	0	0
Fink, p.	0	0	0	0	0	0
Upchurch, p.	1	0	0	0	0	0
bHayes	1	0	0	0	0	0
Total	**33**	**2**	**7**	**27**	**8**	**0**

aBatted for Dietrich in fourth.
bBatted for Upchurch in ninth.

New York ....0 5 0 5 6 1 2 6 0—25
Philadelphia ....2 0 0 0 0 0 0 0 0— 2

Runs batted in—Higgins, Lazzeri 11, DiMaggio 2, Gehrig, Dickey 2, Selkirk 2, Pearson 2, Crosetti 3. Two-base hits—DiMaggio, Chapman 2, Dean. Three-base hits—Dickey 2, Lazzeri. Home runs—Lazzeri 3, DiMaggio, Crosetti. Double plays—Newsome, Warstler and Finney; Crosetti and Gehrig. Left on bases—Philadelphia 7, New York 9. Bases on balls—Off Turbeville 5, Pearson 3, Dietrich 5, Bullock 4, Upchurch 2. Struck out—By Dietrich 3, Pearson 3, Upchurch 2. Hits—Off Turbeville 1 in 1 1-3 innings, Dietrich 6 in 2 2-3, Bullock 1 in 1-3, Fink 3 in 2-3, Upchurch 8 in 4. Wild pitches—Pearson, Bullock 2. Losing pitcher—Turbeville. Umpires—Summers and Johnston. Time of game—2:34.

May 25, 1936

INDIANS' ROOKIE FANS 15 TO SCORE

Feller, 17, Is One Short of Modern League Record in Subduing Browns, 4-1.

TROSKY SMASHES 4 HITS

CLEVELAND, Aug. 23 (AP).—Seventeen-year-old Bob Feller, making his first start for Cleveland, fanned fifteen batters in pitching the Indians to a 4-to-1 victory over the Browns today.

Feller's strike-out was one short of the modern American League record, set by Rube Waddell of Philadelphia in 1908, and two short of Dizzy Dean's National League record set in 1933.

The Adelle, Iowa, rookie, who vaulted into the headlines when he struck out eight Cardinals in three innings during an exhibition game on July 6, restricted the Gashouse Gang's fellow townsmen to six hits. He held St. Louis scoreless except in the sixth inning, when Lyn Lary doubled and Roy (Beau) Bell followed suit.

Hal Trosky led the Indian attack, wtih four hits. Cleveland reached three pitchers for nine hits and put over three runs in the sixth and one in the seventh inning.

The box score:

ST. LOUIS (A.)	ab.	r.	h.	po.	a.	e.
Lary, ss	4	1	1	2	3	0
Clift, 3b.	2	0	1	2	1	0
Solters, lf.	4	0	0	0	0	0
Bell, rf.	4	0	2	1	0	0
West, cf.	4	0	0	0	0	0
Bottomley, 1b.	3	0	1	7	1	0
Bejma, 3b.	4	0	1	1	2	1
Guillani, c.	4	0	1	6	1	0
Caldwell, p.	2	0	0	3	3	0
aColeman	1	0	0	0	0	0
Van Atta, p.	1	0	0	0	0	0
Liebhardt, p.	0	0	0	0	0	0
bPepper	1	0	0	0	0	0
Total	**33**	**1**	**6**	**24**	**11**	**1**

CLEVELAND (A.)	ab.	r.	h.	po.	a.	e.
Hughes, 2b.	4	1	1	0	1	1
Hale, 3b.	2	1	0	1	0	0
Averill, cf.	3	1	1	1	0	0
Trosky, 1b.	4	1	4	5	0	0
Weatherly, rf.	3	0	2	0	0	0
Vosmik, lf.	4	0	1	1	0	0
George, c.	4	0	1	15	1	0
Knickrbckr, ss.	4	0	0	1	0	0
Feller, p.	3	0	1	0	0	0
Total	**31**	**4**	**9**	**27**	**4**	**1**

aBatted for Caldwell in seventh.
bBatted for Liebhardt in ninth.

St. Louis ....0 0 0 0 0 1 0 0 0—1
Cleveland ....0 0 0 0 0 3 1 0 x—4

Runs batted in—Trosky 2, Vosmik 3, Bell. Two-base hits—Lary, Bell, Trosky. Stolen base—Clift. Double play—Caldwell and Lary. Left on bases—St. Louis 9, Cleveland 7. Bases on balls—Off Caldwell 3, Van Atta 1, Feller 4. Struck out—By Caldwell 4, Van Atta 1, Feller 15. Hits—Off Caldwell 6 in 6 innings, Van Atta 2 in 1, Liebhardt 1 in 1. Wild pitch—Feller. Losing pitcher—Caldwell. Umpires—Geisel, Ormsby and Basil. Time of game—2:20.

August 24, 1936

Hubbell Adds No. 24 to String

Giants Capture Sixth in a Row, Ott's Home Run Beating Reds, 3-2

Wallop in Ninth Wins for Hubbell, Who Succeeds Coffman With Score Tied—Mel Also Drives Triple—Bartell Gets Two Doubles—Victors One Game Behind Pirates

By JOHN DREBINGER
Special to THE NEW YORK TIMES.

CINCINNATI, May 27.—Unexpectedly entering a fray which in the beginning was not at all of his choosing, Carl Hubbell today came up with his twenty-fourth consecutive National League victory in a two-year string as the Giants, riding handsomely on the crest of Melvin Ott's seventh homer of the year, brought down the Reds, 3 to 2.

The famous Hub came into the game in the last half of the eighth with the score deadlocked at 2-all, and with no more effort than one would employ in dusting off a shelf, he retired three Reds on infield grounders.

In the upper half of the ninth he sat placidly in the Giant dugout as his no less distinguished roommate, Master Melvin, swung desperately at the slanting shoots served up by the left-handed Lee Grissom. Earlier in the day Mel had cracked a triple off the screening in front of the right-field bleachers, and so the odds were slightly against him on this occasion.

Ball Flies Over 400 Feet

But there is a strange bond of comradeship among these older Giants who date back to the days of John J. McGraw, and Mel swung with tremendous fervor. The result was a towering smash that cleared the screening and dropped into the bleachers more than 400 feet from the plate.

Presently the Giants' inning ended with no further scoring and Hubbell sedately marched out to the mound. He retired three more Reds, this time on pop flies, and it was over. It was as easy as that.

For the screwball maestro it marked his eighth successive pitching victory of 1937 against not a single setback, and this, added to the sixteen straight with which he concluded the 1936 campaign, gives him the amazing all-time mark.

It was also only the second time in this unprecedented string that saw Hubbell receive credit for a game in which he did not start.

Triumph Completes Series Sweep

The victory gave the Giants a clean sweep of the three-game series with the Reds and ran their winning streak to six as they headed back tonight toward the East. It also left them only one game behind the league-leading Pirates, whose game with the Dodgers was called off.

Sharing the spotlight with the spectacular team of Hubbell and Ott was Dashing Dick Bartell, whose bat exploded a pair of doubles which drove in the other two Giant tallies, the second one tying the score in the eighth.

Hal Schumacher started the game on the mound for the Giants and for four innings had a no-hit, no-run effort on the wing. A single by Whitehead and Bartell's first double had given Schumie a one-run lead in the third.

The first Red hit did not come until two had been retired in the fifth. Lew Riggs pumped a blow to right that went for two bases because Ott returned the ball to first instead of second.

Five Hits Rout Schumacher

In the sixth the Reds staged a strenuous uprising that might have been more damaging but for some sleepy work on the bases. Alex Kampouris opened with a double, only to get caught off the bag by the alert Gus Mancuso and Bartell. But after Grissom grounded out, Harvey Walker, Kiki Cuyler, Ival Goodman and Baxter Jordan weighed in with successive line singles that scored two runs and drove Schumie to cover.

Dick Coffman held the Reds in check until he vacated for a pinch hitter in the eighth, when doubles by Whitehead and Bartell tied the score.

After that it was just a case of the old master stepping up, chalking his cue and continuing his unbroken run.

May 28, 1937

The Box Score

NEW YORK (N.)	ab.	r.	h.	po.	a.	e.
Bartell, ss.	4	0	2	4	3	0
Chiozza, 3b.	3	0	0	0	0	0
aDanning	1	0	0	0	0	0
Hubbell, p.	0	0	0	0	1	0
J. Moore, lf.	4	0	1	2	0	0
Ripple, cf.	4	0	1	1	0	0
G. Davis, cf.	0	0	0	1	0	0
Ott, rf.	3	1	2	4	0	0
Mancuso, c.	4	0	1	4	2	0
McC'thy, 1b.	3	0	0	10	0	0
Wh'head, 2b.	4	2	2	1	3	0
Sch'cher, p.	2	0	0	0	0	0
Coffman, p.	0	0	0	0	0	0
Haslin, 3b.	1	0	0	0	2	0
Total	33	3	9	27	11	0

aBatted for Chiozza in eighth.

CINCINNATI (N.)	ab.	r.	h.	po.	a.	e.
Walker, lf.	4	1	1	1	0	0
Cuyler, cf.	4	1	1	3	0	0
Goodman, rf.	4	0	1	3	0	0
V. Davis, c.	4	0	0	5	3	0
Riggs, 3b.	3	0	1	0	2	0
Myers, ss.	3	0	1	3	4	0
K'pouris, 2b.	3	0	1	1	5	0
Grissom, p.	3	0	0	0	1	0
Total	32	2	7	27	15	0

```
New York.................0 0 1  0 0 0  0 1 1—3
Cincinnati...............0 0 0  0 0 2  0 0 0—2
```

Runs batted in—Bartell 2, Ott, Goodman, Jordan.

Two-base hits—Bartell 2, Whitehead, Riggs, Kampouris. Three-base hit—Ott. Home run—Ott. Sacrifices—McCarthy, Haslin. Double play—Bartell, Whitehead and McCarthy. Left on bases—New York 6, Cincinnati 3. Bases on balls—Off Grissom 1, Struck out—By Schumacher 4, Grissom 5. Hits—Off Schumacher 6 in 5 2-3 innings, Coffman 1 in 1 1-3, Hubbell 0 in 2. Winning pitcher—Hubbell. Umpires—Ballanfant, Klem and Sears. Time of game—1:57.

YORK, TIGERS, SETS HOME-RUN RECORD

Clips Ruth Mark With Nos. 17 and 18 in a Month in 12-3 Conquest of Senators

RUDY HITS IN SEVEN RUNS

He and Gehringer Have Perfect Day at Bat—Lawson Hurls 17th Triumph

DETROIT, Aug. 31 (P).—Rookie Rudy York, hitting his twenty-ninth and thirtieth home runs of the season, topped one of Babe Ruth's records today as he led the Tigers in a 12-to-3 victory over Washington.

Ruth hit seventeen homers in a single month in September, 1927. York's two circuit smashes over the scoreboard at Navin Field were his seventeenth and eighteenth during August.

In addition, York collected two singles for a perfect day at bat, and drove in seven runs. Two

Times Wide World
RUDY YORK

mates, were on base when York hit each homer, one in the first and another in the sixth. Pete Fox, Detroit right fielder, hit one over the left field fence with the bases empty in the sixth.

Charlie Gehringer, the American League's leading batsman, also had a perfect record at the plate with a double and two singles. Gehringer walked twice and York once.

Both of York's home runs were hit off Pete Appleton, the Senators' starting pitcher. Roxie Lawson, who won his seventeenth game of the season, gave eleven safeties, but scattered them through every inning, and left thirteen Washington runners stranded.

The box score:

WASHINGTON (A.)	ab.	r.	h.	po.	a.	e.
Almada, cf.	5	0	2	3	0	1
Lewis, 3b.	5	1	2	3	6	0
Travis, ss.	4	1	0	2	0	1
Stone, rf.	3	0	2	0	1	0
Kuhel, 1b.	5	0	1	10	1	0
Myer, 2b.	4	0	2	0	0	0
Simmons, lf.	2	0	1	0	0	0
aSington, lf.	2	1	0	2	0	0
R. Ferrell, c.	4	0	0	6	1	0
Appleton, p.	3	0	1	0	3	0
bMilles, c.	1	0	0	0	0	0
Jacobs, p.	0	0	0	0	0	0
Total	33	3	11	24	14	1

aRan for Simmons in fourth.
bBatted for Appleton in eighth.

DETROIT (A.)	ab.	r.	h.	po.	a.	e.
Walker, lf.	5	2	1	4	0	0
Fox, rf.	4	2	2	1	0	1
G'ringer, 2b.	3	3	3	2	4	0
Greenb'g, 1b.	5	1	2	8	1	0
York, c.	4	2	4	3	0	0
Laabs, cf.	3	0	0	5	0	0
Owen, 3b.	5	0	0	1	0	0
Gelbert, ss.	4	1	1	3	3	0
Lawson, p.	3	1	1	0	2	0
Total	36	12	14	27	10	1

```
Washington ..............1 0 1  1 0 0  0 0 0— 3
Detroit .................3 0 0  4 0 4  1 0.—12
```

Runs batted in—York 7, Gehringer 2, Fox 2, Greenberg, Almada, Kuhel. Two-base hits—Walker, Simmons, Lawson, Gehringer, Lewis. Three-base hit—Myer. Home runs—York 2, Fox. Stolen bases—Gehringer 2, Walker. Sacrifice—Lawson. Left on bases—Washington 13, Detroit 8. Bases on balls—Off Lawson 5, Appleton 6, Jacobs 1. Struck out—By Lawson 3, Appleton 13, Jacobs 1. Hits—Off Appleton 13 in 7 innings, Jacobs 1 in 1. Balk—Lawson. Losing pitcher—Appleton. Umpires—Summers, Geisel and Basil. Time of game—2:00.

September 1, 1937

40,000 See Vander Meer of Reds Hurl Second No-Hit, No-Run Game in Row

DODGERS BOW, 6-0, IN NIGHT INAUGURAL

Vander Meer, Reds' Ace, Makes Baseball History — Hitless String Now 18⅓ Innings

FILLS BASES IN THE NINTH

But Completes Feat Unscathed at Ebbets Field—Fans Rush to Acclaim Young Hurler

By ROSCOE McGOWEN

Last night they turned on the greatest existing battery of baseball lights at Ebbets Field for the inaugural night major league game

in the metropolitan area. A record throng for the season there, 40,000, of whom 38,748 paid, came to see the fanfare and show that preceded the contest between the Reds and the Dodgers.

The game, before it was played, was partly incidental; the novelty of night baseball was the major attraction.

But Johnny Vander Meer, tall, handsome 22-year-old Cincinnati southpaw pitcher, stole the entire show by hurling his second successive no-hit, no-run game, both coming within five days, and making baseball history that probably never will be duplicated. His previous no-hitter was pitched in daylight at Cincinnati last Saturday against the Bees, the Reds winning, 3—0. Last night the score was 6—0.

The records reveal only seven pitchers credited with two no-hitters in their careers and none who achieved the feat in one season.

More drama was crowded into the final inning than a baseball crowd has felt in many a moon. Until that frame only one Dodger had got as far as second base, Lavagetto reaching there when Johnny issued passes to Cookie and Dolf Camilli in the seventh.

But Vandy pitched out of that easily enough and the vast crowd

was pulling for him to come through to the end.

The Crucial Inning

Johnny mowed down Woody English, batting for Luke Hamlin; Kiki Cuyler and Johnny Hudson in the eighth, fanning the first and third men, and when Vito Tamulis, fourth Brooklyn hurler, treated the Reds likewise in the ninth, Vandy came out for the crucial inning.

He started easily, taking Buddy Hassett's bounder and tagging him out. Then his terrific speed got out of control and, while the fans sat forward tense and almost silent, walked Babe Phelps, Lavagetto and Camilli to fill the bases.

All nerves were taut as Vandy pitched to Ernie Koy. With the count one and one, Ernie sent a bounder to Lew Riggs, who was so careful in making the throw to Ernie Lombardi that a double play wasn't possible.

Leo Durocher, so many times a hitter in the pinches, was the last hurdle for Vander Meer, and the crowd groaned as he swung viciously to line a foul high into the right-field stands. But a moment later Leo swung again, the ball arched lazily toward short center field and Harry Craft camped under it for the put-out that brought unique distinction to the young hurler.

The box score:

CINCINNATI (N.)	ab.	r.	h.	po.	a.	e.
Frey, 2b	5	0	1	2	2	0
Berger, lf	5	1	3	3	0	0
Goodman, rf	3	2	1	3	0	0
McC'mick, 1b	5	1	1	9	1	0
Lombardi, c	3	1	0	9	0	0
Craft, cf	5	0	3	1	0	0
Riggs, 3b	4	0	1	0	3	0
Myers, ss	4	0	0	0	1	0
V. Meer, p	4	1	1	2	4	0
Total	**38**	**6**	**11**	**27**	**11**	**0**

BROOKLYN (N.)	ab.	r.	h.	po.	a.	e.
Cuyler, rf	2	0	0	1	0	0
Coscarart, 2b	2	0	0	1	2	0
aBrack	1	0	0	0	0	0
Hudson, 2b	1	0	0	1	0	0
Hassett, lf	4	0	0	3	0	0
Phelps, c	3	0	0	9	0	0
bRosen	0	0	0	0	0	0
Lavagetto, 3b	2	0	0	2	2	
Koy, cf	4	0	0	4	0	0
Durocher, ss	4	0	0	1	2	0
Butcher, p	0	0	0	0	1	0
Pressnell, p	2	0	0	0	0	0
Hamlin, p	0	0	0	0	1	0
cEnglish	1	0	0	0	0	0
Tamulis, p	0	0	0	0	0	0
Total	**27**	**0**	**0**	**27**	**8**	**2**

aBatted for Coscarat in sixth.
bRan for Phelps in ninth.
cBatted for Hamlin in eighth.

Cincinnati ....0 0 4 0 0 0 1 1 0—6
Brooklyn ....0 0 0 0 0 0 0 0 0—0

Runs batted in—McCormick 3, Riggs, Craft, Berger.
Two-base hit—Berger. Three-base hit—Berger. Home run—McCormick. Stolen base—Goodman. Left on bases—Cincinnati 9, Brooklyn 8. Bases on balls—Off Butcher 3, Vander Meer 8, Hamlin 1. Struck out—By Butcher 1, Pressnell 3, Vander Meer 7, Hamlin 3. Hits—Off Butcher 5 in 2 2-3, Hamlin 2 in 1 2-3, Pressnell 4 in 3 2-3, Tamulis 0 in 1. Losing pitcher—Butcher. Umpires—Stewart, Stark and Barr. Time of game—2:22.

It brought, also, a horde of admiring fans onto the field, with Vandy's team-mates ahead of them to hug and slap Johnny on the back and then to protect him from the

EBBETS FIELD UNDER THE FLOODLIGHTS DURING ITS FIRST NIGHT GAME

Times Wide World

mob as they struggled toward the Red dugout.

The fans couldn't get Johnny, but a few moments later they got his father and mother, who had accompanied a group of 500 citizens from Vandy's home town of Midland Park, N. J. The elder Vander Meers were completely surrounded and it required nearly fifteen minutes before they could escape.

Enhances His Record

The feat ran the youngster's re-markable pitching record to eighteen and one-third hitless and scoreless innings and a string of twenty-six scoreless frames. This includes a game against the Giants, his no-hitter against the Bees and last night's game.

Vander Meer struck out seven Dodgers, getting pinch hitters twice, and of the eight passes he issued two came in the seventh and three in the tense ninth.

Added to his speed was a sharp-breaking curve that seldom failed to break over the plate and at which the Dodger batsmen swung as vainly as at his fireball.

On the offense, well-nigh forgot-ten as the spectacle of Vander Meer's no-hitter unfolded, the Reds made victory certain as early as the third frame, when they scored four times and drove Max Butcher away.

Frank McCormick hit a home run into the left-field stands with Wally Berger and Ival Goodman aboard, while a pass to Lombardi and singles by Craft and Riggs added the fourth run.

Craft's third straight single scored Goodman in the seventh, the lat-ter's blow off Tot Pressnell's right kneecap knocking the knuckleball-er out and causing him to be car-ried off on a stretcher. Berger tripled off Luke Hamlin in the eighth to score Vander Meer with the last run.

June 16, 1938

GREENBERG DRIVES HOMERS 57 AND 58

Detroit Star Needs Three In Five Remaining Games to Eclipse Ruth's Record

---

TIGERS WIN DOUBLE BILL

Turn Back Browns by 5 to 4 and 10 to 2—Hank Collects Both Blows in Nightcap

---

By The Associated Press.

DETROIT, Sept. 27.—Hank Green-berg, distance-clouting first base-man of the Tigers, poled two tremendous drives to center for his fifty-seventh and fifty-eighth home runs of the season today as Detroit swept a double-header with the Browns, 5 to 4 and 10 to 2.

With five games left to play, Greenberg is within striking dis-tance of Babe Ruth's 1927 major league record of sixty homers in a single season.

Today's two circuit blows, hit off Pitcher Bill Cox in the first and third innings of the abbreviated nightcap, marked the eleventh time this season Greenberg has hit two or more round-trippers in a single game, thus bettering his own big league record for that feat. Dark-ness halted the second game after seven innings.

Greenberg's first homer was a 440-foot liner inside the park, and Hank had to slide home to beat the relay from center. Mark Christ-man, Detroit third baseman, hit a home run inside the park in the first game, and Dixie Walker and Charlie Gehringer also connected. Gehringer's was his twentieth of the season.

The box scores:

FIRST GAME

ST. LOUIS (A.)	ab. r. h. po. a. e	DETROIT (A.)	ab. r. h. po. a. e
Almada, cf.	4 0 1 1 0 0	Morgan, cf.	5 0 0 0 0 0
McQuinn, 1b	4 0 1 8 0 0	Walker, lf.	5 2 2 1 0 0
Mazzera, lf.	5 1 1 3 0 0	Gehr'ger, 2b	2 1 0 3 7 0
Clift, 3b	4 1 1 1 1 0	Gre'nb'g, 1b	0 1 0 1 0 0
Grace, rf.	5 1 2 4 0 0	Fox, rf.	4 0 2 3 0 0
Kress, ss.	5 0 1 2 2 1	Rogell, ss.	3 1 0 6 3 0
Sullivan, c.	2 1 2 4 1 1	Tebbetts, c.	4 0 1 4 0 0
Heffner, 2b.	3 0 1 1 2 0	Ch'stm'n, 3b.	3 1 1 1 1 0
Walkup, p.	3 0 2 0 2 0	Benton, p.	3 0 0 1 1 0
aBell	1 0 0 0 0 0	Lawson, p.	2 0 0 1 2 0
Johnson, p.	0 0 0 0 0 1		
Total	36 4 12 24 8 3	Total	31 5 7 27 14 0

aBatted for Walkup in eighth.

St. Louis ...... 0 0 0 2 0 2 0 0 1—4
Detroit .... 2 2 0 0 0 0 0 1 .—5

Runs batted in—Greenberg, Fox, Christman, Walker, Kress, Sullivan 2, Heffner.

Home runs—Christman, Walker. Stolen bases—Sullivan, Rogell. Sacrifice—Heffner. Double plays—Gehringer, Rogell and Greenberg; Rogell and Greenberg. Left on bases—St. Louis 11, Detroit 9. Bases on balls—Off Walkup 5, Johnson 2, Benton 2, Lawson 3. Struck out—By Walkup 2, Lawson 2. Hits—Off Walkup 6 in 7 innings, John-son 1 in 1, Benton 9 in 5 2-3, Lawson 3 in 3 1-3. Passed ball—Tebbetts. Winning pitcher—Lawson. Losing pitcher—Johnson. Umpires—Hubbard, Rom-mell and Kolls. Time of game—2:10.

SECOND GAME

ST. LOUIS (A.)	ab. r. h. po. a. e	DETROIT (A.)	ab. r. h. po. a. e
Almada, cf.	4 0 1 1 0 0	Morgan, cf.	3 1 0 6 0 0
M'Quinn, 1b.	4 0 1 10 0 0	Walker, lf.	4 2 2 2 0 0
Mazzera, lf.	2 0 1 0 0 0	Geh'ger, 2b.	3 2 1 2 1 0
M'Quin, lf.	1 0 0 4 0 0	Gr'nberg, 1b.	4 2 2 2 1 0
Clift, 3b.	2 0 0 1 0 0	Fox, rf.	4 1 1 2 0 0
Lu'dello, 3b.	1 1 1 0 0 0	Rorell, ss.	4 0 0 2 3 0
Grace, rf.	4 1 1 3 2 0	Tebbetts, c.	4 0 1 4 0 0
Kress, ss.	4 0 0 1 3 1	Ch'tman, 3b.	3 1 1 1 0 0
Ha'shany, c.	4 0 1 2 0 0	Coffman, p.	3 0 0 1 0 0
Heffner, 2b.	3 0 0 0 5 0		
Cox, p.	2 0 0 2 0 0	Total	31 10 9 21 5 0
aBell	0 0 0 0 0 0		
Cole, p.	0 0 0 0 0 0		
Total	29 2 8 21 10 2		

aBatted for Cox in sixth.

St. Louis .... 0 0 0 0 0 1 1—2
Detroit .... 2 2 3 0 0 0 3 .—10

Runs batted in—Greenberg 4, Christman, Coff-man, Gehringer 3, Heffner, Grace.

Two-base hit—Lucadello. Three-base hit—Christ-man. Home runs—Greenberg 2, Gehringer. Dou-ble play—Heffner, Kress and McQuinn. Left on bases—St. Louis 10, Detroit 2. Bases on balls—Off Cox 1, Cole 1, Coffman 4. Struck out—By Coffman 3. Hits—Off Cox 7 in 5 innings, Cole 2 in 2. Losing pitcher—Cox. Umpires—Rommel, Kolls and Hubbard. Time of game—1:40.

September 28, 1938

Hartnett's Homer With 2 Out in 9th Beats Pirates

CUBS HALT PIRATES FOR 9TH IN ROW, 6-5

34,465 See Chicago Supplant Losers in League Lead With a Half-Game Advantage

---

ROOT WINS IN RELIEF ROLE

By The Associated Press.

CHICAGO, Sept. 28.—In the thick-ening gloom, with the score tied and two out in the ninth inning to-day, red-faced Gabby Hartnett blasted a home run before 34,465 cheering fans to give his Cubs a dramatic 6-to-5 victory over the Pirates and a half-game lead in the furious National League pen-nant battle.

That is the story of one of the most sensational games ever played at Wrigley Field—a game which saw the fighting Chicagoans charge from behind to knot the score and then win on a slashing drive to the left field bleachers to oust Pitts-burgh from the No. 1 position it had held since July 12.

Hartnett's smash, against Mace Brown with the count two strikes and no balls, probably saved the Cub pennant chances. Had he failed, the game would have been called because of darkness, neces-sitating a double bill tomorrow which would have almost insur-mountably handicapped the over-taxed Cub pitching staff.

The Chicago manager, whose team was nine games out of first place a little more than a month ago, had to fight his way through a swirling, hysterical mob to touch all the bases and had trouble reach-ing the dugout. He called the vic-tory and his homer "the two greate-est things that ever happened to me."

Bryant Driven to Cover

A hit and two errors helped the Cubs to a run in the second and, with Clay Bryant pitching master-fully, they stayed in front until the sixth. Then the Pirates, combin-ing Johnny Rizzo's twenty-first homer of the season with two other hits and a pair of walks, chased Bryant with a three-run blast. Jack Russell replaced him.

The Bruins came roaring right back to score in their half of the inning on doubles by Hart-nett and Rip Collins and a bunt which Billy Jurges beat out.

In the seventh a furiously dis-puted double play pulled the Cubs out of another hole. The Pirates charged Vance Page, who had re-placed Russell, had committed a balk on the pitch Rizzo hit into the double killing, but succeeded only in using up time as darkness gath-ered.

Battling desperately, the Corsairs went back to work in the eighth. Arky Vaughan walked and Gus Suhr singled. Larry French re-placed Page. Heinie Manush bat-ted for Pep Young and singled, scoring Vaughan.

Big Bill Lee, who had finished yesterday's game, went in for French and was greeted by Lee Handley's single which scored Suhr. Manush was nailed at the plate when Al Todd grounded to Jurges, but after wild pitching Handley to third, Lee restored order by forcing Bob Klinger to hit into a double play.

Collins opened the Cub eighth with a single which sent Klinger to the showers, Bill Swift taking his place. Jurges walked and Tony Lazzeri, former Yankee star, slashed a pinch double to right, scoring Collins and putting Jurges on third.

Stan Hack was passed and Billy Herman singled, sending in Jurges with the tying run. However, on the play Joe Marty, running for Lazzeri, was out at the plate, Paul Waner to Todd. Mace Brown replaced Swift and forced Frank Demaree to hit into a double play.

Charlie Root pitched for the Cubs in the ninth and held the Pirates to a single by Paul Waner. Phil Cavarretta and Carl Reynolds were easy outs before Hartnett won the battle and put his team on top for the first time since June 8. It was the Cubs' ninth straight victory and their nineteenth in their last twenty-two games.

Tomorrow, in the concluding game of a thrill-packed series, Lee will be Hartnett's pitching hope, with the jittery Pirates banking on Russ Bauers.

The box score:

PITTSBURGH (N.)	ab.	r.	h.	po.	a.	e.		CHICAGO (N.)	ab.	r.	h.	po.	a.	e.
L.Waner, rf	4	1	0	2	1	0		Hack, 3b	3	0	0	3	1	0
P.Waner, rf	5	0	2	3	1	1		Herman, 2b	5	0	3	2	2	0
Rizzo, lf	4	1	1	1	0	0		Demaree, rf	5	0	2	0	0	0
Vaughan, ss	2	2	1	2	5	1		Cavarretta, rf	5	0	0	2	0	0
Suhr, 1b	3	2	1	5	0	0		Reynolds, cf	5	0	1	5	0	0
Young, 2b	2	0	0	1	1	0		Hartnett, c	4	2	3	4	1	0
aManush	1	0	1	0	0	0		Collins, 1b	4	1	3	8	5	0
Thevenow, 2b	0	0	0	1	3	0		Jurges, ss	3	1	1	4	4	0
Handley, 3b	5	0	3	2	1	1		Bryant, p	2	0	1	0	0	0
Todd, c	4	0	0	9	2	1		Russell, p	0	0	0	0	0	0
Klinger, p	4	0	0	0	2	0		bO'Dea	1	0	0	0	0	0
Swift, p	0	0	0	0	0	0		Page, p	0	0	0	0	0	0
Brown, p	0	0	0	0	0	0		French, p	0	0	0	0	0	0
								Lee, p	0	0	0	0	0	0
								cLazzeri	1	0	1	0	0	0
								dMarty	0	0	0	0	0	0
								Root, p	0	0	0	0	0	0
Total	35	5	10	26	18	4		Total	38	6	12	27	9	0

*Two out when winning run scored.

aBatted for Young in eighth.
bBatted for Russell in sixth.
cBatted for Lee in eighth.
dRan for Lazzeri in eighth.

Pittsburgh .... 0 0 0 0 0 3 0 3 0—5
Chicago .... 0 1 0 0 0 2 0 2 1—6

Runs batted in—Manush, Rizzo, Handley 3, Hack, Herman, Collins, Hartnett, Lazzeri. Two-base hits—L.Waner, Hartnett, Collins, Lazzeri. Home runs—Rizzo, Hartnett. Double plays—Thevenow and Suhr; Jurges, Herman and Collins; Hack, Herman and Collins; Lee, Jurges and Collins. Left on bases—Pittsburgh 7, Chicago 10. Bases on balls—Off Klinger 2, Swift 2, Bryant 5, Page 1. Struck out—By Klinger 6, Bryant 1, Page 1. Hits—Off Klinger 8 in 7 innings (none out in eighth); French 0 in 1-3; Page 3 in 1 (none out in eighth); Lee 1 in 1; Root 1 in 1. Wild pitch—Lee. Passed ball—Todd. Winning pitcher—Root. Losing pitcher—Brown. Umpires—Barr, Stark, Goetz and Campbell. Time of game—2:37.

September 29, 1938

FELLER SETS MARK BY STRIKING OUT 18

But Indians Bow to Tigers, 4-1, 10-8—Greenberg Finishes With Homer Total 58

CLEVELAND, Oct. 2 (P).—Bob Feller, young Cleveland marvel, enhanced his fame today, but the Indians bowed twice to the Tigers, 4 to 1 and 10 to 8.

Feller fanned eighteen batters in the opener to topple the major league record for strike-outs in one game, but couldn't pull the game out of the fire.

In 1937 Feller fanned seventeen Athletics to set an American League record and tie Dizzy Dean, who was then with the Cardinals, for the major league mark.

Feller's eighteenth victim today was Chet Laabs, who struck out for the fifth time in the ninth. He fanned Pete Fox twice, McCoy twice, Hank Greenberg twice, Tony Piet once, Mark Christman three times and his mound rival, Harry Eisenstat, three times.

Bob allowed seven hits, walked seven men and hit Piet. Detroit scored twice in the seventh on Greenberg's double, Roy Cullenbine's single and George Tebbetts's double. Two walks, a sacrifice and Christman's single gained the other two Detroit runs. There were two men on base when Feller fanned Laabs for strike-out No. 18. He disregarded the runners and pitched with a full wind-up.

Today's feat raised Feller's strike-out total for the season to 240, which leads both major leagues in that department, and gave him a margin of fifteen over Buck Newsom of the Browns, who fanned ten today for a total of 225.

Eisenstat held the Indians scoreless until the ninth of the opener, allowing only four hits.

Greenberg failed to hit a homer and finished the season with fifty-eight, two under Babe Ruth's mark.

The box scores:

FIRST GAME

DETROIT (A.)	ab.	r.	h.	po.	a.	e.		CLEVELAND (A.)	ab.	r.	h.	po.	a.	e.
McCoy, 2b	5	0	0	1	3	1		Irwin, ss	3	0	0	0	1	0
Fox, rf	5	0	0	0	0	0		Witherly, cf	4	0	1	0	0	1
Cullenbine, lf	4	2	3	4	0	0		Campbell, rf	4	1	1	1	0	0
Greenberg, 1b	3	1	2	11	0	0		Heath, lf	3	1	0	0	0	0
Tebbetts, c	4	1	2	6	0	0		Grimes, 1b	4	2	2	7	0	0
Laabs, cf	5	0	2	3	0	0		Heffner, 2b	4	0	0	4	1	0
Piet, 3b	3	0	0	2	0	0		Pytlak, c	4	0	1	3	0	0
Christman, ss	4	0	1	3	1	0		Grimes, 2b	3	0	0	2	1	0
Eisenstat, p	4	0	1	0	4	0		Feller, p	3	0	0	0	1	0
Total	33	4	7	27	9	1		Total	30	1	4	27	3	0

Detroit .... 0 0 0 0 0 2 0 2 0—4
Cleveland .... 0 0 0 0 0 0 0 0 1—1

Runs batted in—Tebbetts 2, Christman 2, Trosky. Two-base hits—Greenberg, Tebbetts. Stolen bases—Cullenbine, Piet. Sacrifice—Tebbetts. Double play—McCoy, Christman and Greenberg. Left on bases—Detroit 11, Cleveland 5. Bases on balls—Off Feller 7, Eisenstat 3. Struck out—By Feller 18, Eisenstat 3. Hit by pitcher—By Feller (Piet). Umpires—Hubbard, Grieve and Moriarty. Time of game—2:07.

SECOND GAME

DETROIT (A.)	ab.	r.	h.	po.	a.	e.		CLEVELAND (A.)	ab.	r.	h.	po.	a.	e.
McCoy, 2b	4	2	2	1	0	0		Irwin, ss	4	2	3	0	1	0
Fox, rf	4	1	2	0	0	0		Witherly, cf	4	0	1	3	0	1
Cullenbine, lf	3	2	1	1	0	0		Workman, lf	3	1	0	0	0	0
Greenberg, 1b	3	2	3	6	1	1		Heath, lf	3	1	1	0	0	0
Tebbetts, c	4	1	2	5	0	0		Grimes, 1b	4	2	2	7	0	0
Laabs, cf	3	0	1	2	0	0		Heffner	4	0	0	4	1	0
Piet, 3b	4	0	1	2	0	0		Webb, 3b	3	0	1	0	4	0
Christman, ss	3	0	1	2	1	0		Mack, 2b	4	2	2	5	4	0
Harris, p	3	1	1	2	3	0		Humphries, p	3	1	1	0	1	0
								Smith, p	3	0	0	0	1	0
Total	31	10	13	21	8	1		Total	32	8	11	21	12	2

Detroit .... 5 0 1 3 0 0 1—10
Cleveland .... 0 0 0 3 1 1 3— 8

Runs batted in—Laabs 4, Fox, Cullenbine, Greenberg, Tebbetts, Christman, Grimes 2, Mack 2, Weatherly, Heath. Two-base hits—McCoy, Fox. Three-base hits—Grimes, Mack. Stolen bases—Fox, Cullenbine. Double play—Irwin and Grimes. Left on bases—Detroit 3, Cleveland 7. Base on balls—Off Harris 4, Humphries 2, Smith 1. Struck out—Harris 4, Humphries 1, Smith 1. Hits—Off Humphries 5 in 1 inning, Smith 8 in 6. Wild pitch—Harris. Losing pitcher—Humphries. Umpires—Hubbard, Grieve and Moriarty. Time of game—1:57.

October 3, 1938

LOU, NOT HITTING, ASKS REST ON BENCH

Gehrig's String, Started June 1, 1925, Snapped as Yanks Start Series in Detroit

RETURN OF ACE INDEFINITE

By JAMES P. DAWSON
Special to THE NEW YORK TIMES.

DETROIT, May 2.—Lou Gehrig's matchless record of uninterrupted play in American League championship games, stretched over fifteen years and through 2,130 straight contests, came to an end today.

The mighty iron man, who at his peak had hit forty-nine home runs in a single season five years ago, took himself out of action before the Yanks marched on Briggs Stadium for their first game against the Tigers this year.

With the consent of Manager Joe McCarthy, Gehrig removed himself because he, better than anybody else, perhaps, recognized his competitive decline and was frankly aware of the fact he was doing the Yankees no good defensively or on the attack. He last played Sunday in New York against the Senators.

When Gehrig will start another game is undetermined. He will not be used as a pinch-hitter.

The present plan is to keep him on the bench. Relaxing and shaking off the mental hazards he admittedly has encountered this season, he may swing into action in the hot weather, which should have a beneficial effect upon his tired muscles.

Dahlgren Gets Chance

Meanwhile Ellsworth (Babe) Dahlgren, until today baseball's greatest figure of frustration, will continue at first base. Manager McCarthy said he had no present intention of transferring Tommy Henrich, the youthful outfielder whom he tried at first base at the Florida training camp. Dahlgren had been awaiting the summons for three years.

It was coincidental that Gehrig's string was broken almost in the presence of the man he succeeded as Yankee first baseman. At that time Wally Pipp, now a business man of Grand Rapids, Mich., was benched by the late Miller Huggins to make room for the strapping youth fresh from the Hartford Eastern League club to which the Yankees had farmed him for two seasons, following his departure from Columbia University. Pipp was in the lobby of the Book Cadillac Hotel at noon when the with-

Record of Gehrig's Streak

	G.	AB.	R.	H.	RBI.	HR.	PC.
1925....	*126	437	73	129	68	21	.295
1926....	155	572	135	179	107	16	.313
1927....	155	584	149	218	175	47	.373
1928....	154	562	139	210	142	27	.374
1929....	154	553	127	166	126	35	.300
1930....	154	581	143	220	174	41	.379
1931....	155	619	163	211	184	46	.341
1932....	156	596	138	208	151	34	.349
1933....	152	583	138	198	139	32	.334
1934....	154	579	128	210	165	49	.363
1935....	149	535	125	176	119	30	.329
1936....	155	579	167	205	152	49	.354
1937....	157	569	138	200	159	37	.351
1938....	157	576	115	170	114	29	.295
1939....	8	28	2	4	1	0	.143
Total ..	2,141	7,953	1,880	2,704	1,976	493	.340

*Includes eleven games before consecutive run started.

drawal of Gehrig was effected.

"I don't feel equal to getting back in there," Pipp said on June 2, 1925, the day Lou replaced him at first. Lou had started his phenomenal streak the day before as a pinch-hitter for Peewee Wanninger, then the Yankee shortstop.

This latest momentous development in baseball was not unexpected.

64

Bob Feller follows through on one of the pitches that brought him a no-hitter on the opening day of the 1940 season.

Hank Greenberg of the Detroit Tigers had 58 home runs with five games to go in the 1938 season. He hit no more that year and Babe Ruth's record of 60 was to stand for another 23 years.

Joe DiMaggio waits his turn at bat in the eighth inning at Cleveland. It's his last chance to extend his 56-game hitting streak. It ended here—he hit into a double play.

There had been signs for the past two years that Gehrig was slowing up. Even when a sick man, however, he gamely stuck to his chores, not particularly in pursuit of his all-time record of consecutive play, although that was a big consideration, but out of a driving desire to help the Yankees, always his first consideration.

Treated for Ailment

What Lou had thought was lumbago last year when he suffered pains in the back that more than once forced his early withdrawal from games he had started was diagnosed later as a gall bladder condition for which Gehrig underwent treatment all last Winter, after rejecting a recommendation that he submit to an operation.

The signs of his approaching fadeout were unmistakable this Spring at St. Petersburg, Fla., yet the announcement from Manager McCarthy was something of a shock. It came at the end of a conference Gehrig arranged immediately after McCarthy's arrival by plane from his native Buffalo.

"Lou just told me he felt it would be best for the club if he took himself out of the line-up," McCarthy said following their private talk. "I asked him if he really felt that way. He told me he was serious. He feels blue. He is dejected.

"I told him it would be as he wished. Like everybody else I'm sorry to see it happen. I told him not to worry. Maybe the warm weather will bring him around.

"He's been a great ball player.

Fellows like him come along once in a hundred years. I told him that. More than that, he's been a vital part of the Yankee club since he started with it. He's always been a perfect gentleman, a credit to baseball.

"We'll miss him. You can't escape that fact. But I think he's doing the proper thing."

Lou Explains Decision

Gehrig, visibly affected, explained his decision quite frankly.

"I decided last Sunday night on this move," said Lou. "I haven't been a bit of good to the team since the season started. It would not be fair to the boys, to Joe or to the baseball public for me to try going on. In fact, it would not be fair to myself, and I'm the last consideration.

"It's tough to see your mates on base, have a chance to win a ball game, and not be able to do anything about it. McCarthy has been swell about it all the time. He'd let me go until the cows came home, he is that considerate of my feelings, but I knew in Sunday's game that I should get out of there.

"I went up there four times with men on base. Once there were two there. A hit would have won the ball game for the Yankees, but I missed, leaving five stranded as the Yankees lost. Maybe a rest will do me some good. Maybe it won't. Who knows? Who can tell? I'm just hoping."

Gehrig's withdrawal from today's game does not necessarily mean the

end of his playing career, although that seems not far distant. When that day comes Gehrig can sit back and enjoy the fortune he has accumulated as a ball player. He is estimated to have saved $200,000 from his earnings, which touched a high in 1938, when he collected $39,000 as Yankee salary.

When Gehrig performed his duties as Yankee captain today, appearing at the plate to give the batting order, announcement was made through the amplifiers of his voluntary withdrawal and it was suggested he get "a big hand." A deafening cheer resounded as Lou walked to the dugout, doffed his cap and disappeared in a corner of the bench.

Open expressions of regret came from the Yankees and the Tigers. Lefty Vernon Gomez expressed the Yankees' feelings when he said:

"It's tough to see this thing happen, even though you know it must come to us all. Lou's a great guy and he's always been a great baseball figure. I hope he'll be back in there."

Hank Greenberg, who might have been playing first for the Yanks instead of the Tigers but for Gehrig, said: "Lou's doing the right thing. He's got to use his head now instead of his legs. Maybe that Yankee dynasty is beginning to crumble."

Scott Former Record Holder

Everett Scott, the shortstop who

held the record of 1,307 consecutive games until Gehrig broke it, ended his streak on May 6, 1925, while he was a member of the Yankees. However, Scott began his string, once considered unapproachable, with the Red Sox.

By a strange coincidence, Scott gave way to Wanninger, the player for whom Gehrig batted to start his great record.

With only one run batted in this year and a batting average of .143 representing four singles in twenty-eight times at bat, Lou has fallen far below his record achievements of previous seasons, during five of which he led the league in runs driven home.

Some of his more important records follow:

Most consecutive games—2,130.

Most consecutive years, 100 games or more—14.

Most years, 150 games or more—12.

Most years, 100 runs or more—13.

Most consecutive years, 100 runs or more—13.

Most home runs with bases full—23.

Most years, 300 or more total bases—13.

Most years, 100 runs or more driven in—13.

Most games by first baseman in one season—157.

Most home runs in one game—4 (modern record).

Most runs batted in, one season—184 (American League).

May 3, 1939

61,808 FANS ROAR TRIBUTE TO GEHRIG

Captain of Yankees Honored at Stadium—Calls Himself 'Luckiest Man Alive'

By JOHN DREBINGER

In perhaps as colorful and dramatic a pageant as ever was enacted on a baseball field, 61,808 fans thundered a hail and farewell to Henry Lou Gehrig at the Yankee Stadium yesterday.

To be sure, it was a holiday and there would have been a big crowd and plenty of roaring in any event. For the Yankees, after getting nosed out, 3 to 2, in the opening game of the double-header, despite a ninth-inning home run by George Selkirk, came right back in typical fashion to crush the Senators, 11 to 1, in the nightcap. Twinkletoes Selkirk embellished this contest with another home run.

But it was the spectacle staged between the games which doubtless never will be forgotten by those who saw it. For more than forty minutes there paraded in review two mighty championship hosts—the Yankees of 1927 and the current edition of Yanks who definitely are winging their way to a fourth straight pennant and a chance for another world title.

From far and wide the 1927 stalwarts came to reassemble for Lou Gehrig Appreciation Day and to pay their own tribute to their former comrade-in-arms who had carried on beyond all of them only to have his own brilliant career come to a tragic close when it was revealed that he had fallen victim of a form of infantile paralysis.

In conclusion, the vast gathering, sitting in absolute silence for a longer period than perhaps any baseball crowd in history, heard Gehrig himself deliver as amazing a valedictory as ever came from a ball player.

So shaken with emotion that at first it appeared he would not be able to talk at all, the mighty Iron Horse, with a rare display of that indomitable will power that had carried him through 2,130 consecutive games, moved to the microphone at home plate to express his own appreciation.

And for the final fadeout, there stood the still burly and hearty Babe Ruth alongside of Gehrig, their arms about each other's shoulders, facing a battery of camera men.

All through the long exercises Gehrig had tried in vain to smile, but with the irrepressible Bambino beside him he finally made it. The Babe whispered something to him and Lou chuckled. Then they both chuckled and the crowd roared and roared.

Late Rally Fails

The ceremonies began directly after the debris of the first game had been cleared away. There had been some vociferous cheering as the Yanks, fired to action by Selkirk's homer, tried to snatch that

opener away from the Senators in the last few seconds of the ninth. But they couldn't quite make it and the players hustled off the field.

Then, from out of a box alongside the Yankee dugout there spryly hopped more than a dozen elderly gentlemen, some gray, some shockingly baldish, but all happy to be on hand. The crowd recognized them at once, for they were the Yanks of 1927, not the first Yankee world championship team, but the first, with Gehrig an important cog in the machine, to win a world series in four straight games.

Down the field, behind Captain Sutherland's Seventh Regiment Band, they marched—Ruth, Bob Meusel, who had come all the way from California; Waite Hoyt, still maintaining his boyish countenance; Wally Schang, Benny Bengough, Tony Lazzeri, Mark Koenig, Jumping Joe Dugan, Bob Shawkey, Herb Pennock, Deacon Everett Scott, whose endurance record Gehrig eventually surpassed; Wally Pipp, who faded out as the Yankee first sacker the day Columbia Lou took over the job away back in 1925, and George Pipgras, now an umpire and, in fact, actually officiating in the day's games.

At the flagpole, these old Yanks raised the world series pennant they had won so magnificently from the Pirates in 1927 and, as they paraded back, another familiar figure streaked out of the dugout, the only one still wearing a Yankee uniform. It was the silver-haired Earle Combs, now a coach.

Old-Timers Face Plate

Arriving at the infield, the old-timers strung out, facing the plate. The players of both Yankee and Senator squads also emerged from

their dugouts to form a rectangle, and the first real ovation followed as Gehrig moved out to the plate to greet his colleagues, past and present.

One by one the old-timers were introduced with Sid Mercer acting as toastmaster. Clark Griffith, venerable white-haired owner of the Senators and a Yankee himself in the days when they were known as Highlanders, also joined the procession.

Gifts of all sorts followed. The Yankees presented their stricken comrade with a silver trophy measuring more than a foot and a half in height, their thoughts expressed in verse inscribed upon the base.

Manager Joe McCarthy, almost as visibly affected as Gehrig himself, made this presentation and hurried back to fall in line with his players. But every few minutes, when he saw that the once stalwart figure they called the Iron Horse was swaying on shaky legs, Marse Joe would come forward to give Lou an assuring word of cheer.

Mayor La Guardia officially extended the city's appreciation of the services Columbia Lou had given his home town.

"You are the greatest prototype of good sportsmanship and citizenship," said the Mayor, concluding with "Lou, we're proud of you."

Postmaster General Farley also was on hand, closing his remarks with "for generations to come, boys who play baseball will point with pride to your record."

When time came for Gehrig to address the gathering it looked as if he simply would never make it. He gulped and fought to keep back the tears as he kept his eyes fastened on the ground.

But Marse Joe came forward again, said something that might have been "come on, Lou, just rap out another," and somehow those magical words had the same effect as in all the past fifteen years when the gallant Iron Horse

Times Wide World

Members of previous great Yankee teams: Joe Dugan, Waite Hoyt, Herb Pennock, Benny Bengough, Wally Schang, Everett Scott, Wally Pipp, Babe Ruth, George Pipgras, Bob Meusel, Tony Lazzeri, Mark Koenig and Bob Shawkey grouped near flagpole in center field between games.

would step up to the plate to "rap out another."

Gehrig Speaks Slowly

He spoke slowly and evenly, and stressed the appreciation that he felt for all that was being done for him. He spoke of the men with whom he had been associated in his long career with the Yankees—the late Colonel Jacob Ruppert, the late Miller Huggins, his first manager, who gave him his start in New York; Edward G. Barrow, the present head of baseball's most powerful organization; the Yanks of old who now stood silently in front of him, as well as the players of to-day.

"What young man wouldn't give anything to mingle with such men, for a single day as I have for all these years?" he asked.

"You've been reading about my bad break for weeks now," he said. "But today I think I'm the luckiest man alive. I now feel more than ever that I have much to live for."

The gifts included a silver service set from the New York club, a fruit bowl and two candlesticks from the Giants, a silver pitcher from the Stevens Associates, two silver platters from the Stevens employes, a fishing rod and tackle from the Stadium employes and ushers, a silver

cup from the Yankee office staff, a scroll from the Old Timers Association of Denver that was presented by John Kieran, a scroll from Washington fans, a tobacco stand from the New York Chapter of the Baseball Writers Association of America, and the silver trophy from his team-mates.

The last-named present, about eighteen inches tall with a wooden base, supported by six silver bats with an eagle atop a silver ball, made Gehrig weep. President Barrow walked out to put his arms about Lou in an effort to steady him when this presentation was made. It appeared for an instant that Gehrig was near collapse.

On one side of the trophy were the names of all his present fellow-players. On the other was the following touching inscription:

TO LOU GEHRIG

We've been to the wars together,
We took our foes as they came,
And always you were the leader
And ever you played the game.

Idol of cheering millions,
Records are yours by the sheaves,
Iron of frame they hailed you,
Decked you with laurel leaves.

But higher than that we hold you,

We who have known you best,
Knowing the way you came
through
Every human test.

Let this be a silent token
Of lasting friendship's gleam,
And all that we've left unspoken,
Your pals of the Yankee team.

As Gehrig finished his talk, Ruth, robust, round and sun-tanned, was nudged toward the microphone and, in his own inimitable, blustering style, snapped the tears away. He gave it as his unqualified opinion that the Yanks of 1927 were greater than the Yanks of today, and seemed even anxious to prove it right there.

"Anyway," he added, "that's my opinion and while Lazzeri here pointed out to me that there are only about thirteen or fourteen of us here, my answer is, shucks, we only need nine to beat 'em."

Then, as the famous home-run slugger, who also has faded into baseball retirement, stood with his arms entwined around Gehrig's shoulders, the band played "I Love You Truly," while the crowd took up the chant: "We love you, Lou."

All Tributes Spontaneous

All given spontaneously, it was without doubt one of the most

touching scenes ever witnessed on a ball field and one that made even case-hardened ball players and chroniclers of the game swallow hard.

When Gehrig arrived in the Yankee dressing rooms he was so close to a complete collapse it was feared that the strain upon him had been too great and Dr. Robert E. Walsh, the Yankees' attending physician, hurried to his assistance. But after some refreshment, he recovered quickly and faithful to his one remaining task, that of being the inactive captain of his team, he stuck to his post in the dugout throughout the second game.

Long after the tumult and shouting had died and the last of the crowd had filed out, Lou trudged across the field for his familiar hike to his favorite exit gate. With him walked his bosom pal and teammate, Bill Dickey, with whom he always rooms when the Yanks are on the road.

Lou walks with a slight hitch in his gait now, but there was supreme confidence in his voice as he said to his friend:

"Bill, I'm going to remember this day for a long time."

So, doubtless, will all the others who helped make this an unforgettable day in baseball.

July 5, 1939

GAMES ARE TELEVISED

Major League Baseball Makes Its Radio Camera Debut

Major league baseball made its television debut here yesterday as the Dodgers and Reds battled through two games at Ebbets Field before two prying electrical "eyes" of station W2XBS in the Empire State Building. One "eye" or camera was placed near the visiting players' dugout, or behind the right-

hand batters' position. The other was in a second-tier box back of the catcher's box and commanded an extensive view of the field when outfield plays were made.

Over the video-sound channels of the station, television-set owners as far away as fifty miles viewed the action and heard the roar of the crowd, according to the National Broadcasting Company.

It was not the first time baseball was televised by the NBC. Last May at Baker Field a game between Columbia and Princeton was

caught by the cameras. However, to those who, over the television receivers, saw last May's contest as well as those yesterday, it was apparent that considerable progress has been made in the technical requirements and apparatus for this sort of outdoor pick-up, where the action is fast. At times it was possible to catch a fleeting glimpse of the ball as it sped from the pitcher's hand toward home plate.

August 27, 1939

Feller Opens Season With No-Hit Shutout

INDIANS' ACE BEATS WHITE SOX BY 1-0

Feller Is Only One in Modern Major League History to Hurl Opening No-Hitter

FANS EIGHT, WALKS FIVE

By The Associated Press.

CHICAGO, April 16—Bob Feller of the Indians carved a niche for himself in baseball's hall of fame as the American League season opened today, pitching an amazing no-hit game to defeat the White Sox, 1 to 0, before 14,000 roaring fans.

It was the first opening day no-hit contest in modern major league history. It ended after 2 hours and 24 minutes of play as Ray Mack, Cleveland second sacker, made a great knockdown of Taft Wright's grounder and tossed him out at first by a step.

Feller, who struck out eight batsmen and walked five, earned the decision on two timely Indian safeties in the fourth inning. Jeff Heath singled to left with one out, and after Ken Keltner had flied out, Heath scored on a triple to right by Feller's catcher and friend, Rollie Hemsley.

Three Earlier One-Hitters

It was Feller's first no-hitter, although he has had three one-hit performances in his brilliant major league career. The 21-year-old star won twenty-four games last season.

The White Sox, even though they enjoyed six-hit pitching by the southpaw Edgar Smith, threatened seriously only once. In the second they had the bases filled with two out. Feller, using his blazing fast ball, then struck out rookie Bob Kennedy.

Feller, who put on his great show before his parents, Mr. and Mrs. William Feller, and his sister, Marguerite, retired fifteen men in a row from the fourth inning through the eighth.

He got the first two men in the ninth easily, but Luke Appling, White Sox shortstop, gave him and the cheering fans several anxious moments. Appling drove four foul smashes to right before drawing a walk on the tenth pitch.

Nice Stop by Mack

Then Mack made his fine play on Wright's drive on the ground. The ball was to Mack's left and the infielder, with a fine stab, knocked it to the ground, picked up the rolling ball and shot it to First Baseman Hal Trosky for the putout.

The last no-hitter in the major leagues was hurled by Monte Pearson of the Yankees, who beat the Indians in the second game of a double-header in New York on Aug. 27, 1938.

The last no-hit game in Comiskey Park was pitched by Bill Dietrich in beating the Browns on June 1, 1937. Records show that Eddie Cicotte of the Sox pitched a no-hitter as early in the season as April 14, in 1917.

The box score:

CLEVELAND (A.)	ab.	r.	h.	po.	a.	e.		CHICAGO (A.)	ab.	r.	h.	po.	a.	e.
Boudreau, ss.	3	0	0	1	2	0		Kennedy, 3b.	4	0	0	1	2	0
Weatherly, cf	4	0	1	2	0	1		Kuhel, 1b.	3	0	0	11	0	0
Chapman, rf.	3	0	0	6	0	0		Kreevich, cf.	3	0	0	3	0	0
Trosky, 1b.	4	0	0	5	0	0		Solters, lf.	4	0	0	2	0	0
Heath, lf.	4	1	1	0	0	0		Appling, ss.	3	0	0	2	2	0
Keltner, 3b.	4	0	1	0	2	0		Wright, rf.	4	0	0	3	0	0
Hemsley, c.	4	0	2	8	0	0		McNair, 2b.	3	0	0	2	2	1
Mack, 2b.	4	0	1	2	3	0		Tresh, c.				2	0	5	0	0
Feller, p.	3	0	0	0	0	0		Smith, p.				1	0	0	2	0
								aRosenthal	1	0	0	0	0	0
								Brown, p.	0	0	0	0	1	0
Total	33	1	6	27	7	1		Total	28	0	0	27	9	1

aBatted for Smith in eighth.

Cleveland .... 0 0 0 1 0 0 0 0 0—1
Chicago .... 0 0 0 0 0 0 0 0 0—0

Run batted in—Hemsley.
Two-base hit—Mack. Three-base hit—Hemsley. Stolen base—Kuhel. Double play—Kuhel (unassisted). Left on bases—Cleveland 7, Chicago 6. Bases on balls—Off Feller 5, Smith 2. Struck out—By Feller 8, Smith 5. Hits—Off Smith 6 in 8 innings, Brown 0 in 1. Umpires—Geisel, McGowan and Kolls. Time of game—2:24. Attendance 14,000.

April 17, 1940

American League's 4-Run Rally in Ninth Tops National in All-Star Contest

WILLIAMS'S HOMER DECIDES 7-5 GAME

Ted's Hit With Two On, Two Out in Last of Ninth Wins for American League

VAUGHAN NATIONAL'S HERO

His Two 4-Baggers, All-Star Contest Mark, Tally 4 Runs —54,674 at Detroit

By JOHN DREBINGER

Special to THE NEW YORK TIMES.

DETROIT, July 8—Coming up with a last-minute electrifying charge that floored a foe at the very moment he appeared to have a signal triumph within his grasp, the American League snatched victory from defeat today. Scoring four runs in the last half of the ninth inning, the Harridge forces overcame the National League, 7 to 5, in the ninth annual All-Star game.

A blistering home-run smash by Ted Williams, lanky outfielder of the Red Sox, with two colleagues on base sent the final three tallies hurtling over the plate, while a crowd of 54,674, predominantly American League in its sympathies, acclaimed the shot with a thunderous roar.

Only a few moments before this blow landed with stunning and devastating force, the National League cohorts, led by Deacon Bill McKechnie, Reds' manager, appeared to have the battle tucked away.

Conflict Appears Ended

They had entered the final round leading by two runs, thanks to a pair of circuit blows by Arky Vaughan. When, with one out and the bases full, Claude Passeau, Chicago Cubs' pitcher, appeared to have induced the mighty Joe DiMaggio to slam vigorously into a double play, the contest, played for the benefit of the United Service Organizations, looked to be over.

But a rather hurried peg to first base by Billy Herman, Dodger second sacker, went a trifle wide of its mark and Jolting Joe escaped by a stride. It left Passeau still striving for one more out to clinch the struggle, but Claude never caught up with it. For a few seconds later Williams, leading batsman of the American League,

Ted Williams, whose circuit blow with two on won the game.

bashed the ball almost on a line against the upper parapet of the right-field stands of Briggs Stadium.

Thus the squad directed by Del Baker, Tiger pilot, brought to the American League its sixth triumph in the nine All-Star games played since 1933.

Up to the time of this culminating assault, however, the National Leaguers certainly looked to be riding high, wide and handsome. Joe DiMaggio, though his current forty-eight-game hitting streak was not at stake, nevertheless had to wait until the eighth inning before he lashed out with a double to save, at least, his prestige.

Employs 1940 Tactics

Resorting to much the same tactics that he employed at St. Louis a year ago when he fired the National League's vaunted pitching talent into the foe with bewildering rapidity for a shut-out victory, McKechnie, for the first six innings again hurled three crack moundsmen—Whitlow Wyatt, Paul Derringer and Bucky Walters—at the foe, each working only two innings apiece.

But in the home stretch, McKechnie veered from his course. Perhaps the two homers which Vaughan, the Pirate shortstop, had unleashed in the seventh and eighth innings, each with a man on base, lulled the National League skipper into a feeling of false security.

Bill permitted Passeau, who had entered the fray in the seventh, to remain on the mound through the ninth, and with this, by the margin of Williams's staggering clout, the wily Cincinnati leader overreached himself.

Passeau had seen one run shot.

away from him in the eighth when Joe DiMaggio unfurled his double for his first and only hit and presently scored when brother Dominic DiMaggio, who had entered the battle in its later stages, whistled a single to right.

This still lef' Passeau with a two-run margin. When Claude concluded the eighth by fanning the renowned Jimmy Foxx with two aboard the bases, McKechnie apparently saw no reason why the Chicago right-hander could not safely navigate through the ninth as well.

As the last of the ninth opened with Frank Hayes popping out, there still seemed no danger lurking around in the last few strides to the wire.

Pass Fills the Bases

But Ken Keltner, batting for Edgar Smith, the fourth and last American League hurler, bounced a single off Eddie Miller, the Braves' shortstop who had just replaced Vaughan in the field. Joe Gordon of the Yankees singled to right, and when Cecil Travis drew a pass, filling the bases, a feeling that something dramatic was about to come to pass gripped the crowd.

Joe DiMaggio stepped to the plate. But Joe's best was a grounder at Miller that just missed ending the struggle, but Herman's wide peg, though not an error, let in one tally and missed DiMaggio at first for what would have been the final out, and Williams did the rest.

Despite the early fine pitching efforts of Wyatt, Walters and Derringer, the National Leaguers also had to wait until the struggle moved well on its way before they assumed what promised to be a commanding lead. For during the first six rounds the American Leaguers likewise flashed some brilliant hurling.

Bobby Feller, youthful Cleveland ace and ranked as the foremost pitcher of his time, blazed through the first three rounds to face only nine men. He allowed one single and that was all. The hitter was trapped off first.

Then came the left-handed Thornton Lee of the White Sox to hurl the next three rounds and it was not until the sixth that the National Leaguers managed to break through with their first tally.

Walters sparked this one by banging a double to left, advancing to third on Stanley Hack's sacrifice and then skipping home on Terry Moore's long fly to Williams in left.

That matched the run which the American Leaguers had marked up in the fourth off Derringer, although the tally was scarcely big Paul's fault. Travis, crack third sacker of the Senators, had doubled with one out and moved to third on Joe DiMaggio's fly to deep right.

Catches Spikes in Turf

Williams then followed with a sharp liner toward right that seemed to be moving straight for where Bob Elliott, Pirate outfielder, was standing, for the third out. But Elliott momentarily misjudged the ball, rushed in a few steps, caught his spikes in the turf as he tried to back-track and wound up rather inelegantly sprawled on the grass. The ball shot over his head against the stand for a double and Travis scored.

However, though Walters managed to erase this run in the sixth, the American League went ahead again in the same inning by clipping Bucky for a tally. The Cincinnati ace right-hander paved the way for his own difficulties here by walking Joe DiMaggio and Jeff Heath, and then Lou Boudreau smacked a single to center, scoring DiMaggio.

In the seventh the tide veered sharply toward the National League legions. Sid Hudson, youthful right-hander of the Senators, came on to pitch for the American Leaguers and for a few minutes threatened to have himself annihilated.

Enos Slaughter, who had replaced the hapless Elliott in the McKechnie outfield, singled to left and grabbed an extra base when Williams stumbled over the ball for an error. The misplay, however, had no bearing on what followed, for Vaughan arched his first homer into the upper right tier of the grand stand.

Herman followed with a double and it promised another tally when Al Lopez deftly sacrificed Billy to third and Joe Medwick came up to bat for Walters. Just to show that seven long years scarcely tax the memory of a baseball fan, there was again a fine round of boos for Muscles Joe, who, as a Cardinal on this same field in the 1934 world series, had seen himself shelled from the arena with a barrage of vegetables.

But though Medwick tried hard to add a little more to the general discomfiture of his old friends, he grounded to the infield and Hudson luckily escaped without any further scoring being charged against him.

However, with the eighth, the National Leaguers jacked up their lead with another pair of runs and again it was the booming bat of Vaughan that jarred the opposition.

The southpaw Smith had supplanted Hudson on the mound as this round opened and fanned Pete Reiser for a starter. But Johnny Mize, silenced up to now, rifled a two-bagger to right. His Cardinal team-mate, Slaughter, struck out, but Vaughan again belted the ball into that inviting target offered by the upper right stand and the National lead was now 5 to 2.

Hero of the Hour

It marked the first time a player ever had managed to belt two homers in an All-Star game and Vaughan decidedly was the hero of the hour.

And he still was all of that until

Box Score of the Game

NATIONAL LEAGUE

	ab.	r.	h.	tb.	2b.	3b.	hr.	sh.	sb.	bb.	so.	po.	a.	e.
Hack, Chicago, 3b.........	2	0	1	1	0	0	0	1	0	1	1	3	0	0
Lavagetto, Brooklyn, 3b........	1	0	0	0	0	0	0	0	0	0	1	0	0	0
Moore, St. Louis, lf..........	5	0	0	0	0	0	0	0	0	0	1	0	0	0
Reiser, Brooklyn, cf............	4	0	0	0	0	0	0	0	0	0	2	6	0	2
Mize, St. Louis, 1b........	4	1	1	2	1	0	0	0	0	0	5	0	0	
McCormick, Cincinnati, 1b.......	0	0	0	0	0	0	0	0	0	0	0	0	0	
Nicholson, Chicago, rf..........	1	0	0	0	0	0	0	0	0	0	1	1	0	0
Elliott, Pittsburgh, rf..........	1	0	0	0	0	0	0	0	0	0	1	0	0	0
Slaughter, St. Louis, rf.........	2	1	1	1	0	0	0	0	0	0	1	0	0	0
Vaughan, Pittsburgh, ss.........	4	2	3	9	0	0	2	0	0	0	1	2	0	
Miller, Boston, ss..........	0	0	0	0	0	0	0	0	0	0	0	1	0	
Frey, Cincinnati, 2b..........	1	0	1	1	0	0	0	0	0	0	1	3	0	
Herman, Brooklyn, 2b.........	3	0	2	3	1	0	0	0	0	0	3	0	0	
Owen, Brooklyn, c...........	1	0	0	0	0	0	0	0	0	0	0	0	0	
Lopez, Pittsburgh, c..........	1	0	0	0	0	0	0	1	0	0	3	0	0	
Danning, New York, c.........	1	0	0	0	0	0	0	0	0	0	3	0	0	
Wyatt, Brooklyn, p..........	0	0	0	0	0	0	0	0	0	0	1	0	0	
aOtt, New York............	1	0	0	0	0	0	0	0	0	0	1	0	0	
Derringer, Cincinnati, p.........	0	0	0	0	0	0	0	0	0	0	1	0	
Walters, Cincinnati, p........	1	1	2	1	0	0	0	0	0	0	0	0	0	
cMedwick, Brooklyn.........	1	0	0	0	0	0	0	0	0	0	0	0	0	
Passeau, Chicago, p.........	1	0	0	0	0	0	0	0	0	0	0	0	0	
Total	35	5	10	19	3	0	2	2	0	1	7	*26	7	2

AMERICAN LEAGUE

	ab.	r.	h.	tb.	2b.	3b.	hr.	sh.	sb.	bb.	so.	po.	a.	e.
Doerr, Boston, 2b............	3	0	0	0	0	0	0	0	0	0	1	0	0	0
Gordon, New York, 2b.......	2	1	1	1	0	0	0	0	0	0	2	0	0	
Travis, Washington, 3b.......	4	1	2	2	1	0	0	0	0	1	0	1	2	0
J. DiMaggio, New York, cf.....	4	3	1	2	1	0	0	0	0	1	0	1	0	0
Williams, Boston, lf.........	4	1	2	6	1	0	1	0	0	1	1	3	0	1
Heath, Cleveland, rf.........	2	0	0	0	0	0	0	0	0	1	1	0	1	
D. DiMaggio, Boston, rf.......	1	0	1	1	0	0	0	0	0	0	1	0	0	
Cronin, Boston, ss...........	2	0	0	0	0	0	0	0	0	0	1	3	0	0
Boudreau, Cleveland, ss.......	2	0	2	2	0	0	0	0	0	0	1	6	2	0
York, Detroit, 1b..........	3	0	1	1	0	0	0	0	0	0	1	2	2	0
Foxx, Boston, 1b...........	1	0	0	0	0	0	0	0	0	0	4	2	0	
Dickey, New York, c.........	3	0	1	1	0	0	0	0	0	0	2	0	0	
Hayes, Philadelphia, c.........	1	0	0	0	0	0	0	0	0	0	1	0	0	
Feller, Cleveland, p..........	0	0	0	0	0	0	0	0	0	0	1	0	
bCullenbine, St. Louis.........	1	0	0	0	0	0	0	0	0	0	1	0	
Lee, Chicago, p............	1	0	0	0	0	0	0	0	0	0	0	1	0	
Hudson, Washington, p........	1	0	0	0	0	0	0	0	0	0	1	0	0	
dKeller, New York............	0	0	0	0	0	0	0	0	0	0	1	0	1	
Smith, Chicago, p............	0	0	0	0	0	0	0	0	0	0	0	0	0	
eKeltner, Cleveland............	1	1	1	1	0	0	0	0	0	0	0	0	0	
Total	36	7	11	17	3	0	1	0	0	4	6	27	11	3

*Two out when winning runs were scored.
aBatted for Wyatt in third.
bBatted for Feller in third.
cBatted for Walters in seventh.
dBatted for Hudson in seventh.
eBatted for Smith in ninth.

SCORE BY INNINGS

National League................0 0 0 0 0 1 2 2 0—5
American League..................0 0 0 1 0 1 0 1 4—7

Runs batted in—Williams 4. Moore, Boudreau, Vaughan 4, D. DiMaggio, J. DiMaggio.

Earned runs—National League 5, American League 7. Left on bases—National League 6, American League 7. Double plays—Frey, Vaughan and Mize; York and Cronin. Struck out—By Feller 4 (Hack, Reiser, Nicholson, Ott); by Derringer 1 (Heath); by Walters 2 (Cronin, Doerr); by Hudson 1 (Moore); by Smith 2 (Reiser, Slaughter); by Passeau 3 (Keller, Williams, Foxx). Bases on balls—Off Wyatt 1 (Williams); off Walters 2 (J. DiMaggio, Heath); off Hudson 1 (Hack); off Passeau 1 (Travis). Hits—Off Feller, 1 in 3 innings; off Lee, 4 in 3 innings; off Hudson, 3 in 1 inning; off Smith, 2 in 2 innings; off Wyatt, 0 in 2 innings; off Derringer, 2 in 2 innings; off Walters, 3 in 2 innings; off Passeau, 6 in 2 2-3 innings. Winning pitcher—Smith. Losing pitcher—Passeau. Umpires—Summers (A. L.), Jorda (N. L.), Grieve (A. L.) and Pinelli (N. L.). Time of game—2:23. Attendance—54,674.

the DiMaggio brothers whittled one tally away from Passeau's lead in the last of the eighth and Williams swept away the rest with his closing smash in the ninth.

Wyatt's pitching in the first two innings was practically as flawless as was Feller's work in the first three. The slim Brooklyn right-hander faced only six batters and, though he gave one a pass, he immediately snuffed this fellow off the base line by inducing the next man to slap into a double play.

Feller, fanning four during his three scoreless rounds, was equally invincible. Lonnie Frey opened the third with a single, but almost immediately got himself trapped off first base because somebody apparently had failed to tell Lonnie that Rapid Robert no longer is the easy mark for base runners that he used to be.

Ted Williams, simply one of the greatest hitters ever.

Jackie Robinson crosses the plate after hitting his first major league home run.

DiMaggio's Streak Ended at 56 Games

SMITH AND BAGBY STOP YANKEE STAR

DiMaggio, Up for Last Time in Eighth, Hits Into a Double Play With Bases Full

M'CARTHYMEN WIN BY 4-3

Stretch Lead Over Indians to 7 Lengths Before Biggest Crowd for Night Game

By JOHN DREBINGER

Special to THE NEW YORK TIMES.

CLEVELAND, July 17 — In a brilliant setting of lights and before 67,468 fans, the largest crowd ever to see a game of night baseball in the major leagues, the Yankees tonight vanquished the Indians, 4 to 3, but the famous hitting streak of Joe DiMaggio finally came to an end.

Officially it will go into the records as fifty-six consecutive games, the total he reached yesterday. Tonight in Cleveland's municipal stadium the great DiMag was held hitless for the first time in more than two months.

Al Smith, veteran Cleveland lefthand and a Giant cast-off, and Jim Bagby, a young right-hander, collaborated in bringing the DiMaggio string to a close.

Jolting Joe faced Smith three times. Twice he smashed the ball down the third-base line, but each time Ken Keltner. Tribe third sacker, collared the ball and hurled it across the diamond for a put-out at first. In between these two tries, DiMaggio drew a pass from Smith.

Then, in the eighth, amid a deafening uproar, the streak dramatically ended, though the Yanks routed Smith with a flurry of four hits and two runs that eventually won the game.

Double Play Seals Record

With the bases full and only one out Bagby faced DiMaggio and, with the count at one ball and one strike, induced the renowned slugger to crash into a double play. It was a grounder to the shortstop, and as the ball flitted from Lou Boudreau to Ray Mack to Oscar Grimes, who played first base for the Tribe, the crowd knew the streak was over.

However, there were still a few thrills to come, for in the ninth, with the Yanks leading, 4 to 1, the Indians suddenly broke loose with an attack that for a few moments threatened to send the game into extra innings and thus give DiMaggio another chance.

Gerald Walker and Grimes singled, and, though Johnny Murphy here replaced Gomez, Larry Rosenthal tripled to score his two colleagues. But with the tying run on third and nobody out the Cleveland attack bogged down in a mess of bad base-running and the Yanks' remaining one-run lead held, though it meant the end of the streak for DiMaggio, who might have come up fourth had there been a tenth inning.

Started May 15

It was on May 15 against the White Sox at the Yankee Stadium

Jim Bagby Jr.

that DiMaggio began his string, which in time was to gain nationwide attention. As the great DiMag kept clicking in game after game, going into the twenties, then the thirties, he became the central figure of the baseball world.

On June 29, in a double-header with the Senators in Washington, he tied, then surpassed the American League and modern record of forty-one games set by George Sisler of the Browns in 1922. The next target was the all-time major league high of forty-four contests set by Willie Keeler, famous Oriole star, forty-four years ago under conditions much easier then for a batsman than they are today. Then there was no foul-strike rule hampering the batter.

But nothing hampered DiMaggio as he kept getting his daily hits, and on July 1 he tied the Keeler mark. The following day he soared past it for game No. 45, and he kept on soaring until tonight. In seeking his fifty-seventh game, he finally was brought to a halt.

Actually, DiMaggio hit in fifty-seven consecutive games, for on July 8 he connected safely in the All-Star game in Detroit. But that contest did not count in the official league records.

Did Better on Coast

DiMaggio's mark ends five short of his own Pacific Coast League record of sixty-one consecutive games, which he set while with San Francisco in 1933. The all-time minor league high is sixty-seven, set by Joe Wilhoit of Wichita in the Western League in 1919.

The contest tonight was a blistering left-handed mound duel between Gomez and Smith, with Gomez going ahead one run in the first on Red Rolfe's single and Tommy Henrch's double.

A tremendous home run inside the park, which Walker outgalloped, tied the score in the fourth and the battle remained deadlocked until Joe Gordon untied it with his fifteenth homer of the year into the left-field stand in the seventh.

In the eighth the Yanks seemingly clinched victory when Charlie Keller rifled a triple to center past Roy Weatherly, who played the ball badly, needlessly charging in when he might just as well have played it safe for a single.

In its wake came singles by Gomez and Johnny Sturm. A double by Rolfe and two runs were in. Smith walked Henrich to fill the bases, and in this setting, with one out, the result of a harmless grounder by Phil Rizzuto, Bagby stepped in to face the great DiMag. A moment later the streak was over.

Traffic Snarl on Bases

The Indians were guilty of atrocious work on the bases in the ninth after Rosenthal had cracked Murphy for a triple to drive in two. Hal Trosky, pinch hitting, grounded out to first. Then Soup Campbell, batting for Bagby, splashed a grounder to Murphy. Rosenthal tried to score, was run down between third and home.

To make matters worse, Campbell, dashing past first base, never looked to see what was going on and so made no attempt to grab second during the run-up. Weatherly, amid no end of hoots and jeers, grounded out for the final play.

The victory was Gomez's eighth, his sixth in a row. It was the Yanks' seventeenth in their last eighteen games and thirty-first in their last thirty-six contests. Their lead over the thoroughly demoralized Tribe was stretched to seven games.

DiMaggio's Record Streak

Date	Opponent	ab.	r.	h.	2b.	3b.	hr.	Date	Opponent	ab.	r.	h.	2b.	3b.	hr.
May 15—White Sox....		4	0	1	0	0	0	June 17—White Sox....		4	1	1	0	0	0
May 16—White Sox....		4	2	2	0	1	1	June 18—White Sox....		3	0	1	0	0	0
May 17—White Sox....		3	1	1	0	0	0	June 19—White Sox....		3	2	3	0	0	1
May 18—Browns		3	3	3	1	0	0	June 20—Tigers		5	3	4	1	0	0
May 19—Browns		3	0	1	0	0	0	June 21—Tigers		4	0	1	0	0	0
May 20—Browns		5	1	1	0	0	0	June 22—Tigers		5	1	2	1	0	1
May 21—Tigers		4	0	1	0	0	0	June 24—Browns		4	1	1	0	0	0
May 22—Tigers		5	0	1	0	0	0	June 25—Browns		4	1	1	0	0	1
May 23—Red Sox......		5	0	1	0	0	0	June 26—Browns		4	0	1	0	0	0
May 24—Red Sox......		4	2	1	0	0	0	June 27—Athletics		3	1	2	0	0	1
May 25—Red Sox......		4	0	2	1	0	0	June 28—Athletics		5	1	1	0	0	0
May 27—Senators		5	3	4	0	0	1	June 29—Senators		4	1	1	0	0	0
May 28—Senators		4	1	1	0	1	0	June 29—Senators		5	1	1	0	0	0
May 29—Senators		3	1	1	0	0	0	July 1—Red Sox......		4	0	2	0	0	0
May 30—Red Sox......		2	1	1	0	0	0	July 1—Red Sox......		3	1	1	0	0	0
May 30—Red Sox......		3	0	1	1	0	0	July 2—Red Sox......		5	1	1	0	0	1
June 1—Indians		4	1	1	0	0	0	July 5—Athletics		4	2	1	0	0	1
June 1—Indians		4	0	1	0	0	0	July 6—Athletics		5	2	4	1	0	0
June 2—Indians		4	2	2	1	0	0	July 6—Athletics		4	0	2	0	1	0
June 3—Tigers		5	1	1	0	1	0	July 10—Browns		2	0	1	0	0	0
June 5—Tigers		5	1	1	0	1	0	July 11—Browns		5	1	4	0	0	1
June 7—Browns		4	3	2	0	0	2	July 12—Browns		5	1	2	1	0	0
June 8—Browns		4	2	4	1	2	1	July 13—White Sox....		4	2	3	0	0	0
June 8—Browns		4	1	2	1	0	1	July 13—White Sox....		4	0	1	0	0	0
June 10—White Sox....		5	1	1	0	0	0	July 14—White Sox....		3	0	1	0	0	0
June 12—White Sox....		4	1	2	0	0	0	July 15—White Sox....		4	1	2	1	0	0
June 14—Indians		2	0	1	0	0	0	July 16—Indians		4	3	3	1	0	0
June 15—Indians		3	1	1	0	0	1								
June 16—Indians		5	0	1	1	0	0	Total		223	56	91	16	4	15

Batting Mark of .4057 for Williams

STAR GETS 6 HITS AS RED SOX SPLIT

Williams Becomes First Big Leaguer in 11 Years to Bat .400 or Better

WALLOPS 37TH HOME RUN

PHILADELPHIA, Sept. 28 (AP)— Ted Williams of the Red Sox today became the first American Leaguer to hit .400 or higher for a season since 1923, when Harry Heilmann batted .403 for Detroit. Bill Terry was the last National League player to turn the trick. He batted .401 for the Giants in 1930.

Making six hits in eight times at bat while Boston and the Athletics split a double-header, Williams finished with a mark of .4057. He started the twin bill with an average of .39955. Williams played in 143 games this season, getting 185 hits in 456 times at bat.

Boston won the first game, 12 to 11, and the second was called on account of darkness after eight innings, with Philadelphia on top, 7 to 1.

Williams made his thirty-seventh home run and three singles in five chances in the opener, and a double and single in three attempts in the second encounter.

For the season he batted in 120 runs, scored 135 and walked 151 times. He struck out twenty-six times. Williams is the sixth American Leaguer to bat .400. Nap Lajoie, Ty Cobb, George Sisler, Joe Jackson and Heilmann were the others. Jackson hit .408 for Cleveland in 1911, but lost the batting title to Cobb, who finished with .420.

The first game saw the Sox rally after the Mackmen had scored nine runs in the fifth inning.

In the nightcap Fred Caligiuri held the Sox to six hits, one a homer by Frank Pytlak. Hal Wagner homered for the Athletics.

FIRST GAME

BOSTON (A.)	ab.	r.	h.	po.	a.	e.
DiMag'o, cf	5	1	3	4	0	1
Finney, rf	4	1	0	3	0	1
Flair, 1b	5	2	1	5	0	0
Williams, lf	5	3	4	3	0	0
Tabor, 3b	4	2	2	1	2	1
Doerr, 2b	5	3	2	3	3	0
L.News'e, ss	3	0	1	2	2	0
aFoxx	0	1	0	0	0	0
Carey, ss	0	0	0	0	0	0
Pytlak, c	4	0	1	6	1	0
H.News'e, p	2	0	1	0	1	0
Wagner, p	3	0	1	0	0	0
Total	40	12	16	27	9	3

PHILADELPHIA (A.)	ab.	r.	h.	po.	a.	e.
Collins, rf	5	2	2	3	0	0
Valo, lf	5	3	2	2	0	0
Richmond, 3b	5	3	2	2	0	0
Johnson, 1b	4	1	3	15	1	0
Chapman, cf	5	0	2	1	0	0
Davis, 2b	4	1	1	2	6	2
Suder, ss	5	1	2	2	4	1
Hayes, c	3	0	0	1	0	0
bFowler, p	2	0	0	2	0	0
bMiles	1	1	1	0	0	0
Vaughan, p	1	0	0	1	0	0
cShirley, p	0	0	0	2	0	0
cMcCoy	1	0	0	0	0	0
Total	41	11	15	27	18	3

aBatted for L. Newsome in ninth.
bBatted for Fowler in fifth.
cBatted for Shirley in ninth.

Boston .... 0 0 0 0 3 1 6 0 2—12
Philadelphia .... 0 0 2 0 9 0 0 0 0—11

Runs batted in—Richmond, Johnson 2, Williams 2, Tabor, Pytlak, Chapman, Davis, Miles, Collins, Valo 2, Doerr 3, Flair 2, L. Newsome, Wagner 2. Two-base hits—Johnson, Tabor. Three-base hits —Richmond, Valo, Flair, Doerr. Home runs— Williams, Tabor. Sacrifices—L. Newsome, Davis. Double plays—Suder and Johnson; Richmond, Davis and Johnson 2; Davis, Suder and Johnson. Left on bases—Boston 7, Philadelphia 9. Bases on balls—Off H. Newsome 3, Wagner 2, Vaughan 3, Shirley 2. Struck out—By H. Newsome 5. Hits— Off H. Newsome 15 in 4 2-3 innings, Vaughan 5 in 1 2-3, Shirley 3 in 2 1-3. Winning pitcher— Wagner. Losing pitcher—Shirley. Umpires—Mc-Gowan, Quinn and Grieve. Time of game—2:02.

SECOND GAME

BOSTON (A.)	ab.	r.	h.	po.	a.	e.
DiMaggio, cf	4	0	1	4	0	1
Finney, rf	2	0	0	0	0	0
Fox, rf	2	0	1	0	0	0
Flair, 1b	4	0	0	11	1	0
Williams, lf	3	0	2	0	0	0
Tabor, 3b	3	0	0	1	2	0
Carey, 2b	3	0	1	2	3	0
Newsome, ss	3	0	0	3	1	1
Peacock, c	2	0	1	2	0	0
Pytlak, c	1	1	1	2	0	0
Grove, p	0	0	0	0	1	0
Johnson, p	2	0	0	1	2	0
Total	29	1	6	24	13	1

PHILADELPHIA (A.)	ab.	r.	h.	po.	a.	e.
Valo, lf	3	1	1	1	0	0
Mack'wicz, cf	4	1	1	1	0	0
Miles, rf	4	1	2	2	0	0
Davis, 1b	3	1	0	11	0	0
McCoy, 2b	3	1	2	3	3	0
Brancato, 3b	4	0	1	2	2	0
Suder, ss	4	1	1	1	1	0
Wagner, c	4	1	3	3	0	0
Caligiuri, p	4	0	0	0	0	0
Total	32	7	11	24	9	0

Boston .... 0 0 0 0 0 0 0 1—1
Philadelphia .... 3 1 0 1 1 0 1 0—7

Runs batted in—Miles, Brancato 2, Wagner 2, Pytlak.

Two-base hit—Williams. Three-base hits—Suder, Mackiewicz. Home runs—Wagner, Pytlak. Double plays—Tabor, Carey and Flair; McCoy, Suder and Davis. Left on bases—Boston 5, Philadelphia 5. Bases on balls—Off Johnson 4, Caligiuri 1. Struck out—By Johnson 2, Caligiuri 1. Hits—Off Grove 4 in 1 inning, Johnson 7 in 7. Wild pitches— Grove, Johnson. Losing pitcher—Grove. Umpires —Quinn, Grieve and McGowan. Time of game— 1:21. Attendance—10,268.

September 29, 1941

YANKS WIN IN 9TH, FINAL 'OUT' TURNS INTO 4-RUN RALLY

By JOHN DREBINGER

It couldn't, perhaps, have happened anywhere else on earth. But it did happen yesterday in Brooklyn, where in the short space of twenty-one minutes a dazed gathering of 33,813 at Ebbets Field saw a world series game miraculously flash two finishes before its eyes.

The first came at 4:35 of a sweltering afternoon, when, with two out and nobody aboard the bases in the top half of the ninth inning, Hugh Casey saw Tommy Henrich miss a sharp-breaking curve for a third strike that for a fleeting moment had the Dodgers defeating the Yankees, 4 to 3, in the fourth game of the current classic.

But before the first full-throated roar had a chance to acclaim this brilliant achievement there occurred one of those harrowing events that doubtless will live through all the ages of baseball like the Fred Snodgrass muff and the failure of Fred Merkle to touch second.

Makes Frantic Dash

Mickey Owen, topflight catcher of the Dodgers, let the ball slip away from him and, before he could retrieve it in a frantic dash in front of his own dugout, Henrich had safely crossed first base.

It was all the opening Joe McCarthy's mighty Bronx Bombers, shackled by this same Casey ever since the fifth inning, needed to turn defeat for themselves into an amazing victory which left a stunned foe crushed.

For in the wake of that excruciating error came a blazing single by Joe DiMaggio, a two-base smash against the right-field barrier by Charley Keller, a pass to Bill Dickey by the now thoroughly befuddled Casey and another two-base clout by the irrepressible Joe Gordon.

Flatbush's Darkest Hour

Four runs hurtled over the plate and, though the meteorological records may still contend that this was the brightest, sunniest and warmest day in world series history, it was easily the darkest hour that Flatbush ever has known.

For this astounding outburst gave the Yankees the game, 7 to 4, and with this victory McCarthy's miraculous maulers moved to within a single stride of another world championship. Their lead, as the series enters the fifth encounter at Ebbets Field today, now stands at three games to one, and the Bombers need to touch off only one more explosion to bring this epic interborough struggle to a close.

Almost from the moment Mayor La Guardia threw out the first ball this battle was one that had the crowd seething and sizzling under an emotional strain that at times threatened to burst out the sides of the arena in the heart of Flatbush.

Higbe First to Go

Neither of the starting pitchers, Kirby Higbe for the Dodgers and Atley Donald, survived the fierce fighting under the blistering midsummer sun. Kirby, twenty-two-game winner of the National League champions, making his delayed first appearance in the series, was the first to go. He was driven to cover in the fourth inning, by which time the Yanks had run up a lead of 3 to 0.

But this merely provided the setting for the making of a couple of Brooklyn heroes who last night would have been the toast of the borough had victory remained where it momentarily perched at 4:35 o'clock.

One was Jimmy Wasdell, who hit a pinch double in the last of the fourth to drive in two runs. The other was Pete Reiser, freshman star of the Dodgers, who, finally coming into his own, whacked a homer over the rightfield wall with Dixie Walker on base in the fifth inning to give the Brooklyn host its 4-to-3 lead.

That blow finished Donald and, though Relief Pitchers Marvin Breuer and Johnny Murphy gave the Dodgers no more runs, they appeared to need no more to clinch this victory that would have squared the series at two games apiece. For Casey, the same round-faced Hugh whose brief relief turn had opened the floodgates for a Yankee triumph in Saturday's third game, looked this time to have the Bombers firmly in hand. Casey replaced a wavering Johnny Allen in the fifth inning to repulse the Yanks with the bases full and he kept repelling them right on and up through the ninth until Owen's crowning misfortune turned the battle and the arena upside down.

Johnny Sturm, Yankee lead-off man, had opened that last-ditch stand in the ninth by grounding out to Pete Coscarart, who again was at second base for Brooklyn in place of the injured Billy Herman. Red Rolfe proved an even easier out. He bounced the ball squarely into Casey's hands and was tossed out at first with yards to spare.

Two were out, nobody was on, the Yanks looked throttled for the second time in the series and the Brooklyn horde scarcely could contain itself as it prepared to hail the feat with a tumultuous outburst of pent-up enthusiasm.

A Swing and a Miss

Casey worked carefully on Henrich and ran the count to three balls and two strikes. Then he snapped over a low, sharp-breaking curve. Henrich swung and missed. A great Flatbush triumph appeared clinched. But in the twinkling of an eye the victory was to become an even greater illusion.

As the ball skidded out of Owen's mitt and rolled toward the Dodger bench with Mickey in mad pursuit, police guards also came rushing out of the dugout to hold back the crowd which at the same moment was preparing to dash madly out on the field.

Owen retrieved the ball just in front of the steps, but Henrich, who the moment before had been at the point of throwing his bat away in great disgust, now was tearing like wild for first and he made the bag without a play.

The Yanks, of course, had not yet won the game. They were still a run behind and, though they had a man on first, Casey needed to collect only one more out to retain his margin.

But there was an ominous ring to the manner in which DiMaggio bashed a line-drive single to left that sent Henrich to second. A moment later Keller belted the ball high against the screening on top of the right-field fence. It just missed being a home run.

It was recovered in time to hold the doughty King Kong on second for a double, but both Henrich and DiMaggio streaked around the bases and over the plate. The dreaded Yanks were ahead, 5—4. To make matters even more excruciating, Casey had had a count of two strikes and no balls on Keller when King Kong pasted that one.

Down in the Brooklyn bullpen Curt Davis was warming up with great fury, but the Dodger board of strategy appeared paralyzed by the cataclysm and Manager Leo Durocher did nothing.

Casey pitched to Dickey and walked him. Again the Yanks had two on base. Casey stuck two strikes over on Gordon, then again grooved the next one. Ironically, Joe the Flash smacked the ball into left field, where Wasdell, who might have been one of the heroes, was left to chase it while Keller and Dickey raced for home with two more runs to make it four for the round.

This was enough, more than enough. Few clubs in major league history have ever had an almost certain victory snatched from them under more harrowing circumstances.

Snuffing out the final three Dodgers in the last half of the ninth was almost child's play for the relief hurler whom the Yanks affectionately call Grandma Murphy. Indeed, the kindly Grandma appeared motivated by only the most humane feelings as he put those battered Dodgers out of their misery.

Like Casey in the top half of that ninth, Murphy had to face the head of the batting order. But at that moment the Dodgers didn't know whether they were standing on their heads or their heels. Peewee Reese fouled out to Dickey and Walker and Reiser ended the game by never getting the ball out of the infield.

At the outset of the conflict, as Donald and Higbe squared away on the mound, evidence came early as to why Durocher had deferred starting his so-called second ace as long as he had. Higbe went down a run in the very first inning on a single by Rolfe, a pass to DiMaggio and another sharp single to right by Keller.

Slaps Into Force Play

Keller, by far the batting star of the day with four hits, two of them doubles, started Higbe on his final downfall in the fourth by polling his first two-bagger against the right-field barrier. A walk to Dickey and a Gordon single filled the bases with none out. For a moment Higbe promised to squirm out of the difficulty by inducing Phil Rizzuto to slap into a force play at the plate and striking out Donald.

But Sturm, one of those lesser lights in the Yankee attack who occasionally strike damaging blows, struck one now. He drove a sharp single to center. Dickey and Gordon scored and Higbe gave way to Larry French who, in facing only one batter, had checked the Yanks' eighth-inning victory rally on Saturday.

This time the veteran left-hander of the National League did even better. He delivered only one ball to Rolfe. It was almost a wild pitch, Owen blocking it with considerable difficulty, but it ended the inning, for the two Yanks on the bases cut loose from their moorings and Rizzuto was trapped and run down between second and third.

However, the Yanks were ahead, 3 to 0, and with Donald working smoothly, the rest of the blistering afternoon held little excitement in prospect.

But in the last of the fourth came the first jolt when Donald, after retiring two batters, walked Owen and Coscarart. Wasdell was sent in to pinch hit for French. He caught an outside pitch on the end of his bat and the ball soared high down the left-field foul line. It fell safely in the extreme left-hand corner of the playing field, just out of Keller's desperate reach, and the stands swayed as Owen and Coscarart dashed around the bases and scored. The Yanks were now leading by only 3 to 2.

Nor was this a patch to the uproar that went up in the Dodger fifth when the aroused Flatbush Flock routed Donald before he had retired a man. Walker banged a double to left and the next instant the arena became an outdoor madhouse as Reiser, batting champion of the National League in his freshman campaign, rammed the ball over the right-field wall. It was the first Dodger home run hit in a world series in Brooklyn since 1916, when Hy Myers clouted one for the late Wilbert Robinson, and the folks really went to town on this shot.

At the same time Donald went to the clubhouse and Breuer took

the mound for the McCarthy forces. He put a quietus on the show in short order and kept things quiet until he vacated for a futile pinch hitter, George Selkirk, in the eighth.

In the meantime, Casey, who had replaced Allen in the upper half of the fifth with the bases full and then retired Gordon on an easy fly for the third out, was doing his share to keep the Yankees quiet.

But this game apparently was never meant to remain quiet and the uproar and events in that bizarre ninth will doubtless remain a nightmare in Flatbush in all the years to come.

And so the Yanks once again stand poised as they have stood in every world series they have played since 1927—seven in all. They have three victories in the bag, their opponents on the ropes and only one more encounter is needed to haul down the lion's share of the spoils.

As usual, McCarthy can continue to gamble with his inexhaustible supply of mound talent. He used three hurlers yesterday, with Murphy the winner. In the first

three games he started Charley Ruffing, Spud Chandler and Marius Russo. Today, at Ebbets Field, still a fifth starter will make his debut, the husky Tiny Bonham, a strapping right-hander with a tantalizing fork ball.

Tiny came up from the farm system in August of 1940. He has never pitched a world series game before. But then neither had Russo, who spun a masterful four-hitter to win on Saturday.

In contrast with this, Durocher is strictly up against it. He must call on the veteran Whit Wyatt to keep the fading Dodgers in the struggle. And though Whit scored the only Brooklyn victory to date when he won the second game on Thursday, he has had, even with a day of postponement, only three full days of rest since.

The Flock, then, indeed is in a mighty tight spot, and all because it had a pitcher yesterday who threw such a curve it not only fooled the batter but his catcher as well.

Box Score of the Fourth Game

NEW YORK YANKEES

	ab.	r.	h.	tb.	2b.	3b.	hr.	bb.	so.	sh.	sb.	po.	a.	e.
Sturm, 1b.	5	0	2	2	0	0	0	0	0	0	0	9	1	0
Rolfe, 3b.	5	1	2	2	0	0	0	0	0	0	0	2	0	0
Henrich, rf.	4	1	0	0	0	0	0	1	0	0	0	3	0	0
DiMaggio, cf.	4	1	2	2	0	0	0	1	0	0	0	2	0	0
Keller, lf.	5	1	4	6	2	0	0	0	0	0	0	1	0	0
Dickey, c.	2	2	0	0	0	0	0	3	0	0	0	7	0	0
Gordon, 2b.	5	1	2	3	1	0	0	0	0	0	0	2	3	0
Rizzuto, ss.	4	0	0	0	0	0	0	1	0	0	0	2	3	0
Donald, p.	2	0	0	0	0	0	0	0	1	0	0	0	1	0
Breuer, p.	1	0	0	0	0	0	0	0	0	0	0	0	0	0
aSelkirk	1	0	0	0	0	0	0	0	0	0	0	0	0	0
Murphy, p.	1	0	0	0	0	0	0	0	0	0	0	1	0	0
Total	39	7	12	15	3	0	0	5	2	0	0	27	11	0

BROOKLYN DODGERS

	ab.	r.	h.	tb.	2b.	3b.	hr.	bb.	so.	sh.	sb.	po.	a.	e.
Reese, ss.	5	0	0	0	0	0	0	0	0	0	0	2	4	0
Walker, rf.	5	1	2	3	1	0	0	0	0	0	0	5	0	0
Reiser, cf.	5	1	2	5	0	0	1	0	1	0	0	1	0	0
Camilli, 1b.	4	0	2	3	1	0	0	0	0	0	0	10	1	0
Riggs, 3b.	3	0	0	0	0	0	0	1	1	0	0	0	2	0
Medwick, lf.	2	0	0	0	0	0	0	0	0	0	0	1	0	0
Allen, p.	0	0	0	0	0	0	0	0	0	0	0	0	3	0
Casey, p.	2	0	1	1	0	0	0	0	1	0	0	0	0	0
Owen, c.	2	1	0	0	0	0	0	2	0	0	0	4	2	1
Coscarart, 2b.	3	1	0	0	0	0	0	1	2	0	0	2	1	0
Higbe, p.	1	0	1	1	0	0	0	0	0	0	0	0	0	0
French, p.	0	0	0	0	0	0	0	0	0	0	0	0	0	0
Wasdell, lf.	3	0	1	2	1	0	0	0	0	0	0	2	0	0
Total	35	4	9	15	3	0	1	4	5	0	0	27	14	1

aBatted for Breuer in eighth.

SCORE BY INNINGS

New York Yankees .... 1 0 0   2 0 0   0 0 4—7
Brooklyn Dodgers .... 0 0 0   2 2 0   0 0 0—4

Runs batted in—Keller 3, Sturm 2, Wasdell 2, Reiser 2, Gordon 2.

Earned runs—Yankees 3, Dodgers 4.

Left on bases—Yankees 11, Dodgers 8. Double play—Gordon, Rizzuto and Sturm. Struck out—By Donald 2, Higbe 1, Breuer 2, Casey 1, Murphy 1. Bases on balls—Off Higbe 2, Casey 2, Donald 3, Breuer 1, Allen 1. Pitching summary—Off Higbe 6 hits, 3 runs in 3 2-3 innings; French 0 hits, 0 runs in 1-3; Allen 1 hit, 0 runs in 2-3; Casey 5 hits, 4 runs in 4 1-3; Donald 6 hits, 4 runs in 4 (none out in fifth); Breuer 3 hits, 0 runs in 3; Murphy 0 hits, 0 runs in 2. Hit batsman—By Allen (Henrich). Winning pitcher—Murphy. Losing pitcher—Casey. Umpires—Goetz (N. L.), plate; McGowan (A. L.), first base; Pinelli (N. L.), second base; Grieve (A. L.), third base. Time of game—2:54.

Cards Win Pennant on Final Day; Series Starts in St. Louis

By JOHN DREBINGER
Special to THE NEW YORK TIMES.

ST. LOUIS, Sept. 27—Sweeping inexorably on toward their goal, the Cardinals, on this. the final day of the championship season, brought to a triumphant close their spectacular seven-week pennant drive by clinching the National League flag with a smashing victory over the Cubs in the first game of the afternoon's double-header.

The end came at 3:12 o'clock, amid the thunderous roars of 32,-330 frenzied enthusiasts. Billy Southworth's high-flying Redbirds, behind the steady hurling of Ernie White and after routing Lon Warneke with a four-run blast in the fifth inning, crushed the Chicagoans, 9 to 2.

After that it no longer mattered ow the still desperately striving Dodgers fared in Philadelphia or what the outcome of the second game here would be. Just to keep the records, however, it might be added that the forlorn flock of Flatbush went on to win that final game, while the Cards, with most of their regulars on the sidelines, won again, 4 to 1, to give Johnny Beazley, their freshman star righthander, his twenty-first victory. That made it a two-game lead to the finish line.

And so, with all speculation at an end, arrangements for the forthcoming world series, in which the new National League titleholders will face the formidable Yankees of the American League, moved ahead tonight with feverish haste.

The first wartime classic since 1918, in which the United Service Organizations are to share in the receipts, will start here on Wednesday. The second game also will be staged at Sportsman's Park, which has a seating capacity of 34,000.

Following an open date Friday for traveling, the struggle will switch to the Yankee Stadium in New York for the third game on Saturday, as well as the fourth Sunday and the fifth, if needed, on Monday.

If by then neither side has gained the required four victories, the conflict will return here for the sixth game on Oct. 7 and the seventh on Oct. 9.

Caps Sensational Battle

The triumph of the Redbirds today capped one of the most sensational uphill pennant battles the National League, rich in struggles of this sort, has seen in some years. Not since 1934 has a major league race been in doubt until the final day, and that year, oddly, saw the Cardinals win their last pennant as they swept by the faltering Giants.

Trailing by ten games on the morning of Aug. 6 last and still nine and a half lengths back of the front-running Dodgers as late as Aug. 15, the Cards were given little chance of making even a close race of it.

But day after day they kept hammering away until on Sept. 12 they drew even by sweeping a two-game series with the now thoroughly panic-stricken leaders in Brooklyn. On the following day St. Louis forged ahead.

From then on the Cards were never headed, and even when the Dodgers regained their stride to close with an eight-game winning string these surprising young men, directed by the quietly efficient Southworth, never took their eyes off that flag. From the day they moved into the lead on Sept. 13 until they clinched it they won ten out of eleven games.

An Amazing Record

But most amazing of all was their record for their last fifty-three games, more than a third of a season, in which they won forty-three, lost only nine and tied one.

Thus to the Mound City comes its first National League pennant in e ght years and its sixth in the history of the senior loop. It was in 1926. under the leadership of Rogers Hornsby, that the Cardinals won their first flag. That year the Cards also vanquished the Yankees in a memorable seven-game world series which also was to remain as the last Yankee defeat in an October classic.

With Hornsby traded to the Giants in 1927, the Cards did not repeat that year, but in 1928, under Bill McKechnie, they won their second flag. With Gabby Street in command they bagged two more pennants in 1930 and 1931, topping the 1931 victory with another world series triumph in seven games over the formidable Athletics of that era.

In the two following campaigns the Redbirds were vanquished for the flag by the Cubs and then the Giants, but in 1934. with the dynamic Frankie Frisch in the driver's seat, the Cards came roaring back. That was the famous Gas House Gang which, with the two pitching Deans almost incessantly on the firing line, shot by the staggering Giants and then went on to wrest the world championship from the Tigers in a tempestuous seven-game series.

With the Cardinals' famed chain-store farm system then operating at its peak, many feared at the time that the Redbirds would remain invincible for many years. But for one reason or another, no pennants flew at Sportsman's Park for the next seven years.

With the possibility looming that the pennant race still would be plunged into a deadlock by nightfall, there were just a few anxious moments in the first game today when the Cubs forged a run ahead in the fourth on a pair of singles by Stanley Hack and Dom Dallessandro and an overthrow to the plate by Jimmy Brown.

But in the next round there again came one of those brief rifts in the enemy defenses which seem all these swift-moving Redbirds ever need. and when old Warneke went down under four runs every one knew the fight was over.

Whitey Kurowski walked. Len Merullo booted Marty Marion's sharp grounder and in the wake of that came a trio of singles by White, Terry Moore and Enos Slaughter.

In the seventh the Cub defenses cracked again and, off Hiram Bithorn and Vern Olsen, the pennant-bound Redbirds grabbed four more runs and that more than settled it.

As Clyde McCullough ended it with a long fly to Stan Musial in left, a jubilant band of Redbirds dashed from the bench and joined their comrades on the field in hoisting White on their shoulders while the crowd cheered for several minutes.

```
            FIRST GAME
 CHICAGO (N.)           ST. LOUIS (N.)
      ab.r.h.po.a.e          ab.r.h.po.a.e
Hack, 3b...4 1 2 3 2 0  Brown, 2b...3 1 1 2 1 1
Merullo, ss..1 0 0 2 4 1 Moore, cf...5 2 3 1 0 0
Nicholson, rf..1 0 0 0 0 0 Slaughter, rf5 1 2 2 0 0
McCull'gh, c.4 0 0 2 2 1 Musial, lf...4 0 1 4 0 1
Novikoff, lf..3 0 0 0 0 0 W. Cooper, c.3 0 0 10 1 0
Cavar'tta, 1b.3 0 1 6 3 0 Hopp, 1b....4 1 3 5 0 0
Sturgeon, 2b.3 0 0 7 3 1 Kurowski, 3b3 1 1 1 3 0
Warneke, p...1 0 0 1 1 0 Marion, ss...4 2 0 2 0 0
Bithorn, p...1 0 0 0 0 0 White, p....3 2 2 0 0 0
Olsen, p.....0 0 0 0 0 0
aRussell ....1 0 0 0 0 0   Total....34 9 11 27 5 2
Mooty, p.....0 0 0 0 1 0

Total....31 2 5 24 16 4
aBatted for Olsen in eighth.

Chicago .........0 0 0  1 0 0  1 0 0—2
St. Louis ........0 0 0  0 4 0  4 1..—9
Runs batted in—While. Moore 3, Musial. Cavar-
retta, Dalessandro. Slaughter, W. Cooper, Hopp.
Two-base hit.—Cavarretta, Musial. Sacrifices—
Brown, White. Double play—Sturgeon. Merullo nd
Cavarretta. Left on bases—Chicago 3. St. Louis 6.
Bases on balls—Off Warneke 2. Olsen 1. White 1.
Struck out—By Bithorn 2. White 8. Hits—Off
Warneke 6 in 4 1-3 innings, Bithorn 3 in 2, Olsen
1 in 2-3, Mooty 1 in 1. Losing pitcher—Warneke.
Umpires—Barlick, Ballanfant, Conlan and Reardon.
Time of game—2:13.

            SECOND GAME
 CHICAGO (N.)           ST. LOUIS (N.)
      ab.r.h.po.a.e          ab.r.h.po.a.e
Block, 3b...3 1 2 0 0 0  Crespi, 2b..3 1 2 3 3 1
Russell, 3b..1 0 0 0 0 0 Walker, cf...4 0 1 4 0 0
Merullo, ss..4 0 0 4 1 0 Musial, rf...4 0 1 1 0 0
Nich'ls'n, rf.4 0 1 1 0 0 Sanders, 1b.4 0 1 9 0 0
Dal's'dro, cf.3 0 1 0 0 0 O'Des, c....4 0 2 6 0 0
Scheffing, c3 0 0 5 1 0 Triplett, lf..3 1 0 4 0 0
Novikoff, lf.4 0 2 3 0 0 Dusak, 3b...4 2 2 0 5 0
Cavar'ta, 1b.3 0 0 5 0 0 Cross, ss....4 0 0 0 3 0
Foxx, 1b....1 0 0 1 0 0 Beazley, p..4 0 1 0 1 0
Stringer, 2b.4 0 1 2 3 0
Passeau, p..3 0 0 2 3 0   Total ...34 4 11 27 12 1
aGilbert ....1 0 0 0 0 0

Total ....34 1 7 21 7 0
aBatted for Passeau in ninth.

Chicago ...............1 0 0  0 0 0  0 0 0—1
St. Louis ..............1 2 0  0 0 1  0 0.—4
Runs batted in—Dallessandro. Sanders. Cross.
Crespi. Beazley.
Two-base hits—Walker, O'Des, Musial, Dusak,
Beazley. Double play—Dusak, Crespi and San-
ders. Left on bases—Chicago 8. St. Louis 8.
Bases on balls—Off Passeau 2. Beazley 2. Struck
out—By Passeau 6, Beazley 3. Passed ball—
O'Des. Umpires—Ballanfant, Conlan, Reardon and
Barlick. Time of game—1:49. Attendance—32,386.
```

September 28, 1942

No Errors for Litwhiler

PHILADELPHIA, Sept. 28 (P)— Danny Litwhiler of the last-place Phils, set a new major league fielding record for outfielders by playing the entire season without making an error, Phils' officials said tonight. The previous record for outfielders for fewest boots in a season is two, made jointly by Edgar Hahn of the White Sox in 1907, and equaled by Pete Fox of Detroit in 1938.

September 29, 1942

BIG LEAGUE TEAMS TO TRAIN NEAR HOME

Potomac and Ohio Rivers in South, Mississippi in West Fixed as Camp Limits

EASTMAN PRAISES ACTION

Majors, Meeting With Landis, Retain 154-Game Schedule While Revising Dates

By The Associated Press

CHICAGO, Jan. 5—The major leagues, in emergency joint session with Commissioner Kenesaw Mountain Landis, decided today to set back the opening of the 1943 baseball season eight days to April 21, but voted to extend the playing period one week, closing on Oct. 3, instead of Sept. 26.

They also drew up a sharply defined area in which they may do their Spring training, with the understanding each club would condition at home, or as close as possible, in the interest of curtailing rail travel.

Teams, they decided, must train north of the Potomac and Ohio Rivers and east of the Mississippi, with the exception of the two St. Louis clubs, which have the option of using Missouri as a site. This decision ruled out as training bases the South Atlantic seaboard States and Hot Springs, Ark., mentioned as possible alternate sites after Florida and California earlier had been listed as "out of bounds."

Statement by Eastman

In Washington, Director Joseph B. Eastman of the Office of Defense Transportation was "greatly pleased by the action which the major leagues have taken." His statement, released here by the Office of War Information, follows:

"I am greatly pleased with the action which the major leagues have taken today to reduce their travel requirements for the coming season. The only request I made of them was, in effect, a general request that they hold travel to the necessary minimum. At no time have I undertaken to say what the minimum is, because I do not know enough about the baseball industry to pass judgment on that matter.

"In these circumstances, the action which the major leagues have taken on their own initiative is most gratifying. It shows a real and keen appreciation of the very troublesome travel problem which our country has under present war conditions, a problem which is bound to grow in difficulty and seriousness.

"The example which such an important national industry has thus set will have, I am sure, a most beneficial influence hroughout the nation. I hope and believe there will be many who will follow this fine example."

Meeting Delayed Two Hours

The meeting, hailed as baseball's most important since Landis quit the Federal bench in 1921 to become commissioner after the 1919 world series scandal, was delayed nearly two hours because representatives of several Eastern clubs were aboard trains late in arriving.

Landis personally announced results of the two-hour parley. He said the 154-game schedule would remain in effect, including three East-West trips, previously agreed upon. Since 1936, each club has made the cross-country junket four times.

"Transportation during Spring training will be held to a minimum," Landis said, "and after Spring training there will be need for utmost cooperation on the part of the various clubs to cut manmileage as much as possible."

He said the question of reduced personnel on road trips would be left up to the individual clubs. The player limit for each club still is 25, but there have been suggestions that each team take fewer men on trips, possibly no more than 20.

The commissioner, who had conferred last week in Washington with Eastman, presided over the meeting, which was attended by men from fifteen of the sixteen major league clubs.

Washington was the only team without a representative, although Joe Cambria, head scout, was in the anteroom waiting to report back to President Clark Griffith of the Senators.

The determination of a set area wherein clubs may train makes it possible for all to proceed at once with Spring workout plans. The Chicago Cubs and White Sox, already set to go to French Lick Springs, Ind., and the Boston Red Sox, who will train at Tufts College, Medford, Mass., are the only ones certain where they are going.

The decision to open the season approximately one week later apparently was a compromise between the American League, understood to have wanted an April 27 start, and the National, which had favored retaining the original April 13 opening.

Traditionally the major league season has opened on a Tuesday, with Washington getting a one-day start every other year, but the new schedule will call for the campaign to open on a Wednesday. No reason was announced for this shift.

Landis was "utterly astounded at the number of miles saved by condensing Spring training trips within a specific radius." He did not reveal precisely how many man miles would be saved by the new restricted travel program.

Some of the team representatives, before scurrying home to set up their Spring camps, drew this sketchy picture:

The two Philadelphia teams will train "right around home," said President Gerry Nugent of the Phils and Connie Mack of the Athletics.

The St. Louis Cardinals will look around, but may explore Excelsior Springs, Mo., Owner Sam Breadon said.

The Boston Braves will hunt for a college field house near home, Secretary John J. Quinn hinted.

The Cleveland Indians "are looking around," commented President Alva Bradley.

The Pittsburgh Pirates are "uncertain," President Bill Benswanger reported.

The Brooklyn Dodgers probably will work out at Yale University, New Haven, Conn., said General Manager Branch Rickey.

The Detroit Tigers may do part of their conditioning at Benton Harbor, Mich., General Manager Jack Zeller stated.

The Cincinnati Reds are in a spot, President Warren Giles lamented. The new training zone limits clubs to areas north of the Ohio River. "Right now," Giles said, "our ball park is precisely three feet u-n-d-e-r the Ohio River because of flood waters."

January 6, 1943

'HELP WANTED' SIGN OUT

Baseball 'Ad' Reveals Openings on Cards' Farm Clubs

ST. LOUIS, Feb. 23 (AP)—The world champion Cardinals, who once did a booming business selling surplus players from their far-flung farm system, today put out a "help wanted" sign.

An advertisement, probably without precedent in the history of baseball, said the Cardinals had openings on their minor league clubs for free agents with previous professional experience. It appeared in this week's issue of The Sporting News, national baseball weekly.

"These are unusual times," said President Sam Breadon in explanation of the unusual advertisement.

The Cardinal organization, which formerly supplied nearly all major league teams with players, has had a different customer since the war. The armed forces have taken more than 265 athletes from the team's coast-to-coast system.

Memphis of the Southern Association and Toronto of the International League also had advertisements for players in The Sporting News.

February 24, 1943

Negroes Allowed in Grandstand

ST. LOUIS, May 4 (AP)—The St. Louis major league baseball teams, the Cardinals and Browns, have discontinued their old policy of restricting Negroes to the bleachers and pavilion at Sportsman's Park. Negroes now may purchase seats in the grandstand.

May 5, 1944

RULING ON GRAY CATCHES

Umpires Get Instructions on Browns' One-Armed Player

ST. LOUIS, March 14 (AP)—Special instructions for ruling on catches by Pete Gray will be given to umpires if the one-armed outfielder makes the grade this year with the Browns, President Will Harridge of the American League has advised The Post-Dispatch.

After making a catch, Gray places the ball against his chest and moves his left hand to the stub of his right arm. In this motion the ball rolls out of his glove and up his wrist as if it were a ball-bearing between the arm and body. When the glove is tucked under the stub, Gray draws his arm back across his chest until the ball rolls back into his hand, ready for a throw.

Harridge said umpires would be instructed to give credit to Gray for momentary catches. In the event he drops the ball after starting the process of removing his glove, the catch will not be ruled out.

This is the same regulation umpires in the Southern Association used in governing plays by Gray when he was with Memphis last season.

March 15, 1945

SENATOR CHANDLER GETS BASEBALL POST

'Immediately Available,' New Commissioner Accepts for Seven Years at $50,000

NAMED ON FIRST BALLOT

M'Phail, Stoneham Lead Fight for Choice of 46-Year-Old Successor to Landis

CLEVELAND, April 24 (AP)—Baseball's five-month quest for a commissioner ended today with election of Senator Albert B. (Happy) Chandler of Kentucky to fill the position vacated by the death of Kenesaw Mountain Landis.

By unanimous vote of the sixteen major league club owners or their representatives, and on the first ballot, the 46-year-old junior Senator from the Bluegrass State was named for a seven-year term at an annual salary of $50,000. Leslie M. O'Connor, secretary to the late commissioner and chairman of the three-man advisory council that has ruled the sport since the death of Judge Landis last Nov. 25, said Senator Chandler would take office within a reasonable time. In Washington, however, Mr. Chandler said he would be "immediately available."

The former Governor of Kentucky from Versailles was selected after a four-hour discussion in which expected fireworks failed to materialize. The group that favored naming a commissioner at once, and was ready to prolong the argument as long as necessary,

found enough support without extended debate after the major leagues' steering committee of four —Alva Bradley of Cleveland, Don Barnes of the St. Louis Browns, Sam Breadon of the St. Louis Cardinals and Phil Wrigley of the Chicago Cubs—had made its report.

Others Considered for Post

Other men were discussed but club owners declined to identify them, pointing out that Senator Chandler was their man from the time they knew that he was available. From another source, however, it was learned that the names of Gov. Frank J. Lausche of Ohio; Bob Hannegan, chairman of the Democratic National Committee; former Postmaster General James A. Farley and President Ford C. Frick of the National League had been mentioned prominently.

Selection of Mr. Chandler as baseball's second commissioner since the office was established in 1920 was in line with the contention of many baseball men that they should go outside their ranks to fill so important a position.

Senator Chandler, a graduate of the University of Kentucky and Harvard Law School, also is baseball's second lawyer commissioner. Judge Landis was picked off the Federal bench to take over the job following the Chicago White Sox scandal in 1919.

One group of club representatives went into the meeting with the idea of retaining the three-man commission composed of Messrs. O'Connor and Frick and President Will Harridge of the American League, or the selection of a duration commissioner.

They found themselves outnumbered, however, as Larry MacPhail of the Yankees and Horace Stoneham of the Giants rallied a force that called for immediate action.

War Situation Guides Action

At first, Senator Chandler had said he couldn't leave his present job, but, after accepting the position in a telephone conversation, he added: "Now that the war with Germany is virtually over I can conscientiously leave my other duties."

Senator Albert B. Chandler

Before the club representatives got down to the task of selecting Mr. Chandler, they arranged for eight games to be played for the benefit of the Red Cross and National War Fund on July 9, 10 or 11. To save all travel possible and subject to approval of the Office of Defense Transportation, there will be five games in cities having more than one big league club and the other teams will play in towns en route to regularly scheduled games.

In New York it will be the Giants and Yankees; in Boston, Braves and Red Sox; in Chicago, Cubs and White Sox; in Philadelphia, Athletics and Phils, and in St. Louis, Cards and Browns. Detroit will play at Pittsburgh, Brooklyn at Washington and Cincinnati at Cleveland.

At an earlier business session the owners decided that a player reinstated from the National Defense List who had participated in one league game could be retained on the roster for fifteen days without affecting the player limit. Previously a player who had partici-

pated in one game was considered a member of the team.

The magnates also agreed that an athlete undecided about playing baseball this year would be permitted to apply for the voluntary retired list so as not to be included in a club's player limit.

MacPhail Notifies Chandler

WASHINGTON, April 24 (U.P.)—Senator Chandler tonight was informed of his appointment as Baseball Commissioner by Larry MacPhail, who telephoned from Cleveland. The Yankee president put Ford Frick, Will Harridge and representatives of the sixteen major league clubs on the telephone and Mr. Chandler talked to them one by one.

The Senator said that he expected Mr. Frick in Washington within the next few days to discuss when he could take over. He added that league officials had given from thirty to sixty days for him to get his affairs straightened.

Mr. Chandler's hotel room was a bedlam as well-wishers dropped in to extend best wishes and reporters flocked in for an interview. Conversation was interrupted continually by telephone calls. Relating how Mr. MacPhail had broken the news, the Senator said:

"Larry told me that the decision finally was made on the basis of who among all the candidates loved baseball the best. They decided on me. I'm tickled to death and think that is one of the highest tributes ever paid to me in my life."

He said he expected to have full authority as commissioner: that he would not accept if there were any strings attached. "It never occurred to me that it would be anything less," he added. "I can't go in there standing in the shadow of Judge Landis and not have authority to do a good job."

Another telephone call was from Leslie O'Connor, Judge Landis' secretary. Senator Chandler said he had asked Mr. O'Connor to "stand by and we'll do the job."

April 25, 1945

TIGERS ANNEX FLAG ON FOUR-RUN HOMER

Greenberg's Blow With Bases Filled in 9th Tops Browns, 6-3, to Clinch Pennant

NEWHOUSER WINS NO. 25

ST. LOUIS, Sept. 30 (AP)—A mighty home run by Hank Greenberg with the bases filled in the ninth inning proved the championship punch for the Tigers today as

they beat the Browns by 6 to 3 in the first game of a concluding double-header at Sportsman's Park and sewed up the American League pennant.

Never was a title won in more dramatic fashion. Premature darkness was settling over the field and a light mist was falling as big Hank stepped up with his team a run behind and gave one of Nelson Potter's screwballs a tremendous ride into the bleachers just inside the left-field foul line.

The Tigers, the long strain of the flag race suddenly ended by Hank's big whack, raced out of their dugout in a body to meet the tall fellow as he trotted across the plate. One after another they wrung his hand and pounded his broad back as they escorted him joyously to the bench. It was Hank's thirteenth circuit blow since he rejoined the club in July and probably was the most important one he ever has hit.

Play on Muddy Field

It came just in time, too, as the clubs barely had begun the second game a few minutes later when the rain, which had delayed the opener nearly an hour, started coming down in sheets and washed out any further play for the day. It rained off and on throughout the decisive contest and the field was so muddy at times the players had difficulty wading around.

Greenberg's wallop buried the Senators' last hope of finishing in a tie and squared the Tigers away for the opening game of the world series against the Cubs Wednesday in Detroit. After having "backed" close to the title in recent weeks, the Bengals finally won it like true champions, coming from behind to assert their leadership.

Hal Newhouser was credited with the triumph, his twenty-fifth of the season against nine defeats. He relieved Virgil Trucks in the

DETROIT (A.)						ST. LOUIS (A.)					
	ab.	r.	h.	po.	a. e.		ab.	r.	h.	po.	a. e.
Webb, ss	.3	1	1	3	3 0	Gutte'ge, 2b.	.3	1	1	6	3 0
Mayo, 2b	.4	0	1	3	3 0	Finney, if	.2	0	2	1	0 0
Cramer, cf	.5	1	2	0	0	Byrne, rf	.2	0	2	0	0 0
Greenb'g, lf.	.5	1	2	1	1 0	cChristman	.1	0	0	0	0 0
Cullen'e, rf.	.4	1	1	0	0 0	Gray, c	.1	1	0	2	0 0
York, 1b	.5	0	0	6	1 0	McQui'n, 1b.	.4	0	1	5	2 0
Outlaw, 3b.	.2	0	1	1	1 0	Moore, rf	.4	1	1	0	0 0
Richards, c	.4	0	1	10	1 0	Stephens, ss	.4	0	2	2	2 0
Trucks, p	.2	1	0	1	1 0	Mancuso, c	.4	0	0	5	0 0
Newhou'r, p.	.0	0	0	0	0 0	Schulte, 3b	.4	0	0	3	4 0
aWalker	.1	0	1	0	0 0	Potter, p	.3	0	1	1	0 0
bBorom	.0	0	1	0	0 0						
Benton, p	.0	0	0	0	0 0	Total	...32	3	8	27	11 0

Total ...35 6 9 27 11 0
aBatted for Newhouser in ninth.
bRan for Walker in ninth.
cBatted for Byrnes in sixth.

Detroit ....000 011 004—6
St. Louis ....100 000 110—3

Runs batted in—Finney, Mayo, Richards, Stephens, McQuinn, Greenberg (4). Two-base hits—Gutteridge, Potter, McQuinn, Moore. Home run—Greenberg. Sacrifice hits—Webb, Mayo. Double plays—Richards and Mayo; Outlaw, Mayo and York. Left on bases—St. Louis 5, Detroit 9. Bases on balls—Off Trucks 2, Potter 5, Newhouser 1. Struck out—By Trucks 2, Potter 4, Newhouser 5. Hits—Off Trucks 3 in 5 1-3 innings, Newhouser 1 in 2-3, Benton 1 in 1 inning, Potter 9 in 9. Winning pitcher—Newhouser. Umpires—Pingras, Berry, Rue and Hubbard. Time of game—2:33. Attendance—5,582.

sixth inning after the recent Navy dischargee got into trouble.

Double Play Helpful

Al Benton hurled the last inning for the champions and. with the aid of a slick double play, easily protected the club's lead.

It was a tense battle all the way until Hank hit the jackpot, with first one club and then the other forging ahead. The Browns jumped into the lead in the first inning, when Don Gutteridge and Lou Finney, first two batters to face Trucks, ganged on him for a double and a single before he could get his bearings.

The Tigers clawed back to score one off Potter in the fifth on a walk to Trucks and successive sin-

gles by Skeeter Webb and Eddie Mayo, and they pulled ahead, 2—1, in the sixth on a pair of walks and Catcher Paul Richards' clean single to left.

When Trucks weakened in the last of the sixth, giving up a double to Potter and a walk to Gutteridge, Newhouser was rushed in from the bullpen. Hal escaped damage as he struck out Milt Byrnes and caused George Mc- Quinn to fly out to center, but the Browns got to him for the tying run in the seventh on Gene Moore's double off the rightfield wall and Vernon Stephens' single.

Two-Bagger by McQuinn

After the Tigers had failed to

score off Potter in the eighth. even though their first two batters sin- gled, the Browns pushed over an- other run in their half on Finney's single and McQuinn's two-base blast off the screen in deep right center.

Things looked extremely gloomy for Manager Steve O'Neill's cham- pions when they came up for the last time. Hub Walker batted for Newhouser and plunked a single into center field. Webb laid down a bunt toward first, and both run- ners were safe when the throw to second was not in time to get Walker, though the Browns kicked hard on the decision. Red Borom went in to run for Walker.

Mayo sacrificed, moving both runners along, and then, after

a mid-diamond conference, the Browns decided to pass Roger Cramer purposely to get to Green- berg. It was a fatal mistake. The big man rubbed his bat vigorously with a hunk of bone he had carried out to the plate for the purpose, looked at a ball and then got the one he wanted.

There was never a doubt the wallop was going into the stands, but it was so close to the foul line that the crowd of 5,582 paid admis- sions gave the umpires a rousing raspberry for calling it a fair ball. The drive gave the Tigers the game they needed for the championship.

The box score:

October 1, 1945

Cards Win Pennant

BROOKS LOSE, 8-4, DESPITE 3-RUN 9TH

By JOHN DREBINGER

Incredible as it may sound, the National League's pennant race finally has ended.

It drew to a close about 15 minutes after 4 o'clock yesterday afternoon at Ebbets Field when the Cardi- nals, after battering their foe with a bruising thirteen-hit attack, smothered a last-ditch demonstra- tion by a desperate band of Dodgers to finish on top, 8 to 4.

That gave the Redbirds from St. Louis the first pennant play-off series in major league history in two straight victories and the right to engage the American League's champion Red Sox in the long de- ferred and almost forgotten World Series, which will get under way in St. Louis next Sunday.

Remaining in character to the end, the Flatbush Flock went down swinging with one last despairing, electrifying flourish. Held to one run and two hits by Murry Dick- son, crack right-hander, for eight

innings—with both the run and the hits coming in the first— Brooklyn's Beloved Bums thrilled what was left of a gathering of 31,437 of the faithful in the ninth inning by routing Dickson and con- tinuing their attack against Harry Brecheen until they had three tal- lies in and the bases full.

Two Strike-Outs End Game

With the tying run at the plate and only one out, Brecheen hung up two searing strike-outs that doubtless will leave their scars for years to come. Then it was that the Bums, who had escaped seem- ingly inevitable extinction so many times this year, finally breathed their last.

Starting with left-handed Joe Hatten, who was blasted out in- side of five rounds, by which time he had given as many runs, Leo Durocher hurled six pitchers into the struggle, but all to no avail.

So the Cardinals bagged their ninth National League pennant over a span of twenty years and for the sixth time under a differ- ent manager. Rogers Hornsby was the first one for the Redbirds in 1926. Two years later Bill Mc- Kechnie piloted them home in front. In 1930 and 1931, Gabby Street, who came all the way from St. Louis to see yesterday's en- counter, was the winning skipper. Frankie Frisch led the famed Gas- house Gang in 1934 and then came Billy Southworth's three straight winning campaigns from 1942 to 1944.

Now quiet, soft-spoken Eddie Dyer, who used to operate the Cardinal farm system, retired a few years ago and returned when Southworth left for Boston, has guided St. Louis home in front in his first year as a major league manager and after one of the most thrilling campaigns in history.

Good World Series Record

Five of eight previous Cardinal pennant winners went on to take world championships, if that is or any encouragement to the present Redbirds as they prepare for the redoubtable Red Sox. who for

weeks and weeks have been wait- ing for this big moment.

As yesterday's battle got under way under a cloudless sky, the crowd, doomed to spend most of the afternoon in stony silence, got an early chance to whoop it up a bit when the Dodgers in a surprise foray after their first two batters had been retired tore into Dickson for a run.

Augie Galan, who in a last-min- ute switch was moved to third while Dick Whitman started in left, outgalloped an infield hit to Red Schoendienst. On the heels of this came a single by Dixie Walker and when Ed Stevens lashed a single through the mound and into center field Galan romped home amid considerable noise.

At that, it didn't sound quite like a genuine Flatbush roar, giving rise to the suspicion that in the general shuffle for reserved seats most of the faithful must have suf- fered a complete shut-out. It seemed more like a sedate world series gathering than the boister- ous Flatbush host one might have expected for the occasion.

Marion Drives in Dusak

Then the Dodger lead vanished almost as quickly as the cheers in that first inning had subsided. With one out in the second, Erv (four-sack) Dusak smacked one against the left-field wall and while he didn't get all four sacks on that shot he did get three. Came a fly by Marty Marion to Carl Furillo in center and Dusak scored.

A moment later two surprise blows snapped the tie almost in the twinkling of an eye. Clyde Kluttz, whom the Giants had tossed away last May for some- thing less than a song, considering the fact that Vince DiMaggio never could sing, slammed a single into center. That, of course, didn't seem so damaging, as the next batter was Dickson.

But the slim right-hander has a habit of producing a damaging blow when least expected. He won one of those important Cub games in the West with a single and this time he did infinitely better. He belted a line triple into right center. It fetched home Kluttz and the Cards were in front to remain there.

To be sure, the margin at that point was only 2 to 1, but somehow the folks seemed to feel it was all over and when the Redbirds went

on another rampage in the fifth, routing Hatten with a three-run blast, even the last die-hard on the premises realized the Bums had run out their string of miraculous achievements. They were just in there to take a beating and they absorbed it, one must say, with ex- ceptionally good grace.

It was quite an unexpected blow that leveled the flock in the fifth round, for there were two out and the bases were empty when Stan Musial, batting champion of the league, banged a double over Dixie Walker's head in right. Hatten then was instructed to pass Whitey Kurowski, but this was to prove a sad day for Durocher's usually successful strategems.

Enos Slaughter, who isn't a fel- low to take lightly the imputation

Dodgers' Box Score

ST. LOUIS (N.)	ab.	r.	h.	po.	a.	e.
Schoen't, 2b.	5	1	1	1	5	0
Moore, cf.	5	1	2	2	0	0
Musial, 1b.	4	1	1	14	1	0
Kurow'i, 3b.	2	1	1	1	1	0
Slaugh'r, rf.	3	1	1	0	0	0
Dusak, lf.	3	1	2	1	0	0
H. Wal'r, lf.	1	0	0	0	0	0
Marion, ss.	3	0	1	4	3	0
Kluttz, c.	5	1	2	3	2	0
Dickson, p.	5	0	2	1	5	0
Brecheen, p.	0	0	0	0	0	0
Total	36	8	13	27	17	0

BROOKLYN (N.)	ab.	r.	h.	po.	a.	e.
Stanky, 2b.	5	0	0	3	4	0
Whitman, lf.	4	0	0	2	0	0
aSchults	1	0	0	0	0	0
Galan, 3b.	4	2	2	1	0	0
F. Wal'r, rf.	3	0	0	1	0	0
Stevens, 1b.	4	1	2	11	0	0
Furillo, cf.	4	1	1	4	0	0
Reese, ss.	2	0	0	2	3	0
Edwards, c.	2	0	1	3	1	0
Hatten, p.	0	0	0	0	0	0
Behrman, p.	0	0	0	0	0	0
aHerm'ski	1	0	0	0	0	0
Lomb'rdi, p.	0	0	0	0	1	0
Higbie, p.	0	0	0	0	0	0
Melton, p.	0	0	0	0	0	0
bMedwick	1	0	0	0	0	0
Taylor, p.	0	0	0	0	0	0
cLevagetto	0	0	0	0	0	0
Total	32	4	6	27	14	0

aBatted for Beh'man in fifth.
bBatted for Melton in eighth.
cBatted for Taylor in ninth.
dBatted for Whitman in ninth.

St. Louis .... 0 2 0 0 3 0 1 2 0—8
Brooklyn .... 1 0 0 0 0 0 0 0 3—4

Runs batted in—Stevens 2, Marion 2, Dickson, Slaughter 2, Dusak, Kurowski 2, Furillo, Edwards.

Two-base hits—Musial, Moore, Galan. Three- base hits—Dusak, Dickson, Slaughter, Stevens. Sacrifices—Schoendienst, Dusak, Marion. Double plays—Dickson, Marion and Musial; Stanky, Reese and Stevens. Left on bases—St. Louis 11, Brook- lyn 7. Bases on balls—Off Dickson 5 (F. Walker, Edwards 2, Reese 2); Hatten 3 (Kurowski 2, Mar- ion); Lombardi 2 (Kurowski, Slaughter); Higbie 2 (Musial, Slaughter); Brecheen 1 (Levagetto). Struck out—By Dickson 3 (Stanky, Reese, Her- manski); Brecheen 2 (Stanky, Schultz); Higbie 1 (Dickson); Taylor 1 (Dickson).

Pitching summary—Hatten 7 hits 5 runs in 4 2-3 innings; Behrman 1 hit 0 runs in 1-3; Lom- bardi 1 hit 1 run in 1 1-3; Higbie 3 hits 2 runs in 1; Melton 0 hits 0 runs in 2-3; Taylor 1 hit 0 runs in 1; Dickson 5 hits 3 runs in 8 1-3 in- nings; Brecheen 1 hit 1 run in 2-3. Wild pitch— Dickson. Winning pitcher—Dickson. Losing pitcher—Hatten.

Umpires—Pinelli (plate); Goetz (1b); Boggess (2b); Reardon (3b). Time of game—2:44. At- tendance—31,487.

that he can't hit a left-hander as well as any right-handed batsman, smashed a terrific drive into deep right center and by the time the ball had been retrieved Slaughter was on third for another Redbird triple while Musial and Kurowski were over the plate.

Next came a single to center by Dusak, Slaughter raced in with the third tally of the inning and Hatten went out to be replaced by Hank Behrman, who finally brought the round to a close without further damage.

There was no checking those Redbirds for long, though. With Behrman passing out almost immediately for the first of four pinch-hitters Durocher tossed into the battle, little Vic Lombardi appeared in the sixth.

Lombardi Loses Control

The diminutive southpaw got by well enough in that inning, but he walked Kurowski and Slaughter to open the seventh. After a sacrifice by Dusak, Durocher made another frantic wave to the Dodger bull pen.

It called out the indefatigable Kirby Higbe and his familiar "13," but the numeral brought no particular luck on this momentous occasion. Marion executed a deft sacrifice squeeze bunt that sent Kurowski streaking home from third and while this was the only tally the Redbirds got in this round,

they smacked Higbe lustily in the eighth, routing him with a three-hit splurge that accounted for their final pair of tallies.

Many Fans Leave Before Rally

Schoendienst opened this brisk assault with a single and a moment later swept around to third on a double to left by Terry Moore. Again came an intentional pass, this time to Musial, and again the move failed to meet requirements.

Kurowski, walked three times in a row, slammed a single into right and Schoendienst and Moore counted. The Redbirds now had eight runs, while the Dodgers, though still on their feet, appeared hopelessly out.

After their brief first inning demonstration against Dickson, they had been utterly unable to do a thing for seven tortuous rounds. In fact, in that stretch they got only one ball beyond the confines of the infield, a fly to left by Stevens in the fourth. They never were close to a hit, drew three passes and not a Dodger advanced to second.

It was too much for even the hardiest of Flatbush habitues and so it was that when the Dodgers, with an effort born of despair, launched their belated ninth-inning rally the stands were almost one-quarter empty.

The attack began with Galan ramming a double into right, but when the beloved Dixie Walker, hitless throughout this play-off series, flied harmlessly to centre, the folks just knew this was the bitter end. Even when Stevens followed with a three-base smash to center, scoring Galan, it caused only a feeble cheer, but soon it became evident that both the Dodgers and the noise were not to be shut down with this for a final gesture.

Furillo plunked a single in centre driving in Stevens. Then Dickson unfurled a wild pitch and walked Peewee Reese and the folks plucky enough to remain let out a full-throated roar.

Ideal Setting for Homer

Dyer, unable to stand the suspense any longer, bustled out of his dugout for the second time in the inning and called in Brecheen, a left-hander, but the Cat wasn't to solve the problem at once. Bruce Edwards greeted Brecheen with a single to left, driving in Furillo with the third run of the inning, and when Cookie Lavagetto, batting for Harry Taylor, walked, filling the bases, Flatbush could not have asked for a better setting.

There was the tying run at the plate and a homer into the stands really would have turned things upside down, but at that point the fates must have decided that

Brooklyn's hour of miraculous deeds had run far enough. Either that, or Brecheen decided he had better put a little more stuff on the ball.

Stanky fanned, taking the third strike and then tall Howie Schultz, who had hit a homer in that first play-off game on Tuesday in St. Louis, batted for Dick Whitman. He swung with tremendous fervor but disturbed nothing save the atmosphere, for his strike-out ended the struggle. The Flock, at least, went down swinging to provide some measure of comfort for those who remained to the last.

With this triumph the Cards closed the season's book against their most determined foes with a record of sixteen triumphs against eight for the Flock. Never conceded the barest pennant chance at the outset of the race last April, Brooklyn remained in the running until battered down in this unprecedented play-off series.

The victory was Dickson's fifteenth against only six setbacks. It was also his fourth over the Brooks, who beat him once. Hatten, going into the battle seeking his fifteen triumph and with a six-game winning streak, went down for his eleventh reverse and fourth at the hands of the Redbirds.

October 4, 1946

PENSION PROGRAM FOR PLAYERS VOTED BY MAJOR LEAGUES

By JOHN DREBINGER

The most elaborate and complicated pension program ever undertaken by a professional sport was adopted yesterday when the National and American Leagues, sitting in joint session in the Waldorf-Astoria Hotel, agreed to a plan assuring veteran baseball players an income ranging from $50 to $100 a month on reaching

fifty years of age.

In making the announcement Commissioner A. B. (Happy) Chandler, who presided at the meeting, said the two leagues approved in full the plan worked out by a special committee. Dixie Walker of the Dodgers and Johnny Murphy of the Yankees sat as player representatives on the committee. It meets, Chandler said, virtually all the original requests made by the players.

Under the provisions of the program a player, after serving five seasons in the major leagues, shall receive, on reaching 50, an income of $50 a month for the rest of his life. Each additional year of service will increase the pension amount $10 a month until a maximum of $100 a month is reached for ten-year men and over.

Those Who Are Eligible

All players, coaches and trainers on the rosters of the sixteen major league clubs on opening day of the 1947 season shall be eligible. Also, all players who served in the war shall be permitted to include that time in service, provided they were in the major leagues for three years prior to their entrance into the armed forces.

To insure this huge pension program, which within a few years will involve several thousand players, it is estimated by its underwriters, the Equitable Life Assur-

ance Society of the United States, that an annual pool of approximately $675,000 will be required.

This amount will be raised by dues from players, contributions by the ball clubs, the total receipts from the annual All-Star game and the $150,000 which some sponsor pays annually for the world series radio broadcasting rights.

Victory For the Players

It was estimated yesterday that the ball clubs will carry approximately 80 per cent of the burden of upkeep, thereby yielding another signal victory to the players who, when they started their movement for better working conditions last year, included a pension request among their demands.

Dues from players will operate on a sliding scale. A player must pay $45.45 the first year he subscribes to the plan, and $90.90 the second year. Thereafter the payments increase each year until the tenth year when the fee will be $454.75. However, when a player's total payments aggregate $2,500, his yearly payments shall be reduced to $250 annually.

In the event a player does not remain in the majors at least five years to qualify for the lowest income the money he has put in shall be returned to him. Also, should a player die before drawing any benefits, a group insurance plan provides that his beneficiaries

shall be paid for 120 months at the rate applying to the player.

Obligation of Owners

The club owners' contributions shall consist of a flat payment of $250 by each club for every player on its roster subscribing to the plan and there will be no refunds on these subscriptions. The owners further committed themselves to make up the difference should there still be insufficient funds on hand to finance the plan. There is at present $352,000 being held in escrow by Commissioner Chandler for the fund, part of this amount including last year's All-Star receipts and the money from the sale of the world series radio rights.

It is stipulated, however, that for the plan to operate a 75 per cent membership will be required from an entire league, and each club must have at least 60 per cent of its players participating. If less than this quota on a club takes part, none can be permitted to do so.

Feeling in a surprisingly magnanimous mood, the club owners also adopted a rule which provides a minimum world series players' pool of $250,000 whenever the receipts do not come up to that amount. Last fall the players of the Cardinals and Red Sox shared in only $212,000, with the result that the individual players of the losing Boston club received less money than the umpires. Under the new arrangement a player on a winning team will be guaranteed approximately $5,000.

Slight Curb Adopted

At the same time the owners moved to put a slight curb on post-season barnstorming with the adoption of a rule which prohibits barnstorming games to start until the conclusion of the world series. The 30-day limit, however, still prevails.

At the insistence of the Commissioner, the magnates also acted to curb the practice of a club rewarding its pennant winning players with a bonus such as Owner Tom Yawkey conferred on his Red Sox players last season. Actually, a rule barring the practice has been on the books but it failed to carry a penalty. Now teeth have been added and any club giving its players such group awards shall be fined the equivalent of the total bonus.

Official recognition also was given to the "bonus player" clause which provides that any free agent player who receives more than $5,000 for signing a contract shall be known as a "bonus player" and thus subjected to numerous restrictions. Actually, the leagues adopted the rule last year, but numerous changes had to be made to make it conform with the demands of the minor leaguers.

Just before the joint meeting went into session George Traut-

man, new president of the National Association, governing body of the minors, appeared before the owners. He assured them that the vigorous campaign launched by his predecessor, William G. Bramham, to stamp out gambling evils would be continued and that he was confident present plans would meet the situation fully.

February 2, 1947

Chandler Bars Durocher For 1947 Baseball Season

By LOUIS EFFRAT

Leo Durocher, manager of the Brooklyn Dodgers, yesterday was suspended for the 1947 season by Commissioner A. B. (Happy) Chandler in the most drastic action ever taken against a major league baseball pilot.

From his offices in Cincinnati, where the diamond czar had been weighing evidence, Chandler announced also that Charley (Chuck) Dressen, New York Yankee coach, had been suspended for thirty days. Fines of $2,000 each were levied against the Dodger and Yankee clubs and one of $500 against Harold Parrott, Brooklyn road secretary.

The Durocher and Dressen suspensions are effective next Tuesday.

All Quiet in Brooklyn

The outgrowth of a feud that has been seething between the Brooklyn and Yankee organizations since L. S. (Larry) MacPhail, former Dodger president, moved over to the Yankees in the rival American League, the ruling by Chandler brought a strange stillness to Brooklyn yesterday. In Durocher case the severity of the penalty was without precedent in all-time baseball history, covering more than a century.

Durocher, oft-entangled, fiery field manager who in eight seasons at the helm of the Dodgers master-minded his team into first-division finishes seven times and won Brooklyn's first National League pennant in twenty-one years in 1941, was charged by Commissioner Chandler with being guilty of "conduct detrimental to baseball."

Durocher and President Branch Rickey of the Dodgers had accused MacPhail, Leo's one-time boss and friend, of having alleged gamblers in his box at an exhibition game between the Dodgers and Yankees at Havana last month. MacPhail, perturbed, to put it mildly, filed charges against both and the commissioner held hearings at Sarasota and at St. Petersburg. Chandler listened to testimony from numerous baseball persons, but did not disclose his decision until yesterday.

Standards Not Met

The commissioner, in his decision at Cincinnati, said:

"Durocher has not measured up to the standards expected or required of managers of our baseball teams.

"This incident in Havana, which brought considerable unfavorable comment to baseball generally, was one of a series of publicity-producing affairs in which Manager Durocher has been involved in the last few months.

"Managers of baseball teams are responsible for the conduct of players on the field. Good managers are able to insure the good conduct of the players on the field and frequently their example can influence players to be of good conduct off the field.

"As a result of the accumulation of unpleasant incidents detrimental to baseball, Manager Durocher is hereby suspended from participating in professional baseball for the 1947 season."

Dressen was suspended because in Chandler's opinion, the crafty coach, himself a former major-league pilot, had broken a verbal agreement to remain with the Dodgers as aide to Durocher, Chuck now serves in a similar capacity under Stanley (Bucky) Harris of the Yankees.

Reason for Parrott Fine

Parrott, ex-baseball writer for The Brooklyn Daily Eagle, was fined because, as Durocher's "ghost writer," he had written derogatory statements in Durocher's column in the Eagle. Incidentally, he was ordered by Chandler to stop writing the column at once.

The $2,000 fines against each club were "because their officials engaged in a public controversy damaging to baseball."

Dejected, confused, bewildered in fact, Durocher received the news in Rickey's office yesterday morning. Aside from a "For what?" outburst. The Lip, as he is called, remained quiet, as it were. That Leo is to be sidelined for the season was a shock to everyone in Brooklyn—the front office and the man-on-the-street.

Durocher, President Rickey, coaches and other executives were in conference in the Brooklyn offices early yesterday. They were engaged in a round-table discussion concerning the immediate future of Jackie Robinson, Negro star with the Montreal farm club. Rickey's phone rang. It was a long distance emergency call from Cincinnati and Commissioner Chandler was on the opposite end.

Silent on His Plans

The commissioner informed Rickey of his action and when the Dodger president told Durocher, the latter's reaction was "For what?" Throughout the afternoon, Leo's only remarks were repeatedly "For what?" He had nothing to say about future plans, how long he would remain here, where he would go or what his next move might be. He just didn't know. Nor did Rickey.

Would there be an appeal?

"To whom?" Rickey replied. "Mr. Chandler is the commissioner. No, I don't think we will appeal."

Will Durocher's salary—estimated to be in the neighborhood of $57,000 annually, including bonuses—be paid during the period of suspension?

"I haven't gone into that," Rickey said.

Will Durocher be returned as manager in 1948?

"Obviously, I can't talk about that now," Rickey answered.

It was evident that none directly or indirectly concerned in the most spectacular off-the-field baseball development in years was in the mood to talk about it. At the offices of the Yankees, MacPhail had "nothing at all to say." Instead, he scheduled a press conference for 11 A. M. today at the midtown offices of the Yankees.

No Comment From Frick

Ford Frick, National League president, hastily summoned to Brooklyn by Rickey, had no comment, and at Chicago, Will Harridge, American League head, was similarly noncommittal. Anyway, Commissioner Chandler had warned:

"All parties to this controversy are silenced from the time this order is issued."

Totally unexpected, Chandler's action was most stunning. It left the Dodgers without a manager a

week before the regular season's start. Four exhibition games are to be played at Ebbets Field, one with Montreal today and three with the Yankees over the weekend. For today only, Clyde Sukeforth, one of Durocher's trio of coaches, will handle the Dodgers against the Royals.

Of Durocher's successor, Rickey merely said: "We'll have a manager on the field next Tuesday." Who that person will be still is a matter of conjecture. Among the experts, there was considerable speculation yesterday. The names of Ray Blades, currently a Brooklyn coach and former manager of St. Louis Cardinals; Dixie Walker, veteran outfielder of the Dodgers; Bill Terry, former Giant leader; Frankie Frisch, ex-St. Louis Cardinal and Pittsburgh Pirate pilot, now a radio broadcaster, and three or four others were mentioned as possibilities.

Target of Criticism

Commissioner Chandler, who exonerated MacPhail and Rickey in yesterday's action, showed that he is determined to rule with a firm hand. The target of much criticism since he succeeded the late Judge Kenesaw Mountain Landis two years ago, the former Governor and Senator from Kentucky made his biggest and certainly his most important decision yesterday.

Not even Landis, who once suspended Babe Ruth and Bob Meusel for forty days back in 1921, dealt so heavily with a suspended player. The judge later barred Jimmy O'Connell and Cozy Dolan of the Giants for life, but on the matter of suspension yesterday's move was tops.

Durocher celebrated his fortieth birthday last July. He was involved in a fracas with a fan at Ebbets Field last season, but was cleared in court of fracturing the man's jaw. Durocher and Chandler had a long chat after the season and it is rumored that the commissioner warned Leo to watch his step, to choose his company.

Last winter Durocher married Laraine Day, movie star, and legal complications followed. Miss Day, here now, was scheduled to fly to Hollywood last night, but delayed the trip after learning of her husband's suspension.

Some persons — none officially connected with baseball—yesterday were inclined to remove Durocher permanently from the picture. They, however, were strictly guessing. It is not that easy to read Rickey's mind.

April 10, 1947

Dodgers Purchase Robinson, First Negro in Modern Major League Baseball

ROYALS' STAR SIGNS WITH BROOKS TODAY

International League Batting Champion Will Bid for Job in Big League Infield

MONTREAL TRIPS DODGERS

Lund and Campanis Hit 2-Run Homers Against Branca in Fourth for 4-3 Triumph

By LOUIS EFFRAT

Jackie Robinson, 28-year-old infielder, yesterday became the first Negro to achieve major-league baseball status in modern times. His contract was purchased from the Montreal Royals of the International League by the Dodgers and he will be in a Brooklyn uniform at Ebbets Field today, when the Brooks oppose the Yankees in the first of three exhibition games over the week-end.

A native of Georgia, Robinson won fame in baseball, football, basketball and track at the University of California at Los Angeles before entering the armed service as a private. He emerged a lieutenant in 1945 and in October of that year was signed to a Montreal contract. Robinson's performances in the International League, which he led in batting last season with an average of .349, prompted President Branch Rickey of the Dodgers to promote Jackie.

The decision was made while Robinson was playing first base for Montreal against the Dodgers at Ebbets Field. Jackie was blanked at the plate and contributed little to his team's 4-3 victory before 14,282 fans, but it was nevertheless, a history-making day for the well-proportioned lad.

An Inopportune Moment

Jackie had just popped into a double-play, attempting to bunt in the fifth inning, when Arthur Mann, assistant to Rickey, appeared in the press box. He handed out a brief, typed announcement: "The Brooklyn Dodgers today purchased the contract of Jackie Rosevelt Robinson from the Montreal Royals."

Robinson will appear at the Brooklyn offices this morning to sign a contract. Rickey does not anticipate any difficulty over terms.

According to the records, the last Negro to play in the majors was one Moses Fleetwood Walker, who caught for Toledo of the American Association when that circuit enjoyed major-league classification back in 1884.

The call for Robinson was no surprise. Most baseball persons had been expecting it. After all, he had proved his right to the opportunity by his extraordinary work in the AAA minor league, where he stole 40 bases and was the best defensive second baseman. He sparked the Royals to the pennant and the team went on to annex the little world series.

Robinson's path in the immediate future may not be too smooth, however. He may run into antipathy from Southerners who form about 60 per cent of the league's playing strength. In fact, it is rumored that a number of Dodgers expressed themselves unhappy at the possibility of having to play with Jackie.

Jackie, himself, expects no trouble. He said he was "thrilled and it's what I've been waiting for." When his Montreal mates congratulated him and wished him luck, Robinson answered: "Thanks, I'll need it."

Whether Robinson will be used at first or second base is not known. That will depend upon the new manager, yet to be named by Rickey.

Rickey, in answer to a direct query, declared he did not expect trouble from other players, because of Robinson. "We are all agreed," he said, "that Jackie is ready for the chance."

Several thousand Negroes were in the stands at yesterday's exhibition. When Robinson appeared for batting practice, he drew a warm and pleasant reception. Dixie Walker, quoted in 1945 as opposed to playing with Jackie, was booed on his first turn at bat. Walker answered with a resounding single.

If, however, Robinson is to make the grade, he will have to do better than he did against the Brooks. Against Ralph Branca, Jackie rolled meekly to the mound, walked and then popped an intended sacrifice bunt into a double play. At first base—a new position for him—he handled himself flawlessly, but did not have a difficult chance.

Six Hits for Each Club

The biggest crowd to watch the Dodgers this spring saw the Brooks, under Clyde Sukeforth (he's the pro tem manager, Rickey said), go down to defeat before the sound pitching of Ervin Palica and Jack Banta, who combined for a six-hit effort. The Royals collected the same number of safeties against Branca, Hank Behrman and Lefty Paul Minner, but two were round-trippers.

The homers, both in the fourth inning at the expense of Branca, accounted for all the Montreal runs. After Robinson had walked and Jack Jorgensen had flied out, Don Lund blasted a liner into the lower left-field stand. Then a pass to Earl Naylor and a longer four-bagger to left center by Al Campanis made it 4—0.

The Dodgers retrieved two runs in the same stanza. Walker walked and Duke Snider doubled to center. Walker tallied and when Lou Welaj, Montreal shortstop, threw wild on the relay, Snider went all the way around. A walk to Stan Rojek and Gene Hermanski's double netted the last Brooklyn run in the seventh.

While Lund's and Campanis' round-trippers were well tagged, both would have been caught last year. The walls are fourteen feet closer to home plate this season.

"I'm for Robinson" buttons were sold outside the park.

The box score:

MONTREAL	ab.	r.	h.	po.	a.	e.
Welaj, ss.	3	0	0	2	1	1
Rob'son, 1b.	3	1	0	7	0	0
Jorg'sen, 3b.	4	0	1	0	1	0
Lund, rf.	3	1	1	0	0	0
Naylor, cf.	3	1	1	3	0	0
Pluss, lf.	3	0	1	1	0	0
C'panis, c.	2b.	4	1	3	3	0
Sandlock, c.	2	0	0	7	0	0
U'p'an'la.	c.	1	0	0	3	1	0
Palica, p.	2	0	1	0	0	0
ashuba	1	0	0	0	0	0
Banta, p.	1	0	0	0	3	0
Total	29	4	6	27	10	1

DODGERS (N.)	ab.	r.	h.	po.	a.	e.
Stanky, 2b.	3	0	0	3	2	0
Mauch, 2b.	2	0	0	2	0
La'g'to, 3b.	2	0	0	1	1	0
Rojek, 3b.	1	1	0	0	0	0
Herm'ki, lf.	3	0	2	5	0
Walker, rf.	2	1	1	0	0
Woyt, rf.	1	0	0	0	0
Snider, cf.	4	1	2	9	0	0
Stevens, 1b.	1	0	0	8	0	0
rTatum	0	0	0	0	0	0
Miksis, ss.	3	0	2	3	2	0
Brazan, c.	3	0	0	2	2	0
dReiser	0	0	0	0	0	0
Anderson, c.	0	0	0	1	0	0
Branca, p.	2	0	0	2	0
bWhitman	1	0	0	0	0	0
Behrman	0	0	0	0	0	0
eVaughn	1	0	1	0	0
Minner, p.	0	0	0	1	1
Total	30	3	6	27	13	1

aGrounded out for Palica in seventh.
bFanned for Branca in seventh.
cRan for Stevens in eighth.
dWalked for Bragan in eighth.
eSingled for Behrman in eighth.

Montreal .... 0 0 0 4 0 0 0 0 0—4
Brooklyn .... 0 0 0 2 0 0 1 0 0—3

Runs batted in—Lund 2, Campanis 2, Snider, Hermanski. Two-base hits—Hermanski 2, Snider, Jorgensen. Home runs—Lund, Campanis. Sacrifices—Miksis, Pluss. Double plays—Lavagetto and Miksis; Mauch, Miksis and Stevens; Banta, Campanella and Robinson. Left on bases—Montreal 5, Brooklyn 10. Bases on balls—Off Palica 4, Branca 6, Banta 4. Struck out—By Palica 6, Branca 2, Banta 2, Minner 1. Hits—Off Palica 4 in 6 innings, Banta 2 in 3, Branca 4 in 7, Behrman 1 in 1, Minner 1 in 1. Winning pitcher—Palica. Losing pitcher—Branca. Umpires—Tabacchi and Goetz. Time of game—2:20. Attendance—14,282.

April 11, 1947

Says Cards' Strike Plan Against Negro Dropped

Ford Frick, National League president, said last night a threatened strike by the St. Louis Cardinals against the presence of Negro First Baseman Jackie Robinson in a Brooklyn Dodger uniform has been averted, The Associated Press reported.

Frick said that Sam Breadon, owner of the Cardinals, came to New York last week and informed him that he understood there was a movement among the Cardinals to strike in protest during their just-concluded series with the Dodgers if Robinson was in the line-up.

"I didn't have to talk to the players myself. Mr. Breadon did the talking to them. From what Breadon told me afterward the trouble was smoothed over. I don't know what he said to them, who the ringleader was, or any other details," Frick said.

Asked if he intended to take any action, Frick said he would have to investigate further before he could make any decision.

The National League president said he had not conferred with Baseball Commissioner A. B. (Happy) Chandler concerning the matter.

May 9, 1947

DODGERS' ONLY HIT BEATS YANKEES, 3-2, WITH 2 OUT IN NINTH

Lavagetto's Pinch Double Bats in 2 Runs. Evens Series and Spoils Bevens' No-Hitter

10 WALKS HELP BROOKLYN

Casey Wins in Relief Second Day in Row With Lone Pitch Resulting in Double Play

By JOHN DREBINGER

With the first no-hitter in world series history in the making at Ebbets Field yesterday, Cookie Lavagetto rewrote the script with two out in the ninth inning to establish the Dodgers as the first club in baseball's autumnal classic ever to win a game on just one hit.

In his familiar role of pinch hitter, the veteran Lavagetto slammed a two-bagger off the right-field wall against Floyd (Bill) Bevens that drove in two runners put on by walks. That floored the Yankees on the spot for a 3-to-2 Brooklyn triumph, tied the series at two victories apiece, stunned about half the crowd of 33,443 and sent the other half— the faithful of Flatbush—screaming hysterically on to the field in an endeavor to lay fond hands on their hero.

Bevens, stalwart right-hander, was within one short stride of baseball immortality until he lost all in the twinkling of an eye to Burt Shotton's unpredictable Dodgers.

For eight and two-thirds innings of this nerve-tingling fourth game Bevens, a strong, silent man from Salem, Ore., held the bats of Brooklyn's Bums even more silent than a tomb. No series pitcher ever had gone that far without allowing a hit.

An Unenviable Record

On the way, Bevens established another world series mark, though he will never reflect upon that one in his later years with any feeling of gratification. He gave ten bases on balls, one more than Colby Jack Coombs of the Athletics permitted in 1910.

Two of those passes helped the Dodgers to their first run in the fifth inning to whittle away one of

two tallies the Yanks had counted earlie.. And the final two were indirectly to cause his defeat, though the last one was not wholly of his choosing. It was ordered by Manager Bucky Harris, who by that decision left himself open to sharp criticism. Most observers seemed to feel the usually astute Yankee skipper had pulled something of a strategic "rock."

As the final half of the ninth opened, with the Bombers leading, 2 to 1. Bruce Edwards went out when Johnny Lindell hauled down his lofty shot in front of the left-field stand with a leaping catch. But Carl Furillo walked for Bevens' ninth pass before Shotton fairly sprayed the summery afternoon with a maze of masterminding.

Jorgensen Fouls Out

After Spider Jorgensen had fouled out to George McQuinn back of first, Shotton sent Al Gionfriddo, rookie outfielder, to run for Furillo. Only one more batter need be retired then to clinch the victory for Bevens as well as that world series no-hit goal which has eluded some of baseball's greatest hurlers since 1903.

The batter was Pete Reiser, whom Shotton sent up for Hugh Casey, relief ace who had entered the contest in the top half of the ninth with the bases full and one out to end the inning on one pitch. Pistol Pete, limping painfully on a swollen ankle which he had

sprained the previous day, had sat this one out up to that moment.

Shotton's strategy flashed again with one strike and two balls on Reiser as Gionfriddo streaked for second and stole the bag on an eyelash play. That pitch, too, was wide, making the count three and one.

There Harris made his questionable move. He ordered Bevens to toss the next one wide, thereby walking the lame Reiser. It seemed a direct violation of one of baseball's fundamental precepts which dictates against putting the "winning run" on base in such a situation.

Shotton followed with two more moves on the field, which seemed suddenly converted into a chessboard. He sent Eddie Miksis in to run for Reiser, an obvious shift, and then called on Lavagetto to bat for Ed Stanky.

The swarthy-complexioned veteran, a right-handed batter, swung viciously at the first pitch and missed. Then he swung again and connected, the ball sailing toward the right-field wall.

Over raced Tommy Henrich. The previous inning the brilliant Yankee gardener had made a glittering leaping catch of a similar fly ball to rob Gene Hermanski of a blow and keep the no-hitter alive.

There was nothing Tommy could do about this one, though it soared over his head and struck the wall. Desperately he tried to clutch the ball as it caromed off the boards in order to get it home as quickly as possible, but that sloping wall

is a tricky barrier and as the ball bounced to the ground more precious moments were lost.

Finally Henrich hurried the ball on its way. McQuinn caught it and relayed it to the plate, but all too late. Gionfriddo and Miksis already were over the plate while in the center of the diamond Dodger players and fans were all but mobbing Lavagetto in their elation.

First to Lose One-Hitter

While that was going on Bevens, the silent man from the northwest, was walking silently from the field. In a matter of seconds a priceless no-hit victory had been wrenched from his grasp and converted into a galling one-hit defeat. Only two other pitchers had tossed world series one-hitters before with both, of course, winning. They were Ed Reulbach of the Cubs in 1906 and Claude Passeau, a later day Cub, in 1945.

Big Casey, relief pitcher who had won for the Flock in that stirring 9-8 game the previous day, also was returned the winner of this one, though he pitched only one ball. The Flock was still behind when he went in and under the rules he automatically became the victor, the first pitcher in world series history to take two games on successive days.

Huge Hughey entered the struggle when Hank Behrman, third of Shotton's hurlers in this extraordinary conflict, got into trouble. A single by Lindell, a belated throw to second by Edwards on Bevens' sacrifice and a single by George Stirnweiss filled the bases with one out in the ninth.

Gionfriddo stealing second in ninth inning as Rizzuto takes Berra's throw. Pinelli is the umpire.

Casey Replaces Behrman

Casey replaced Behrman. Henrich slapped his first pitch right back into Casey's hands. Hughey fired to Catcher Edwards at the plate for one out and Edwards winged to Jackie Robinson at first for the double play.

That inning, too, was typical of the Yanks' play throughout. Actually they lost by wasting myriad chances to sew it up decisively. In the opening round, Harry Taylor, an experimental starter for the Dodgers, offered to roll up the series on the spot for the Bombers when he faced only four batters and forced in a run with a walk.

That tally was all the Yanks made out of their flying start. They didn't get another until the fourth when Bill Johnson cracked Hal Gregg for a triple to open the inning and Lindell followed with a double. They never did get another with Gregg pitching brilliantly from the first through the seventh and though they totaled eight blows they lost when their hurler allowed only one.

The Yanks started as if they meant to annihilate the Dodgers piecemeal and mesh the parts into the Gowanus. The opportunity lay before them to tear the game wide open as the youthful Taylor, carrying for the moment Shotton's despairing hopes, faced four batters and got none out, although he would have retired one except for a misplay.

Rookie Sensation Fails

Taylor had been one of the rookie sensations of the National League, winning ten and losing five until he tore a tendon in his right elbow in the process of beating the Cardinals. Handsome Harry, however, simply had nothing to carry into this combat beyond the best wishes of the Flatbush faithful and about the only mystifying feature was the fact that the Brooks' board of strategy never became aware of that until he started laboring on the mound.

Stirnweiss greeted Taylor's first pitch with a sharp single into left field. Henrich allowed the count to reach two and two before he smacked a single into center,

Snuffy holding up at second.

Then followed a play that might have helped Taylor over the rough spot but instead put him deeper in the hole. Larry Berra, back behind the plate as the Yanks' starting catcher, slapped a grounder to Robinson. Jackie fired the ball to Reese for a force play on Henrich, but Peewee dropped the throw.

The error filled the bases so that Taylor, within a few minutes of the start, was up to his elbows in trouble. Moreover, he was confronted by the wholly uninviting situation of facing Joe DiMaggio with the bases full and nobody out.

At that, it is quite possible he did about the best circumstances would permit. He tossed four wide pitches for a base on balls and while that forced in a run it could have been a lot worse.

With that walk Taylor was asked to walk out himself under orders from the bench, and Gregg, who had started warming up on Taylor's third pitch, took over. McQuinn popped to Reese for the first out and a moment later Johnson slapped a grounder at Reese. In a flash, Peewee, Stanky and Robinson completed one of their gilt-edged double plays.

One run was all the vaunted Bombers extracted from that wide open position and in the third they blew another opportunity. With two down, DiMaggio drew his second pass and McQuinn tapped a ball in front of the plate. Edwards grabbed it and when his fast peg shot wide of first to bounce off the temporary boxes running down the right-field side, DiMaggio and McQuinn tore around the bases.

Rounding third, DiMaggio was waved on by the usually coldly calculating Coach Chuck Dressen, who miscued this time. Out in right Dixie Walker, who otherwise played an inconspicuous role, collared the ball and fired it to the plate in ample time for the third out.

After the extra-base blows by Johnson and Lindell in the fourth, the Yanks got no more hits until the ninth. Then Behrman, who had started pitching in the eighth, gave up two.

In the meantime Bevens was weaving in and out of trouble, but only because of the endless walks he kept serving up. Only a few fine plays were needed to help him, so invincible was his stuff. Lindell made a miraculous diving catch of a foul fly off Robinson in the third and DiMaggio faded way back to haul down a shot in dead center by Hermanski in the fourth.

Bevens walked two in the first, one in the second and another in the third, to which he added a wild pitch. When he passed two in the fifth, they led to the Dodgers' first tally.

Jorgensen received the first of those to open the round and Gregg followed with the next. Stanky sacrificed the runners to second and third and on Reese's grounder to Phil Rizzuto, which resulted in Gregg being tossed out at third on a fielder's choice, Jorgensen counted.

Bevens walked one in the sixth and one in the seventh. Not until the eighth, which Henrich ended with his great catch off Hermanski, did big Bill pitch a perfect inning. Then he walked two more in the ninth, inviting disaster just once too often. He opened four of the nine innings with passes.

So this most amazing series, starting as a gay jaunt for the Yanks, threatens to develop into a real dog fight that must return to the Yankee Stadium for final decision after today's fifth game at Ebbets Field. Frank Shea, who won the opener for the Bombers, though he tossed only five innings, is slated to make his second start today. Viv Lombardi, mite southpaw whom the American Leaguers belted out in the second game, is Shotton's mound choice.

October 4, 1947

Series Box Score

FOURTH GAME
NEW YORK YANKEES

	AB.	R.	H.	PO.	A.	E.
Stirnweiss, 2b	4	1	2	2	1	0
Henrich, rf	5	0	1	2	0	0
Berra, c	4	0	1	2	0	0
DiMaggio, cf	2	0	0	6	1	1
McQuinn, 1b	4	0	1	7	0	0
Johnson, 3b	4	1	1	3	2	0
Lindell, lf	3	0	2	3	0	0
Rizzuto, ss	4	0	1	1	2	0
Bevens, p	3	0	0	0	1	0
Total	33	2	8	*26	7	1

BROOKLYN DODGERS

	AB.	R.	H.	PO.	A.	E.
Stanky, 2b	1	0	0	2	3	0
eLavagetto	1	0	1	0	0	0
Reese, ss	4	0	0	3	5	1
Robinson, 1b	4	0	0	11	0	0
Walker, rf	2	0	0	1	1	0
Hermanski, lf	4	0	0	2	0	0
Edwards, c	4	0	0	7	1	1
Furillo, cf	3	0	0	2	0	0
bGionfriddo	0	1	0	0	0	0
Jorgensen, 3b	2	1	0	1	1	0
Taylor, p	0	0	0	0	0	0
Gregg, p	1	0	0	0	1	0
aVaughan	0	0	0	0	0	0
Behrman, p	0	0	0	0	1	0
Casey, p	0	0	0	0	1	0
cReiser	0	0	0	0	0	0
dMiksis	0	1	0	0	0	0
Total	26	3	1	27	15	3

*Two out when winning run scored.
aWalked for Gregg in seventh.
bRan for Furillo in ninth.
cWalked for Casey in ninth.
dRan for Reiser in ninth.
eDoubled for Stanky in ninth.

New York ...... 1 0 0 1 0 0 0 0 0—2
Brooklyn ...... 0 0 0 0 1 0 0 0 2—3

Runs batted in—DiMaggio, Lindell, Reese, Lavagetto 2.

Two-base hits—Lindell, Lavagetto. Three-base hit—Johnson. Stolen bases—Rizzuto, Reese, Gionfriddo. Sacrifices—Stanky, Bevens. Double plays—Reese, Stanky and Robinson; Gregg, Reese and Robinson; Casey, Edwards and Robinson. Earned runs—New York 1, Brooklyn 3. Left on bases—New York 9, Brooklyn 8. Bases on balls—Off Taylor 1 (DiMaggio), Gregg 3 (DiMaggio, Lindell, Stirnweiss), Bevens 10 (Stanky 2, Walker 2, Jorgensen 2, Gregg, Vaughan, Furillo, Reiser). Struck out—By Gregg 5 (Stirnweiss 2, Henrich, McQuinn, Bevens), Bevens 5 (Edwards 3, Gregg, Robinson). Pitching summary—Off Taylor 1 run, 2 hits in 0 innings (none out in first); Gregg 1 run, 4 hits in 7; Behrman 0 runs, 2 hits in 1 1-3; Casey 0 runs, 0 hits in 2-3. Wild pitch—Bevens. Winning pitcher—Casey. Umpires—Goetz (NL), plate: McGowan (AL), first base; Pinelli (NL), second base; Rommel (AL), third base; Boyer (AL), left field; Magerkurth (NL), right field. Time of game—2:20. Attendance—33,443.

DODGERS SET BACK YANKEES BY 8 TO 6 FOR 3-3 SERIES TIE

Rout Page With Four in Sixth to Win Before 74,065, New Crowd Mark for Classic

By JOHN DREBINGER

Incredible as it may seem to a bewildered world at large, the 1947 world series is still with us, and so are the Dodgers.

For in one of the most extraordinary games ever played, one that left a record series crowd of 74,065 limp and exhausted, Burt Shotton's unpredictable Flock fought the Yankees in a last-ditch stand at the Stadium yesterday and defeated them, 8 to 6.

As a consequence, the classic, which in this same park last Tuesday had started as a soft touch for Bucky Harris' American League champions, now stands tied at three victories apiece. The seventh and deciding game will be played at the Stadium today.

It was a conflict that lasted three hours and nineteen minutes, the longest on record for nine innings in a world series. Had it gone into an extra inning, another series precedent would have been set, as permission had been obtained to turn on the floodlights.

As for the gathering, which had shelled out record gross receipts of $393,210, it was to thrill to a show that scarcely left a moment's breathing spell. The Yanks tossed twenty-one players into the fray, six of them hurlers, while the battling Bums countered with seventeen, four of them flingers, the last of all being the astounding Hugh Casey.

The game also was marked by one of the greatest catches in series history—Al Gionfriddo's collaring of Joe DiMaggio's 415-foot drive in the sixth inning.

The fans saw the aroused Dodgers fighting to keep the series alive, rout Allie Reynolds inside of three rounds, getting two runs in the first and two in the third. It saw the Bombers roar back in the lower half of the third to blast Vic Lombardi from the mound with a four-run demonstration.

The Yanks added one more tally off Ralph Branca in the fourth to take a 5-4 lead, while the Bums screamed to the high heavens that the umpires were blind in calling Yogi Berra's single down the right-field foul line a fair ball.

This was not a patch to what followed as the Flock, in the sixth, crushed the incomparable Yankee relief hurler. Joe Page, with a withering four-run attack, a single by Peewee Reese off Bobo Newsom driving in the final pair.

In the lower half of the same round the crowd was to witness the Bombers come within an eyelash of tying the score again. With two on, DiMaggio sent a tre-

Allie Reynolds almost didn't get the no-hitter he is shown here pitching in 1951. With two out in the ninth, Yogi Berra dropped a pop foul off the bat of the feared Ted Williams. But Williams hit the same thing on the next pitch and this time Berra caught it.

Yankee pitcher Floyd Bevens watches helplessly as the Dodger's Cookie Lavagetto ruins his bid for a no-hitter in the 1947 World Series. Bevens lost the game as well as the no-hitter on the ninth inning double.

mendous smash in the direction of the left-field bullpen only to see Gionfriddo, a rookie outfielder, rob Jolting Joe of his greatest moment.

Dashing almost blindly to the spot where he thought the ball would land and turning around at the last moment, the 25-year-old gardener, who had been merely tossed as an "extra" into the deal that shipped Kirby Higbe to the Pirates earlier this year, leaned far over the bullpen railing and, with his gloved hand, collared the ball.

It was a breathtaking catch for the third out of the inning. It stunned the proud Bombers and jarred even the usually imperturbable DiMaggio. Taking his position in center field with the start of the next inning, he was still walking inconsolably in circles, doubtless wondering whether he could believe his senses.

Casey Takes the Mound

And then came the last of the ninth when the Yanks, still three runs in arrears, sought desperately to make their last-ditch stand. Joe Hatten, the southpaw who had come in for the Flock in the sixth, had managed to squirm out of one difficulty when the Bombers filled the bases in the seventh. However, when Bill Johnson opened the Yankee ninth with a single and George McQuinn walked, big Casey came out of that left-field bullpen to make his fifth appearance in the series.

Casey retired Phil Rizzuto on a fly to center, but Aaron Robinson plunked a single into left, filling the bases, and the already exhausted fans rallied once more to this last dramatic surge. Lonnie Frey, pinch-hitting, grounded to Jackie Robinson, who threw to second for a force play while Johnson scored.

The tying runs were still on base, but they never got any farther. Casey in person handled George Stirnweiss' feeble grounder to the mound, tossed the ball to Jackie Robinson and the epic struggle was over.

The Yankees, setting a series record with their twenty-one players and tying another with their six pitchers, had amassed fifteen hits. But they left thirteen men stranded on the bases, one short of the record, and this is where they left the battle. The southpaw Page, who had saved and won so many games for them this year, failed them at a most vital moment to become the losing pitcher.

Another casualty was Johnny Lindell who, after getting two singles, had to leave the field when it was discovered he was suffering from a fractured rib. That forced Harris, who had started so confidently with Sherman Lollar behind the plate and the rookie Jack Phillips on first, to throw in all his manpower, winding up with Berra, his jittery catcher, in right and Tommy Henrich in left.

As for the Dodgers, the battle was of a sort in which they reveled all summer as they outscrambled their National League rivals so many times. They collected twelve blows. These included a trio of doubles by Reese, Robinson and Dixie Walker that sank Reynolds in the third and the pair of two-baggers by Carl Furillo and pinch-hitter Bob Bragan that sparked the four-run rally which brought down Page in that hysterical sixth.

Their winning pitcher was Ralph Branca, who, relieving little Lombardi in the Yanks' explosive third, hurled only two and one-third innings. He yielded six hits, not to mention the tally that put the Yanks ahead for the only time in the fourth. However, the four runs with which the Flock tore off the roof in the sixth went to his credit and that gave him the triumph.

Other Yankee hurlers to get into the fray were Karl Drews, who relieved Reynolds in the third; Vic Raschi and Charlie Wensloff who, all too late, held the Dodgers hitless and runless in the final three rounds. The ten hurlers for the two teams set another series mark.

It was again a cloudless, summery day such as had prevailed in the games in Brooklyn. When the first three batters got on base the picture bore an even closer resemblance to that of the two previous afternoons in Flatbush.

This time, however, it was the Brooks who looked as though they meant to rip things wide open at the outset. Though they didn't quite extract all that the situation invited, they did do a little better than the Bombers. For where the Yanks had squeezed only one run from a similar first-inning set-up on Friday and none at all on Saturday, the Flock came up with two tallies, although neither was scored with any particular degree of elegance.

The strains of "The Star-Spangled Banner" had scarcely floated away over the adjoining Bronx housetops, which also were jammed to capacity, than Eddie Stanky brought the crowd up with a roar as he rammed a single into left. On the heels of that Reese stroked a one-base thump into center, and at that moment it seemed everyone in the park was for the underdog Dodgers.

Then Jackie Robinson sent a towering fly down the left-field foul line. Lindell seemed at first to have trouble sighting the ball, got it and then lost it in the blinding sun. It fell to the ground but, as both runners had remained tagged up, Robinson got only a single, filling the bases.

Reynolds, an easy mound victor in the second game, was really up to his neck in trouble and yet, like Harry Taylor and Rex Barney in the previous two encounters, he almost managed to make a similar escape.

Walker swung vigorously but succeeded only in thumping into a double play that rubbed out him-

Composite Score of World Series Games

BROOKLYN DODGERS

	G	AB	R	H	2B	3B	HR	RBI	BB	SO	Bat Avg	PO	A	E	Fldg Avg
Stanky 2b	6	21	4	5	1	0	0	2	3	2	.238	15	18	1	.971
J. Robinson, 1b	6	23	3	7	2	0	0	3	2	3	.304	46	4	0	1.000
dReiser, cf-lf	5	8	1	2	0	0	0	0	3	1	.250	7	0	1	.875
Walker, rf	6	24	1	6	1	0	1	4	2	1	.250	6	1	0	1.000
Hermanski, lf	6	17	3	2	0	0	0	1	3	3	.118	13	0	0	1.000
Furillo, cf	6	14	2	5	2	0	0	3	3	0	.357	10	1	1	.917
Edwards, c	6	23	2	4	1	0	0	1	2	7	.174	39	4	1	.977
Jorgensen, 3b	6	18	1	3	1	0	0	2	2	4	.167	8	11	2	.905
eLavagetto, 3b	4	6	0	1	1	0	0	3	0	2	.167	0	1	0	1.000
Reese, ss	6	20	5	7	1	0	0	4	5	2	.350	8	14	1	.957
Branca, p	3	5	0	0	0	0	0	0	0	1	.000	0	1	0	1.000
Behrman, p	4	0	0	0	0	0	0	0	0	0	.000	0	3	0	1.000
Casey, p	5	1	0	0	0	0	0	0	0	1	.000	2	3	0	.000
fLombardi, p	3	2	0	0	0	0	0	0	0	0	.000	0	0	0	.000
Gregg, p	2	1	0	0	0	0	0	0	1	1	.000	0	3	0	1.000
Barney, p	2	1	0	0	0	0	0	0	0	0	.000	0	1	0	1.000
Hatten, p	3	3	1	1	0	0	0	0	0	0	.333	0	0	0	.000
aMiksis, 2b-lf	4	2	1	0	0	0	0	0	0	1	.000	1	1	1	.667
bVaughan	3	2	0	1	1	0	0	0	1	0	.500	0	0	0	.000
gBragan	1	1	0	1	1	0	0	1	0	0	1.000	0	0	0	.000
cGionfriddo, lf	3	3	2	0	0	0	0	0	1	0	.000	1	0	0	1.000
hBankhead	1	0	1	0	0	0	0	0	0	0	.000	0	0	0	.000
Total		195	27	45	12	0	1	24	28	29	.231	156	66	8	.965

NEW YORK YANKEES

	G	AB	R	H	2B	3B	HR	RBI	BB	SO	Bat Avg	PO	A	E	Fldg Avg
Stirnweiss, 2b	6	25	3	7	0	1	0	3	5	8	.280	13	17	0	1.000
Henrich, rf	6	26	2	9	2	0	1	4	2	2	.346	10	0	0	1.000
Berra, c-rf	5	16	2	3	0	0	1	2	1	2	.188	20	2	2	.917
DiMaggio, cf	6	23	4	6	0	0	2	5	5	2	.261	19	0	0	1.000
McQuinn, 1b	6	21	2	3	0	0	0	1	4	7	.143	41	4	1	.978
Johnson, 3b	6	23	6	6	0	2	0	2	2	4	.261	10	13	0	1.000
Lindell, lf	6	18	3	9	3	1	0	7	5	2	.500	11	0	0	1.000
Rizzuto, ss	6	22	1	5	1	0	0	1	4	0	.227	16	13	0	1.000
Lollar, c	2	4	3	3	2	0	0	1	0	0	.750	2	1	0	1.000
A. Robinson, c	2	7	2	2	0	0	0	0	1	0	.286	9	0	1	.900
Shea, p	2	5	0	2	1	0	0	1	0	2	.400	1	3	0	1.000
Page, p	3	2	0	0	0	0	0	0	0	0	.000	1	2	0	1.000
Reynolds, p	2	4	2	2	0	0	0	1	0	0	.500	1	0	0	1.000
Newsom, p	2	0	0	0	0	0	0	0	0	0	.000	0	1	0	1.000
Raschi, p	2	0	0	0	0	0	0	0	0	0	.000	0	0	0	.000
Drews, p	2	2	0	0	0	0	0	0	0	2	.000	0	3	0	1.000
Chandler, p	1	0	0	0	0	0	0	0	0	0	.000	0	0	0	.000
Bevens, p	1	3	0	0	0	0	0	0	0	1	.000	0	1	0	1.000
Wensloff, p	1	0	0	0	0	0	0	0	0	0	.000	0	1	0	1.000
iBrown	3	2	2	2	1	0	0	2	1	0	1.000	0	0	0	.000
jClark	2	1	1	0	0	0	0	0	1	0	.000	0	0	0	.000
kPhillips, 1b	2	2	0	0	0	0	0	0	0	0	.000	4	0	0	1.000
lHouk	1	1	0	1	0	0	0	0	0	0	1.000	0	0	0	.000
mFrey	1	1	0	0	0	0	0	0	0	0	.000	0	0	0	.000
Total		208	33	60	10	4	4	30	31	32	.288	158	61	4	.982

a Struck out for Behrman in seventh of first game and ran for Reiser in ninth of fourth game.
b Flied out for Gregg in seventh of second game, walked for Gregg in seventh inning of fourth game, and doubled for Behrman in seventh of fifth game.
c Forced Jorgensen for Barney in ninth of second game, ran for Furillo in ninth of fourth game, and walked for Hatten in sixth of fifth game.
d Walked for Casey in ninth of fourth game, and walked for Stanky in seventh of fifth game.
e Doubled for Stanky in ninth of fourth game, and fanned for Casey in ninth of fifth game.
f Ran for Edwards in ninth of fifth game.
g Doubled for Branca in sixth of sixth game.
h Ran for Bragan in sixth of sixth game.
i Walked for Shea in fifth of first game, doubled for Chandler in sixth of third game, and singled for Phillips in third of sixth game.
j Walked for Raschi in third of third game, and lined out for Newsom in sixth of sixth game.
k Flied out for Drews in fourth of third game.
l Singled for Raschi in seventh of sixth game.
m Forced A. Robinson for Wensloff in ninth of sixth game.

COMPOSITE SCORE BY INNINGS

Brooklyn	3	6	4	3	1	6	1	0	3	—27
New York	2	0	7	6	10	2	5	0	1	—33

PITCHING SUMMARY

	G	CG	IP	H	R	ER	BB	SO	HB	WP	W	L	Pct	Era
Casey	5	0	8 1/3	4	0	0	1	2	1	0	2	0	1.000	0.00
Branca	3	0	8 1/3	12	8	8	5	9	1	0	1	1	.500	8.64
Lombardi	2	0	6 2/3	14	9	9	1	5	0	1	0	1	.000	12.15
Barney	2	0	6 1/3	4	2	2	10	3	0	2	0	1	.000	2.84
Behrman	4	0	4 2/3	7	4	4	2	2	0	1	0	0	.000	7.71
Hatten	3	0	8 2/3	11	7	7	7	4	0	0	0	0	.000	7.27
Gregg	2	0	9	6	2	2	4	7	0	0	0	0	.000	2.00
Taylor	1	0	0	2	1	0	1	0	0	0	0	0	.000	0.00
Shea	2	1	14	6	2	2	7	10	0	0	2	0	1.000	1.29
Reynolds	2	1	11 1/3	15	7	6	3	6	0	0	1	0	1.000	4.74
Bevens	1	1	8 2/3	1	3	3	10	5	0	1	0	1	.000	3.12
Newsom	2	0	2 1/3	6	5	5	2	0	0	0	0	1	.000	19.29
Page	3	0	8	11	6	6	2	6	0	2	0	1	.000	6.75
Raschi	2	0	1 1/3	2	1	1	0	1	0	0	0	0	.000	6.75
Drews	2	0	3	2	1	1	0	0	1	1	0	0	.000	3.00
Chandler	1	0	2	2	2	2	4	1	0	0	0	0	.000	9.00
Wensloff	1	0	2	0	0	0	0	0	0	0	0	0	.000	0.00

Earned runs—Brooklyn 26, New York 32. Left on bases—Brooklyn 42, New York 54. Stolen bases—J. Robinson 2, Reese 3, Walker, Rizzuto, Gionfriddo. Sacrifices—Henrich, J. Robinson, Stanky, Bevens, Furillo. Double plays—Johnson and McQuinn; Jorgensen, Stanky and J. Robinson; Stirnweiss, Rizzuto and McQuinn; Reese, Stanky and J. Robinson 3; Stanky and J. Robinson; Gregg, Reese and J. Robinson; Casey, Edwards and J. Robinson; Reese, Miksis and J. Robinson; Rizzuto and Phillips. Hit by Pitcher—By Branca (Johnson); Drews (Hermanski); Casey (Lindell). Balk—Shea. Passed balls—Lollar 2, Edwards 2. Umpires—McGowan (AL); Pinelli (NL); Rommel (AL); Goetz (NL); Magerkurth (NL) and Boyer (AL). Attendances—First game, 73,365; second game, 69,865; third game, 33,098; fourth game, 33,443; fifth game, 34,379; sixth game, 74,065. Times of games—2:20, 2:36, 3:05, 2:20, 2:46, 3:19.

self and Robbie at second. However, Stanky counted and Reese moved to third on the play which was further enlivened by Jackie Robinson crashing heavily into Rizzuto at the midway bag. It knocked the wind out of Li'l Phil and it required almost five minutes for him to get it back.

Yanks Go on Rampage

Then came a passed ball as Lollar failed to block one of Reynolds' shots, and Reese raced over with the second tally. The Flock had come up with only two runs but it grabbed two more in the third for a 4-0 lead as Reese, Robinson and Walker hit successive two-baggers that sent Reynolds to the showers.

But the hub-bub caused by the Flatbush faithful had barely subsided than the Yanks went on a rampage in the third and finished Lombardi. Lollar opened with a double. Drews, left to bat for himself, fanned, but Spider Jorgensen's fumble of Stirnweiss' grounder, and singles by Henrich, Lindell and DiMaggio followed for three runs.

Then Branca replaced Lombardi, the mite left-hander. Bill Johnson greeted him with a single that drove in the fourth run before the big right-hander could get things under control.

In the fourth, however, Branca faltered and was nicked for singles by Aaron Robinson, who had now become the Yankee backstop; Henrich and Berra. The Dodgers put up a terrific uproar when Umpires Pinelli and Rommel, who at first made no signal at all, ruled the Berra hit a fair ball.

That shot put the Yanks in front by a tally, but the margin endured only until the Dodgers swung into action with their tempestuous sixth. Bruce Edwards opened it with a single and moved to third on Furillo's double.

Scores Tying Run

Here, for the third successive day, Cookie Lavagetto was called on to pinch hit. Friday he had delivered his epic two-run two-bagger that had sunk the Yanks in the ninth and robbed Bill Bevens of a

no-hitter. Saturday, in an almost similar ninth-inning situation, he had fanned. This time he came sort of "in between." He lifted a fly to Berra in right and Edwards galloped in with the tying run.

Then Bragan, a catcher, slammed a pinch double to left to score Furillo. Dan Bankhead, the Dodgers' Negro pitcher, entered the struggle as a runner for Bragan.

Page, who had entered the game the previous round to relieve Drews, now appeared visibly shaken. Stanky pounded a single into right and as Berra fired the ball home, Bankhead skidded back to third. But here Aaron Robinson fumbled it and that enabled Stanky to take second on the misplay. It was a slip that was to provide the Flock with an additional run.

For after Newsom replaced the stunned and crestfallen Page, Reese promptly greeted Bobo with a single, his third hit of the afternoon, and both Bankhead and Stanky scored. That made it four for the round and an 8-5 lead.

After that it became a matter

of hanging on for dear life, and this the Dodgers did with the help of their amazing Casey. In this unprecedented struggle of the bullpens Hugh seemed to score a great personal triumph over his American League rival, Page.

And so, with the classic all even once more, the Dodgers, though still not favorites in the betting, nevertheless have precedent heavily in their corner for the first time. This marks the eleventh time the struggle has gone down to the final encounter of a seven-game series. Of the ten already played, the National Leaguers have won seven.

Also to be remembered is the fact that Harris must counter today with Bevens, who has had only two days' rest since losing that heart-breaking one-hitter Friday. As for Shotton, his hurling staff seems no more badly scrambled than at any time in the series. He will start with Hal Gregg and doubtless follow with a string of others that eventually will get down to one more appearance for the inimitable Casey.

October 6, 1947

Indians Win American League Flag, Beating Red Sox in Play-Off, 8-3

By JOHN DREBINGER
Special to THE NEW YORK TIMES.

BOSTON, Oct. 4—Cleveland is to have its first world series in twenty-eight years.

This became an actuality today as the Indians, fired by the inspirational leadership of their talented skipper, Lou Boudreau, crushed Joe McCarthy's Red Sox in the single game that had been found necessary to break the deadlock in the American League 1948 pennant scramble.

The play-off, first in the history of the junior circuit and witnessed by a crowd of 33,957 shivering fans, most of whom watched it in glum silence, was decided by an 8-to-3 score, and as a consequence the Indians will oppose the National League champion Braves when the world series opens here Wednesday.

It marked only the second American League flag to be won by Cleveland and the first since 1920, when Tris Speaker, the famed Grey Eagle, led another band of Indians to a pennant as well as a subsequent world championship.

There never was much doubt of the outcome on this crisp autumnal afternoon. For the Tribe, which in the last few days of one of the most thrilling pennant races in major league history, had flubbed a couple of chances to win the flag outright over the regular 154-game schedule, this time shot

straight for the mark.

Behind the stout-hearted five-hit hurling of Gene Bearden, 27-year-old southpaw freshman who last year was toiling on the Pacific Coast, Manager Boudreau blazed the trail with two home runs. Ken Keltner blasted another with two comrades aboard to spark a bruising four-run fourth inning, and that about tells the story.

Boudreau's play throughout was truly phenomenal. The personable graduate of the University of Illinois who in 1942 at the age of 25 became the youngest manager ever to direct a major league club, gave a performance seldom matched by any player in a struggle of such vast importance.

Playing his own position at shortstop flawlessly, maneuvering his men hither and yon with rare judgment and watching like a hawk every pitch of his youthful moundsman, Lou still found time not only to larrup two homers over the left field barrier, but added two singles, each of which figured in further scores.

Against this demonstration Joe McCarthy, completing his first year as manager of the Red Sox, and winner of eight American League pennants as field general of the Yankees, suddenly found himself completely out of ammunition.

For the battering Bosox, whose electrifying spurt in the last two days of the regular campaign had overcome a two-game deficit, failed Marse Joe rather badly.

Denny Routed In Fourth

In a surprise move McCarthy started his veteran righthander, Dennis Galehouse, and lived to regret it within four innings. For Denny was put to rout with the Keltner three-run homer. Then he followed with Ellis Kinder, who fell victim of the final fourth-inning tally, gave up three more in the fifth, eighth and ninth.

Even the renowned Ted Williams cast a rather sorry figure in this sudden-death struggle which the pleading Hub fans had hoped would produce the first All-Boston world series in history.

The Kid's mighty bat, which the two previous days had helped blast the Yankees out of the race, connected for only one single in four tries today. To add further to the woes of the disconsolate Boston fans, Williams capped his day by muffing a fly ball that gave the Clevelanders their tally in the eighth.

Of all the Sox, Bobby Doerr alone remained about the only "hero in defeat." With Williams on base, the result of the Indians' only misplay of the day, Doerr whacked his twenty-seventh homer of the year in the sixth.

But after this slip, Bearden kept the Sox tightly bottled the rest of the way.

Seventh Victory in Row

Inasmuch as all records compiled today go into the season's final statistics, this also marked the twentieth mound victory for the tall Coast southpaw against only seven defeats, and his seventh triumph in row.

Amid a world series setting which saw Commissioner A. B. Chandler in a "ringside" box and correspondents on hand from virtually all major league towns, the conflict had progressed only a few minutes when the indomitable Boudreau fired his first shot.

On his arrival this morning with his team from Cleveland, where

the Indians had suffered an excruciating Sunday defeat at the hands of the Tigers to plunge the race into a last-day tie, Boudreau appeared a bit drawn and tired.

But there was nothing wrong with his flashing, clear eyes as he whipped into a Galehouse pitch and sent it sailing over the left-field barrier for his seventeenth homer of the year. It came with two out and nobody on and gave the Indians a one-run lead.

The margin was wiped out almost immediately when Johnny Pesky doubled in the lower half of the first and galloped home on Vern Stephens' single just inside the third-base line.

For the next two rounds Bearden and Galehouse kept the one-all deadlock intact. But in the fourth the Indians struck again and once more it was Boudreau who showed the way. This time the Cleveland pilot plunked a single into left. Joe Gordon followed with another into the same sector and a feeling of uneasiness swept through the crowd.

A moment later Keltner exploded a towering shot and as the ball streaked against the clear blue sky the Hub fans, who so often have seen enemy hopes dashed against the perilous left-field wall of historic Fenway Park, knew on the spot the worst was about to happen.

No. 31 Over the Wall

The ball soared over the wall for Keltner's thirty-first homer of the campaign and three Tribal runs scored. That was all for Galehouse and Kinder, one of the lesser lights on the Bosox staff, acquired from the St. Louis Browns last winter, emerged from the bullpen.

The former Brownie righthander didn't quell the uprising at once. Lary Doby, the Negro star, rifled a double off the wall in left center, the first of two two-baggers he was to hit during the afternoon. A sacrifice bunt by Bob Kennedy advanced Doby to third and he streaked over the plate while Stephens was tossing out Jim Hegan at first.

The Indians were four tallies in front and the stunned gathering, now looking on in stony silence, seemed to sense that final disaster was not far away.

The fifth was almost a repetition of the first. Kinder had just retired the top two batters of the Cleveland line-up when Boudreau unfurled his second circuit smack of the afternoon and eighteenth of the campaign. That made it 6—1.

Gordon Muffs Ted's Fly

In the last of the sixth, however, came a faint flurry of Boston hope. With one out, Williams, who had grounded out in the first and fouled out in the third, lifted a towering fly back of second base.

The crowd groaned but cheered a moment later as Gordon, staggering under the ball as he tried to sight it against a blinding sun, momentarily caught it, then dropped it for an error.

Unruffled, Bearden fanned Stephens for the second out, but Doerr was not to be disposed of so easily. He, too, sent the ball winging over the left field wall and as the two runners jogged around the basepaths, Boston spirits flared again. The score was now 6 to 3.

But the Bosox were never to get any closer. Bearden quickly brought the sixth to a close by fanning Stan Spence and in the seventh the chilled spectators were to put in another harrowing period as a pair of singles by Bearden and Dale Mitchell, a sacrifice and an intentional pass to Boudreau filled the bases for Cleveland with only one out.

More Trouble in Eighth

But Kinder revived hopes by retiring Gordon on the end of an infield pop-up and holding Keltner to a fly that Williams caught in left. The folks breathed again, but not for long. For there was more trouble in the eighth. Doby lashed another double into left center. Kennedy sacrificed him to third and Hegan drew a pass.

For an instant it looked as though Kinder would again effect a miraculous escape when Doby got himself picked off third for the second out, Hegan taking second during the run-up.

But on the heels of that Bearden lifted a high fly to left center

Play-off Box Score

CLEVELAND INDIANS

	AB.	R.	H.	PO.	A.	E.
Mitchell, lf	5	0	1	1	0	0
Clark, 1b	2	0	0	5	0	0
Robinson, 1b	2	1	1	9	0	0
Boudreau, ss	4	3	4	3	5	0
Gordon, 2b	4	1	1	2	3	1
Keltner, 3b	5	1	3	0	6	0
Doby, cf	5	1	2	1	0	0
Kennedy, rf	2	0	0	0	0	0
Hegan, c	3	1	0	6	1	0
Bearden, p	3	0	1	0	2	0
Total	35	8	13	27	17	1

BOSTON RED SOX

	AB.	R.	H.	PO.	A.	E.
D. DiMaggio, cf	4	0	0	3	0	0
Pesky, 3b	4	1	1	3	4	0
Williams, lf	4	1	1	3	0	1
Stephens, ss	4	0	1	2	4	0
Doerr, 2b	4	1	1	5	2	0
Spence, rf	1	0	0	1	0	0
aHitchcock	0	0	0	0	0	0
bWright	0	0	0	0	0	0
Goodman, 1b	3	0	0	7	1	0
Tebbetts, c	4	0	1	3	1	0
Galehouse, p	0	0	0	0	1	0
Kinder, p	2	0	0	0	1	0
Total	30	3	5	27	14	1

which Williams, verging on the ball with Dom DiMaggio, elected to take. Ted, however, dropped it and Hegan scored easily.

In the ninth came the Tribe's final thrust. Ed Robinson singled and so did Boudreau for his fourth hit in four official times at bat. Came a wild pitch that advanced the runners to second and third and this forced an intentional pass to Gordon.

At that, only one run scored, Robinson skipping home while

aHitchcock walked for Spence in ninth.

bWright ran for Hitchcock in ninth.

Cleveland .1 0 0 4 1 0 0 1 1—8
Boston ...1 0 0 0 0 2 0 0 0—3

Runs batted in—Boudreau 2, Keltner 3, Hegan, Stephens, Doerr 2.

Two-base hits—Doby 2, Keltner, Pesky. Home runs—Boudreau 2, Keltner, Doerr. Sacrifices—Kennedy 2, Robinson. Double plays—Hegan and Boudreau; Gordon, Boudreau and Robinson; Bearden, Gordon and Robinson; Stephens, Doerr and Goodman 2. Left on bases—Cleveland 7, Boston 5.

Bases on balls—Off Bearden 5 (Spence 2, Galehouse, Goodman, Hitchcock); Kinder 3 (Boudreau, Hegan, Gordon). Struck out—By Bearden 5 (Goodman, Doerr, Stephens, Spence, Pesky); Galehouse 1 (Hegan); Kinder 2 (Hegan, Doby).

Hits—Off Galehouse 5 in 3 innings (none out in fourth); Kinder 8 in 6. Wild pitch—Kinder. Losing pitcher—Galehouse.

Umpires— McGowan (plate); Summers (first base); Rommel (second base); Berry (third base). Time of game—2:24. Attendance —33,957.

Keltner was pounding into a double play. But the Indians needed no more.

There was nothing the Sox could do with Bearden's baffling slider and knuckler. Bill Goodman drew a pass in the seventh only to see Birdie Tebbetts ground into a twin killing.

After Dom DiMaggio, hitless all day, had grounded out in the eighth and Pesky had fanned, Williams connected with a well-placed single into left. But Stephens ended this threat by forcing Ted at second.

In the ninth came one more pass, the fifth to be given up by Bearden. But the tall lefty made Goodman his sixth strike-out victim. Then Tebbetts grounded to Keltner and the American League's thrilling flag race, which early in August had seen four entries virtually locked in a tie and which still had three in the running up to the next to the last day of the regular season, finally had come to an end.

And so the Indians, after nearly three decades of bitter disappointments and in the third year of Bill Veeck's spectacular tenure as club president, at long last brought a second pennant to Cleveland.

Veeck, whose glamorous feats of showmanship produced attendance figures in the lakefront city which surpassed even the fabulous record of the Yankees, had once threatened this summer to jump off the "highest bridge in Cleveland" if the Indians failed to win the flag. Tonight he was all smiles as jubilant American Leaguers showered him with congratulations and best wishes for success in the forthcoming world series.

October 5, 1948

Ban on Major Leaguers Who Jumped to Mexico Lifted by Chandler

WELCOME ASSURED ON EXILES' RETURN

WASHINGTON, June 5 (AP)— Major league baseball tonight welcomed back all players who presently are under five-year suspensions for jumping to the outlawed Mexican League in 1946.

Commissioner A. B. (Happy) Chandler said he was forwarding by mail an offer to reinstate all players "who were placed on the ineligible list in 1946 for breaking their player contracts and jumping to Mexico."

Chandler said that all the league jumpers have to do to return to the majors is apply in writing to the president of their league—the American or the National as the case may be. In each case, he said, reinstatement will be automatic.

"Application for reinstatement," he told a reporter, "is tantamount to reinstatement itself."

"In fact, I just talked with Mickey Owen, who is in Winner, S. D., and he's leaving immediately to join the Brooklyn Dodgers."

Owen, one of the best-known players who jumped to Mexico,

talked with Chandler by telephone in the presence of newsmen. The commissioner was heard to tell Owen:

"Get your bag packed, boy, and get to your club right away."

Owen replied that he would join the Dodgers within 48 hours.

In reply to questions, Chandler said the reinstatement action had been talked over between all the club owners in both leagues and all are willing to take their players back.

"That is why application is automatic reinstatement," Chandler said.

"This is being done at this time because, under all the circumstances, it seems a fair thing to do, and because the threat of compulsion by court action has now been removed by recent unanimous decisions of the Circuit Court of Appeals in New York."

Judge Conger's Decision

In the New York court last Thursday, the Appeals bench unanimously affirmed District Court Judge Conger's decision of last April pointing out that to compel reinstatement of the players through the court "would restore them to positions they resigned voluntarily."

The Court ruled that in jumping

to the Mexican League in the spring and summer of 1946, the players thereby violated their contracts, in effect resigning from their positions.

This verdict was rendered in the case of two former St. Louis Cardinal pitchers—Rookie Fred Martin and Max Lanier.

Former New York Giant outfielder Danny Gardella also has an action before the courts. Both cases are new pending before the Federal District Court in New York and no time has been set as to when they will be heard.

In addition to the four, mentioned the outstanding players affected by the ruling are:

Second baseman Lou Klein of the St. Louis Cardinals; Napoleon Reyes and hurler Adrian Zabala of the New York Giants; outfielder Roberto Ortiz and Chile Gomez of the Washington Senators; Luis Olmo of the Brooklyn Dodgers; Bobby Estalela of the Philadelphia Athletics; Chico Hernandez of the Chicago Cubs and Rene Monteagudo of the Philadelphia Phillies.

Lanier, reached by telephone in Canada, said he was "delighted" by Chandler's action and would apply for reinstatement immediately. Lanier is playing with Drummondville in the Quebec Provincial League.

Letter to the Players

Chandler's letter to each of the players concerned read as follows:

"This is to notify you that I have decided to permit you and other players placed on the ineligible list for violation of contractual obligations to apply for reinstatement. Accordingly, if you desire to be reinstated you should file your application at once with the president of your league in accordance with the provisions of major league rule 16."

In a statement to reporters, Chandler added:

"In 1946 when our players were being induced to break their contracts and jump to Mexico by glowing promises and enormous cash bonuses, I announced that I would suspend for five years those players who violated their player contracts by jumping to Mexico and who did not return to their clubs before the beginning of the season.

"In Havana, Cuba, in March I personally told those players who had jumped to come back to the majors and report to their clubs or they would be suspended.

"This action (suspension for five years) was then necessary in order to make these young men fully realize the serious nature of their contractual obligations and because of the threat to the integrity of the game resulting from their wrongful action.

"Some eighteen men in all were nevertheless persuaded to break their contracts and to play baseball in the Mexican League, and I accordingly notified each of these men that he would be placed on the ineligible list for five years. Shortly afterwards, Major league rule 15 (A) was enacted to make compulsory the five year ineligibility of players who jumped their contracts after that time. No more did so. (To support Chandler's action, the American and the National League adopted the five-year rule in July of 1946 at their annual meeting.)

"Following the failure of the Mexican League to live up to the glowing promises made for it, many of these men petitioned me for reinstatement. In fairness to those players who had, in spite of large cash offers, remained with their clubs and carried out their obligations, I refused to reinstate them at that time. I always intended to give consideration for their reinstatement at a later date, after I had become convinced that the seriousness of their action in disregarding solemn obligations had been sufficiently brought home.

"In October, 1947, however, the Gardella suit was filed for the purpose, among others, of forcing the reinstatement of these players on the ground that baseball's contracts and in fact its entire structure was an illegal violation of the anti-trust laws. Another action was later filed by Martin and Lanier.

"If these suits had been successful in compelling the immediate reinstatement of these players, my authority, as commissioner, to enforce rules designed to preserve the honesty and integrity of the game would have been seriously impaired, if not destroyed. I have been confident throughout that no court would order the immediate reinstatement of these players, who have properly been declared ineligible for contract violation.

"While this question was still before the courts and could be interpreted as a threat, however, I could not even consider taking such action voluntarily. Baseball will not ever surrender to threats of force, and it cannot afford to take any action which could be interpreted as such a surrender."

Forcing Action Fails

"The attempt to force immediate reinstatement through the courts has now failed. In denying the plaintiffs this relief in April, Judge Conger pointed out that to compel reinstatement of these players 'would restore them to positions they resigned voluntarily.' On appeal the Circuit Court of Appeals last Thursday unanimously affirmed this decision. This is a definite determination that baseball cannot be compelled to reinstate these players now, and it accordingly appears to remove the possibility that a court will order any change in their status during the term of the five-year ineligibility period originally ordered.

"The threat of compulsion by a court order having been ended, I feel justified in tempering justice with mercy in dealing with all of these players. They have been ineligible for more than three years, and nearly all of them have admitted their original mistake and have expressed regret at their submission to the temptation to violate their contracts. In addition, the president of the Mexican League has met with me in Cincinnati, and satisfactory relations have been established which should end the efforts of that league to induce our players to break their contracts.

"In the interest, therefore, of fair play to all and in the hope that the misguided young men who once so lightly disregarded their obligations will now be able to make a fresh start, I have decided to permit them to be restored, on application, to the eligible list."

Chandler pointed out that the major league clubs concerned are not bound to keep the reinstated players in the big time.

They will be reinstated to all the rules of baseball and under such can be optioned and waivered to the minor leagues, he said.

Chandler said that if any of the players don't ask for reinstatement now, they will automatically be reinstated in July, 1951, when the five-year suspension ends.

June 6, 1949

KINER HITS NO. 50, SETS LOOP RECORD

But Giants Nip Pirates, 6-4, as Williams Gets a 2-Run Homer in the Tenth

PITTSBURGH, Sept. 19 (P)—Ralph Kiner, Pittsburgh left fielder, smashed his fiftieth home run of the year tonight to establish a National League record but the Giants nipped the Pirates, 6—4, as Dave Williams hit a homer in the first of the tenth with one on.

Kiner, who got his circuit clout in the second inning, became the first player in the National League twice to hit fifty or more homers in a season.

Williams' homer came off relief pitcher Harry Gumbert, the fourth Buc hurler.

A rhubarb developed in the seventh after the Bucs had gone into a 4-3 lead. Tom Saffell was caught in a rundown by Infielder Bill Rigney and Pirate players rushed onto the field when they thought Rigney pushed the ball into Saffell's face. However, order was restored quickly.

A crowd of 11,452 was on hand to see Kiner hit his homer. He now is only one behind his own record of fifty-one established in 1947.

The box score:

NEW YORK (N.)							PITTSBURGH (N.)						
	ab	r	h	o	a	e		ab	r	h	o	a	e
Williams, 2b	4	1	2	1	4	0	Reyes, ss	4	0	1	3	1	0
Lockman, lf	4	1	1	1	0	0	Saffell, rf	4	0	1	2	0	0
Gordon, 3b	4	0	0	1	0	1	Hopp, 1b	5	1	2	7	2	0
Marshall, rf	5	1	2	0	0	0	Kiner, lf	5	2	1	4	0	0
Thomson, cf	5	1	1	2	0	0	Westlake, cf	3	0	1	0	0	0
Lafata, 1b	3	1	1	9	1	0	Castiglione, 2b	4	0	0	2	3	0
Rigney, ss	4	0	2	3	2	0	McCullough, c	4	1	1	5	1	0
Westrum, c	3	0	1	5	0	0	Walsh, 3b	1	0	0	1	0	0
Higbe, p	2	0	0	0	1	0	Poat, p	1	0	0	0	1	0
aThompson	1	0	0	0	0	0	bWalker	1	0	0	0	0	0
Jones, p	2	0	1	0	1	0	Sewell, p	0	0	0	0	1	0
							Gumbert, p	0	0	0	0	1	1
Total	35	6	7	30	16	1	Total	34	4	9	30	16	1

aSingled for Higbe in eighth
bSacrificed for Poat in seventh

New York .... 0 2 0 0 0 1 0 1 0 2—6
Pittsburgh .... 0 0 1 0 2 1 0 0 0—4

Runs batted in—Westrum 2, Kiner, Higbe, Westlake, McCullough, Saffell, Williams 2. Two-base hits—Westlake, Kiner. Home run—Kiner, Williams. Stolen bases—Thomson, Hopp, Lockman. Sacrifice—Walker, Jones, Lafata. Double play—Rojek, Bragall and Hopp. Left on bases—New York 11, Pittsburgh 6. Bases on balls—Off Walsh 4, Higbe 2, Poat 1, Sewell 1, Jones 1, Gumbert 1. Struck out—By Higbe 4, Walsh 3, Poat 1, Jones 1. Hits—Off Walsh 2 in 4 1-3 innings, Poat 1 in 2 2-3, Sewell 1 in 0, Gumbert 1 in 2, Higbe 7 in 7, Jones 1 in 2. Passed ball—Westrum. Winner—Jones (11-10), Loser—Gumbert (5-2). Umpires—Goetz, Reardon and Jorda. Time of game—2:41. Attendance—11,342.

September 20, 1949

YANKEES AND DODGERS WIN PENNANTS IN FINAL GAMES; 68,055 CHEER IN STADIUM

RED SOX DEFEATED

By WILLIAM J. BRIORDY

It will be the New York Yankees against the Brooklyn Dodgers in the 1949 edition of the world series starting Wednesday at Yankee Stadium.

In pulse-quickening finishes to the keenest major-league races in forty-one years, the battered Yanks staved off a last-inning rally to beat the Boston Red Sox, 5—3, to win the American League pennant before 68,055 Yankee Stadium onlookers, while the Dodgers collared the National League flag by halting the Phillies, 9—7, in ten innings at Philadelphia's Shibe Park yesterday.

When the Yanks and Dodgers come to grips Wednesday, it will mark the third world series meeting of the interborough rivals and the second in three years. The Yanks won both previous series—in 1941 and 1947. The triumph was the sixteenth in the American League for the Yanks. Starting with 1890, the Dodgers have annexed the National League championship eight times. The Yanks' margin over the Dodgers in 1941 was 4—1 and in 1947 it was 4—3.

The Yanks and Red Sox were in a flat-footed tie when the teams took the field at the Stadium yesterday. The Dodgers entered the final day with a one-game lead over the St. Louis Cardinals, who snapped out of a four-game losing streak to beat the Chicago Cubs, 13—5.

The Cards pulled out of their

MANAGERS OF THE CHAMPIONS

Casey Stengel, Yankees

Burt Shotton, Dodgers

tailspin too late to catch the Brooks. The Yanks and Dodgers annexed their respective league titles by one game and, interestingly enough, the winners and runners-up in each circuit finished with identical records, 97 and 57 for the champions and 96 and 58 for the second-place clubs.

The Dodgers will be at Yankee Stadium Wednesday and Thursday and then the Brooks will be hosts to the Bombers Friday, Saturday and Sunday, at Ebbets Field, barring a sweep. In the event the series lasts that long, the final two games are listed for the Stadium on Monday and Tuesday, Oct. 10 and 11.

Stout-hearted hurling by their big righthander, Vic Raschi, enabled the gallant Yanks to defeat Joe McCarthy's Red Sox. It was a bitter pill, too, for the 62-year-old McCarthy, who saw his pennant hopes smashed in the same sta-

dium where he led the Bombers to eight American League pennants and seven world championships. Moreover, itt was the second straight season the Bosox were beaten out in the last stage of the campaign. Last year the Red Sox lost in a play-off with Cleveland.

Raschi held Boston in check for eight innings behind a one-run lead which a triple by Phil Rizzuto had given him in the first inning. The Bomber hurler, up to the ninth, had the Bosox blanked on two hits in a tense mound battle with Ellis Kinder, who was trying for his twenty-fourth decision of the year.

Game Decided in Eighth

In the last of the eighth the Yanks put on the rally that won the flag. With Kinder going out for a pinch-hitter, the desperate McCarthy nominated Mel Parnell, his 25-game winning southpaw, to hold the Bombers until his own

power hitters could have one last fling at Raschi.

Old Reliable Tommy Henrich greeted Parnell with a home run into the right field stands. Yogi Berra singled and Tex Hughson was called on to relieve Parnell. Joe DiMaggio hit into a double play but the Yanks proceeded to fill the bases. Then Jerry Coleman, rookie second baseman, cleared them with a pop fly two-bagger to short right field. That four-run outbreak carried the day, for the aroused Bosox lashed back for three runs in the ninth.

The first two Red Sox runs in the ninth came in on Bobby Doerr's triple over the head of Joe DiMaggio, running on shaky legs. The Clipper then called time and dramatically took himself out of the game. Joltin' Joe, a sick man these past three weeks, received a great ovation as he walked off the field.

BOSTON (A.)							NEW YORK (A.)						
	ab.	r.	h.	po.	a.	e.		ab.	r.	h.	po.	a.	e.
D.DiM'gio,cf4		0	0	5	0	0	Rizzuto, ss..4		1	2	1	7	0
Pesky, 3b...	3	0	0	1	4	0	Henrich, 1b.3		1	1	0	0	0
Williams, lf.2		1	0	0	0	1	Berra, c....4		0	1	5	0	0
Stephens, ss.4		1	1	2	3	0	J.DiMa'gio,cf4		0	1	3	0	0
Doerr, 2b...	4	1	2	0	5	0	Woodling lf..0		0	0	0	0	0
Zarilla, rf ..4		0	1	1	0	0	Lindell, lf ...2		0	1	1	0	0
Goodman, 1b.3		0	1	9	1	0	Bauer, lf-rf..0		0	0	0	0	0
Tebbetts, c..4		0	0	6	0	0	Johnson, 3b..4		1	2	0	0	0
Kinder, p...	2	0	0	0	2	0	Mapes, rf-cf.3		1	0	3	0	0
aWright 0		0	0	0	0	0	Coleman, 2b.4		0	1	3	1	0
Parnell, p...	0	0	0	0	0	0	Raschi, p....3		0	0	1	0	0
Hughson, p..0		0	0	0	0	0							
Total....30	3	5	24	12	1		Total....31	5	9	27	0		

aWalked for Kinder in eighth.

Boston . . . . .000 000 003—3
New York . . . . .100 000 04x—5

Runs batted in—Henrich 2, Coleman 3, Doerr 2, Goodman.

Two-base hit—Coleman. Three-base hits—Rizzuto, J. DiMaggio, Doerr. Home run—Henrich. Stolen bases—Goodman, Lindell. Double plays—Coleman and Henrich; Rizzuto and Henrich; Doerr, Stephens and Goodman. Left on bases—Boston 5, New York 6. Bases on balls—Off Raschi 5, Kinder 3, Hughson 1. Struck out—By Raschi 4, Kinder 5. Hits—Off Kinder 4 in 7 innings, Parnell 2 in 0 (pitched to 2 batters); Hughson 3 in 1. Wild pitch—Raschi. Passed ball—Berra. Winner—Raschi (21—10). Loser—Kinder (23—6). Umpires — Hubbard, Rommel, Berry, Summers, Honochick and Hurley. Time of game—2:30. Attendance—68,055.

Dusk was settling over Shibe Park as the Dodgers put over their rousing tenth-inning rally to down the Phillies. Jack Banta, young relief pitcher, handcuffed the dangerous Philadelphia hitters for four innings after the Brooks had dissipated a 5-0 bulge.

Peewee Reese, who in five previous visits to the plate hadn't hit the ball out of the infield, dropped a single into left to open the top half of the tenth. Then the Dodgers proceeded to rush their two tallies across like real champions. Reese moved to second on Eddie Miksis' sacrifice and big Duke

Snider sent the Dodger captain home when he rapped a sizzler through the legs of Pitcher Ken Heintzelman, nemesis of the Brooks all season.

With 36,765 fans cheering them on, the Brooks sewed it up. After Jackie Robinson had been purposely passed, Luis Olmo smashed a single past Willie Jones into left field to drive Snider across. Duke had taken second on the throw to the plate as Reese counted.

The jubilant Dodgers mobbed Banta at the end of the game. It was the tenth victory of the season for the big righthander, but none of his successes was as important as this one. He had come into the game after Don Newcombe and Rex Barney had been driven to the showers.

The Box Score

BROOKLYN (N.)							PHILADELPHIA (N.)						
	ab.	r.	h.	po.	a.	e.		ab.	r.	h.	po.	a.	e.
Reese, ss...	5	1	1	0	1	0	Ashburn, cf.6		0	2	4	0	0
Jorg'en, 3b	3	1	1	2	2	0	eSanicki ...1		0	0	0	0	0
aEdwards ..1		0	0	0	0	0	Hamner, ss.5		1	1	4	5	0
Miksis, 3b..0		0	0	1	2	0	Sisler, 1b...4		0	1	11	2	1
Snider, cf..4		1	2	2	0	0	Ennis. lf...4		2	2	0	0	0
Robi'son, 2b.5		1	1	2	2	0	Seminick, c.5		0	1	1	1	0
H'm'nski, lf.3		1	1	2	0	0	Nich'son, rf.4		1	1	2	0	0
Olmo, lf...2		0	1	2	0	0	Jones, 3b...5		1	1	1	4	0
Furillo, rf..6		2	4	4	0	1	Goliat, 2b...5		1	2	5	0	0
Camp'ella, c.3		0	1	7	0	0	Meyer, p....0		0	0	1	0	0
Hodges, 1b..4		2	2	10	1	0	Roberts, p...0		0	0	0	0	0
N'combe, p..2		0	1	1	0	0	bBlatner ...1		1	1	0	0	0
Barney, p...1		0	0	0	0	0	Th'mpson, p.0		0	0	0	0	0
Banta, p....1		0	0	0	1	0	cHollmig ...1		0	1	0	0	0
							Simmons, p.0		0	0	0	0	0
Total 38	9	13	30	9	1	K'nstanty, p.0		0	0	0	0	0
							dBlaink 1		1	1	1	0	0
							H'zelman, p.1		0	0	0	2	0
							Trinkle, p...0		0	0	0	0	0
							Total ...42	7	12	30	14	2	

aFiled out for Jorgensen in seventh.
bWalked for Roberts in third.
cDoubled for Thompson in fourth.
dSingled for Konstanty in sixth.
eStruck out for Trinkle in tenth.

Brooklyn . . . . .0 05 020 000 2—9
Philadelphia . . . . .0 00 412 000 0—7

Runs batted in—Robinson, Furillo, Hodges, Newcombe 2, Campanella 2, Snider, Olmo, Jones 3, Ashburn, Nicholson, Hamner, Ennis.

Two-base hits—Hollmig, Campanella, Nicholson. Home run—Jones. Sacrifices—Banta, Robinson. Miksis. Stolen bases—Robinson 2. Double plays—Hamner and Sisler. Left on bases—Brooklyn 12, Philadelphia 9. Bases on balls—Off Meyer 3, Roberts 1, Newcombe 2, Thompson 1, Barney 1, Konstanty 1, Heintzelman 4, Banta 1. Struck out—By Newcombe 2, Barney 1, Konstanty 1, Banta 3. Hits—Off Meyer 5 in 2 2-3 innings, Roberts 1 in 1-3, Thompson 0 in 1, Simmons 2 in 0, Newcombe 6 in 3 1-3, Barney 4 in 2 1-3, Banta 4 in 4 1-3, Konstanty 1 in 2, Heintzelman 4 in 3 1-3, Trinkle 0 in 2-3. Wild pitch—Meyer 2. Winner—Banta (10—6). Loser—Heintzelman (17—10). Umpires—Goetz, Reardon, Barlick and Jorda. Time of game—3:17. Attendance—36,765.

October 3, 1949

Phils Beat Dodgers for Flag; Win 4-1 on Homer in Tenth

By ROSCOE McGOWEN

The Philadelphia Whiz Kids, who came so close to winning the ignominious title of the Fizz Kids, captured the first National League pennant for the Quaker City in thirty-five years when they beat the Dodgers, 4—1, yesterday at Ebbets Field before the greatest outpouring of Flatbush fans—35,073—of the 1950 season.

The Brooklyn pennant bubble exploded in the top of the tenth inning when Dick Sisler, son of

the Hall of Fame fellow who has been a Branch Rickey employe for years, swung with a mixture of power and desperation and drove a three-run homer into the lower left field stands.

Don Newcombe, who pitched and lost the first game of the 1950 campaign in Philadelphia, was the victim of Sisler's flag-winning wallop and Robin Roberts, the same chap who bested Newk in the season's opener, was the winning pitcher.

Roberts gained his twentieth triumph—the most important No. 20

he'll ever win — and became the first Phil hurler to win that many since the great Grover Cleveland Alexander turned in his third

straight thirty-game season in 1917.

The courageous young righthander, who had failed in six previous starts to nail down No. 20, although pitching some fine games, deserved this big triumph, for he held the Brooks to five hits and would have had a shut-out but for a freakish home run by Peewee Reese, the gallant Brooklyn captain and shortstop.

In the sixth inning, with two out and the Phils leading, 1—0, Reese hit a towering fly to right field and the ball came down to the top of the wall and lodged in the screen.

Reese, assuming the ball had bounced off the screen or wall, raced around to third before he learned that the ball was out of play, while the crowd screamed its delight. That, they thought, would send the Brooks on to vic.ory—and they were wrong only by a little bit, at thåt.

In the ninth inning the Dodgers appeared certain to push over the winning tally, but it was thrown out at the plate, and from now on through the winter it will be hard to convince a lot of Flatbush fanatics that Coach Milt Stock didn't make a bad decision.

That momentous inning started with Cal Abrams, the lead-off man, drawing his second pass from Roberts on a three-and-two pitch. Reese tried twice to bunt and, with two strikes against him, lined a clean single into left center field, Abrams stopping at second.

Naturally, the Phils had to look for a bunt from Duke Snider, and were playing fairly close, but Duke rifled the first pitch into center—and the stands exploded in a vast roar. This was it.

But Richie Ashburn, coming in fast, fielded the hit clearly and fired it with deadly accuracy to Stan Lopata at the plate. Meanwhile, Stock was waving Abrams around third, with the disappointing, but certainly not unexpected result that Lopata was waiting with the ball when Cal arrived.

Robinson Purposely Passed

Even then, since Reese and Snider had advanced on the throw, the Dodgers had a big chance for the victory that would have sent them into a play-off today.

Jackie Robinson, of course, was purposely passed to fill the bases. Then Carl Furillo swung at the first pitch and the fans groaned as Eddie Waitkus camped under the feeble foul near first base.

The last hope faded when Gil Hodges, the Brooks' leading home

run hitter, drove a high fly to right that Del Ennis took near the center field side of the scoreboard.

Then came the Phils' tenth and one could almost sense the feeling in the stands that this was all for the Dodgers. This feeling became more pronounced when Roberts started the winning frame with a single through the middle.

Waitkus, making one attempt to bunt, then swung and dropped a pop-fly single into short center out of everybody's reach, Roberts stopping at second. The bunt was on again but Ashburn, a good bunter and a fast runner, bunted into a force out at third, Newcombe making a good play on the attempted sacrifice.

Tp came the extremely dangerous Sisler, who already had driven three consecutive singles into right field off Newcombe's slants. Dick swung at the first two pitches, missing one and fouling one, then looked at a wide one.

Biggest and Shortest

When he let go at the next one and the ball arched high toward left field, Abrams stood for a split second, then ran madly toward the wall. But it was no use. The biggest home run—and possibly one of the shortest—the stands are only 348 feet from home plate—that young Sisler ever hit, was on the records and the Whiz Kids had won the pennant that had been eluding them so exasperatingly for the longest week of their lives.

What followed was anticlimax. Newcombe striking out Ennis and getting Puddin' Head Jones on a simple grounder to Reese.

The Dodger tenth was a breeze for Roberts. Roy Campanella hit a solid liner to deep left but t was caught easily by Jack Mayo, who had just been sent into left field in place of Sisler as a defensive move —one which Manager Eddie Sawyer frequently has made this year.

Then Jim Russell, pinch-hitting for Billy Cox, struck out and Tommy Brown, taking Newcombe's place at bat, lifted a high one to Waitkus at first.

The first break for the Phils came in the fifth inning, when they scored their first and all-important run, which might have been averted.

Waitkus and Ashburn had been retired on a couple of fine plays by Hodges, with Newcombe covering

first base in each instance, when the tough young Sisler slashed his second single just out of Gil's reach.

Here Ennis lifted a high fly to right center and it appeared it could be caught. But Snider, playing deep for the Phil slugger in left center, couldn't race in fast enough, and Jackie Robinson didn't get out under the ball.

Whether Jackie could have made the catch is something that won't be known. Certainly Robby must have thought Snider would get under it, because Dou was running at top speed all the way.

Anyway, immediately following that, Sisler, having moved around to third, Jones swung at Newcombe's first pitch and rifled the ball through to Reese's left for the single that brought in the run.

Reese delivered three of the five Brooklyn hits, opening the fourth inning with a line double to left that bounced around in the densely populated Phil bullpen. But here the Dodgers got a bad break when Snider tapped a ball toward first that he probably would have beaten out for a hit.

Marooned at Second

That would have put men on first and third with none out, but the ball just brushed Duke's leg as he dashed for first and the alert Larry Goetz, calling balls and strikes for the second straight day, promptly called Duke out and Reese had to return to second.

That's where the Little Colonel stayed, for Robinson bounced out to Roberts and Furillo lifted one of the few flies to the outfield hit by the Brooks, Ashburn taking it in right center.

As an indication of the caliber of Roberts' pitching, the big bonus boy had six assists and one putout, while his first baseman had seventeen putouts.

Newcombe, on the other hand, was rather soundly smacked, even when he got his man out. A double play following Ennis' single to open the second frame, started by Reese, got Don out of trouble then, and at the start of the Phils' ninth Abrams made a spectacular leaping catch of Gran Hamner's drive against the left-field wall.

When Andy Seminick followed with a single and the fleet Ralph Caballero ran for him, Newcombe was helped out again by the fine

collaboration of Campanella and Robinson, who nailed Ralph trying to steal.

Altogether the Phils made eleven hits, which helps to indicate that, on one important day, at least, the better pitcher and the better team won.

Thirteenth for Dick

A touch of irony may be noted in the fact that Sisler's homer was his thirteenth of the year, his third off Brooklyn pitching, and that all three were struck at Ebbets Field.

Seminick came into second with considerable vigor in the seventh when Mike Goliat bunted into a force play, Campanella to Reese, and Pee Wee had his right foot spiked slightly. Robinson was observed making a few comments to the big Phil catcher as Andy was heading for the dugout.

A small boy risked life and limb to clamber atop the right-field wall to get Reese's home-run ball. The kid tossed it to a friend in the stands below, apparently fearing a cop would take it away from him.

For the record, which doesn't matter much now, the Dodgers, starting from third place nine games back on Sept. 19, won 13 of 16 games to come close to the Phils, who won only three of twelve in that period.

The box score:

PHILADELPHIA (N.)							BROOKLYN (N.)						
	ab.	r.	h.	po.	a.	e.		ab.	r.	h.	po.	a.	e.
Waitkus, 1b.	5	1	1	15	0	0	Abrams, lf.	2	0	0	2	0	0
Ashburn, cf.	5	1	0	2	1	0	Reese, ss.	4	1	3	3	5	0
Sisler, lf.	5	2	4	0	0	0	Snider, cf.	4	0	1	3	0	0
Mayo, lf.	0	0	0	1	0	0	Rob'son, 3b.	3	0	0	4	3	0
Ennis, rf.	5	0	2	2	0	0	Furillo, rf.	4	0	0	3	0	0
Jones, 3b.	5	0	1	0	3	0	Camp'lla, c.	4	0	1	2	1	0
Hamner, ss.	4	0	1	2	4	0	Hodges, 1b.	4	0	0	9	3	0
Seminick, c.	3	0	1	3	1	0	Cox, 3b.	3	0	0	1	2	0
aCaballero	0	0	0	0	0	0	bRussell	1	0	0	0	0	0
Lopata, c.	0	0	0	1	0	0	N'combe, p.	3	0	0	0	2	0
Goliat, 2b.	4	0	1	1	3	0	cBrown	1	0	0	0	0	0
Roberts, p.	2	0	1	1	6	0							
Total....	38	4	11	30	16	0	Total....	33	1	5	30	17	0

aRan for Seminick in ninth.
bStruck out for Cox in tenth.
cFouled out for Newcombe in tenth.

Philadelphia ....0 0 0 0 0 1 0 0 0 3—4
Brooklyn ....0 0 0 0 0 1 0 0 0 0—1

Runs batted in—Jones, Reese, Sisler 3. Two-base hit—Reese. Home runs—Reese, Sisler. Sacrifice—Roberts. Double plays—Reese, Robinson and Hodges; Roberts and Waitkus. Left on bases—Philadelphia 7, Brooklyn 5. Bases on balls—Off Roberts 3, Newcombe 3. Struck out—By Roberts 2, Newcombe 3. Winning pitcher—Roberts (20—11). Losing pitcher—Newcombe (19—11). Umpires—Goetz, Dascoli, Jorda and Donatelli. Time of game—2:35. Attendance—35,073.

October 2, 1950

Mack Quits as Athletics' Manager After 50 Years; Dykes Gets Post

By WILLIAM G. WEART
Special to THE NEW YORK TIMES

PHILADELPHIA, Oct. 18— Connie Mack, known the world over as the grand old man of baseball, retired today as manager of the Athletics, the Philadelphia team he founded and managed since he helped organize the American League in 1901.

After sixty-seven years of playing the game and leading his White Elephants, the genial 87-year-old patriarch of the national game an-

nounced his resignation as field boss of the club at a hastily called luncheon press conference.

As two score newspaper men and sportscasters sat in stunned silence, Mr. Mack revealed that Jimmy Dykes, one of his most famous protégés, had been selected to succeed him in the dugout and that Arthur Ehlers, as general manager, would be in complete charge of the club's business affairs.

Speaking from his place at the center of the head table, with Dykes on one side and Ehlers on the other, Connie, tall and erect, smiled and said:

"It's a pleasure for me to be here today. I'm retiring from baseball and this is the way I'm retiring— as manager of the baseball club. I'm not quitting because I'm too old, but because I think the people want me to."

Continuing without the usual long pauses and "ah's," Mr. Mack added:

"I know you realize I have been connected with the game for a long time. There are two men sitting here beside me—one is the new general manager. The other is the real (team) manager." He pointed to Ehlers and Dykes in

turn and then went on:

"It is a pleasure for me to make the announcement. While I have not given Philadelphia all that was expected of me, I do know your future manager will do a great job if we get him the players—with the material he will have."

Although he will remain as president of the club, Mr. Mack emphasized that Ehlers would handle all future deals and, in the future, also would give out all news concerning the team.

Even in retiring, Connie still hopes for that "one more" pennant for the A's. During his half-century as manager, the team captured nine pennants and won five world series, among his golden years were 1929, 1930 and 1931 when the club, on which Dykes was the third baseman, came roaring home with successive pennants.

"You know," Connie observed, "we all like a winner and I feel that in our new manager we are going to have a winner—at least we are going after the material to make a winner."

Rumors that Mr. Mack would retire have been prevalent over the last decade, but each time he spiked them by saying that he would manage the Athletics as long as he was physically able.

His retirement from the bench follows closely the reorganization of the club, both officially and financially. Two of his sons, Roy and Earle, gained control of the club recently by buying out Connie Mack Jr., a half-brother, and other stockholders, excepting the interest held by Connie himself.

Mr. Mack's decision to retire as manager, it was learned, was reached on Monday after a series of discussions with Roy and Earle, who are vice president and secretary-treasurer, respectively.

The sons did not bring any pressure to force their father to withdraw from the bench. On the contrary, they announced a few weeks ago that their father would remain in the dugout as long as he wanted to. He will retain his post as club president and plans to make some of the road trips with the team, "because that's a habit hard to break."

In expressing thanks for his appointment as general manager, Ehlers said he intended to call upon Mr. Mack and his sons for advice "whenever I need it."

"I'm no different from any other person in baseball," he added. "I have the deepest respect and admiration for Mr. Mack. He is the most lovable and kindly man I ever knew and it is an honor to be associated with him.

Dykes then warned that he would tolerate no loafing on the ball club next season. "If any of the players read what I say," he added, "I want them to know that the honeymoon is over."

"Until last night," Jimmy said. "I had no idea where I'd be next year. In fact I was dickering for a job with Detroit.

"If as manager of the Athletics. I can ever receive one-millionth of the praise and respect that Mr. Mack has, I'll think I have acquired something."

WON FIRST FLAG IN 1902

Mackmen Beat Cubs for Initial Series Triumph in 1910

Connie Mack was born Dec. 23. 1862, in East Brookfield. Mass. His name then was Cornelius McGillicuddy, but sports writers whittled that down to Connie Mack. It fitted better in the box scores. The telephone directory still lists his name as "McGillicuddy."

The 6 foot 2 'string bean' quit a factory job in 1883 to play professional baseball. He was a catcher for eighteen years before organizing the Athletes in the newly formed American League in 1901.

As the "tall tactician" of baseball, Mack brought Philadelphia its first league title in 1902. Again in 1905, with Chief Bender and Eddie Plank as the leading pitchers, the Mackmen dominated baseball's junior circuit.

The first Mack victory in a world series came in 1910 when the Athletes turned back the Chicago Cubs. They retained the world title in 1911, whipping the New York Giants.

Again in 1913 and 1914 the Athletics won the American League

flag, taking the world series in 1913. But in 1914 George Stallings' amazing Boston Braves defeated the Athletics in the post-season series.

Scraps $100,000 Infield

Mack then sold many of his stars, including Eddie Collins and the remainder of the fabulous $100,000 infield.

After finishing seven successive years in the cellar. Mack began rebuilding. Gradually the Athletics moved into contention, until in 1929 they won the first of three straight pennants.

Spearheads of what Mack has often called his greatest team were such great players as Lefty Grove, George Earnshaw, Rube Walberg. Jimmy Foxx, Al Simmons, Mule Haas, Bing Miller, Max Bishop, Joe Boley, Mickey Cochrane and Dykes.

Mack then unloaded his entire team in another sale. Since then Connie's efforts to build another serious pennant contender have proved futile.

Won Edward Bok Prize

One of the most respected men connected with sports, Connie was awarded the $10,000 Edward W. Bok prize for distinguished service to Philadelphia in 1929. Before that, the award had gone only to artists, scientists, educators and philanthropists.

He was wined and dined in countless pre-season gatherings before the opening of the 1950 season. All were focused on another pennant in Mack fiftieth year of managing.

The pitching staff, a bulwark for several years, fell apart, however, and the club was unable to make up for the mound deficiency at the plate.

October 19, 1950

Connie Mack's Record
By The United Press.

PLAYER

Year. Club and League.	Pos.G. AB. R. H. BA.FA.
1884, Meriden (Ct.St.)	.c.
1885, Hartford (So.N E.)	
Conn. St.)	.c. 1 4 1 2 .500 .917
'86, Hartford (E.)	.c.inf. 69 278 44 69 .248 .953
'86, Wash. (Nat.)	.c. 10 36 4 13 .361 .932
'87, Wash. (Nat.)	.c.c 322 35 71 .220 .904
1888, Wash. (Nat.)	.c. 85 300 49 56 .187 .916
1889, Buff.(Plyrs.)	.c.inf. 123 506 95 136 .268 .939
1890, Pitt. (Nat.)	.c. 71 271 41 57 .210 .933
1891, Pitt. (Nat.)	.c. 102 48 97 386 51 113 .292 .903
1892, Pitt. (Nat.)	.c. 36 120 22 39 .325 .885
1893, Pitt. (Nat.)	.c. 63 230 32 59 .257 .938
1894, Pitt. (Nat.)	.c. 66 338 39 87 .257 .949
1895, Pitt. (Nat.)	.c. 14 47 12 17 .362 .916
1896, Pitt. (Nat.)	.c. 30 116 7 24 .207 .981
1897, Milw. (West.)	.c.1b. 27 71 12 18 .254 .963

Major league total...695 2,672 387 672 .251 .925
(Mack hit only two home runs during his playing career, both for Pittsburgh in 1892).

MANAGER

Year. Club and League.	Fin.	Games W. L.
*1894 Pittsburgh (Nat.)	7th	11 11
1895, Pittsburgh	7th	11 11
1896, Pittsburgh	6th	66 63
1897, Milwaukee (West.)	4th	83 57
1898, Milwaukee	3d	82 57
1899, Milwaukee	6th	55 68
1900, Milwaukee (Amer.)	2d	79 58

(American League)

Year Club	Fin.	Games W. L.	Year Club	Fin.	Games W. L.
1901. Phila.	4th	74 62	1926. Phila.	3d	83 67
1902. Phila.	1st	83 53	1927. Phila.	2d	91 63
1903. Phila.	2d	75 60	1928. Phila.	2d	98 55
1904. Phila.	5th	81 70	1929. Phila.	1st	104 46
1905. Phila.	1st	92 56	1930. Phila.	1st	102 52
1906. Phila.	4th	78 67	1931. Phila.	1st	107 45
1907. Phila.	2d	88 57	1932. Phila.	2d	94 60
1908. Phila.	6th	68 84	1933. Phila.	3c	79 72
1909. Phila.	2d	95 58	1934. Phila.	5th	68 82
1910. Phila.	1st	102 48	1935. Phila.	8th	58 91
1911. Phila.	1st	101 50	1936. Phila.	8th	53 100
1912. Phila.	3d	90 62	1937. Phila.	7th	54 97
1913. Phila.	1st	96 57	1938. Phila.	8th	53 99
1914. Phila.	1st	99 53	1939. Phila.	7th	55 97
1915. Phila.	8th	43 .09	1940. Phila.	8th	54 100
1916. Phila.	8th	36 .17	1941. Phila.	8th	64 90
1917. Phila.	8th	55 98	1942. Phila.	8th	55 99
1918. Phila.	8th	52 76	1943. Phila.	8th	49 105
1919. Phila.	8th	36 104	1944. Phila.	5th	72 82
1920. Phila.	8th	48 106	1945. Phila.	8th	52 98
1921. Phila.	8th	53 100	1946. Phila.	8th	49 105
1922. Phila.	7th	65 89	1947. Phila.	5th	78 76
1923. Phila.	6th	69 83	1948. Phila.	4th	84 70
1924. Phila.	5th	71 81	1949. Phila.	5th	81 73
1925. Phila.	2d	88 64	1950. Phila.	8th	52 102

*Took over as manager on Sept. 3 with club in seventh place.

WORLD SERIES
(ALL WITH PHILADELPHIA)

Year and Opponent.	Games W. L.	Year and Opponent.	Games W. L.
1905. New York.1	4	1914. Boston...0	4
1910. Chicago..4	1	1929. Chicago..4	1
1911. New York.4	2	1930. St. Louis..4	2
1913. New York.4	1	1931. St. Louis..3	4

Feller Hurls Third No-Hitter for Indians

ACE HELPS TRIBE TAKE TWO, 2-1, 2-0

Errors Enable Tigers to Tally in Feller's No-Hitter That Makes Baseball History

CLEVELAND, July 1 (UP)—Bobby Feller, who had to talk a coach into letting him stay in the game, pitched the third no-hitter of his career — and became the first pitcher in modern times to do so — as the Indians beat the Tigers, 2—1, today. The Indians also won the second game of the double-header, 2—0, on Bob Chakales' four-hitter.

The venerable fireballer, who was tossed aside as "through" only a few months ago and left off the American League All-Star team, said he was never better than when he set down the Tigers this afternoon. The one run he gave up was the result of two errors, one of

them Feller's.

In the third inning Coach Mel Harder went out to the mound and asked Feller, "Do you feel okay? You don't look too good."

But Feller insisted that he was good enough to stay in — and then he proved it in historic fashion. Only four men reached base — three on walks, one on an error.

Throws Sliders, Curves

"I didn't even have a very good fast ball," Feller mused after the game. "I threw mostly sliders and curves. It was a wonderful thrill, but I still think my second no-hitter — against the Yankees — was better."

He is the first modern pitcher in history to throw three no-hitters. The legendary Cy Young pitched one in 1897, another in 1904 and the third in 1908.

Feller pitched his first no-hitter against the White Sox on opening day in 1940, his second against the Yankees on April 30, 1946, and then today he did it again before 42,891 nearly hysterical fans.

The Tigers got their run in the fourth inning. It came as the result of Ray Boone's error, a stolen

base, a wild pick-off throw and a fly ball.

It's all part of a monumental comeback for the Iowa farm boy who broke into the majors in 1936 at the age of 17. He had a 16-11 record last season and that—for him—was dismal.

His No. 219 in Majors

But he started like a whirlwind this season, winning four straight.

losing a game, then winning six straight. The triumph today was his eleventh of the season against two losses, and the 219th of his career—more than any other active major league pitcher. Both of his previous no-hitters were by 1—0 scores.

The crowd rocked huge Cleveland Stadium as Feller slipped a third strike past Vic Wertz with the count 3—2 for the last out of

Feller's Pitching Masterpieces

	NO-HIT GAMES			
Date.	Opponent.	Score.	Strikeouts.	Walks. *Spoiler.
April 16, 1940	Chicago	1—0	8	5
April 30, 1946	New York	1—0	11	5
July 1, 1951	Detroit	2—1	5	3

	ONE-HIT GAMES				
April 20, 1938	St. Louis	9—0	6	6	Sullivan
May 25, 1939	Boston	11—0	10	5	Doerr
June 27, 1939	Detroit	5—0	13	6	Averill
July 12, 1940	Philadelphia	1—0	13	2	Siebert
Sept. 26, 1941	St. Louis	3—2	6	7	Ferrell
Sept. 19, 1945	Detroit	2—0	7	4	Outlaw
July 31, 1946	Boston	4—1	9	9	Doerr
Aug. 8, 1946	Chicago	5—0	5	3	Hayes
April 22, 1947	St. Louis	5—0	10	1	Zarilla
May 2, 1947	Boston	2—0	8	6	Pesky

*All hits were singles.

the game.

Feller was forced to go at top form all of the way against Bob Cain, who threw a six-hitter, and the Indians did not win until the eighth when Sam Chapman tripled and Luke Easter slashed a single off Dick Kryhoski's glove to score Milt Nielsen who ran for Chapman.

The Tigers hit only five flies to the outfield and Feller struck out five. He walked only three men and retired the first nine hitters in order.

Cain allowed a run in the first inning on singles by Dale Mitchell and Bob Avila and Easter's infield out. The last time Cain pitched against Cleveland Bob Lemon beat him with a one-hitter.

Second No-Hitter of Year

Feller's no-hitter was the second of the year in the majors. Cliff Chambers pitched one for the Pirates against the Boston Braves

on May 6. The last no-hitter by an American League pitcher was turned in by Lemon on June 30, 1948, and the victims were the same Tigers.

The Indians completed the humiliation of the Tigers in the second game as they made it ten victories in a row for the season. In the ten games, the Tigers have scored a total of eight runs against Cleveland pitching. They were shut out three times, scored one run in six games and two runs in one game.

The Indians collected seven hits off Ted Gray and Virgil Trucks and scored their runs in the sixth on a walk to Avila, singles by Chapman and Easter and a double by Bob Kennedy.

In New York, Yankee Manager Casey Stengel, who will pilot the American League All-Stars in the annual dream game with the Na-

tional League, said he left Feller off the team "because I think Lemon would relieve better."

Casey shook his head and added: "That cooks me. How could I know the guy was gonna pitch a no-hitter?" The box scores:

FIRST GAME

DETROIT (A.)	ab.r.h.po.a	CLEVELAND (A.)	ab.r.h.po.a
Lipon, ss	.3 1 0 1 3	Mitchell, lf	.3 1 1 3 0
aHutchinson	.1 0 0 0 0	Avila, 2b	.4 0 1 0 3
Berry, ss	.0 0 0 0 0	Chapman, cf	.4 0 1 1 0
Priddy, 2b	.3 0 0 2 1	cNeilsen	.0 1 0 0 0
bKeller	.1 0 0 0 0	Easter, 1b	.4 0 1 13 0
Kell, 3b	.4 0 0 1 1	Doby, cf	.0 0 0 0 0
Wertz, rf	.3 0 0 1 0	Simpson, 1b	.0 0 0 0 0
Evers, lf	.3 0 0 5 0	Rosen, 3b	.4 0 0 0 4
Kryhoski, 1b	.3 0 0 8 1	Kennedy, rf	.4 0 0 3 0
Ginsberg, c	.3 0 0 3 1	Boone, ss	.2 0 0 2 5
Groth, cf	.2 0 0 2 0	Hegan, c	.3 0 2 5 0
Cain, p	.2 0 0 1 1	Feller, p	.2 0 0 0 0
Total	.28 1 0 24 8	Total	.30 2 6 27 12

aFlied out for Lipon in eighth.
bFlied out for Priddy in ninth.
cRan for Chapman in eighth.

Detroit .... 0 0 0 1 0 0 0 0 0—1
Cleveland .... 1 0 0 0 0 0 0 1 .—2

Errors—Boone, Feller. Runs batted in—Easter, Kell.
Three-base hit—Chapman. Stolen base—Lipon. Left on bases—Detroit 3, Cleveland 7. Bases on balls—Off Cain 3. Feller 3. Struck out—By

Cain 3. Feller 5. Winning pitcher—Feller (11-2). Losing pitcher—Cain (6-6). Umpires—Berry, Napp, Hurley and Passarella. Time of game—2:06.

SECOND GAME

DETROIT (A.)	ab.r.h.po.a	CLEVELAND (A.)	ab.r.h.po.a
Lipon, ss	.4 0 2 1 1	Mitchell, lf	.4 0 2 1 0
Priddy, 2b	.4 0 1 5 5	Avila, 2b	.2 1 0 1 4
Kell, 3b	.4 0 1 2 2	Chapman, cf	.4 1 2 1 0
Wertz, rf	.3 0 1 1	Easter, 1b	.3 0 2 8 0
Evers, lf	.4 0 1 0 1	Simpson, cf	.0 0 0 0 0
Kryhoski, 1b	.3 0 0 10 0	Rosen, 3b	.4 0 0 1 1
Groth, cf	.2 0 0 2 0	Kennedy, rf	.2 0 1 3 0
Robinson, c	.2 0 0 3 0	Boone, ss	.3 0 0 2 5
Gray, p	.2 0 1 1 2	Tebbetts, c	.2 0 0 5 0
aGinsberg	.1 0 1 0 0	Chakales, p	.3 0 0 0 1
Trucks, p	.0 0 0 0 1		
Total	.29 0 4 24 16	Total	.26 2 7 27 8

aSingled for Gray in eighth.

Detroit .... 0 0 0 0 0 0 0 0 0—0
Cleveland .... 0 0 0 0 0 2 0 0 .—2

Runs batted in—Easter, Kennedy.
Two-base hit—Kennedy. Sacrifices—Kennedy, Avila. Double plays—Gray and Kryhoski; Avila, Boone and Easter 2. Left on bases—Detroit 5, Cleveland 6. Bases on balls—Off Gray 3. Trucks 1. Chakales 3. Struck out—By Gray 1, Trucks 1. Chakales 4. Hits—Off Gray 6 in 7 innings. Trucks 1 in 1. Winning pitcher—Chakales (3-2). Losing pitcher—Gray (3-8). Umpires—Napp, Hurley, Passarella and Berry. Time of game—1:41. Attendance—42,561.

July 2, 1951

Frick Elected Commissioner Of Baseball for Seven Years

National League Head Gets Job at $65,000 Annually When Giles Withdraws

By JOSEPH M. SHEEHAN
Special to The New York Times.

CHICAGO, Sept. 20—Ford C. Frick, 56-year-old president of the National League, tonight was elected commissioner of baseball.

His appointment, accepted over the phone from Bronxville, N. Y., was for a seven-year term at an annual salary of $65,000. It was to go into effect at midnight.

Warren C. Giles, president of the Cincinnati Reds and chief rival of Mr. Frick for the post vacated last July 15 by Albert B. (Happy) Chandler, withdrew his name from consideration after an around-the-clock voting deadlock between two career baseball men.

So on the final ballot of a number that reached at least fifty, Mr. Frick was the unanimous choice of the voting representatives of the sixteen major league clubs. The decision was announced shortly after 11 P. M. (New York time) following morning and afternoon sessions that had failed to produce a result. The vacancy left by the necessary resignation of Mr. Frick as president of baseball's senior circuit will be dealt with in the near future by the National League owners, probably during the world series, scheduled to open Oct. 3 or 4. An excellent guess is that Mr. Giles will get that job.

The choice of Mr. Frick, a teacher, sports writer, newspaper columnist and radio commentator before he became president of the National League in 1934, marks the first time that the sport has named a baseball man to the national pastime's highest adminis-

Ford C. Frick
The New York Times

trative post.

The first commissioner was the late Judge Kenesaw Mountain Landis, nominated to the office in 1921 after the infamous Chicago Black Sox scandal had rocked the spot to its foundations. In 1945, following the death of Judge Landis, Mr. Chandler, then United States Senator from Kentucky, was voted into the job.

After a tempestuous reign, Mr. Chandler failed by three votes to muster the twelve votes required for re-election at St. Petersburg, Fla., last December. He was repudiated again in Miami last March. and he stepped down last July.

In considering a successor, the owners weighed the qualifications of many prospective candidates from all walks of life. There was much debate concerning whether another outsider of public stature and administrative experience would not be the wisest choice.

However, the final showdown was between two members of baseball's family circle—Mr. Frick and Mr. Giles.

No other names, of all those that have been bandied about for the last few months, figured in the picture in this executive session at the Palmer House, the first and only official joint meeting of the leagues on the commissionership since Mr. Chandler lost out.

Going into today's marathon session, Mr. Giles was generally considered to have the edge. The personable 55-year-old Cincinnati president had the backing of the owners who had supported Mr. Chandler, which gave him a nine-vote start toward the required twelve votes.

However, Mr. Frick had strong support also and some of those who were for Mr. Giles were satisfied that the National League president, who had run the affairs of his circuit with smooth efficiency, was equally qualified for the big job.

With the voting conducted on an "aye" and "nay," rather than man-against-man basis, with Mr. Giles and Mr. Frick considered alternately, neither man was able to muster a three-fourths majority. It was learned after the meeting that ten votes was the highest either polled on any ballot, and their fortunes fluctuated throughout.

Webb Only Non-Voter

Asked how many ballots were taken, Del Webb said, "a lot of them," then added, "at least fifty." The vice president of the New York Yankees served as non-voting chairman of the joint meeting. As chairman of the screening committee, he had devoted months of laborious effort to narrowing the field of candidates to workable proportions.

After disposing of a few routine matters, the club officials went into executive session at 12:30 P. M. (New York time). Attendance was restricted to voting representatives, except for Mr. Webb.

As a large corps of lobby-watchers roamed restlessly about the corridors, the meeting dragged on behind locked doors. Now and then officials would pop out but only to cancel transportation reservations.

Announcement by Mr. Webb, before the dinner-time break, that "numerous ballots were taken on two candidates, Mr. Frick and Mr. Giles" without decisive result marked the first official identification of candidates.

Identity of the survivors after the narrowing of the field to eleven, then five at informal joint meetings in New York on Aug. 7 and 21, had been carefully guarded, although subsequent leaks had brought most of the names out into the open.

Other prospective candidates prominently mentioned along the tortuous route to selecting a successor to Mr. Chandler were Gen. of the Army Douglas MacArthur, James A. Farley, former Postmaster General and currently chairman of the board of the Coca Cola Export Company, and Gov. Frank Lausche of Ohio.

Vice President Gabe Paul represented Cincinnati, Mr. Giles withdrawing to await the decision at a neighboring hotel. However, the president of the Reds was recalled to the meeting at the start of the night session.

Shortly after he had entered the room, a burst of applause was heard. This first was taken to mean that he had been elected. It later proved to have been an accolade in appreciation of his sportsmanship in stepping down and thus ending the long deadlock.

Earl Hilligan and Charles Segar, respective publicity directors of the American and National Leagues, then were called into the room. In a short while Mr. Hilligan emerged to read the official announcement of Mr. Frick's election.

Representing the National League clubs were Horace Stoneham, Giants; Walter O'Malley, Dodgers; Robert Carpenter, Phillies; Lou Perini, Braves; Philip K. Wrigley, Cubs; Fred Saigh, Cardinals; John Galbreath, Pirates, and Gabe Paul, Reds.

American League electors were Dan Topping, Yankees; Roy Mack, Athletics; Tom Yawkey, Red Sox; Calvin Griffith, Senators; Walter O. Briggs Jr., Tigers; Ellis Ryan, Indians; Charles Comiskey, White Sox, and Bill DeWitt, Browns.

September 21, 1951

Yanks Clinch Flag, Aided by Reynolds' No-Hitter

BOMBERS CONQUER RED SOX, 8-0, 11-3

Yanks Take 3d Flag in Row, Reynolds' 2d No-Hitter of Year Winning Opener

RASCHI'S 21ST IS CLINCHER

7-Run Second Inning Decides Second Game—Joe DiMaggio Drives 3-Run Homer

By JOHN DREBINGER

In a brilliant display of all-around skill that included a nerve tingling no-hitter in one encounter and a seven-run explosion in the other, the Yankees yesterday clinched the 1951 American League pennant. It was their third flag in a row and eighteenth in thirty years.

With Allie Reynolds tossing his second no-hitter of the year—a feat previously achieved by only one other hurler in history—the Bombers vanquished the Red Sox in the opener of the double-header at the Stadium, 8 to 0.

Then, behind big Vic Raschi, the Stengeleers crushed the already eliminated Bosox, 11 to 3, to the cheers of 39,038 fans. Joe DiMaggio further embellished the triumph with a three-run homer as another flag was nailed to the Yankee masthead.

Tribe Clinches Second

Even were the Bombers to lose their three remaining games to the Steve O'Neill's Red Sox, they could not be overtaken by the last to survive. Cleveland's doleful Indians, three and a half games out, have only two more encounters to play. The Tribe clinched second place as a result of Boston's two defeats.

Thus there remains nothing more for the Bombers to do now but await the outcome of the seething National League race between the Giants and the Dodgers to determine which club they shall meet in the world series. Unless the National's struggle ends in a deadlock tomorrow, necessitating a best-two-of-three game play-off, the big series will start at the Stadium on Wednesday.

In yesterday's smashing Yankee triumph, Reynolds' masterful performance provided most of the thrills, making even the clinching of the pennant somewhat anticlimactic.

Those who sat in on the show are not likely to forget those last

Allie Reynolds

tense moments when Reynolds, who had walked four batters during the game, had to collect "twenty-eight outs" before reaching his goal.

Berra Goes Sprawling

With two out in the ninth and the still fearsome Ted Williams at bat, a high foul was struck back of home plate. Yogi Berra, usually sure on these, scampered under it, but in the next agonizing moment the ball squirmed out of his glove as the Yanks chunky backstop went sprawling on his face.

It meant Williams would have to be pitched some more. But Reynolds, an amazingly good-natured competitor under the most trying circumstances, patted Berra consolingly on the back and said, "Don't worry, Yogi, we'll get him again."

And, sure enough, up went another high, twisting foul off to the right side of the plate. It looked tougher than the first one. But Yogi meant to catch this one if it burst a girth rope and as he finally froze to the ball directly in front of the Yankee dugout, Reynolds first, and virtually all the other Yanks jubilantly piled on top of him. For a moment it

looked as if Berra, not Reynolds, was the hero of the occasion.

Only one other major league hurler has ever fired two no-hitters in one season, and none ever in the American League. In 1938, Johnny Vander Meer, Cincinnati southpaw, turned in two on successive mound appearances, holding the Braves hitless on June 11 and repeating the trick on June 15 against the Dodgers in the first night game played in Ebbets Field. This was the fourth no-hitter recorded in the majors this season. Aside from Reynolds, Bob Feller of the Indians hurled one against the Tigers on July 1, and Cliff Chambers of the Pirates posted one on May 6 against the Braves.

Reynolds' first no-hitter this year was tossed on the night of July 12 against the Indians at Cleveland. After the forthcoming world series, the Chief expects to undergo an operation on his right elbow.

Apart from the four batters who drew walks, the passes coming singly in the first, fourth, seventh and ninth innings, no other member of the Sox reached first base. No one reached second. The ace right-hander struck out nine and not one Boston batter seemed to

come even close to a hit.

Behind this superlative hurling, which gave Reynolds his seventeenth triumph of the season against eight defeats, the Yanks lost no time getting the upper hand. They counted twice in the first off Mel Parnell, their conqueror in Boston last week, and added two more in the third with the help of a Dom DiMaggio error.

Then Ray Scarborough came on to be clubbed for a two-run homer by Joe Collins in the sixth and in the eighth Gene Woodling larruped his No. 15 into the right field seats off Harry Taylor.

With this victory, the Yanks were assured of at least a first-place tie. Then they went after the clincher.

Some Anxious Moments

At the start there were some anxious moments as the Sox, with Williams out of their line-up, clipped Raschi for two runs in the first and another in the second with the aid of two surprising wild pitches. Williams, it was explained, had suffered a painful bruise when hit by a foul tip on the right leg in the first game.

Trailing by three, the Bombers made their move in the last of the second. With Commissioner-elect Ford C. Frick looking on, they crushed the Bosox with a seven-

The Box Scores

FIRST GAME

BOSTON (A.)	ab.	r.	h.	po.	a.
D.DiM'gio, cf.	2	0	0	2	0
Pesky, 2b.	4	0	0	1	2
Williams, lf.	3	0	0	3	0
Vollmer, rf.	2	0	0	0	0
Goodman, 1b.	3	0	0	12	0
Boudreau, ss.	3	0	0	0	1
Hatfield, 3b.	3	0	0	3	2
Robinson, c.	3	0	0	3	0
Parnell, p.	1	0	0	0	2
Scarb'gh, p.	1	0	0	0	1
Taylor, p.	0	0	0	0	2
aMaxwell	1	0	0	0	0

| Total | 26 | 0 | 0 | 24 | 10 |

NEW YORK (A.)	ab.	r.	h.	po.	a.
Rizzuto, ss.	5	1	1	1	2
Coleman, 2b.	3	2	1	2	3
Bauer, rf.	4	0	1	5	0
J.DiM'gio, cf.	4	0	1	0	0
McD'gald, 3b.	3	1	1	0	1
Berra, c.	4	0	1	9	1
Woodling, lf.	4	2	2	2	0
Collins, 1b.	4	2	2	8	0
Reynolds, p.	3	0	0	0	1

| Total | 34 | 8 | 10 | 27 | 8 |

aGrounded out for Taylor in ninth.

Boston .... 0 0 0 0 0 0 0 0 0—0
New York .... 2 0 2 1 0 2 0 1 x—8

Errors—D. DiMaggio, Vollmer, Hatfield, Berra. Runs batted in—Bauer, Berra, McDougald, Coleman, Collins 2, Woodling. Two-base hit—Collins. Home runs—Collins, Woodling. Stolen base—Coleman. Sacrifice—Reynolds. Double plays—Hatfield and Goodman; Rizzuto and Collins. Left on bases—Boston 3, New York 5. Bases on balls—Off Parnell 2, Reynolds 4. Struck out—By Parnell 2, Reynolds 9. Hits—Off Parnell 5 in 3 innings, Scarborough 3 in 3, Taylor 2 in 2. Winning pitcher—Reynolds (17–8). Losing pitcher—Parnell (18–11). Umpires—Hubbard, McGowan, Berry and Hurley. Time of game—2:12.

SECOND GAME

BOSTON (A.)	ab.	r.	h.	po.	a.
D.D'M'gio, cf.	5	2	2	4	0
Pesky, 2b.	4	1	1	2	3
Maxwell, lf.	3	0	2	0	0
Vollmer, rf.	4	0	1	0	0
Goodman, 1b.	3	0	0	5	0
Boudreau, ss.	4	0	2	1	2
Hatfield, 3b.	3	0	1	1	1
Moss, c.	3	0	0	7	0
aRichter	1	0	0	0	0
Wright, p.	0	0	0	0	0
Masterson, p.	0	0	0	0	0
Stobbs, p.	2	0	0	1	0
Nixon, p.	0	0	0	0	0
bWright	0	0	0	0	0

| Total | 33 | 3 | 6 | 24 | 6 |

NEW YORK (A.)	ab.	r.	h.	po.	a.
Rizzuto, ss.	5	1	3	1	4
Coleman, 2b.	1	3	1	1	2
Bauer, rf.	5	2	1	3	0
J.D'M'gio, cf.	5	2	1	1	0
McD'gald, 3b.	5	0	1	2	3
Berra, c.	4	0	1	8	1
Woodling, lf.	4	1	2	6	0
Collins, 1b.	4	1	2	6	0
Raschi, p.	3	1	0	0	0

| Total | 36 | 11 | 13 | 27 | 6 |

aFouled out for Moss in ninth.
bWalked for Nixon in ninth.

Boston .... 2 1 0 0 0 0 0 0 0—3
New York .... 0 7 0 0 0 3 0 1 .—11

Errors—Goodman, Boudreau. Runs batted in—Boudreau, Maxwell, McDougald 2, Rizzuto 2, Bauer 2, J. DiMaggio 4, Collins.

Two-base hits—Bauer, Coleman. Three-base hit—McDougald. Home run—J. DiMaggio. Stolen base—D. DiMaggio. Sacrifice—Coleman. Double plays—Boudreau, Pesky and Goodman. 2. Left on bases—Boston 7. New York 6. Bases on balls—Off Wight 3, Stobbs 1, Raschi 4. Struck out—By Stobbs 2, Nixon 4, Raschi 5. Hits—Off Wight 4 in 1 1-3 innings, Masterson 2 in 1-3. Stobbs 5 in 4 1-3. Nixon 2 in 2. Wild pitches—Raschi 2, Nixon. Passed ball—Moss. Winning pitcher—Raschi (21–10). Losing pitches Wight (7–7). Umpires—McGowan, Berry, Hubbard and Huly. Time of Game—2:32.

run demonstration, raking Bill Wight and Walt Masterson for five blows, the last a tremendous triple by Gil McDougald.

Commissioner Frick had missed the no-hitter, but he was in at the "kill" of the flag race. It probably marked the first time since his days as a baseball scribe covering the Yankees that the man who for seventeen years has been the National League president, saw an American League pennant decided.

From the third inning on, Raschi swung into his usually flawless style and so rolled on to his twenty-first victory against ten defeats. The closing crusher for the crestfallen Bosox came in the sixth, when Joe DiMaggio, not to be denied a share in the final spotlight, belted Chuck Stobbs for his twelfth homer with two runners aboard.

And so, to this most successful organization in baseball history not only comes its eighteenth pennant but for the fourth time the Bombers have annexed three in a row. Once they stretched the string to four and the chance to repeat this feat lies before them in 1952.

Also to the astounding Charles Dillon Stengel, who never had spent a day in the American League prior to 1949, when he succeeded Bucky Harris as Yankee manager, comes the distinction of being the third pilot to win pennants in his first three years in a league. The fabulous Frank Chance did it with the Cubs in 1906-07-08. In the American League Hughey Jennings did it with the Tigers in 1907-08-09.

It was on this same corresponding Friday date that Bombers clinched their pennant last year, although on that occasion they had it much easier. The Yanks sitting idly in their hotel quarters in Boston while the runner-up Tigers were eliminated by the Indians. The most difficult victory came in 1949, when the Yanks, trailing the Red Sox by one with two games to go, vanquished the Sox in both games to win on the last day.

The span of Yankee triumphs covers only three decades. They won their first pennants under the late Miller Huggins in 1921-22-23, and with the little Miller still added three more in 1926-27-28.

After Huggins' death in 1929, the Bombers lapsed for a few years, but Joe McCarthy had them back with a flag in 1932 and then with 1936 followed the greatest sustained effort of winning in baseball history.

The Bombers, under McCarthy, won four in a row from 1936 through 1939. They were nosed out in a close finish in 1940. But in 1941 were back to reel off three more through 1943. In eight years, Marse Joe had bagged seven flags, a feat without precedent in the majors. But Professor Casey, with three victories in three tries, may give that record a terrific go.

September 29, 1951

BROOKS BEAT PHILS IN FOURTEENTH, 9-8

By ROSCOE McGOWEN
Special to THE NEW YORK TIMES.

PHILADELPHIA, Sept. 30—Jackie Robinson made the most vital put-out of his career in the twelfth inning today, then hit the most important home run of his life in the fourteenth to give the embattled Dodgers a 9-8 triumph over the Phils and put the Brooks into a pennant play-off with the Giants.

Two more dramatic events probably never have been seen in such a ball game, and the record Shibe Park crowd of 31,755—thousands of them from Brooklyn—reacted accordingly.

Don Newcombe, the sixth pitcher Manager Chuck Dressen had tossed into the game, had the bases filled and two out in the twelfth when a hit would have sent the Dodgers tumbling into the most disastrous flag loss in National League history.

Eddie Waitkus apparently had made that hit with a low line drive to the right field side of second base. But Robinson raced over, dived to clutch the ball just off the ground and Umpire Lon Warneke's arm went up signaling the saving put-out.

Robbie fell hard on his shoulder and collapsed after tossing the ball weakly toward the infield. Anxious Dodgers clustered around the second baseman and several minutes later he rose groggily and walked slowly and uncertainly toward the dugout, while fans in every part of the stands rose and cheered him.

Out After Passing Two

The game went on, with both Robin Roberts, third Phil pitcher, and Newcombe constantly threatened. Roberts was having something the better of the tense duel. In the thirteenth Newcombe walked two after two were out and Dressen took him out and brought in Bud Podbelian. Bud ended the inning easily.

Roberts set the Dodgers down in the thirteenth and had retired Pee Wee Reese and Duke Snider on pop-ups in the fourteenth when Robinson came to the plate.

Roberts got one ball and one strike on Robby, then Jack swung with all his power and the ball sailed high into the upper left field stands. Jackie trotted slowly around the bases and was overwhelmed by the entire Brooklyn team as he approached the dugout.

President Walter O'Malley, his wife, General Manager Buzzie Bavasi and his wife, who had been alternately despairing and hopeful throughout the game, rose from their rail box and became as nearly hysterical as such normally composed people can be.

But the tension wasn't ended. Podbielan, who previously had won one game and lost two, still had to get the Phils out in their half. Bud was threatened immediately by the best hitter among the Phils, Richie Ashburn, who lined a single to left just a few inches from Reese's gloved hand and was promptly sacrificed to scoring position by Puddin' Head Jones.

Easy Pop to Hodges

Podbielan went to a full-count against Del Ennis and a great sigh of relief came from the Dodger fans when Del lifted an easy pop to Gil Hodges.

Waitkus, the fellow who almost won the game in the twelfth, didn't prolong the agony. Eddie lifted a simple fly to Andy Pafko, and there was a wild scene around the Brooklyn dugout.

Hundreds of fans swarmed out of the stands and Dodgers in the field had to fight their way through to get to their dressing rooms.

The feeling of relief for the Dodgers and for their harried supporters was terrific, considering the handicap the Brooks had to overcome even to get into the ball game.

By the end of the third inning they were trailing, 1—6, with Preacher Roe knocked out in the second and Ralph Branca giving up two runs in the third.

Robinson had been an early "bust," slapping into an inning-ending double play in the first inning with Reese on third and Duke Snider on first base, and looking at a third strike from Bubba Church in the fourth. Jackie also had failed to snare a grounder from Ashburn in the Phils' four-run second inning, which became a two-run single—but not in Jackie's book. He thought he should have had the ball.

Driven Home by Pafko

Robbie redeemed himself in the fifth with a triple to right that drove in Snider and sent Church away, and Pafko singled Robby home with the third run of the inning that reduced the Phils' lead to 6—5.

But in the fifth Brooklyn hopes suffered another blow when Clyde King, who had taken over at the start of the fourth, was knocked out by Gran Hamner's bad-hop triple, which led to two more runs.

Bill Nicholson had opened with a single to right and Hamner hit what appeared to be another one. But the ball took a sudden hop over Carl Furillo's head and went for three bases, scoring Nicholson.

With Clem Labine pitching, Ed Pellagrini singled the second run across and the Dodgers faced another struggle to get even.

Meanwhile the scoreboard, showing the Giants leading the Braves, 3—1, continued to drop a row of ciphers in the Boston column and the Dodgers, who couldn't avoid noticing this, more and more were being put in a hopeless position.

It was 3:35 by the scoreboard clock and Jones was at bat against Carl Erskine in the sixth inning when the final score at Boston was posted. At the roar of the Phils' partisans Robinson looked over his shoulder and he—and every other Dodger—knew certainly then that they had to win this one, or else.

Erskine did his job competently for two innings, preventing any scoring, then left to let Rube Walker bat for him in the all-important eighth—when the Brooks really got into the game for the first time by tying the score at 8-all.

Walker came through nobly, walloping a long double to left center off Karl Drews after the pitcher had two strikes against him. This blow scored Hodges, who had beaten out a hit to Hamner, and Cox, who had dumped a single just inside the right-field foul line.

At this point Roberts replaced Drews and Furillo, who perhaps should be rated the gilt-edged hero ahead of Robinson, lined a one-and-one-pitch into left center for the single that scored Don Thompson, running for Walker, with the run that tied the count.

Newcombe came out amid a tremendous burst of cheers to start pitching in the eighth and, while he was constantly threatened in every inning, still allowed only one hit. That was a single to center by Ashburn, the first man he faced.

Don had put two strikes over on Ashburn and the next pitch sent Richie into the dirt, which brought a warning from Plate Umpire Lou Jorda. Dressen came from the dugout on the double-quick to protest the umpire's action. But Newcombe emerged safely from that and every succeeding inning until, apparently, his arm stiffened or tired and Dressen finally took him out.

The Dodgers had Roberts wobbling a bit in the ninth, which Snider opened with a single, and in the tenth, which Hodges started with a single. But the Brooks couldn't score. Following Hodges' blow Cox bunted into a double play—second time in two games a Dodger had done that.

Reese bounced a single through the middle with one out in the eleventh but neither Snider nor Robinson could harm Roberts then and Robin had retired ten Dodgers in a row when Robinson connected for what could be a $165,000 home run—an estimate of a world series winning pot.

Pafko also came through with a game-saving catch on Seminick in the eleventh inning with Hamner on via a pass and two out. Andy raced toward the left-field foul line and made a gloved-hand grab of the vicious liner that seemed ticketed for two bases.

The box score:

BROOKLYN (N.)	ab	r	h	po	a
Furillo, rf	7	1	2	2	0
Reese, ss	6	0	3	3	3
Snider, cf	7	1	3	3	0
Robinson, 2b	6	2	2	6	5
Campanella, c	7	1	2	8	0
Pafko, lf	7	0	1	7	2
Hodges, 1b	5	1	2	10	5
Cox, 3b	6	1	1	2	3
Roe, p	0	0	0	0	0
Branca, p	0	1	0	0	0
aRussell	1	0	0	0	0
King, p	0	0	0	0	0
Labine, p	0	0	0	0	0
bBelardi	1	0	0	0	0
Erskine, p	0	0	0	0	0
cWalker	1	0	1	0	0
dThompson	0	1	0	0	0
Newcombe, p	2	0	0	1	0
Podbielan, p	0	0	0	0	0
Total	56	9	17	42	18

PHILADELPHIA (N.)	ab	r	h	po	a
Pellagrini, 2b	6	1	2	5	5
Ashburn, cf	8	0	4	2	0
Jones, 3b	4	0	1	3	3
Ennis, lf	8	0	1	6	1
Brown, 1b	2	1	1	3	1
Waitkus, 1b	6	0	0	10	1
Clark, rf	1	0	0	1	0
Nicholson, rf	6	2	2	2	0
Hamner, ss	5	3	2	2	6
Seminick, c	2	1	0	7	1
Church, p	2	0	1	1	0
Drews, p	2	0	1	0	1
Roberts, p	1	0	0	0	1
Total	53	8	15	42	21

aStruck out for Branca in fourth.
bStruck out for Labine in sixth.
cDoubled for Erskine in eighth.
dRan for Walker in eighth.

Brooklyn	001	130	030	000	01	—9
Philadelphia	042	020	000	000	00	—8

Errors—Jones, Robinson.

Runs batted in—Brown, Pellagrini 2, Ashburn 2, Church 2, Hamner, Reese, Pafko 2, Snider, Robinson 2, Walker 2, Furillo.

Two-base hits—Jones, Hamner, Pellagrini, Snider, Walker, Campanella. Three-base hits—Reese, Campanella, Robinson, Hamner. Home runs—Brown, Robinson. Sacrifices—Jones 2, Robinson, Pellagrini. Double plays—Hamner, Pellagrini and Brown; Ennis, Pellagrini and Waitkus; Seminick, Hamner and Pellagrini. Left on bases—Brooklyn 9, Philadelphia 18. Bases on balls—Off Church 3, Roe 1, Branca 2, Labine 1, Newcombe 6. Struck out—By Church 3, Drews 2, Roberts 1, Roe 1, Branca 1, Labine 2, Newcombe 3. Hits—Off Roe 5 in 1 2-3 innings, Branca 2 in 1 1-3, King 3 in 1 (none out in fifth), Labine 1 in 1, Church 6 in 4 1-3, Drews 5 in 3, Roberts 6 in 6 2-3, Erskine 2 in 2, Newcombe 1 in 5 2-3, Podbielan 1 in 1 1-3. Hit by pitcher—By King (Jones), Newcombe (Pellagrini). Wild pitch—Branca. Winning pitcher—Podbielan (2—2). Losing pitcher—Roberts (21—15). Umpires—Jorda, Gore, Warneke and Goetz. Time of game—4:30. Attendance—31,755.

October 1, 1951

GIANTS CAPTURE PENNANT, BEATING DODGERS 5-4 IN 9TH ON THOMSON'S 3-RUN HOMER

BROOKLYN'S BRANCA LOSER

Yields Homer on Second Pitch After Relieving Newcombe in the Play-Off Final

By JOHN DREBINGER

In an electrifying finish to what long will be remembered as the most thrilling pennant campaign in history, Leo Durocher and his astounding never-say-die Giants wrenched victory from the jaws of defeat at the Polo Grounds yesterday, vanquishing the Dodgers, 5 to 4, with a four-run splurge in the last half of the ninth.

A three-run homer by Bobby Thomson that accounted for the final three tallies blasted the Dodgers right out of the world series picture and this afternoon at the Stadium it will be the Giants against Casey Stengel's American League champion Yankees in the opening clash of the world series.

Seemingly hopelessly beaten, 4 to 1, as the third and deciding game of the epic National League play-off moved into the last inning, the Giants lashed back with a fury

routed big Don Newcombe while scoring one run.

Then, with Ralph Branca on the mound and two runners aboard the bases, came the blow of blows. Thomson crashed the ball into the left-field stand. Forgotten on the instant was the cluster of three with which the Brooks had crushed Sal Maglie in the eighth.

For a moment the crowd of 34,320, as well as all the Dodgers, appeared too stunned to realize what had happened. But as the long and lean Scot from Staten Island loped around the bases behind his two team-mates a deafening roar went up, followed by some of the wildest scenes ever witnessed in the historic arena under Coogan's Bluff.

Mobbed at Home Plate

The Giants, lined up at home plate, fairly mobbed the Hawk as he completed the last few strides to the plate. Jubilant Giant fans, fairly beside themselves, eluded guards and swarmed on the field to join the melee.

When the players finally completed their dash to the center-field clubhouse, the fans, thousands

deep on the field, yelled themselves purple as Thomson repeatedly appeared in the clubhouse windows in answer to the most frenzied "curtain calls" ever accorded a ballplayer.

And so, as this extraordinary campaign moves on in a flow of diamond drama, it will be the Giants and Yankees meeting for the sixth time in world series history. They last were rivals in the classic of 1937.

The second game also will be staged in the Bronx arena that so quietly looked down on the scene yesterday from the other side of the Harlem.

On Saturday the action will shift to the Polo Grounds, where the third and fourth games will be played, as well as the fifth, if necessary. Should neither side have four victories racked up by then, the struggle will return to the Stadium for the sixth and seventh games.

A Long Uphill Battle

As soon as Durocher was able to regain his voice he announced that Dave Koslo, his lone southpaw of any account, will be the starter against the Bombers today. Casey Stengel announced, following the clinching of the American League pennant last Friday, that Allie Reynolds, hero of two no-hitters the past season, would be his mound choice for the opener.

The pennant, which the Giants so dramatically won in the second play-off series in National League history and the first to go the full three games, brought to a climax one of the most astonishing uphill struggles ever waged in the annals of the sport.

Off to an atrocious start in the spring when they blew eleven in a row, the Giants plugged away grimly for weeks to make up the lost ground. But as late as Aug. 11 they were still thirteen and a half games behind the high-flying Brooks who, hailed by experts as the "wonder team" of the modern age, threatened to win by anywhere from fifteen to twenty lengths.

Then, on Aug. 12 began the great surge. Sixteen games were won in a row and from there the Polo Grounders rolled on to finish in a deadlock with the Dodgers at the close of the regular schedule. Majestically they swept ahead on Monday in the opener of the three-game play-off series in Brooklyn. Then disaster engulfed them as they came to the Polo Grounds Tuesday to be buried under a 10-0 score.

And they were still struggling to get out from under as late as the ninth inning yesterday when Thomson, whose two-run homer had won on Monday, exploded his No. 32 of the year that ended it all.

In the stretch from Aug. 12 until yesterday's pennant-clincher Durocher's minions hung up the almost incredible record of thirty-nine victories, against only eight defeats, an achievement to match that of the Miracle Braves of 1914.

The pennant is the sixteenth in the long history of the Giants, who captured their first two flags back in the late Eighties under Jim Mutrie, who also gave them their nickname. Under John J. McGraw they won ten in a span that began in 1904 and ended in 1924, when the Little Napoleon became the first manager in history to win four in a row.

In 1933 Bill Terry, a spectator at yesterday's game, piloted the Giants to the top again and repeated it in 1936 and 1937. Since then, however, the years have been lean and bleak, until the fiery Leo the Lip came through for them this year. The Giants thus tied the sixteen-pennant record of the Chicago Cubs in the National League.

The clincher was a struggle that should live long in the memory of the fans who saw it, as well as those who had it portrayed for them by radio and television in a coast-to-coast hook-up.

And many a night will Bob Thomson recall that, despite his game-winning homer, his third hit of the day, he might well have wound up the "goat" of the game by reason of some blind base running back in the second inning, when the Giants were trailing, 1—0.

Nor will Sal Maglie, the Barber, soon forget those agonizing moments he spent directly after the Giants had wrenched a run away from Newcombe in the seventh to tie the score at one-all. The Dodgers laced him for three runs in the top of the eighth, the first coming in on a wild pitch.

But the most poignant memory of all will be that which hapless Chuck Dressen, the Brooks' pilot, will carry with him for years to come. His club had blown a thirteen-and-a-half game lead. But all this would have been forgotten and forgiven had Branca held that margin in the last of the ninth.

He Follows the "Book"

But with one out and runners on second and third Dressen, as daring a gamester as Durocher, chose to follow the "book." He refused to walk Thomson because that would have represented the "winning run." Yet behind Bobby was Willie Mays, a dismal failure throughout the series and behind that the Giants had even less to offer. It's something the second guessers will hash over through many a winter evening.

The Box Score

BROOKLYN DODGERS

	AB.	R.	H.	PO.	A.
Furillo, rf.	5	0	0	0	0
Reese, ss.	4	2	1	2	5
Snider, cf.	3	1	2	1	0
Robinson, 2b.	2	1	1	3	2
Pafko, lf.	4	0	1	4	1
Hodges, 1b.	4	0	0	11	1
Cox, 3b.	4	0	2	1	3
Walker, c.	4	0	1	2	0
Newcombe, p.	4	0	0	1	1
Branca, p.	0	0	0	0	0
Total	34	4	8	*25	13

NEW YORK GIANTS

	AB.	R.	H.	PO.	A.
Stanky, 2b.	4	0	0	0	4
Dark, ss.	4	1	1	2	2
Mueller, rf.	4	0	1	0	0
cHartung	0	0	0	0	0
Irvin, lf.	4	1	1	1	0
Lockman, 1b.	3	1	2	7	0
Thomson, 3b.	4	1	3	4	1
Mays, cf.	3	0	0	1	0
Westrum, c.	0	0	0	7	1
aRigney	1	0	0	0	0
Noble, c.	0	0	0	0	0
Maglie, p.	2	0	0	1	2
bThompson	1	0	0	0	0
Jansen, p.	0	0	0	0	0
Total	30	5	8	27	11

*One out when winning run scored
aStruck out for Westrum in eighth
bGrounded out for Maglie in eighth
cRan for Mueller in ninth

Brooklyn .....100001 030—
New York .....000 000 104—

Runs batted in—Robinson, Thomson 4, Pafko, Cox, Lockman (Reese scored on Maglie's wild pitch in eighth.

Two-base hits—Thomson, Irvin, Lockman. Home run—Thomson. Sacrifice—Lockman. Double-plays—Cox, Robinson and Hodges; Reese, Robinson and Hodges. Left on base—Brooklyn 7, New York 3. Bases on balls—Off Maglie 4 (Reese, Snider, Robinson 2), Newcombe 2 (Westrum 2). Struck out—By Maglie 6 (Furillo, Walker 2, Snider, Pafko, Reese), Newcombe 2 (Mays, Rigney). Hits—Off Maglie 8 in 8 innings, Jansen 1 in 1, Newcombe 7 in 8 1/3, Branca 1 in 0 (pitched to one batter in ninth). Wild pitch—Maglie. Winning pitcher—Jansen (23-11). Losing pitcher—Branca (13-12). Umpires—Lou Jorda (plate), Jocko Conlan (first base), Bill Stewart (second base) and Larry Goetz (third base). Time of game—2:28. Attendance—34,320 (paid).

For seven innings this was a bitter mound duel between Newcombe, seeking his twenty-first victory, and Maglie, gunning for his twenty-fourth. In the end neither figured in the decision. For it was Branca who was tagged with the defeat while the triumph went to Larry Jansen, who pitched for the Giants in the ninth when the cause seemed lost.

Larry retired three batters in a row and the Dodgers, three runs in front, thought absolutely nothing of it. They were certain they had this one in the bag.

But a few minutes later Jansen was jubilantly stalking off the field in possession of his twenty-third triumph, fitting tribute at that, considering that the tall right-hander from Oregon had pitched the 3-2 victory over the Braves last Sunday to send the race into the play-offs.

A momentary break in control put Maglie a run behind in the first inning when, with one out, he walked Pee Wee Reese and Duke Snider, the latter on four straight pitches. Jackie Robinson followed with a single to drive in the Dodger captain.

From then through the seventh, Maglie pitched magnificently. But not until the last of the seventh were the Giants able to match that Brooklyn run that kept taunting them on the scoreboard. With one out in the second, Whitey Lock-

AFTER THE GAME WAS OVER

man singled and Thomson blasted a line drive down the left field line.

Lockman had to pull up at second, but Thomson kept on running until he, too, was almost on top of second. He was promptly run down and that wrecked that rally.

In the fifth the indomitable Thomson got a double because there was no one in front of him to watch. But that availed nothing. For there was one out and Mays fanned. After Wes Westrum walked, Maglie grounded out.

Finally in the seventh the Giants made it and again it was Thomson's bat that played the decisive stroke.

Monte Irvin opened with a double. He advanced to third on Whitey Lockman's attempted sacrifice on which the Dodgers retired nobody and a moment later Thomson lifted a high fly to Snider in dead center to bring Irvin over the plate.

The Giants at long last were even, but victory was shunted far into the background when Maglie faltered in the eighth. Reese singled, went to third on Snider's single and scored on a wild pitch.

Following an intentional pass to Robinson came a scratch hit off Thomson's glove by Andy Pafko to drive in another run and then Bill Cox rifled one past Thomson to fetch in the third tally of the inning.

The Scot, converted into a third baseman by Durocher in midseason, certainly seemed to be moving in the center of everything in this great struggle.

In the last of the eighth the stunned Giants were three easy outs for Newcombe, who had a four-hitter going. In the top of the ninth hardly anyone paid attention as Jansen polished off three Dodgers in a row.

Wait for Final Outs

Through eight innings the Dodgers gave Newcombe brilliant support afield. Cox was a stone wall

Bobby Thomson and Manager Leo Durocher of the Giants in the clubhouse after the victory over the Dodgers. Associated Press

at third. Reese was an artist at short. Robinson made a great play on a wide throw from left by Pafko to save a run. Hodges made a leaping catch of a rifled shot over first. In the ninth of course, the Dodgers couldn't do much about it. There's no defense against home runs.

Jubilant Brooklyn fans were waiting for just "three more outs." Even the most devout of Giant diehards were preparing to slink out as quietly as possible. Their pets had waged a great uphill fight, but to win it all, perhaps, was just a trifle too much to expect.

Then Alvin Dark raised a feeble hope as he opened this last ditch stand by banging a sharp single off Gil Hodges' glove. Don Mueller, who was to wind up a casualty in the inning, slammed another single into right. To a deep groan, Monte Irvin popped out. But Whitey Lockman rammed a double into left, with Mueller racing to third. As Don slid into the bag he sprained his left ankle and the Giant outfielder had to be carried off the field on a stretcher.

At this point Dressen made his two most momentous decisions. Deciding that Newcombe, who had hurled fourteen and two-third innings to keep the flock in the race over Saturday and Sunday in Philadelphia, could go no further, he called in Branca.

Then, following a further consultation, it was decided that though first base was open, Big Ralph was to pitch to the Scot.

It was a decision that in a few more minutes was to bring to a suprising end the tremendous struggle which had been going on for 157 games.

Branca fearlessly fired the first strike past Robert.

What he tossed on the next pitch brought a varied assortment of opinion even from those most involved. But there was no doubt about where it went.

It sailed into the lower left-field stand a little beyond the 315 foot mark. The ball, well tagged, had just enough lift to clear the high wall.

And with that Leo Durocher almost leaped out of his shoes as he shrieked and danced on the coaching line.

Now Leo the Lip, who as manager of the Dodgers fought the Yankees in 1941 in a world series and lost, will try it again, and with one of the most extraordinary Giant teams in the long history of baseball on the banks of the Harlem.

October 4, 1951

CAIN, FELLER YIELD ONLY 1 BLOW EACH

Browns Score by 1-0 to Take First Place From Indians and Drop Tribe to Third

NEW LEAGUE RECORD SET

Young's Triple in 1st Helps Win as Two One-Hitters Establish a Low Total

ST. LOUIS, April 23 (AP)—Bobby Cain outpitched Bob Feller tonight in a unique duel in which the Browns defeated the Indians, 1 to 0, and took over first place in the

American League.

Feller, like Cain, allowed only one hit, but the safety off the Cleveland veteran was a first-inning triple by Bobby Young, good for a run, whereas the only hit off Cain's delivery was a harmless single by Luke Easter in the fifth.

Young's triple opened the Brown's first inning and when the third baseman, Al Rosen, fumbled Marty Marion's grounder, Young scored the only run of the game.

It was Feller's eleventh one-hit game and the only one-hitter he ever lost. The game was played in 50 degree cold, before 7,110 shivering and delighted fans.

Second Victory for Cain

Cain, who came to the Browns last Valentine's Day in a seven-player deal with the Tigers, hasn't known a winning season as a major leaguer since breaking in with the White Sox in 1949. With tonight's excellent performance he now has a 2-0 record, one of three Browns as yet undefeated.

In two games the Browns have toppled the Indians out of a one-and-a-half game lead, breaking the Tribe's seven-game winning streak and reducing Cleveland to third place.

Ironically, Cain was Feller's victim when Bob pitched his third no-hitter last year. On July 1 the Cleveland right-hander defeated Cain and Detroit, 2—1, holding the Tigers hitless. Cain allowed six hits.

Tonight's game marked the second time in modern baseball history that each pitcher allowed the opposition only one hit. On July 4, 1906, Mordecai (Three-Fingered) Brown of Chicago and Lefty Leifield of Pittsburgh permitted only one hit each as the Cubs defeated the Pirates, 1—0.

On May 2, 1917, Jim Vaughn of Chicago and Fred Toney of Cincinnati hurled a no-hitter each through nine innings. The Reds, however, nicked Vaughn for two hits and a run in the tenth to win, 1—0, as Toney hurled a ten-inning no-hitter.

The 33-year-old Feller and Cain, 27, battled on even terms all the way through the duel which goes into the record books as the lowest-hit game in the fifty-one-year history of the American League.

The box score:

CLEVELAND (A.)							ST. LOUIS (A.)						
	ab.	r.	h.	po.	a.			ab.	r.	h.	po.	a.	
Simpson, rf.	4	0	0	1	0		Young, 2b.	4	1	1	2	4	
Berardino, 2b.	2	0	0	1	5		Marion, ss.	2	0	0	2	3	
Reiser, cf.	3	0	0	3	0		Rivera, cf.	2	0	0	4	0	
Easter, 1b.	3	0	1	10	0		Wright, lf.	3	0	0	1	0	
Rosen, 3b.	2	0	0	0	0		Rapp, rf.	3	0	0	1	0	
Fridley, lf.	3	0	0	3	0		Delsing, rf.	0	0	0	0	0	
Boone, ss.	2	0	0	0	2		Goldsb'ry, 1b.	3	0	0	8	0	
Tebbetts, c.	3	0	0	5	0		Thomas, 3b.	3	0	0	1	3	
Feller, p.	2	0	0	1	1		Courtney, c.	3	0	0	8	1	
aAvila	1	0	0	0	0		Cain, p.	3	0	0	0	0	
Total	25	0	1	24	8		Total	26	1	1	27	11	

aFiled out for Feller in ninth.

```
Cleveland ............. 0 0 0  0 0 0  0 0 0—0
St. Louis ............. 1 0 0  0 0 0  0 0 .—1
```

Error—Rosen. Run batted in—Marion. Three-base hit—Young. Double plays—Courtney and Young; Young, Marion and Goldsberry; Marion, Young and Goldsberry. Left on bases—Cleveland 1, St. Louis 3. Bases on balls—Off Cain 3, Feller 2. Struck out—By Cain 7, Feller 5. Runs and earned runs—Feller 1 and 1. Winning pitcher—Cain (2-0). Losing pitcher—Feller (1-1). Umpires—Honochick, Rommel and Berry. Time of game—1:58. Attendance—7,110.

1913 Record Is Erased

The former American League record for the least amount of hits by both teams in one game was three, set by Washington, with one safety, and Detroit, with two, on June 10, 1913, and equaled by

Robin Roberts, classy right-hander of the Philadelphia Phillies, won 28 games in 1952.

Washington (2) and Cleveland (1) July 27, 1915.

Cain, a southpaw, fanned seven and walked three. Feller struck out five and gave up two passes. The big strikeout for Cain came when he fanned Harry Simpson to end the game.

Only four Browns reached base.

The Tribe put men on base the same number of times.

It was a stunning defeat for Cleveland, still staggered by Tuesday night's 8-3 Brownie victory.

There was much debate about whether Young's all-important triple could have been caught. Most writers believed it could have been.

Perhaps figuring that the wind would stall the ball in flight, Rookie Jim Fridley moved to his left in left field and stood hopeless as the ball sailed over his head.

The lone run was ruled an earned tally by the official scorekeeper despite the fact Rosen muffed Marion's grounder to allow

Young to cross the plate. According to the official scorer, Young would have been able to score with or without Rosen's assistance.

April 24, 1952

Roberts Beats Giants for No. 28

12-BLOW ASSAULT TAKES FINALE, 7-4

Phils Rout Harshman of the Giants and Roberts Equals Dean's Record of 1935

JONES, NICHOLSON EXCEL

Their Homers Spark Winners' Drive at Polo Grounds— Thompson Also Hits One

By JAMES P. DAWSON

The Giants closed the 1952 championship season at the Polo Grounds yesterday by serving as the victims of Robin Roberts' twenty-eighth triumph of the campaign. This gave the right-handed stalwart of the Phillies the distinction of being the first National League pitcher to count so many successes since Dizzy Dean won twenty-eight and lost twelve for the Cards in 1935. The score was 7 to 4.

A twelve-hit assault, topped by home-runs by Willie Jones and Bill Nicholson, aided Roberts to his victory. Three Giant hurlers were pounded.

The loser was Jack Harshman. He gave up nine of the Phillies' hits and six of their runs in his second unsuccessful attempt to prove that he is a better pitcher than he was a first baseman.

Hit by Batted Ball

Harshman hobbled off the field with one out in the fifth after Stan Lopata had caromed a freak double off his left leg. Al Corwin checked the Phils briefly. The left-handed Montia Kennedy, hurling the last four innings, was around long enough to yield Nicholson's homer in the ninth.

Henry Thompson walloped a homer for the Giants in the second inning. A gift run followed when Jones booted Bobby Thomson's rap. But this lead was shortlived.

After Harshman had fanned six while blanking the Phils with two

Associated Press

WINS 28TH ON THE 28TH: Robin Roberts, Phillies' ace, wears Curt Simmons' No. 28 uniform to denote number of mound victories. With him in dressing room after game with Giants at Polo Grounds are Bill Nicholson, left, and Willie Jones, whose homers helped him to win.

---

hits through three innings, he weakened. Del Ennis opened the fourth with a single. Granny Hamner tripled. With one out Jones sent his eighteenth homer into the upper left field stand.

In the fifth Dick Young opened with a walk and stole second. Richie Ashburn sacrificed. Successive singles by Nicholson, Ennis and Hamner preceded the Lopata double. That finished Harshman.

One Hit in Five Innings

Robert steadied after the second and yielded but one hit in the next five innings. In the eighth, however, he wavered and the Giants got a run on two singles, a pass and a force out. They clustered three singles for their final run in the ninth.

A crowd of 5,933 turned out for the finale, boosting Giant home attendance for the season to 985,-011.

Whitney Lockman rounded out the entire 154-game schedule by playing the first inning. He was the only Giant to do so.

The box score:

PHILADELPHIA (N.)	ab.	r.	h.	po.	a.
Ryan, 2b	0	0	0	0	0
Young, 2b	3	1	0	2	1
Ashburn, cf	4	0	1	1	0
Nicholson, rf	2	2	2	0	0
Ennis, lf	3	2	2	0	0
Hamner, ss	5	1	3	2	3
Lopata, c	5	0	2	6	1
Jones, 3b	5	1	2	2	2
Waitkus, 1b	3	0	0	11	1
Roberts, p	4	0	1	1	1
Total	37	7	12	27	9

NEW YORK (N.)	ab.	r.	h.	po.	a.
Mueller, rf	5	1	3	1	0
D.Spencer, ss	5	0	3	1	4
Lockman, 1b	1	0	0	0	0
Wilson, 1b	4	0	0	11	0
Thompson, 3b	3	1	1	1	1
Thomson, cf	4	1	0	2	0
Rhodes, lf	4	0	1	2	0
Williams, 2b	2	0	0	0	1
Hofman, 2b	1	0	0	2	4
Katt, c	4	1	1	7	3
Harshman, p	1	0	0	0	1
Corwin, p	0	0	0	0	0
aHartung	1	0	0	0	0
Kennedy, p	1	0	0	0	1
bIrvin	1	0	0	0	0
Total	37	4	9	27	15

aStruck out for Corwin in fifth.
bStruck out for Kennedy in ninth.

Philadelphia ....000 330 001—7
New York ....020 000 011—4

Errors—Jones, Young. Runs batted in—Thompson. Williams. Hamner 2 Jones 2, Nicholson 2, Lopata, Thomson, D. Spencer. Two-base hit—Lopata. Three-base hit—Hamner. Home runs—Thompson. Jones, Nicholson. Stolen base—Young. Sacrifice—Ashburn. Double play—Hamner and Waitkus. Left on bases—New York 5. Philadelphia 9. Bases on balls—Off Harshman 2. Corwin 1. Roberts 1. Kennedy 2. Struck out—By Harshman 6. Kennedy 2. Roberts 6. Hits—Off Harshman 9 in 4 1-3 innings. Corwin 0 in 2-3. Kennedy 3 in 4. Runs and earned runs—Harshman 6 and 6. Kennedy 1 and 1. Roberts 4 and 3. Hit by pitcher—By Roberts (Hofman). Winning pitcher—Roberts (28—7). Losing pitcher—Harshman (0—2). Umpires—Boggess. Jackowski. Pinelli and Engeln. Time of game—2:31. Attendance—5,933.

September 29, 1952

CHAPTER 3

AN ERA OF EXPANSION

This man is not directing traffic. He is Carlton Fisk of the Boston Red Sox and he has just hit a long fly ball in the 12th inning of the sixth game of the 1975 World Series. He is urging the ball to stay fair for a game-winning home run. It did.

Braves Move to Milwaukee; Majors' First Shift Since '03

National League Lets Perini Transfer Club From Boston After 77 Years' Stay

By LOUIS EFFRAT
Special to The New York Times.

ST. PETERSBURG, Fla., March 18—Unlike Bill Veeck, who had failed to effect an American League transfer of his Browns from St. Louis to Baltimore two days ago, Lou Perini succeeded today in shifting his National League baseball franchise from Boston to Milwaukee.

After a meeting of senior circuit club owners, Warren Giles, the league president, announced the unanimous approval of Perini's plan. Although the discussions lasted three and a half hours, Giles said "there was no real opposition" to the first shift of a major-league baseball franchise in half a century.

Minor details, including the rescheduling of night games, remain; but the package was wrapped, sealed and delivered to Perini. To gain his point, the contractor-sportsman, a native New Englander, had to receive all eight votes of the National League club owners.

One negative ballot would have brought rejection, but once Walter O'Malley of the Dodgers had moved for approval of the Braves' transfer and Horace Stoneham of the Giants had seconded the motion, every hand, including Perini's went up in approval in the open vote.

It then became necessary to satisfy and compensate the American Association, the Triple-A minor league in which the Milwaukee Brewers had been playing and from which they would have to be moved. Perini convinced the association's leaders that Toledo, Ohio, an "open city," was ready to

Associated Press Wirephoto
Lou Perini, Braves president, after the decision yesterday.

welcome the Milwaukee club, which he owns, in the same association, and agreed to pay the group $50,000. The vote to accept Perini's proposition was 7—1 in favor of the move. Only Kansas City, the Yankees' farm, voted "no."

At 2:39 P. M., Giles emerged from the meeting room with the following announcement:

"The National League has unanimously approved the transfer of the Boston franchise to Milwaukee on condition that the American Association takes the necessary steps, so that the move can be made."

Within a half hour, the "necessary steps" were taken and for the first time since 1901, when the Red Sox set up American League business at the Hub, Boston became a one-team city. The Braves, who, along with the Cubs, are uninterrupted charter members of the National League, had been there since 1876. For five years prior

to 1876, Boston had been in the National Association of Professional Baseball Clubs.

The nickname of the team will continue to be the "Braves." However, it no longer will be an Eastern outfit. It was agreed that Pittsburgh would hereafter be in the Eastern Division, while Milwaukee would be in the Western Division. Each will absorb the other's original schedule, with only the night game dates to be shuffled. Thus, opening day, April 13, will find Milwaukee at Cincinnati and on the following afternoon it will be Pittsburgh at Brooklyn.

'Fine Standing' Held Factor

Some observers thought Perini's success was almost as great a surprise as was Veeck's failure. It had been felt that the American League had set the precedent at Tampa Monday, when the Browns' plea was turned down. But Perini never lost confidence and Giles later declared that "the fine standing and prestige of Perini in our league was a great factor." The president conceded that questions were asked, but these mostly concerned schedules, commitments and other minor matters.

"These were answered most satisfactorily by Perini," Giles said. "He has received written releases from radio and television contracts and all is cleared. It is a good move for our league to go into as thriving a Midwestern city as Milwaukee. We wanted to do what Perini wanted to do. The time element is inconvenient, but if it's right, it's right."

At Milwaukee, the Braves' new home will be in County Stadium, a $5,000,000 structure that at the moment has 28,011 grandstand seats and 7,900 bleachers.

According to 1950 census figures, Milwaukee has a total population of 871,047 in its metropolitan district, with 637,392 in the city area. However, there is a potential of 1,500,000 fans within a radius of a hundred miles.

Perini expressed appreciation for the "vote of confidence" extended to him by the National League and for the cooperation of the American Association. He had taken active control of the Braves at Boston in 1945 and in 1948, the year his club won the pennant, 1,455,439 fans saw the home games.

Last year, though, the fans did not support the Braves, who finished seventh, and attracted only 281,000. It was said that Perini

had lost more than $700,000 in 1952. That financial loss, however, was not the motivating factor in Perini's decision to move.

"I definitely feel that since the advent of television Boston has become a one-team city," Perini said, "and the enthusiasm of the fans for the Boston National League club has waned. The interests of baseball can best be served elsewhere and Milwaukee has shown tremendous enthusiasm."

He said that he had foreseen the trend of transferring franchises and that "other cities can take a page from the Milwaukee book by providing for major-league facilities."

Perini said "naturally, I regret having to disappoint a great many New England fans and apologize for discommoding so many members of the press and radio."

Perini was congratulated by all of the baseball men present, including Bill Dewitt, vice president of the Browns. O'Malley said he was "dubious at first, but I have high regard for Perini's judgment and went with him." Stoneham said, "I was with him all the way."

Gabe Paul, the vice president of the Reds, also voiced confidence in Perini.

The all-star game, listed for July 14 at Braves' Field, will be played at Crosley Field, Cincinnati, on the same date. Cincinnati's turn would have come in 1954, but today's action moved the Ohio city up. The game was last played there in 1938.

The American Association had gone into session this morning before the National League owners assembled. At the request of Giles the minors group recessed until the completion of the big league's session. Then the association members completed their business.

Branch Rickey, who flew here from Havana, where his Pirates are training, agreed to absorb the original Boston schedule, though his team's first fifteen games will be against the Dodgers, Giants and Phillies.

Before today the last change in the major-league map occurred in 1903, when the Baltimore Orioles became the New York Highlanders, now the Yankees. In 1902 Milwaukee, then in the American League, became the St. Louis Browns and in 1898 Louisville moved to Pittsburgh.

March 19, 1953

Towering Drive by Yank Slugger Features 7-3 Defeat of Senators

By LOUIS EFFRAT
Special to The New York Times.

WASHINGTON, April 17—Unless and until contrary evidence is presented, recognition for the longest ball ever hit by anyone except Babe Ruth in the history of major league baseball belongs to Mickey

Mantle of the Yankees. This amazing 21-year-old athlete today walloped one over the fifty-five-foot high left-field wall at Griffith Stadium. That ball, scuffed in two spots, finally stopped in the backyard of a house, about 565 feet away from home plate.

This remarkable homer, which helped the Yankees register a 7-3 victory over the Senators, was Mickey's first of the season, but he will have to go some, as will anyone else, to match it.

Chuck Stobbs, the Nat southpaw, had just walked Yogi Berra after two out in the fifth, when Mantle strode to the plate. Batting right-handed, Mickey blasted the ball toward left center, where the base of the front bleachers wall is 391 feet from the plate. The distance to the back of the wall is sixty-nine feet more and

then the back wall is fifty feet high.

Bounces Out of Sight

Atop that wall is a football scoreboard. The ball struck about five feet above the end of the wall, caromed off the right and flew out of sight. There was no telling how much farther it would have flown had the football board not been there.

Before Mantle, who had cleared the right-field roof while batting left-handed in an exhibition game at Pittsburgh last week (only

Babe Ruth and Ted Beard had ever done that) had completed running out the two-run homer, Arthur Patterson of the Yankees' front-office staff was on his way to investigate the measure.

Patterson returned with the following news:

A 10-year-old lad had picked up the ball. He directed Patterson to the backyard of 434 Oakdale Street and pointed to the place where he had found it, across the street from the park. The boy, Donald Dunaway of 343 Elm Street N. W., accepted an undisclosed sum of money for the prize, which was turned over to Mantle. The Yankee was to send a substitute ball, suitably autographed to the boy.

Until today, when Mantle made it more or less easy for Lefty Ed Lopat, who worked eight innings, to gain his first triumph, no other batter had cleared the left-field wall here. Some years ago, Joe DiMaggio bounced a ball over, but Mickey's accomplishment was on the fly.

Longest Bunt as Well

Later in the contest, Mickey dragged a bunt that landed in front of second base and he outsped it for a single. Thus, in the same afternoon, it would appear, the young man from Commerce, Okla., fashioned one of the longest homers and the longest bunt on record.

Everything else that occurred in this contest was dwarfed by Mantle's round-tripper, which traveled 460 feet on the fly. There was a third-inning homer by Bill Martin, which gave the Yankees' the lead.

The Nats tied it against Lopat in the same frame on a single by Wayne Terwilliger, a sacrifice by Stobbs and Eddie Yost's single to left.

However, Hank Bauer doubled and counted on a single by Joe Collins for a 2-1 edge in the fourth then it was that Mickey connected with a fast ball and wrote diamond history. Other things happened, including Tom Gorman's appearance for the last inning, but no one appeared to be interested.

April 18, 1953

The Box Score

NEW YORK (A.)						WASHINGTON (A.)					
	ab	r	h	po	a		ab	r	h	po	a
Martin, 2b..	4	1	2	3	4	Yost, 3b..	5	0	2	1	4
Rizzuto, ss..	5	0	1	3		Busby, cf..	4	0	1	4	1
Berra, c..	4	1	1	2	2	Vernon, 1b..	3	0	0	13	1
Mantle, cf..	3	1	2	0	0	Jensen, rf..	4	0	0	3	0
Bauer, rf..	4	2	1	2	0	Runnels, ss..	3	1	1	0	2
Woodling, lf..	5	1	2	5	0	Wood, lf..	4	0	1	0	2
Lopat, p..	4	0	1	1	1	Ter'liger, 2b..	4	2	3	2	3
Collins, 1b..	4	0	1	11	1	Peden, c..	4	0	1	0	1
Carey, 3b..	4	1	1	1	1	Stobbs, p..	1	0	0	2	1
Lopat, p..	4	0	1	0	4	aHoderlein..	1	0	1	0	0
Gorman, p..	0	0	0	0	0	Moreno, p..	0	0	0	0	0
						bVerble..	1	0	0	0	0
Total	37	7	12	27	15	Total	34	3	10	27	15

aSingled for Stobbs in seventh.
bFlied out for Moreno in ninth.

New York ....001 120 030—7
Washington ....001 000 110—3

Errors—None.

Runs batted in—Martin 2, Yost, Collins, Mantle 2, Hoderlein, Carey, Woodling, Terwilliger. Two-base hits—Bauer, Terwilliger, Woodling. Home run—Martin, Mantle. Stolen base—Martin. Sacrifice—Stobbs. Double play—Lopat, Martin and Collins. Left on bases—New York 9, Washington 8. Bases on balls—Off Stobbs 4, Lopat 3, Moreno 2. Struck out—By Lopat 2. Hits—Off Lopat 10 in 8 innings, Stobbs 7 in 7, Gorman 0 in 1, Moreno 5 in 2, Runs and earned runs—Stobbs 4 and 4, Lopat 3 and 3, Moreno 3 and 3. Winning pitcher—Lopat (1—0). Losing pitcher—Stobbs (0—1). Umpires—Honochick, McGowan, Paparella and McKinley. Time of game—2:27. Attendance—4,206.

Baltimore Gets St. Louis Browns As Syndicate Buys Veeck Interest

American League Unanimously Approves Move—Controlling Stock Brings $2,475,000

By JOSEPH M. SHEEHAN

The major league baseball map, unchanged for fifty years, underwent its second revision in a little more than six months last night when the American League unanimously approved the transfer of the St. Louis Browns to Baltimore.

To effect the American League's first franchise shift since 1903, when Baltimore dropped out and New York was admitted, a Baltimore syndicate paid $2,475,000 to buy Bill Veeck's controlling interest in the Browns.

At Tampa, Fla., last March 15, two days before the National League had approved the transfer of the Braves from Boston to Milwaukee, and here only last Sunday, the American League had rejected the Browns-to-Baltimore proposals in which Veeck would have retained administrative control and considerable financial interest in the franchise he acquired in July, 1951.

The decisive action that will return to big league baseball one of its most glamorous names of the past—that of the Baltimore Orioles—was accomplished behind locked doors at the Hotel Commodore within the space of ninety minutes. This was in sharp contrast to proceedings of Sunday and Monday, when the American League owners had grappled for hours without effective result with the problem of what to do with the moribund Browns, who had a checkered past and a completely hopeless future in St. Louis.

Baltimore won its unflagging battle to take over the Browns, who finished last in the campaign that just closed with fifty-four victories and 100 defeats, because it alone of the numerous cities under consideration had the enthusiasm, the resources and the facilities to swing the deal.

When it became obvious after last Sunday's adverse 4-4 vote (six affirmative votes are needed to approve a franchise shift) that his fellow-owners wanted nothing more to do with Veeck, the Baltimore syndicate headed by Clarce W. Miles went to work and raised the additional money to buy Veeck out.

Originally, the Miles syndicate had proposed to acquire, for $1,-115,000, half of the 79 per cent stock interest in the Browns that Veeck controlled for Chicago and St. Louis interests. In this situation, Veeck was to continue in the picture as general manager of the club.

There were objections to Baltimore's entry also on the grounds that it was situated too close to Philadelphia and Washington, none too secure financially themselves, and that the traditional East-West balance of the league would be upset.

Mayor Plays Key Role

These objections foundered in the face of the fact that "Baltimore is ready to play ball," as Mayor Thomas D'Alesandro, who played a key role in his city's winning fight, succinctly put it the other day. No other candidate city could make that claim.

Baltimore's reconstructed municipal stadium, on which the Orioles already hold a lease-option at favorable terms, is now being double-decked and will be ready for baseball use, with nearly 52,000 seats, next April. Only Cleveland's Municipal Stadium (73,500) and New York's Yankee Stadium (67,000) and the Polo Grounds (55,000), of the present major league parks have a larger seating capacity.

Despite Baltimore's location between Philadelphia and Washington, both of which are in the Eastern division, the Orioles will be a "Western club" in the American League. Every effort will be made not to have Baltimore and Washington playing at home at the same time, since it is felt many persons living between the two cities may be attracted to games in both.

Los Angeles, San Francisco, Kansas City, Minneapolis, St. Paul, Montreal and Toronto, the other cities most prominently mentioned before yesterday as possible new homes for the Browns, did not have the existing facilities to stage major league baseball properly. Nor were they, in the showdown, willing to put up the cash necessary to acquire the St. Louis franchise.

However, the American League made clear its continuing interest in acquiring Pacific Coast representation. Simultaneously with the news of the shift of the Browns, the circuit announced the adoption of a constitutional amendment providing for expansion to a ten-club league "in the event it should become desirable to bring major league baseball to the Pacific Coast."

Concession to Webb

This amendment, duplicating similar action taken by the National League several years ago, represented a concession to the views of Del E. Webb. The vice president and co-owner of the Yankees, convinced that the future of the American League lies to the West, had fought a successful delaying action against the admission of Baltimore in the hope of bringing Los Angeles into the circuit.

When Los Angeles' financial support failed to materialize, Webb bowed to the exigencies of the situation and withdrew his objections to Baltimore and, in fact, made the motion to admit that city with the ten-club rider, which was accepted.

The news break came shortly before 6 P. M., when Earl Hilligan, director of the American League Service Bureau, emerged from the conference room, into which the owners had closeted themselves at 4:30 P. M.

Surrounded by reporters, cameramen and radio people, Hilligan read this statement: "The American League today approved the transfer of the St. Louis franchise to Baltimore. At the same time, the American League constitution was amended to provide for a ten-club league in the event it should be desirable to expand major league baseball to the Pacific Coast."

With the announcement that Baltimore at last had been accepted, a spontaneous cheer broke out from the corps of newspaper men from that city, who had waited three anxious days with their delegation. They were joined, by others whose sympathies had been won over by the gallant fight, against odds that seemed overwhelming, of the Miles group and Mayor D'Alesandro.

Pennant for Team Forecast

Probably the happiest man of all was Mayor D'Alesandro. Spotting Webb after the break-up of the meeting, he approached the Yankee executive and exclaimed, "Mr. Webb, I promise you when the Yankees come to Baltimore we'll have a record crowd out to see them. But I must warn you that we're out to break your monopoly on winning pennants. We are going to be in the World Series in 1954."

Then turning to the assembled newsmen, he said, "This is a great day for Baltimore and the big leagues. We have been fighting a long time to bring this about and it was worth it. I want to thank all my friends who supported me and helped bring it about."

The jubilation of Mayor D'Alesandro was echoed in Baltimore. Wire service reports from the nation's sixth-ranking city (population 940,000) carried exultant quotes by civic leaders and the "man-in-the-street" on the rebirth of the Orioles.

As organizer of the purchasing syndicate, Miles, an attorney who

101

is chairman of the Maryland State Bar Association, will become chairman of the Orioles' board of directors. His associates, not identified yesterday, include a number of Baltimore's leading industrialists and business men.

While neither Miles nor any of his group have previously been identified with baseball, "we are all sports-minded and intensely interested," he said.

"I feel confident that this will be a successful operation because of the tremendous public interest our efforts have aroused. There is a keen appetite and desire for major league baseball in Baltimore."

Without specifying any figure, Miles said that his group was prepared to spend "as much as we can" to make the Browns a contender. Under the terms of the sale, Baltimore acquires all the St. Louis players and minor league properties.

To clear the way for the American League to come into Baltimore, the Miles syndicate purchased the Baltimore Orioles International League franchise from Jack Dunn for $350,000. Dunn has been invited to join the new organization.

Miles will meet soon with Frank Shaughnessy, president of the International League, to decide what will become of the Baltimore franchise in that circuit. The belief is that the International League will operate as a six-team circuit, with Springfield as well as Baltimore out.

Veeck Expresses Satisfaction

Although the transaction knocked him out of baseball, Veeck expressed satisfaction with the results of the meeting.

"Yes, I sold everything—lock, stock and barrel," he said. "It was the only satisfactory solution and

the only way we could fulfill our promises and bring the club to Baltimore.

"The Browns obviously were in bad shape and these people, with strictly local backing, are in a much better position to do a job than we were."

Although he admittedly was in desperate financial straits after reportedly losing nearly a million dollars in two and a half seasons at St. Louis, Veeck insisted that he had not made a "'distress sale." "The price obviously was satisfactory or it would not have been accepted," he said.

There was no stipulation that Veeck remain out of baseball. "In fact, like a bad penny, I'll probably turn up again somewhere," he quipped. In response to queries as to whether he believed that anyone had been "out to get him," Veeck replied "I do not choose to think so—which is my privilege."

The former owner of the Browns has no immediate plans except to stay here for the world series and then "sneak off and spend some of my ill-gotten gains, which aren't much, I can assure you."

Before his ill-fated venture in St. Louis, Veeck had spectacular success at Milwaukee, then in the American Association, from 1941 through 1945, and with the Cleveland Indians of the American League, from 1946 through 1949.

The curly haired ex-Marine, who affects open-collared sport shirts, was a dynamic baseball executive, who kept things hummig on and off the field. He specialized in daring trades and bizzare promotion stunts. At Cleveland, he gave out orchids to female fans, hired baby sitters for ticket-purchasers, put on colorful sideshows on special occasions, etc. Under his di-

rection, the Indians set a major league attendance record of 2,620,-627 in 1948.

Even at St. Louis, long since discredited as a two-team city, attendance rose from 293,790 in 1951 to 518,796 in 1952 under his guidance. However, when his attempt to move the Browns to Baltimore last spring backfired, he was dead in St. Louis—and knew it. Playing out the string, as Veeck described it, the Browns drew 310,914 this season.

Three Two-Club Cities

With the demise of the Browns as a St. Louis entry, New York, Chicago and Philadelphia (where the days of the Athletics may be numbered) are the only two-club cities remaining in major league baseball.

The shift of the Braves to Milwaukee (a step taken in part out of desperation by Owner Lou Perini and in part to block Veeck's entry into a city where he was known and respected), looms more than ever as the touch-off of a chain-reaction. Additional changes in the set-up of the two major leagues seem inevitable in the near future.

Milwaukee demonstrated the crowd-drawing potential of new territory by establishing a National League attendance record of 1,-826,397 in its first season of operation.

It is somewhat coincidental that St. Louis, Milwaukee and Baltimore all were involved in the only previous franchise shifts since the two present major leagues shook down into stable form with the organization of the American League in 1901.

St. Louis joined the junior circuit in 1902, as a replacement for Milwaukee, an original member.

Baltimore, as previously cited, dropped out in 1903 and Milwaukee, of course, came back into the majors, as a National League team, last spring.

In its fifty-two years in the American League, St. Louis won only one pennant, in the World War II season of 1944, and managed only twelve first-division finishes.

Despite its long absence from the major league scene, Baltimore has a rich and glowing baseball tradition. Identified with professional baseball since 1871, the Maryland city was the home of one of the famous teams of history, the Orioles of 1894-96.

This swaggering group, which included such Hall of Famers as John J. McGraw, Wee Willie Keeler, Wilbert Robinson, Hughey Jennings and Fred Clarke, won three straight National League pennants and twice beat American Association rivals in the Temple Cup competition, which was a forerunner of the modern world series. Even today the description "old Oriole" typifies the peak of dash and spirit in a player.

It also was in Baltimore that baseball's most famous player of all, Babe Ruth, was born and made his start.

The return of major league baseball to Baltimore marked that city's second big sports success of the year. In January, Baltimore won a battle to be readmitted to the National Football League. With the completion of its new stadium, the city also looks to staging such big football attractions as Navy-Notre Dame and perhaps major fights.

September 30, 1953

Yanks Take 5th Series in Row, a Record; Martin's Hit in 9th Beats Dodgers, 4 to 3

Furillo's Last-Inning Homer Ties Score, Then Bomber Star Gets 12th Safety

By JOHN DREBINGER

In a whirlwind, breath-taking finish that doubtless will be remembered as long as baseball is played, Casey Stengel's Yankees yesterday became the first club in history to win five world series championships in a row.

The extraordinary feat was achieved at the Stadium before a crowd of 62,370 roaring fans. They saw the American League's amazing Bombers vanquish a fighting band of Dodgers, 4 to 3, to clinch the 1953 classic by a margin of four games to two.

For one throbbing moment in a thrill-packed ninth inning, Chuck

Dressen's Flatbush Flock stood even. This came when Carl Furillo blasted a two-run homer off Allie Reynolds. It deadlocked the score at 3-all.

Minutes later, in the last half of the ninth, amazing Bill Martin, doubtless cast from the start to fill the hero's role, slammed a single into center field off relief hurler Clem Labine. That shot, which gave Billy a series record of twelve hits, sent Hank Bauer racing over the plate with the decisive tally.

Sixteen in Thirty Years

And so to 63-year-old Charles Dillon Stengel, who in some forty-odd years has just about touched all the bases in an astounding career, now goes the distinction of becoming the first manager to match five straight

pennants with five successive world titles. He did it, too, in his first five years in the American League. For prior to 1949 the Ol' Perfessor, as the gravel-voiced philosopher, sage and wit of the diamond is fondly known, had never so much as played, coached or managed a single inning in the junior circuit.

As a fitting climax to the classic's fiftieth anniversary, the Yankees chalked up their sixteenth world championship against only four defeats. This achievement is all the more remarkable in that all sixteen triumphs were gained in a span of thirty years. Also, it boosted the American League's lead over the rival loop to a margin of thirty-three series victories to seventeen.

On the other hand, Brooklyn's record of gloom took on an even

darker hue. For this was the seventh time that a Dodger team had tried and failed to bring to that hotbed of diamond fanaticism its first world series crown. But even the most sorely disappointed Flatbush fan could not complain about the way Dressen's National Leaguers, on this occasion, fought off defeat until the last gasp.

Chuck had started Carl Erskine, the trim righthander who on Friday had set a world series record with fourteen strikeouts to win the third game in Ebbets Field. But Carl had only two days of rest and the Bombers got a three-run lead in the first two rounds behind their own Whitey Ford.

If there were any mistakes up to now it was the Yanks who made them. They tossed away an extra tally in the second inning when Ford, in an astounding mental lapse, failed to score on a fly ball that traveled almost 400 feet.

Though Dressen was later to get superb relief hurling from Bob Milliken and Labine until Clem's final cave-in in the last of the ninth, overhauling that three-run deficit proved a herculean effort. Off Ford the Dodgers never did make it.

They knicked the young south-

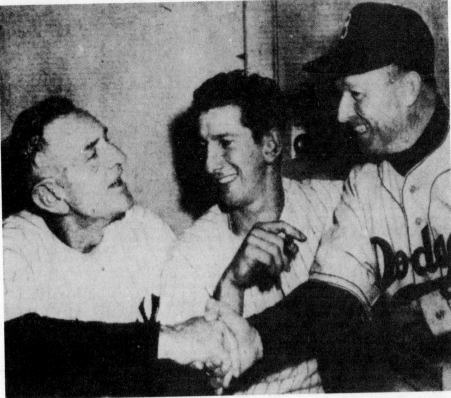

The New York Times

With a brave smile, Chuck Dressen congratulates Casey Stengel on the Yankees' fifth straight world series victory. In center is Billy Martin, who won last game with ninth-inning hit.

The Box Score

SIXTH GAME
BROOKLYN DODGERS

	AB.	R.	H.	PO.	A.
Gilliam, 2b	4	0	0	4	4
Reese, ss	4	0	1	1	4
Robinson, lf	4	1	2	3	0
Campanella, c	4	0	1	4	0
Hodges, 1b	4	0	0	7	0
Snider, cf	3	1	0	4	1
Furillo, rf	4	1	3	2	0
Cox, 3b	4	0	1	0	1
Erskine, p	1	0	0	0	0
aWilliams	0	0	0	0	0
Milliken, p	0	0	0	0	0
bMorgan	1	0	0	0	0
Labine, p	1	0	0	0	1
Total	34	3	8x	25	11

NEW YORK YANKEES

	AB.	R.	H.	PO.	A.
Woodling, lf	4	1	2	1	0
Collins, 1b	3	0	1	5	1
cMize	1	0	0	0	0
Bollweg, 1b	0	0	0	0	0
Bauer, rf	3	2	1	3	0
Berra, c	5	0	2	10	0
Mantle, cf	4	0	1	5	0
Martin, 2b	5	0	2	1	0
McDougald, 3b	4	0	0	0	0
Rizzuto, ss	4	1	2	2	2
Ford, p	3	0	1	0	1
Reynolds, p	1	0	1	0	0
Total	37	4	13	27	4

xOne out when winning run scored.
aWalked for Erskine in fifth.
bFlied out for Milliken in seventh.
cGrounded out for Collins in eighth.

Dodgers ....000 001 002—3
Yankees ....210 000 001—4

Errors—Gilliam, Erskine, Cox.

Runs batted in—Berra, Martin 2, Woodling, Campanella, Furillo 2, Robinson. Two-base hits—Berra, Furillo, Martin, Robinson. Home runs—Furillo. Stolen base—Robinson. Double plays —Cox, Gilliam and Hodges; Snider, Gilliam and Campanella; Labine, Gilliam and Hodges. Left on bases— Dodgers 6, Yankees 13. Bases on balls—Ford 1 (Williams), Reynolds 1 (Snider), Erskine 3 (Woodling, Mantle, Bauer), Milliken 1 (Collins), Labine 1 (Bauer). Strike outs—Ford 7 (Snider 3, Cox, Erskine, Campanella, Gilliam), Reynolds 3 (Campanella, Cox, Labine), Erskine 1 (Collins), Labine 1 (McDougald). Hits—Off Erskine 6 in 4 innings, Milliken 2 in 2, Ford 6 in 7, Labine 5 in 2 1/3, Reynolds 2 in 2. Runs and earned runs—Erskine 3 and 3, Milliken 0 and 0, Ford 1 and 1, Labine 1 and 1, Reynolds 2 and 2. Winning pitcher —Reynolds. Losing pitcher—Labine. Umpires—Bill Stewart (N. L.), plate; Ed Hurley (A. L.), first base; Art Gore (N. L.), second base; Bill Grieve (A. L.), third base; Frank Dascoli (N. L.), left field; Hank Soar (A. L.), right field. Time of game— 2:55. Paid attendance—62,370.

paw from Astoria for one tally in the sixth which Jackie Robinson personally conducted around the paths by stroking a two-bagger, stealing third and scoring on an infield out. But the pair that tied it in the ninth on Furillo's homer was not made off Ford at all.

Actually, all that final drama began with the eighth inning. It was then that Stengel, in a move as startling as any in his brilliant managerial career, withdrew Ford. The bull-pen gates opened to reveal the confidently striding figure of Reynolds. The redoubtable Chief, who had started the opener for the Yanks, had strained a muscle in his back in that game. He came back to stop the Flock in its tracks in the ninth inning of the fifth game in Brooklyn Sunday. Now he was being called upon to lock up the clincher.

Ford, in his seven innings, had given up only six hits. He was leading 3 to 1, and there seemed to be no particular reason for making a change. Still, the Ol' Perfessor often makes alterations that defy analysis by baseball's outstanding academic minds.

Ford had made a spectacular comeback after his ill-starred one-inning effort which had cost the Bombers the fourth game. Perhaps the shot which pinch hitter Bob Morgan had streaked toward the right field stands in the seventh with a runner aboard helped Casey to make up his mind.

Bauer had caught that one off Morgan's bat as it was about to fall into the seats. Anyway, little did anyone suspect that Reynolds, now entering the game simply to

save it for the youthful Ford, would wind up the winner himself, for it was his seventh world series mound triumph, tying the record of another Yankee stalwart of another period, Red Ruffing.

Robinson singled in the eighth, but there were two out and Roy Campanella, striving desperately to answer the prayers of the Flatbush faithful, went down swinging on a third strike.

Big Jawn Called to Bat

In the last of the eighth Stengel made another move, startling yet withal a nice gesture. Phil Rizzuto and Reynolds had singled with one out. A close play at the plate had rubbed out Rizzuto when he tried to score on Gene Woodling's grounder, but there were still two on base.

So the Ol' Perfessor called in Johnny Mize to pinch hit. A year ago the big Georgian had been the hero. This year there had not been much occasion to call on him and at the age of 41 this easily could prove his farewell as an active player. His best was a grounder down the first base line that ended the round.

But the Yanks were still two in front and they were still that way when Gil Hodges, first Dodger up in the ninth, flied out. But Duke Snider, whom Ford had fanned three times earlier in the battle, now worked Reynolds for a pass after running the count to three and two.

Then came Furillo. He, too, worked it to three and two. Then he lashed one on a line into the lower right field stand and the

Flatbush host was beside itself. The score was deadlocked and one could see Reynolds felt keenly disappointed.

The Chief fairly burned the ball across the plate as he next struck out Billy Cox and Labine to end the inning. But the score was tied.

Now the grand finale. Bauer, first up in the last of the ninth, walked. Yogi Berra flied out but Mickey Mantle topped a ball to the left of the diamond which skipped off Cox's glove and went for a hit. This set up the break in the game.

For up came that incredible 25-year-old star. Martin, a .257 hitter through the regular season who was now emerging as the grand hero. His base clearing first inning triple had sent the Yanks off to a flying start at the outset of the series. He later was to hit two homers and up to this moment he had made eleven hits, tops for the series.

One Smack to Glory

Labine worked carefully, got the count to one and one. Then Billy smacked it. Right over second base it went and that was it.

It was the twelfth hit of the series for the peppery Californian who once played for Stengel when the latter managed Oakland in the Coast League before coming to the Yanks. In fact, it was largely on the insistance of Casey that Martin came to the Yanks at all. They never did think too much of him. Now he can name his own price. Those twelve hits gave Martin the record for a six-game series and tied the mark of a dozen blows made in a seven-game classic.

For the first time since the series began, the weatherman, who so obligingly had provided a mid-summer setting for the first five games, walked out on the show. A gray sky that threatened rain almost from the first, blotted out every trace of the sun, so that the fielders had nothing to worry about on that score. Shirt sleeves also went out of fashion overnight for the fans. It was, in fact, more than a trifle chilly.

However, though the weather slumped, not so those toughened pioneers of that first world series fifty years ago who have been rotating in tossing out the first ball. Yesterday it was Fred Parent, 1903 Red Sox shortstop, who took his turn. Fred really put something on it as he fired into Berra's big mitt. Then the stars of today took over.

It soon became evident that Erskine wasn't the pitcher of the third game of last Friday and that the two intervening days had not given him sufficient rest.

In Trouble From the Start

He was in trouble right from the start and but for some blundering by the Bombers on the basepaths in the second inning, the handsome Hoosier righthander would have plunged deeper in the hole.

He walked Woodling, who again was leading off in the Stengel batting order. He fanned Joe Collins, one of his four-time victims last Friday at Ebbets Field, but Bauer lined a single to left and Berra hammered a drive down the right field line that hopped by Furillo and bounced into the stand for an automatic two-bagger.

In a way that helped the Dodgers since Bauer, who almost certainly would have scored had the ball remained in play, had to hold up at third, while only Woodling was permitted to count. The break didn't help much, however.

Erskine, who also fanned Mantle four times the last time he faced him, was not permitted to embellish that record. He was instructed to pass the Oklahoma Kid intentionally and that filled the bases.

This strategy might have paid off. Martin sent a blistering one hopper to the right of second base.

Junior Gilliam momentarily collared the ball only to let it get away. Had he held it, it most likely would have resulted in an inning-ending double play.

Scored as an Error

Instead, it was scored an error, although this verdict did not meet with the general approval of the press box occupants. Quite a few of the experts were of the opinion it should have been called a hit, since it looked to have Gilliam handcuffed all the way.

Be that as it may, it allowed Bauer to come home with the second tally and though Gil McDougald here slapped into a double play, the Bombers for the fourth time in the series had skipped off to a first inning lead.

And in the second they got with another run. They should have had two, but lost one on an incredible bit of base running—or lack of it—on the part of Master Ford.

Rizzuto opened the inning with a single to center and Whitey lined one into right that swept Li'l Phil around to third. Woodling followed with a long fly to Jackie Robinson in left and Rizzuto scampered over the plate with one run.

Now came some harrowing moments for the Dodgers. They seemed about to blow sky high. But the Bombers themselves bun-

gled it. Collins, in backing away from a pitch, accidentally bunted one down the third-base line that could not have been more scientifically placed.

Erskine tracked it down and fired the ball to first, but too late and too wide. In fact, Carl threw the ball right over Hodges' head and it went for a hit and an error, the play winding up with Ford on third, Collins on second and still only one out.

Pitching cautiously to Bauer, Erskine walked him to fill the bases. Then Berra lifted a towering fly that Snider caught in deep right center. It was so deep that no one even thought Ford would fail to score from third. All eyes were focused on Collins as he tagged up at second and lit out for third the moment the ball landed in Duke's glove.

But as Gilliam received Snider's throw-in someone in the infield yelled, "Home, home, throw it home." Gilliam whirled around, fired the ball to Campanella at the plate and, lo and behold, was Ford, still leisurely jogging home and never making it. For Campy tagged him with the ball for the third out. That "lost" run was almost to come up and haunt the Bombers in the end.

It probably was destined right from the beginning that the Yanks should win this series if only in re-

sponse to an overwhelming force of habit.

It was in 1923 that the Yanks won their first world title under the late Miller Huggins. They had won their first league pennants in 1921 and 1922, but had been turned back by the Giants in the series. Since 1923 they have been stopped only twice, by the Cardinals in 1926 and again by the Redbirds in 1942.

After '23 they triumphed again under Huggins in 1927 and 1928. They won next in 1932 under Joe McCarthy, who then led them through four successive series triumphs from 1936 to 1939, a mark that stood until Stengel tied it last year and surpassed it this year.

Two more titles went to the Yanks under McCarthy in 1941 and 1943. Then Marse Joe stepped out, but in 1947 the Yanks were back with another world crown under Bucky Harris and in 1949 there began the present act of five in a row under Stengel.

For Brooklyn, the defeat was the seventh in world series play. The Dodgers of Uncle Wilbert Robinson's day bowed to the Red Sox in 1916 and to the Indians in 1920. Since then it's been five setbacks in a row at the hands of the Yankees, in 1941, 1947, 1949, last October and finally the one in yesterday's cold and biting wind.

October 6, 1953

Stan Musial

Musial Sets Record With 5 Homers

ST. LOUIS SLUGGER PACES 10-6 VICTORY

Musial Belts 3 Homers, Then Adds 2 for Twin-Bill Mark as Giants Triumph, 9-7

By JOHN DREBINGER
Special to The New York Times.

ST. LOUIS, May 2—Stan Musial set one major league record and tied another today as he walloped five home runs in the course of a double-header. But all it got the Cardinals was an even break with the Giants in a bruising twin bill that kept 26,662 roaring fans in a dither for the better part of seven hours.

In the opener the Redbirds downed the Polo Grounders, 10 to

6, with an outburst of five circuit drives to three for the New Yorkers. Stan the Man hit three in this game, his final blast, off Jim Hearn, coming with two aboard in the last of the eighth to break a 6-all tie.

Then, in the nightcap, practically all of it played under lights, Musial hit two more. But Leo Durocher's minions, erupting for eight runs in the fourth inning, managed to hang on to win this one, 9 to 7.

Cards Get 12 Homers

In all the Cards hit three homers in the second encounter to one for the Giants, making a grand total of twelve round trippers for the day.

Musial set a new mark with his five for the twin bill, the previous high for most homers in a double-header being four.

Musial also tied the major league record of five homers for two consecutive games.

The second game was, indeed, a bruising affair. When it wound up, Musial had a season's total of eight home runs.

At the outset it looked as though the Giants were headed for another drubbing when Tom Alston clubbed Don Liddle for a base-clearing double in the first inning. But in the fourth, the Polo Grounders came back with their cluster of eight as they battered Joe Presko, Royce Lint and Mel Wright for eight hits.

Mueller, who came up with five blows in this game, got two in this inning, one a triple, while Bobby Hofman contributed a three-run homer. But Hoyt Wilhelm, who replaced Liddle, ran into a three-run squall in the fifth on homers by Musial and Ray Jablonski and in the seventh Musial whacked him for another.

Both of the shots by Stan were tremendous wallops clear out of the park into Grand Avenue. They drove in three runs which, along with six in the first game, gave Musial a total of nine runs-batted-in for the day.

But at this point, Larry Jansen came on to stop the Redbirds cold. He blanked them through the eighth and ninth, and for good measure drove in an extra run for the Giants in the top of the ninth with a single.

Stan the Man was pretty much the whole show in the opener, which saw Alpha Brazle, the ancient southpaw replace Starter Gerry Staley in the sixth inning

to notch his first victory of the season.

Warming up on a base on balls off Johnny Antonelli in the first inning, Musial then proceeded to ring up a perfect game at bat for himself.

He hit homers in successive times at bat off Antonelli in the third and fifth, the first of these shots coming with the bases empty, the second with one on. He singled off Hearn in the sixth and in the eighth whacked the big right-hander for his game-clinching clout with two runners aboard.

It was, in fact, pretty much a home-run or no count affair most of the way, with eight of the ten tallies by the Cards coming as the result of circuit clouts.

Antonelli was slapped for six runs and four homers before being belted out in the fifth. In addition to Musial's first two, the former Brave lefty saw Wally Moon hit his third four-bagger of the season in the first and Tom Alston his third in the fourth.

The Giants, however, weren't exactly standing still. They reached Staley for three runs in the fourth with the aid of a couple of doubles by Henry Thompson and Irvin. Successive homers by Lockman and Westrum produced two more tallies in the fifth and in the sixth Irvin's No. 4 off Brazle deadlocked

the score at 6-all.

From here on Brazle held firm while Hearn blew wide open in the eighth and went down to his second setback of the year.

Giants' Box Scores

FIRST GAME

NEW YORK (N.)	ab.	r.	h.	po.	a
Williams, 2b	4	1	1	2	1
Dark, ss	4	0	1	0	2
Tho'son, 3b	4	1	1	1	4
Irvin, lf	3	2	2	2	0
Mueller, rf	4	0	1	0	0
Mays, cf	3	0	0	2	0
Lockm'n, 1b	4	1	1	9	1
Westrum, c	4	1	2	7	2
An'nelli, p	2	0	0	1	1
Hearn, p	0	0	0	0	0
Picone, p	0	0	0	0	0
cHofman	1	0	0	0	0
Total	**33**	**6**	**9**	**24**	**11**

ST. LOUIS (N.)	ab.	r.	h.	po.	a
Moon, cf	5	2	2	2	0
S'dienst, 2b	3	3	0	3	3
Musial, rf	4	3	4	4	0
Jab'ski, 3b	5	0	1	0	2
Repulski, lf	4	1	1	2	0
Alston, 1b	4	1	4	8	1
Gram'as, ss	3	0	0	1	1
Rice, c	3	0	0	6	1
aHemus, ss	3	0	1	0	0
Staley, p	1	0	0	1	2
bLowrey	1	0	0	0	0
Brazle, p	1	0	0	0	0
Total	**37**	**10**	**14**	**27**	**10**

aHit into force out for Grammas in fifth.
bStruck out for Staley in fifth.
cStruck out for Picone in ninth.

New York .... 000 321 000—6
St. Louis .... 201 120 04.—10

Errors—Thompson. Dark.
Runs batted in—Moon, Alston 2. Musial 6. Hemus, Thompson, Irvin 2. Mueller. Lockman, Westrum.
Two-base hits—Thompson, Irvin, Repulski. Home runs—Moon, Musial 3. Alston, Lockman, Westrum, Irvin. Sacrifices—Staley, Hearn. Double plays—Schoendienst, Grammas and Alston: Jablonski. Schoendienst and Alston. Left on bases—New York 3, St. Louis 9. Bases on balls—Antonelli 3. Hearn 2. Brazle 2. Struck out—By Antonelli 4. Hearn 2, Staley 3. Brazle 3. Hits—Off Antonelli 6 in 4 innings (faced three men in fifth). Hearn 8 in 3 1-3. Picone 0 in 2-3. Staley 7 in 5. Brazle 2 in 4. Runs and earned runs—Off Antonelli 6 and 5, Hearn 4 and 4. Staley 5 and 5. Brazle 1 and 1. Winning pitcher—Brazle (1—0). Losing pitcher—Hearn (0—2). Umpires—Donatelli, Ballanfant, Barlick and Warneke. Time of game—2:48.

SECOND GAME

NEW YORK (N.)	ab.	r.	h.	po.	a
Lockman, 1b	2	1	0	10	1
Dark, ss	.5	0	0	2	1
Thompson, 3b	4	1	1	0	2
Irvin, lf	4	1	1	0	0
Mueller, rf	.5	3	5	2	0
Mays, cf	4	0	1	6	0
St. Claire, c	4	1	2	3	1
bAmalsitano	0	0	0	0	0
Poholsky, p	0	0	0	0	1
gLowrey	0	0	0	0	0
Westrum, c	0	0	0	1	0
Samford, 2b	1	0	0	0	0
aRhodes	1	1	1	0	0
Wilhelm	1	0	0	0	1
Jansen, p	2	0	1	0	2
Liddle, p	1	0	0	1	0
bTaylor	1	0	0	0	0
cHofman, 2b	4	1	1	2	3
Total	**38**	**9**	**13**	**27**	**12**

ST. LOUIS (N.)	ab.	r.	h.	po.	a
Moon, cf	.4	0	1	2	0
Sch'ienst, 2b	5	2	2	2	2
Musial, rf	4	3	2	4	1
Jablonski, 3b	5	1	3	1	0
Repulski, lf	4	1	0	3	0
Alston, 1b	2	0	1	7	0
Grammas, ss	3	0	0	2	3
Poholsky, p	0	0	0	0	1
gLowrey	0	0	0	0	0
Sarni, c	2	0	0	2	0
dHemus, ss	2	0	0	0	0
Presko, p	.1	0	0	0	1
Lint, p	.0	0	0	0	1
Wright, p	.1	0	0	0	0
eFrazier	.1	0	0	0	0
fMiller	.0	0	0	0	0
Rice, c	.1	0	0	4	0
Total	**35**	**7**	**10**	**27**	**8**

aSingled for Samford in fourth.
bWalked for Liddle in fourth.
cHit home run for Taylor in fourth.
dFlied out for Sarni in sixth.
eDoubled for Wright in sixth.
fRan for Frazier in sixth.
gWalked for Poholsky in seventh.
hRan for St. Claire in ninth.

New York .... 000 800 001—9
St. Louis .... 300 030 100—7

Errors—None.

Runs batted in—Alston 3. Musial 3. Jablonski. Mays 3. Hofman 3. Mueller 2. Jansen. Two-base hits—Schoendienst. Alston, Mueller. Thompson. Three-base hits—Mueller, Schoendienst. Home runs—Hofman. Musial 2. Jablonski. Stolen base—Thompson. Sacrifice fly—Mays. Double plays—Thompson. Hofman and Lockman; Jansen. Dark and Lockman. Left on bases—New York 9, St. Louis 7. Bases on balls—Off Wilhelm 3. Jansen 2, Presko 3. Lint 2. Struck out—By Wilhelm 3, Jansen 1. Wright 1. Hits—Off Liddle 3 in 3 innings. Wilhelm 6 in 3 (none out in seventh). Jansen 1 in 3, Presko 4 in 3 1-3. Lint 3 in 1-3. Wright 4 in 2 1-3, Poholsky 0 in 1. Deal 2 in 2. Runs and earned runs—Off Liddle 3 and 3. Wilhelm 4 and 4. Presko 3 and 3. Lint 5 and 5. Deal 1 and 1. Hit by pitcher—By Moon (Liddle); St. Claire (Deal). Winning pitcher—Jansen (1—0). Losing pitcher—Lint (1—1). Umpires—Ballanfant, Barlick. Warneke and Donatelli. Time of game—2:56. Attendance—26.662.

May 3, 1954

PLAYERS ORGANIZE AND RETAIN LEWIS

CLEVELAND, July 12 (P)—Big league baseball players today organized formally into a group known as the Major League Baseball Players Association. They also adopted by-laws and a constitution.

J. Norman Lewis, the players' attorney, will be paid a reported $30,000 for services rendered while helping the players negotiate revisions in their pension set-up with the owners. The money, to come from the majors' central fund, will cover the lawyer's fee through October, 1954.

Lewis said the matter of any retaining fee after October was not discussed.

The sixteen-player representatives from the American and National League clubs met for three and a half hours.

The group will elect player representatives from each of the sixteen clubs beginning in July, 1955. These men in turn will elect a league representative from each circuit.

Lewis denied that the player action could be construed as the forming of a union. He pointed out that no dues would be paid into the association. Previously, the player representatives group, which was formed informally in 1946, preferred to be known as a "players' fraternity."

There will be four meetings a year of the new organization—the second week of April; All-

Star game week; world series time and the first week of December.

All expenses, including the attorney's salary will be paid from baseball's central fund. This fund consists of the gate receipts of the All-Star game and the TV-radio receipts of the All-Star game and the world series.

The present league player representatives, Ralph Kiner of the Chicago Cubs and Allie Reynolds of the New York Yankees, and the current player representatives from each major league club, will continue to serve until the new delegates are elected in 1955.

Lewis will meet tomorrow with the American and National League attorneys to discuss the question of preparing contracts on a revised pension agreement.

The central fund, after the present contract on the players' pension expires in 1955, will earmark 60 per cent of the money for the players and 40 per cent for the owners.

The player discussions brought up these proposals to be submitted at the July 26 meeting of club owners in New York:

¶That players be permitted to deal directly for winter league baseball play themselves and that no limit be placed on the number of players in winter ball.

¶That the owners start spring training no earlier than March 1, play no games earlier than March 10 and keep one day per week open in the spring training.

¶That the clubs pay their players on a monthly basis over 12 months instead of the general practice of five and a half months a year.

July 13, 1954

ADCOCK'S 4 HOMERS HELP BRAVES ROUT DODGERS, 15-7

TEN 4-BAGGERS HIT

By ROSCOE McGOWEN

Joe Adcock, the Braves' first baseman, hit four home runs and a double at Ebbets Field yesterday to tie three major league records and establish two others.

The Braves won the game, 15—7, running their winning streak to nine. Milwaukee is only five games out of second place and the Brooks are four games back of the first-place Giants.

Adcock was the seventh player to hit four homers in a game. Bobby Lowe of Boston in 1894, Ed Delahanty of Philadelphia in 1896, Chuck Klein of the Phils in 1936 and Gil Hodges of the Dodgers in 1950 were the National Leaguers sharing the record previously. Lou Gehrig of the Yankees in 1932 and Pat Seerey of the Chicago White Sox in 1948 were the American League players to turn the trick.

Klein and Seerey required extra innings to match the mark. Klein belted his fourth homer in the tenth inning and Seerey connected for No. 4 in the eleventh.

The Braves' star, who connected in the fourth inning on Friday against the Brooks, equalled the major league mark for five homers in two consecutive games.

Joe's total of eighteen bases put a new record in the book, the seventeen-base total previously having been shared by Lowe, Delahanty and Hodges. Adcock's other mark was for the most extra bases on long hits, thirteen.

The two teams tied the National League record for homers by both clubs, ten, the Braves belting seven and the Brooks three. The American League record is eleven, set by the Yankees (six) and Detroit (five), in 1950.

Four Pitchers Belted

Adcock's homers were made off four pitchers, Don Newcombe, the loser; Erv Palica, Pete Wojey and Johnny Podres. His two-bagger was belted off Palica on Joe's second trip to the plate in the third inning.

Two of his homers and the double were hit on first pitches, the other two big blows on sec-

ond pitches. The second homer bounced off the façade, but the others went into the lower stands in left center field.

The other major league record tied by Adcock was five extra base hits in a nine-inning game. Lou Boudreau, with Cleveland in 1946, set the modern record with four doubles and a homer in one game.

The other Milwaukee home run hitters were Eddie Mathews, who hit two in a row off Newcombe and Palica, in the first and third innings; and Andy Pafko, who hit his into the left field stands in the seventh off Wojey.

For the Dodgers, Don Hoak and Gil Hodges smacked solo homers in the sixth and eighth and Rube Walker a two-run blast in the eighth, all off Lew Burdette. The Braves' hurler gained his ninth triumph, but had to be relieved in the Brooks' four-run eighth.

Burdette had taken over for Charley Grimm's undefeated starter, Jim Wilson, in the second inning. And in the first two innings, the Dodgers gave their season's greatest exhibition of futility.

In both innings they had the bases filled with none out and managed to score only one run

in the first inning. Thereafter, Burdette held the Brooks at bay until Hoak broke through with his homer. Probably the intense heat—the mercury officially registered 95.3—took its toll from Burdette.

Adcock drove in seven runs, his second homer in the fifth being belted with two on, his third in the seventh with one aboard. All other Milwaukee homers were solo shots. One run, in the ninth, when Podres was on the mound, scored on a wild pitch and another when Dave Jolly, the final Braves' pitcher, hit into a double play.

Although the Dodgers made sixteen hits, only three under the Milwaukee output, they never were really in the ball game after being frustrated in the first two innings.

With four runs across in the eighth, they had the bases filled on Podres' second straight single, another by Junior Gilliam and a pass to Don Zimmer.

But with the 17,263 fans, including 5,000 Knothole kids—excepting 460 Milwaukeeans who came here on an excursion to root for their heroes—pleading for a grand slam, George Shuba popped to Mathews and Hodges grounded out to short.

Newcombe suffered his sixth loss and now has two straight knockouts.

SEVEN HOMERS AMONG THEM: Milwaukee players hold up fingers to indicate home runs hit by each one of them in game with Dodgers. Left to right: Ed Mathews, Joe Adcock, who tied a major league record with four homers in a nine-inning game, and Andy Pafko.

Associated Press

The Box Score

MILWAUKEE (N.)	ab.	r.	h.	po.	a.	BROOKLYN (N.)	ab.	r.	h.	po.	a.
Bruton, cf..	6	0	4	4	0	Gilliam, 2b.	4	1	4	3	1
O'C'nell, 2b..	5	0	0	4	4	Reese, ss.	3	0	1	1	1
Mathews, 3b..	4	1	2	3	2	Zimmer, ss..	1	0	0	1	1
Aaron, lf .	5	2	2	0	0	Snider, cf..	4	0	1	0	0
Adcock, 1b..	5	5	5	10	0	Shuba, lf..	1	0	0	0	0
Pafko, rf....	4	2	3	0	0	Hodges, 1b..	5	1	1	7	0
P'ndleton, rf.	1	1	0	0	0	Amoros.lf-cf.	5	2	3	6	0
Logan, ss...	2	1	1	1	1	Robin's'n, 3b.	0	0	0	0	0
Smalley, ss..	2	1	1	0	1	Hoak, 3b.	2	1	1	0	1
Crandall, c..	4	0	0	3	1	Furillo, rf..	5	1	2	3	0
Calderone, c.	1	0	1	2	0	Walker, c..	5	1	1	6	1
Wilson, p....	1	0	0	0	0	Newc'mbe, p.	0	0	0	0	0
Burdette, p..	4	0	0	0	4	Palica, p....	0	0	0	0	0
Buhl, p.....	0	0	0	0	0	aMoryn	1	0	0	0	0
Jolly, p.....	0	0	0	1	0	Wojey, p....	1	0	0	0	1
						bPodres, p..	2	0	2	0	1
Total..	44	15	19	27	13						
						Total....	39	7	16	27	7

aHit into double play for Labine in second.
bSingled for Wojey in seventh.

Milwaukee .... 1 3 2 0 3 0 3 0 3—15
Brooklyn .... 1 0 0 0 0 1 0 4 1— 7
Error—Hoak.
Runs batted in—Mathews 2, Snider, Adcock 7, Logan, Bruton, Hoak 2, Pafko 2, Hodges, Furillo, Walker 2.
Two-base hits—Gilliam, Pafko, Bruton 3, Amoros, Adcock, Aaron. Three-base hit—Amoros. Home runs—Mathews 2, Adcock 4, Hoak, Pafko, Hodges, Walker. Sacrifice—O'Connell. Sacrifice fly—Hoak. Double plays —Mathews, O'Connell and Adcock; O'Connell, Logan and Adcock; Zimmer, Gilliam and Hodges. Left on bases—Milwaukee 6, Brooklyn 10. Bases on balls—Off Burdette 2, Jolly 1, Palica 2, Wojey 3, Podres 1, Jolly 1; Palica 1, Wojey 3, Podres 1. Hits—Off Wilson 5 in 1 inning (pitched to three batters in second); Burdette 8 in 6 1-3, Buhl 2 in 0 (pitched to two batters in eighth), Jolly 1 in 1 2-3; Newcombe 4 in 1 (pitched to three batters in second), Labine 1 in 1, Palica 5 in 2 1-3, Wojey 4 in 2 2-3, Podres 5 in 2. Runs and earned runs—Off Wilson 1 and 1, Burdette 5 and 5, Jolly 1 and 1, Newcombe 4 and 4, Palica 5 and 5, Wojey 3 and 3, Podres 3 and 2. Wild pitch—Podres. Hit by pitcher—By Wilson (Robinson). Winning pitcher—Burdette (10—11). Losing pitcher—Newcombe (6—6). Umpires—Boggess, Engeln, Stewart and Pinelli. Time of game—2:53. Attendance—12,263.

Indians Take 111th For Record Season

By The United Press.

CLEVELAND, Sept. 25—Early Wynn missed a no-hitter in the ninth but the Cleveland Indians set an American League record of 111 victories in a single season by defeating the Detroit Tigers 11 to 1, today.

Wynn missed what would have been the first American League no-hitter of the season when Fred Hatfield singled to open the ninth inning. Steve Souchock tripled one out later to deprive Wynn of a shutout.

It was Wynn's fourth two-hitter of the year and he remains a possibility to open the world series against the Giants. He was pitching today with a sore left foot, the result of an ingrown toenail on the big toe of that leg. By gaining his

twenty-third triumph, Wynn tied his teammate, Bob Lemon, for the league lead in victories. Either Wynn or Lemon will face the Giants at the Polo Grounds next Wednesday.

Today's 111th victory broke the league record of 110, established in 1927 by the New York Yankees.

The Indians pounded three Tiger pitchers, starting with George Zuverink, for fourteen hits. These included three by Bob Avila, who improved his average to .340 and who is certain to be crowned batting champion of his league.

Larry Doby drove in a run to increase his runs-batted-in total to 125, giving him the lead over Yogi Berra of the Yankees.

Wynn had a perfect game until one man was out in the sixth, but then he walked Red Wilson on a 3-2 pitch. He passed four men in all, and struck out four.

Hatfield ran the count to 3—1 before he rapped his clean single to right field.

The box score:

DETROIT (A.)						CLEVELAND (A.)					
	ab.	r.	h.	po.	a.		ab.	r.	h.	po.	a.
Kuenn, ss.	3	0	0	0	3	Smith, lf. rf.	4	3	3	0	0
Herbert, p.	0	0	0	0	0	Avila, 2b.	4	3	3	5	2
dNieman	.1	0	0	0	0	Doby, cf.	3	1	2	3	0
Marlowe, p.	0	0	0	0	0	Rosen, 3b.	1	0	1	1	0
Hatfield, 3b.	3	1	2	4	2	aRega'do,3b	1	0	1	1	2
Delsing, lf.	3	0	0	1	0	bMitchell	.1	1	1	0	0
Boone, 3b.	2	0	0	1	0	Majeski, 3b.	2	0	0	0	2
Souchock,3b	2	0	1	0	3	Glynn, 1b.	3	1	1	7	0
Kaline, rf.	4	0	0	1	1	Philley,rf.	5	1	1	2	0
Tuttle, cf.	3	0	0	1	0	Strickland,ss	2	1	1	2	1
Wilson, c.	0	0	0	3	2	Hegan, c.	4	0	0	6	0
Streull, c.	0	0	0	1	0	Wynn, p.	4	0	0	0	1
Zuverink, p.	1	0	0	1	1						
Lary, p.	0	0	0	0	0						
cKing	.1	0	0	0	0						
Bullard, ss.	1	0	0	2	2						
Total	29	1	2	24	17	Total	36	11	14	27	8

aRan for Rosen in first.
bDoubled for Regalado in fifth.
cFlied out for Lary in sixth.
dHit into force play for Herbert in eighth.
Detroit .... 0 0 0 0 0 0 0 0 1—1
Cleveland .... 1 0 2 0 4 0 4 0 .—11
Errors—Kaline, Bullard.
Runs batted in — Regalado 2, Mitchell 2, Philley 2, Strickland, Wynn, Smith, Souchock, Doby.
Two-base hits—Doby, Avila, Mitchell, Philley. Three-base hit—Souchock. Double play—Wilson and Hatfield. Left on bases—Detroit 5, Cleveland 7. Bases on balls—Off Zuverink 3, Lary 1, Herbert 2, Wynn 4. Struck out—By Zuverink 2, Marlowe 1, Wynn 4. Hits—Off Zuverink 7 in 4 1-3 innings, Lary 2 in 2-3, Herbert 5 in 2, Marlowe 0 in 1. Runs and earned runs—Off Zuverink 6 and 6, Lary 1 and 1, Herbert 4 and 0, Wynn 1 and 1. Wild pitch—Wynn. Winning pitcher—Wynn (23—11). Losing pitcher—Zuverink (9—13). Umpires—Runge, Summers, McKinley and Hurley. Time of game—2:28. Attendance—8,647.

September 26, 1954

GIANTS WIN IN 10TH FROM INDIANS, 5-2, ON RHODES' HOMER

Pinch-Hitter Decides World Series Opener With 3-Run Wallop at Polo Grounds

---

52,751 SEE LEMON LOSE

Grissom Is Victor in Relief—Mays' Catch Saves Triumph —Wertz Gets 4 Hits

---

By JOHN DREBINGER

At precisely 4:12 o'clock by the huge clock atop the center-field clubhouse at the Polo Grounds yesterday afternoon, Leo Durocher peered intently at his hand and decided it was time to play his trump card.

It was the last half of the tenth inning in the opening game of the 1954 world series. The tense and dramatic struggle had a gathering of 52,751, a record series crowd for the arena, hanging breathlessly on every pitch.

The score was deadlocked at 2-all. Two Giants were on the base paths and on the mound was Bob Lemon, twenty-three-game

winner of the American League, who had gone all the way and was making a heroic bid to continue the struggle a little further. Then Leo made his move.

He called on his pinch-hitter extraordinary, James (Dusty) Rhodes from Rock Hill, S. C., to bat for Monte Irvin. Lemon served one pitch. Rhodes, a left-handed batsman, swung and a lazy pop fly sailed down the right-field foul line.

Ball Just Clears Wall

The ball had just enough carry to clear the wall barely 270 feet away. But it was enough to produce an electrifying three-run homer that enabled the Giants to bring down Al Lopez' Indians, 5 to 2.

It was a breath-taking finish to as nerve-tingling a struggle as any world series had ever seen. The game had started as a stirring mound duel between 37-year-old Sal Maglie and the Tribe's brilliant Lemon.

It saw Vic Wertz, sturdy first sacker, rake Giant pitching for four of the Indians' eight hits. His first one was a triple that drove in two first-inning runs off Maglie. In the third the Polo Grounders wrenched those two tallies back from Lemon.

Then, in the eighth, Maglie faltered and Don Liddle, a mite of a southpaw, went in, almost to lose the game on the spot. With two runners on base, Wertz connected for another tremendous drive that went down the center of the field 450 feet, only to have Willie Mays make one of his

most amazing catches.

Traveling on the wings of the wind, Willie caught the ball directly in front of the green boarding facing the right-center bleachers and with his back still to the diamond.

That brought on Marvin Grissom, another Giant relief ace, who was to go the rest of the way fending off one Cleveland threat after another. And in the tenth it was Willie the Wonder who again moved into the picture.

Mays Gets a Walk

For though Mays was to go hitless throughout the afternoon, here he made an offensive maneuver that presently was to set the stage for Rhodes' game-winning homer. With one out, Mays drew a pass, his second walk of the day.

Then, with Lemon pitching carefully to Henry Thompson, Willie stole second. That immediately changed Cleveland's strategy. Thompson received an intentional pass, doubtless in the hope that Irvin, whom Durocher had insisted on playing in left field and who had been ineffective, would obligingly slap into a double play. But Monte never went to bat.

Instead, up went Dusty. An instant later he leaned into the first pitch and produced a shot that doubtless was heard around the world, though for distance it likely could go as one of the shortest homers in world series history.

The ball hit the chest of a fan

in the front row about seven feet from the foul line and bounced back on the playing field. It would have made no difference if the ball had been ruled in play, for Mays undoubtedly would have scored the winning run on the blow.

At any rate, the clout, which was only the fourth pinch homer hit in a modern fall classic, served its purpose. It sent the National Leaguers roaring out of the arena.

It was a steaming, summery afternoon right out of a July calendar. As Perry Como, accompanied by Artie White's orchestra, led the crowd in the singing of the national anthem, white shirts were the fashion in the sun-bathed seats along the left side of the park. Then the spotlight turned on 12-year-old Jimmy Barbieri, captain of Schenectady's champion team of Little Leaguers, who at this moment doubtless was the proudest youngster in all the land.

They had conferred the honor of tossing out the first ball upon Jimmy and there were lusty cheers as he fired it with a thud into the big mitt of Wes Westrum, the Giants' catcher. A moment later the fifty-first modern world series was on its way and in no time at all it became evident that not all in the packed stands were Giant partisans.

The American League had its representation, too, including disgruntled Yankee fans, not to mention a few disguised National Leaguers from Brooklyn.

And they made their presence known in no mistaken tones as Maglie got off to a shaky start that sent the Indians off to a two-run lead.

The Barber, whose control is his chief stock in trade and is usually razor sharp, confounded nearly everyone by serving three wide pitches to Al Smith, Cleveland's lead-off batter.

The fourth pitch was even wider, hitting Smith in the side, and the first man up was on Bobby Avila, the American League's batting champion, followed. Maglie served another ball, making it five in a row that missed the plate. A feeling of uneasiness swept through the stands.

Finally Maglie sent over a strike. It brought a cheer, but the applause was short-lived. For Avila stroked the next one into right field for a single and when Don Mueller, charging the ball, fumbled it, Smith raced to third. The Indians had runners on first and third with nobody out.

Here, the Barber of old asserted himself. He snuffed out Larry Doby, the American League's top home-run clouter, on the end of a pop foul that Thompson gobbled up back of third, and the slugging Al Rosen went out on an infield pop-up to Whitey Lockman.

But Maglie's opening-round troubles weren't over yet and a moment later the situation became serious as Wertz lined a powerful drive over Mueller's head in deep right-center. The ball caromed off the wall and bounded gaily past the Giant bullpen before the fleet-footed Mays collared it and started it on its way toward the infield.

Liddle Warms Up

When order was restored, Wertz was on third with a triple. Smith and Avila had crossed the plate to put the Tribe two in front and Liddle started warming up with feverish haste in the Giant bullpen. But Maglie wasn't needing any help yet. He got Dave Philley to line the ball to Mueller for the third out, and Giant fans breathed again.

In fact, in a few more minutes the New York fans were setting up quite a din of their own as, in the lower half of the first, the Polo Grounders launched their first threat against Lemon. With one down, Alvin Dark drew a pass and Mueller punched a single to right, sweeping Dark around to third.

But Lemon quickly quelled the uprising. With the crowd imploring Mays to square matters, Willie went out on a pop fly to George Strickland, Cleveland shortstop, and Thompson ended it by grounding to Wertz down the first-base line.

With the third, however, the Giants did draw even as they lashed into Lemon for three singles which, along with a pass, gave them two tallies. Lockman, the blond North Carolinian, opened the assault on the Cleveland right-hander with a single to right and a moment later was on his way to third as Dark blasted a single through the mound and into center field.

Mueller followed with a grounder to Avila that resulted in a force play at second, but it permitted Lockman to score. Mays walked and Thompson singled to right to drive in Mueller, and the contest was tied at 2—all.

What is more, the Giants had

Dusty Rhodes

runners on first and third, there was only one out and it was now Cleveland's turn to show uneasiness in the dugout. In the Tribe bullpen Art Houtteman started warming up.

But Lemon stopped the assault himself. He fanned Irvin, who patrolled left field in place of Rhodes, and Davey Williams ended matters with a grounder to short.

But the Giant fans were happy. Maglie was back on an even footing with the American League's top winning pitcher and from here on it was touch and go.

Westrum Gets Two Hits

For a time both hurlers steadied. There were two Giant singles in the fourth. One was by Westrum, the Polo Grounders' supposedly weak-hitting receiver, who contributed two blows to the New York final total of nine. But the second safety of the inning by Dark fell with two out, and Lemon got out of that spot.

Meanwhile, Maglie was staging a fine recovery, even though Wertz clipped him for a single to left in the fourth, and it wasn't until the sixth that the Barber seemed headed for more trouble. Again his tormentor was Wertz, who this time singled to right, with Mueller adding another error. Don tried to nip the runner off first, but his throw shot by Lockman and Vic wound up on second. An infield out put him on third with one down.

But Maglie got Strickland to pop up and then was saved when Thompson came up with the first of several sparkling plays he made at third. Knocking down Jim Hegan's hard smash over the bag, Henry had to recover the ball in foul territory. Yet he fired it to first in time to make the third out, and in the seventh Thompson again made a fine stop. Henry was really playing a great defensive game at the hot corner.

In the eighth, however, Maglie

faltered again. He walked Doby, and Rosen, hitless to this point, banged a scorching single off Dark's bare hand. That brought in Liddle, who saw Wertz almost wreck everything with his tremendous bid for a fourth straight hit. Mays alone saved Don with his miraculous catch in center.

Grissom went in immediately as both managers now surcharged the air with masterminding maneuvers. Lopez already had sent up Hank Majeski to pinch-hit for Philley, but when Leo switched to the right-handed Grissom, Lopez countered with Dale Mitchell, a left-handed batter. This duel of wits ended with Mitchell drawing a pass, filling the bases with one out.

The Indians were poised for a big killing, and as another lefty swinger, Dave Pope, capable of hitting a long ball, stepped up to bat for Strickland, the National League enthusiasts scarcely were able to breathe.

But Grissom slipped a third strike over on an astonished Indian and that doubtless was the turning point of the battle. A moment later the inning and big threat ended with Hegan flying out.

In the last of the eighth the Giants crowded Lemon for the first time since the third. Thompson walked and presently got around to third on a sacrifice and a wild pitch. But Westrum ended this threat with a long fly to Doby in center.

In the ninth Giant hearts stopped beating when, with two out, Irvin dropped Avila's pop fly for a two-base error. That put Grissom in a jam again, but he got out of it by giving Doby an intentional pass and rubbing out Rosen on another fly to left, which Irvin this time froze to with a great sigh of relief.

In the top of the tenth the desperately straining Clevelanders made another bid and once more Wertz started it. Vic blasted a double into left-center that even Mays couldn't track down. As Wertz jogged off the field after being replaced by a pinch-runner, Rudy Regalado, the crowd generously gave him an ovation.

Sam Dente's sacrifice put Regalado on third with only one out. But Grissom fanned Glynn after Pope walked, and Lemon, striving to win his own game, lined the ball squarely into Lockman's glove inches off the ground.

That was to prove the Indians' last threat, for in the last of the tenth it all vanished on the end of Rhodes' poke.

The pinch home run, which so spectacularly had won for the Giants all summer, had paid off again. During the regular season the Polo Grounders had set a major league record with ten pinch home runs. Rhodes contributed two of these.

In world series play the only previous pinch homers ever hit were those by Yogi Berra of the Yanks in 1947, Johnny Mize, another Yank, in 1952 and George Shuba of the Dodgers last year. And yesterday's game was the first extra-inning affair since Oct. 5, 1952, when the Dodgers beat the Yankees, 6—5, in eleven innings.

And so Leo the Lip considered

himself sitting pretty last night as he prepared to fire his southpaw ace, Johnny Antonelli, against the Clevelanders in the second game at the Polo Grounds this afternoon.

There were, to be sure, some critics unkind enough to remark that had Leo played Rhodes in left field from the beginning, victory might have come easier. Perhaps so, but then just look at the tremendous thrill the crowd, which had to pay a net sum of $316,957 into the till, would have missed.

As for Lopez, the Cleveland skipper's big hope was that his other twenty-three-game winner, Early Wynn, would fare better than Lemon and square the series before it moves to Cleveland tomorrow.

Kansas City's American League Bow a Success

32,844 FANS WATCH TEAM TRIUMPH, 6-2

Transplanted A's Top Tigers With 3-Run Sixth—Truman Makes Opening Pitch

By JOSEPH M. SHEEHAN
Special to The New York Times.

KANSAS CITY, April 12— Kansas City made a festive, happy bow into major league baseball today. To the boundless delight of an overflow crowd of 32,844 at the sparkling new Municipal Stadium, the transplanted Athletics turned back the Detroit Tigers, 6—2, in their opening game.

A three-run rally in the sixth settled matters in favor of Lou Boudreau's charges. Don Bollweg's pinch single with the bases full brought home the last two runs after Elmer Valo, also up as a pinch-hitter, had worked a pass to force home Bill Renna with the tally that put the Athletics in front.

Ewell Blackwell, recently purchased from the New York Yankees, preserved the lead for Kansas City with three scoreless innings of relief pitching. However, the official credit for the victory went to Alex Kellner, who started for the Athletics and was still the pitcher of rec-ord when they moved ahead to stay.

Many notables were on hand to join in the celebration of Kansas City's entrance into the big leagues. Former President Harry S. Truman made the ceremonial first pitch. It was a sizzling, left-handed fast ball that smacked into Joe Astroth's mitt.

Kansas Governor at Game

Gov. Fred Hall of Kansas, Lieut. Gov. James C. Blair of Missouri, Mayor H. Roe Bartle of Kansas City, the mayors of numerous surrounding communities and other high state and city officials also attended.

Ford C. Frick, the commissioner of baseball; Will Harridge, president of the American League, and Earl Hilligan, his assistant, looked on.

So did Walter O. (Spike) Briggs Jr., president of the Tigers, and Del E. Webb, co-owner of the Yankees and co-builder of the handsome new stadium here.

A particularly warmly received guest of Arnold Johnson, the new owner of the Athletics, was 92-year-old Connie Mack, under whose direction the club had operated in Philadelphia for more than half a century. Roy Mack and other members of the Mack family also came on from Philadelphia for the historic event.

Reacting to the situation, the Athletics, rather an apathetic crew in finishing last, with a 51-103 won-loss record in Philadelphia last season, put on a sprightly show for their new followers.

Kansas City has no illusions about the merits of the ball club it has adopted.' But there was obvious elation' in the stands that, on this occasion at least, the home athletes gave a major-league performance.

'Big' Inning a Hit

Certainly Boudreau, who took over the management of the Athletics after the transfer of the franchise, won friends and influenced people here by his unhesitating decision to go for the "big" inning with the score tied in the sixth.

The Athletics had scored first. A double by Bill Wilson, who had a perfect day at bat with a homer, single and a walk in addition, and a single by Joe DeMaestri gave them a run in the second. They picked up another in the third on a double by Jim Finigan and a single by Gus Zernial.

But the Tigers quickly caught up. Ray Boone's walk, a double by J. W. Porter and a long fly to right by Bill Tuttle produced a run for the visitors in the fourth. They tied the score in the fifth on Bob Wilson's homer over the left-field wall.

There will be a lot of homers hit over this twelve-foot barrier, only 330 feet from the plate at the foul line and 375 feet in left center.

In the decisive sixth, Renna greeted Ned Garver with a line double off the left-field wall. Bill Wilson walked and, after DeMaestri had advanced both runners with a grounder to third that Boone bobbled, a pass to Astroth filled the bases.

Here Boudreau made his move. He sent Valo to hit for Kellner and Elmer worked Garver for a pass. Lou then called on Boll-weg, another left-handed hitter, to bat for Vic Power. Don responded with a solid single to right that drove in Wilson and Astroth.

The Athletics added a security tally in the eighth when Bill Wilson smashed his homer, also a left-field wallop, off Van Fletcher, who had succeeded Garver in the seventh.

Keeping the Tigers off balance with assorted sweeping side-arm curves, Blackwell did the rest for Kansas City. The big right-hander, out of action all last season with a dead arm, yielded two singles and three walks, but wrapped up each of his three innings by inducing an unwary Tiger to hit into a double play.

April 13, 1955

DETROIT (A.)						KANSAS CITY (A.)					
	ab.	r.	h.	po.	a		ab.	r.	h.	po.	a
Kuenn, ss.	4	0	1	2	1	Power, 1b.	3	0	0	6	1
Hatfield, 2b.	4	0	1	2	1	bBollweg, 1b.	1	0	1	3	0
Kaline, rf.	4	0	2	3	1	Suder, 2b.	5	0	0	4	4
Boone, 3b.	2	1	0	2	5	Finigan, 3b.	4	1	1	0	3
Porter, 1b.	4	0	1	7	0	Zernial, lf.	4	0	1	2	0
Tuttle, cf.	3	0	0	1	0	Renna, rf.	4	1	1	3	0
B. Phil'ps, lf.	3	0	0	2	0	W. Wilson, cf.	3	3	3	3	0
eDelsing	0	0	0	0	0	Dema'tri, ss.	4	0	2	2	1
R. Wilson, c.	4	1	3	4	1	Astroth, c.	1	1	0	4	0
Garver, p	2	0	0	0	0	Kellner, p.	2	0	0	0	4
cFain	0	0	0	0	0	aValo	0	0	0	0	0
dMalmberg	0	0	0	0	0	Blackwell, p	0	0	0	0	0
Fletcher, p	0	0	0	1	0						
Total	30	2	8	24	9	Total	31	6	9	27	13

aWalked for Kellner in sixth.
bSingled for Power in sixth.
cWalked for Garver in seventh.
dRan for Fain in seventh.
eWalked for Phillips in ninth.
Detroit ....0 0 0 1 1 0 0 0 0—2
Kansas City .....0 1 1 0 0 3 0 1.—6
Error—Boone.
Runs batted in—Tuttle, R. Wilson, DeMaestri, Zernial, Valo, Bollweg 2, W. Wilson.
Two-base hits—Hatfield, W. Wilson, Finigan, Porter, Renna. Home runs—R. Wilson, W. Wilson. Sacrifice—Blackwell. Sacrifice fly—Tuttle. Double play—Hatfield and Kuenn, DeMaestri, Suder and Bollweg; Finigan, Suder and Bollweg; Suder and Bollweg. Left on bases—Detroit 6, Kansas City 8. Bases on balls—Off Garver 4, Fletcher 1, Kellner 1, Blackwell 3. Struck out—By Garver 3, Kellner 4. Hits—Off Garver 7 in 5 innings, Kellner 6 in 6, Fletcher 2 in 2, Blackwell 2 in 3. Runs and earned runs—Off Garver 5 and 5, Kellner 2 and 2, Fletcher 1 and 1. Hit by pitcher—By Garver (Astroth). Winning pitcher—Kellner (1-0). Losing pitcher—Garver (0-1). Umpires—Summers, Hurley, Runge and Soar. Time of game—2:38. Attendance—32,147 (paid).

National All-Stars Win in Twelfth, 6-5

By JOHN DREBINGER
Special to The New York Times.

MILWAUKEE, July 12— Short of winning a world championship, which it some day hopes to achieve, this seething baseball metropolis of the Midwest experienced its greatest baseball thrill today.

A gathering of 45,314 roaring fans watched a grimly fighting band of National Leaguers rally to draw even with the American League and carry the 1955 All-Star game into extra innings.

The fans saw, in the top half of the twelfth, their own Gene Conley, the beanpole right-hander of the Braves, step to the mound to fan three batters in a row.

In the last half of the inning they saw Stan Musial of the St. Louis Cardinals blast a home run into the right field bleachers.

The blow gave the Nationals the game, 6 to 5. It also gave Leo Durocher, who directed the National League forces, another signal triumph over Cleveland's skipper, Al Lopez, who led the American Leaguers and who last October bowed to Leo in the world series.

Lopez, during the early stages of the battle, had directed his forces well. But then he seemed to lose command in the closing rounds as the Nationals closed with a rush.

The Americans had ripped into Robin Roberts for four runs in the opening round. Three tallies rode in on a homer by the Yankees' Mickey Mantle. By the sixth the Americans had increased the advantage to 5—0.

But as the game progressed, Durocher, who hadn't been doing so well with the starting line-up the fans had voted him in the nationwide poll, began making changes of his own. The Giant manager inserted his own Willie Mays, who in the seventh inning made an electrifying catch that robbed Ted Williams of a homer, which would have given the Americans two additional runs.

On the heels of that, the Say Hey Kid, with a pair of singles, helped ignite two rallies that enabled the Nationals to draw even. They counted twice in the seventh and three times in the eighth to make it 5-all.

Meanwhile, Don Newcombe blanked the Americans in the seventh. In the eighth, the Cubs' Sam Jones got into difficulties and filled the bases with two out. But here Cincinnati's left-hander, Joe Nuxhall, entered the struggle to turn in some of the day's best pitching.

The Redlegs' hurler struck out Whitey Ford of the Yanks, a development that later was to cause some more second guessing on Lopez. Most experts seemed to feel Lopez, even though still three runs ahead, should have called on a pinch hitter, since he had ample pitching strength in Bob Turley, Herb Score and Dick Donovan.

Nuxhall held the Americans scoreless through the ninth, tenth and eleventh. Then Conley put on his magnificent performance in the twelfth as he fanned Kaline, Mickey Vernon and Al Rosen to become the eventual winner.

Sullivan Yields Homer

In gaining their winning tally, which Musial hammered out of bounds, the Nationals had to overcome an equally rugged foe-

Duke Snider watches Mickey Mantle's three-run homer for the American Leaguers disappear over the fence in the first inning.

Box Score of All-Star Game

AMERICAN LEAGUE

	ab	r	h	po	a	e
Kuenn, ss	3	1	1	1	0	0
Carrasquel, ss	3	0	2	1	3	1
Fox, 2b	3	1	1	2	0	0
Avila, 2b	1	0	0	1	2	0
Williams, lf	3	1	1	1	0	0
Smith, lf	1	0	0	0	0	0
Mantle, cf	6	1	2	3	0	0
Berra, c	6	1	1	8	2	0
Kaline, rf	4	0	1	8	2	0
Vernon, 1b	5	0	1	6	0	0
Finigan, 3b	3	0	0	1	8	0
Rosen, 3b	2	0	0	2	0	1
Pierce, p	0	0	0	0	0	0
bJensen	1	0	0	0	0	0
Wynn, p	0	0	0	0	1	0
gPower	1	0	0	0	0	0
Ford, p	1	0	0	0	1	0
Sullivan, p	1	0	0	0	0	0
Total	44	5	10	*33	9	2

NATIONAL LEAGUE

	ab	r	h	po	a	e
Schoendienst, 2b	6	0	2	3	2	0
Ennis, lf	1	0	0	1	0	0
cMusial, lf	4	1	1	0	0	0
Snider, cf	2	0	0	3	0	0
Mays, cf	3	2	2	3	0	0
Kluszewski, 1b	5	1	2	9	1	0
Mathews, 3b	2	0	0	0	3	1
Jackson, 3b	3	1	1	0	0	0
Mueller, rf	2	0	1	0	0	0
dAaron, rf	2	1	2	0	0	0
Banks, ss	2	0	0	2	1	0
Logan, ss	3	0	1	1	1	0
Crandall, c	1	0	0	1	0	0
eBurgess, c	1	0	0	2	0	0
hLopata, c	3	0	0	10	0	0
Roberts, p	0	0	0	1	1	0
aThomas	1	0	0	0	0	0
Haddix, p	0	0	0	0	2	0
fHodges	1	0	0	1	0	0
Newcombe, p	0	0	0	0	0	0
iBaker	1	0	0	0	0	0
Jones, p	0	0	0	0	0	0
Nuxhall, p	2	0	0	0	1	0
Conley, p	0	0	0	0	0	0
Total	45	6	13	36	12	1

*None out when winning run was scored.
aPopped out for Roberts in third.
bPopped out for Pierce in fourth.
cStruck out for Ennis in fourth.
dRan for Mueller in fifth.
eHit into force out for Crandall in fifth.

fSingled for Haddix in sixth.
gPopped out for Wynn in seventh.
hSafe on error for Burgess in seventh.
iFlied out for Newcombe in seventh.

```
American ............ 4 0 0   0 0 1   0 0 0   0 0 0—5
National ............ 0 0 0   0 0 0   2 3 0   0 0 1—6
```

Runs batted in—Mantle 3, Vernon, Logan, Jackson, Aaron, Musial. Two-base hits—Kluszewski, Kaline. Home runs—Mantle, Musial. Sacrifices—Pierce, Avila. Double plays—Kluszewski, Banks and Roberts; Wynn, Carrasquel and Vernon. Left on bases—American 12, National 8. Bases on balls—Roberts 1 (Williams), Ford 1 (Aaron), Jones 2 (Vernon, Rosen), Nuxhall 3 (Smith, Kaline, Avila), Sullivan 1 (Musial). Strike outs—Pierce 3 (Ennis, Snider, Banks), Haddix 2 (Kaline, Finnigan) Wynn 1 (Musial), Newcombe 1 (Avila), Jones 1 (Mantle), Nuxhall 5 (Ford, Vernon, Rosen, Sullivan, Smith), Sullivan 4 (Mays, Jackson, Logan, Lopata), Conley 3 (Kaline, Vernon, Rosen). Hits—Off Roberts 4 in 3 innings, Pierce 1 in 3, Haddix 3 in 3. Wynn 3 in 3, Newcombe 1 in 1, Jones 0 in 2-3, Ford 5 in 1 2-3, Nuxhall 2 in 3 1-3, Sullivan 4 in 3 1-3 (faced one batter in twelfth), Conley 0 in 1. Runs, earned runs—Roberts 4 and 4, Haddix 1 and 1, Ford 5 and , Sullivan 1 and 1. Hit by pitcher—By Jones (Kaline). Wild pitch—Roberts. Passed ball—Crandall. Winning pitcher—Conley. Losing pitcher—Sullivan. Umpire—Barlick (N.), Soar (A.), Boggess (N.), Summers (A.), Secory (N.), Runge (A.). Time—3:17. Attendance—45,314. Receipts (gross)—$179,545.50.

man. Frank Sullivan, the Red Sox right-hander, after relieving Ford in the eighth, had held the Nationals at bay through three and one-third innings before Musial's blow laid him low.

It was the fourth All-Star home run of his career for Stan the Man, a record for the competition. Like Mays, Musial was a late starter in the game, since he was not one of the originals chosen by the fans. Although a first sacker all this season, Stan replaced the Phils' Del Ennis in left field to allow Cincinnati's mighty Ted Kluszewski to play the entire game at first.

Musial's appearance also made him the dean of all present-day active players in All-Star competition. This was his twelfth classic, one more than Williams, who today played in his eleventh.

Williams, however, did not finish and the move doubtless was one that Lopez long will regret. He permitted the Red Sox slugger, who had singled earlier in the day, to retire after Mays made his spectacular catch to end the Americans' seventh. The Americans were still leading by five and the victory seemed safe.

Just before the battle got under way the crowd, which had tossed $179,545.50 into the till, stood in silent tribute to the memory of Arch Ward, the Chicago Tribune sports editor, who had founded the All-Star game in 1933. Funeral services for Ward were held in Chicago this morning.

Then, scarcely had the fans settled back in their seats after the singing of the National Anthem, than the American Leaguers opened fire on Roberts. The right-handed ace of the Phillies was starting his fifth mid-summer classic.

Harvey Kuenn singled to left. Nellie Fox singled to right and runners were on first and third. Next occurred a wild pitch as Roberts worked on Williams. Kuenn scored on the slip.

Roberts, who seemed to be having unusual trouble with his control, wound up walking Williams. A moment later, Mantle sent a tremendous smash straight down the middle. It cleared the barrier between the bleachers and bullpens, more than 400 feet away. It also gave the American Leaguers a 4-0 lead.

For all of five innings after that, the game became one of the most silent All-Star struggles in history. The crowd, predominantly National League in its sympathies, watched the futile efforts of its favorites to cut down the margin.

Billy Pierce, the crack southpaw of the White Sox, blanked the Nationals and allowed only one hit in the first three innings. In fact, he faced only nine batters.

Red Schoendienst, leading off the Durocher batting order, singled in the first. But the Cardinal second sacker was then rubbed out trying to steal second on a pitch that bounced out of Catcher Yogi Berra's glove.

Early Wynn, the star righthander of Lopez' Indians, then blanked the Nationals for three more innings. He gave up three blows. In the fifth, Kluszewski doubled and Don Mueller singled to left. But Kluszewski couldn't score on the hit and Wynn worked his way out of the jam.

In the sixth, the gloom of the Milwaukee fans went even a shade deeper. Harvey Haddix, a Cardinal left-hander, yielded a tally after blanking the American Leaguers in the fourth and fifth.

Berra singled and Al Kaline banged a double off Ed Mathews' wrist. The injury later sent the Braves' third sacker to the hospital for X-rays. The examination showed no fracture.

Berra went to third on Kaline's blow. Vernon bounced a grounder to Kluszewski and Yogi scooted home. The Americans were ahead, 5 to 0.

Mays Takes Over

With the seventh, however, the Nationals began to bestir themselves. The Dodgers' Duke Snider had not overly distinguished himself when he gave way in center field to Mays. Willie made his presence felt almost immediately.

Two were out and Chico Carrasquel was on first in the American's seventh when Williams stroked a powerful smash toward right center. But Willie gave chase and just as the ball appeared to clear the wire railing, the Say Hey Kid leaped up to snare the ball in his glove.

First up in the last of the seventh, Mays greeted Ford with a single to left. The Yankee southpaw had just taken the mound. He got the next two, but Hank Aaron of the Braves, in as the result of another belated, though popular, move by Durocher, drew a pass.

A moment late. the Braves' Johnny Logan singled to right and one run scored. Then Stan Lopata grounded to Carrasquel, who had just taken over at short for the Americans. Chico booted the ball, threw wide to second and a second run scored on the error.

Two were out in the eighth when the Nationals launched another offensive against Ford. Again it was Mays who started it with a single. Kluszewski and Randy Jackson, who had replaced Mathews, also singled. That scored Willie and Ford went out for Sullivan.

Before the Red Sox righthander got matters under control, Lopez was to receive another jolt as two runs tallied to tie the score.

Aaron blasted a single to right and when Kaline's throw toward third got away from Rosen for an error, both Kluszewski and

Jackson tallied. The Indians' Rosen had another delayed entry by Lopez that did not pan out so well.

The aroused Nationals appeared set for a killing in the ninth when, with two down, Schoendienst singled and Musial walked. But Sullivan this time mastered Mays and got him on a third strike.

Nuxhall drew thunderous cheers when, after walking Kaline in the tenth, he fanned three in a row, but he had a close call in the eleventh. A pass to Avila and a single by Mantle had two on with two out when

Berra bounced a grounder over second.

Schoendienst made a miraculous stop and fired the ball over his shoulder toward first. A mighty close play followed and when Yogi was called out, he protested vehemently. That, too, was to prove the American Leaguers' last gasp.

The cheering for Conley in the twelfth had barely subsided when Musial hit Sullivan's first pitch in the lower half. With that, another stirring interleague classic had gone into the records. The Americans still lead in the series, thirteen games to

nine, but the Nationals have won five of the last six contests.

For the vanquished, Berra set a record by becoming the first catcher to work five complete All-Star games. He had previously been tied with Roy Campanella at four. Three other American Leaguers went all the way today, Mantle, Kaline and Vernon. Kluszewski and Schoendienst were the two "iron men" for the triumphant National League 3.

July 13, 1955

Banks Breaks Majors' Record for Shortstops With 40th Homer as Cubs Crush Cards, 12-2

Stephens' Mark of 39 Circuit Blows for Red Sox in 1949 Season Is Surpassed

CHICAGO, Sept. 2 (UP)—Ernie Banks broke the major league record for home runs by a shortstop today. He walloped his fortieth homer of the year to lead the Chicago Cubs to a 12-2 triumph over the St. Louis Cardinals. A ladies' day crowd of 14,693 saw the game.

Banks' blow, his first homer in eighteen games since Aug. 11, came with Dee Fondy and Gene Baker on base and capped the Cubs' eight-run second inning against Tom Poholsky and Paul LaPalme. The hit was made off LaPalme on a 2-and-1 pitch and it went into the wire net behind the left-field runway.

The previous record for homers by a shortstop was thirty-

nine set by Vern Stephens with the Boston Red Sox in 1949. Banks hit his thirty-ninth against the Cincinnati Redlegs.

Chicago Home Stand Opens

The game today opened a Cubs' home stand in Wrigley Field after a fifteen-game road trip.

The victory went to Paul Minner. It was his sixth without defeat against the Cardinals this season and the twenty-first of his career over St. Louis, against seven losses.

The Cubs clinched the decision in the second when Banks, Ransom Jackson and Eddie Miksis opened with singles. Two runs scored when Alex Grammas bobbled Jim Bolger's ground ball and the bases were full again when Walker Cooper was safe on a fielder's choice.

Miksis scored on Fondy's infield single and Baker doubled for two more runs before Banks batted for the second time and knocked the ball over the fence.

The three runs batted in lifted Ernie's season total to 101.

Jackson later collected his eighteenth homer and Cooper his seventh. The triumph was the sixth for the Cubs in the last seven games and the Cards' fourth straight loss.

Poholsky suffered his tenth defeat against seven successes.

Tight Inside Pitch

After the game, Banks said, "I had a feeling that I ought to get one today. All the time we were on the road they were pitching me outside and I was hitting the ball to center field or right field.

"But the Cardinals always pitch me tight inside, and that's where LaPalme threw it. I was tired out on the road and I couldn't get around well on the outside pitches. Maybe the half-day rest before today's game did me some good."

The homer was Banks' eighth of the year off Cardinal pitch-

ing, but his first off LaPalme.

Banks has collected four grand-slam homers this season to tie the major league record.

September 3, 1955

The Box Score

ST. LOUIS (N.)	ab.	r.	h.	po.	a.	CHICAGO (N.)	ab.	r.	h.	po.	a.
Boyer. 3b.	4	1	4	2	2	Fondy. 1b.	5	1	4	10	0
S'dienst. 2b.	2	0	1	0	1	Baker. 2b.	5	1	1	3	5
Steph'n. 2b.	2	0	1	1	3	B'mholtz. lf.	4	0	0	1	0
Musial. rf.	2	0	1	0	0	Merriman.lf	1	0	0	0	0
Elliott. rf.	1	0	0	2	0	Banks. ss.	4	2	3	5	3
Wh'nant. lf.	4	0	3	0		Jackson. 3b.	5	3	2	2	0
Sarni. c.	2	0	0	3	1	Miksis. rf.	4	1	1	0	0
Burbrink. c	2	0	0	1	1	Cooper. c.	4	2	1	2	0
Virdon. cf.	4	0	1	2	0	Cooper. c.	4	2	1	5	0
Moon. 1b.	3	1	1	10	0	Minner. p.	4	1	1	1	4
Grammas.ss	4	0	2	0	3						
Poholsky. p.	1	0	0	0	1	Total	40	12	14	27	13
LaPalme. p.	0	0	0	0	1						
Mack'son. p.	1	0	0	0	0						
aRepulski	1	0	0	0	0						
McDaniel. p.	0	0	0	0	0						
bHemus	1	0	0	0	0						

Total . 34 2 11 24 12

aPopped out for Mackinson in seventh.
bGrounded out for McDaniel in ninth.

St Louis .... 0 0 1 0 0 0 0 0 1—2
Chicago .... 0 8 2 0 0 1 1 0 .—12

Errors—Grammas. Moon.
Runs batted in—Bolger. Fondy 3. Baker 2. Banks 3. Jackson. Cooper. Moon.
Two-base hits—Boyer. Musial. Baker. Bolzer. Fondy 2. Grammas. Home runs—Banks. Jackson. Cooper. Moon. Double plays—Minner and Baker: Baker. Banks and Fondy 2; Baker and Fondy. Left on bases—St. Louis 7. Chicago 5. Bases on balls Minner 2. McDaniel 1. Struck out—By Minner 5. Poholsky 2. Mackinson 1. Hits—Off Poholsky 5 in 1 1-3 innings. La Palme 1 in 2-3. Mackinson 6 in 4. McDaniel 2 in 2. Runs and earned run—Off Minner 2 and 2. Poholsky 7 and 4. La Palme 1 and 0. Mackinson 3 and 3. McDaniel 1 and 1. Winning pitcher—Minner (8-8). Losing pitcher—Poholsky (7-10). Umpires Pinelli. Gorman. Boggess and Engeln. Time of game—2:20. Attendance—8,160 (paid).

DODGERS CAPTURE 1ST WORLD SERIES; PODRES WINS, 2-0

He Beats Yanks Second Time as Team Takes Classic in 8th Try, 4 Games to 3

HODGES DRIVES IN 2 RUNS

By JOHN DREBINGER

Brooklyn's long cherished dream finally has come true. The

Dodgers have won their first world series championship.

The end of the trail came at the Stadium yesterday. Smokey Alston's Brooks, with Johnny Podres tossing a brilliant shutout, turned back Casey Stengel's Yankees, 2 to 0, in the seventh and deciding game of the 1955 baseball classic.

This gave the National League champions the series, 4 games to 3. As the jubilant victors almost smothered their 23-year-old left-handed pitcher from Witherbee, N. Y., a roaring crowd of 62,465 joined in sounding off a thunderous ovation. Not even the stanchest American League diehard could begrudge Brooklyn its finest hour.

Seven times in the past had the Dodgers been thwarted in

their efforts to capture baseball's most sought prize—the last five times by these same Bombers.

When the goal finally was achieved the lid blew off in Brooklyn, while experts, poring into the records, agreed nothing quite so spectacular had been accomplished before. For this was the first time a team had won a seven-game world series after losing the first two games.

Victor in Third Game

And Podres, who had vanquished the Yankees in the third game as the series moved to Ebbets Field last Friday, became the first Brooklyn pitcher to win two games in one series.

Tommy Byrne, a seasoned campaigner who was the Yanks'

"comeback hero of the year," carried the Bombers' hopes in this dramatic struggle in which victory would have given them their seventeenth series title. But Byrne, whose southpaw slants had turned back the Dodgers in the second encounter, could not quite cope with the youngster pitted against him.

In the fourth inning a two-bagger by Roy Campanella and a single by Gil Hodges gave the Brooks their first run.

In the sixth a costly Yankee error helped fill the bases. It forced the withdrawal of Byrne, though in all he had given only three hits.

Stengel called on his right-handed relief hurler, Bob Grim. Bob did well enough. But he couldn't prevent Hodges from lifting a long sacrifice fly to center that drove in Pee Wee Reese with the Brooks' second run of the day.

Fortified with this additional tally, Podres then blazed the way through a succession of thrills while a grim band of Dodgers fought with the tenacity of inspired men to hold the advantage to the end.

Fittingly, the final out was a grounder by Elston Howard to Reese, the 36-year-old shortstop and captain of the Flock. Ever since 1941 had the Little Colonel from Kentucky been fighting these Yankees. Five times had he been forced to accept the loser's share.

Many a heart in the vast arena doubtless skipped a beat as Pee Wee scooped up the ball and fired it to first. It was a bit low and wide. But Hodges, the first sacker, reached out and grabbed it inches off the ground. Gil would have stretched halfway across the Bronx for that one.

Thus to the 43-year-old Walter E. Alston of Darrtown, Ohio, goes the distinction of piloting a Dodger team to its first world title. As a player, Smokey had appeared in the majors only long enough to receive one time at bat with the Cardinals. What is more, he ruefully recalls, he struck out.

Dropped back to the minors soon after that, Alston didn't appear in the majors again until he was named manager of the Brooks in 1954.

Yet, in his second year he not only led the Dodgers to an overwhelming triumph for the National League pennant but also attained a prize that had eluded such managerial greats as the late Uncle Wilbert Robinson, Leo Durocher, Burt Shotton and Chuck Dressen.

The Dodgers made their first world series appearance in 1916. They lost to the Boston Red Sox. In 1920 they bowed to the Cleveland Indians. Then in 1941, '47, '49, '52 and '53 they went down before the mighty Bombers.

As for the Yanks, the defeat brought to an end a string of world series successes without parallel. Victors in sixteen classics, they suffered only their fifth setback. It was their first defeat under Charles Dillon Stengel, who bagged five in a row from 1949 through 1953.

Giants, Cards Did Trick

Back in 1921 and 1922 the Bombers lost to John McGraw's Giants. Until yesterday the Cardinals had been the only other National League champions to stop them. St. Louis won in 1926 and again in 1942. Since then the Yankees had bagged seven classics until the Brooks broke their spell.

Perfect baseball weather again greeted the belligerents as the battle lines were drawn for this final conflict.

The crowd, though smaller than for the three previous Stadium games, contributed $407,-549 to the series pool, to help set a world series "gate" total of $2,337,515. This, of course,

The New York Times

BATTERY IS CHARGED WITH VICTORY: Johnny Podres is hoisted aloft by Catcher Roy Campanella after pitching the Dodgers to triumph over Yankees yesterday in seventh game of the world series. Don Hoak, third baseman, rushes over to join the festivities.

is apart from the addition revenues derived from radio and television.

As the players took the field there was a final check on the invalids, of whom both sides provided more than a fair share.

Duke Snider was back in the Dodger line-up. Duke had gone out of the sixth game on Monday with a twisted knee when he stepped in a small hole fielding a pop fly in center field.

But Jackie Robinson, who had fought so valiantly for the Brooks in the three straight games they won in Ebbets Field, had to remain on the sidelines. He was suffering from a strained Achilles tendon in his right leg. So Don Hoak played third.

Bauer in Right Field

In the Yankee camp, Hank Bauer, the ex-marine, was in right field again despite a pulled thigh muscle. But Mickey Mantle, a serious loss to the Bombers throughout the series, was still out with his painfully torn leg muscle. He did manage to get into the game for one pinch-hit performance. His best was a towering, though

harmless, pop fly.

Since the Yanks, who on Monday had squared the series by crushing the left-handed Karl Spooner with a five-run first-inning blast, were again being confronted by a southpaw, Stengel strung along with his right-handed batting power. But defensively this was to prove costly. For it was Bill Skowron, his first-sacker, who made the damaging fielding slip in the sixth.

For three innings Podres and Byrne maintained a scoreless deadlock. Skowron, a right-handed hitter who had stunned the Brooks with his three-run homer into the right-field stands Monday, gave them another mild jolt in the second.

This time he bounced a ground-rule double into the same stands. But there already were two out and Podres quickly checked this scoring bid.

There again were two out when the Yanks strove to break through in the third with a threat that had a freakish end. Phil Rizzuto walked. Incidentally, this was Li'l Phil's fifty-

second world series game, topping by one the record held by Joe DiMaggio.

Behind that pass Billy Martin singled to right, Rizzuto pulling up at second. Gil McDougald then chopped a bounding ball down the third-base line. Had Hoak fielded it he doubtless would have been unable to make a play anywhere.

But Don didn't get his hands on it. The ball struck Rizzuto at the moment L'il Phil was sliding into third base. McDougald, of course, received credit for a hit. But Rizzuto was declared out for getting hit by a batted ball and the inning was over.

In the fourth the Dodgers broke through for the first run and they did it with their first two hits off Byrne.

The 35-year-old lefty from Wake Forest, N. C., had just fanned Snider for the first out when Campanella slammed a double into left. Roy moved to third on Carl Furillo's infield out and a moment later Campy was over the plate on Hodges' solid single into left.

In the last of this round

Podres had to turn back a serious Yankee threat. A mix-up of signals in the usually smooth operating Dodger outfield had Johnny in a hole.

Yogi Berra lifted an easy fly slightly to the left of center. It appeared to be a simple catch for Snider. But Junior Gilliam, who had started the game in left, also dashed for the ball. As a result the Duke at the last second shied away from the ball and it fell to the ground for a flukey two-bagger.

Since this happened on the first play of the Yankee inning, Podres had his work cut out for him. But he got Bauer on a fly to right. Skowron grounded to Zimmer and Bob Cerv ended it with a pop to Reese.

A single by Reese started the drive against Byrne in the sixth. Ill fortune then overtook Tommy in a hurry. Snider laid down a sacrifice bunt. Byrne fielded it and flipped it to Skowron, who had an easy out at first. But Moose, who had been the big hero on Monday, now became the goat.

Seeking to make the out on Snider by way of a tag, Skowron had the ball knocked out of his hand and the Dodgers had two aboard. Campanella then sacrificed and the runners were on second and third.

Byrne was allowed to remain long enough to give Furillo an intentional pass. Then Tommy gave way to Grim. But Bob couldn't keep Hodges from hitting a long fly to center that scored Reese with the second run of the game.

For a moment it looked as if the Dodgers would pile up more since Grim, before steadying, unfurled a wild pitch and gave a pass to Hoak to fill the bases a second time.

But here Alston called on Shotgun George Shuba to pinchhit for Zimmer. George grounded to Skowron to end the round.

However, this maneuver indirectly was to play a prominent part in what followed. For, just as on Monday Stengel's move to replace Skowron by the betterfielding Joe Collins at first had resulted in the nipping of a

Dodger threat, something of the sort now worked for Alston.

For with Zimmer out, Gilliam was switched to second base and Sandy Amoros went in as the left fielder. Minutes later Sandy was to make a glittering catch and throw that were to save the Brooks some mighty bad moments.

Martin walked in the last of the sixth and McDougald outgalloped a bunt for a hit to put two on with nobody out. Berra then stroked an outside pitch, the ball sailing down the leftfield foul line.

It appeared to be a certain hit. But Amoros, racing at top speed, stuck out his glove and caught the ball in front of the stand. Martin, meanwhile had played it fairly safe and was only a few feet up from second.

But McDougald had gone well down from first, with the result that when Sandy fired the ball to Reese, who in turn relayed it to Hodges at first, McDougald was doubled off the bag by inches. It was a killing play for the Yanks.

Then in the eighth the Bombers made their last bid. Rizzuto, fighting heroically to the last, singled to left. Martin flied out. But McDougald slashed a fierce hopper down the third-base line that struck Hoak on the shoulder and bounded away for a single.

The Yanks again had two on and with the still dangerous Berra and Bauer the next two batters. Podres now turned on his finest pitching of the afternoon. He got Berra on a short pop-up that Furillo snared in right. He then fanned Bauer amid a deafening salvo of cheers.

That about clinched it. For even though Bob Turley tossed two scoreless rounds for the Yanks in the eighth and ninth, Stengel's best stretch of relief pitching in the entire series had come too late and to no purpose.

Podres, who had just turned 23 on Friday when he tripped the Yanks the first time in this series, made short work of the Bombers in the last of the ninth.

He allowed eight hits in bagging his second triumph of the series but he was always in command.

This also was only the third time a Brooklyn pitcher had scored a series shutout. Burleigh Grimes did it in 1920 against the Indians and Preacher Roe tossed one against the Yanks in 1949.

Thus an amazing season came to a close for Brooklyn. Earlier in the year those beloved "Bums" had ripped the National League flag race apart by winning twenty-two of their first twenty-four games. It was a runaway pace that enabled them to clinch the flag on Sept. 8 by a margin of seventeen games.

And now the Dodgers are the world champions after as extraordinary a series as has been played. For six days the home team won. The Yanks won the first two games with their lefthanded pitchers, Whitey Ford and Byrne, at the Stadium. Then the Brooks tore off three in a row in Brooklyn.

But when Stengel tried to make it again with his two lefties he slipped up. Ford came through to win a second time on Monday to square it at 3-all. But in this final test, Byrne, a tower of strength to the Yanks in their stirring pennant fight, wasn't up to taking the youthful Podres.

Johnny, recovering from a sore arm, which had plagued him in midseason, more than took up the slack caused by the loss of Don Newcombe's services.

Far into the night rang shouts of revelry in Flatbush. Brooklyn at long last has won a world series and now let someone suggest moving the Dodgers elsewhere!

National Leaguers, too, were rejoicing. For, coming after the Giants' triumph over the Indians last October, this marks the first time since 1933 and 1934 that the senior loop has been able to put together two successive series winners. In 1933 and 1934 the Giants and Cardinals did it.

The Box Score

SEVENTH GAME

BROOKLYN DODGERS

	AB.	R.	H.	PO.	A.
Gilliam, lf., 2b.....	4	0	1	2	0
Reese, ss..........	4	1	1	2	6
Snider, cf..........	3	0	0	2	0
Campanella, c......	3	1	1	5	0
Furillo, rf.........	3	0	0	3	0
Hodges, 1b........	2	0	1	10	0
Hoak, 3b..........	3	0	1	1	1
Zimmer, 2b........	2	0	0	0	2
aShuba	1	0	0	0	0
Amoros, lf........	0	0	0	2	1
Podres, p.........	4	0	0	0	1
Total	29	2	5	27	11

NEW YORK YANKEES

	AB.	R.	H.	PO.	A.
Rizzuto, ss........	3	0	1	1	3
Martin, 2b........	3	0	1	1	6
McDougald, 3b.....	4	0	3	1	1
Berra, c..........	4	0	1	4	1
Bauer, rf.........	4	0	0	1	0
Skowron, 1b......	4	0	1	11	1
Cerv, cf.........	4	0	0	5	0
Howard, lf........	4	0	1	2	0
Byrne, p..........	2	0	0	0	2
Grim, p..........	1	0	0	0	0
bMantle	1	0	0	0	0
Turley, p........	0	0	0	0	0
Total	33	0	8	27	14

aGrounded out for Zimmer in sixth.

bPopped out for Grim in seventh.

Brooklyn ......0 0 0 1 0 1 0 0 0—2
New York......0 0 0 0 0 0 0 0 0—0

Error—Skowron.
Runs batted in—Hodges 2.
Two-base hits—Skowron, Campanella, Berra. Sacrifices—Snider, Campanella. Sacrifice fly—Hodges. Double play—Amoros, Reese and Hodges. Left on bases—Brooklyn 8. New York 8. Bases on balls—Off Byrne 3 (Hodges, Gilliam, Furillo), Grim 1 (Hoak), Turley 1 (Amoros), Podres 2 (Rizzuto, Martin). Struck out—By Byrne 2 (Snider, Zimmer), Grim 1 (Reese), Turley 1 (Snider), Podres 4 (McDougald), Byrne 2, Bauer). Hits—Off Byrne 3 in 5 1/3 innings, Grim 1 in 1 2/3, Turley 1 in 2. Runs and earned runs—Off Byrne 2 and 1. Wild pitch—Grim. Losing pitcher—Byrne.

Umpires—Honochick (A.), plate; Dascoli (N.), first base; Summers (A.), second base; Ballanfant (N.), third base; Flaherty (A.), left field; Donatelli (N.), right field. Time of game—2:44. Paid attendance—62,465.

October 5, 1955

BERRA IS NAMED MOST VALUABLE IN LEAGUE AGAIN

By JOHN DREBINGER
Special to The New York Times.

CHICAGO, Dec. 3—Yogi Berra, a potent factor in the seven pennants the Yankees have won in the last nine campaigns, again has been named the American League's most valuable player.

The Bombers' stout-hearted and strong-armed catcher was declared the winner today of the twenty-four-man-committee poll of the Baseball Writers Association that decided the disposition of the Kenesaw Mountain Landis Trophy for 1955.

The election, however, was a tight one. Yogi finished on top with 218 points. Second place went to Al Kaline, the Detroit Tigers' slugging young outfielder and the season's American League batting champion.

Kaline polled 201 points against an even 200 for Al Smith, the Cleveland Indians' fine outfielder and utility infielder.

Each member of the committee rated ten players on his ballot, points being scored on a basis of 14 for first place, 9 for second, 8 for third and so on down to one for tenth.

Foxx Pioneer in Feat

Berra thus becomes the third player in American League history to win the award three times. Jimmy Foxx, powerful home run clouter of the then Philadelphia Athletics, won it in 1932 and 1933 and again in 1938 as a member of the Boston Red Sox.

That mark was not equaled until Joe DiMaggio, the Yankee

Clipper, came along to win the prize in 1939, 1941 and 1947. Berra gained his previous crowns in 1951 and 1954. Only one other player, besides Foxx and Berra, has won the award in two successive years. The Tigers' Hal Newhouser made it in 1944 and 1945.

The first writers' poll was conducted in 1931, with the Athletics' Bob Grove the American League victor. In the National League, only one player has captured the award three times, the Cardinals' Stan Musial having taken it in 1943, 1946 and 1948.

Ted Williams, famed Red Sox

player and a former winner, placed fourth in the 1955 poll with 143, followed by the Yankees' Mickey Mantle with 113 points.

Rounding out the first ten were Ray Narleski, the Indians' indefatigable relief hurler, with 90; Nellie Fox, Chicago White Sox, 84; Hank Bauer, Yankees, 64; Vic Power, Kansas City Athletics, 53, and Jackie Jensen, Red Sox, 39. In all, twenty-nine players received votes.

Berra, Kaline and Smith were the only candidates to be named on all twenty-four ballots. Oddly, though Smith finished only third in the point score, he tied Berra for first-place ballots with seven apiece. Kaline drew four first-place votes, but rolled up points with six seconds and six fourths.

Berra received only two second-place counts, but followed with six thirds, four fourths, three fifths, one sixth and one eighth.

In addition to the first three, the only players to receive first-place ballots were Williams, Narleski, Bauer and Power, each of whom was named once, and Gil McDougald. Gil had a curious count. The Yankee infielder picked up two first-place ballots, but was named on only one other, for fifth place.

The 30-year-old Berra has been a New York stalwart since 1947. In the ensuing years he has compiled a lifetime batting average of .293, with a total of 208 home runs and 898 runs batted in for an even 1,200 games. Last season, catching 147 games, Yogi's batting mark slipped to .272, his lowest since he entered the majors.

But there was no denying he was still the great driving force of the American League champions, their most dependable clutch hitter, in addition to being an almost flawless receiver. He hit twenty-seven homers and drove in 108 runs to make 1955 his fourth year over the 100 mark.

In Service Two Years

Berra, who was born in St. Louis, began his professional career in 1943 with Norfolk in the Yankee farm system. He just missed becoming a St. Louis Cardinal because Branch Rickey, then head man of the Redbirds, refused to pay him an additional $500. Following two years in service, Yogi was promoted to the Newark club in 1946 and in 1947 was a full-time Yankee.

He was also a part-time outfielder, but he soon established himself as a receiver and as such has been rated tops in the American League since 1949.

Last October saw Yogi in his seventh world series. He has been the American League's catcher in seven All-Star games.

The point totals in the voting: Yogi Berra, New York, 218; Al Kaline, Detroit, 201; Al Smith, Cleveland, 200; Ted Williams, Boston, 143; Mickey Mantle, New York, 113; Ray Narleski, Cleveland, 90; Nellie Fox, Chicago, 84; Hank Bauer, New York, 64; Vic Power, Kansas City, 53; Jackie Jensen, Boston, 39; Sherman Lollar, Chicago, 37; Gil McDougald, New York, 34; Billy Klaus, Boston, 24; Tommy Byrne, New York, 24; Whitey Ford, New York, 21; Ray Boone, Detroit, 16; Roy Sievers, Washington, 9; Harvey Kuenn, Detroit, 8; Billy Pierce, Chicago, 8; Dave Philley, Cleveland and Baltimore, 6; Early Wynn, Cleveland, 6; Elmer Valo, Kansas City, 5; Mickey Vernon, Washington, 4, and Billy Hoeft, Detroit; Don Mossi, Cleveland; Frank Sullivan, Boston; Gus Triandos, Baltimore; Jose Valdivielso, Washington, and Sammy White, Boston, 1 each.

December 4, 1955

Campanella Is Named as Most Valuable in National League

DODGERS' CATCHER PICKED THIRD TIME

Campanella Captures Honors by 5 Points Over Snider— Banks of Cubs Is Next

By ROSCOE McGOWEN

For the third time in his eight-year National League career, Roy Campanella won the most valuable player award yesterday The other great local catcher, Yogi Berra of the Yankees, recently gained the American League honors for 1955, also his third such citation.

It was a close race between the star Brooklyn catcher and his center-field team-mate, Duke Snider. Each received eight first-place votes, but the balloting by the twenty-four-member committee of the Baseball Writers Association from second place on down decided the issue.

Campanella's total was 226 points and the Duke received 221. The point system was based on 14 for a first-place ballot, 9 for second, 8 for third and so on, down to 1 for tenth.

Campanella received six second-place votes, three third-place, four for fifth and three for seventh place. Snider, who, amazingly, was omitted from one ballot, drew four seconds, two thirds, five fourths, three fifths and one seventh.

Reese and Roberts Cited

Ernie Banks of the Chicago Cubs, who set a record for home runs by a shortstop with 44, drew six first-place ballots. The other candidates who received first-place votes were Robin Roberts, ace right-handed pitcher of the Phillies, and Pee Wee Reese, captain and shortstop of the Dodgers, who drew one each.

Banks finished third with 195 points and the Giants' Willie Mays was fourth with 165. Roberts finished fifth with 159 and Reese tied for ninth with Henry Aaron, Milwaukee Braves' outfielder, at 36.

Brooklyn's twenty-game winning pitcher, Don Newcombe, had 89 points in seventh place, behind Ted Kluszewski, Cincinnati Redlegs' first baseman, who scored 111.

Three players, in addition to Campanella and Berra, have been three-time winners of the most valuable player award in the majors. In the American League Jimmy Foxx of the then Philadelphia Athletics won it in 1932, 1933 and 1938, and Joe DiMaggio of the Yankees in 1939, 1941 and 1947. Stan Musial, St. Louis Cardinal star, was the National League winner in 1943, 1946 and 1948.

Berra and Campy both captured the honors in 1951. Berra repeated in 1954 and Campanella in 1953.

Campy had a sad season in 1954. His injured left hand reduced him to a .207 batting average, with only nineteen homers and fifty-one runs batted in, and he didn't receive a single vote for the award that year. His hand was operated on twice in 1954, in May and after the season ended.

Despite an injury to his left kneecap, which put him out of action for more than two weeks in midseason, Roy caught in 123 games and was one of the big reasons the Dodgers won the 1955 flag.

He finished fourth in the National League batting averages with a mark of .318, a fraction of a point behind Musial and Mays, but all were several points below the batting champion, Richie Ashburn, Philly outfielder.

Scored Decisive Series Run

Campy belted thirty-two home runs in 1955. That put his major league total at 209, twenty-seven below the mark for catchers set by Gabby Hartnett of the Cubs.

Roy whacked twenty doubles and one triple and batted in 107 runs this year. Perhaps his most important double, however, was one that didn't figure in the season statistics. That two-bagger came in the seventh and deciding game of the world series against the Yankees.

Following that blow Campy scored on a single to left by Gil Hodges. It proved enough to win for the glittering young pitching hero of the series, Johnny Podres.

Campy scored eighty-one runs during the regular season and his hits totaled 142.

Roy has had three seasons with Brooklyn in which he has batted in 100 or more runs and four campaigns in which he has hit thirty or more homers. It was in 1953 that Campanella set a record for runs batted in by a catcher with 142.

December 9, 1955

Long Extends Homer Streak

FRIEND'S 2-HITTER TOPS BROOKS, 3-2

Pirates' Pitcher Helped in Posting No. 8 by Long's 8th Homer in 8 Games

By JOHN DREBINGER
Special to The New York Times.

PITTSBURGH, May 28—There was no stopping Dale Long or the Pirates tonight.

Responding to the roars of 32,221 fans, the Bucs' spectacular first sacker exploded another home run for his eighth four-bagger in eight consecutive games. The blow broke the record of seven homers in seven games set by Long in Philadelphia last Saturday.

And while he was about this, the rambunctious Pirates, behind the two-hit pitching of Bob Friend, brought down Carl Erskine and the Dodgers, 3 to 2, in the opener of a two-game series.

The outcome enabled the Pirates to retain their hold on third place and it dropped the stunned world champions deeper in the second division. Friend scored his eighth mound triumph of the year against two defeats. The Pittsburgh right-hander has won five in a row, the last four being complete games.

Homer for Snider

Jarred in the first inning by Duke Snider's 450-foot two-run homer, the Bucs fought heroically for this game. And they made it when two of Long's colleagues, Lee Walls and Hank Foiles, weighed in with triples, each productive of a tally.

Long hit his homer in the fourth and it was something more than ornamental. Leading off the inning, it tied the score at 2—all.

It was a well stroked ball that sailed into the lower right-field stands beyond the 375-foot marker. It was also No. 14 for the six-foot four-inch, 30-year-old Long who, prior to last season, had spent most of his first eleven years in baseball in the minor leagues.

Fans were still streaming into the arena when Junior Gilliam, leading off for the Brooks in the first, drew a pass. After Pee Wee Reese, trying to bunt, had gone out on a pop foul, Snider sent a mighty drive down the center of the fairway. It cleared the wall just alongside of the 436-foot marker. The homer was the Duke's seventh of the year.

Five Dodgers Walk

However, after that blow Friend was to give up only one more hit, a single by Gilliam in the third. Five other Dodgers got to first on walks.

The Bucs scored their first tally in the second when Walls sent Snider chasing his long triple in left center. Walls scored on Gene Freese's sacrifice fly.

Then, after Long had sent the crowd wild by tying the score with his record shot in the fourth, Foiles tossed the gathering into another uproar in the fifth.

First up, the Pirate catcher hit a foul on an attempted bunt. Then he smacked the ball over Snider's head in deep center for another three-bagger. A pinch single by Bob Skinner sent Hank home and Friend made the run stand up to the end.

Long's homer was his only blow of the night. He grounded out the first time up and fanned on his last two tries. Clem Labine, who pitched the eighth for the Dodgers, got Dale for the second strike-out.

The defeat was Erskine's fourth against two victories. It also marked the third time the Hoosier right-hander had failed to go the distance after his no-hitter against the Giants on May 12.

BROOKLYN (N.)						PITTSBURGH (N.)					
	ab.	r.	h.	po.	a.		ab.	r.	h.	po.	a.
Gilliam, 2b	3	1	1	1	1	Virdon, cf	4	0	1	3	0
Reese, ss	3	0	0	3	4	Groat, ss	4	0	0	1	7
Snider, cf	3	1	1	3	1	Long, 1b	4	1	1	14	0
C'mp'nella,c	4	0	0	5	0	Thomas, lf	4	0	2	1	0
Hodges, 1b	3	0	0	9	2	cClem'nte,lf	0	0	0	0	0
Robinson,3b	3	0	0	1	1	Walls, rf	4	1	1	1	0
Amoros, lf	3	0	0	0	0	Freese, 3b	3	0	0	0	3
Furillo, rf	3	0	1	0	0	Foiles, c	2	1	1	5	1
Erskine, p	2	0	1	3	0	J.O'Brien,2b	1	0	0	1	2
bJackson	1	0	0	0	0	aSkinner	1	0	1	0	0
Labine, p	0	0	0	0	1	Roberts, 2b	0	1	1	2	1
						Friend, p	2	0	0	0	1
Total	26	2	2	24	13	Total	30	3	8	27	16

aSingled for J. O'Brien in fifth.
bGrounded out for Erskine in eighth.
cRan for Thomas in eighth.

Brooklyn	2 0 0	0 0 0	0 0 0—2
Pittsburgh	0 1 0	1 1 0	0 0 .—3

Error—Gilliam.
Runs batted in—Snider 2, Freese, Long, Skinner.
Two-base hit—Roberts. Three-base hits—Walls, Foiles. Home runs—Snider, Long. Sacrifice—Friend. Sacrifice fly—Freese. Double plays—Erskine, Reese and Hodges; Groat, J. O'Brien and Long; Groat, Roberts and Long. Left on bases—Brooklyn 3, Pittsburgh 6. Bases on balls—Off Erskine 1, Friend 6. Struck out—By Erskine 3, Labine 1, Friend 3. Hits—Off Erskine 7 in 7 innings, Labine 1 in 1. Runs and earned runs—Off Erskine 3 and 3, Friend 2 and 2. Winning pitcher—Friend (8-2). Losing pitcher—Erskine (2-4). Umpires—Ballanfant. Gore, Jackowski and Crawford. Time of game—2:13. Attendance—32,221.

May 29, 1956

Mantle Hits 19th and 20th Homers

BOMBERS RECORD 4-3, 12-5 VERDICTS

Mantle's First-Game Homer 18 Inches Short of Going Over Roof at Stadium

By JOSEPH M. SHEEHAN

Mickey Mantle clouted two homers, including one of colossal proportions, as the Yankees, with five four-baggers in all, downed the Washington Senators, 4—3, and 12—5, before a throng of 29,825 at the Stadium yesterday.

As a result of their double triumph, Casey Stengel's rampaging Bombers stretched to six games their lead over the second-place White Sox, who beat the Indians twice.

No more than eighteen inches of elevation kept the muscular Mantle from achieving the distinction of being the first player to hit a fair ball out of the Stadium.

Mickey's nineteenth homer, hit off Pedro Ramos on a 2-2 count in the fifth inning of the opener, was a skyscraper wallop to right that hit just below the top of the roof cornice high above the third deck.

Even though Mantle did not quite get enough loft to clear everything, he reached previously unplumbed territory with his mighty drive. No one previously got close to hitting the roof facade at the home of champions.

A check of Stadium blueprints disclosed that the ball struck at a point about 370 feet from the plate some 117 feet above the ground. While it obviously was descending when it hit the cornice, it retained enough velocity to rebound on to the field.

"I've never seen anything like it before," the Yankees said between games.

Mickey allowed, "it was the best I ever hit a ball left-handed."

There was nothing modest, either, about the dimensions of Mantle's twentieth homer, which he clouted off Pascual in the fifth inning of the nightcap. It carried halfway up into the right-field bleachers, just to the left of the bullpen.

With sixteen homers in this merry month of May, Mickey is eleven games ahead of Babe Ruth's record sixty-homer pace of 1927. The Babe hit No. 20 in his fifty-second game on June 11, and had only fourteen on Memorial Day.

By way of demonstrating his versatility, Mantle also contributed a nifty third-strike drag bunt single, a right-handed line single, a stolen base and a rifle throw in the first game and drew a pass in the second game.

Excused after seven innings of the second game, Mantle ended the day leading the majors in six offensive departments: Runs (45), hits (65), total bases (135), homers (20), runs batted in (50) and batting average (.425).

Hank Bauer and Eddie Robinson joined Mantle as homer

Yankees' Box Scores

FIRST GAME

WASHINGTON (A.)						NEW YORK (A.)					
	ab.	r.	h.	po.	a.		ab.	r.	h.	po.	a.
Yost, 3b	4	0	0	1	1	Bauer, rf	4	1	1	1	0
Luttrell, ss	4	0	2	5	5	McD'g'd, ss	3	1	1	2	5
Herzog, lf	3	0	1	3	0	Mantle, cf	4	1	3	3	0
Sievers, 1b	4	0	0	10	0	Berra, c	2	0	0	6	1
Lemon, rf	2	0	2	0	0	Collins, lf	3	0	0	2	1
K'brew, 2b	4	1	0	1	1	bHoward	1	0	0	0	0
Olson, cf	1	1	3	1	0	Rob'son, 1b	3	0	0	6	0
Berberet, c	2	0	0	1	0	Martin, 2b	1	0	0	7	2
Courtney, c	2	0	1	0	0	Carey, 3b	4	0	1	0	3
Ramos, p	2	0	0	0	0	Kucks, p	2	1	1	0	0
aRunnels	1	1	1	0	0	Morgan, p	1	0	0	0	0
Stewart, p	0	0	0	0	0						
cPaula	1	0	0	0	0	Total	31	4	7	27	12
Total		33	3	8	24	8						

aTripled for Ramos in seventh.
bGrounded out for Collins in seventh.
cFlied out for Stewart in ninth.

Washington	0 1 0	0 0 0	2 0 0—3
New York	0 0 0	0 3 1	0 0 .—4

Errors—Killebrew, Mantle 3, Bauer.
Runs batted in—Berberet, Runnels, Luttrell, Mantle 3, Bauer.
Two-base hits—Herzog, Runnels. Home run—Mantle. Sacrifice—Herzog. Double play—Martin, McDougald and Robinson. Left on bases—Washington 7, New York 8. Bases on balls—Off Ramos 5, Kucks 4. Struck out—By Ramos 1, Kucks 4. Hits—Off Ramos 5 in 6 innings, Kucks 4 in 7 1-3, Stewart 2 in 2, Morgan 1 in 1 2-3. Runs and earned runs—Off Ramos 4 and 4, Kucks 3 and 3. Winning pitcher—Kucks (6-2). Losing pitcher—Ramos (3-2). Umpires—Summers, McKinley, Flaherty and Rice. Time—2:36.

SECOND GAME

WASHINGTON (A.)						NEW YORK (A.)					
	ab.	r.	h.	po.	a.		ab.	r.	h.	po.	a.
Yost, 3b	2	9	1	2	3	Bauer, rf	6	3	3	2	0
Luttrell, ss	3	0	1	0	0	Martin, 2b	3	1	1	4	2
Herzog, lf	2	0	1	1	0	cJ.C'man, 2b	1	0	0	1	0
Sievers, 1b	4	0	0	5	0	Mantle, cf	4	1	1	1	0
Courtney, c	3	2	1	7	0	Howard, lf	4	1	1	1	0
Olson, cf	5	0	1	3	0	Berra, c	3	1	2	6	1
Lemon, rf	2	1	0	3	0	Col'ns, lf-cf	4	1	1	2	1
Kill'brew, 2b	3	1	1	3	2	Rob'son, 1b	4	2	1	10	0
Pascual, p	2	1	1	0	0	M'D'gald, ss	3	3	1	1	4
aPaula	1	0	0	0	0	Carey, 3b	3	2	1	1	3
Stewart, p	0	0	0	0	0	Turley, p	4	0	2	1	2
bOravetz	0	0	0	0	0	Stur'vant, p	1	0	0	0	0
Clev'nger, p	0	0	0	0	1						
Total		30	5	8	24	7	Total	37	12	13	27	13

aFouled out for Pascual in seventh.
bWalked for Stewart in eighth.
cGrounded out for Martin in eighth.

Washington	0 1 1	0 0 0	0 2 0—5
New York	1 2 0	0 1 5	0 3 .—12

Errors—Sievers, Lemon.
Runs batted in—Bauer 3, Lemon, Robinson 2, Herzog, Killebrew, Collins 3, Turley, Oravetz, Yost, Carey.
Two-base hits—Yost, Berra, McDougald, Collins, Carey. Home runs—Bauer 2, Robinson, Killebrew, Mantle. Stolen bases—Carey 2. Sacrifice—Luttrell. Sacrifice fly—Lemon. Double plays—Berra and Martin; McDougald, Martin and Robinson. Left on bases—Washington 10, New York 12. Bases on balls—Off Turley 9, Pascual 3, Stewart 1, Sturdivant 1, Clevenger 1. Struck out—By Turley 6, Pascual 1, Clevenger 1. Hits—Off Pascual 10 in 6 innings, Stewart 1 in 1, Clevenger 2 in 1, Turley 7 in 7 2-3, Sturdivant 1 in 1 1-3. Runs and earned runs—Off Pascual 9 and 7, Turley 5 and 5, Clevenger 3 and 3. Wild pitch—Turley. Winning pitcher—Turley (2—1). Losing pitcher—Pascual (2—6). Umpires—McKinley, Flaherty, Rice and Summers. Time of game—3:10. Attendance—29,825.

hitters in the second game, in which the Bombers pounded Camilo Pascual, Bunky Stewart and Truman Clevenger for thirteen hits. Hank hit two, No. 10 leading off in the first, and No. 11, inside-the-park in the eighth. Eddie rapped his second leading off in the second.

Mantle's fifth-inning homer put the Bombers ahead to stay

and they settled matters with a five-run outburst in the sixth, marked by Joe Collins' three-run double.

Bob Turley was the beneficiary of this assorted slugging. However, Bob became wild and needed help from Tom Sturdivant to bag the victory.

Besides being a conversation piece, Mantle's homer was the

chief factor in the Yankee's opening-game victory. Mickey touched off his big blast with two mates aboard to erase a 1-0 lead Washington had taken on Johnny Kucks in the second.

The Bombers added a tally in the sixth on a single by Kucks and Hank Bauer's long double to center. However, Kucks apparently cooked himself scoring

from first on Bauer's blow.

The Senators ripped into Johnny for three hits and two runs in the seventh. When Kucks got into further difficulties in the eighth, Casey Stengel called in Tom Morgan to preserve the youngster's sixth victory.

May 31, 1956

MUSIAL FIRST IN POLL

Cards' Star Named Player of Decade—DiMaggio Second

ST. LOUIS, July 7 (AP)—Stan Musial, St. Louis Cardinals' outfielder-First baseman who owns a hatful of National League records, today was named the player of the decade by the Sporting News.

The national baseball weekly reported Musial won the honor for the period 1946-55 in a poll of 260 players, club officials, umpires, writers and sportscasters.

Joe DiMaggio, former topflight outfielder of the New York Yankees, was second in the balloting and Ted Williams, the Boston Red Sox slugging outfielder, was third.

Musial received 2,654 points,

DiMaggio 2,433 and Williams 2,312 on the basis of fourteen points for a first-place vote, nine for second and running down to one for tenth.

Musial will receive the prize award, a grandfather's clock, at a luncheon of the Touchdown Club in Washington on Monday, the day before he appears in his thirteenth All-Star game.

July 8, 1956

Ted Williams Fined $5,000 in Outburst

Special to The New York Times.

BOSTON, Aug. 7—Ted Williams, the Boston Red Sox' slugging outfielder, was fined $5,000 by the baseball club today for spitting at fans and newspaper men during a game with the New York Yankees.

Williams, who had put on similar exhibitions earlier in the season, showed his contempt at the end of the eleventh inning of the game, won by the Red Sox, 1 to 0. Williams first missed a fly ball and then made an outstanding catch for the third out on another drive. He started spitting as he neared the Red Sox dugout amid a mixture of cheers and jeers. An hour and a half after the game Joe Cronin, the Red Sox' general manager, announced the club was fining Williams "for his conduct on the field." Williams, whose annual salary is $100,000, was notified of the fine by phone in his hotel suite.

"We just can't condone that sort of thing," said Cronin. "It

Associated Press

Ted Williams

was a great game and a great crowd. After he muffed that ball he made a great catch on Yogi Berra to end the inning. It was too bad he had to spoil it.

"When I got him on the phone and told him of the fine, he said, 'I was sorry I did it a minute

later. I just have no explanation as to why I did it'."

[The United Press reported Williams as saying, "I'm not a bit sorry for what I did. I'd spit again at the same fans who booed me today. If I had the money, I wouldn't be out there tomorrow."]

Williams gained the distinction of matching one Babe Ruth record, though in his spectacular career he has missed most of the others. In 1925 the Bambino was fined $5,000 by Miller Huggins, then the Yankee manager, for insubordination and breaking training rules. This remained baseball's highest player fine until equaled today by Williams.

Temperamental Ted has been fined twice before by the Red Sox. Each previous fine was for $100, one for throwing a ball over the roof in an exhibition game in Atlanta in 1939, and the other in 1941 for rattling a hit off Fenway Park's left field wall, then walking in a pet to second base because Umpire Bill McGowan had irritated him.

This season his outburst of spitting has had Boston newspapermen as its principal target. Several times Williams has referred to Hub writers as being a "gutless" lot.

On one occasion Ted commented:

"Nobody's going to make me stop spitting. The newspaper guys in this town are bush. And some of those fans are the worst in the world."

Williams first spit this season as he crossed home plate following the 400th home run of his major league career.

Ted made another spitting gesture July 20, the night Cronin was honored for his election to baseball's Hall of Fame.

Cronin said Tom Yawkey, the club owner, "was listening to the game on the radio and was very upset by Ted's actions."

Umpire Ed Runge said that he would include in his official report a description of Williams' action of throwing his bat in the air after drawing the walk that decided the game. However, Runge did not say whether the spitting incident would be included in the report.

Will Harridge, the American League president, had talked to umpires after an earlier game marked by Williams' spitting and they reported "nothing to the incident."

"If there is anything at all to it, I presume it will be handled by the Boston club," Harridge said.

That is what the Red Sox did.

August 8, 1956

Larsen Beats Dodgers in Perfect Game; Yanks Lead, 3-2, on First Series No-Hitter

By JOHN DREBINGER

Don Larsen is a footloose fellow of whom Casey Stengel once said, "He can be one of baseball's great pitchers any time he puts his mind to it." Larsen had his mind on his work yesterday.

He pitched the first no-hit game in world series history. Not only that, but he also fired the first perfect game—no batter reaching first base—to be posted in the major leagues in thirty-four years.

This nerve-tingling perform-

ance, embellished with a Mickey Mantle home run, gained a 2-0 triumph for the Yankees over the Dodgers and Sal Maglie at the Stadium. It enabled Casey Stengel's Bombers to post their third straight victory for a 3-2 lead in the series. The Bombers

are within one game of clinching the series as it moves back to Ebbets Field today.

Crowd Roars Tribute

With every fan in a gathering of 64,519 hanging breathlessly on every pitch, Larsen, a 27-year-old right-hander, slipped over a third strike on Dale Mitchell to end the game.

Dale, a pinch hitter, was the twenty-seventh batter to face Larsen. As he went down for the final out, the gathering set up a deafening roar, while jubilant Yankees fairly mobbed the big pitcher as he struggled to make his way to the dugout.

The unpredictable Larsen had triumphed at a time when the Bombers needed it most with one of the most spectacular achievements in diamond history. Last spring the' tall, handsome Hoosier, who now makes his home in San Diego, Calif., had caused considerable to-do in the Yankees' St. Petersburg training camp. In an early dawn escapade, Don wrapped his automobile around a telephone pole. He later explained he had fallen asleep at the wheel.

Yesterday big Don remained wide-awake through every moment of the nine innings as he wrapped his long fingers around a baseball to make it do tricks never seen' before in world series play.

He did it, too, with a most revolutionary delivery, which might account for his sudden rise to fame. Don takes no wind-up at all. Each pitch is served from a standing delivery that he adopted only a little over a month ago.

In the history of baseball this was only the seventh perfect game ever hurled in the major leagues and only the fifth in baseball's modern era, which dates back to the beginning of the present century. A perfect game is one in which a pitcher faces exactly twenty-seven men with not one reaching first base through a hit, base on balls, error or any other means.

The last perfect game in the majors was achieved by Charlie Robertson of the Chicago White Sox on April 30, 1922, when he vanquished the Detroit Tigers, 2—0.

No-hitters during the season, of course, have been common enough. In fact, Maglie, beaten yesterday despite a commendable five-hitter, tossed one earlier this year for the Dodgers.

In modern world series play, which started in 1903, three pitchers missed no-hitters by one blow. Ed Reulbach of the Cubs fired a one-hitter against the White Sox on Oct. 10, 1906. Jiggs Donohue, the White Sox first baseman, wrecked that no-hit bid.

Rudy York of the Tigers made the only hit off Claude Passeau of the Cubs on Oct. 5, 1945. In that game Passeau allowed only one other Tiger to reach first base, that one on a pass.

Bevens' Bid Fails

On Oct. 3, 1947, Floyd Bevens, a Yankee right-hander, got closest of all to the no-hit goal, when, against the Dodgers at Ebbets Field, he moved within one out of his objective. Then Cookie Lavagetto rattled a pinch two-bagger off the right-field wall that not only broke the no-hit spell but also defeated the Yankees.

So amazing was Larsen's feat that only four batted balls had a chance of being rated hits. One was a foul by inches. Three drives were converted into outs

by miraculous Yankee fielding plays.

In the second inning, Jackie Robinson banged a vicious grounder off Andy Carey's glove at third base for what momentarily appeared a certain hit. But Gil McDougald, the alert Yankee shortstop, recovered the ball in time to fire it for the put-out on Jackie at first base.

In the fifth, minutes after Mantle had put the Yanks ahead, 1—0, with his blast into the right field stand, Gil Hodges tagged a ball that streaked into deep left center, seemingly headed for extra bases.

But Mantle, whose fielding in the series has at times been a trifle spotty, more than made amends. He tore across the turf to make an extraordinary glove-fanned seven.

On the next play, Sandy Amoros leaned into a pitch and rocketed a towering drive toward the right field stand. This drive promised to tie the score, but at the last moment the ball curved foul.

And then, in the eighth, Hodges once again was victimized by a thrilling Yankee fielding play. Gil drove a tricky, low liner to the left of Carey. The Yankee third sacker lunged for the ball and caught it inches off the ground.

For a moment it was hard to say whether he had caught the ball or scooped it up. Andy, just to make certain, fired the ball to first in time to make the putout doubly sure. Officially, it was scored as a caught ball.

So accurate was Larsen's control that of the twenty-seven batters to face him, only one managed to run the count to three balls. That was Pee Wee Reese, the doughty Dodger captain and shortstop, in the first inning. Pee Wee then took a third strike. In all, Larsen fanned six.

For Maglie, the performance by his youthful rival was a heartbreaker. The 39-year-old Barber, whose astounding comeback this year had reached its peak when he hurled the Dodgers to victory in the series opener last Wednesday, did a pretty good job of pitching, too.

For three and two-third innings the one-time Giant star right-hander matched Larsen batter for batter, turning back the first eleven Yankee batters. But with two out in the fourth and the bases empty, Mantle blazed his homer into the lower right stand.

A moment later Yogi Berra appeared to have connected for another hit as he stroked a powerful low drive toward left center. However, Duke Snider tore over from center field and snared the ball with a headlong dive.

In the sixth, the Yanks tallied their second run when they ganged up on the Barber for three singles, although they needed only two of them to produce the tally. Larsen had a hand in the scoring.

Carey had opened the inning with a single over second for

only the second blow off Maglie. Then Larsen, one of several accomplished batsmen Stengel lists among his pitchers, laid down a perfect bunt sacrifice.

That sent Carey to second. On the heels of the sacrifice, Hank Bauer drove another single to center to send Carey scampering over the plate. For a moment it looked as though the Yanks would pile up some more runs as Joe Collins followed with a single into right that swept Bauer around to third.

A rather freakish double play put a quick finish to this rally. Mantle crashed a sharp grounder down the first base line. Hodges scooped up the ball and stepped on the bag almost in the same instant to retire Mantle. Then, seeing Bauer heading for home, Hodges got the ball to the plate in time to head off Hank, who was tagged in a rundown between third and home.

Double Play Helps Maglie

Another double play had saved the Barber in the fifth. Enos Slaughter had opened with a pass only to be forced at second on Billy Martin's sacrifice attempt. Then McDougald followed with a drive that appeared headed for left center.

But Reese, who leaped in the air, deflected the ball with his glove, then caught it. Martin, certain the drive was a hit, had gone too far off first to get back and was doubled off the bag.

With two out in the seventh, the irrepressible Martin singled to left and McDougald walked to receive the second and last pass given up by Maglie. But the Barber ended this threat by inducing Carey to slap into a force play at second.

Just to show he still had plenty left, the ancient Barber swept through the eighth by fanning three Yanks in a row. Maglie got Larsen, Bauer and Collins and as he walked off the mound toward the Dodger dugout he received a rousing ovation.

Nevertheless, the noise then was barely a whisper compared with the din set up minutes later when Larsen finished his perfect game.

One could have heard a dollar bill drop in the huge arena as Carl Furillo got up as the first Dodger batter in the ninth. Carl lifted a fly to Bauer in right and one roar went up. Roy Campanella slapped a grounder at Martin for out No. 2 and the second roar followed.

Then only Mitchell, batting for Maglie, remained between Larsen and everlasting diamond fame. The former American League outfielder, for years a sure-fire pinch hitter with the Cleveland Indians, ran the count to one ball and two strikes.

Mitchell fouled off the next pitch and as the following one zoomed over the plate Umpire Babe Pinelli called it strike three. At this point the Stadium was in an uproar.

Mitchell whirled around to protest the call and later he said

The Box Score

FIFTH GAME
BROOKLYN DODGERS

	AB.	R.	H.	PO.	A.
Gilliam, 2b.	3	0	0	2	0
Reese, ss.	3	0	0	4	2
Snider, cf.	3	0	0	1	0
Robinson, 3b.	3	0	0	2	4
Hodges, 1b.	3	0	0	5	1
Amoros, lf.	3	0	0	3	0
Furillo, rf.	3	0	0	0	0
Campanella, c.	3	0	0	7	2
Maglie, p.	2	0	0	0	1
a-Mitchell	1	0	0	0	0
Total	27	0	0	24	10

NEW YORK YANKEES

	AB.	R.	H.	PO.	A.
Bauer, rf.	4	0	1	4	0
Collins, 1b.	4	0	1	7	0
Mantle, cf.	3	1	1	4	0
Berra, c.	3	0	0	7	0
Slaughter, lf.	2	0	0	1	0
Martin, 2b.	3	0	1	3	4
McDougald, ss.	2	0	0	0	2
Carey, 3b.	3	1	1	1	1
Larsen, p.	2	0	0	0	1
Total	26	2	5	27	8

a—Called out on strikes for Maglie in ninth.

Brooklyn ......0 0 0 0 0 0 0 0 0—0
New York......0 0 0 1 0 1 0 0 .—2

Errors—None.
Runs batted in—Mantle, Bauer.
Home run—Mantle.
Sacrifice—Larsen.
Double plays—Reese and Hodges; Hodges, Campanella. Robinson, Campanella and Robinson.
Left on bases—Brooklyn 0, New York 3.
Bases on balls—Off Maglie 2 (Slaughter, McDougald).
Struck out—By Larsen 7 (Gilliam, Reese. Hodges, Campanella, Snider, Maglie, Mitchell); Maglie 5 (Martin, Collins 2, Larsen, Bauer).
Runs and earned runs—Off Maglie 2 and 2.
Winning pitcher—Larsen.
Losing pitcher—Maglie.
Umpires—Pinelli (N.), plate; Soar (A.), first base; Boggess (N.), second base; Napp (A.), third base; Gorman (N.), left field, and Runge (A.), right field.
Time of game—2:06.
Attendance—64,519 (paid).

it was a fast ball that was outside the strike zone. But Dale was in no spot to gain any listener. The Yanks were pummeling Larsen and the umpires were hustling off the field.

Doubtless for Pinelli, this, too, could have provided his greatest thrill in his long career as an arbiter. For after this series, Babe, as the dean of the National League staff of umpires, is to retire.

And so, with this most spectacular of all world series spectaculars, the pattern, in reverse of last October's series between these two rivals continues to hold. Last fall the Dodgers blew the first two games at the Stadium, then swept the next three in Ebbets Field. Returning to the Stadium, they lost the sixth game to tie it at three-all, but then bagged the seventh to gain Brooklyn's first world championship.

This time the Yanks hold the 3-2 advantage. They need only one more victory to clinch it. But that victory will have to be gained either today or tomorrow in the lair of the Dodgers and the Yanks haven't won a world series game at Ebbets Field since Oct. 4, 1953.

Stan Musial hits the third of his record-breaking five home runs in a double-header in 1954.

The Yankees' Don Larsen throws a ''perfect'' pitch to strike out Dale Mitchell of the Dodgers for the final out of the fifth game of the 1956 World Series—a game in which Larsen did not permit any Brooklyn batter to reach first.

Even Larsen, yesterday's no-hit hero, couldn't win there when he pitched the second game of the series last Friday. In fact, Don started that game, which wound up with the Yanks going down to a 13-8 defeat. He went out in the second inning after the Bombers had got him off to a 6-0 lead.

However, with two out, the Dodgers had scored only one run when Stengel removed Larsen with the bases filled. What followed was the doing of others and some experts had hinted

Casey had been a bit hasty in hauling Don out so soon.

All's Well That Ends Well

Stengel later admitted this could have been the case. "However," added the philosophical skipper of the Bombers, "it might also help to get him really on his toes the next time he starts." And that it most certainly did yesterday.

At a late hour last night, Stengel was still undecided whether in today's encounter,

which could win it all for him, he would start Johnny Kucks or Bob Turley.

Johnny, a 23-year-old sopho-m're right-hander and an eighteen-game winner the past season, also appeared briefly in that Friday rout in Flatbush. He followed Larsen and gave up the bases-filled single to Reese that drove in two runs. He then gave way to Tommy Byrne, who was tagged for Snider's three-run homer.

Turley is the right-hander who also joined the Yanks along

with Larsen in the Baltimore eighteen-player deal.

Walter Alston of the Dodgers, now fighting desperately to remain alive in the series, will stake all on his prize relief specialist, Clem Labine. Clem has been used only sparingly as a starter this year, but in this trying hour Alston suddenly seems to have no other choice.

October 9, 1956

GIANTS WILL SHIFT TO SAN FRANCISCO FOR 1958 SEASON

Board of Directors Approves, by 8-1 Vote, Coast Offer of 35-Year Stadium Lease

TEAM HERE SINCE 1883

Move From Polo Grounds Is Independent of Any Action Planned by Dodgers

By BILL BECKER

They'll be the San Francisco Giants in 1958.

The board of directors of the National Exhibition Company, the corporation operating the New York Giants, voted yesterday, 8 to 1, to move the baseball franchise to San Francisco next spring. The Giants have been a New York institution for seventy-four years.

Horace C. Stoneham, the club president, said he planned to fly to San Francisco within the next week for the formal signing of the contract. Mayor George Christopher of the Coast city indicated the contract would be drawn up within a few days.

Mr. Stoneham announced the transfer at the Giants' executive offices, 100 West Forty-second Street.

"It's a tough wrench," he said. "We're very sorry we're leaving. I'm very sentimental about the Giants and New York City. But conditions were such we had to accept now or they might not be so favorable again."

The twelve-point San Francisco plan includes construction

of a stadium seating between 40,000 and 45,000. It will be rented to the Giants on a thirty-five-year lease. The rental was set by the city at 5 per cent of receipts after taxes and other deductions, with a minimum annual rental guarantee of $125,-000 by the Giants.

Asked what forced the decision to move, Mr. Stoneham said: "Lack of attendance. We're sorry to disappoint the kids of New York, but we didn't see many of their parents out there at the Polo Grounds in recent years."

He declined comment on the transfer of the Brooklyn Dodgers to Los Angeles, which has been hanging fire for months. But he did venture a prediction that both the National and American Leagues—and perhaps a third major league—would continue to expand westward.

Seals' Stadium Available

Warren C. Giles, the president of the National League, said that the Giants' move would in no way affect the Dodgers if the Brooklyn club decided to remain in New York.

"I have studied the language of the resolution concerning the moves (adopted by the league in May) and it was my understanding that either one or both could go," Mr. Giles said in Cincinnati. "While consent was given on a roll-call vote, that is the way I interpreted the language in my study of the resolution," he said.

Mayor Christopher, who has been the prime mover in promoting big league baseball for the West Coast, was on the phone to congratulate the Giants' directorate immediately after they had taken the action.

The Mayor said the contractors were hopeful that the new stadium could be completed by the opening of the 1958 season. But, he said, in the event it was not finished, the Giants could arrange the rental of the 22,000-seat Seals Stadium temporarily.

The Mayor said the city had reached a tentative agreement with Paul Fagan, the owner of Seals Stadium, where the Pacific Coast League team has played for years.

Mr. Stoneham indicated that the club was willing to start the season in Seals Stadium and probably would move into its new Bayview Park home later in the year.

The director who voted against the move was M. Donald Grant, a partner in the Wall Street firm of Fahnestock & Co.

"It just tears my heart to see them go," said Mr. Grant. "I've been a Giant rooter all my life. Then, too, as a business man, I think they would do better staying here. I would rather have a National League franchise here than in any other city."

Mr. Grant said he couldn't see any sense in relinquishing New York to the Yankees, especially with four more years to go on the Polo Grounds lease. The Giants are obligated to pay $131,254.40 a year for rental and taxes there through 1961.

The directors voting for the transfer were Mr. Stoneham, his son, Charles H. (Petey) Stoneham, and his nephew, Charles S. (Chub) Feeney, vice presidents; Edgar P. Feeley, treasurer; Joseph J. Haggerty, Max Schneider, Dr. Anthony M. Palermo and Charles Aufderhar, Horace Stoneham's brother-in-law.

They undoubtedly were swayed by Mr. Stoneham's recent report to stockholders that he could assure an annual profit of $200,000 to $300,000 if the club moved to San Francisco. The Giants reportedly have lost money in all except two of the last eight years.

Proposal Is Outlined

Here is what San Francisco offered the Giants:

1. A new stadium seating from 40,000 to 45,000 in the Bayview Park area, south of San Francisco, to be constructed as to permit expansion if desired.

2. The city will operate and collect revenue from a parking area holding from 10,000 to 12,000 cars.

3. The Giants will operate and receive revenue from all concessions, including a club

and restaurant similar to the Yankees' Stadium Club.

4. The Giants will have exclusive occupancy for roughly six months of the year, although the city may rent the stadium for special events when the team is on the road.

5. Rental shall be 5 per cent of gross receipts after deducting taxes, visiting clubs' and the National League's shares. The Giants are to guarantee a minimum of $125,000 against the rental.

6. The city shall equip the stadium with everything needed for operation, including the lights for night games.

7. Office space will be provided for the Giant executives at the stadium.

8. The city will maintain the physical property, but the club is to pay for maintenance during the baseball season.

9. A thirty-five-year lease. Mayor Christopher said the city could not legally give an option now to renew this lease, but said he saw "no reason why a new lease cannot be negotiated" later.

10. Final plans for the stadium—to cost about $5,000,000—are subject to the Giants' approval. Other developments in the Bayview sector will cost at least another $5,000,000, the Mayor estimates.

11. The Giants will have exclusive advertising privileges on the stadium fences; the city will have the same under the stands.

12. The Mayor will appoint a Northern California Citizens Committee to promote the sale of season tickets before the 1958 season opens.

Damages Not Mentioned

The terms of San Francisco's offer were spelled out in a letter of intent signed by the Mayor and Francis McCarty, a member of the Board of Supervisors, which governs the City and County of San Francisco.

Mr. Stoneham had nothing to say about the amount of damages that the club and/or league will have to pay the Pacific Coast League for the invasion of its territory. It has been reported that this figure might be in the neighborhood of $1,000,000.

The Giants' president also declined comment on whether the club would indemnify the Boston Red Sox to move the San Francisco franchise, which the

American League club owns. Some reports have stated that the Giants would pay $125,000 to have the Seals transferred, possibly to Salt Lake City. Other versions have the Giants trading their Minneapolis franchise to the Red Sox for full rights to San Francisco.

The promise of closed-circuit television was a factor—"but not a big one," Mr. Stoneham said.

The Giants will play all day games in San Francisco, Mr. Stoneham said, with the exception of Tuesday and Friday nights. The spring and early summer nights are chill and damp in San Francisco—not to mention the traditional fog. A heating system will be installed in the stadium.

The club president also assured employes of the organization that they "will certainly be welcome" to accompany the team to San Francisco. He said he had not yet decided whether he and his family would move to the Coast.

Mr. Stoneham made it plain that the team—despite its 3,000-mile shift from the Harlem River—would still be called the Giants.

This probably afforded scant consolation to the faithful of Coogan's Bluff who have followed the team through its salad days—seventeen pennants, five world's championships—and its recent skim-milk diet.

Few teams in the history of baseball so captured the sports public's imagination as the Giants under the late John (Muggsy) McGraw. The team, first known as the Nationals, entered the National League in 1883, and has called the present Polo Grounds home since 1911.

Pennants were won in 1888, 1889, 1904, 1905, 1911, 1912, 1913, 1917, 1921, 1922, 1923, 1924, 1933, 1936, 1937, 1951, 1954. World series victories were recorded in 1905, 1921, 1922, 1933 and 1954.

Mr. McGraw managed the team from 1902 to 1932. Christy (Big Six) Mathewson was the pitching nonpariel of the 1911-13 pennant winners. A decade later such stars as Frankie Frisch and Bill Terry were the mainstays of the team.

Mr. Terry succeeded Mr. McGraw and managed until 1941.

Mel Ott, another Giant great, ran the team from 1941 to 1948. He was followed by Leo Durocher, who was the manager from 1948 to 1955. The incumbent, Bill Rigney, took over in 1955.

The transfer of the Giants will be the fourth—and farthest—move made by the major leagues in the last four years.

The Braves shifted from Bosto to Milwaukee in 1953. The St. Louis Browns became the Baltimore Orioles in 1954 and the Athletics moved from Philadelphia to Kansas City in 1955.

All transfers have been successful financially, particularly in Milwaukee, which has set league attendance records.

August 20, 1957

Spahn's 41st Shutout Sets Mark As Braves Subdue Cubs by 8-0

Milwaukee Hurler Tops Loop Record for Left-Handers— Aaron Belts No. 39

CHICAGO, Sept 3 (AP)—Warren Spahn pitched the pennant-bound Milwaukee Braves to a 8-0 victory over the Chicago Cubs today, registering the forty-first shutout of his career for a National League record for left-handers.

The 36-year-old hurler, rounding out thirteen years in the league, stifled the Cubs on six hits for his fourth blanking job of the season, his eighth straight decision and his eighteenth victory against eight defeats.

Spahn increased his shutout total over the previous record of forty, shared by Eppa Rixey and Larry French. The league record is ninety, set by a right-hander, Grover Cleveland Alexander.

The Braves were blanked for six innings by Dick Littlefield, who gave four hits and struck out seven in that span. However, he was blasted for five runs in the seventh inning, three of them unearned.

In the eighth inning, Hank Aaron slammed his thirty-ninth homer of the year into the left-field seats with two on, to hike his runs-batted-in total to 118.

Spahn retired the first eleven men he faced and yielded the first Chicago hit, a blooper into short center by Walt Moryn, in the fourth.

The Box Score

MILWAUKEE (N.)						CHICAGO (N.)					
	ab.	r.	h.	po.	a.		ab.	r.	h.	po.	a.
Schoen't,2b	3	1	1	4	4	Adams,3b	4	0	1	1	1
Jones, 1b	4	2	2	8	1	Walls, lf	4	0	1	1	0
Mathews,3b	5	2	2	1		Moryn, lf	4	0	2	3	0
Pafko, rf	5	2	3	0		Banks, ss	4	0	1	0	c.
Mantilla, ss	4	0	0	1	0	Bolger, cf	4	0	0	2	0
Mantilla, ss	4	1	1	2	4	Long, 1b	3	0	0	7	0
Cov'gton, lf	4	0	1	1	0	Neeman, c	3	0	0	9	0
Crandall, c	5	0	1	6	1	Morgan, 2b	3	0	0	4	1
Spahn, p	5	0	0	1	0	Littlef'ld, p	2	0	0	0	1
						aKin'all	1	0	0	0	0
Total	39	8	11	27	11	Poholsk'2,p	0	0	0	0	1
						Total	32	0	6	27	4

aPopped out for Littlefield in eighth.
Milwaukee .... 0 0 0 0 0 0 5 3 0—8
Chicago .... 0 0 0 0 0 0 0 0 0—0
E ror—Adams.
Runs batted in—Mathews, Aaron 4, Mantilla, Covington, Crandall.
Two-base hits—Schoendienst, Adams. Home run—Aaron. Double play—Mantilla, Schoendienst and Jones. Left on bases—Milwaukee 10, Chicago 6. Bases on balls—Off Littlefield 6, Spahn 1. Struck out—By Littlefield 8, Spahn 3, Poholsky 1. Hits—Off Littlefield 11 in 8 innings, Poholsky 0 in 1. Runs and earned runs—Off Littlefield 8 and 5. Wild pitch—Littlefield 2. Winning pitcher—Spahn (18-8). Losing pitcher—Littlefield (5-2). Umpires—Delmore, Smith, Conlan and Donatelli. Time of game—2:31. Attendance—7,490.

September 4, 1957

DODGERS ACCEPT LOS ANGELES BID TO MOVE TO COAST

Team Will Play in California in '58 After Representing Brooklyn Since 1890

CITY TO SEEK NEW CLUB

By EMANUEL PERLMUTTER

The Dodgers will play their baseball in Los Angeles next year.

The Brooklyn Baseball Club announced yesterday it was proceeding with the necessary steps to move to Los Angeles.

Warren C. Giles, president of the National League, hailed the Dodger move to the West Coast as proof of the league's "professional" nature. He said he and the league would miss New York, however.

Thus ended a colorful and often zany baseball era in Brooklyn. The Dodgers had represented Brooklyn in the National League since 1890. They had become world famous, first because of their erratic baseball and then because of their winning teams. In their flight to the Pacific, they join the New York Giants, who are moving to San Francisco.

The Yankees, who will now have the New York baseball territory to themselves, issued a public statement of regret at the departure of the Dodgers.

"We are sorry to see the Dodgers go, and we wish them the best of luck in Los Angeles," Dan Topping, co-owner of the American League club, said. "Now that they have definitely gone, there are so many things to be considered that we will have no further comment until after the next American League and joint major league meetings in December."

Meanwhile, the Yankees have more pressing problems. They meet the Milwaukee Braves today at the Yankee Stadium in the sixth game of the world series. Bob Turley is scheduled to pitch for the Yankees and Bob Buhl for the National League club.

Upon learning of the Dodgers' decision to move, Mayor Wagner immediately announced at City Hall that he soon would appoint a committee of citizens to try to get another National League team for New York.

New York and Los Angeles had engaged in a tug-of-war for the Dodgers since early in the year. A plan by which the city hoped to condemn a slum area in downtown Brooklyn and build a stadium there collapsed when the cost of the over-all project was estimated at $30,000,000. Offers by Nelson A. Rockefeller to help defray the costs also were fruitless.

The announcement of the Dodger move was cheered yesterday by residents of Los Angeles. Their City Council had approved an ordinance on Monday that embodies an agreement with the Brooklyn club.

The Los Angeles ordinance was officially signed last night by Mayor Norris Poulson, making it an official city statute. The signing took place in the Mayor's office, and was witnessed by the ten Councilmen who voted for it Monday. Four Councilmen had been opposed.

In Brooklyn, the news was received with mixed reaction. Business men in the vicinity of Ebbets Field, where the Dodgers had played since 1913, were hopeful that apartment houses would be built there and bring economic gain to the area. Fans interviewed generally felt the Dodger owners had bickered so long for a site that they had lost the esteem of Brooklyn rooters.

Cashmore Disappointed

Borough President John Cashmore expressed disappointment at the Dodgers' decision to leave. He said that he had worked hard to get the Dodgers to stay here and that he would "leave nothing undone" to get another team for Brooklyn.

Although both the Dodgers and the Giants are leaving because they assertedly feel the financial pickings are better in California, Brooklyn has been a profitable place for the Dodger owners.

The Dodgers hav. made more money in recent years than any other National League club. However, the Giants, who have finished poorly in the league standings, have suffered in gate receipts.

The end of New York as a National league baseball city was announced at 4 P.M. by publicity representatives for both the Dodgers and the league in the world series press room at the

Team's Managers

Following is a list of Dodger managers since 1890:
1890—William McGunnigle
1891192—John Montgomery Ward
1893-96—Dave Foutz
1897—William Barnie
1898—Barnie, Mike Griffin and C.H. Ebbets
1899-1905—Ned Hanlon
1906-8—Patsy Donovan
1909—Harry Lumley
1910-13—Bill Dahien
1914-31—Wilbert Robinson
1932-33—Max Carey
1934-36—Casey Stengel
1937-38—Burleigh Grimes
1939-46—Leo Durocher
1947—Burt Shotton
1948—Durocher and Shotton
1949-50—Shotton
1951-53—Charlie Dressen
1954 to present—Walter Alston

Waldorf-Astoria Hotel. Neither Mr. Giles, nor Walter F. O'Malley, the Dodger president, was present.

The Dodgers' statement was brief. It read:

"In view of the action of the Los Angeles City council yesterday and in accordance with the resolution of the National League made Oct. 1, the stockholders and directors of the Brooklyn Baseball Club have today met and unanimously agreed that necessary steps be taken to draft the Los Angeles territory."

Mr. Giles issued the following statement:

The National League has again demonstrated it is a professional organization. The transfer of the giants and the Dodgers means that

two more great municipalities are to have major league baseball without depriving another city of that privilege.

"The National League, and I, personally, will miss New York, but it is only human nature to want to reach new horizons. We look forward to 1958, when National League baseball will be played on the West Coast."

A spokesman for Ford C. Frick, Commissioner of Baseball, announced that Mrs. O'Malley had already filed with the commissioner his formal "notice of intent to acquire the Los Angeles terriB tory for the purpose of operating a National League club therein."

"Following the rules of baseball, Mr. O'Malley's communication has been forwarded to the President of the Pacific Coast League, the president of the Los Angeles ball club, the president of the National Association of Professional Baseball leagues and the president of the American League," Mr. Fricks' statement concluded.

Before the Dodgers can start playing baseball in Los Angeles, they will have to iron out territorial rights to that area. At present, both Los Angeles and Hollywood have teams in the Pacific Coast League.

Although the Dodgers own the Los Angeles team, they must reach an agreement with the minor league. Should they fail to reach an understanding, the matter will be settled by arbitration. The Giants must follow similar procedures in their move to San Francisco.

The question of which ball park the Dodgers will use next year is still undecided. Harold (Red) Patterson, assistant general manager and publicity man for the team, said it would be either Wrigley Field, the Los Angeles Coliseum, or both. The Dodgers own Wrigley Field, but its capacity is only 22,00

Under terms of their agreement with Los Angeles, the Dodgers are to construct a $10,000,000 stadium in Chavez Ravine, seating 50,000 persons. They will also give Wrigley Field to the city. However, the new stadium will not be ready next year.

The Dodger management said that the team would have spring training again next year at its Vero Beach, Fla. camp. However, the spring training schedule has not yet been worked out, the club added.

New York's official efforts to get a ball club to replace the Dodgers and the Giants may be impeded by the American League. Last week, the American League offered the National the borough of Queens as a future baseball site, reserving the other boroughs for itself. The matter is to be discussed at the December meeeting of the two leagues in Colorado Springs.

Although Mayor Wagner has indicated that the city might be willing to build a stadium in Flushing Meadow Park, Queens, for use by a major league team, this might not prove as attractive as Manhattan, the Bronx or Brooklyn to an out-of-town prospect.

The Mayor was asked at his press conference yesterday whether he thought Mr. O'Malley had acted in good faith in his negotiations with the city.

"I can only say that in my conversations with him he said that he had no commitments, and I have to take the man's word," Mr. Wagner replied.

In another development, Gordon Gray, executive vice president and general manager of WOR-TV, which televised the Dodger games, announced that the station would return to its "regular programming schedule."

October 9, 1957

Braves Beat Yanks, 5-0, to Win Series

Burdette Hurls 7-Hit Shutout in 7th Game for His 3d Victory

By JOHN DREBINGER

Milwaukee, which less than five years ago didn't even boast a major league club, bestrides the baseball universe today.

Manager Fred Haney's Braves, playing inspired ball behind another brilliant pitching effort by their tireless Lew Burdette, smothered the supposedly invincible Yankees, 5 to 0, in the seventh and deciding world series game at the Stadium yesterday.

The victory, generously

cheered by a gathering of 61,-207 as Burdette gained his third mound triumph of the classic, gave the National Leaguers the series, 4 games to 3. It brought to Milwaukee a world championship in its first crack at the title.

Inversely, it wound up a damaging campaign for New York. In little more than a month Old Gotham had lost two ball clubs, the Dodgers and Giants. Yesterday it was shorn of the world series crown it had held, with one or another of its three entries, since 1949.

Takes It From Both Sides

One sharp, decisive four-run thrust in the third inning yesterday gave the Milwaukeans a stranglehold they never relin-

quished. There just wasn't a thing the inexhaustible baseball brain of Casey Stengel could do about it.

Haney, a one-time pint-sized infielder who was appearing in a world series for the first time, had Stengel licked from the start of the game.

A costly error by Tony Kubek, rookie star of the Bombers during the earlier stages of the series, opened the gates for the Braves in the third. Before the inning was over, Don Larsen. Casey's starting pitcher, had been put to rout.

The big fellow, hero of last year's epic perfect game against the Dodgers, had been carefully groomed for this one. But he couldn't weather the punish-

ment he took from bo'h sides.

Eddie Mathews unloaded a two-run two-bagger. Bobby Shantz replaced Larsen, but the Braves rolled on. Hank Aaron and Wes Covington singled. Before the little Yankee southpaw could stem the tide, four runs were in and the American Leaguers were about out on their feet.

For good measure and by way of giving his team additional security, Del Crandall, Burdette's catcher, dropped a home run into the left-field stand in the eighth. But that shot was not needed.

For by then one Selva Lewis Burdette Jr., 30-year-old righthander and one-time farm hand in the Yankee chain, was putting the finishing touches to one of the most astounding exhibitions of sustained pitching mastery in more than a half-century of world series competition.

Burdette vanquished the Yankees in the second game, 4 to 2, last Thursday in New York. Last Monday in Milwaukee he shut them out, 1 to 0, in the fifth game to put the Braves in front. Yesterday, with his second dazzling shutout after only two days of rest, he completed a stretch of twenty-four scoreless innings. In the twenty-seven innings of his three complete games he allowed only two runs.

Only one hurler, perhaps the greatest of all, topped this. In 1905, the immortal Christy Mathewson rolled up twenty-seven innings of scoreless hurling to win three shutouts for the Giants.

Seven 3-Game Winners

Burdette yesterday became the seventh pitcher to gain three victories in a world series. The last was Harry Brecheen in 1946. But the Cardinal southpaw gained one in a relief role.

Four, besides Burdette, posted three complete-game victories. They were Mathewson, Jack Coombs of the Philadelphia Athletics in 1910, Babe Adams of the Pittsburgh Pirates in 1909 and Stanley Coveleskie of the Cleveland Indians in 1920.

The only other pitcher to win three games was Urban Faber of the Chicago White Sox in 1917. But in one of his triumphs he was removed for a relief hurler.

For Milwaukee, of course, yesterday easily was the day of days. That metropolis, home of the brew, the Braves and the finest of cheeses, doubtless will remain in a daze for some time to come.

Milwaukee entered the National League officially on March 18, 1953, when Owner Lou Perini moved his Braves from Boston. It was the first franchise shift in the senior league in more than half a century.

The transfer started a chain of upheavals. The Athletics moved from Philadelphia to Kansas City, the Browns from St. Louis to Baltimore, where they became the Orioles, and next year will see the New York Giants playing in San Francisco and the Brooklyn Dodgers in Los Angeles.

Four seasons of frustration followed the shift to Milwaukee. The Braves, despite a tremendous improvement from their sixth-place finish in Boston, were second in 1953, third in 1954, and second again the next two years. The 1956 season was the most bitter disappointment, for Haney's men let the pennant slip away in the last few days.

Sixth Yankee Setback

For New York, defeat perhaps was not too difficult to take. Seventeen times in the past have the Yankees brought the title here. This was only their sixth series setback.

For Stengel, the defeat was only his second in his nine seasons as manager of the Bombers. He has been the winner

six times.

He fought hard to save this one. In desperation he even returned Mickey Mantle to action in a surprise move. The Oklahoma slugger had gone to the sidelines with a shoulder injury after the fourth game and almost everyone thought he had made his last appearance save for a possible role as pinch-hitter.

But there he was, out in center field, playing the entire game. He singled for one of the seven hits permitted by Burdette.

Even Bill Skowron, out since the first game with a lame back, got into it in the closing innings.

The Braves, on the other hand, played without their wounded. Red Schoendienst, crippled in the fifth game with a groin injury, remained on the sidelines. Warren Spahn sat it out in the bullpen. The ace lefty was to have hurled this game but had to be sidetracked because of a mild influenza attack on Wednesday.

The incredible Burdette, however, needed no help once the Yankees let the game fall apart in the third inning.

Larsen had just retired his mound adversary, Burdette, on a foul back of third for the first out in the fateful inning when Bob Hazle, a rookie outfielder, stroked a "wrong field" single to left. Then came a play that doubtless will remain seared in Stengel's amazing memory through many a wintry night.

Peg to Second Wide

For the player who gummed it up had been the apple of Casey's eye all season—the brilliant and versatile Kubek. Tony had started the series last week at third, then switched to left field and center when Mantle went out of action. With Mantle back in center, Tony was on third again and that's where all the trouble started.

Johnny Logan slammed a grounder at Kubek. It looked like a sure-fire double play. But Tony's peg to second was wide. It pulled Jerry Coleman off the bag and there was no out there. Desperately, Jerry fired the ball to first in an effort to get at least one man. But Logan beat the throw and the Braves, instead of having been retired, had two on with one out.

It reminded one of what Uncle Wilbert Robinson of early Brooklyn baseball vintage, once described as the "phantom double play."

A moment later Mathews lined a two-bagger down the right-field foul line. Before the ball could be brought back to the infield both Hazle and Logan had scored. That was all for the crestfallen Larsen. Shantz went in.

Aaron, one of the Braves' top hitters in the series, punched a single into center and Mathews scored. Covington singled to left, sending Hank to third. Then when the Yanks failed to complete a double play by way of second base on Frank Torre's grounder to Coleman, Aaron

streaked home with the fourth tally.

After that nothing really mattered as Burdette kept firing his bewildering assortment of screwballs, sliders and sinkers.

So perfect was his control he walked only one batter, and that was intentional. It came after Hank Bauer had opened the Yankee first inning by belting Burdette's first pitch for a double.

This gave Hank the distinction of having connected in fourteen consecutive games for a world series record. Bauer had hit in each of the seven games in last October's classic.

He topped by one the former mark of thirteen games held jointly by Frank Schulte of the Cubs fifty years ago and Harry Hooper of the Red Sox of 1915, 1916 and 1918. To add luster to the record was the fact that the Yanks' ex-Marine had compiled his mark in only two series.

However, nothing else came of this blow even though there was a slight mix-up by the Braves on the next play. Enos Slaughter grounded to Burdette. This hung up Bauer between second and third.

But the Brave inner defense didn't play well and Hank scrambled back to second. However, the situation still was saved for Milwaukee since by then Slaughter had ambled down to second and so was an easy out.

Mantle, taking his first turn at bat since the tenth inning of the fourth game, then went out on a grounder to the mound. Yogi Berra was intentionally passed and Gil McDougald ended the inning with an infield pop-up.

Following the four-run third, Art Ditmar and Tom Sturdivant held the Braves scoreless for two innings apiece and Tommy Byrne did well enough in the last two.

But in the eighth, with two out and the bases empty, Byrne was guilty of one errant pitch. Crandall lifted it into the left-field seats, the ball just going beyond Slaughter's frantic reach.

After the Yanks' brief first-inning splurge, they didn't get a man on base until Coleman singled in the fifth.

In the sixth the Bombers made another bid, which didn't get started until two were out. Here Mantle singled and Mathews fumbled Berra's grounder. But McDougald then grounded to Mathews, who this time froze to the ball.

Game to the end, the Bombers made a despairing effort to break through Burdette in the last of the ninth. With one away, McDougald singled. After Kubek flied out, Coleman outgalloped an infield tap for his second hit.

Byrne then smashed a hard grounder over second base. It threatened to ruin Burdette's shutout. But Felix Mantilla, again substituting at second for Schoendienst, threw himself

The Box Score

SEVENTH GAME

MILWAUKEE BRAVES

	AB	R	H	PO	A
Hazle, rf	4	1	2	3	0
dPafko, rf	1	0	0	0	0
Logan, ss	5	1	2	1	4
Mathews, 3b	4	1	1	3	4
Aaron, cf	5	1	2	3	0
Covington, lf	3	0	1	2	0
Torre, 1b	2	0	0	8	0
Mantilla, 2b	2	0	0	2	0
Crandall, c	4	1	2	4	0
Burdette, p	2	0	0	0	3
Total	34	5	9	27	11

NEW YORK YANKEES

	AB	R	H	PO	A
Bauer, rf	4	0	1	2	0
Slaughter, lf	4	0	0	2	0
Mantle, cf	4	0	1	2	0
Berra, c	3	0	0	4	1
McDougald, ss	4	0	1	2	1
Kubek, 3b	4	0	1	3	4
Coleman, 2b	4	0	2	4	3
Collins, 1b	2	0	0	5	0
Sturdivant, p	0	0	0	0	0
cHoward	1	0	0	0	0
Byrne, p	1	0	1	0	0
Larsen, p	0	0	0	0	1
Shantz, p	0	0	0	0	1
aLumpe	1	0	0	0	0
Ditmar, p	0	0	0	0	0
bSkowron, 1b	3	0	0	3	2
Total	35	0	7	27	12

aStruck out for Shantz in third.
bHit into force out for Ditmar in fifth.
cStruck out for Sturdivant in seventh.
dFouled out for Hazle in eighth.

Milwaukee ......004 000 010—5
New York ......000 000 000—0

Errors—Kubek, McDougald, Berra, Mathews.
Runs batted in—Mathews 2, Aaron, Torre, Crandall.
Two-base hits—Bauer, Mathews.
Home run—Crandall.
Sacrifices—Covington, Burdette, Mathews.
Double play—McDougald, Coleman and Skowron.
Left on bases—Milwaukee 8, New York 9.
Bases on balls—Off Larsen 1 (Torre), Byrne 2 (Torre, Burdette), Burdette 1 (Berra).
Strike outs—By Larsen 2 (Hazle, Mathews), Ditmar 1 (Burdette), Sturdivant 1 (Aaron), Burdette 3 (Collins, Lumpe, Howard).
Hits—Off Larsen 3 in 2⅓ innings. Shantz 2 in ⅔, Ditmar 1 in 2, Sturdivant 2 in 2, Byrne 1 in 2.
Runs and earned runs—Off Larsen 3 and 3, Shantz 1 and 0, Byrne 1 and 1.
Losing pitcher—Larsen.
Umpires—McKinley (A), plate; Donatelli (N.), first base; Paparella (A.), second base; Conlan (N.), third base; Secory (N.), left field; Chylak (A.), right field.
Time of game—2:34.
Attendance—61,207.

headlong at the ball and blocked its path. It was a hit, but merely filled the bases. The Yanks still were looking for a run. Skowron banged a sharp one-hopper down the third-base line. Mathews scooped it up, stepped on third and the series was over.

A record attendance of 394,712 was set for a seven-game series. This topped the former mark of 389,763 set by the Yankees and Dodgers in 1947. The total receipts, exclusive of revenues from radio and television, reached $2,475,978, also a record.

But perhaps its greatest record was the bringing of the first world championship to what could well develop into the most fanatic baseball center in the nation. At least it has given the newcomers, Los Angeles and San Francisco, something to shoot at.

On March 15, 1953, when the prospect of Milwaukee getting the Braves' franchise was still

a rumor, a crowd of 15,000, unmindful of wind and snow, gathered at Milwaukee's Municipal Stadium. They undoubtedly dreamed of the day when perhaps they might win a pennant and world series. Last night in that sizzling midwestern metropolis that dream came

true.

Back in 1914 another Braves' team made history. That was when the "Miracle Braves" came out of the National League cellar on July 4 to win the pennant and then down the then formidable Athletics four straight in the world series. But

that was out of Boston. Thirty-nine years later Boston was to give up on the Braves.

Now Milwaukee rules the roost. It will be many a year before they'll forget the pitching of Lew Burdette.

October 11, 1957

Haddix Hurls 12 Perfect Innings But Loses to Milwaukee in 13th

Pirate Southpaw Retires 36 in Row—Double by Adcock Wins for Braves, 2 to 0

By United Press International.

MILWAUKEE, May 26 — Harvey Haddix of the Pittsburgh Pirates pitched twelve perfect innings tonight but lost in the thirteenth. The first hit he yielded, to Joe Adcock, gave a 2-0 victory to the Milwaukee Braves.

Haddix, who retired thirty-six men in a row, became the first major league pitcher to carry a perfect performance past nine innings.

Seven major league pitchers have hurled, and won, nine-inning perfect games. Don Larsen of the Yankees did it most recently, in the 1956 world series against the Dodgers. The longest previous no-hitter, eleven innings, dated back to Oct. 4, 1884. It was pitched by Edward J. Kinber of Brooklyn against Toledo.

Felix Mantilla was the first man to face the slender, 33-year-old curveball specialist in the thirteenth. He hit a grounder to the Pirates' third baseman, Don Hoak, who threw into the dirt at the feet of the first baseman, Rocky Nelson.

Mantilla was safe on the throwing error. Haddix' perfect string was snapped but the no-

hitter was intact.

Ed. Mathews, the next man up, sacrificed the fleet Mantilla to second. Hank Aaron, the major' leading batter, received an intentional base on balls.

Then Adcock connected. The hit barely cleared the right-center-field fence and the big first baseman hesitated a moment before starting around the bases. Then two boys crawled under the barricade and snatched the ball.

Adcock at first was credited with a home run, and the final score was announced as 3—0. But then he was declared out for passing Aaron between second and third base and his home run became a double. The jubilant Aaron, who had cut across the diamond without touching third, was sent back by his mates to touch third and then home.

Confusion developed immediately after Adcock's blow cleared the fence. The umpires stopped the action as players swarmed out on the field. Aaron and Mantilla were ordered to retrace their steps and cross the plate. It was not until some minutes after the game was over that Umpire Frank Dascoli handed down his ruling on the play.

The putout of Adcock was Skinner lined out to Adcock with men on first and third and third and two out.

The National League president, Warren Giles, said later in Cincinnati that he believed the final score of the game eventually would be changed by official ruling to 1—0.

Giles said he could make "no official ruling" until he studied

reports on the game, but expressed the opinion that only the number of runs sufficient to win the game for Milwaukee should have been allowed to count by the umpires.

Until his downfall in the thirteenth Haddix had used a fast ball that was always on target and a curve that cleverly nipped the corners. The closest thing to a base hit during the regulation nine innings was Johnny Logan's line drive in the third that the shortstop, Dick Schofield, speared on a leaping catch. Haddix fanned eight men.

Virdon Hauls Down Drives

In the eleventh inning, both Wes Covington and Del Crandall sent towering drives to center field that the center center field that Bill Virdon, hauled down at the fence.

Haddix' loss was his third this season and the toughest in baseball history.

Several pitchers have gone nine hitless innings and then lost the game in extra innings among them Bobo Newsom of the old St. Louis Browns in 1934. Tom Hughes of the Yankees in 1910, Leon Ames of the Giants in 1909 and Earl Moore of the Indians in 1901.

Fred Toney of the Reds and Jim Vaughn of the Cubs matched hitless pitching for nine innings on May 2, 1917. Toney won when the Reds pushed across a run in the tenth.

Lew Burdette went the route for the Braves. He won his eighth game of the season against two losses, allowing twelve hits, walking none, and striking out two batters.

The Pirates bunched three hits in the third inning, two of them infield singles, but failed to score. They got two hits in the ninth inning but again failed to push across a run. Bob Skinner lined out to the first

baseman, Adcock, with men on first and third and two out.

Haddix, a native of Medway, Ohio, was obtained last winter by the Pirates in a deal with the Cincinnati Reds. He won eight games and lost seven with the Reds last season.

He broke in with the St. Louis Cardinals in 1952 and in 1953 had his best record in the majors—twenty victories and nine losses with a 3.06 earned-run average.

He had an 18-13 record the next year but slumped to 12-16 in 1955 and the Cardinals traded him to the Phillies on May 11, 1956. He had a 13-8 record that season, and was 10—13 with the Phillies in 1957.

The box scores:

PITTSBURGH (N.)					MILWAUKEE (N.)				
	ab.	r.	h.	rbi		ab.	r.	h.	rbi
Schofield, ss.	6	0	3	0	O'Brien, 2b	3	0	0	0
Virdon, cf	6	0	1	0	bRice	1	0	0	0
Burgess, c	5	0	0	0	Mantilla, 2b	1	1	0	0
Nelson, 1b	5	0	2	0	Mathews, 3b	4	0	0	0
Skinner, lf	5	0	1	0	Aaron, rf	4	1	0	0
Mazeroski, 2b	5	0	1	0	Adcock, 1b	5	0	1	2
Hoak, 3b	5	0	2	0	Covington, lf	4	0	0	0
Mejias, rf	3	0	1	0	Crandall, c	4	0	0	0
aStuart	1	0	0	0	Pafko, rf	4	0	0	0
Christopher, p	1	0	0	0	Logan, ss	4	0	0	0
Haddix, p	5	0	1	0	Burdette, p	4	0	0	0
Total	47	0	12	0	Total	38	2	1	2

aFlied out for Mejias in 10th; bFlied out for O'Brien in 10th.

Pittsburgh .000 000 000 000 0—0
Milwaukee .000 000 000 000 2—2

Two out when winning runs scored.
E—Hoak. A—Pittsburgh 13, Milwaukee 21. DP—Logan and Adcock; Mathews, O'Brien, Adcock; Adcock, Logan. LOB—Pittsburgh 8, Milwaukee 0.
2B Hit—Adcock. Sacrifice—Mathews.

	IP.	H.	R.	ER.	BB.	SO.
Haddix (L, 3—3)	12⅔	1	2	1	0	8
Burdette (W, 8—2)	13	12	0	0	0	2

Umpires—Smith, Dascoli, Secory, Dixon.
Time—2:54. Attendance—19,194.

May 27, 1959

3D LEAGUE HURLS CURVE AT MAJORS

By HOWARD M. TUCKNER

After more than half a century as a two-league operation, big-time baseball this week was faced with the prospect of a third major league. Although

it had been rumored for some time, the formation of the new league—called the Continental —caused considerable surprise among both fans and major league officials.

Since 1901, when the American League was formed — the National has been in business since 1876—there have been only two major leagues. The third league, with founding teams in New York, Houston, Denver, Toronto and the Twin Cities of Minneapolis-St. Paul,

expects to begin operating as an eight, ten or even a twelve-team circuit by 1961.

Each franchise owner of the founding teams has deposited $50,000 in the league's treasury. Each owner is prepared to spend between $2,500,000 and $3,000,000, exclusive of stadium construction costs.

Some of the teams in the Continental League are planning to erect new stadiums, the construction of which will run into the millions. New York's

stadium—a 52,000-seat ballpark that will cost $12,000,000—is to be erected at Flushing Meadow, Queens, the site of the old World's Fair grounds. Players whose salaries average $15,000 and can run to over $100,000 a year must be purchased from the existing major league teams.

Big Business

Baseball is a big business, although not always a profitable one.

Most major league teams operate at a subsistence level, and the "have-nots" in each league often end their seasons with a deficit. It is estimated that the sixteen major league clubs—eight in the National and eight in the American—have a total income not exceeding $50,000,000. After operating expenses and taxes are paid, total profit is not more than $5,000,000.

While still below the post-war peaks of more than 20,000,000, major league attendance has made a modest comeback from its low of 14,400,000 in 1953, and has leveled off at around 16,500,000 a year.

Unlike the minor leagues, which as a group lost $2,900,000 in 1956 and are still losing vast sums, the majors have been able to boost their take from radio and television rights to their games.

Senate Study

Aside from attendance worries and rising costs, professional baseball today is faced with other problems. The business is under Congressional investigation to decide just what kind of business it is. Last week the Senate's Antitrust and Monopoly subcommittee, headed by Estes Kefauver, Democrat from Tennessee, heard testimony in an attempt to clarify the status of professional baseball, football, basketball and hockey under the antitrust laws. On Friday Senator Kefauver, a

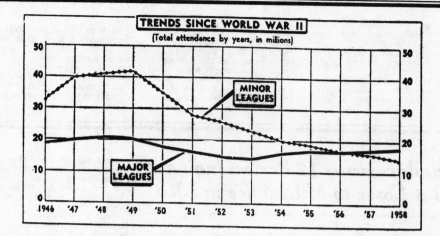

strong advocate of the third major league, warned baseball executives that their attitudes toward the proposed new league would be watched closely.

What led to the formation of the third major league?

In December, 1957, a few months after the Giants and Dodgers transferred to California, Mayor Wagner selected a committee to study ways to bring another major league team to New York. William A. Shea, a New York corporation lawyer, was picked to head the committee. After almost a year's efforts to attract another team had failed, Mr. Shea last November went ahead with plans for a third league.

Owners Opposed

Most owners of big-league clubs are against the formation of a third league. Competition is the chief reason. Instead of bidding against fifteen teams for the services of potential stars, they would compete against twenty-three or even more clubs. The stadiums of some major league teams — such as Shibe Park in Philadelphia and Griffith Stadium in Washington — are run down and have poor parking facilities. What will be the reaction of Philadelphia and Washington fans, for example, when the Continental League begins building modern stadiums or spacious sites?

A meeting between the found-

ers of the Continental League and a seven-man committee from the National and American League is set for Aug. 16.

For the Continental League to begin operations in 1961—or ever, for that matter—it must receive the blessings of the major league committee on Aug. 18. It is doubted that the majors will invite the Continental League into its camp at that meeting. If they do, though, the third league's problems — in such things as money raising, player acquisition, stadium building and revamping long-established traditions like the World Series—will be just beginning.

August 2, 1959

Dodgers Beat Braves in 12th, 6-5, To Win Pennant Play-Off Series

By JOHN DREBINGER
Special to The New York Times.

LOS ANGELES, Sept. 29—The Dodgers today brought a National League pennant to Los Angeles in the city's second year in major league baseball.

Before a roaring crowd of 36,528, Walter Alston's Angelenos made it a two-game sweep of the pennant play-off series as they conquered the Milwaukee Braves, 6 to 5, in a tense, dramatic, twelve-inning struggle. They will meet the White Sox in the first game of the world series in Chicago on Thursday.

Trailing by three runs in the last of the ninth, the Dodgers drew even in a frenzied spurt that had Fred Haney frantically throwing three of his hurlers into the fray.

And in the last of the twelfth, it was fittingly enough, 37-year-old Carl Furillo, a veteran of six

Dodger pennant triumphs in the days when the club performed in Brooklyn, who helped break up today's torrid conflict.

It was an infield hit by Furillo, coupled with a wide throw to first base by Felix Mantilla, that enabled Gil Hodges to go tearing in from second base with the deciding run.

With two out and Bob Rush on the mound for the Braves, Hodges drew a pass. Joe Pignatano singled to left and the Dodgers had runners on first and second.

Rush had snuffed out a Dodger threat in the eleventh, going to the mound with the bases loaded and two out. But this time the Angelenos were not to be denied.

Furillo then drilled a sharp grounder over second. Mantilla, who had been forced to shift from second to short because of

an injury to Johnny Logan earlier in the day, really made a brilliant stop. However, his desperate peg to first not only arrived too late, but also shot past Frank Torre, Milwaukee's first baseman.

That sent Hodges scooting over the plate and the encounter was over. The Dodgers, who had won the first play-off game by 3-2 in Milwaukee yesterday, thus bagged their thirteenth National League pennant.

In National League history, there have been only three play-offs and the Dodgers appeared in all of them. But not until today were they able to win one. They bowed to the Cardinals in 1946 and to the Giants in 1951.

But today, with the aid of a towering, 23-year-old right-hander, Stan Williams, they made it. Williams was the sixth pitcher to be used by Manager Alston. He entered the game in the tenth, reeled off three scoreless innings and received credit for the victory.

Williams had one tight squeeze in the eleventh when he walked three, but he fired his way out of that one.

And so the Dodgers capped a comeback that must be ranked as one of the most astounding in major league history. For the Dodgers, after

their sad seventh-place finish in their first year in Los Angeles last season, were picked by few to finish in the first division, let alone win the title.

Yet, curiously enough, they never were far from the top, though they only occasionally held the lead. After the early April skirmishing—they were in first place on April 26—they never were on top again until Sept. 20. On that day they swept a three-game series with the Giants in San Francisco.

The Giants, season-long front-runners, thus dropped out of the lead and virtually out of contention. It then became touch and go between the Dodgers and Braves, with these two finally finishing in a tie on Sunday.

Mathews Belts Homer

The Braves, with the aid of Eddie Mathews' homer, which helped bring about the rout of Don Drysdale in the fifth, were holding a three-run lead and Lew Burdette appeared to have his twenty-second victory of the year all wrapped up when the Dodgers suddenly went on their frenzied spurt in the ninth.

Up to that moment only Charley Neal had been able to do anything with the Braves' starter. Neal accounted for the Dodgers' first two runs, the first with a triple, the second with a homer.

Wally Moon opened that last-ditch stand with a single to center. Duke Snider followed with another to the same sector and Hodges singled to left.

Don McMahon replaced Burdette, only to be slapped for a two-run single by Norm Larker. In came Warren Spahn, the Braves' stalwart southpaw.

But Spahn couldn't prevent a pinch hitter, Furillo, from lifting a sacrifice fly to right, which scored Hodges with the tying run. Then Maury Wills singled for the fifth hit of the inning, sending Pignatano, running for Larker, to second. Here Haney made another mound switch.

He called in Joey Jay, who got a pinch hitter, Ron Fairly, to ground into a force play at second. This moved Pignatano to third but Joe got no further. For Hank Aaron in right made a fine running catch of Jim Gilliam's bid for a hit that would have ended it.

The struggle then went into overtime, with Jay on the firing line for the Braves and Williams for the Dodgers.

Played under a cloudless sky and with the temperature in the sun-baked arena around 80, the game had scarcely begun when the Braves jumped into a two-run lead.

An Early Disagreement

With one out, Drysdale walked Mathews and Hank Aaron followed with a two-bagger to left center. Aaron slid into second just ahead of Duke Snider's throw, and Neal, the Dodger second sacker, did some loud squawking. But this in no way influenced Umpire Augie Donatelli and the Braves had runners on second and third.

A moment later both were over the plate on Torre's well-placed single through the hole between short and third. The inning ended with Lee Maye

grounding into a double play. The Dodgers got a run back in their half when Neal connected for his first extra-base blow of the game. It was a triple that sailed over Bill Bruton's head in center. The run followed when Wally Moon stroked a single into left.

Burdette then fanned Snider and retired six more Dodgers in a row through the second and third before the Angelenos scored their next tally. Neal delivered this one with a towering fly that sailed over the trick forty-foot barrier in left field. It was Charley's nineteenth of the year and thirteenth in the Coliseum.

That cut the Braves' margin to one run, but not for long. In the fifth Mathews hooked one of Drysdale's deliveries down the right-field foul line. It skirted just inside the foul pole and into the stand.

The homer was Mathews' forty-sixth of the season, breaking his tie with Ernie Banks of the Chicago Cubs for the major league leadership. The American League leaders were Rocky Colavito of the Cleveland Indians and Harmon Killebrew of the Washington Senators, with forty-two each.

When Drysdale walked Aaron, Alston decided to take no further chances with his erratic hight-hander. He called on his southpaw, Johnny Podres, whom he had passed up as a starter yesterday in Milwaukee. The lefty quickly retired the side.

For a time Podres did all right, although it took a spectacular catch by Norm Larker to prevent Logan from getting a hit to left center in the sixth. But in the seventh Johnny appeared headed for trouble when Mathews and Aaron weighed in with singles.

However, a fine throw by Moon to Jim Gilliam nipped Mathews as he tried to reach

third base on the Aaron blow and that helped. For Podres unfurled a wild pitch that put Aaron on third and he also walked Torre.

That had Alston bringing in his rookie right-hander, Clarence Nottingham Churn, called Chuck, who managed to ward off further trouble there. But in the eighth Chuck yielded a run. Del Crandall clubbed him for a triple and Mantilla fetched the Braves' catcher home with a sacrifice fly.

In the seventh the Braves ran into a bad scare when for a moment it looked as though their shortstop, Logan, had met with a serious mishap. After Larker had opened with a single, John Roseboro grounded to Torre, who fired the ball to second just as Larker came slamming into Logan, intending, of course, to break up a double play.

Logan Goes Sprawling

In this he failed, for Logan got the ball away in time to complete the twin killing on Roseboro at first. But the Brave shortstop had been knocked sprawling and every Milwaukee player rushed to Logan's side as he rolled on the ground, apparently in considerable pain.

However, after Logan had been carried off the field on a stretcher, it was disclosed that he had suffered nothing beyond having the wind knocked out of him. The Braves finished the inning with Mantilla shifting from second to short, while Red Schoendienst, recently returned to the active list after a siege of tuberculosis, went to his old position at second.

Meanwhile, Burdette seemed merely to be toying with the Dodgers. So it came as a jolt when the Dodgers suddenly routed the Brave right-hander with three successive singles that eventually were to plunge the struggle into overtime.

The Box Score

MILWAUKEE (N.)	ab.r.h.rbi	LOS ANGELES (N.)	ab.r.h.rbi
Bruton, cf	6 0 0 0	Gilliam, 3b	5 0 1 0
Mathews, 3b	4 2 2 1	Neal, 2b	6 2 2 1
Aaron, rf	4 1 2 0	Moon, rf, lf	6 1 3 1
Torre, 1b	3 0 1 2	Snider, rf	4 0 1 0
Maye, lf	2 0 0 0	eLillis	0 1 0 0
aPafko, lf	1 0 0 0	Williams, p	2 0 0 0
bSlaughter, lf	1 0 0 0	Hodges, 1b	5 2 2 0
DeMerit, lf	0 1 0 0	Larker, rf	4 0 2 2
kSpangler, lf	0 0 0 0	fPignatano, c	1 0 1 0
Logan, ss	3 1 2 0	Roseboro, c	3 0 0 0
Schoend'st, 2b	1 0 0 0	gFurillo, rf	2 0 2 1
dVernon	1 0 0 0	Wills, ss	5 0 1 0
Cottier, 2b	0 0 0 0	Drysdale, p	1 0 0 0
lAdcock	1 0 1 0	Podres, p	1 0 0 0
Avila, 2b	0 0 0 0	Churn, p	0 0 0 0
Crandall, c	6 1 1 1	cDemeter	1 0 0 0
Mantilla, 2b, ss	5 0 1 1	Koufax, p	0 0 0 0
Burdette, p	3 0 0 0	Labine, p	0 0 0 0
McMahon, p	0 0 0 0	hEssegian	0 0 0 0
Spahn, p	0 0 0 0	jFairly, cf	2 0 0 0
Jay, p	1 0 0 0		
Rush, p	1 0 0 0		
Total	44 5 10 4	Total	48 6 15 5

aFlied out for Maye in 5th; bPopped out for Pafko in 7th; cLined out for Churn in 8th; dStruck out for Schoendienst in 9th; eRan for Snider in 9th; fRan for Larker in 9th; gHit sacrifice fly for Roseboro in 9th; hAnnounced for Labine in 9th; jHit into forceout for Essegian in 9th; kWalked for DeMerit in 11th; lHit into forceout for Cottier in 11th.

Milwaukee	2 1 0	0 1 0	0 1 0	0 0 0—5
Los Angeles	1 0 0	1 0 0	0 0 3	0 0 1—6

Two out when winning run was scored.

E—Snider, Neal, Mantilla 2. DP—Wills, Neal, Hodges; Torre, Logan, Torre. LOB—Milwaukee 13, Los Angeles 11.

PO—Milwaukee 35: Bruton 4, Mathews 2, Aaron 3, Torre 10, Spangler 3, Logan 2, Avila, Crandall 6, Mantilla. Los Angeles 36: Gilliam 4, Neal 3, Moon 3, Snider, Hodges 11, Larker 2, Pignatano 3, Roseboro 5, Wills 3, Drysdale, Fairly. A—Milwaukee 13: Mathews 2, Torre 2, Logan 5, Crandall, Mantilla, Burdette 2. Los Angeles 11: Gilliam 3, Neal 2, Moon, Roseboro, Wills 5, Drysdale, Churn.

2B Hit—Aaron. 3B—Neal, Crandall. HR—Neal, Mathews. SF—Mantilla, Furillo.

	IP.	H.	R.	ER.	BB.	SO.
*Burdette	8	10	5	5	0	4
†McMahon	0	1	0	0	0	0
Spahn	1/3	0	0	0	0	0
Jay	2 2/3	1	0	0	1	1
Rush (L, 5—6)	2	1	1	1	0	0
Drysdale	4 1/3	6	4	3	2	3
Podres	2 2/3	2	0	0	1	1
Churn	1 1/3	1	1	1	0	0
Koufax	2 2/3	0	0	0	3	1
Labine	1/3	0	0	0	0	1
Williams (W, 5—5)	3	0	0	0	3	0

*Faced 3 batters in 9th; †Faced 1 batter in 9th.

HBP—By Jay (Pignatano). Wild pitch—Podres. PB—Pignatano. Umpires—Barlick, Boggess, Donatelli, Conlan, Jackowski, Gorman. Time—4:06. Attendance—36,528.

September 30, 1959

PIRATES WIN, 10-9, CAPTURING SERIES ON HOMER IN 9TH

By JOHN DREBINGER
Special to The New York Times.

PITTSBURGH, Oct. 13—The Pirates today brought Pittsburgh its first world series baseball championship in thirty-five years when Bill Mazeroski slammed a ninth-inning home run high over the left-field wall of historic Forbes Field.

With that shot, Danny Murtaugh's astounding Bucs brought down Casey Stengel's

Yankees, 10 to 9, in a titanic struggle that gave the National League champions the series, four games to three.

Minutes later a crowd of 36,683 touched off a celebration that tonight is sweeping through the city like a vast conflagration. For with this stunning victory, which also had required a five-run Pirate eighth, the dauntless Bucs avenged the four-straight rout inflicted by another Yankee team in 1927.

First Title Since 1925

The Steel City thus had its first world title since 1925, when the Corsairs of Bill McKechnie conquered the Washington Senators.

As for the 70-year-old Stengel, if this is to be his exit—his retirement has been re-

peatedly rumored—the Ol' Professor scarcely could have desired a more fitting setting short of a victory.

For this was a terrific, nerve-tingling struggle that saw a dazzling parade of heroes who followed on the heels of one another in bewildering profusion.

It saw the Bucs dash off to a four-run lead in the first two innings as they clobbered Bob Turley and Bill Stafford. The first two runs scored in the first inning on a homer by Rocky Nelson.

Berra Hits 3-Run Homer

But in the sixth the Bombers suddenly opened fire on their two arch tormentors of the series, Vernon Law and the Bucs' ace reliever, ElRoy Face,

Law, with the help of Face, was seeking his third victory over the Bombers, but the Yanks scored four times in this round, three riding in on a homer by the incomparable Yogi Berra.

These four tallies, along with one which they had picked up in the fifth on a Bill Skowron homer, had the Yanks in front, 5 to 4. When they added two off Face in the eighth for a 7-4 lead, Stengel appeared to have his eighth world series title wrapped up, along with the Bombers' nineteenth autumn triumph.

But in the eighth the Corsairs suddenly erupted for five runs, the final three scampering across on an electrifying homer by Hal Smith. That had the Bucs two in front, but still the conflict raged.

In the ninth the embattled Yanks counted twice as once again they routed Bob Friend. Then left-handed Harvey Haddix, winner of the pivotal fifth game, brought them to a halt.

In the last of the ninth it was the clout by Mazeroski, first up, that ended it. Ralph Terry, the fifth Yankee hurler, was the victim. It made him the losing pitcher and Haddix the winner.

So, instead of the Bombers winning the nineteenth title, they had to accept their seventh world series defeat. As for Stengel, he remains tied with Joe McCarthy, a former Yankee manager, with seven series triumphs. The setback was his third. McCarthy lost two, one with the Yanks and one with the Chicago Cubs.

Bobby Shantz, a diminutive left-hander, who had gone to the box in the third to do some brilliant relief hurling for five innings, was one victim of the Bucs' startling five-run eighth.

The assault opened with Gino Cimoli, hitting for Face, cracking a single to right. Bill Virdon followed with a vicious grounder to short that resulted in doubtless the crucial play of the entire series.

It looked like a double play until the ball took a freak hop and struck Tony Kubek in the larynx. Instead of a double play, Tony was stretched on the ground. Virdon was on first with a single and Cimoli was on second. Kubek had to leave the game and was rushed to a hospital.

Meanwhile the Pirate attack rolled on. Dick Groat followed with a single to left, scoring Cimoli. That was all for Shantz and Jim Coates, a lean right-hander, took the mound.

Bob Skinner, back in the Buc line-up despite a still swollen left thumb, sacrificed the runners to second and third. Nelson flied out, leaving the position unchanged, and then came another rough break for the Stengeleers.

Bob Clemente dribbled a grounder to the right of the mound. Skowron scooped up the ball and this should have been the third out of the inning had Coates covered first base. But the tall Virginian failed to get to the bag in time. Clemente thus got an infield hit that enabled Cimoli to score the second run of the inning.

Three more followed as Smith, a one-time Yankee prospect, belted the ball high over the left-field wall. The Bucs were in front, 9—7, and the fans were in a delirium.

They cooled perceptibly in the top of the ninth. Murtaugh called on Friend, twice knocked out earlier in the series, to protect that two-run lead. But Bobby Richardson singled, as did Dale Long, a pinch-hitter, and Murtaugh lost no time in hustling in his fifth-game winner, Haddix.

The little lefty retired Roger Maris on the end of a foul back

of the plate, but Mickey Mantle singled to right, scoring Richardson and sending Long to third.

Another bewildering play followed. Berra grounded sharply down the first-base line. Nelson grabbed the ball, stepped on the bag for one out, then made a lunge for Mantle who, seeing he had no chance to make second, darted back to first. Mickey made it with a headlong dive that sent him under Rocky's tag.

Meanwhile, Gil McDougald, in as a runner for Long, crossed the plate and the score was 9-all. Haddix, getting Skowron to ground to Groat, brought the round to a close. Minutes later the game was over.

Although the weather again was warm and summery, the sun for the first time had difficulty breaking through a haze which enveloped the park with something akin to a Los Angeles smog.

However, no one was paying much attention to the weather and once the game got on the way it could have snowed without anyone paying the slightest attention.

For this was Pittsburgh's first big chance to win a world championship in three and a half decades and the fans were out to make the most of it. Nor did the Bucs keep their cohorts long in suspense.

The cheers, following the setting down of the first three Yankees in the first inning by Law, barely had subsided before they broke out afresh.

Turley, Stengel's starting choice over the youthful Stafford, got by the first two Pirates, but Skinner walked.

Next came Nelson. Before the series returned here, Murtaugh had been emphatic that, regardless of Yankee pitching, Dick Stuart would be his first baseman. Yet here was the 36-year-old Nelson in the starting line-up as the first baseman.

Rocky, a left-handed swinger who began his professional baseball career eighteen years ago and spent most of the intervening time trying to convince managers he was a major league ball player, waited for Turley to run up a count of two balls and one strike. Then he lifted one that had just enough carry to clear the thirty-foot screen in front of the lower right-field stand at a point about 350 feet from home plate.

The fans went wild with joy as Nelson rounded the bases behind Skinner. Rocky had appeared in one series before this one. That was as a Brooklyn Dodger in 1952, when he was up four times as a pinch-hitter, but got no hits.

In the second, the Bucs went to work on Turley again, but this time not for long. For after Smoky Burgess had opened with a single to right, Stengel called on Stafford, the 22-year-old right-hander who had pitched five scoreless innings in relief in a hopeless Yankee cause in the fifth game.

In fact, Stengel had to weather

some rough second-guessing after that defeat because he didn't start the youngster in that game instead of Art Ditmar.

This time Stafford spared his manager further embarrassing moments so far as this game was concerned. He walked Don Hoak and allowed Mazeroski to outgallop a bunt for a hit that filled the bases.

Stafford momentarily did get a grip on the situation when he induced Law to slap a roller to the mound. Stafford converted this one into a double play via the plate.

However, the Bucs still had runners on second and third and a moment later Virdon drove both home with a single to right, to which Maris added a fumble to put Virdon on second. The error didn't matter, but the Bucs were four in front.

Meanwhile Law, making a heroic bid to pitch his third victory of the series, held the Yanks in a tight grip. Like Ford yesterday, Law was back with only three days' rest, but he certainly didn't show it in the first four innings.

A dazzling stop and throw by Hoak took a possible hit away from Berra in the second. Hector Lopez delivered a pinch single in the third and Mantle singled with two down in the fourth.

In the fifth inning, the first tinge of uneasiness swept through the stands. Skowron stroked an outside pitch into the upper right deck. It was the Moose's second homer of the series and his sixth in series competition.

An inning later almost the entire arena was enveloped in a deep and profound silence. The Yanks ripped into both Law and Face for their cluster of four to take the lead.

Richardson, a thorn in the side of the Bucs throughout the series, opened the assault with a single. When Kubek drew a pass Murtaugh decided the moment had arrived for Face to do his usual flawless relief work.

He had done the rescue work in the three Pirate victories preceding this game, saving Law twice and Haddix in the fifth game.

This time he encountered trouble. He retired Maris on a foul back of third, but Mantle punched a single over second which a diving Groat just missed flagging down. The hit scored Richardson and sent Kubek to third.

Up stepped Berra, who again was in left field for the Bombers while a rookie, John Blanchard, worked behind the plate in place of the injured Elston Howard. The latter had gone out with a fractured hand when hit by a stray pitch in the sixth game. Yogi fouled off one pitch. Then he unfurled a lofty shot that sailed into the upper right-field deck close to the foul pole, which at the base measures only 300 feet from the plate. Mantle and Kubek scored ahead of Berra.

It was Yogi's eleventh homer

The Box Score

SEVENTH GAME
NEW YORK YANKEES

	AB.	R.	H.	RBI.	PO.	A.
Richardson, b.	5	2	2	0	2	5
Kubek ss.	3	1	0	0	3	2
DeMaestri, ss.	0	0	0	0	0	0
dLong	1	0	1	0	0	0
eMcD'gald, 3b.	0	1	0	0	0	0
Maris, rf.	5	0	0	0	2	0
Mantle, cf.	5	1	3	2	0	0
Berra, lf.	4	2	1	4	3	0
Skowron, 1b.	5	2	2	1	10	2
Blanchard, c.	4	0	1	1	1	1
Boyer, 3b., ss.	4	0	1	1	0	3
Turley, p.	0	0	0	0	0	0
Stafford, p.	0	0	0	0	0	1
aLopez	1	0	1	0	0	0
Shantz, p.	3	0	1	0	3	1
Coates, p.	0	0	0	0	0	0
Terry, p.	0	0	0	0	0	0
Total	40	9	13	9	24	15

PITTSBURGH PIRATES

	AB.	R.	H.	RBI.	PO.	A.
Virdon, cf.	4	1	2	2	3	0
Groat, ss.	4	1	1	1	3	2
Skinner, lf.	2	1	0	0	1	0
Nelson, 1b.	3	1	1	2	7	0
Clemente, rf.	4	1	1	1	4	0
Burgess, c	3	0	2	0	0	0
dChristopher	0	0	0	0	0	0
Smith, c.	1	1	1	3	1	0
Hoak, 3b.	3	1	0	0	3	2
Mazeroski, 2b.	4	2	2	1	5	0
Law, p.	2	0	0	0	0	1
Face, p.	0	0	0	0	0	1
cCimoli	1	1	1	0	0	0
Friend, p.	0	0	0	0	0	0
Haddix, p.	0	0	0	0	0	0
Total	31	10	11	10	27	6

aSingled for Stafford in third.
bRan for Burgess in seventh.
cSingled for Face in eighth.
dSingled for DeMaestri in ninth.
eRan for Long in ninth.

New York.......000 014 022—9
Pittsburgh ....220 000 051—10

None out when winning run was scored.

Error—Maris. Double plays—Stafford, Blanchard and Skowron; Richardson, Kubek and Skowron; Kubek, Richardson and Skowron. Left on bases—New York 6, Pittsburgh 1.

Two-base hit—Boyer. Home runs—Nelson, Skowron, Berra, Smith, Mazeroski. Sacrifice—Skinner.

in world series competition, tying him for third place with the Dodgers' Duke Snider.

The Yanks were now a run in front and in the eighth they clubbed Face for two more tallies.

The trim right-handed reliever had the Yanks' two most formidable clouters, Maris and Mantle, out of the way, when Berra drew a pass. Skowron sent a bounder down the third-base line which Hoak fielded but couldn't play. It went for a single and Berra was on second.

Two sharp thrusts did the rest. Blanchard pulled a single into left, scoring Yogi. Cletis Boyer drove a two-bagger down the left-field line, sending in Skowron. Moose's single was his twelfth hit, thereby tying another world series record.

Meanwhile, with Shantz reeling off one scoreless inning after another, the game looked tucked away for the Bombers. For five innings the little lefty allowed only one hit, a single. But in the Pittsburgh eighth the real pyrotechnics began. They never stopped until Mazeroski, with a count of one ball and no strikes in the ninth, whacked the ball over the left-field brick wall directly over the 402-foot mark.

October 14, 1960

NATIONAL LEAGUE ADMITS NEW YORK, HOUSTON FOR 1962

By LOUIS EFFRAT
Special to The New York Times.

CHICAGO, Oct. 17—New York and Houston received franchises in the National League today.

If all goes well, as baseball officials expect, the new clubs will start playing in the 1962 season. The league, organized in 1876, will have ten clubs under the new arrangement. The National League has had clubs in New York before but never in Texas.

The club owners, in special session at the Sheraton Blackstone Hotel, responded with "unanimous enthusiasm" to the proposal that both cities be accepted for membership. The action surprised no one.

The proposal was made by Walter F. O'Malley, the president of the Dodgers. Ironically, O'Malley was the man who, in October of 1957, took the Dodgers out of Brooklyn and moved them to Los Angeles.

O'Malley also convinced Horace Stoneham to take the New York Giants out of the Polo Grounds and into San Francisco at the same time. Stoneham was one of the eight who voted in favor of today's action.

Giles Discloses Move

Warren C. Giles, the president of the National League, disclosed the expansion move after the owners had taken a break for lunch.

He said the following resolution was approved by the National League in the morning:

"Resolved that the National League approve and adopt the recommendations of its expansion committee in the following respects:

"1—That the National League expand effective with the 1962 season to add two clubs, each additional club to be a member club of the Continental League which meets the qualifications for membership in the National League.

"2—That within a period of four years, the National League shall reappraise the situation with a view to carrying out its policy of further expansion."

New York and Houston were members of the proposed Continental League, which aspired to be the third major league. It disbanded when the National and American Leagues agreed

to admit four of its eight members.

Giles, in identifying the franchise winners, referred to New York as the "Payson group" and Houston as the "Cullinan group." Mrs. Charles Shipman Payson of New York and Manhasset, L. I., heads the New York club. Craig F. Cullinan Jr. is the leader of the Texas club.

The owners felt that both groups qualified for membership in every way and that certain obligations, including indemnification to minor-league clubs, would be met.

Other details are to be ironed out, including the amount of money—"They are going to have to have a lot of money," Giles said—the two groups must spend.

There may or may not be a membership fee. Each new club must deposit a still unspecified sum to gain equity in the league treasury. It is believed that the National League reserve fund holds $1,500,000.

The site and size of the stadium each city will call home, and the method of acquiring playing personnel were among items occupying the owners' attention this afternoon.

American League Has a Say

Perhaps the most important item, though, concerned New York. Formal approval for entry into the city, thereby infringing on the territorial rights of the Yankees, must be considered by the American League.

Whether the American League goes along with the proposition is not likely, however, to affect the situation. The National League is certain it will have the support of Ford Frick, Commissioner of Baseball.

Baseball law dictates that the commissioner cast the deciding vote if the two major leagues

cannot agree. The National League will propose at the joint meeting of the majors at St. Louis on Dec. 7 a change in Rule 1-C. This deals with territorial rights and calls for unanimous approval of all sixteen clubs before a second team may invade a city.

"It is possible the American League will vote along with us on this proposition," Giles said. "They have been very cooperative. However, if they vote in the negative we are confident that the commissioner will decide in our favor. He has stated publicly as well as to me that he is in favor of New York being open territory."

No New Yorkers Present

New York was not represented by any active member of its group today. Mrs. Payson, M. Donald Grant, Dwight Davis Jr., G. H. Walker Jr. and William Simpson, identified by Giles as the "Payson group," remained in New York. This was done upon the advice of O'Malley.

"I talked with Grant, as well as with Bill Shea, the chairman of Mayor Wagner's Baseball Committee, in New York," O'Malley said. "We talked it over and I felt there would be no point in any of them coming here. I said I would represent them, and I guess I did a pretty fair job of representing them."

The "Cullinan group" is made up of Cullinan, Judge Roy Hofheinz, R. E. Smith, K. S. (Bud) Adams and George Kirksey. Adams was a founder of the American Football League, which began operations this season. Cullinan, Hofheinz and Kirksey were on hand, and Cullinan, an oil man and sportsman, said all were elated.

"This climaxes four years of hard work," he said. "Now we must really prove we're big league. We will work harder than even before."

Construction of a $14,500,000 stadium in Harris County in Houston will begin on Feb. 1. It will have 43,197 seats.

Where the New York club will play its home games is a matter for its owners to decide. "We feel that's their own problem and that they will solve it," Giles said.

The construction of a 55,000-seat stadium at Flushing Meadow, Queens, has been assured by Mayor Wagner. Until then, the New York club could move into the Polo Grounds or share Yankee Stadium with the Yankees.

O'Malley and Stoneham were happy over today's developments.

"When we left New York," O'Malley said, "we tried to get a National League club to go in at that time. Now it has a fair chance of working out, if they come up with some fair players."

How that is to be accomplished is a matter for conjecture. Some feel the player limit for each club will be reduced from twenty-five to twenty-three for 1962. There is likely to be a plan offering three players from each present club to the new members. Houston already has acquired a dozen players from the Western Carolina League.

"I am happy that New York is back in the National League," Stoneham said. "I'm certain that in the near future they will have a fine, representative team. Mrs. Payson and the new people will do well by their franchise and for the fans of New York. She was an avid Giant fan and I am happy for her sake, too."

The possibility of an American League club now moving into Los Angeles was mentioned to O'Malley.

"I don't think that would be very smart," the president of the Dodgers said. "I believe they will go to the Coast eventually. San Diego and Seattle are wonderful cities. Right now, the American League faces a realignment problem before expansion."

The National League has operated with six, eight and twelve clubs, but never with ten. Originally made up of eight teams, the circuit expelled New York and Philadelphia in 1877 because both clubs refused to make the last Western trip that season.

Numerous franchise shifts were made through 1900. From 1892 through 1899 there were twelve teams in the league.

From 1900 through 1952 eight clubs played. They were Boston, Brooklyn, Chicago, Cincinnati, New York, Philadelphia, Pittsburgh and St. Louis.

The shift of Boston to Milwaukee by Lou Perini, the Braves' principal owner, was the first break-through major league franchise shift of the century. After the 1957 season, Brooklyn became Los Angeles and New York became San Francisco. Until today's action, that was the way the National League lined up.

Excluding suburban areas, New York City has a population of 7,710,346 and Houston 932,680, according to preliminary figures from the 1960 Federal census.

New York ranks first among the nation's cities in population. Houston is sixth, following Chicago, Los Angeles, Philadelphia and Detroit. Los Angeles is the only city in the nation with a larger area than Houston.

The club representatives were Philip K. Wrigley and John Holland of Chicago, Gabe Paul of Cincinnati, O'Malley of Los Angeles. Perini, John McHale and Birdie Tebbetts of Milwaukee; Bob Carpenter of Philadelphia, John Galbreath and Joe L. Brown of Pittsburgh, August A. Busch Jr., Dick Meyer and Anthony Buford of St. Louis and Stoneham of San Francisco.

October 18, 1960

American League, in '61, to Add Minneapolis and Los Angeles

By JOHN DREBINGER

The American League, taking the most revolutionary step in its history, voted yesterday to become a ten-club circuit.

What is more, the league will begin the expanded operation in 1961, getting a jump of a year on the rival National League.

These lightning moves made the expansion possible:

¶Calvin Griffith, owner of the Washington Senators, received permission to move his franchise to Minneapolis - St. Paul.

¶A new club for Washington was approved, assuring the capital of continued major league baseball. The owners of the new franchise will be disclosed later.

¶Still another new franchise was approved for Los Angeles, also under owners to be identified later.

The announcement was made by the league president, Joe Cronin, after a day-long session of the top executives of the eight present clubs at the Savoy Hilton Hotel.

The news startled the baseball world. While there had been endless speculation on the league's expansion plans, few had expected such speedy action.

But the American Leaguers apparently were determined to beat the National League to the punch. Last week the National League had announced it was expanding to ten clubs with the addition of New York and Houston. However, the new teams will not begin play until 1962.

Thus, for the first time since the American League was founded in 1900, the two leagues will present uneven alignments next year.

The American League will operate with New York, Boston, Washington, Baltimore and Cleveland in the East and Los Angeles, Minneapolis-St. Paul, Kansas City, Chicago and Detroit in the West. It will play a 162-game schedule.

Each club will play eighteen games against every other club. The eight clubs in the National League will adhere to the usual 154-game schedule, with twenty-two meetings between each club.

So swiftly did the American Leaguers move that not even Commissioner Ford C. Frick seemed prepared for it.

"I haven't seen anything officially yet," said the Commissioner at his office. "There are so many angles to be considered, such as ball parks and what to do regarding players, that I cannot make any comment until I have talked to the people involved officially."

However, the American Leaguers already appeared assured that ball parks would offer no problem even if the new ownerships in Washington and Los Angeles remained a secret for a few more weeks.

The Senators will move into Metropolitan Stadium in Minneapolis, which was built in 1956 and has a seating capacity of 22,000. However, the Twin Cities organization already has started increasing this to 40,000 for the 1961 football season. Some new seats should be ready for the baseball season.

Washington already has started work on a new stadium, a Federal project that will be completed by September, 1961. It will seat 40,000 persons and is near the National Guard Armory, only about five minutes by cab from the Capitol.

Until the new stadium is ready, the new Washington club will play at Griffith Stadium, which up to now has been the home of the Senators. Calvin Griffith, the Senators' owner, will retain ownership of the park for the present. He said he would rent it to the new club.

In Los Angeles the situation is less settled, although Cronin said everything would be worked out satisfactorily well before the opening of the 1961 season.

Los Angeles Prepared

It is presumed that the American League entry in Los Angeles will play in the Coliseum, now the home of the National League Dodgers. If this cannot be worked out, Wrigley Field is available, according to Del Webb, the chairman of the American League expansion committee.

Whether the new club eventually will move in with the Dodgers when the latter's Chavez Ravine stadium is completed cannot be answered at this time, said Webb.

Immediately after the meeting, the general managers of the eight clubs went into another session to draw plans that will help the Washington and Los Angeles clubs stock their rosters. The Minneapolis-St. Paul club will be manned by the Washington Senator players of 1960.

The player plans will be submitted for ratification at another league meeting on Nov. 17. It is possible that the league will make additional expansion announcements at that time.

For in disclosing the new ten-club set-up, Cronin called it "only the first step."

"The American League is considering other fine baseball cities," said Cronin, "for a possible future expansion to twelve clubs."

It was, in all, a bewildering day. Scrapped, apparently, and with no attempt made to explain why, was the so-called commitment made by the two leagues to the defunct Continental League last summer.

A joint expansion committee

of the two leagues assured the Continental League then that each league would absorb two Continental cities if the Continental League dissolved.

However, none of the Continental League groups figured in yesterday's moves. Minneapolis-St. Paul does get a ball club, but it will be operated by Griffith's organization.

Out of the picture completely go Dallas-Fort Worth and Toronto, which had been optimistic about gaining entry to the American League. However, there seemed to be no hard feelings.

Eliminated but Elated

"We are elated over what has happened," said Wheelock Whitney of the Twin City Continental group. "Our major object has from the first been to get the Twin Cities into a major league. Now that that is assured, we are ready to do everything possible to help Griffith make a success of his new move."

Griffith had tried for many years to get into Minneapolis but the American league had always balked him. He said he wanted the shift for the "betterment of our corporation."

The Twin Cities organization, Griffith said, was guaranteeing him 1,000,000 attendance for each of the next five years. Revenues from radio and television also will be substantially higher than in Washington.

"In Washington," said Griffith, "our radio-TV brought us about $180,000. Our new contract in Minneapolis should bring us about $500,000 annually."

Although no vote totals were disclosed, it was understood that the shift from Washington had been approved by 6 to 2, just enough to make it. The vote was unanimous on the franchise for Los Angeles and the new ownership for Washington.

The identity of the new owners will likely remain a mystery for at least two or three weeks. However, the Washington group will not include Hank Greenberg, who had frequently been mentioned as a possible buyer. Greenberg is the vice president of the Chicago White Sox.

Greenberg, who attended the meeting, declined to commit himself on whether he might be involved in the Los Angeles venture. Webb also has been mentioned frequently in connection with the Los Angeles club.

Though Webb is a Yankee co-owner, most of his other business interests are in the West. He said yesterday, however, that there was nothing to the reports that he was interested in a Los Angeles operation.

Although disappointed that for the present they had been sidetracked, the Dallas - Fort Worth group, headed by Amon Carter Jr. and Joseph A. W. Bateson, apparently took comfort in Cronin's statement that the American League wasn't stopping at ten clubs.

Another indication of how strikingly sure the American Leaguers were of themselves was the fact that they never even bothered to advise the National League in advance of their plans.

"We didn't feel it was neces-

sary to discuss it with them," said Cronin. "They made their move last week, today we've made ours. We made our move into Los Angeles with the assurance from Commissioner Frick that he was declaring Los Angeles an open city just as he did New York."

In Cincinnati, Warren C. Giles, the National League president, appeared to show no resentment over the American League action.

"I still think it more practical to expand to ten clubs in

1962, as we've announced. However, they know what's best for their league," he said.

This marks the fifth time the American League has shifted its field, with this one the most drastic. Until now the league always has operated with eight clubs. The last franchise shift was in 1955, when the Philadelphia Athletics were moved to Kansas City.

October 27, 1960

Mays Wallops Four Home Runs

RECORD EQUALED IN 14-4 CONTEST

Mays, Ninth to Connect 4 Times in One Game, Paces 8-Homer Giant Offense

MILWAUKEE, April 30 (AP) —Willie Mays today became the ninth player in major league history to hit four home runs in one game as the San Francisco Giants routed the Milwaukee Braves, 14—4.

Mays, who drove in eight runs, connected in the first, third, sixth and eighth innings. In the ninth, with the crowd of 13,114 cheering for him to get another turn at bat, Willie advanced to the on-deck circle. But Jim Davenport, the Giant immediately preceding him in the batting order, ended the suspense by grounding out.

The effort by Mays contributed to the setting or tying of five home-run records. Hitting

eight home runs in all, the Giants accomplished the following:

¶Set a National League record of thirteen home runs in two consecutive games. They had hit five yesterday.

¶Equaled the major league record for home runs in two consecutive games.

¶Equaled the major league record of eight homers in one game.

¶Equaled, with the help of Milwaukee's two homers, the National League record of ten four-baggers in one game by two teams.

Mays, who had hit only two homers previously this season, tied a mark shared by Lou Gehrig, among others.

Mays Put Out Once

The last major league player to hit four homers in one game had been Rocky Colavito, who belted four in a row for the Cleveland Indians on June 10, 1959. The last National Leaguer had been Joe Adcock of the Braves, who connected on July 31, 1954. Colavito is now with the Detroit Tigers.

Mays did not connect in succession. The string was broken in the fifth, when Moe Drabowsky retired him on a line drive

to the center fielder.

Lew Burdette, who started for the Braves and pitched three innings, yielded the first two homers to Mays. The Giant center fielder hit his third off Seth Morehead and his fourth off Don McMahon.

Mays hit one homer with two men on base, two with one on and the other with the bases empty. His eight runs batted in fell four short of the one-game record.

Henry Aaron was the Braves' batting star, hitting both Milwaukee homers.

Pagan Hits 2 Homers

José Pagan hit two of the San Francisco home runs, the first of his major league career. He entered the game with a batting average of .056 and made four hits in five tries. Orlando Cepeda and Felipe Alou hit the other four-baggers.

The club's thirteen homers in two games broke the league record of twelve set by the Braves in a double-header at Pittsburgh on Aug. 30, 1953, and tied the major league high set by the New York Yankees in a double-header on June 28, 1939.

Other major leaguers who hit four homers in one game were

Gil Hodges for the Brooklyn Dodgers; Pat Seerey, Chicago White Sox; Chuck Klein, Philadelphia Phillies; Ed Delahanty, Phillies, and Bob Lowe of the old Boston Braves.

SAN FRANCISCO (N.)					MILWAUKEE (N.)				
	ab.r.h.rbi					ab.r.h.rbi			
Hiller, 2b	6	2	3	1	McMillan, ss	4	1	1	0
Davenport, 3b	4	3	1	1	Bolling, 2b	4	1	2	0
Mays, cf	5	4	4	8	Mathews, 3b	4	0	1	0
McCovey, 1b	3	0	0	0	Aaron, cf	4	2	2	4
Marshall, 1b	3	0	0	0	Roach, rf	4	0	1	0
Cepeda, lf	5	1	1	1	Adcock, 1b	4	0	0	0
M. Alou, lf	4	1	1	1	Lau, c	3	0	1	0
F. Alou, rf	4	1	1	1	McMahon, p	0	0	0	0
Bailey, c	4	0	0	0	Brunet, p	0	0	0	0
Pagan, ss	5	3	4	2	cMaye	1	0	0	0
Loes, p	3	0	0	0	DeMerit, rf	0	0	0	0
					Burdette, p	1	0	0	0
Total	39	14	14	14	Willey, p	0	0	0	0
					Drabowsky, p	0	0	0	0
					aMartin	1	0	0	0
					Morehead, p	0	0	0	0
					MacKenzie, p	0	0	0	0
					bLogan	1	0	0	0
					Taylor, c	0	0	0	0
					Total	34	4	8	4

aFlied out for Drabowsky in 5th; bFanned for MacKenzie in 7th; cWalked for Brunet in 9th.

San Francisco ... 1 0 3 3 0 4 0 3 0—14
Milwaukee .... 3 0 0 0 0 1 0 0 0— 4

E—Mathews. A—San Francisco 9, Milwaukee 15. DP—Davenport, Hiller, Marshall; Burdette, McMillan, Adcock; Bolling, McMillan, Adcock. LOB—San Francisco 6, Milwaukee 7.
2B Hits—Hiller 2. 3B—Davenport. HR—Mays 4, Pagan 2, Cepeda, F. Alou, Aaron 2. Sacrifices—Loes 2.

	IP.	H.	R.	ER.BB.SO.		
Loes (W, 2—1)	9	8	4	4	1	3
Burdette (L, 1—1)	.3	5	5	5	0	0
Willey	.1	3	2	2	0	0
Drabowsky	.1	0	0	0	1	0
Morehead	.1	2	4	4	1	1
MacKenzie	.1	0	0	0	0	1
McMahon	.1	3	3	3	2	0
Brunet	.1	1	0	0	0	0

*Faced 1 batter in 4th.
HBP—By Burdette (Davenport), by MacKenzie (Bailey). Umpires—Pelekoudas, Forman, Conlan, Donatelli, Burkhart. Time—2:40. Attendance—13,114.

May 1, 1961

Maris Hits 61st in Final Game

Yank First to Exceed 60 Home Runs in Major Leagues

By JOHN DREBINGER

Roger Maris yesterday became the first major league player in history to hit more than sixty home runs in a season.

The 27-year-old Yankee outfielder hit his sixty-first at the Stadium before a roaring crowd of 23,154 in the Bombers' final game of the regular campaign.

That surpassed by one the sixty that Babe Ruth hit in 1927. Ruth's mark has stood in the record book for thirty-four years.

Artistically enough, Maris' homer also produced the only

run of the game as Ralph Houk's 1961 American League champions defeated the Red Sox, 1 to 0, in their final tune-up for the world series, which opens at the Stadium on Wednesday.

Maris hit his fourth-inning homer in his second time at bat. The victim of the blow was Tracy Stallard, a 24-year-old Boston rookie right - hander. Stallard's name, perhaps, will in time gain as much renown as that of Tom Zachary, who delivered the pitch that Ruth slammed into the Stadium's right-field bleachers for No. 60 on the next to the last day of the 1927 season.

Along with Stallard, still another name was bandied about at the Stadium after Maris' drive. Sal Durante, a 19-year-old truck driver from Coney Island, was the fellow who caught the ball as it dropped into the lower right-field stand, some ten rows back and about ten feet to the right of the Yankee bull pen.

For this achievement the young man won a $5,000 award and a round trip to Sacramento, Calif., offered by a Sacramento restaurant proprietor, as well as a round trip to the 1962 World's Fair in Seattle.

Maris was fooled by Stallard on an outside pitch that he stroked to left field for an out in the first inning. He let two pitches go by when he came to bat in the fourth with one out and the bases empty. The first one was high and outside. The second one was low and appeared to be inside.

Waist-High Fast Ball

The crowd, interested in only one thing, a home run, greeted both pitches with a chorus of boos. Then came the moment for which fans from coast to coast had been waiting since last Tuesday night, when Maris hit his sixtieth.

Stallard's next pitch was a fast ball that appeared to be about waist high and right down the middle. In a flash, Roger's rhythmic swing, long the envy of left-handed pull hitters, connected with the ball.

Almost at once, the crowd sensed that this was it. An ear-splitting roar went up as Maris, standing spellbound for just an instant at the plate, started his triumphant jog around the bases. As he came down the third-base line, he shook hands joyously with a young fan who had rushed onto the field to congratulate him.

Crossing the plate and arriving at the Yankee dugout, he was met by a solid phalanx of team-mates. This time they made certain the modest country lad from Raytown, Mo., acknowledged the crowd's plaudits.

He had been reluctant to do so when he hit No. 60, but this time the Yankee players wouldn't let Roger come down the dugout steps. Smiling broadly, the usually unemotional player lifted his cap from his blond close-cropped thatch and waved it to the cheering fans. Not until he had taken four bows did his colleagues allow him to retire to the bench.

Ruth's record, of course, will not be erased. On July 17, Commissioner Ford C. Frick ruled that Ruth's record would stand unless bettered within a 154-game limit, since that was the schedule in 1927. Maris hit fifty-nine homers in the Yanks' first 154 games to a decision. He hit his sixtieth four games later.

Maris Homers Day by Day

HR NO.	GAME NO.	DATE APRIL	OPPOSING PITCHER AND CLUB.	WHERE MADE.
1.	10	26	Foytack, Detroit (R)	Detroit
		MAY		
2.	16	3	Ramos, Minnesota (R)	Bloomington
3.	19	6	Grba, Los Angeles (R)	Los Angeles
4.	28	17	Burnside, Washington (L)	New York
5.	29	19	Perry, Cleveland (R)	Cleveland
6.	30	20	Bell, Cleveland (R)	Cleveland
7.	31	21	Estrada, Baltimore (R)	Cleveland
8.	34	24	Conley, Boston (R)	New York
9.	37	28	McLish, Chicago (R)	New York
10.	39	30	Conley, Boston (R)	New York
11.	39	30	Fornieles, Boston (R)	Boston
12.	40	31	Muffett, Boston (R)	Boston
		JUNE		
13.	42	2	McLish, Chicago (R)	Chicago
14.	43	3	Shaw, Chicago (R)	Chicago
15.	44	4	Kemmerer, Chicago (R)	Chicago
16.	47	6	Palmquist, Minnesota (R)	New York
17.	48	7	Ramos, Minnesota (R)	New York
18.	51	9	Herbert, Kansas City (R)	New York
19.	54	11	Grba, Los Angeles (R)	New York
20.	54	11	James, Los Angeles (R)	New York
21.	56	13	Perry, Cleveland (R)	Cleveland
22.	57	14	Bell, Cleveland (R)	Cleveland
23.	60	17	Mossi, Detroit (L)	Detroit
24.	61	18	Casale, Detroit (R)	Detroit
25.	62	19	Archer, Kansas City (L)	Kansas City
26.	63	20	Nuxhall, Kansas City (L)	Kansas City
27.	65	22	Bass, Kansas City (R)	Kansas City
		JULY		
28.	73	1	Sisler, Washington (R)	New York
29.	74	2	Burnside, Washington (L)	New York
30.	74	2	Klippstein, Washington (R)	New York
31.	76	4	Lary, Detroit (R)	New York
32.	77	5	Funk, Cleveland (R)	New York
33.	81	9	Monbouquette, Boston (R)	Boston
34.	83	13	Wynn, Chicago (R)	Chicago
35.	85	15	Herbert, Chicago (R)	Chicago
36.	91	21	Monbouquette, Boston (R)	Boston
37.	94	25	Baumann, Chicago (L)	New York
38.	94	25	Larsen, Chicago (R)	New York
39.	95	25	Kemmerer, Chicago (R)	New York
40.	95	25	Hacker, Chicago (R)	New York
		AUG.		
41.	105	4	Pascual, Minnesota (R)	New York
42.	113	11	Burnside, Washington (L)	Washington
43.	114	12	Donovan, Washington (R)	Washington
44.	115	13	Daniels, Washington (R)	Washington
45.	116	13	Kutyna, Washington (R)	Washington
46.	117	15	Pizarro, Chicago (L)	Washington
47.	118	16	Pierce, Chicago (L)	New York
48.	118	16	Pierce, Chicago (L)	New York
49.	123	20	Perry, Cleveland (R)	New York
50.	124	22	McBride, Los Angeles (R)	Los Angeles
51.	125	26	Walker, Kansas City (R)	Kansas City
		SEPT.		
52.	134	2	Lary, Detroit (R)	New York
53.	134	2	Aguirre, Detroit (L)	New York
54.	139	6	Cheney, Washington (R)	New York
55.	140	7	Stigman, Cleveland (L)	New York
56.	142	9	Grant, Cleveland (R)	New York
57.	150	16	Lary, Detroit (R)	Detroit
58.	151	17	Fox, Detroit (R)	Detroit
59.	154	20	Pappas, Baltimore (R)	Baltimore
60.	158	26	Fisher, Baltimore (R)	New York
		OCT.		
61.	162	1	Stallard, Boston (R)	New York

Recapitulation: 49 homers off right-handed pitchers; 12 off left-handed pitchers. (Maris bats left-handed, throws right-handed.)

Game numbers do not include a tie game played by the Yankees in 1961. It was the eighth game of the year, April 22, against Baltimore. Maris did not hit a homer in the game.

However, Maris will go into the record book as having hit the sixty-first in a 162-game schedule.

Maris finished the season with 590 official times at bat. Ruth, in 1927, had 540 official times at bat. Their total appearances at the plate, however, were nearly identical—698 for Maris and 692 for Ruth.

According to the official baseball rules, a batter is not charged with an official time at bat when "he hits a sacrifice bunt or sacrifice fly, is awarded first base on four called balls, is hit by a pitched ball or is awarded first base because of interference or obstruction."

Though it had taken 162 games (actually, 163, since the Yankees played one tie) a play-

Yanks' Score

deed, Greenberg had the best chance of all to crack the record. When he hit No. 58, he still had five games to play in a 154-game schedule.

When Stallard came to bat in the fifth the fans, who earlier had booed him when it seemed he might walk Maris, now generously applauded the hurler.

In the sixth, Maris, coming up for the third time, tried mightily to oblige the crowd with another home run. This time, however, Stallard struck him out on a 3-and-2 pitch.

With the Boston right-hander then stepping out for a pinch-hitter, Chet Nichols, an experienced 30-year-old left-hander, opposed Maris on his last turn at bat in the eighth. Roger ended the inning with a pop fly that the second baseman, Chuck Schilling, caught for the third out.

Apart from Maris, the Yankee hitters did not overly distinguish themselves, but Manager Ralph Houk saw enough to satisfy him. Superlative pitching made the biggest home run of 1961 stand up to the end.

Bill Stafford, who is to pitch the third game of the series against the Reds, hurled the first six innings and allowed only two hits, both by Russ Nixon. The first was a single, the second a triple. Hal Reniff then retired three Red Sox in the seventh and Luis Arroyo held them to one single in the last two innings.

er finally had risen from the ranks to pass Ruth's majestic record. Maris himself missed only two of these games, although he sat out a third without coming to bat when, after playing the first inning in the field, he was bothered by something in his eye.

For thirty-four years the greatest sluggers in baseball had striven to match Ruth's mark. Mickey Mantle fought Maris heroically through most of the season, but in the closing weeks he fell victim to a virus attack and his total stopped at fifty-four.

The two who came closest in the past were Jimmy Foxx and Hank Greenberg. In 1932, Foxx hit fifty-eight. In 1938, Greenberg matched that figure. In-

Thirty four years after Babe Ruth set the record of 60 home runs in a season, Roger Maris breaks it.

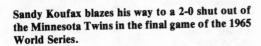

Sandy Koufax blazes his way to a 2-0 shut out of the Minnesota Twins in the final game of the 1965 World Series.

YANKS BEAT REDS A THIRD TIME, 7-0; FORD SETS RECORD

Pitcher Raises Series Mark to 32 Scoreless Innings Before Injury in 6th

O'TOOLE LOSES AGAIN

New York Team One Game Away From Final Victory —Richardson Gets 3 Hits

By JOHN DREBINGER
Special to The New York Times.

CINCINNATI, Oct. 8 — The Yankees defeated the Cincinnati Reds, 7 to 0, today and moved within a game of winning the 1961 world series.

Babe Ruth's forty-three-year-old pitching record of twenty-nine and two-thirds scoreless innings fell along with the Reds. The record was broken by the skillful Whitey Ford.

Ford was able to pitch only five innings before leaving with a bruised toe. But he departed with a world series mark of thirty-two consecutive scoreless innings. Before today, he had pitched three successive series shutouts.

The victory gave Ralph Houk's American League champions a 3-to-1 lead in games. They need only one more in the four-of-seven-game struggle to end it.

Reds on the Brink

They can end it here tomorrow, when Cincinnati gets its last view of the show. Should the Reds escape another defeat, the series will return to New York for the sixth game on Wednesday.

But there were few who felt Freddy Hutchinson's National Leaguers could salvage the series.

Roger Maris, whose homer won yesterday's game, hit no homers today. In fact, he got no hits in three official times at bat. His last time up, he struck out. On two other appearances he was walked, once intentionally.

Mickey Mantle, playing with a painful right hip, had to retire in the top half of the fourth, but not before he had delivered a damaging single.

Mantle's hit paved the way for the Yanks' first run.

That run, and a run in the fifth, were scored off Jim O'Toole, the crack young left-hander who was beaten by Ford's two-hitter in New York last Wednesday and was opposing Whitey a second time.

Coates Wraps It Up

When Ford withdrew after facing one batter in the sixth, Jim Coates, a tall right-hander from Virginia, took over. He held the shutout to the end before a crowd that totaled 32,589 for the second successive day.

The frustrated Reds never knew from which side the next blow would fall.

After O'Toole had yielded the fifth-inning tally, Hutchinson gambled with a pinch-hitter who didn't hit. The relief pitcher who followed, Jim Brosnan, didn't pitch well either.

The Yanks cuffed Brosnan for six hits in the sixth and seventh innings, scoring twice in the sixth, three times in the seventh.

There were no Yankee homers, but there were eleven hits. Bobby Richardson, who somehow needs a world series to inspire him, came up with three hits, one a double. This brought his series total of hits to eight. Bill Skowron also connected for three hits.

Ford hit himself on the right foot with a foul tip in the sixth. When he retired in the bottom of the inning after Elio Chacon had opened with a single, Ford received a rousing round of applause from the fans.

With his five scoreless innings, Ford had erased a record cherished by Ruth. The Bambino always had been mighty proud of that mark, which he rolled up in the series of 1916 and 1918 for the Boston Red Sox before he became the Sultan of Swat.

Last October Ford had pitched nine-inning shutouts against the Pittsburgh Pirates in the third and sixth games of the world series. In the opener of this series last Wednesday, he tossed another shutout.

Since Ford received credit for today's victory, he increased to nine his own world series record of most pitching triumphs. However, because he did not complete the game, he did miss tying Christy Mathewson's record of four world series shutouts.

Mathewson, the former great right-hander of the Giants, pitched three of his shutouts against the Athletics in 1905 and the fourth against the Athletics in 1913.

Fans in Shirt Sleeves

This was another day right out of July, with not a cloud in the sky, the temperature around 80 and the fans sitting in their shirt sleeves in the sun-drenched right-field bleach-ers and lower left-field stand.

The Reds dug into the past for another notable figure to toss out the first ball. Yesterday it had been the oldest living former major league player, 99-year-old Dummy Hoy. Today it was Bill McKechnie, the popular Deacon, who managed the last Cincinnati pennant-winning teams in 1939 and 1940.

Ford passed Ruth's pitching record in the third inning.

After retiring six Reds in a row in the first two innings, Whitey had one away in the third when Darrell Johnson, who was back in the Cincinnati lineup as the catcher, caused a mild flurry. The former third-string receiver of the Bombers plunked a single into left.

However, the suspense didn't last for long. O'Toole forced Johnson at second and Chacon ended the inning with a grounder to Richardson.

In connection with Ruth's record, there has always been a question whether the two-thirds of an inning should have counted.

In the first game of the 1916 World Series between the Red Sox and the Dodgers Ruth was tagged for a first-inning homer with two out by Hi Myer.

He then held the Dodgers scoreless until the Sox won the game, 2—1, in fourteen innings. The Babe thus received credit for thirteen and one-third innings of scoreless pitching.

In the 1918 series against the Cubs, Ruth pitched a nine-inning shutout in the opener. In the fourth game the Chicagoans for seven and one-third innings before they scored twice. Many contend that in a record of this sort fractions of an inning should not count.

O'Toole, as in the first game of the series, kept pace with Ford for three innings, then gave a tally in the fourth. It was Whitey's bosom pal, Mantle, who struck the decisive blow.

Skowron's Hit Wasted

Maris, who had fouled out in the first inning, drew a pass in opening the fourth. Mantle followed with a single to left center and Maris raced to third.

Mantle might have made it a double but he was limping badly as he ran to first. Houk immediately took him out of the game.

Hector Lopez was sent to run for Mickey, and when Elston Howard grounded into a double play, Maris scored.

In the fifth the Bombers picked up their second tally, although Skowron's inning-opening single was wiped out when Cletis Boyer slammed into a double play.

Ford drew a pass, however. Richardson and Tony Kubek weighed in with singles and Whitey scored. Richardson, one of the surprise hitting stars in last year's world series, also had hit a double in the third.

With O'Toole's departure for a pinch hitter in the fifth, Bros-

The Box Score

FOURTH GAME
NEW YORK YANKEES

	AB.	R.	H.	RBI.	PO.	A.
Richardson, 2b.	5	1	3	0	4	4
Kubek, ss.	5	0	1	1	0	4
Maris, rf. cf.	3	2	0	1	3	0
Mantle, cf.	2	0	1	0	3	0
aLopez, rf.	3	1	1	2	3	0
Howard, c.	4	1	1	0	3	0
Berra, lf.	2	1	1	0	4	0
Skowron, 1b.	3	0	3	1	9	0
Boyer, 3b.	4	0	1	2	0	2
Ford, p.	2	1	0	0	0	0
Coates, p.	1	0	0	0	0	0
Total	34	7	11	6	27	10

CINCINNATI REDS

	AB.	R.	H.	RBI.	PO.	A.
Chacon, 2b.	4	0	1	0	4	4
Kasko, ss.	4	0	1	0	1	2
Pinson, cf.	4	0	0	0	4	1
Robinson, rf.	1	0	0	0	2	0
Post, lf.	4	0	1	0	1	0
Freese, 3b.	4	0	0	0	1	2
Coleman, 1b.	4	0	0	0	5	0
D. Johnson, c.	2	0	2	0	5	0
cBell	1	0	0	0	0	0
Zimmerman, c.	1	0	0	0	3	0
O'Toole, p.	1	0	0	0	1	0
bGernert	1	0	0	0	0	0
Brosnan, p.	0	0	0	0	0	0
dLynch	1	0	0	0	0	0
Henry, p.	0	0	0	0	0	0
Total	31	0	5	0	27	9

aRan for Mantle in fourth.
bHit into force play for O'Toole in fifth.
cGrounded out for D. Johnson in seventh.
dStruck out for Brosnan in eighth.

New York......000 112 300—7
Cincinnati ......000 000 000—0

Error—Pinson. Double plays—Kasko, Chacon and Coleman; Kubek, Richardson and Skowron; Freese, Chacon and Coleman; Coleman (unassisted). Left on bases—New York 6, Cincinnati 7. Two-base hits—Richardson, Howard, Boyer.

	IP.	H.	R.	ER.
O'Toole (L)	5	5	2	2
Brosnan	3	6	5	5
Henry	1	0	0	0
*Ford (W)	5	4	0	0
Coates	4	1	0	0

*Faced one batter in sixth.

Bases on balls—Off O'Toole 3 (Skowron, Maris, Ford), Brosnan 3 (Berra 2, Maris), Coates 1 (Robinson). Struck out—By O'Toole 2 (Kubek, Howard), Brosnan 3 (Lopez, Howard, Coates), Henry 2 (Kubek, Maris), Ford 1 (Chacon), Coates 2 (Lynch, Freese). Hit by pitcher—By Ford (Robinson), by Coates (Robinson). Wild pitch—Brosnan.

Umpires—Donatelli (N). plate; Runge (A). first base; Conlan (N). second base; Umont (A). third base; Crawford (N). left field; Stewart (A). right field. Time of game—2:27; Attendance—32,589.

nan, the distinguished author and relief specialist, entered for the Reds in the sixth. He was promptly roughed up for two runs.

With one down, Howard doubled, Yogi Berra walked and Skowron outgalloped an infield hit. Then Boyer doubled to left, Howard and Berra scoring and Skowron stopping at third.

The inning ended on an odd note. Ford grounded out to the first baseman, Gordy Coleman, who tore across the diamond to track down Skowron between third and home. He completed the double play on the Moose single-handed.

It was also in this inning that Ford, just before grounding out, fouled off the ball that hit his toe.

The Reds had made only three hits in the first five innings, all singles. There wasn't much apprehension when Chacon opened the sixth with a single, except that for a moment it was feared that Berra, in making a diving stab for the ball, had hurt himself.

However, after receiving ministrations from Trainer Gus Mauch, Yogi found himself still in one piece and able to continue. He did have a slight cut over the right eye.

Meanwhile Houk had gone to the mound to confer with Ford and before anyone seemed aware a change was about to be made, Coates ambled up from the bull pen.

Apart from hitting Frank Robinson with a pitched ball, Coates had no difficulty making this a scoreless round, so that Ford's string of thirty-two scoreless innings remains intact. He can add more to it this year or in any future series.

Another Hit for Bobby

Finding Brosnan still around, the Yanks romped off with three more runs in the seventh while the home fans looked on in glum silence. Richardson's third hit began this assault. It was a single, with Bobby grabbing an extra base when Vada Pinson fumbled the ball.

Kubek flied out but Maris drew an intentional pass, and after a wild pitch had put the runners on second and third, Lopez scored both with a single to center.

Lopez took second on a futile throw to the plate. This, after Howard had fanned, induced Brosnan to give Berra an intentional pass. But that didn't help either.

Skowron's third straight single, a smash that rifled through the box and into center field, fetched home the third and final tally.

In suffering this second shutout of the series, the Reds collected only five hits, four off Ford, one off Coates. All were singles. Ford and Coates each hit one batter (Robinson both times) and Coates walked one (Robinson again). Only three Cincinnatians reached second base. None got to third.

October 9, 1961

Cheney of Senators Fans Record 21 in 16 Innings

BALTIMORE, Sept. 12 (UPI) —Tom Cheney, a baldish, much-traveled 27-year-old right-hander, set a record of twenty-one strikeouts for a game of any duration in pitching the Washington Senators to a 2-1 victory in sixteen innings over the Baltimore Orioles tonight.

But Zippel won the game with one out in the sixteenth when he hit a home run off Dick Hall.

Cheney, who had only three complete games in his twenty previous starts this season, had thirteen strikeouts in the regulation nine innings. He added two in each of the tenth and eleventh innings.

He equaled the modern record of eighteen by fanning Marv Breeding for the second out in the fourteenth inning. He made Hall his nineteenth victim for the third out of the fourteenth and got No. 20 to surpass even pre-1900 marks when he fanned Russ Snyder for the second out of the fifteenth inning. He wound up the game by getting a pinch hitter, Dick Williams, on a called third strike.

Feller, Koufax Hold Mark

Bob Feller and Sandy Koufax share the mark of eighteen strikeouts for a nine-inning game. The record for extra innings in the modern era was also eighteen and was held by Jack Coombs, who did it twice, and Warren Spahn. A pre-1900 record of nineteen strikeouts in a nine-inning game was set by Charles Sweeney and one-armed Hugh Daley in 1884.

Cheney, who gave ten hits, in all, didn't allow a hit between Boog Powell's single with one out in the eighth and Dave Nicholsons single with one out in the sixteenth for a string of eight hitless innings.

Baltimore made the score 1—1 in the seventh when Breeding doubled and Charlie Lau, batting for the Oriole starter, Milt Pappas, singled him home.

The Senators had scored in the first when Ron Stillwell got an infield single, went to third on Chuck Hinton's double and scored on Zipfel's grounder.

Cheney, who broke into the major leagues with the St. Louis Cardinals in 1957, has had a checkered career. After failing to win a game for St. Louis he pitched in the Pittsburgh Pirate chain, appeared in the 1960 world series with the Pirates and was purchased by the Senators from Columbus of the International League on June 29, 1961.

Tonight's victory was only his ninth in the majors against thirteen losses. For the season he is 6—8.

The Washington manager, Mickey Vernon, has always maintained that Cheney had as much equipment as any other member of the Senators' staff.

WASHINGTON (A.)				BALTIMORE (A.)			
	ab r h rbi				ab r h rbi		
Kennedy, ss	6 0 1 0			Adair, ss	6 0 2 0		
Stillwell, 2b	3 1 1 0			Snyder, rf	7 0 2 0		
bKing	1 0 1 0			Robinson, 3b	5 0 1 0		
Cottier, 2b	2 0 0 0			Gentile, 1b	7 0 1 0		
Hinton, rf	7 0 1 0			Powell, lf	6 0 1 0		
Zipfel, 1b	7 1 3 2			Nicholson, cf	7 0 1 0		
Retzer, c	7 0 0 0			Lancrith, c	6 0 0 0		
cOsteen	0 0 0 0			eBrandt	1 0 0 0		
Schmidt, c	0 0 0 0			Breeding, 2b	6 1 1 1		
Hicks, cf	5 0 1 0			fWilliams	1 0 0 0		
dSchaive	1 0 0 0			Pappas, p	2 0 0 0		
Piersall, cf	0 0 0 0			aLau	1 0 1 1		
Lock, lf	7 0 1 0			Hall, p	3 0 0 0		
Brinkman, 3b	5 0 1 0			Hoeft, p	0 0 0 0		
Cheney, p	6 0 0 0			Stock, p	0 0 0 0		
Total	57 2 10 2			Total	58 1 10 1		

aSingled for Pappas in 7th; bSingled for Stillwell in 10th; cRan for Retzer in 16th; dFouled out for Hicks in 16th; eFlied out for Landrith in 16th; fStruck out for Breeding in 16th.

Washington 1 0 0 0 0 0 0 0 0 0 0 0 0 0 0 1—2
Baltimore 0 0 0 0 0 0 1 0 0 0 0 0 0 0 0 0—1

E—Adair, Breeding A—Washington 12, Baltimore 16 LOB Washington 13, Baltimore 13. 2B Hits—Hinton, Snyder, Adair, Breeding HR Zipfel SB—Adair Sacrifice Cheney

	IP	H	R	ER	BB	SO
Cheney (W, 6-8)	16	10	1	1	4	21
Pappas	7	4	1	1	3	4
Hall (L, 6—6)	8⅓	5	1	1	1	4
Hoeft	⅓	1	0	0	0	0
Stock	⅓	0	0	0	1	0

Wild pitch—Cheney Balk—Pappas Umpires—McKinley, Chylak, Umont, Stewart. Time—3 59. Attendance—4,098.

September 13, 1962

Wills Sets Mark as Dodgers Lose

He Steals 96th and 97th Bases, but the Cards Win, 12-2

ST. LOUIS, Sept. 23 (UPI)—Maury Wills of the Los Angeles Dodgers stole two bases today to bring his total to 97 for 156 games, but the St. Louis Cardinals defeated the league leaders, 12—2.

Wills went one ahead of Ty Cobb's modern stolen base mark in the seventh inning. After reaching base on a single, he stole second easily. The throw, high over the bag, was not held.

He tied Cobb in the third after reaching base on a hit. With a crowd of 20,743 roaring its approval, Wills stole second as Carl Sawatski's throw bounced past Dal Maxvill.

Wills was retired when he tried to go to third base on a grounder to short. He received an ovation while he trotted off the field into the Dodger dugout where he was congratulated by waiting teammates.

When he went to the plate in the ninth, the game was stopped and the public address announcer presented a base to Wills, saying, "And you won't have to steal this one." After the game, Wills received the actual base that he had stolen to pass Cobb. Cobb had also amassed his total in 156 games.

The Cards had little trouble handling the stumbling Dodgers their fifth defeat in seven games. They collected 15 hits off five Dodger pitchers, putting together two three-run innings and one four-run inning.

Don Drysdale was pinned with his eighth loss, his third to the Cards, against his league high of 25 victories. He yielded three runs in the first and single runs in the third and fourth innings before leaving in the Cardinals' four-run fourth.

LOS ANGELES (N.)				ST. LOUIS (N.)			
	ab r h rbi				ab r h rbi		
Wills, ss	5 0 2 0			Javier, 2b	4 3 2 1		
Gilliam, 2b	4 1 3 0			Flood, cf	4 3 3 2		
Snider, lf	5 1 3 1			Musial, lf	3 1 2 3		
T. Davis, 3b	5 0 3 1			aShannon, lf	1 0 0 0		
Fairly, 1b	4 0 0 0			White, 1b	5 0 2 3		
Howard, rf	4 0 0 0			Boyer, 3b	5 0 3 1		
W. Davis, cf	3 0 1 0			Sawatski, c	4 0 0 1		
Roseboro, c	4 0 0 0			Kolb, rf	5 1 1 0		
Drysdale, p	2 0 0 0			Maxvill, ss	3 3 1 0		
Perranoski, p	0 0 0 0			Jackson, p	3 1 1 0		
J. Smith, p	0 0 0 0			Total	37 12 15 11		
Richert, p	0 0 0 0						
bHarkness	1 0 0 0						
Koufax, p	0 0 0 0						
cMoon	1 0 0 0						
Total	38 2 12 2						

aRan for Musial in 5th; bGrounded out for Richert in 7th; cStruck out for Koufax in 9th.

Los Angeles .... 2 0 0 0 0 0 0 0 0—2
St. Louis .... 3 0 1 4 3 0 1 0 .—12

E—T. Davis. A—Los Angeles 7, St. Louis 12. DP—Wills, Fairly. LOB—Los Angeles 11, St. Louis 9. 2B Hits—Gilliam, Snider, Flood, White, Boyer, Musial. SB—Wills 2. Sacrifice—Jackson. SF—Sawatski.

	IP	H	R	ER	BB	SO
Drysdale (L, 25—8)	3⅓	6	8	6	2	2
Perranoski	1	5	3	3	0	1
J. Smith	⅓	0	0	0	0	0
Richert	1⅓	2	0	0	1	3
Koufax	2	2	1	1	3	2
Jackson (W, 15—11)	9	12	2	2	1	6

HBP—By Drysdale (Flood), by Jackson (W. Davis). Umpires—Donatelli, Secory, Venzon, Pryor. Time—2 52. Attendance—20,743.

September 24, 1962

Giants Win Playoff, 6-4, in 9th; Oppose Yanks in Series Today

LOS ANGELES, Oct. 3—One of the most dramatic and nerve-racking pennant races in years came to an astounding end today when the San Francisco Giants vanquished the Dodgers, 6 to 4, in the third and deciding game of the National League playoff.

Before an incredulous crowd of 45,693 the Dodgers, holding a 4-2 lead in the ninth inning, came apart. Al Dark's San Franciscans jammed four runs across the plate that inning on two singles, four walks and a Dodger error.

Thus the Giants, moving into their 17th National League pennant, will face the American League champion Yankees in the World Series, which will open in San Francisco tomorrow.

Game time will be noon (3 P.M., New York time) as the Giants and Yankees meet for the seventh time in a World Series.

Ironically, just 11 years ago the Giants brought the Dodgers down in the ninth inning of the deciding playoff game on the wings of Bobby Thomson's electrifying three-run homer.

Today, however, the Giants' triumph wasn't quite so dramatic. Rather, in the earlier stages of the game, Walter Alston's Dodgers supplied most of the thrills.

With Johnny Podres and Juan Marichal the starting pitchers, the Dodgers had one jittery spell in the third inning when three ghastly errors gave Marichal a two-run lead. But here the Dodgers dug in and held firm.

They wrenched one run from Marichal in the fourth. In the sixth came what almost everyone in the steaming arena believed to be the turning point. After the Giants had filled the bases on three hits with nobody out, Ed Roebuck went to Podres's rescue and stopped the Giants cold on four pitches.

In the last of the sixth the crowd went into a frenzy as the Dodgers swept ahead on a two-run homer by Tommy Davis. The mercurial Maury Wills added a run in the seventh.

Connecting for a single, his fourth hit of the day, Maury, who already had stolen a base, now stole second. He then stole third, and when a frustrated throw by the catcher, Ed Bailey, sailed by that base, the fleet Dodger kept running and scored. Wills closed the season with 104 stolen bases, a modern

major league record.

That seemed to wrap it up. The Dodgers were leading, 4—2, and with Roebuck moving serenely along with brilliant relief pitching, preparations already were under way for the opening of the World Series in Chavez Ravine.

But then came the Giants' decisive ninth. It opened with Matty Alou batting for Larsen and singling. He was forced by Harvey Kuenn for the first out.

Roebuck's control deserted him. He walked a pinch-hitter, Willie McCovey, who gave way to a pinch-runner, Ernie Bowman. Felipe Alou also walked, filling the bases.

Now Willie Mays, hitless up to here though he had drawn two walks, slammed a single that caromed off Roebuck. The ball remained in the infield, but Kuenn scored and the bases remained filled.

Roebuck gave way to Stan Williams, who saw Orlando Cepeda lift a sacrifice fly to right that scored Bowman with the tying run. The fly also advanced Felipe Alou to third.

When a wild pitch that rolled only a few feet from the plate sent Mays to second, Alston ordered an intentional walk to Bailey, again filling the bases.

But that also backfired, for Williams, never noted for his control, also walked Jim Davenport. This forced in the tie-breaking run.

Left-handed Ron Perranoski relieved Williams and appeared to have brought matters under control with the Dodgers still trailing by only one run. But Larry Burright, who had taken over as the Dodgers second baseman in a late-inning defensive maneuver, fumbled José Pagan's grounder behind second. Mays raced across the plate on the play, and the Giants had a 6-4 lead.

The Giants never needed that extra margin. Dark, recalling how his Giants had frittered away yesterday's second game after holding a 5—0 lead, was taking no chances this time.

To pitch the last of the ninth he called in his brilliant left-hander, Billy Pierce, who had blanked the Dodgers on three hits in the playoff opener on Monday. The stunned Dodgers were helpless again.

A grounder, two fly balls that Willie the Wonder caught in dead center, and to paraphrase the immortal words of Chuck Dressen, there was nothing to say but "The Dodgers is dead."

Podres was the third pitcher to go to the mound in this playoff with only two days of rest—Don Drysdale and Jack Sanford were the others. Podres got by well enough in the first two innings. But in the third, the Dodgers suddenly took to tossing the ball around in a manner that would have had the Mets green with envy.

Podres himself committed one of three errors. When the Giants added three hits to the mixture, the astonishing part was the Dodgers escaped with only two runs scored against them.

After Pagan had opened the third with a single, Marichal followed with a bunt that Podres fielded, then fired into center field in a bold attempt to force Pagan at second. That put Pagan on third and Marichal at first.

Kuenn then singled to left, scoring Pagan and moving Marichal to second. Then came another butter-fingered play. As Chuck Hiller missed a bunt attempt, Marichal appeared hopelessly trapped off second. But John Roseboro's throw sailed into center field and allowed Marichal to reach third.

A bizarre play followed. When Hiller flied to Duke Snider in short left, Marichal remained glued to third. But Kuenn broke for second and drew a throw to Jim Gilliam, who fired the ball to first in the hope of nailing the retreating Kuenn. But the ball cracked Harvey on the back of the head, and Marichal scored on this error.

Behind all this came a single by Felipe Alou that sent Kuenn to third. Felipe took second on the throw-in. But Podres finally got matters under control by intentionally walking Mays, then getting Cepeda to slap into a double play.

Those two runs had most of the crowd glum, but not for long. In the fourth the Dodgers got back one run after Snider, their old reliable, had opened with a double to right. Tommy Davis singled sharply to left,

but the Duke had to hold at third. He was still there after Wally Moon had lifted a fairly long fly to right.

However, when the Giant infield failed to convert Frank Howard's grounder into a double play by way of second, Snider finally crossed the plate.

In the sixth the Giants finished Podres, but before this inning was over it was the San Franciscans who were groaning. A big Giant killing appeared in the making as singles by Cepeda and Bailey and a beautifully executed bunt single by Davenport filled the bases with nobody out.

Roebuck emerged from the Dodger bull pen, and the Giant threat vanished with the smog. Pagan grounded to Wills for a force play at the plate. Marichal also grounded to Maury, who stepped on second, then whipped the ball to first for an inning-ending double play.

Minutes later, the sun really shone for the home folks as the Dodgers swept ahead on Tommy Davis' homer. Snider opened the Dodger sixth with a single to left, his second hit of the day. Then, with the count 3 and 1, Tommy drove the ball 400 feet into the bleachers in left center.

It was homer No. 27 for this Davis, who also wound up the season as the National League's leading batter.

The Dodgers fattened their lead to 4-2 on Wills's heroics in the seventh. But Maury's derring-do was forgotten as the Giants rallied in the ninth and made it good-by pennant race, hello World Series.

Box Score of 3d Playoff Game

SAN FRANCISCO (N.)	AB.	R.	H.	RBI.	PO.	A.
Kuenn, lf.	5	1	2	1	2	0
Hiller, 2b.	3	0	1	0	4	1
bMcCovey	0	0	0	0	0	0
cBowman, 2b.	0	1	0	0	0	0
F. Alou, rf.	4	1	1	0	4	0
Mays, cf.	3	1	1	1	3	0
Cepeda, 1b.	4	0	1	1	8	0
Bailey, c.	4	0	2	0	3	0
Davenport, 3b.	4	0	1	1	2	4
Pagan, ss.	5	1	2	0	1	2
Marichal, p.	5	2	1	1	0	0
Larsen, p.	0	0	0	0	0	0
aM. Alou	1	0	1	0	0	1
dNieman	1	0	0	0	0	0
Pierce, p.	0	0	0	0	0	0
Total	36	6	13	4	27	7

LOS ANGELES (N.)	AB.	R.	H.	RBI.	PO.	A.
Wills, ss.	5	1	4	0	3	0
Gilliam, 2b-3b.	5	0	0	0	3	1
Snider, lf.	3	2	2	0	2	1
Burright, 2b.	1	0	0	0	3	2
eWalls	1	0	0	0	0	0
T. Davis, 3b-lf.	3	1	2	2	1	0
Moon, 1b.	3	0	0	0	8	0
Fairly, 1b-rf.	0	0	0	0	2	0
Howard, rf.	4	0	1	0	0	0
Harkness, 1b.	0	0	0	0	0	0
Roseboro, c.	3	0	0	0	3	1
W. Davis, cf.	3	0	0	0	2	0
Podres, p.	2	0	0	0	0	2
Roebuck, p.	2	0	0	0	0	2
Williams, p.	0	0	0	0	0	0
Perranoski, p.	0	0	0	0	0	0
Total	35	4	8	3	27	14

aSingled for Larsen in 9th; bWalked for Hiller in 9th; cRan for McCovey in 9th; dStruck out for M. Alou in 9th; eLined out for Burright in 9th.

San Francisco Giants	0	0	2	0	0	0	0	4—6
Los Angeles Dodgers	0	0	0	1	0	2	1	0 0—4

Errors—Marichal, Podres, Roseboro, Gilliam, Pagan, Bailey, Burright. Double plays—Gilliam, Wills and Moon; Wills and Moon; Wills, Burright and Fairly. Left on bases—San Francisco 12, Los Angeles 8.

Two-base hits—Snider, Hiller. Home run—T. Davis. Stolen bases—Wills 3, T. Davis. Sacrifices—Hiller, Marichal, Fairly. Sacrifice fly—Cepeda.

	IP.	H.	R.	ER.	BB.	SO.	HBP.	WP.	Balks
*Marichal	7	3	4	3	1	2	0	1	0
Larsen (W. 5–4)	1	0	0	0	2	1	0	0	0
Pierce	1	0	0	0	1	0	0	0	0
†Podres	5	9	2	2	1	2	0	0	0
Roebuck (L, 10–2)	3⅓	4	4	3	3	0	0	0	0
Williams	⅓	0	0	0	2	0	0	1	0
Perranoski	⅓	0	0	0	1	0	0	0	0

*Faced one batter in 8th. †Faced three batters in 6th.

Bases on balls—Off Marichal 1 (T. Davis), Larsen 2 (Roseboro, W. Davis), Podres 1 (Mays), Roebuck 3 (Mays, McCovey, F. Alou), Williams 2 (Bailey, Davenport). Struck out—By Marichal 2 (Roseboro, Podres), Larsen 1 (Howard), Perranoski 1 (Nieman). Wild pitch—Williams. Umpires—Boggess (plate), Conlan (second base), Barlick (third base). Time of game—3:00. Attendance—45,693.

Spahn Beats Phils for No. 20 And Ties Mathewson's Record

Braves' Left-Hander Becomes 20-Game Winner for 13th Time With 3-2 Victory

PHILADELPHIA, Sept. 8 (AP). — Warren Spahn, Milwaukee's 42-year-old pitching great, hurled the Braves to a 3-2 victory over the Philadelphia Phils today and became a 20-game winner for the 13th time. He tied Christy Mathewson for the most 20-victory seasons in National League history.

The major league record for 20-victory seasons is 16 held by Cy Young. He pitched for Cleveland and Boston in the American League and St. Louis in the National League, mostly before the turn of the century. Mathewson compiled his record with the New York Giants.

Gene Oliver produced the deciding blow with a two-run homer that broke a 1—1 tie in the top of the eighth.

Spahn, who recently took over seventh place among baseball's career winners, earned his 347th victory by scattering nine hits.

For six innings it appeared Spahn might hurl his 61st shutout. But in the seventh, Tony Gonzalez lined a ball to center that took a weird hop past Lee Maye for a triple. Gonzalez scored on a sacrifice fly by Roy Sievers.

Spahn, who has lost only five games this season, gave two singles following the run, but retired Bob Oldis and Bob Wine on infield outs to end the inning.

In the ninth, Don Demeter hit a homer to bring the Phillies within one run and Don Hoak followed with a double. But Spahn bore down and got Oldis on a grounder and Wes Covington on a fly to end it.

Milwaukee scored its first run in the first inning on a single by Maye, who took second on an overthrow by the Phillie pitcher, Dallas Green. Frank Bolling sacrificed Maye to third and he scored as Hank Aaron grounded out.

MILWAUKEE (N.)					PHILADELPHIA (N.)				
	ab	r	h	rbi		ab	r	h	rbi
Maye, cf, lf	5	1	2	0	Taylor, 2b	4	0	0	0
Bolling, 2b	4	0	0	0	Callison, rf	4	0	1	0
Aaron, rf	5	0	0	1	Gonzalez, lf	4	1	2	0
Mathews, lf	3	1	2	0	Sievers, 1b	3	0	1	1
Cline, cf	1	0	0	0	Demeter, cf	4	1	2	1
J. Torre, c	4	0	0	0	Hoak, 3b	4	0	3	0
Oliver, 1b	4	1	1	2	Oldis, c	4	0	0	0
Menke, 3b	4	0	3	0	Wine, ss	3	0	0	0
McMillan, ss	3	0	2	0	Short, p	0	0	0	0
Spahn, p	3	0	1	0	aCovington	1	0	0	0
					Green, p	2	0	0	0
Total	36	3	11	3	Amaro, ss	1	0	0	0
					Total	34	2	9	2

aFlied out for Short in 9th.

Milwaukee .... 1 0 0   0 0 0   0 2 0—3
Philadelphia ...... 0 0 0   0 0 0   1 0 1—2

E—Green. A—Milwaukee 15, Philadelphia 14. DP—Menke, Bolling, Oliver. LOB—Milwaukee 10, Philadelphia 6.
2B Hit—Hoak. 3B—Mathews, Gonzalez. HR—Oliver, Demeter. SB—Menke. Sacrifice—Bolling. SF—Sievers.

	IP.	H.	R.	ER.	BB.	SO.
Spahn (W, 20—5)	9	9	2	2	0	0
Green (L, 5—4)	7⅓	11	3	3	3	1
Short	1⅔	0	0	0	0	2

Umpires—Walsh, Jackowski, Crawford, Burkhart. Time—2:22. Attendance—8,807.

September 9, 1963

Giants Top Mets Twice as 7-Hour-23-Minute, 23-Inning 2d Game Sets Mark

NEW YORK DROPS 5-3, 8-6 CONTESTS

57,037, Season's Top Crowd in Majors, Attend Games— Mets Make Triple Play

By JOSEPH DURSO

Baseball's transcontinental archrivals—the New York Mets and San Francisco Giants—battled through 10 hours and 23 minutes of a titanic doubleheader at Shea Stadium yesterday that included the longest game on a time basis ever played in the major leagues.

Endurance records, attendance records and performance records fell through nine innings of the first game and 23 innings of the second before the largest crowd of the baseball season anywhere—57,037.

The huge throng saw the Giants square the spectacular holiday weekend series with the Mets by winning, 5-3 and 8-6. And the 8,000 to 10,000 still on hand when the action ended at 11:25 P.M. saw 41 players struggle for 7 hours and 23 minutes, a record, in the second game.

They saw baseball rarities like a two-man triple play executed in the 14th inning of the second game by Roy McMillan and Ed Kranepool, the second triple play in Met history.

Two Strike-Out Records

They saw 12 pitchers share in two strike-out records—36 in one game and 47 in one day.

They saw the Mets carry the second game into extra innings on Joe Christopher's three-run seventh-inning home run. Then, 16 innings later, they saw a pinch-hitter, Del Crandall, the 40th man in the game, break the tie with a double into the right-field corner.

Finally, they saw history repeat itself for two pitchers, Gaylord Perry of the Giants and Galen Cisco of the Mets. Tht pitched an entire game in relief—10 innings for Perry and nine for Cisco—in a duplicate of the 15-inning struggle in San Francisco two weeks ago. A home run by Willie Mays sent that game into extra innings before the Giants won, 6—4, with Perry the winner and Cisco the loser.

But most of the performance records pale alongside the monumental endurance records that the Giants and Mets set:

¶They played the longest game in time elapsed in major-league history: 7 hours 23 minutes. This was 23 minutes longer than the 22-inning struggle between the New York Yankees and Tigers at Detroit on June 24, 1962, won by the Yankees, 9—7.

¶They played the longest double-header in history: 9 hours 52 minutes on the field. Many fans sat for about 10½ hours, including the intermis-

sion, and many small boys who hate to miss batting practice doubtless sat for a dozen hours.

¶They played the most innings ever played by big-league teams in one day: 32. This surpassed the 29 innings that the Boston Red Sox and Philadelphia Athletics labored through in a double-header on July 4, 1905.

¶They played the fourth longest game in baseball history. Brooklyn and Boston hold the marathon record, 26 innings to a 1-1 tie on May 1, 1920. There were two 24-inning games in the American League and a 23-inning tie, again between Brooklyn and Boston.

So the Giants and Mets played the longest National League game to a decision when the Giants made the decisive moves with two out and nobody on base in the 23d inning.

By that time the lights had been on nearly four hours; Alvin Dark, the Giants' manager, had been ejected from the game, and Mays had gone back to center field after playing shortstop.

The first blow was struck by Jim Davenport, whose home run had ended the 15-inning game in San Francisco. This time he drove a long liner into the right-field corner for a triple. The Mets then gave Cap Petersen an intentional base on balls. The Giants countered by calling Crandall in from the bull pen to swing for Perry, their fifth pitcher.

Crandall responded with a whistler into the right-field cor-

First Game Score

SAN FRANCISCO (N.)					NEW YORK (N.)				
	ab	r	h	rbi		ab	r	h	rbi
Kuenn, lf	5	0	3	1	Kanehl, 2b	4	0	1	0
cM. Alou, lf	0	0	0	0	McMillan, ss	4	0	0	0
Crandall, c	4	0	0	0	Gonder, c	4	0	1	0
Mays, cf	3	1	1	0	Thomas, lf	4	0	1	0
Hart, 3b	4	1	1	0	bR. Smith, lf	0	0	0	0
Cepeda, 1b	4	2	3	1	Christpher, rf	4	1	1	0
Davenport, 2b	3	0	1	1	Kranepool, 1b	4	1	1	0
J. Alou, rf	4	1	2	1	Hickman, cf	4	1	2	3
Garrido, ss	3	0	1	0	C. Smith, 3b	3	0	2	0
Marichal, p	4	0	0	0	Jackson, p	1	0	0	0
					Sturdivant, p	0	0	0	0
Total	34	5	12	4	aAltman	1	0	0	0
					Bearnarth, p	0	0	0	0
					dStephenson	1	0	0	0
					Total	34	3	8	3

aStruck out for Sturdivant in 7th; bRan for Thomas in 8th; cRan for Kuenn in 9th; dStruck out for Bearnarth in 9th.

San Francisco ...... 0 0 0   1 0 3   0 0 1—5
New York .... 0 3 0   0 0 0   0 0 0—3

E—Hickman, Hart. A—San Francisco 10, New York 14. DP—Garrido, Davenport; Cepeda; McMillan, Kranepool. LOB—San Francisco 6, New York 6.
2 B Hits—Cepeda, C. Smith. HR—Hickman. SB—Cepeda. Sacrifices—Crandall, Jackson, Garrido. SF—Davenport.

	IP.	H.	R.	ER.	BB.	SO.
Marichal (W, 8—1)	9	8	3	3	0	7
*Jackson (L, 3—7)	5	8	4	4	1	3
Sturdivant	2	2	0	0	0	0
Bearnarth	2	2	1	1	0	1

*Faced 3 batters in 6th.
HBP—By Marichal (C. Smith). Umpires—Burkhart, Sudol, Pryor, Secory. Time—2:29.

ner that went for a ground-rule double, scoring Davenport and breaking a deadlock that had persisted for 16 innings.

For good measure on this day of incredible baseball, Jesus Alou outgalloped a topper to the right of the mound and Petersen scored, making it 8—6.

For the Mets, Chris Cannizzaro and John Stephenson struck out and Amado Samuel hit a fly to right field. The clock read 11:25 and the scoreboard read Giants 8, Mets 6.

Before the end, both sides had

Baseball's Longest Game

SAN FRANCISCO GIANTS (N.)				
	ab.	r.	h.	rbi
Kuenn, lf	5	1	0	0
Perry, p	3	0	0	0
jCrandall	1	0	1	0
Hendley, p	0	0	0	0
J. Alou, rf	10	1	4	2
Mays, cf, ss	10	1	1	1
Cepeda, 1b	9	1	3	0
Haller, c	10	1	4	1
Hiller, 2b	8	1	1	1
Hart, 3b	4	0	1	1
hM. Alou, cf, lf	6	0	0	0
Garrido, ss	3	0	0	0
fMcCovey	1	0	0	0
Davenport, ss, 3b	4	1	1	1
Bolin, p	2	0	1	0
MacKenzie, p	0	0	0	0
Shaw, p	0	0	0	0
gSnider	1	0	0	0
Herbel, p	0	0	0	0
iPeterson, 3b	4	1	0	0
Total	81	8	17	8

NEW YORK METS (N.)				
	ab.	r.	h.	rbi
Kanehl, 2b	1	0	0	0
cGonder	1	0	0	0
Samuel, 2b	7	0	2	0
McMillan, ss	10	1	2	0
Thomas, lf	10	1	2	0
Christopher, rf	10	2	4	3
Kranepool, 1b	10	1	3	1
Hickman, cf	10	1	2	0
C. Smith, 3b	9	0	4	1
Cannizzaro, c	7	0	1	1
Wakefield, p	0	0	0	0
aAltman	1	0	0	0
bJackson	0	0	0	0
Anderson, p	0	0	0	0
Sturdivant, p	0	0	0	0
dD. Smith	1	0	0	0
Lary, p	0	0	0	0
eTaylor	1	0	0	0
Bearnarth, p	3	0	0	0
Cisco, p	2	0	0	0
kStephenson	1	0	0	0
Total	83	6	20	6

aWalked intentionally for Wakefield in 2d; bRan for Altman in 2d; cFlied out for Kanehl in 2d; dGrounded out for Sturdivant in 5th; eStruck out for Lary in 7th; fStruck out for Garrido in 8th; gGrounded out for Shaw in 9th; hGrounded out for Hart in 10th; iLined out for Herbel in 13th; jDoubled for Perry in 23d; kStruck out for Cisco in 23d.

San Francisco 204 000 000 000 000 000 000 02–8
New York 010 002 300 000 000 000 000 00–6

Errors—Garrido, Haller, Cepeda, Cisco. Putouts and assists—San Francisco 69-14, New York 69-31. Double plays—Perry, Davenport, Cepeda; Davenport, Cepeda; Christopher, Kranepool. Triple play—McMillan, Kranepool. Left on bases—San Francisco 16, New York 14. Two-base hits—J. Alou, Kranepool, Cepeda, Crandall. Three-base hits—Kranepool, Haller, Davenport. Home run—Christopher. Sacrifices—Herbel, Hiller, C. Smith, Cisco.

	IP.	H.	R.	ER.	BB.	SO.
Bolin	6 2/3	8	6	5	2	7
*MacKenzie	0	1	0	0	0	0
Shaw	1 1/3	1	0	0	0	1
Herbel	4	3	0	0	0	3
Perry (W, 3–1)	10	7	0	0	1	9
Hendley	1	0	0	0	0	2
Wakefield	2	2	2	2	2	1
Anderson	1/3	4	4	4	0	0
Sturdivant	2 2/3	3	0	0	1	2
Lary	7	0	0	0	0	2
Bearnarth	9	3	0	0	4	4
Cisco (L, 2–5)		5	2	2	2	5

*Faced 1 batter in 7th.
Hit by pitcher—By Shaw (Samuel); by Cisco (Cepeda). Passed ball—Cannizzaro. Umpires—Sudol, Pryor, Secory, Burkhart. Time—7:23. Attendance—57,037.

performed wild feats of thwarting rallies as they toiled overtime.

San Francisco had started strong against Bill Wakefield, giving Bob Bolin, their first pitcher, a cushion of six runs.

The major power was displayed in the third inning when the Giants shook off a two-week batting slump during which they had hit .173, pushing across four runs. These were produced by singles by Alou, Orlando Cepeda, Tom Haller, Chuck Hiller, Jim Hart and Bolin.

The Mets nibbled away, however, narrowing the margin to 6—3 and finally, in the seventh, sending the game into extra innings on one tremendous drive.

McMillan and Frank Thomas were aboard with singles when the lightning struck with a count of 3 balls and no strikes. Bolin came in with a fast ball over the plate and Christopher powered it 400 feet over the fence in left-center beyond a mighty leap by Mays.

For the next 16 innings extraordinary defensive play and relief pitching on both sides kept the score at 6-6.

McMillan supplied the most dramatic play in the 14th after Alou had singled and Mays walked. Cepeda then hit a liner behind second base that McMillan speared as Alou and Mays ran full speed ahead. McMillan stepped on second, doubling off Alou, who was halfway to third, and fired the ball to Kranepool to catch Mays.

It was the second triple play of the season, the Philadelphia Phillies having executed one against the Houston Colts. The Mets made their first on Memorial Day, 1962, when Elio Chacon, Charlie Neal and Gil Hodges collaborated.

Davenport Ends Threats

In the 15th and 17th innings.

Davenport made dazzling tags at second base in starting double plays that held off the Mets. And among the relief pitchers Larry Bearnarth worked seven innings after going two in the first game, while Cisco added nine to seven he had pitched on Thursday.

The first game had had its moments, too, although they seemed remote by the time the day ended.

For one thing, the Mets broke one of their most frustrating streaks of the year—they had gone 37 innings without providing any runs for Al Jackson. Then, they provided three, but it was not enough.

The Mets scored their three runs off Juan Marichal in one cluster after Christopher and Kranepool, just back from Buffalo, had singled. Jim Hickman then lined his third home run of the season and his second of the weekend into the left field stand.

But in the sixth, the Giants retaliated. Captain May walked,

Jim Hart singled and Cepeda doubled to left. Tom Sturdivant relieved Jackson at this point. Davenport's long fly to center scored Hart with the typing run and sent Cepeda to third.

After one strike to Gil Garrido, Cepeda came thundering down the base line as Sturdivant threw a low, outside knuckleball. Cepeda slid across the plate to steal home before Jesse Gonder could make the tag. Ironically, Garrido then singled to left, but the Giants had a 4-3 lead they never relinquished.

The double victory for the Giants evened the four-game series with the Mets, but left the Mets one-up in nine games played for the year.

The crowd raised attendance for the three days this weekend to 150,571—a figure that is believed safe until next weekend, when the Los Angeles Dodgers come to town.

June 1, 1964

Bunning Pitches a Perfect Game; Mets Are Perfect Victims, 6 to 0

By GORDON S. WHITE Jr.

Jim Bunning of the Philadelphia Phillies pitched the first perfect game in the National League in 84 years yesterday when he retired all 27 New York Met batters.

The Phils won the contest, the first game of a doubleheader at Shea Stadium, by 6—0 before 32,904 fans who were screaming for Bunning during the last two innings.

The lanky right-hander became the eighth man in the 88-year history of major league baseball to pitch a perfect game. He is the first man to pitch one in the majors since

Don Larsen of the New York Yankees did not permit a Brooklyn Dodger to reach base in the fifth game of the 1956 World Series. That was the only perfect game ever pitched in a World Series game.

Bunning also became the first pitcher in the modern era (since 1901) to hurl a no-hit game in each major league. The former Detroit Tiger pitcher held the Boston Red Sox hitless on July 20, 1958. That performance, during which he walked two batters and hit one, came in the first game of a Sunday double-header on a

hot day at Fenway Park in Boston.

Yesterday's perfect pitching turned the usually loyal Met fans into Bunning fans in the late innings. From the seventh inning on, the 32-year-old Bunning had the crowd virtually 100 per cent behind him as he toiled in the 91-degree heat.

When Bunning struck out a rookie, John Stephenson, the 27th and last Met hitter, he received a standing ovation that lasted for many minutes. He was mobbed by his teammates, and when he went to the dugout, the crowd began calling, "We want Bunning! We want Bunning!"

He returned to the field to be interviewed behind home plate by Ralph Kiner on a television show. The crowd, still standing, gave him one of the biggest ovations ever heard in the Mets' new stadium.

The last National League pitcher to hurl perfect ball was

John M. Ward for Providence against Buffalo on June 17, 1880. Five days before that, John Lee Richmond of Worcester hurled the first perfect game against Cleveland in the National League (The American League was established in 1901.)

Many rules have been changed since the achievements of Ward and Richmond. In 1880, the distance from the pitcher to batter was 45 feet. The distance now is 60 feet 6 inches. Also in 1880, it took nine balls to gain a base on balls and a batter was out if a foul ball was caught on the first bounce.

Since the turn of the century, five American League pitchers have recorded perfect games. Larsen's achievement was the first since Charlie Robertson of the Chicago White Sox pitched one against the Detroit Tigers on April 30, 1922. Thus Bunning's was the first regular-season major league perfect game in 42 years.

Bunning, who became disenchanted last season with the Detroit Tigers' manager Chuck Dressen, was traded with a catcher, Gus Triandos, to the Phillies for Don Demeter, an outfielder, and Jack Hamilton, a pitcher, last Dec. 4. Bunning has been a star this season in the Phillies' bid for their first pennant in 14 years. Triandos caught the perfect game yesterday.

It was Bunning's seventh victory of the season against two defeats.

Bunning threw only 86 pitches with his customary three-quarter motion. The Mets were baffled by his fast curve, and by the slider he used now and then as he struck out 10.

Only three Mets came close to getting a hit. One, Jesse Gonder, nearly broke up the perfect game with a hard shot toward right field in the fifth inning.

Gonder slammed one half way between Tony Taylor, the second baseman, and John Herrnstein, the first baseman. It was Taylor's play, and he made it.

With a diving stab at the hard-hit ball, Tony slapped it to the ground. He quickly recovered it then easily tossed out Gonder. The ball was hit so hard that by the time Taylor had control of it, Gonder was only about a third of the way to first base.

In the third inning, Amado Samuel lined a ball over shortstop, but Cookie Rojas jumped about two or three feet and caught the liner for the out.

In the fourth, Ron Hunt, the Mets' leading hitter, popped a fly ball along the right-field line. The ball was out of the reach of Johnny Callison, who was playing toward right-center for the right-handed Hunt.

The ball landed a foot in foul territory, however, and the perfect game was saved. Hunt then struck out after getting the count to three balls and two strikes.

Bunning fanned Jim Hickman, the Mets' lead-off batter, three times.

Hawk Taylor, who was called out on strikes in the eighth, ran the count to 3 and 2, as did Hunt in the fourth. But after Taylor was called out by the plate umpire, Ed Sudol, Triandos dropped the ball. But Triandos jumped on the ball quickly and tossed to Herrnstein to put out Taylor.

The Phils who also won the second game, 8—2, had an easy time in the opener against three pitchers, collecting eight hits, one a home run by Callison leading off the four-run sixth inning.

The Met pitching victim in the sixth was the starter, Tracy Stallard. Bunning's double drove in the last two runs and drove out Stallard. Bill Wakefield took the mound.

Tom Sturdivant pitched the last three innings without permitting a run. Stephenson was hitting for Sturdivant in the ninth when he fanned for the final out.

In the second game, the Mets were held to three hits by a rookie, Rick Wise, and John Klippstein. Frank Lary, who was traded from the Tigers to the Mets only three weeks ago, and was once a team-mate of

Bunning's, was the Mets' starter and loser.

Johnny Briggs started Lary to defeat with a lead-off homer in the first inning. Callison also hit another homer with the bases empty.

The sweep of the twin bill increased the Phils league lead to two games.

Met Scores

Perfect Game

PHILADELPHIA PHILS (N.)

	AB.	R.	H.	PO.	A.	Bi.
Briggs, cf	4	1	0	2	0	0
Herrnstein, 1b	4	0	0	7	0	0
Callison, rf	4	1	2	1	0	1
Allen, 3b	3	0	1	0	2	1
Covington, lf	2	0	0	1	0	0
aWine, ss	1	1	0	2	1	0
T. Taylor, 2b	3	2	1	3	0	0
Rojas, ss, lf	3	0	1	3	0	0
Triandos, c	4	1	2	11	1	2
Bunning, p	4	0	1	0	0	2
Totals	32	6	8	27	7	6

NEW YORK METS (N.)

	AB.	R.	H.	PO.	A.	Bi.
Hickman, cf	3	0	0	2	0	0
Hunt, 2b	3	0	0	3	2	0
Kranepool, 1b	3	0	0	8	0	0
Christopher, rf	3	0	0	4	0	0
Gonder, c	3	0	0	7	1	0
R. Taylor, lf	3	0	0	1	0	0
C. Smith, ss	3	0	0	1	1	0
Samuel, 3b	2	0	0	0	1	0
cAltman	1	0	0	0	0	0
Stallard, p	1	0	0	0	3	0
Wakefield, p	0	0	0	0	0	0
bKanehl	1	0	0	0	0	0
Sturdivant, p	0	0	0	1	0	0
dStephenson	1	0	0	0	0	0
Totals	27	0	0	27	8	0

a—Ran for Covington in 6th; b—Grounded out for Wakefield in 6th; c—struck out for Samuel in 9th; d—Struck out for Sturdivant in 9th.

Philadelphia ... 110 004 000—6
New York ..... 000 000 000—0

Errors—None. Left on Bases—Philadelphia 5, New York 0.
Two Base Hits—Triandos, Bunning. Home Run—Callison. Sacrifices—Herrnstein, Rojas.

	IP.	H.	R.	ER.	BB.	SO.
Bunni'g (W. 7-2)	9	0	0	0	0	10*
Stallard (L, 4-9)	5 2-3	7	6	6	4	3
Wakefield	1-3	0	0	0	0	0
Sturdivant	3	1	0	0	0	3

*Bunning struck out Hickman 3, C. Smith, Hunt, Kranepool, Christopher, R. Taylor, Altman, Stephenson.

Wild Pitch—Stallard. Time—2:19. Umpires— Sudol, Pryor, Secory, Burkhart. Attendance—32,026.

SECOND GAME

PHILADELPHIA (N.)

	ab.	r.	h.	bi.		**NEW YORK (N.)**	ab.	r.	h.	bi.
Briggs, cf	5	1	1	1		Hickman, cf	5	0	0	0
Herrnstein, 1b, rf	5	0	0	0		Hunt, 2b	5	0	0	0
						Kranepool, 1b	3	0	0	0
Callison, rf	3	1	1	1		Christopher, rf	5	0	1	1
Sievers, ph, 1b	2	0	1	0		Gonder, c	3	1	1	0
Allen, 3b	3	1	0	0		B. Taylor, lf	4	0	1	0
Amaro, 3b	1	0	1	0		C. Smith, ss	3	0	0	0
Covington, lf	3	1	2	0		Samuel, 3b	2	0	0	0
Wine, pr, ss	2	1	1	0		Altman, ph	1	0	0	0
T. Taylor, 2b	4	2	2	2		Stephenson, 3b	0	0	0	0
Rojas, ss, lf	2	1	1	1		Lary, p	0	1	0	0
Dalrymple, c	2	0	1	2		Kanehl, ph	1	0	0	0
Wise, p	2	0	0	1		Cannizzaro, ph	0	0	0	0
						D. Smith, ph	1	0	0	0
Totals	34	8	11	8		Totals	33	2	3	1

Philadelphia .... 3 0 1 1 3 0 0 0 0—8
New York .... 0 1 1 0 0 0 0 0 0—2

E—T. Taylor, Allen 2, Wine. DP—New York 1. LOB—Philadelphia 7, New York 11. 2B—Covington, T. Taylor. HR—Briggs (1), Callison (10). SF—Dalrymple, Wise.

	IP.	H.	R.	ER.	BB.	SO.
Wise (W, 1-0)	6	3	2	0	2	0
Klippstein	3	0	0	0	2	2
Lary (L, 0-2)	4	7	6	6	3	2
Sturdivant	1	1	2	2	0	0
Hunter	2	2	0	0	0	0
Wakefield	1	0	0	0	0	0
Cisco	1	1	0	0	0	0

*Faced 1 man in 5th; †Faced 1 man in 7th.

HBP—By Lary (Rojas), by Sturdivant (Rojas), by Klippstein (Kranepool, Stephenson). WP—Wise, Sturdivant, Hunter, Klippstein 2. PB—Gonder. Time—2:51. Attendance—32,026.

June 22, 1964

The New York Times (by Ernest Sisto)

Tony Taylor, second baseman of the Phillies, leaping to knock down a line drive hit by Jesse Gonder of Mets in the fifth inning. Taylor's play saved perfect game for Bunning.

The Greatest Pitcher Of Them All

By LEONARD KOPPETT

FOR the last four years, the brilliant pitching feats of Sandy Koufax, Brooklyn's gift to Los Angeles and to contemporary American folklore, have given new life to an old diversion: choosing a designee for the title of "The Greatest Pitcher in the History of Baseball."

Not even the interruptions caused by two serious injuries—a damaged finger which kept him idle for two months in 1962, and an injured elbow which ended the current season for him seven weeks early—have altered Sandy's status as a prime stimulant for such discussion.

Last year, Koufax capped a sensational regular-season performance by striking out 15 New York Yankees in the first game of the World Series, and then beating them again four days later for a startling four-game sweep by his Los Angeles Dodgers. The World Series about to start is not likely to offer anything half as exciting.

This June, he pitched a no-hitter for the third straight year (an unprecedented feat) against the Philadelphia Phillies, who were well on their way to succeeding the Dodgers as National League champions. Before hurting his elbow in August, he had compiled an all-around record good enough to be called the best in baseball this year: 19 victories, 5 defeats, 223 strikeouts in exactly that many innings, and an earned-run average of 1.74. He breaks some sort of record almost every time he pitches.

Is Koufax, then, "the greatest pitcher?" Or is it someone from the distant, or not so distant, past—someone who is only a name to most present-day baseball fans — like Walter Johnson, Grover Cleveland Alexander, Christy Mathewson, Cy Young? Or someone who remains a vivid memory from a later era, like Lefty Grove or Bob Feller? Or even someone else pitching today?

ANY answer to such a question has to be intensely personal, which is probably why a proposition so basically unprovable remains so popular. As a rule, the younger generation takes for granted that today's "greatest" anything is automatically superior. Older people, or at least those with longer memories, frequently insist that the "really great" ones were

LEONARD KOPPETT is a reporter in the sports section of The New York Times.

the heroes of antiquity—a period which, among sports fans, invariably coincides with the adolescence and early adulthood of the speaker. With such a privately defined "golden age" embedded in each interested party, an objective evaluation is difficult and a thoroughly exhilarating, rip-roaring argument always possible.

My own choice is Johnson—a man I never saw pitch. The best I've ever seen are Feller and Koufax. But Sandy doesn't really qualify for reasons best explained by an exceptionally well-informed source: Sanford Koufax himself.

"To talk of me in such terms is ridiculous," he says, in a typically sincere, analytic speech. "I had a great year, and I'm proud of it. I hope to have many more. I don't feel any false modesty about my natural gifts, and I try to work hard at my job, which is winning games.

"But before you compare me with the great pitchers of all time, let me be around a while. Let me prove I can do some of these things over a long period of time. Don't put me in a class with pitchers like Warren Spahn and Whitey Ford until I've

shown I can win games for 10 or 15 years. Spahn's been doing it for 20. That's what it takes to rate as a great ballplayer, not a couple of good years, but a whole career."

KOUFAX is 28 years old, and the opinion that he is the best pitcher working today is as close to unanimous as anything in baseball can be. Yet this is only his fourth season as an established regular and only his second as a superstar. He signed with the Dodgers in his native Brooklyn in 1955 for a modest bonus (about $14,000) during his freshman year at the University of Cincinnati. Because of rules covering bonus players at that time, he couldn't be sent to the minors to learn his trade. He spent three seasons, therefore, sitting around and pitching infrequently in over-matched situations. Only after the club moved to Los Angeles in 1958 did he begin to work regularly, and only in spring training of 1961 did he acquire the key to his present success.

So Koufax may be, some day, a prime candidate for the title of "greatest"—if he is fortunate enough to retain good health. Pitchers' arms are notoriously fragile; the wear and tear is tremendous, and the risk of injury on a ball field is considerable. Sandy himself has had to face this uncertainty in a particularly vivid manner. Two years ago his career was almost destroyed by a freak accident.

IT was during the first half of the 1962 season, when he had reached his full development and was on his way to a carload of records and honors. One day he bruised his hand while batting. The result was a circulatory

Sandy Koufax, a near-unanimous choice as the best pitcher working today, who in June pitched his third no-hitter and by August, when he was injured, had won 19 games and fanned 223, for an earned-run average of 1.74.

obstruction which gradually numbed the forefinger of his pitching hand. He couldn't pitch at all the second half of the season—and if the last of a series of modern medical treatments hadn't succeeded, amputation might have been necessary. This year's injury was more routine: an inflamed elbow.

LONGEVITY, then, is one of the fundamental standards in judging the "greatest." We are trying to single out one man among the thousands who have pitched in the major leagues over a period of many decades; however distinguished the achievements of any of them may be, only those who could maintain their superiority for the full span of career possibility—about 20 years—can be considered for the No. 1 ranking.

This immediately rules out some famous names whose moments of glory were every bit as bright as Koufax's and somewhat longer. Dizzy Dean, for instance, in 1933-37, was as commanding a figure as any pitcher could be (he won 30 games in 1934, something no one has done since). But in the 1937 All-Star game, a line drive broke his toe; when he tried to resume pitching too soon, he favored the leg and strained his arm, and he was never great again. Less celebrated, and certainly less remembered, is Addie Joss, who won 155 games for Cleveland in his first eight major-league seasons and pitched two no-hitters, one a perfect game. But Joss died of tuberculosis in 1911, at the age of 31.

A MORE recent example is Herb Score. Less than a decade ago, he was the magnet for all the superlatives now heaped on Koufax. After the 1956 season, the Boston Red Sox offered Cleveland $1,000,000 for his contract—and were turned down. But the very next year a line drive hit Score in the eye. His sight was saved, but he never could regain his pitching rhythm and soon developed a sore arm. He kept trying until last year, when he finally retired to become a play-by-play broadcaster for the Chicago White Sox—still only 31 years old.

All right, then; longevity narrows the field to those who lasted 20 years or so. What are the other standards of pitching greatness? There are four: stuff, control, craft and poise. At this point, some

remarks on the art of pitching are in order.

In baseball language, "stuff" refers to the physical element of a pitcher's equipment: How hard can he throw? How much can he make a curve ball break? Basically, exceptional "stuff" is the product of strength and hair-trigger coordination. It seems to be an innate quality, subject perhaps to improvement by practice and technique, but not acquirable.

Control, of course, is exactly what it implies: the ability to throw the ball—with "stuff" on it—where the pitcher wants to with extraordinary accuracy.

CRAFT comprises the knowledge that comes with experience, analytic powers, meticulous observation and resourcefulness. Craft is what tells a pitcher where and how to apply the stuff he can control.

Poise includes the ability to apply one's craft under the most severe competitive conditions, to rise to an occasion, to produce best when the need is greatest.

Fundamentally, a pitcher is trying to keep the batter from hitting the ball squarely. The ball is round; it travels up to 90 miles an hour. The bat is round. Only a tiny area of these two round surfaces is the "right" area for hitting the ball. Anything the pitcher can do to prevent them from meeting is good pitching.

For this, the pitcher has two dimensions to work with: space and time. He can make the batter swing off balance (just a trifle is enough) by making the trajectory of the ball deceptive. Or he can change the speed of the delivery so that the batter's timing is disrupted. And, of course, he can combine the two weapons in a variety of proportions.

A PITCHER with a great fast ball can simply throw it past hitters, but this is never enough by itself to defeat major league hitters. A pitcher with exceptional "breaking stuff"—curves of various types or trick deliveries like knuckleballs—is better equipped provided his fast ball is fast enough to be a useful contrast. A pitcher with pinpoint control is best off, as long as his stuff is moderately good, because he can exploit the weak spot that every batter has.

Naturally, the more stuff a pitcher has, the harder it is

to control, and usually control is acquired at the sacrifice of some power. Furthermore, both the practice that produces control and the experience that produces knowledge and poise are time-consuming. In the process, age and the attrition of muscular strain take their toll. Usually, by the time a pitcher masters his craft, some degree of his physical gift has been lost.

It is very rare, therefore, to find a man who possesses the highest degree of stuff, control and craft simultaneously. It is so rare, in fact, that our list of eligibles for the "greatest pitcher" designation is immediately reduced to quite manageable terms.

Warren Spahn and Whitey Ford are the most distinguished pitchers active today. Spahn, finishing his 20th major league season at the age of 43, already holds the record for most victories by a left-handed pitcher. (He had 350 before this season began.) Ford, who has spent his 14-year career with the perpetually successful Yankees, has the best winning percentage in the history of the game.

BUT neither of them, outstanding as they are, ever had speed and power comparable to that possessed by Johnson, Feller or Koufax. The same was true of Carl Hubbell, Herb Pennock, Ted Lyons and a dozen others. They were artists, worthy of a place in Baseball's Hall of Fame, but not contenders for No. 1 ranking.

Others, like Dean, Lefty Gomez, Dazzy Vance and Rube Waddell, did have overpowering stuff, but they never perfected the craft. Untouchable for a while, they became merely very good pitchers when their exceptional speed was lost.

That narrows our list to Johnson, Alexander, Mathewson, Grove and Feller.

Cy Young must be mentioned. He won 511 games, more than any other pitcher on record. But his career began in 1890, when conditions of play were simply too different to make any comparison meaningful. Major-league baseball was stabilized in its familiar form in 1903, after the American League had shaken down. All those being considered pitched after that (although Young did last until 1911, too).

Feller is next to be eliminated, partially by fate. To a blinding fast ball he added one of the biggest, most be-

wildering curve balls ever used. He joined Cleveland in 1936, at the age of 17, and started breaking strikeout records right away. In all, he won 266 games, pitched three no-hitters and 12 one-hitters, and set a record for strikeouts in one season (348 in 1946) which still stands.

BUT Feller was robbed of almost four full seasons, at the very height of his powers, by World War II. He was only 23 years old when he went into service, and took up where he left off when he returned at 27. Granted peaceful times, he might have posted 100 more victories and 1,000 more strikeouts. He might have made his claim to No. 1 undeniable. Even when his fast ball was long since gone, in 1951, he won 22 games. But the lost years eliminate him.

Grove, according to most testimony, was faster than Feller. "He was the fastest pitcher who ever lived," says Ford Frick, Commissioner of Baseball, who spent the 1920's and early 1930's as a baseball writer. Grove never had Feller's curve, but he kept his fast ball longer. In 17 American League seasons, he won exactly 300 games (losing only 140) and was still the league-leader in earned-run average at the age of 39 (in 1939).

BUT Grove did it all on power. Mathewson had power, too, and more finesse. He threw a famous "fadeaway," a pitch that today would be called a "right-handed screwball." His career with the New York Giants ran from 1900 to 1916. Of his 373 victories, 365 came in a 14-year span, which means an *average* of 26 per year.

Still, Mathewson was usually with a winning team. Alexander and Johnson were not.

"I would have to say," says Casey Stengel, who ought to know, "that Johnson was the most amazing pitcher in the American League and Alexander in the National. Alexander had to pitch in that little Philadelphia ball park, with the big tin fence in right field, and he pitched shutouts, which must mean he could do it. He had a fast ball, a curve, a change of pace and perfect control. He was the best I batted against in the National League."

Alexander was 24 years old when he joined the Phillies in 1911. As a right-hander, that

250-foot right-field barrier in Baker Bowl presented a special hazard, since left-handed hitters were the ones who had a crack at it. It's true, the lively ball was not yet in use but, by the same token, hitters who weren't swinging at the fences were much harder to strike out. In his first seven seasons with the Phillies, Alexander won 190 games.

He moved on to Chicago and St. Louis and in 1926, at the age of 39, was the World Series hero for the Cardinals as they defeated the Yankees in seven games.

Altogether, Alexander won 373 games. He pitched 90 shutouts, still the National League record, and this is a peculiarly significant statistic. "A good pitcher's main job," Sal Maglie, the Giant ace of the 1950's, once observed, "is not to give up the first run." If a pitcher holds the opposition scoreless, his team can't lose. Once his own team scores, the pitcher's job is to give the other side one less. A shutout is proof positive that the pitcher has done his team job to perfection.

Strikeouts are important in this respect, too. Base-runners can't advance on strikeouts. With a man on third, a winning run can be scored on a fly-out or a ground-out—but not on a strikeout. Alexander struck out 2,198 bat-

ters. (Grove, by the way, fanned 2,266; Feller, 2,581; Mathewson, 2,505.) That's why "stuff" is so important. At the same time, control is even more important, and Alexander walked only 951 men — averaging about one walk for every six innings pitched, and he pitched in 696 games.

IF our accolade was to be for "the most complete pitcher of all time," Alexander would be it. But Johnson was greater still.

Walter Perry (Barney) Johnson was primarily a fast-ball pitcher, the fastest of all. He developed a fairly good curve after a while, but mostly he just leaned back and fired the fast ball with a three-quarter-arm motion, almost side-arm.

"You might know it was coming," says Stengel, "but you couldn't hit it. He had perfect control, too."

"When I batted against him, in 1921," says Fred Haney, now general manager of the Los Angeles Angels, but then a Detroit infielder, "he looked so fast I couldn't believe it. When I got back to the bench, they told me, 'You should have seen him 10 years ago; he was twice as fast then.' Heck, I was glad I didn't see him 10 years before; I didn't want to see him the way he was now."

"Johnson," says Frick, "al-

ways worried that his fast ball might kill omeone if it hit him in the head. His control was so perfect, though, that he didn't even have to throw close to hitters. He just kept throwing it over the plate."

Johnson came out of Humboldt, Kan., in 1907 at the age of 19. He went straight to the Washington Senators and never pitched for any other team in organized baseball—except one inning for Newark in the International League in 1928, when he was the manager. The Senators then, as ever, were seldom successful. During his first 16 years with them, they finished in the second division 10 times. They were last or next-to-last seven times. He didn't get a chance to pitch in the World Series until 1924, when he was almost 37 years old. Then he lost two games to the Giants, but won the seventh and deciding game to give Washington its first and only world championship.

DESPITE this minimal support, Johnson won 414 games —more than anyone else in the modern era.

"He was, besides, a wonderful man," says Frick. "The scene that sticks in my memory is the end of the 1925 World Series. Johnson was at the end of his career, and pitching in the seventh and deciding game at Pittsburgh.

Roger Peckinpaugh, a great shortstop who was having a terrible series, made an error, and then KiKi Cuyler hit a bases-loaded double and Johnson was beaten.

"When the inning was over, he waited at the mound until Peckinpaugh came by on the way off the field and he put his arm around Peckinpaugh's shoulders in a comforting and forgiving gesture. That was Johnson the man."

AND this was Johnson the pitcher: He pitched 113 shutouts, a record that stands by itself. He struck out 3,508 batters — about 1,000 more than anyone else. He once pitched 56 consecutive scoreless innings—still a record. He had a 16-game winning streak in 1912, setting an American League record that has been tied but not surpassed. He started, finished and appeared in more games than any other pitcher. From 1910 through 1919 he won 264 games, or more than one-third of all the games won by his team during those 10 years (the Senators won 755).

Statistics in themselves prove little, but Johnson's are beyond quibbling. Anyone might have another candidate for "the greatest pitcher of all," but no one can ever call Johnson an unreasonable choice.

October 4, 1964

Cards Set Back Mets, 11-5, Take Pennant

GIBSON WINS 19TH IN RELIEF EFFORT

Mets Lead, 3-2, in Fifth but Homers by White, Flood Assure Flag Victory

By JOSEPH DURSO
Special to The New York Times

ST. LOUIS, Oct. 4—The St. Louis Cardinals won the most savagely contested pennant in National League history today on the last day of the season by overpowering the New York Mets, 11—5, while the Philadelphia Phillies were knocking the Cincinnati Reds out of a first-place tie.

Before a roaring sellout

throng of 30,146, the Cardinals finally defeated Casey Stengel's 10th-place tigers 48 hours after the Mets had cut the Cardinals' league lead from one game to half a game and 24 hours after they had wiped it out.

The tumult in Busch Stadium mounted with every run scored here and 350 miles away in Cincinnati, where the Phillies were overwhelming the Reds, 10—0. The Phillies, who led the league by 6½ games two weeks ago, thus enjoyed the supreme irony of the season's final hours by thwarting the Reds, who had wrenched first place from them one week ago today only to lose it two days later to the Cardinals.

St. Louis rushed its No. 1 pitcher, Bob Gibson, into the game in relief of Curt Simmons to hold back the Mets and forestall a three-way tie threatened by the Phillies.

Now for the Series

Gibson pitched four solid

innings. St. Louis finished first by one game. the Phils and Reds shared econd place — and the Cardinals open the World Series here Wednesday against the New York Yankees.

There was jubilation in the Cardinals' dressing room after the game and August A. Busch Jr., the president and owner of the club and of Anheuser-Busch, Inc., a brewery, served champagne to Manager Johnny Keane and the players. "This is the happiest day of my life," Busch shouted hoarsely to Keane. "I just want to say hello to you and bring you this glass of champagne."

For almost six innings the outcome was in serious doubt as the Mets tied the Cardinals, 1—1, in the fourth, passed them in the fifth and drew near again in the sixth.

But St. Louis broke the game open with three runs in the fifth, three in the sixth and three in the eighth against half a dozen pitchers dispatched to the scene by Stengel.

Cardinals' Score

NEW YORK (N.)	ab.	r.	h.	bi	ST. LOUIS (N.)	ab.	r.	h.	bi
Klaus, 2b	4	1	2	1	Flood, cf	4	1	1	1
McMillan, ss	4	1	1	2	Brock, lf	4	2	2	0
Ch'topher, rf	4	0	1	0	White, 1b	5	2	2	2
Hickman, cf	4	0	0	0	Boyer, 3b	2	3	1	1
Smith, 3b	5	1	1	1	Groat, 2s	5	2	2	1
Taylor, c	3	1	2	0	McCarver, c	4	1	3	3
Elliot, ph	1	0	0	0	Shannon, rf	5	0	1	1
Kanehl, ph	1	0	1	1	Maxvill, 2b	4	0	2	2
Kranepool, 1b	4	0	1	0	Simmons, p	2	0	0	0
Altman, rf	3	1	1	0	Gibson, p	2	0	0	0
Cisco, p	1	0	0	0					
Gonder, c	1	0	0	0	Totals	36	11	14	11
Totals	34	5	10	5					

New York .... 000 121-001—5
St. Louis .... 010 133 03.—11

E—Hickman, Klaus. DP—New York 1, St. Louis 1. LOB—New York 11, St. Louis 8. 2B—McCarver 2, Groat 2, Boyer. Klaus. HR—Smith (20), White (21), Flood (5). S—Cisco 2.

	IP.	H.	R.	ER.	BB.	SO.
*Cisco (L, 6—19)	4	7	5	5	4	0
Wakefield	⅔	1	0	0	1	0
Fisher	⅓	0	0	0	0	1
Hunter		3	3	3	1	1
Ribant	1⅔	2	3	3	1	2
Locke	⅓	1	0	0	0	0
Simmons	4⅓	7	3	3	1	0
Gibson (W, 19—12)	4	2	2	2	5	2
Schultz		2	2	2	1	0

*Faced 3 batters in 5th. HBP—By Gibson, Christopher. WP—Gibson. PB—McCarver 2. T—3:06. A—30,146.

The Cards broke on top in the second inning, after Tim McCarver hit a liner into the left-field corner for a double. Mike Shannon drove a 2-and-2 pitch into left for a single, and St. Louis was ahead for the first time all weekend, 1—0.

With two out in the fourth, just as three runs were being hoisted on the scoreboard for the Phillies in Cincinnati, Charlie Smith tempered the joy by hitting a towering fly down the right-field line, just fair and onto the roof for his 20th home run.

In the bottom of the fourth,

Dick Groat doubled into the right-field corner and, after the next two men had gone out, Dal Maxvill singled to center and the Cardinals were on top, 2—1.

But in the fifth the first signs of panic appeared when George Altman singled over second, Cisco advanced him with a bunt and Bobby Klaus and Roy McMillan doubled in succession. That put the Mets back in command, 3—2, and caused the Cardinals to call for Gibson, who had pitched eight innings and lost to the Mets Friday, 1—0.

After that Gibson (and Barney Schultz in the ninth) restrained the Mets with three hits and no more runs while the Cardinals exploded for nine runs in four innings. The victory was Gibson's 19th of the year.

In the fifth, Lou Brock walked on a 3-and-2 pitch, Bill White lined a single to right, Ken Boyer doubled into the left-field corner and the game was tied, 3—3, with the Cards finally rolling.

Bill Wakefield relieved Cisco, but Groat scored White on a

shot off Wakefield's glove, Maxvill lined a single to right with two out, Jack Fisher was in for the Mets and the Cards led. 5—3.

In the sixth, Brock doubled to right for his 200th hit of the year and White bombed one over the roof in right for his 21st home run. And in the eighth Curt Flood put one onto the roof in a three-run inning, and the weeks of suspense and upsets were over.

October 5, 1964

LEAGUE REFUSES TO ALLOW BRAVES TO MOVE TILL '66

Team to Stay in Milwaukee Next Season, but May Go to Atlanta Thereafter

By United Press International

PHOENIX, Ariz., Nov. 7— The National League ruled today that the Braves must remain in Milwaukee for the 1965 season but may move to Atlanta in 1966.

Warren Giles, the league president, said the league held a special meeting here to discuss the Milwaukee situation. The Milwaukee representatives were asked to leave the room, and in their absence, the other league representatives voted unanimously to instruct Milwaukee to remain in the Wisconsin city next year, Giles said. The league also ruled, he added, that "it was in the best future interests of baseball to have the club move to Atlanta in 1966."

The Braves stated on Oct. 21 that they hoped to move to Atlanta next season.

Ford Frick, the baseball commissioner, said after the final joint session of both leagues here this morning that it was the concensus of all attending that the regular baseball con-

vention in Houston in December would take up the proposed adoption of a free-agent draft and an unrestricted draft that would include all players once every club had reached its limit of 40 players.

Centralization of Office

Frick said the baseball owners also agreed to the centralization of baseball headquarters, preferably in a two-league city, which would mean New York, Chicago or Los Angeles. However, he said no preference for a city was expressed.

Frick said the owners, who wound up a three-day closed-door meeting at the Arizona Biltmore, also agreed to restore the more sweeping authority of the Commissioner, which was

taken away after the death of Commissioner Kenensaw Mountain Landis.

Frick said at a briefing after the session that the baseball owners had also expressed interest in developing and training umpires and in subsidizing four geographical leagues for college players in which talent could be developed without the players losing their amateur status.

The Milwaukee decision of the National League was the only official action taken at the meeting. Frick said any official decisions on the matters discussed would be made after the Houston baseball convention.

November 8, 1964

---

320 Are Picked in Baseball Draft

Selections Continue Today for Rights to Free Agents

By LEONARD KOPPETT

Baseball's first free-agent draft was conducted with unexpected efficiency at the Hotel Commodore yesterday, with all 20 major league clubs represented by top executives and busy staffs.

Robert James (Rick) Monday, a 19-year-old left-handed hitter at Arizona State at Tempe who is universally acknowledged to be the most desirable prospect available, was the No. 1 choice. He was picked, as expected, by the Kansas City Athletics.

A total of 320 players were selected in about seven hours before the officials adjourned the meeting until today, when the drafting will resume.

Under the regulations adopted last December, teams draft the exclusive right to negotiate with the player named. Choices are made in reverse order of

last year's standings, so that the weaker teams get the earlier selections. The main motive is to eliminate competitive bidding that has led to huge bonus payments; the secondary purpose is to equalize player talent among the teams.

Such drafts will be held each June and January. In practice, each major league club could choose as many men as it wanted, but technically the first round was for major league rosters, the next two for Class AAA teams, the next four rounds for Class AA and the rest for Class A. In all cases, the major league team did the choosing for its minor league affiliates.

Mets Draft Left-Hander

The No. 2 choice in the first round belonged to the New York Mets. They took Leslie Rohr, a 6-foot-5-inch left-handed pitcher from Billings, Mont. He is 19 years old.

The New York Yankees had the 19th turn in the first round. They selected William Burbach; a 17-year-old right-handed pitcher from Dickeyville, Wis.

Each team had compiled a

list of 200 to 500 prospects. Most lists overlapped, but there were plenty of differences among them. The total number of players listed was estimated at 1,500.

"I feel I've taken part in something historic," said Bing Devine, No. 2 in command of the Mets. "As you know, I've been in favor of giving this rule a chance, even though the official position of the club has been against it, and I was very impressed with how the first few rounds went."

George Weiss, the president of the Mets, is one of the baseball officials strongly against the draft. Also opposed are the Yankees and Los Angeles Dodgers.

Devine singled out another aspect of the draft that he considered progress.

"A team can concentrate its effort on evaluating players, and then on negotiating with the players chosen, instead of spending so much time in the frustrating chase of a few high-priced bonus players beyond limit."

Monday, a power hitter who

is a sophomore at Arizona State at Tempe, is playing in the college baseball World Series. Kansas City officials said he would not be approached until that was over. His bonus may be $100,000 because he is so outstanding a prospect.

Devine, Bavasi and Houk all said they would have made Monday their first choice if they had the rights to him.

The teams have six months in which to negotiate with the prospects picked. If terms are not agreed to by then, the player goes into a pool for a special draft (from which the team he rejected is excluded) before the next free-agent draft in January. In any case, it is no longer possible for any player, once drafted, to choose freely which team to sign with.

Leading Draft Choices

By The Associated Press

—KANSAS CITY ATHLETICS—Rick Monday, 19 year old, outfielder from Arizona State University (Tempe) and Santa Monica, Calif. 6 foot 3 inches, 195 pounds.

2—NEW YORK METS—Leslie Rohr, 19, left-handed pitcher from Billings (Mont.) High School, 6-5, 200.

3—WASHINGTON SENATORS—Joe Coleman Jr. 17, right-handed pitcher from Natick (Mass.) High School, 6-3, 165.

141

4—HOUSTON ASTROS—Alex Barrett, 18, right-handed shortstop from Atwater High School, Winton, Calif., 6-0, 175.

5—BOSTON RED SOX—Bill Conigliaro, 17, right-handed outfielder-pitcher from Swampscott (Mass.) High School, 6-0, 175.

6—CHICAGO CUBS—Richard James, 17, right-handed pitcher from Coffee High School, Florence, Ala., 6-0, 200.

7—CLEVELAND INDIANS—Raymond Fosse, 18, right-handed catcher from Marion (Ill.) High School, 6-3, 210.

8—LOS ANGELES DODGERS—John Scott Wyatt, 17, right-handed shortstop from Bakersfield (Calif.) High School, 6-2, 200.

9—MINNESOTA TWINS—Ed Leon, 18, right-handed shortstop from University of Arizona and Tucson, Ariz., 5-11, 165.

10—PITTSBURGH PIRATES—Douglas Dickerson, 17, outfielder from Ensley High School, Birmingham, Ala., 6-1, 188.

11—LOS ANGELES ANGELS—James Spencer, 17, first baseman from Anderson High School, Glen Burnie, Md., 6-0, 190.

12—MILWAUKEE BRAVES—William Grant, 19, first baseman from Watertown High School, Swampscott, Mass. 6-4, 205.

13—DETROIT TIGERS—William Lamont, 18, catcher from Hiawatha High School, Kirkland, Ill., 6-1, 180

14—SAN FRANCISCO GIANTS—Alan Gallagher, 19, third baseman from Santa Clara University Daly City, Calif., 6-0, 182.

15—BALTIMORE ORIOLES—Scott McDonald, 18, right-handed pitcher from Marquette High School, Yakima, Wash. 6-1, 195.

16—CINCINNATI REDS—Bernardo Carbo, 17, third baseman from Livonia (Mich.) High and Garden City, Mich., 5-11, 170.

17—CHICAGO WHITE SOX—Kenneth Plesha, 19, catcher from Notre Dame University and McCook, Ill., 5-11, 185.

18—PHILADELPHIA PHILLIES—John Michael Adamson, 18, right-handed pitcher from Point Loma High School, San Diego, 6-2, 185.

19—NEW YORK YANKEES—William Burbach, 17, right-handed pitcher from Wahlert High School, Dubuque, Iowa and Dickeyville, Wis., 6-4, 195

20—ST. LOUIS CARDINALS—Joe Di Fabrin, 21, right-handed pitcher from Delta State College and Cranford, N.J., 5-11, 195.

NEW YORK AREA CHOICES

CLASS AAA—Frank Pepedino, Wingate H. S., Brooklyn, by Baltimore Orioles (for Rochester).

CLASS AA—George Mercado, Bishop Dubois H. S., New York, by Los Angeles Dodgers

(for Albuquerque); Doug Brittelle, Massapequa H. S., L. I., by New York Mets (for Williamsport); Fred Kamp, Shore Regional H. S., Monmouth Beach, N. J., by Cleveland Indians (for Reading); Robert Chiupsa, Manhattan College, New York, by Philadelphia Phils (for Chattanooga); John Hurley, Port Richmond H. S., Staten Island, by New York Yankees (for Columbus, Ga.).

CLASS A—Thomas Capowski, Fordham, by Phils (for Huron); Jeffrey Albies, Long Island University, Glendale, Queens, by Milwaukee Braves (for Yakima); Donald Conk, L. I. U., Massapequa, L. I., by Phils (for Eugene); George Lauzerique, New York, by Kansas City Athletics (for Burlington); John Dunn, Woodside, Queens, by Athletics (for Leesburg); Bob Crosby, the Bronx, by Los Angeles Angels (for San Jose); Henry Knittel, Franklin Square, L. I., by Chicago Cubs (for Duluth); Gil Torres — New York, by Washington Senators (for Geneva); Paul Giglio, Whitestone, Queens, by Pittsburgh Pirates (for Kingston); Will Beauchemin, Point Pleasant, N. J., by Orioles (for Appleton).

OTHER CHOICES

YANKEES—Class AAA: Danny Thompson, shortstop, Capron, Okla., and Dennis Baldridge, outfielder, Finn Rock, Ore. Class

AA: Stanley Bahnsen, right-handed pitcher, Council Bluffs, Iowa; Leslie Howell, catcher, Louisville, Ky.; John Hurley, right-handed pitcher, Staten Island, and Darcy Fast, first baseman, Olympia, Wash. Class A: Scott Lund, pitcher, Davenport, Iowa; Gary Girouard, pitcher, Woburn, Mass.; Fred Dawson, outfielder, Bernico, La.; James Alvey, first baseman, Leitchfield, Ky.; Donald Alley, catcher, Denver; Robert Hall, third baseman, Villanova U.; Dwain Davidson, third baseman, Mountain Hope, Ark.; Steve Mezich, catcher, Seattle; Morton Zenor, first baseman, Lawton, Iowa.

METS—Class AAA: Randolph Caldwell Kohn, catcher, Greenville, S. C., and Joe Moock, infielder, Baton Rouge. Class AA: Ken Boswell, infielder, Austin, Tex.; Douglas Brittelle, right-handed pitcher, Massapequa, L. I.; Harold Roberson, right-handed pitcher, Alma, Mich., and Mike McClure, infielder, Poth, Tex. Class A: Roger Harrington, pitcher, Sunnyvale, Calif.; Joss Williams, catcher, Baltimore; Roger Stevens, outfielder, Pasadena, Calif.; James McAndrew, pitcher, Iowa City; Nolan Ryan, pitcher, Alvin, Tex.

June 9, 1965

Koufax of Dodgers Hurls Perfect Game

By The Associated Press

LOS ANGELES, Sept. 9—Sandy Koufax of the Los Angeles Dodgers pitched a perfect game tonight in a 1-0 victory over the Chicago Cubs and became the first pitcher in baseball history to pitch four no-hitters in his career.

Outpitching Bob Hendley in a brilliant duel between left-handers, Koufax hurled his fourth no-hitter in four years and surpassed the record for multiple no-hitters held by Bob Feller, Cy Young and Larry Corcoran.

Hendley, who allowed only one hit, yielded a run in the fifth inning when the Dodgers scored without a hit. Lou Johnson walked to open the inning, was sacrificed to second, stole third and raced home when Chris Krug, the catcher, threw wild.

That was enough for the Dodgers, who remained half a game behind San Francisco in the National League pennant race.

The only hit off Hendley — and the only hit of the game — was Johnson's bloop double to right field with two out in the seventh inning.

Koufax, 29 years old, whose career was in jeopardy three years ago because of a circulatory ailment in his pitching hand, retired 27 Cubs in order.

Koufax Strikes Out 14

Koufax struck out 14, lifting his major-league-leading total to 332, as he posted the first perfect game in his 11-year career, the eighth in modern baseball history and only the third in National League annals. Jim Bunning of Philadelphia accomplished the feat last year.

Feller, the long-time Cleveland ace, pitched no-hitters in 1940, 1946 and 1951. Corcoran pitched three pre-1900 no-hitters for the Cubs, in

Sandy Koufax

1880, 1882 and 1884. Young pitched his first no-hitter for Cleveland which was then in the National League, in 1897, and pitched no-hitters for Boston of the American League in 1901 and, 1908.

Koufax, bringing his won-lost record in 22.7 was overpowering with his assortment of fast balls and breaking stuff. He struck out the last six batters he faced and seven of the last nine.

In the eighth he faced two of the clubs *hardest-hitting* players, Ron Santo and Ernie Banks. He struck out both, then ended the inning by fanning Byron Browne, a rookie left fielder.

Tension Mounts

In the ninth as the tension

mounted in the crowd of 29,139, Koufax fired a third strike past the young Cubs' catcher, Krug. A pinch-hitter, Joey Amalfitano, also went down swinging—on three pitches. Then it was up to another pinch-hitter, Harvey Kuenn, the former American League batting champion.

Kuenn also went down swinging—and Koufax had his first perfect game.

He also closed in on another of baseball's most spectacular achievements. Feller's strike-out record of 348 in one season. Koufax now is 16 shy of matching that feat.

There were no tough chances for the Dodger fielders as only seven batters hit the ball well

enough to get it to the outfield.

In the second inning, Browne lofted one to center field. In the third, Krug flied to center and Don Kessinger flied to right. In the fourth, Glenn Beckert flied to right field, and in the fifth Santo flied to left. In the seventh, Beckert flied to right field and Williams to left.

The perfect game with no runner getting to first base—was the first since Bunning accomplished the feat against the New York Mets on June 21 last year. The only other perfect game in modern National League history was by Harvey Haddix.

Haddix, then with Pittsburgh, pitched 12 innings of perfect ball against Milwaukee in 1959. However, he gave up a hit in the 13th and eventually was the loser.

Other perfect games were pitched by Young in 1904, Addie Joss of Cleveland in 1908, Ernie Shore of Boston in 1917, Charles Robertson of Chicago in 1922 and Don Larsen of the New York Yankees in 1956. Larsen pitched his perfect game in the World Series.

Koufax, who won the Cy Young award as the best pitcher in the majors in 1963 when he posted a 25-5 record, pitched his first no-hitter against the New York Mets, June 30, 1962, winning 5-0. His second came May 11, 1963, against San Francisco, with the Dodgers winning 8-0.

The Box Score

CHICAGO (N.)	ab	r	h	bi	LOS ANGELES (N.)	ab	r	h	bi
Young, cf	3	0	0	0	Wills, ss	3	0	0	0
Beckert, 2b	3	0	0	0	Gilliam, 3b	3	0	0	0
Williams, rf	3	0	0	0	Kennedy, 3b	0	0	0	0
Santo, 3b	3	0	0	0	Davis, cf	3	0	0	0
Banks, 1b	3	0	0	0	Johnson, lf	2	1	0	0
Browne, lf	3	0	0	0	Fairly, rf	1	0	0	0
Krug, c	3	0	0	0	Lefebvre, 2b	3	0	0	0
Kessinger, ss	3	0	0	0	Tracewski, 2b	0	0	0	0
Amalfitano, ph	1	0	0	0	Parker, 1b	3	0	0	0
Hendley, p	2	0	0	0	Torborg, c	3	0	0	0
Kuenn, ph	1	0	0	0	Koufax, p	2	0	0	0
Totals	27	0	0	0	Totals	24	1	1	0

Chicago   000 000 000—0
Los Angeles   000 010 00x—1

E—Krug. LOB—Chicago 0, Los Angeles 1. 2B—Johnson. SB—Johnson. S—Fairly.

	IP.	H.	R.	ER.	BB.	SO.
Hendley (L, 2-3)	8	1	1	0	1	3
Koufax (W, 22-7)	9	0	0	0	0	14

T—1:43. A—29,139.

Koufax made it three no-hitters last year, June 4, against Philadelphia, winning 3-0.

The no-hitter was the third in the majors this season. Cincinnati's Jim Maloney pitched two, winning one and losing another. 'n Maloney's losing no-hitter he ve up a hit in the 10th inning.

Koufax, whose career was threatened following the 1962 season, also was presented with another chilling possibility when it developed this spring that he was suffering from arthritis in the elbow of his pitching arm.

Doctors at first feared that

Koufax would be a once-a-week hurler, but the ace left-hander has managed to take his turn every four days. However, he packs his arm in ice after each game to guard against any serious injury.

His no-hitter was the first pitched by a Dodger since Sal

Maglie pitched one against Philadelphia, Sept. 25, 1956.

Hendley also had a perfect game going until Johnson walked in the fifth, and became the game's first base runner.

September 10, 1965

Ashford First Negro Umpire Hired by American League

BOSTON, Sept. 15 (AP)— The American League hired its first Negro umpire today with the purchase of Emmett L. Ashford from the Pacific Coast League.

Joe Cronin, the league president, said that Ashford would join a staff of 23 umpires at spring training next year.

Ashford, who will be 47 years old on Nov. 23, has been in the Pacific Coast League for 12 years, the last three as umpire-in-chief. He began his professional umpiring career in the Southwest International League in 1951. He spent seasons in the Arizona-Texas and Western International Leagues before moving up to the Pacific Coast League.

September 16, 1965

DODGERS TRIUMPH OVER TWINS, 2-0, AND TAKE SERIES

Koufax Fans 10 and Yields 3 Hits in Gaining His 2d Shutout in 4 Days

---

KAAT IS ROUTED IN 4TH

Johnson's Homer and Hits by Fairly and Parker Decide 7th Game

---

By LEONARD KOPPETT
Special to The New York Times

BLOOMINGTON, Minn., Oct. 1 —Sandy Koufax completed a season of incredible personal accomplishment by pitching the Los Angeles Dodgers to a 2-0 victory over the Minnesota Twins today in the seventh and deciding game of the World Series.

Less than seven months ago, the 29-year-old left-hander from Brooklyn was afraid that his brilliant career was prematurely finished. He had discovered that he had a chronic arthritic condition in his left elbow, which was swollen and bent, and one week before the baseball season was to begin no one could tell whether Koufax would ever be

able to pitch again.

Today, pitching with only two days of rest, or one fewer than the ordinary healthy pitcher usually needs, he overpowered the Twins after a shaky beginning. He allowed only three hits walked three men and struck out 10. He retired 14 of the last 15 batters he faced.

It was Koufax's second victory and second shutout of this series, and it put the ultimate embellishment on his year's work. During the regular season, he never missed a starting turn, won 26 games, set a season strike-out record, pitched a perfect game and did his best work during a stretch drive that enabled the Dodgers to win the pennant.

Including the World Series, Koufax pitched 360 innings and struck out 411 batters with an arm that needed constant medication.

His performance today, therefore, involved determination and response to pressure as much as sheer talent and skill. When it was over, he seemed too tired to show elation and even his teammates avoided the usual Series-ending ritual of mob congratulations.

End of Long Season

As Bob Allison swung and missed for the final out, Sandy walked wearily toward the dugout while the crowd of 50,596 a record here at Metropolitan Stadium—seemed silent and depressed. It wasn't until he was across the third-base foul line that Koufax was joined by his fellow victors, and even then there was little leaping and

back-pounding.

The most excited escort was Lou Johnson, who arrived late from his position in left field. It was his home run off Jim Kaat in the fourth inning that had provided the ndispensable run.

A minor-leaguer most of his career, the 32-year-old Johnson went to the Dodgers last May only because Tommy Davis

broke an ankle. He frequently powered the limited Dodger offense throughout the tight pennant race. Today, he made the most important hit of all— and he is not the type of man to hide his emotions.

The second Dodger run came immediately after the homer, which hit the left-field foul-pole screen. It was produced by three other often unappre-

Box Score of 7th Series Game

LOS ANGELES (N.)	AB.	R.	H.	RBI.	PO.	A.		MINNESOTA (A.)	AB.	R.	H.	RBI.	PO.	A.
Wills, ss.	4	0	0	0	2	3		Versalles, ss.	4	0	1	0	0	2
Gilliam, 3b.	5	0	2	0	2	1		Nossek, cf.	4	0	0	0	4	0
Kennedy, 3b.	0	0	0	0	0	0		Oliva, rf.	3	0	0	0	4	0
W. Davis, cf.	2	0	0	0	1	0		Killebrew, 3b.	3	0	1	0	2	2
Johnson, lf.	4	1	1	1	3	0		Battey, c.	4	0	0	0	8	1
Fairly, rf.	4	1	1	0	0	0		Allison, lf.	4	0	0	0	1	0
Parker, 1b.	4	0	2	1	6	0		Mincher, 1b.	3	0	0	0	10	0
Bracewski, 2b.	4	0	0	0	0	0		Quilici, 2b.	3	0	1	0	1	3
Roseboro, c.	3	0	0	0	12	0		Kaat, p.	1	0	0	0	0	1
Koufax, p.	3	0	0	0	0	0		Worthington, p	0	0	0	0	1	1
Total	33	2	7	2	27	7		aRollins	1	0	0	0	0	0
								Klippstein, p.	0	0	0	0	0	0
								Merritt, p.	0	0	0	0	0	0
								bValdespino	1	0	0	0	0	0
								Perry, p.	0	0	0	0	0	0
								Total	30	0	3	0	27	10

aWalked for Worthington in 5th.
bFouled out for Merritt in 9th.

Los Angeles Dodgers.........0 0 0 2 0 0 0 0 0—2
Minnesota Twins............0 0 0 0 0 0 0 0 0—0

Error—Oliva. Left on bases—Los Angeles 9, Minnesota 6. Two-base hits—Roseboro, Fairly, Quilici. Three-base hit—Parker. Home run—Johnson. Sacrifice—W. Davis.

	IP.	H.	R.	ER.	BB.	SO.	HBP.	WP.	Balks
Koufax (W)	9	3	0	0	3	10	0	0	0
Kaat (L)	3	5	2	2	1	2	0	0	0
Worthington	2	0	0	0	1	1	0	0	0
Shopstein	1⅔	2	0	0	3	1	0	0	0
Merritt	1⅓	0	0	0	0	1	0	0	0
Berry	1	0	0	0	1	1	0	0	0

*Faced 3 batters in 4th.

Bases on balls—Off Koufax 3 (Oliva, Killebrew, Rollins), Kaat 1 (Koufax), Worthington 1 (Roseboro) 1, Klippstein 1 (Roseboro), Perry 1 (Wills). Struck out—By Koufax 10 (Versalles, Battey 2, Allison 2, Mincher, Kaat, Oliva 2, Quilici), Kaat 2 (Wills, Tracewski), Klippstein 2 (Tracewski, Koufax), Merritt 1 (Roseboro), Perry 1 (Koufax). Hit by pitcher—By Klippstein (W. Davis).

Umpires—Hurley (A.), plate; Venzon (N.), first base; Flaherty (A.) second base; Sudol (N.), third base; Stewart (A.), left field; Vargo (N.), right field. Time of game—2:27. Attendance—50,596.

ciated Dodgers: Ron Fairly Wes Parker and Manager Walt Alston.

Fairly followed Johnson's drive with one just fair into the other corner of the field for a double. This was with nobody out in the fourth inning, so it was natural to expect the Dodgers to sacrifice Fairly to third, from where he could score on an out.

The Twins set their infield defense for this eventuality, but Alston, speaking to Parker before he went to the plate, told him to swing and try to hit the ball past the charging infield. Parker did exactly that. He bounced a single over the head of Don Mincher, the onrushing first baseman, and Fairly scored.

Thus the Dodgers became champions of the baseball world for the second time in three years, and for the fourth time in five chances under Alston's regime.

Alston became manager of the Dodgers when they were still in Brooklyn, and still had a star-studded line-up, in 1954. The next year, Brooklyn had its first and only world championship, thanks to a 2-0 victory in the seventh game at Yankee Stadium. The man who pitched that one — Johnny Podres — sat in the Dodger bull pen all day today, no longer needed.

In 1956, the Dodgers again battled the Yankees through seven games, but lost the last one. After the 1957 season, they moved to Los Angeles, and in 1959 won the pennant in a post-season playoff with Milwaukee. They then defeated the Chicago White Sox in the World Series, 4 games to 2.

In 1962, with fundamentally the same personnel now playing, the Dodgers lost a pennant playoff to the San Francisco Giants. But in 1963, they won

the pennant handily and swept the Yankees, 4-0, with Koufax pitching two outstanding games. Last year, however, the Los Angeles club couldn't even win half its games and finished in a tie for sixth.

Koufax, Don Drysdale and Claude Osteen, plus Ron Perranoski and Bob Miller as relievers, gave the Dodgers superb pitching this year. And the bunt-run-steal-scamper attack led by Maury Wills produced enough runs.

That was the pattern used in this Series. In the first two games here, the attack didn't function, Drysdale and Koufax were not sharp, and the Twins won easily.

In the next three games in Los Angeles, Osteen pitched a shutout, Drysdale a five-hitter and Koufax a shutout — and the Dodger offense ran wild. Yesterday here, the offense died again and when Osteen made one bad pitch (which Allison hit for a two-run homer) the Series was all even.

It was, therefore, up to Koufax today. Drysdale was ready, however, to take over at any time. And three times in the first five innings it appeared that he would be needed.

Koufax almost had a run to work with at the start. Jim Gilliam singled with one out in the first and was bunted to second by Willie Davis. He was on his way home when Tony Oliva raced in and made a tumbling catch of Johnson's looper to right.

Control was Sandy's problem in the first. He was consistently high as he struck out Zoilo Versalles and retired Joe Nossek on a grounder. He walked Oliva on a full count and Harmon Killebrew on four pitches. Then he fired a third strike past Earl Battey and was out of the inning.

In the third, the Dodgers

failed to score even though John Roseboro led off with a double and Koufax walked. Kaat made Wills bounce out, advancing the runners, and forced Gilliam to fly out to right field, too short for any attempt to score. Then he got Davis to foul out.

In the home half of the inning, Koufax had his second crisis, and he got a break. Versalles singled with one out and was trying to steal second when Nossek swung at a 1-1 pitch. In doing so Nossek clearly interfered with Roseboro's unsuccessful throw to second, so Umpire Ed Hurley declared Nossek out and sent Versalles back to first.

After getting his 2-0 lead, Koufax retired the Twins in order in the fourth, but had to struggle again in the fifth.

Frank Quilici lined a two-base hit off the fence in left-center with one out and Rich Rollins, a pinch-hitter for the pitcher, worked a full-count walk. The tying runs were on with one out and the top of the batting order was up.

Here Koufax got fielding support. Versalles smashed a sharp grounder down the third-base line. Gilliam, with a lunge, smothered it back - handed, scrambled to his feet and got over to the base in time for a forceout. Nossek's grounder to Wills then proved a third-out force at second.

From that point on, Koufax seemed to have much better control. Battey hit a line drive at Wills in the sixth and Versalles flied deep to left in the eighth, but no one got on base until Killebrew lined a single to left with one out in the ninth.

That meant a home run could tie the game and Koufax had to "reach back" for whatever strength he had left in his 360th inning.

He fired two strikes past Battey and hit the outside corner for a called strike three. Allison fouled the first pitch to him and took two balls, both high. Then he swung and missed for strike two. Finally Sandy reached back for the last time and threw strike three as Allison swung and missed.

It might have been an easier task for Koufax, but the Dodgers wasted three scoring opportunities after they had their runs.

In the fourth, Parker's single knocked out Kaat and Parker took second when Oliva bobbled the ball. Al Worthington relieved and made a fine catch on Dick Tracewski's pop bunt along the third-base line. Worthington walked Roseboro semi-intentionally, fielded Koufax's soft tap to the mound while the runners advanced, and made Wills foul out to Killebrew.

Parker tripled off Johnny Klippstein with one out in the sixth, but Tracewski bunted foul for the third strike on an attempted squeeze play. An intentional pass to Roseboro and a strike-out of Koufax ended the inning.

With one out in the seventh, Gilliam singled and Davis was hit on the foot by a pitch. Johnson's slow bounder to third left men on second and third with two out.

At that point Manager Sam Mele called Jim Merritt, a left-hander, in from the bull pen to face Fairly. It was an excellent decision because Fairly, who had been murdering Minnesota's right-handed pitchers, flied meekly to right field.

In the final analysis, then, the old baseball adage was proved true once more: The arm is mightier than the bat.

October 15, 1965

Retired General Replaces Frick As the Commissioner of Baseball

By United Press International

CHICAGO, Nov. 17—William D. Eckert, a 56-year-old retired lieutenant general of the United States Air Force, was named commissioner of baseball today in a surprise move by the major league club owners.

General Eckert's selection was approved unanimously by representatives of the owners of the 20 major league teams. He will succeed Ford C. Frick, who is retiring. The general accepted a seven-year contract at $65,000 a year, the same salary Commissioner Frick received.

Lee MacPhail, the president and general manager of the Baltimore Orioles, who was reported to be among those being considered for the commis-

sioner's job, was named administrator of the commissioner's office, and thus will become General Eckert's executive assistant. Mr. MacPhail received a three-year contract at $40,000 a year.

Joe Cronin, who was also among those considered for the commissioner's job, accepted a new contract extending his term as president of the American League for seven years.

Although General Eckert was one of 150 candidates originally suggested as Frick's successor, his name was not among those recently mentioned publicly in speculation for the job.

General Eckert said he had had "a few weeks" to consider

whether he would accept the job after he was first approached about it by John Galbreath of the Pittsburgh Pirates and John Fetzer of the Detroit Tigers, members of the screening committee assigned by the owners to nominate the commissioner.

'Pleased and Honored'

General Eckert said he was not surprised but "pleased and honored" to be elected. "After 35 years in the Air Force," he said, "I don't think I'm the type to be surprised."

"I'm going to call the signals as I see them in all fairness and equity in the interests of the public, the players and the franchises," he said. "I agree that I have full authority to step in and do the job that needs to be done."

The general said he would rely on Mr. Frick and the commissioner's staff to help him become oriented to baseball and

that he would ask Mr. Frick to "assist, advise and officiate at the coming meeting" of baseball club owners in Miami, Dec. 1.

"I'm ready to go to work now," he said, "and I plan to get in touch with Frick's staff immediately. I want to encourage clean sports and honest competition, but I'll be better prepared in three months to say how I'll handle the job as commissioner of baseball."

The general was asked his opinion of the transfer of the Milwaukee Braves to Atlanta, but before he could answer Mr. Frick intervened and said "let's give the man a chance. It's unfair to ask the new commissioner questions like that."

The new commissioner, however, said he would not evade the question and would attempt to answer all questions to the best of his ability at any time.

"I hope the Milwaukee problem will be worked out to the satisfaction of the communities concerned," he said. "However,

I am not familiar with the legalities of the situation."

Thin Baseball Background

General Eckert, who retired from the Air Force in 1961, said he did not believe he was hired by the club owners because of his baseball background. His only competition was in Madison (Ind.) High School.

"I don't think they hired me to put me out on the field," he said.

Instead he said he believed his business background with the Air Force, in procurement, research and personnel, was a major factor in determining his qualifications for the job. Since his retirement the general has been a member of numerous industry and defense advisory boards, but he said he planned to resign from most of them.

General Eckert graduated from West Point in 1930 and later was a fighter plane pilot. While he served in the Army he received a Master's Degree in Business Administration at Harvard.

During World War II he was a bomb group commander in Europe, and later chief of maintenance and supply for the 9th Air Force Service Command. He later was assigned to Air Force Headquarters and in February, 1960, became Comptroller of the Air Force.

November 18, 1965

Artificial Grass Installed On Astrodome Outfield

HOUSTON, July 9 (AP) — Workmen installed artificial grass in the outfield area of the Astrodome this week.

The infield area was previously covered with the synthetic grass called Astroturf.

An Astro spokesman said the final slice of grass and turf removed from the outfield would be shipped to Leo Durocher, the Chicago Cubs manager, who has been a bitter critic of the artificial grass.

July 10, 1966

National League Wins Longest All-Star Game, 2-1

AMERICAN LEAGUE LOSES 5TH IN ROW

Allen and Brooks Robinson Also Clout Homers — 30 Strike-Outs Set Record

By JOSEPH DURSO
Special to The New York Times

ANAHEIM, Calif., July 11— The National League won baseball's 38th and longest All-Star Game today by defeating the American League, 2-1, on a 15th-inning home run by Tony Perez of the Cincinnati Reds.

It was the fifth straight victory for the National Leaguers and their 16th in the last 21 games. And it required 3¾ hours of overpowering pitching on both sides, plus four records, before a decision was reached.

A crowd of 46,309 sat in hot, sunny weather in the $20-million home of Gene Autry's California Angels in suburban Los Angeles as the pitching parade passed by.

Richie Allen of Philadelphia hit a home run off Dean Chance of Minnesota in the second inning. Brooks Robinson of Baltimore hit one off Ferguson Jenkins of Chicago in the sixth inning. And then nobody else scored until Perez went to bat in the 15th in his first All-Star Game and hit a 375-foot home run to left-center field off Jim (Catfish) Hunter of Kansas City.

Seaver Protects Lead

Then, in the last half of the 15th, a kind of footnote to All-Star history was written when Manager Walter Alston of Los Angeles turned his team's one run lead over to the only man in California wearing a New York Mets uniform.

He called in Tom Seaver, the Mets' 22-year-old rookie, to replace Don Drysdale and protect the National League's margin.

Seaver, who is used to living dangerously, walked one batter, Carl Yastrzemski, but he struck out Ken Berry of Chicago for the final out and for the 30th strike-out of baseball's longest All-Star show.

The following records were set in deciding the issue here in the citrus-and-neon groves of Orange County, the shrine of Mickey Mouse, Donald Duck and other Walt Disney heroes —and today the center of baseball:

¶Length of the game—15 innings, surpassing the previous marathon of 14 innings, which the National League won in 1950 on a home run by Red Schoendienst.

¶Total number of strike-outs —30, demolishing the former record of 20, set in 12 innings in 1955. Today's mark was divided as follows: 17 American Leaguers and 13 National Leaguers fanned. Along the way, they also broke the record for strike-outs in nine innings, which had been a mere 18.

¶Strike-outs by one pitcher— six, by Jenkins, the Canadian prodigy of the Chicago Cubs. He followed Juan Marichal, pitched the three normally middle innings and equaled the six strike-outs of Carl Hubbell in 1934, Johnny Vander Meer in 1943 and Larry Jansen in 1950.

¶Strike-outs by one batter— four, by Roberto Clemente of Pittsburgh. In its way, this was the most astonishing. Clemente, the winner of two batting titles, arrived in the West with an average of .352. But after beating out a minihit in the first inning, he struck out four times in a row.

Marichal Allows One Hit

A record for courage was probably set, too, by the home-plate umpire, Ed Runge. He was officiating when the most poignant moments of the game were reached within a matter of minutes. First, Mickey Mantle pinch-hit for the American League in the fifth inning to a roaring, standing ovation; a few minutes later, Willie Mays pinch-hit for the National League to a similar roaring, standing ovation.

Both had come into the big leagues in 1951 and both had hit more than 500 home runs. Both were bypassed in the voting by the players, and both were named to the All-Star teams by the managers. Runge called both out on strikes.

All these wondrous things were seen for the first time by a "prime time" television audience in the East. The game started at 4:25 P.M., Pacific Daylight Time, putting it on home screens along the Atlantic Seaboard at 7:15 P.M. And the novel arrangement cast a long shadow toward the time when All-Star Games and even World Series would be played (and televised) at night.

The long day's journey into night began with Dean Chance of Minnesota pitching against Marichal, the impresario of San Francisco, a man with one of the fanciest records in All-Star history. In five previous games,

Box Score of All-Star Game

NATIONAL

	AB.	R.	H.	BI.	PO.	A.
Brock, lf	2	0	0	2	0	0
cMays, ph, cf	4	0	0	3	0	0
Clemente, rf	6	0	1	0	6	0
Aaron, cf, lf	6	0	1	0	6	0
Cepeda, 1b	6	0	0	0	6	0
Allen, 3b	4	1	1	1	0	0
Perez, 3b	2	1	1	1	0	3
Torre, c	2	0	0	0	4	1
Haller, c	1	0	0	0	7	0
gBanks, ph	1	0	1	0	0	0
McCarver, c	2	0	2	0	7	1
Mazeroski, 2b	4	0	0	0	7	1
Drysdale, p	1	0	0	0	0	0
kHelms, ph	1	0	0	0	0	0
Seaver, p	0	0	0	0	0	0
Alley, ss	5	0	0	0	1	3
Marichal, p	1	0	0	0	0	0
Jenkins, p	1	0	0	0	0	0
Gibson, p	0	0	0	0	0	0
tWynn, ph	1	0	1	0	0	0
Short, p	0	0	0	0	0	1
iStaub, ph	1	0	1	0	0	0
Cuellar, p	0	0	0	0	0	0
jRose, ph, 2b	1	0	0	0	0	0
Total	51	2	9	2	45	13

a Singled for Chance in 3d; b Struck out for McGlothlin in 5th; c Struck out for Brock in 6th; d Singled for Peters in 8th; e Ran for

AMERICAN

	AB.	R.	H.	BI.	PO.	A.
B. Robi'son, 3b	6	1	1	1	0	6
Carew, 2b	3	0	0	0	2	2
McAuliffe, 2b	3	0	0	0	3	2
Oliva, cf	6	0	2	0	4	0
Killebrew, 1b	6	0	0	0	15	1
Conigliaro, rf	6	0	0	0	4	0
Yastrzemski, lf	4	0	3	0	2	0
Freehan, c	5	0	0	0	13	0
Petrocelli, ss	5	0	0	0	0	1
McGlothlin, p	0	0	0	0	0	0
bMantle, ph	1	0	0	0	0	0
Peters, p	0	0	0	0	0	1
dMincher, ph	1	0	1	0	0	0
eAgee, pr	0	0	0	0	0	0
Downing, p	0	0	0	0	0	0
hAlvis, ph	1	0	0	0	0	0
Hunter, p	1	0	0	0	0	0
iBerry, ph	1	0	0	0	0	0
Chance, p	0	0	0	0	0	0
jFregosi, ph, ss	4	0	1	0	2	3
Total	49	1	8	1	45	16

Mincher in 8th; f Singled for Gibson in 9th; g Singled for Haller in 10th; h Grounded into fielders' choice for Downing in 10th; i Singled for Short in 11th; j Flied out for Cuellar in 13th; k Grounded into double play for Drysdale in 15th; l Struck out for Hunter in 15th.

National	0 1 0	0 0 0	0 0 0	0 0 1—2
American	0 0 0	0 0 1	0 0 0	0 0 0—1

Double play—Robinson, Carew and Killebrew; McAuliffe and Killebrew. Left on bases—National 5, American 7. Two-base hit—Yastrzemski, McCarver. Three-base hit—None. Home runs—Allen, B. Robinson, Perez. Stolen base—Aaron. Sacrifice—Freehan. Sacrifice fly—None.

	I.P.	H.	R.	E.R.	B.B.	S.O.	H.P.P.	W.P.	Blk.
Chance	3	1	1	1	2	4	0	0	0
McGlothlin	2	1	0	0	2	0	0	0	0
Peters	2	0	0	0	0	2	0	0	0
Downing	2	2	0	0	0	2	0	0	0
Hunter (L.)	5	4	1	0	0	2	0	0	0
Marichal	3	1	0	0	0	3	0	0	0
Jenkins	3	1	1	0	6	0	0	0	0
Gibson	2	2	0	0	2	0	0	0	0
Short	2	0	0	0	1	1	0	0	0
Cuellar	2	1	0	0	1	2	0	0	0
Drysdale (W.)	2	1	0	0	0	2	0	0	0
Seaver	1	0	0	0	1	0	0	0	0

Bases on balls—Off Short (Yastrzemski), off Seaver (Yastrzemski). Struck out—By Marichal 3 (Oliva, Yastrzemski, Freehan), Jenkins 6 (Killebrew, Conigliaro, Mantle, Fregosi, Carew, Oliva), Conigliaro, Freehan), Short 1 (Fregosi), Gibson 2 (Conigliaro, Freehan), Short 1 (Fregosi), Gibson 2 (Conigliaro, Freehan), Cuellar 2 (B. Robinson, Oliva), Drysdale 2 (Hunter, Killebrew), Seaver 1 (Berry), Chance 1 (Clemente), McGlothlin 2 (Allen, Alley), Peters 4 (Mays, Clemente, Cepeda, Allen), Downing 2 (Clemente, Allen), Hunter 4 (Alley 2, Clemente, Perez).

Umpires—Runge (A.), plate; Secory (N.), first base; Dimuro (A.), second base; Burkhart (N.), third base; Ashford (A.) and Pelekoudas (N.), foul lines. Time of game—3:41. Attendance—46,309.

the 28-year-old Dominican had allowed only six hits and one run.

For three innings today he showed the American League what has tormented the National for half a dozen years. He retired eight straight batters before Jim Fregosi singled. But then he got Brooks Robinson on a grounder (for the second time), and turned the pitching over to Jenkins, Bob Gibson, Chris Short, Mike Cuellar, Drysdale and Seaver.

Chance, meanwhile, was faring almost as well. Clemente chopped a pitch to the right side in the first and beat it out. Henry Aaron, who forced Clemente, stole second base. But otherwise Chance's only bad moment came in the top of the second inning when Allen led off.

The Philadelphia slugger dorve Chance's third pitch deep in the temporary bleachers in right-center past the 393-foot marker, and the Nationals had a one-run lead.

Chance was succeeded in the fourth by Jim McGlothlin, the 23-year-old redhead who pitches for California. The young right-

hander was nicked for a single by the first batter, Aaron, but he got both Aaron and Orlando Cepeda on a double-play grounder and then struck out Allen.

The American League tried to break through Jenkins's service in the fourth when Tony Oliva singled over second base with one out. But he was caught stealing and Harmon Killebrew of Minnesota looked at a third strike.

McGlothlin, throwing a giant-sized dropping curve, retired Joe Torre, Bill Mazeroski and Gene Alley in order in the fifth. And then the Americans stirred again.

After Tony Conigliaro had struck out, Yastrzemski hit a low line drive to center field. Aaron, normally a right-fielder, appeared to lose the ball in the haze as he ran in, then got his glove on it briefly before it squirted away for a double.

However, Jenkins retired Bill Freehan of Detroit on a pop fly to shortstop and then caught Mantle looking at a fast ball for a third strike.

Robinson Hit Ties Score

In the bottom of the sixth,

the Nationals suddenly lost their lead. Robinson, playing in his 11th straight All-Star Game at third base, lined Jenkins's second pitch into the left-field bull pen for his first home run in the series.

That tied the score, and the score stayed tied for the next eight innings.

McGlothlin was followed by Gary Peters, Al Downing and Hunter, and except for the home-run hitters nobody got past second base until the 13th. At one stretch, between the fourth and ninth innings, McGlothlin and Peters retired 15 batters in a row.

The American Leaguers might have capitalized on this air-tight pitching several times. Yastrzemski, for example, got on base five straight times on three hits and two walks, but four times in extra innings, the American Leaguers ended their time at bat with strike-outs.

Hunter Victim of Perez's Hit

Then, in the bottom of the 15th, just as the teams set the record for endurance, the end came fast.

Hunter was pitching his fifth inning by then, which was a

distinction in itself. He was the first man to pitch more than four innings since Johnny Antonelli in the 1956 game. He is so talented that, at 21 years of age, he already has been on two All-Star teams. But when he tired today, it proved fatal.

Hunter's peak had come two innings earlier when Tim McCarver doubled into the left-field corner with nobody out and was bunted to third. But Catfish struck out Alley and retired Pete Rose on a fly to center.

In the 15th, though, Cepeda opened with a fly to deep right. Conigliaro, who had made the catch of the day in the 10th on Cepeda, got this one, too. Then up came Perez.

The 25-year-old right-handed infielder was born in Cuba, lives in Puerto Rico and works in Cincinnati. He had been filling in for Allen at third base since the 10th inning. He took a strike from Hunter, then drilled the ball 375 feet into the seats in left-center. And after the Mets' Mr. Seaver had held the fort in the bottom of the 15th, the longest All-Star game in history was over.

July 12, 1967

Red Sox Win Pennant

By JOSEPH DURSO
Special to The New York Times

BOSTON, Oct. 1—The Boston Red Sox completed one of baseball's great rags-to-riches stories today by defeating the Minnesota Twins, 5-3, and winning the tightest American

League pennant race in history.

They won it before a roaring crowd of 35,770 persons in the 162d and final game of the season, one year after they had finished ninth in the league and 21 years after they had won their last pennant.

They also won it in a dramatic tale of two baseball cities with help from the California Angels, the final hurdle standing between the Detroit Tigers and a possible playoff.

But when the Tigers lost to the Angels, 8-5, in the second game of their double-header in Detroit—and in the last game of their season—the three-team free-for-all was finally ended. The Tigers and Twins finished in a tie for second, one game behind.

As a result, the Red Sox—

a second-division team for nine years — will open the 64th World Series on Wednesday against the St. Louis Cardinals.

They will open it in Fenway Park, where the Red Sox won their second straight game over Minnesota today behind the seven-hit pitching of Jim Lonborg and four straight hits by Carl Yastrzemski.

Yastrzemski, with three singles and a double, batted across two runs for the Red Sox. They were both scored in the sixth inning of a gripping struggle, when the Red Sox rallied for five runs and overcame a 2-0 lead that Minnesota had built for Dean Chance.

Two innings later, Yastrzemski made a key throw from left field to second base killing a counter-rally staged by Minnesota and ending two days of heroic performance that carried the Red Sox to the top.

For 5½ innings this afternoon, though, the gloom thickened in Fenway Park as the Red Sox and Twins fought it out under their rookie managers, Dick Williams and Cal Ermer.

Lonborg, gunning for his 22d victory, retired the first two batters, then walked Harmon Killebrew. Then came the first of two errors that put Minnesota ahead. Tony Oliva banked a line drive off the left-field fence just over Yastrzemski's head and the ball bounced toward center field.

Reggie Smith, in pursuit, picked it up and fired a good throw toward home plate. But George Scott, the first baseman, cut off the throw 25 feet in front of the plate and flung it high and wide to the screen as Killebrew scored.

In the third, trouble brewed for Boston again with two out. This time Lonborg walked Cesar Tovar, and Killebrew lined a single to left. Tovar normally would have stopped at second base, but when the ball skipped past Yastrzemski to the wall, he scored and it was 2-0, Minnesota.

And that's the way things stood until the sixth. Yastrzemski had singled in the first, Rico Petrocelli had singled in the second, Lonberg had singled in the third and Yastrzemski had doubled in the fourth—but still

Chance had protected his 2-0 lead.

A Lucky Chance

The closest call for Minnesota developed in the fourth, when Yastrzemski led off with a lone drive off the left-field wall, just missing a home run. Ken Harrelson flied out to Oliva, but Scott ripped a vicious liner toward center field. However, Chance instintively reached up, clutched the ball in the netting of his glove, whirled and threw to second base to double up Yastrzemski.

Two innings later, the Red Sox abruptly broke through with a spectacular thrust that may rank with the Brink's robbery as one of the stunning events of Boston history. They sent 10 batters to the plate, four hit safely, one walked, one reached base on a fielder's choice, four advanced on a pair of wild pitches—and five scored.

Lonborg, who was pitching but losing a two-hitter at that point, started it all by curling a perfect bunt down the third-base line for a single. Jerry Adair hit the next pitch past the diving Rod Carew into center for a single. Dalton Jones, after fouling off the first pitch while trying to bunt, lined a single past third and the bases were loaded with nobody out.

The batter was Yastrzemski, who was leading the league in most offensive departments and who had hit two singles and a home run the day before.

Surrounded by deafening noise, he took a ball inside and then lined a single into center as Lonborg and Adair scored to tie the game and Fenway Park went wild.

The hit was the third straight of the game for Yastrzemski and his fifth in a

Rico Petrocelli

row in the series. Before the game was over, he was to single again and run his streak to six hits in a row and seven for eight during the climactic weekend series. He also wound up with 121 runs batted in, and the feeling in Boston was unanimous that Nos. 120 and 121 were his most important.

Versalles Throws Home

While paper and streamers were still swirling through the air, Harrelson followed by chopping a high bouncer over the mound to the left of second base, where Zoilo Versalles grabbed it. He had a play at first but fired the ball instead to home plate, too late to intercept Jones, who was scoring the third run.

Chance, foiled in his bid for his 21st victory, was relieved by Al Worthington while José Tartabull went in as a pinch-run-

ner for Harrelson, who had joined the Red Sox a month ago from the embroiled Kansas City Athletics.

There were still no outs and, when Scott squared away to bunt on the first pitch, Worthington pitched hard on the outside and off his catcher's glove. The runners each moved up a base.

Two pitches later, Worthington delivered another wild pitch into the dirt and, as it bounced into the front row boxes near the Boston dugout, Yastrzemski scored and Tartabull took third. Scott finally struck out.

Minnesota's hour of despair was not over, though. Rico Petrocelli walked, and Reggie Smith cracked a hard grounder off Killebrew's glove at first base. As the ball bounced into foul territory, Tartabull scored the fifth and final run of the inning.

MINNESOTA (A.)					BOSTON (A.)				
	ab	r	h	bi		ab	r	h	bi
Versalles, ss	3	0	0	0	Adair, 2b	4	1	2	0
Reese, lf	1	0	1	0	Andrews, 2b	0	0	0	0
Tovar, 3b	3	1	0	0	Jones, 3b	4	1	2	0
Killebrew, 1b	2	2	2	0	Yastrzemski, lf	4	1	4	2
Oliva, rf	3	0	2	0	Harrelson, rf	3	0	0	1
Allison, lf	4	0	1		Tartabull, rf	1	1	0	0
Hernandez, ss	0	0	0	0	Scott, 1b	4	0	0	0
Uhlaender, cf	4	0	1	0	Petrocelli, ss	3	0	0	0
Carew, 2b	4	0	0	0	Smith, cf	4	0	0	1
Zimmerman, c	2	0	0	0	Gibson, c	2	0	0	0
Nixon, c	1	0	0	0	Siebern, ph	1	0	0	0
Rollins, ph	1	0	0	0	Howard, c	1	0	1	0
Chance, p	2	0	0	0	Lonborg, p	4	1	2	0
Worthington, p	0	0	0	0					
Kosco, ph	1	0	0	0					
Roland, p	0	0	0	0					
Grant, p	0	0	0	0					
Total	31	3	7	1	Total	35	5	12	4

Minnesota .... 1 0 1 0 0 0 0 1 0—3
Boston .... 0 0 0 0 0 5 0 0 x—5
E—Scott, Yastrzemski, Killebrew. DP—Minnesota 3, Boston 2. LOB—Minnesota 5, Boston 7. 2B—Oliva, Yastrzemski.

	IP.	H.	R.	ER.	BB	SO
Chance (L, 20-14)	5	8	5	5	0	2
Worthington	1	0	0	0	1	0
Roland	2	3	0	0	0	0
Grant						
Lonborg (W, 22-9)	9	7	3	2	1	4

WP—Lonborg, Worthington 2.
T—2:25. A—35,770.

American League Approves Shift of Athletics to Oakland

LOOP OF 12 TEAMS SLATED BY 1971

New Franchises Will Be Situated at Kansas City and Possibly Seattle

By LEONARD KOPPETT
Special to The New York Times

CHICAGO, Oct. 18 — The American League voted tonight to allow Charles O. Finley to

move his Kansas City Athletics to Oakland, and to expand the league to 12 teams, "as soon as practicable, but not later than the 1971 season," with the new franchises to be situated in Kansas City and Seattle.

This compromise solution was arrived at after more than 11 hours of hearings and deliberations at the Continental Plaza hotel here. There were a few conditional aspects to the final decision. Seattle's franchise is contingent on the provision of suitable stadium facilities; a bond issue for this purpose will be voted on in Seattle in February.

/ Also, the entire arrangement

is "subject to suitable baseball rules and procedures." Details must be worked out, including the coordination of the expansion plans with the commissioner of baseball and with the National League.

Dallas People Invited

Throughout the day the American League owners and their staffs heard presentations from Finley, Kansas City officials, Oakland officials, the Seattle delegation and two representatives from Dallas (Lamar Hunt and Dick Butler). The Dallas people were invited to attend only yesterday and were, in Hunt's words "surprised to

be here."

Underlying the entire decision process was a rivalry between the American and National League. Both wanted Seattle, the last major marketing area in the country untouched by major league baseball.

American Leaguers felt strongly that the National League beat them in prior moves in California, Houston and Atlanta and were determined not to lose Seattle. That is why they made the commitment to Seattle now although no physical facility exists for fielding a team.

The bond issue will concern a multi-purposed domed stadium and must be carried by a 60 per cent vote. But even if it is beaten there exist possibilities of private development. The Seattle representatives, Johnny O'Brien (well-known former athlete) and David Cohn expressed "delight" at the situation.

From Kansas City's point of view, the granting of a deferred expansion franchise was a bitter disappointment. The Kansas City people, whose delegation included Stuart Symington of Missouri and Mayo Ilus Davis, had stressed of their desire for "uninterrupted baseball."

The Dallas maneuver was widely interpreted as a courtesy move to people who had shown some interest in the past, but did not seem terribly eager or prepared for immediate expansion.

Within the American League, the big battle was between those who advocated immediate expansion for 1968 and those who wanted a more cautious and slower approach. The compromise, then, consisted of a time-table that may extend to 1971 but with an immediate identification of the expansion cities involved.

October 19, 1967

Hunter of A's Pitches Baseball's 10th Perfect Game

OAKLAND HURLER DRIVES IN 3 RUNS

Only 6 Balls Hit to Outfield as Hunter Strikes Out 11, Killebrew Three Times

OAKLAND, Calif., May 8 (AP)—Jim (Catfish) Hunter pitched the American League's first perfect game in regular season play since 1922 tonight and drove in three runs as the Oakland Athletics routed the Minnesota Twins, 4-0.

Hunter, a 22-year-old right-hander in his fourth major league season, set down 27 of the hard-hitting Twins in becoming the 10th man to pitch a perfect game in baseball history.

The 6-foot-5-inch, 195-pound Hunter struck out 11 and needed the help of just one outstanding defensive play—Sal Bando's stab of a fifth inning grounder to third base by Bob Allison. Harmon Killebrew, the Minnesota slugger was a strikeout victim three times.

The last perfect game was pitched by Sandy Koufax of the Los Angeles Dodgers three years ago against the Chicago Cubs.

The last American Leaguer to pitch one was Don Larsen of the New York Yankees, who did it in the 1956 World Series against the Brooklyn Dodgers.

But Charlie Robertson of the Chicago White Sox, in 1922, was the last to pitch one in a regular season contest. He did it against Detroit.

Hunter completed his feat by getting a pinch-hitter, John Roseboro, to ground out in the ninth, then striking out Bruce Look and Rich Reese. The latter had fouled off five straight pitches. Only five balls were hit out of the infield against Hunter.

Delivers Bunt Single

Hunter delivered a run-scoring bunt single in the seventh and a two-run single in the eighth.

Hunter, who signed with the Athletics for a $75,000 bonus in 1964, had a 13-17 won-lost record last year. He has a 2-2 mark this season.

The Athletics, who moved to C   d this year from Kansas City, had not had a no-hitter since Bill McCahan threw one against Washington on Sept. 3, 1947, when the club was in Philadelphia.

Hunter's no-hitter, witnessed by 6,298 spectators, the second smallest turnout this season at Oakland Coliseum, was the second of the season. Tom Phoebus of the Baltimore Orioles pitched a 6-0, no-hit victory against the Boston Red Sox on April 27.

Dave Boswell pitched six scoreless innings for Minnesota.

In the A's seventh Rick Monday doubled, took third on Boswell's second wild pitch, then scored when Hunter beat out a bunt.

With the bases filled in the eighth, Ron Perranoski replaced Boswell and walked Danny Cater, forcing a run. Hunter followed with his two-run single.

Hunter went to a 3-2 count on only six batters. He had a count of 3-0 on Tony Oliva in the second inning, then struck out the dangerous two-time league hitting champion.

"I just tried to throw strikes to everybody; control is the name of the game," Hunter said.

MINNESOTA (A.)					OAKLAND (A.)				
	ab	r	h	bi		ab	r	h	bi
Tovar, 3b	3	0	0	0	Campaneris, ss	4	0	2	0
Carew, 2b	3	0	0	0	Jackson, rf	4	0	0	0
Killebrew, 1b	3	0	0	0	Bando, 3b	3	0	1	0
Oliva, rf	3	0	0	0	Webster, 1b	4	1	2	0
Uhlaender, cf	3	0	0	0	Donaldson, 2b	3	0	0	0
Allison, lf	3	0	0	0	Pagliaroni, c	3	1	0	0
Hernandez, ss	2	0	0	0	Monday, cf	3	2	0	0
Roseboro, ph	1	0	0	0	Rud ss	3	0	0	0
Look, c	3	0	0	0	Cater, lf	0	0	0	2
Boswell, p	2	0	0	0	Cater, lf	3	0	0	2
Perranoski, p	0	0	0	0	Hunter, p	4	0	3	3
Reese, ph	1	0	0	0					
Total	27	0	0	0	Total	34	4	10	4

Minnesota   000 000 000—0
Oakland   000 050 13x—4
E—Boswell. DP—Minnesota 2. LOB—Oakland 9. 2B—Hunter, Monday. SB—Campaneris.

	IP	H	R	ER	BB	SO
Boswell (L, 3-3)	7	9	4	4	3	4
Perranoski	1	0	0	0	1	0
Hunter (W, 3-2)	9	0	0	0	0	11

HBP—By Boswell (Donaldson). WP—Boswell 2.
T—2:28. A—6,298.

May 9, 1968

National League Adds Montreal and San Diego

EXPANSION MOVE EFFECTIVE IN 1969

Shift to Canada for 12th Team Is Surprise—Price Is $10-Million Apiece

By JOSEPH DURSO
Special to The New York Times

CHICAGO, May 27 — Major league baseball crossed its first international frontier tonight when Montreal was voted into the National League along with San Diego.

The vote came on the 16th secret ballot after 10 hours of discussion and argument, and was unanimous. It will bring big league baseball to Canada next April, when the league expands from 10 teams to 12.

Montreal and San Diego beat out three other cities that had campaigned aggressively for franchises. They were Buffalo, Milwaukee and Dallas - Fort Worth, and all expressed "shock" and disappointment tonight when the vote was announced after an all-day closed meeting of the league's club owners.

Conditions Are Suitable

The selection of San Diego was no upset. Though close to Los Angeles and Anaheim, which already have big-league teams, San Diego has a new stadium that seats 45,000 persons. It also has an ideally mild climate and a successful team in the American Football League.

Montreal, though, had been given only an outside chance of surviving the battle of the cities. It is a shrine of ice hockey, but has had no high-level baseball since the Montreal Royals, a one-time International League farm team of the old Brooklyn Dodgers, were disbanded in 1960.

However, Montreal made a strong pitch for admission by promising that a domed stadium—the second in baseball—would be built by 1971 with a capacity of 55,000. Until then, the new team will play in the Expo Stadium, which will be enlarged to seat 45,000 persons.

The cost of passing a baseball milestone will be high for both cities. They will pay $10-million apiece for the privilege. It will cost them $6-million each for 30 players, who will be bought from the 10 other National League clubs plus $4-million for initiation and a split of television revenue.

Follow the Leader

The decision tonight guarantees that the National League will expand precisely on schedule with the American, which voted last October to add two clubs. They are Seattle and Kansas City, which also will field teams in 1969.

The Nationals had been reluctant to be "stampeded" into

expansion. They felt there were insuperable conflicts of geography and scheduling and feared that the available baseball talent would be diluted.

· But the resistance to expansion broke down tonight under the threat that the rival league would cross the bridge to the talent first and would siphon off the best.

· No decision was reached by the National League on whether to divide the 12 teams into two conferences of six teams each. The American League has already drawn such a blueprint and will wind up with two pennant winners each September with a playoff determining who gets into the World Series.

However, both leagues will meet here tomorrow with the commissioner of baseball, William D. Eckert, and a symmetry probably will be established. If not, a lopsided pattern would result, with one league holding a championship playoff, while the other awarded the pennant to the number one team of all 12 at the end of the season.

What Went Wrong?

The losers in the balloting were disconsolate with strong overtones that cities in the United States had been bypassed for a Canadian city.

"It's unthinkable," said Judge Robert Cannon of the Milwaukee delegation, "that baseball would do this to cities in the United States — which made baseball what it is."

"It's a shock," said J. Frederick Schoelkopf 4th of the Buffalo group. "Erie County has already voted money for a domed stadium and we can't understand what went wrong."

Milwaukee had been fighting to return to the major leagues, which abandoned the city in 1966, when the Braves decamped to Atlanta.

The Dallas group, led by oil millionaires such as Lamar Hunt, had made a strong appeal despite the fact that Houston, with its roofed Astrodome, was only 200 miles away.

Buffalo had campaigned as

the "eighth largest television market in North America," with a radius that would include parts of Canada surrounding Toronto.

The Montreal team will be operated by a syndicate of seven men headed by Jean-Louis Levesque, a financier. However, the principal ballcarrier was Jerry Snyder, the vice mayor, and the chief momentum came from Expo '67.

The San Diego group will include E. J. (Buzzie) Bavasi, executive vice president and general manager of the Los Angeles Dodgers.

May 28, 1968

Drysdale Sets Scoreless Record

DODGERS WIN, 5-3

Drysdale Hurls 58 2/3 Innings Without Allowing Run

By The Associated Press

LOS ANGELES, June 8—Don Drysdale set a major-league record by pitching 58⅔ consecutive scoreless innings before being driven from the mound tonight in the Los Angeles Dodgers' 5-3 victory over the Philadelphia Phils.

Drysdale broke Walter John-

son's major-league record of 56 consecutive scoreless innings when he retired Roberto Pena on a grounder opening the third inning. A capacity crowd of 50,060 gave the 31-year-old right-hander a standing ovation.

But the string ended at 58 2/3 when Howie Bedell, a pinchhitter, delivered a sacrifice fly with two out in the fifth, scoring Tony Taylor from third base. Singles by Taylor and Clay Dalrymple set up the run.

Drysdale Departs in 7th

Drysdale allowed a sixth-inning homer to Bill White and was knocked from the box when Cookie Rojas singled home the seventh-inning run that narrowed the Los Angeles lead to 4-3.

The Dodgers got their win-

ning margin with four runs in the first four innings against Larry Jackson.

Ken Boyer singled home a first-inning run. The Dodgers then scored three in the fourth after Tom Haller had doubled and taken third on Boyer's single.

Haller scored on a fielder's choice. Boyer scored on an error by Pena and Zoilo Versalles ended the rally with a run-scoring fly.

Parker Hits Home Run

Wes Parker hit a seventh-inning homer for the Dodgers.

The victory was the Dodgers' sixth straight and their ninth in their last 10 games.

After Drysdale broke the scoreless inning record in the third, the plate umpire, Augie Donatelli, examined the pitch-

er's hair, apparently looking for excess grease. He again checked Drysdale before the fourth inning, but took no action on either occasion.

PHILA. (N.)				LOS ANGELES (N.)			
	ab.r.h.bi				ab.r.h.bi		
Rojas, 2b	5 0 2 1			Parker, 1b	4 1 2 1		
Briggs, cf	2 0 0 0			Davis, cf	4 1 0 0		
Sutherland, ph	1 0 0 0			Gabrielson, lf	4 0 1 0		
Farrell, p	0 0 0 0			Fairey, lf	0 0 0 0		
Gonzalez, lf	4 0 0 0			Haller, c	3 1 3 0		
Callison, rf	3 0 0 0			Boyer, 3b	4 1 2 1		
White, 1b	4 1 1 1			Fairly, rf	4 1 1 1		
Taylor, 3b	4 1 1 0			Popovich, 2b	4 0 1 0		
Dalrymple, c	2 1 1 0			Versalles, ss	3 0 0 1		
Allen, ph	1 0 0 0			Drysdale, p	2 0 0 0		
Ryan, c	0 0 0 0			Aguirre, p	1 0 0 0		
Pena, ss	4 0 0 0						
L. Jackson, p	1 0 1 0			Total	33 5 10 4		
Bedell, ph	0 0 0 1						
G. Jackson, p	0 0 0 0						
Lock, cf	2 0 0 0						
Total	33 3 6 3						

Philadelphia   000 011 100—3
Los Angeles   100 300 10x—5

E—Pena, Versalles, Fairly. DP—Philadelphia 1. LOB—Philadelphia 7, Los Angeles 6. 2B—Haller. HR—White (6), Parker (3). SB—Davis. SF—Versalles, Bedell.

	IP.	H.	R.	ER.	BB.	SO.
L. Jackson (L, 6-6)	4	5	4	3	1	1
G. Jackson	2	5	0	0	0	2
Farrell	2	0	0	0	2	5
Drysdale (W, 8-3)	6⅓	5	3	2	2	5
Aguirre	2	0	0	0	0	2

T—2:29. A—50,060.

June 9, 1968

M'LAIN DEFEATS ATHLETICS FOR 30TH VICTORY

RALLY IN 9TH WINS

By LEONARD KOPPETT
Special to The New York Times

DETROIT, Sept. 14—What no major league pitcher had been able to do since 1934 and what only two had accomplished in the last 48 years was achieved by Dennis Dale McLain of the

Detroit Tigers today when he posted his 30th victory of the season.

The 24-year-old right-handed extrovert won it sitting on the bench, because he had been removed for a pinch hitter in the home half of the ninth inning.

The pinch-hitter, Al Kaline, walked and set off a two-run rally that gave the Tigers a 5-4

victory over the Oakland Athletics.

Grove Did It in '31

But the dramatic finish, typical of a Tiger team that has moved within four victories of clinching the American League pennant, in no way minimized McLain's triumph. He had pitched a strong game, hurt only by two home runs by Reg-

gie Jackson, Oakland's budding star, and by the only walk he issued, which was turned into a run. McLain struck out 10 men and pitched his 27th complete game in 38 starts.

All the significance was packed into the "30." A 20-game winner is a member of baseball's elite. Only a handful of pitchers have won 30. The

Don Drysdale pitches against the Phillies in 1968, the year that he broke the major league record for consecutive scoreless innings.

last had been Dizzy Dean, who hurled the St. Louis Cardinals to the 1934 National League pennant w.th a 30-7 record. Bob (Lefty) Grove of the Philadelphia Athletics was the last in the American League with a 31-4 season in 1931. No one else had won 30 since 1920.

When Willie Horton's drive over the left fielder's head ended the game by knocking in the tie-breaking run with one out, a wild scene erupted. It was an appropriate climax to an event carried by the National Broadcasting Company to millions of home television screens, and no set of scriptwriters could have surpassed what reality had provided.

In the stands were 44,087 people, 33,688 of them paying customers and the rest children admitted in groups, and they became part of the show.

His Mates Mob Him

As Horton's hit fell safe, McLain raced out of the dugout to embrace the teammates who had brought him his prize after it had passed out of his own power to gain. They, in turn, surrounded and lifted him, precariously, in a march to the dugout. Photographers, television crews and fans started to converge on the scene and there was a terrific crush near the third-base dugout.

Finally, McLain was able to say a few words on camera with Dean, who was present for the

occasion, and with Sandy Koufax, who retired two years ago and removed himself from the glory McLain had attained.

On a personal level, there is the record itself, the argument for a $100,000 contract next year and the limitless possibilities for outside income for McLain and his organ-playing career.

But on a team basis, his superb season made possible the pennant the Tigers failed to win last year only on the last day, so the jubilation did not stem merely from statistics.

'We Want Denny!'

When McLain finally disappeared into the clubhouse, the crowd remained, chanting, "We want Denny!" When he heard about it, he insisted on going out again to wave, acknowledge the cheers and pose for more pictures. Half an hour later he was still gleefully answering questions inside while the clubhouse door was besieged by admirers.

The game, which lasted 3 hours 3 minutes, formed a perfect build-up. Jackson's first homer, with a man on, had put Oakland ahead, 2-0, in the fourth inning. But Norm Cash hit one with two on in the Tigers' half, and McLain had a 3-2 lead.

He lost it in the fifth to a leadoff walk, a sacrifice and a single by Bert Campaneris, and with two out in the sixth, Jackson hit another homer, the 28th of his first full major league campaign.

Now it was up to Diego Segui, Oakland's fourth pitcher,

to hold off the Tigers, and he did for three innings.

With two out in the eighth, a walk and an infield single, on which Segui had failed to cover first, gave Detroit two men on with two out. Gates Brown, the Tigers' best pinch-hitter, bounced out on the first pitch. Had he walked, McLain would have had to be removed for a hitter right then, with unknown results.

Kaline Draws a Walk

As it happened, though, McLain breezed through the ninth and Kaline led off for him in the home half. Fouling off two 3-2 pitches, Kaline drew a hard-earned walk. Dick McAuliffe, after fouling back two bunt attempts, popped out on a foul, but Mickey Stanley grounded the next pitch through the box into center for a single and Kaline hustled into third.

Bob Kennedy, the Oakland manager who had checked Detroit's fourth-inning rally by using two relievers to pitch to one man each, now went out to discuss matters with Segui. Jim Northrup, a left-handed pull-hitter, was up, and a home run was a real danger. But Kennedy left Segui in and, from a pitching point of view, events did not prove him wrong.

But with the infield drawn in to try to cut down the tying run at the plate, Northrup bounced to Danny Cater, the first baseman. There was plenty of time to get Kaline, but Cater's throw was high and wild, and while Kaline scored

OAKLAND (A.)						DETROIT (A.)				
	ab.	r.	h.	bi			ab.	r.	h.	bi
Campaneris, ss	4	0	1	1		McAuliffe, 2b	5	0	1	0
Monday, cf	4	0	1	0		Stanley, cf	5	1	2	0
Cater, 1b	4	1	2	0		Northrup, rf	4	1	0	0
Bando, 3b	3	0	0	0		Horton, lf	5	1	2	1
Jackson, rf	4	2	2	3		Cash, 1b	4	1	2	3
Green, 2b	4	0	0	0		Freehan, c	3	0	1	0
Keough, lf	3	0	0	0		Matchick, ss	4	0	1	0
Gosger, lf	0	0	0	0		Wert, 3b	2	0	0	0
Duncan, c	2	1	0	0		Brown, ph	1	0	0	0
Dobson, p	1	0	0	0		Tracewski, 3b	0	0	0	0
Aker, p	0	0	0	0		McLain, p	1	0	0	0
Lindblad, p	0	0	0	0		Kaline, ph	0	1	0	0
Donaldson, ph	0	0	0	0						
Segui, p	1	0	0	0						
Total	30	4	6	4		Total	34	5	9	4

Oakland .... 000 211 000—4
Detroit .... 000 300 002—5

E—Matchick, Bando, Cater. DP—Detroit 1. LOB—Oakland 2, Detroit 10. HR—Jackson 2 (28), Cash (21). S—McLain, Bando, Donaldson.

	IP.	H.	R.	ER.	BB.	SO.
Dobson	3⅔	4	3	3	2	4
Aker	0	0	0	0	1	0
Lindblad	⅓	0	0	0	0	1
Segui (L, 5-5)	*4⅓	5	2	1	2	1
McLain (W, 30-5)	9	6	4	4	1	10

*One out when winning run was scored.
Wild pitch—Aker.
T—3:00. A—33,688.

Stanley raced around to third.

In the dugout McLain, who had been watching quietly most of the inning, leaped up and shouted. He thought Stanley, too, might score on the overthrow.

"Calm down, calm down," drawled Manager Mayo Smith. McLain laughed and calmed down.

Now it was up to Horton. Only the man on third counted, and both the infield and outfield played close, since a long fly-out would be as decisive as a home run. Segui put up quite a battle, until Horton smacked a 2-2 pitch beyond Jim Gosger's reach.

September 15, 1968

Slider Is the Pitch That Put Falling Batting Averages on the Skids

By JOSEPH DURSO

Satchel Paige, a 60-year-old pitcher for the Atlanta Braves, says his best pitch these days is a slider.

Denny McLain, who is young enough to be Satchel's grandson, won over 30 games this year for the Detroit Tigers. His pitching coach, Johnny Sain, reports McLain is throwing an improved slider.

Rocky Colavito, an outfielder who hit 372 home runs in 1,796 games, caused a sensation last month by pitching for the New York Yankees — and announced that his best pitch was a slider.

Baseball has seen the fastball, curveball, slowball, sinkerball, spitball, fadeaway, spinner, screwball, forkball, and even something called the emery ball. But now, in this year of the domineering pitcher and the disappearing hitter, the most talked-about tool of the trade is the slider.

Pitch Denied to Koosman

It has been derided as "a 5-cent curveball," scorned as a junkball, lionized as the greatest "out" pitch of this generation. It

has been banned by the Mets from the repertory of Jerry Koosman, because its captivating quality might cause him to neglect his curveball. Steve Hamilton of the Yankees calls it "a nonexistent pitch." Sain says some pitchers throw it 40 times a game.

Whatever the slider is, it has become the favorite weapon of the strong-armed men who are making pitching the black art of a game that once belonged to the hitters.

To them, it is a ball that approaches home plate like a fastball but that suddenly veers—or slides—a few inches to one side and perhaps even down. It does not "drop off the table" like Sandy Koufax's big curve. It does not "tail away" like Bob Gibson's fastball. It slides—like a fast 5-cent curveball.

Nobody knows for sure who invented the slider or whether it was just there all the time waiting to be harnessed, like electricity.

Frank Crosetti, who joined the Yankees 34 years ago, remembers that old-time pitchers such as George Blaeholder and Johnny Babich threw natural mini-curves.

Sailing Fastball Renamed

Jim Turner, the pitching coach for the Yankees, recalls that a "sailing fastball" or "any short curve" before World War II became known as a slider. Phil Rizzuto thinks that it may have evolved from the "slip pitch" taught by Paul Richards, a smart catcher who now runs the Atlanta Braves.

"When I came up in 1941," Rizzuto said, "Al Milnar of Cleveland was the only pitcher who threw a slider regularly. Then after the war, the young pitchers like Mel Parnell came along and everybody started to throw breaking pitches that we now call sliders."

"I spent four years in the lowest minor leagues, the 'D' leagues," Sain said, "and I never had over-powering speed. So I kept practicing my breaking stuff, big curves and short ones. I started in 1936, and by the time I came up to the big leagues with Boston in 1942 I was throwing sliders."

"When I came up in 1951," Mickey Mantle recalled, "you'd get ahead of the pitcher and you could expect a fastball. If the pitcher was a hard thrower like Virgil

Grip for fastball

Grip for a curve

The New York Times

Grip for a slider

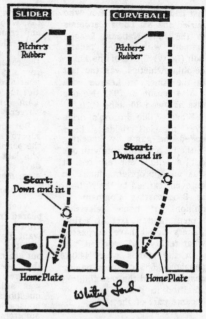

This is how a slider and curve ball break over the plate. The diagram is for left-handed pitcher throwing to right-handed batter. Whitey Ford of Yankees provided diagram and modeled grips in pictures.

Trucks, it was 90 to 1 that you'd get a fastball. But now they nibble you to death with breaking pitches, sliders, curves, even knuckleballs."

"I didn't throw a slider until 1961," said Whitey Ford, who became a Yankee in 1950. "Then I began losing my speed and had to develop new pitches. Johnny Sain joined the club that year as a coach and taught me the slider. I used it all the time. It broke over and down, and the batters would even chase it into the dirt.

"Ted Williams told me this summer that he had only two pitches to worry about when he started—fastball and curveball. And the pitchers knew he could hit fastballs, so his guessing was narrowed to curveballs. Later they started throwing sliders, Ted said, and really had him guessing. It's got to be one of the reasons for lower batting averages these days."

The big difference between a curve and a slider, Ford says, is this:

The curve is thrown with maximum spin, preferably down. It starts high, then about 15 feet from the plate starts to break down and away.

Easy Pitch for Hurler

The slider is thrown more like a fastball, but with the wrist turned to the side. It looks like a fastball until it gets three or four feet from the batter, then breaks just enough to throw him off stride or to miss the fast part of his bat.

Everybody agrees that the slider has grown popular for two reasons: it's relatively easy for the pitcher to throw. But it's relatively hard for the batter to "read" or recognize.

It has the potential danger of not breaking far enough away from the batter, the way a curve should. But it is such an all-purpose pitch that the Mets' coach, Rube

Walker, told Koosman not to use it this year for fear he would stop developing his curveball. Koosman has abstained, with success, but he is an exception.

"Ford learned it one day and used it immediately." Sain said. "If you can throw it, you usually can control it. And if you're in the business of fooling people, you throw it."

September 22, 1968

ST. LOUIS WINS, 4-0, IN SERIES OPENER; GIBSON SETS MARK

Cardinal Hurler Strikes Out 17 Tigers to Break Record of 15 Held by Koufax

M'LAIN LEAVES IN SIXTH

By JOSEPH DURSO
Special to The New York Times

ST. LOUIS, Oct. 2 — Bob Gibson outpitched Denny Mc-Lain, overpowered the rest of the Detroit Tigers and struck out 17 batters today as the St. Louis Cardinals won the opening game of the World Series, 4-0.

The 32-year-old Nebraskan broke the Series strike-out record of 15, set by Sandy Koufax of the Los Angeles Dodgers against the New York Yankees in 1963. He allowed five hits and resolved baseball's "pitching duel of the century" before the game was half over.

He was the man of the hour on this summery afternoon as 54,692 persons in Busch Memorial Stadium and a national television audience watched. He left no questions unanswered as he conquered McLain, the first man to win 31 games in the major leagues in 37 years.

By winning his sixth straight game in three Series in five years, he tied the record set by Lefty Gomez and Red Ruffing of the Yankees between 1932 and 1942.

Another Record Falls

By working his sixth straight complete game in Series competition, he broke the record set by Ruffing for pitchers who finish what they start when the money is on the table.

Gibson, who started life in the slums of Omaha and now earns $90,000 a year, pitched to only 32 Detroit hitters. He also became the National League's No. 1 World Series winner. Other pitchers have won more games—Whitey Ford leads everybody with 10 victories during the Yankee era—but nobody has won more for the senior league than Gibson in 65 World Series.

He got all the runs needed for all this statistical success during one inning. It was the fourth, an inning marked by a fatal loss of control by Mc-Lain, who had walked only 63 batters in 336 innings this season.

This time the fresh-faced extrovert and organist walked two batters on the minimum total of eight pitches. Then Mike Shannon and Julian Javier singled and Gibson suddenly was staked to a three-run lead.

The other run was produced in the seventh inning by Lou Brock, who was Gibson's chief ally in the Cardinals' victory last fall against the Boston Red Sox. He bombed a 3-and-2 pitch into the center-field bleachers off Pat Dobson for a 400-foot home run.

But the essence of the day was Gibson's overwhelming fast ball and his surprisingly sharp curve.

He had won 22 games and lost nine this year, with 15 victories in a row, 13 shutouts and a league record for efficiency — allowing only 1.12 earned runs a game. He also had won three games in the World Series last year, including the final one. So today he was back at the old stand.

He walked one man and gave up four singles and one double. He struck out Dick McAuliffe to open the game, then added Al Kaline. He fanned Norm Cash, Willie Horton and Jim Northrup in the second inning, then got Bill Freehan and McLain in the third. So he struck out seven of the first nine men, including five in a row.

He struck out everybody in the Detroit line-up and he took care of the renowned Kaline three times and the power-hitting left-hander, Norm Cash, three times.

By the ninth inning, he had 14 strike-outs and needed one more to tie Koufax's memorable performance in Yankee Stadium five years ago.

Stanley Delays Inevitable

There was a pause while Mickey Stanley singled to center field, raising some faint thoughts about the Tigers' talent for raising a rumpus late in ball games. Thirty times this year they had won games in their final turn at bat. But not today.

Kaline, playing in his first series in a 16-year career, then swiped at a 1-and-2 pitch and missed for strike-out No. 15. Gibson seemed serenely unaware of the milestone he had reached, but many persons in the crowd knew, especially those with transistor radios.

They rose and gave him a standing ovation. A bit startled, Gibson peered over his shoulder just in time to see the news flashed on the right-field scoreboard.

Then he struck out Cash on a 2-and-2 pitch and got another standing ovation. And finally, for good measure, he threw a curveball past Horton for his 17th strike-out and the final out of the day.

While all this was going on, what of McLain, the 24-year-old man-child of Detroit, the musician and self-styled mercenary soldier, the prime mover in Detroit's first American League title in 23 years?

He had approached his confrontation with Gibson without losing his flair. He was not unduly upset by reports that he had top billing on the Cardinals' clubhouse bulletin board for his remark: "I want to humiliate the Cardinals."

On the eve of battle, he even packed the lobby of a downtown hotel by sitting down at an organ in a lounge and giving an impromptu recital. He played appropriate mood music like "Stardust," then soared into ad-lib rock tempos. Then this afternoon he met Gibson.

The result: McLain pitched five innings before leaving for a pinch-hitter. He allowed three hits and three walks, struck out three Cardinals and saw three runs cross the plate. His "thing" with the number 3 included errors—the Tigers committed three behind him.

He almost jumped off to a fast start when Stanley singled solidly to left field with one down in the first inning.

This was the young Stanley, the best center fielder in the league, who had been switched to shortstop in order to make room for more bats in the Tiger line-up. Playing with a borrowed infielder's mitt, he behaved professionally at shortstop and got two of the five hits off Gibson.

However, Stanley tried to steal second base on the next pitch after his single and was thrown out by Tim McCarver. Then Gibson struck out Kaline, and so much for McLain's fast start.

McLain, meanwhile, retired the first four Cardinals. Then, with one down in the second, McCarver lined the first pitch into the alley in right-center. He gambled that he could beat the relay and he did when McAuliffe's throw to third base went wide and McCarver wound up with a triple. But McLain struck out Mike Shannon and Javier to end the threat.

However, that turned out to be McLain's finest hour. In the third, he flirted with trouble by walking Dal Maxvill. Then Gibson bunted Maxvill to second. Brock followed with a grounder to McLain, who turned and stalked Maxvill between second and third, finally throwing him out with Stanley covering second.

Brock, who had been safe during this maneuvering, promptly stole second base for his eighth steal in eight Series games over the last two years. When Freehan's throw skipped into right field, Brock made it to third. But he was still there when Curt Flood popped up to Stanley.

The inning proved indecisive, though it may haunt the Cardinals before the Series ends. Brock jammed his right shoulder while sliding into second base and required some deep-freeze spray to ease the pain.

Then came the fourth inning and big trouble for the man-child. McLain opened the inning by throwing four straight balls to Roger Maris, who will retire after the Series and become a beer distributor in Florida. Then McLain threw two balls to Orlando Cepeda and immediately had company on the mound—Manager Mayo Smith.

Smith returned to the dugout and Cepeda fouled out. But McLain threw four straight balls to McCarver, Shannon lined a 2-and-2 pitch to left for one run and, when Horton

Handshake for Great Performance

Associated Press

Bob Gibson, Cardinals' pitcher, being congratulated by Tim McCarver after striking out 17 in St. Louis yesterday.

Box Score of First Series Game

DETROIT (A.)	AB.	R.	H.	RBI.	PO.	A.		ST. LOUIS (N.)	AB.	R.	H.	RBI.	PO.	A.
McAuliffe, 2b.	4	0	1	0	3	0		Brock, lf	4	1	1	1	2	0
Stanley, ss	4	0	2	0	3	2		Flood, cf	4	0	1	0	1	0
Kaline, rf	4	0	1	0	2	0		Maris, rf	3	1	0	1	0	0
Cash, 1b	4	0	1	0	7	1		Cepeda, 1b	4	0	0	0	1	1
Horton, lf	4	0	0	0	2	0		McCarver, c.	3	1	1	0	17	1
Northrup, cf.	3	0	0	0	2	0		Shannon, 3b.	4	1	2	1	0	0
Freehan, c.	2	0	0	0	4	1		Javier, 2b.	3	0	1	2	2	0
Wert, 3b	2	0	1	0	0	1		Maxvill, ss.	2	0	0	0	2	0
bMathews, ph.	1	0	0	0	0	0		Gibson, p	2	0	0	0	1	0
Tracewski, 3b.	0	0	0	0	0	0								
McLain, p	1	0	0	0	0	2		Total	29	4	6	4	27	2
aMatchick, ph.	1	0	0	0	0	0								
Dobson, p	0	0	0	0	0	0								
cBrown, ph	1	0	0	0	0	0								
McMahon, p.	0	0	0	0	1	0								
Total	31	0	5	0	24	7								

aGrounded out for McLain in 6th.
bStruck out for Wert in 8th.
cFlied out for Dobson in 8th.

Detroit (A.) .... 0 0 0 0 0 0 0 0 0—0
St. Louis (N.) .... 0 0 0 3 0 0 1 0 x—4

Errors—Freehan, Horton, Cash. Left on bases—Detroit 5, St. Louis 6. Two-base hit—Kaline. Three-base hit—McCarver. Home run—Brock. Stolen bases—Brock, Javier, Flood. Sacrifice—Gibson.

	IP.	H.	R.	ER.	BB.	SO.	HBP.	WP.	Bks.
McLain—L	5	3	3	2	3	3	0	0	0
Dobson	2	2	1	1	1	0	0	0	0
McMahon	1	1	0	0	0	0	0	0	0
Gibson—W	9	5	0	0	1	17	0	0	0

Bases on balls off McLain 3 (Maxvill, Maris, McCarver), Dobson 1 (Javier), McMahon (none), Gibson 1 (Freehan). Struck out by McLain 3 (Shannon, Javier, Gibson), Dobson (none), McMahon (none), Gibson 17 (McAuliffe, Kaline 3, Cash 3, Horton 2, Northrup 2, Freehan 2, McLain, Wert, Stanley, Mathews).

Umpires—Gorman (N.) plate; Honochick (A.) first base; Landes (N.) second base; Kinnamon (A.) third base; Harvey (N.) left field; Haller (A.) right field. Time of game—2:29. Attendance—54,692.

bobbled the ball, McCarver took third base and Shannon second.

On the next pitch, Javier grounded a single into right field and both runners scored. That made it 3-0 and then McLain got Maxvill on a fly to left and Gibson on a strike-out.

Denny was followed by Pat Dobson of Depew, N. Y., who worked the next two innings, and by Don McMahon of Brooklyn, who worked the last two. They kept order except for the seventh-inning home run by Brock, who hit .414 in the Series last year with 12 hits, including a home run.

When it was all over — at least until Gibson and McLain meet again on Sunday—Gibson said he had relied chiefly on his fastball.

"But I had a good breaking ball," he said. "I think I was more of a surprise to them than anything else."

McLain conceded he had hurt himself with eye-high pitches that were called balls.

"That bad inning was typical of me," he said, not quite speechless. "A couple of walks, then the whole thing comes undone."

October 3, 1968

Baseball Rules Committee Makes 3 Decisions to Produce More Hits and Runs

By GEORGE VECSEY
Special to The New York Times

SAN FRANCISCO, Dec. 3— The baseball rules committee made three decisions tonight in the hope of producing more hits and more runs next season. The committee, which has the authority to make changes without further consultations with owners or general managers, voted to lower the pitching mound, to shrink the strike zone and to enforce the current rule about illegal pitches.

The action was taken at the suggestion of the baseball commissioner, William D. Eckert, and following several proposals from a meeting of managers and general managers yesterday. Eckert said today the rules changes were a "good step forward" to producing "more action" in games next year. Last season seemed to be a blur of 1-0 games because of the superiority of the pitchers.

To counteract the dominance of the pitchers, the rules committee voted to drop the mound from 15 inches to 10 instead of the original suggestion of eight inches. Also, all mounds must be sloped gradually so that pitchers will not look as if they are firing from a steep cliff to the batters down below.

Vigilance Is Extended

The second change involved the strike zone, which has been considered anything between the shoulders and the knees. The strike zone next year will be from the tops of the knees to the armpits.

Rather than make the umpires, batters and pitchers adjust to the shift on their own, the committee will have sketches made of hitters in their normal stance. Presumably arrows will note where armpits and tops of knees are situated, so that all men will be prepared when the moment of truth occurs. After all, matadors must learn the anatomy of the bull before entering the ring, so there is a precedent for this move.

The third decision was to keep the vigilance against illegal pitches, or, as Jim Gallagher of the Commissioner's office put it, "those naughty things." It is still illegal to put spit, Vaseline, emery or most any foreign substance on a baseball. If a pitcher throws a ball with a foreign substance on it, the umpire may eject him from the game.

This was the rule last year, and the committee voted to enforce it next year. Also, if a pitcher puts his hands to his mouth while inside the mound area, the umpire shall call an automatic ball, even if the pitcher does not throw the pitch. This is the same rule from last year, and will be enforced.

The committee made two other changes. Next year, a tied, extra-inning game that is stopped for curfew or any other reason will be resumed from that point as soon as possible. Previously, the game was considered a tie and was replayed from the start.

Also, the new type of stud-spike, which Maury Wills was forbidden to wear in league games, has been legalized for next year. The committee realized there was nothing objectionable about the thicker, golf-type spike, and it took them only a year of Maury Wills's life.

The committee also said it had not considered strengthening the 20-second limit for pitchers, or the long-discussed "wild-card pinch-hitter for pitchers."

Finally, the committee appointed a group to study synthetic fields. Bing Devine of St. Louis, Clark Griffith of Minnesota and Dick O'Connell of Boston will work with Spec Richardson of Houston.

Richardson has inside knowledge of synthetic fields since baseballs have been taking unpredictable bounces on the wiggly carpet ever since the Astrodome was opened in 1965. Many baseball executives are interested in synthetic fields so they can do away with mud and maintenance problems, even if they incur a few bad bounces.

December 4, 1968

Bowie Kuhn, Wall St. Lawyer, Named Commissioner

By LEONARD KOPPETT
Special to The New York Times

BAL HARBOUR, Fla., Feb. 4 —Bowie Kuhn, a 42-year-old Wall Street lawyer who has been intimately involved with various baseball problems for more than a decade, was named Commissioner Pro Tem today for a one-year term at a salary of $100,000.

He was selected unanimously on one ballot by the 24 major league clubs as the answer to the deadlock that had arisen with the American League supporting Michael Burke, president of the New York Yankees, and the National League supporting Charles S. (Chub) Feeney, vice president of the San Francisco Giants. No vote was taken on their candidacies.

Instead, Feeney and Burke were added to the planning committee, whose task it is to restructure baseball administration. Jerry Hoffberger of Baltimore is chairman of that committee and Dick Meyer of St. Louis and John Holland of the Chicago Cubs are the other members.

Kuhn's task was defined as providing the leadership for this committee, which went into session immediately after the announcement of Kuhn's election at 5:40 P.M. at the Americana Hotel here. He will also assume all the traditional duties of the commissionership, but the first priority is to carry out a thorough re-examination and reshaping of baseball's structure.

Last Act for Eckert

This ended William D. Eckert's two-month interval of lame duck administration. Eckert, a retired Air Force general with no previous baseball connection, had been given a seven-year contract at $65,000 a year in November, 1965. He was forced to resign last Dec. 6, and will collect the remaining four years' pay due him. But when the clubowners failed to choose between Burke and Feeney on Dec. 20, Eckert's continuance in office led to increasing instability.

Today, therefore, the owners found themselves still unable to unite behind either Burke or Feeney, and they knew it going into the meeting. It was promptly suggested that restructuring should get first consideration, and a seven-man committee went off to recommend means.

The committee was composed of Gabe Paul, of Cleveland, leader of the Burke faction; Walter O'Malley of Los Angeles, leader of the Feeney support; Meyer, Lee MacPhail, vice president of the Yankees; John Galbreath of Pittsburgh, Arthur Allyn of the Chicago White Sox and Frank Dale of Cincinnati.

This group came up with Kuhn's name. When it proposed it to the entire meeting, the reaction was "Why, of course, yes," and Kuhn was elected immediately.

Raised in Washington

Although unknown to the public, Kuhn is not only a known quantity, but an immensely respected figure within the baseball community.

He is a member of Willkie, Farr and Gallagher, a general corporate legal firm that has handled the National League since 1936. He became active in baseball affairs around 1950, on joining the firm out of the University of Virginia Law School, and took over more and more of the load on general baseball business, as well as National League matters, in recent years. He has been involved in franchise shifts (notably the Milwaukee-Atlanta case), pension plans, Player Association negotiations, Congressional hearings, etc.

He comes from Tacoma Park, Md., a suburb of Washington, D. C. He grew up in Washington and attended Theodore Roosevelt High School there before going on to Princeton (Class of '48). He served in the Navy during World War II. His home now is Ridgewood, N. J., and he and his wife Louisa have four children—George, 16; Paul, 12; Alexandra, 9, and Stephen, 7.

"I was always a baseball fan, and sports fan in general," he said, when asked to tell about himself, "and back in 1939 or 1940, I worked inside the scoreboard at Griffith Stadium, where the Senators played. My salary was $1 a day," he added, his eyes twinkling, "and I've been waiting for years to make that public."

The $100,000 he will receive for a one-year term will represent a considerable decrease from his normal income.

"I'll try to terminate my partnership with the firm in some fashion," he explained, "and I will disassociate myself as counsel to the Players Relations Committee. [This is the committee negotiating with the players now.] The Commissioner does have functions as an arbitrator, but I will excuse myself from all pending cases between players and clubs. I will not enter into any of the negotiations now going on with the players."

Breakthrough Seen

Dale, acting as spokesman for the owners, hailed today's action as "a major break-

through in baseball history."

"This may be the last time we meet as separate leagues, having separate caucuses," he said. "We arrived at this in a combined way, among 24 clubs, and the main job now is to restructure as quickly as possible."

Kuhn struck the same note.

"We are major league baseball," he said, "not the major leagues of baseball. A phenomenon is emerging here, a unified operation which is essential today."

In an unusual display of unity and cooperation, all the owners remained seated at their tables while Kuhn conducted his first news conference. Afterward, all who were questioned expressed great satisfaction with the result, and spoke highly of Kuhn's special qualifications. They seemed to feel that a great dividing line had been crossed in solving the Burke-Feeney dilemma, and that with Kuhn's leadership the planning committee could really modernize and strengthen their business.

February 5, 1969

Mets Top Cards, 4-3, Despite Carlton's Record 19 Strike-Outs

SWOBODA CLOUTS PAIR FOR ALL RUNS

His Second Homer in 8th Brings Victory and Widens Lead to 4½ Games

By JOSEPH DURSO
Special to The New York Times

ST. LOUIS, Sept. 15—Steve Carlton of the St. Louis Cardinals set a major league record tonight by striking out 19 New York Mets. But the Mets still won the game, 4-3, on a pair of two-run home runs by Ron Swoboda and extended their lead to 4½ games with 15 to play.

Carlton, a 24-year-old left-hander, struck out the side in four of the nine innings as he surpassed the record of 18 strike-outs set by Sandy Kou-

fax, Bob Feller and Don Wilson. He even fanned Swoboda twice—on his first and third times at bat.

But on his second and fourth trips to the plate, the Maryland muscleman drove home runs into the left-field seats—both times with a man on base, both times with the Mets trailing by one run.

Cubs in a Tailspin

As a result, the Mets swung even higher on their high-flying trapeze with two and a half weeks to play. They put 4½ games between themselves and the Chicago Cubs, who lost to the Montreal Expos and continued one of the stunning tailspins of the baseball season.

The Mets' victory — despite Carlton's virtuoso performance —was No. 27 in their last 34 games. They trailed Chicago by 9½ games on Aug. 13, but since then have soared to the top of the Eastern Division of the National League, and tonight marked the 20th straight game in which their pitchers did did not allow an enemy home run.

Carlton, though, suffered a bittersweet evening precisely

because he threw the home-run pitch twice to the right-handed Swoboda—who had won Saturday's game with a grand-slam home run in Pittsburgh.

The 6-foot-4-inch 200-pounder from Miami pitched his way into the baseball record books by striking out half of the 38 batters he faced. He got 27 outs—19 on third strikes—but allowed nine hits and two walks, and took his 10th defeat against 16 victories.

Three to Go in Ninth

Going into the ninth inning tonight, Carlton had 16 strike-outs, meaning he had to fan the side to establish the record. He had already struck out three Mets in the first, second and fourth innings. He had struck out Amos Otis three times and four other Mets twice apiece.

Then in the final inning, he struck out Tug McGraw, who had relieved Gary Gentry in the seventh inning of a game that had been delayed twice by rain for a total of 81 minutes. That was No. 17.

Next came Bud Harrelson, and he looked at strike three for No. 18. And finally, Otis—just recalled from the minor leagues—swung and missed a

Mets' Box Score

NEW YORK (N.)					ST. LOUIS (N.)				
	ab.	r.	h.	bi		ab.	r.	h.	bi
Harrelson, ss	4	0	1	0	Brock, lf	4	1	2	0
Otis, lf	5	0	0	0	Flood, cf	5	2	2	1
Agee, cf	4	1	1	0	Pinson, rf	4	0	3	1
Clendenon, 1b	3	1	1	0	Torre, 1b	4	0	1	1
Swoboda, rf	4	2	2	4	McCarver, c	4	0	0	0
Charles, 3b	4	0	0	0	Shannon, 3b	4	0	0	0
Grote, c	4	0	2	0	Javier, 2b	4	0	0	0
Weis, 2b	4	0	1	0	Maxvill, ss	3	0	0	0
Gentry, p	2	0	0	0	Browne, ph	1	0	0	0
Pfeil, ph	1	0	1	0	Carlton, p	3	0	0	0
Gosger, pr	0	0	0	0	Gagliano, ph	1	0	0	0
McGraw, p	1	0	0	0	Nossek, pr	0	0	0	0
Total	36	4	9	4	Total	37	3	8	3

New York .... 000 200 020—4
St. Louis .... 001 020 000—3

E—Javier, Charles 2, Clendenon, Harrelson. DP—New York 1. LOB— New York 7, St. Louis 9. HR—Swoboda 2 (9). SB—Pinson, Brock.

	IP.	H.	R.	ER.	BB.	SO.
Gentry	6	7	3	3	1	3
McGraw (W, 8-3)	3	1	0	0	1	3
Carlton (L, 16-10)	9	9	4	4	2	19

Wild pitch—Carlton.
T—2:23. A—13,806.

third strike for No. 19 and the record.

"It was the best stuff I ever had," said Carlton, like a sculptor who has just created a masterpiece and then accidentally chipped it. "When I had nine strike-outs, I decided to go all the way. But it cost me the game because I started to challenge every batter."

Before he began challenging Swoboda, though, the Cardinals provided a one-run lead in the third on a walk to Lou Brock and singles by Curt Flood and Vada Pinson. They might have scored more, but Brock was thrown out at the plate by Tommie Agee when he tried to score from first on a single

that slowed to a stop on the wet outfield grass.

In the fourth, though, Donn Clendenon walked and Swoboda lined the two-strike pitch into the left-field mezzanine for his eighth home run of the season.

Carlton then fanned the side, but he now was behind, 2-1.

However, the Cardinals put him ahead again in the fifth with four straight singles off Gentry with two down. The singles were hit by Brock, Flood, Pinson and Joe Torre, and now Carlton was ahead again, 3-2.

But in the eighth, Agee

singled to center, Clendenon struck out and up came Swoboda. Carlton challenged him again, but on the 2-and-2 pitch Swoboda lined another home run into the same section for the deciding run. ✺

September 16, 1969

Mets Win, 5-3, Take the Series

By JOSEPH DURSO

The Mets entered the promised land yesterday after seven years of wandering through the wilderness of baseball.

In a tumultuous game before a record crowd of 57,397 in Shea Stadium, they defeated the Baltimore Orioles, 5-3, for their fourth straight victory of the 66th World Series and captured the championship of a sport that had long ranked them as comical losers.

They did it with a full and final dose of the magic that had spiced their unthinkable climb from ninth place in the National League — 100 - to - 1 shots who scraped and scrounged their way to the pinacle as the waifs of the major leagues.

At 3:17 o'clock on a cool and often sunny afternoon, their impossible dream came true when Cleon Jones caught a fly ball hit by Dave Johnson to left field. And they immediately touched off one of the great, riotous scenes in sports history, as thousands of persons swarmed from their seats and tore up the patch of ground where the Mets had made history.

Lovable Winners Now

It was 10 days after they had won the National League pennant in a three-game sweep of the Atlanta Braves. It was 22 days after they had won the Eastern title of the league over the Chicago Cubs. It was eight years after they had started business under Casey Stengel as the lovable losers of all sports.

They reached the top, moreover, in the best and most farfetched manner of Met baseball.

They spotted the Orioles three runs in the third inning when Dave McNally and Frank Robinson hit home runs off Jerry Koosman.

But then they stormed back with two runs in the sixth inning on a home run by Donn Clendenon, another in the seventh on a home run by Al Weis and two more in the eighth on two doubles and two errors.

The deciding run was batted home by Ron Swoboda, who joined the Met mystique in 1965 when the team was losing 112 games and was finishing last for the fourth straight time.

But, like most of the Mets' victories in their year to remember, the decision was a collective achievement by the youngest team in baseball, under Manager Gil Hodges—who had suffered a heart attack a year ago after the Mets "surged" into ninth place.

The wild, final chapter in the story was written against the desperate efforts of the Orioles, who had swept to the American League pennant by 19 games as one of the most powerful teams in modern times.

Orioles' Wings Clipped

The Orioles had not won since the opening game last Saturday in Baltimore and needed three straight victories to survive. In the third inning, they lashed out at Koosman with three runs and erased the memory of the six no-hit innings he had pitched against them Sunday.

Mark Belanger led off with a looping single over first base. He was nearly caught off the base by Jerry Grote, the New York catcher, who was backing up the play. But in a brief shoving contest, Belanger was called safe as he scrambled back to the base, where Grote took a throw from Swoboda.

On the next pitch, McNally hit a home run into the Baltimore bull pen in left field and the Orioles led, 2-0.

McNally, who had lost the second game to Koosman, is a 27-year-old left-hander who can hit as well as pitch. He didn't lose a game this season until Aug. 3, then finished with 20 victories. He also hit three home runs last year, including

a grand slam, and another this year.

His drive off Koosman was the first extra-base hit for Baltimore in 35 innings and it cast a pall over the fans who had come to see the Mets reach the stars. Two outs later, Frank Robinson bombed Koosman's first pitch over the center-field fence, Baltimore led by 3-0 and the Mets' magic suddenly seemed remote.

But Koosman settled down after that and checkmated the Orioles on one single for the final six innings. He retired 19 of the last 21 batters, closed with a five-hitter and even swung a mean bat when the Mets began to do their "thing."

They almost revived in the third when Koosman doubled past third base. Nothing came of it because McNally knocked off the next three batters, but it was an omen: Koosman had made only four hits in 84 times at bat all season.

Then, in the sixth, another omen appeared. Each team argued in turn that a batter had been hit by a pitched ball. The Orioles, though, lost their

argument; the Mets won theirs. And the game veered inexorably toward the "team of destiny."

Motion Is Denied

The Orioles pleaded their case first. With one out in the top

of the sixth, an inside fastball plunked Frank Robinson on his right thigh. The home-plate umpire, Lou DiMuro, ruled that it had glanced off the bat first for strike two. Baltimore's volatile manager, Earl Weaver, who had been banished from Wednesday's game argued that it had simply struck Robinson, who already had started for first base.

When the Orioles were overruled, Robinson disappeared in to the runway behind the dug out for five minutes while th trainer sprayed his thigh wit a freezing medication and whil everybody in the stadium waited. Then he returned, was greeted by a sea of waving handkerchiefs and struck out.

In the bottom of the sixth, it was the Mets' turn to plead an identical case and, in the

Box Score of Fifth Series Game

BALTIMORE (A.)	AB.	R.	H.	RBI.	NEW YORK (N.)	AB.	R.	H.	RBI.
Buford, lf	4	0	0	0	Agee, cf	3	0	1	0
Blair, cf	4	0	0	0	Harrelson, ss	4	0	0	0
F. Robinson, rf	3	1	1	1	Jones, lf	3	2	1	0
Powell, 1b	4	0	1	0	Clendenon, 1b	3	1	1	2
Salmon, pr	0	0	0	0	Swoboda, rf	4	1	2	1
B. Robinson, 3b	4	0	1	0	Charles, 3b	4	0	0	0
Johnson, 2b	4	0	1	0	Grote, c	4	0	0	0
Belanger, ss	3	1	1	0	Weis, 2b	4	1	1	1
Etchebarren, c	3	0	0	0	Koosman, p	3	0	1	0
McNally, p	2	1	1	2					
Motton, ph	1	0	0	0	Total	32	5	7	4
Watt, p	0	0	0	0					
Total	32	3	5	3					

Baltimore (A.) .... 0 0 3　0 0 0　0 0 0—3
New York (N.) .... 0 0 0　0 0 2　1 2 .—5

Errors—Powell, Watt. Left on base—Baltimore 3, New York 6. Doubles—Koosman, Jones, Swoboda. Home runs—McNally (1), F. Robinson (1), Clendenon (3), Weis (1). Stolen base —Agee.

	IP.	H.	R.	ER.	BB.	SO.
McNally	7	5	3	3	2	6
Watt (L, 0—1)	1	2	2	1	0	1
Koosman (W, 2—0)	9	5	3	3	1	5

Hit by pitch—by McNally (Jones)
Time of game—2:14. Attendance—57,397.

amazing spirit of their new fortune, they won it on an appeal.

Jones was the leadoff batter and he was struck on the right instep by a dropping curveball. The umpire called it a ball; Jones insisted he had been hit. Hodges, the old hero of Ebbets Field, retrieved the ball from the Mets' dugout, where it had bounced, and executed the old "look-at-the-ball-trick."

DiMuro duly looked at the ball, detected a swatch of shoe polish on its cover, reversed himself and waved Jones to first base. Now Weaver shot out of the dugout to voice his indignation, but lost his point and soon his ball game.

The next batter, Clendenon, went to a count of two balls and two strikes, then whacked a home run off the auxiliary scoreboard on the facing of the left-field loge seats.

It was his third home run in three games (he had hit 16 during the regular schedule) and it punctuated a remarkable season for the 34-year-old ex-student of law.

His homer yesterday, which put him one short of the Series record of four shared by Babe Ruth, Lou Gehrig, Hank Bauer and Duke Snider, put the Mets back in business. In the next inning, Al Weis brought them even on McNally's second pitch.

Weis, the silent supersub, drove the pitch over the 371-foot sign in left-center as the crowd rocked the stadium, and the game was tied, 3-3. It marked another achievement for the right-handed platoon that Hodges deploys against left-handed pitching and it was no mean achievement for Weis.

During Weis's two seasons with the Mets, 212 home runs had been hit in Shea Stadium —none by Al. He had hit only two all year, both in Chicago in July. But in the World Series, the quiet little infielder turned tiger with four walks, four singles and one historic home run.

Finally, the stage was set for the last full measure of Met magic.

In the eighth, with Eddie Watt pitching for Baltimore, Jones looked at three straight balls and then a strike. Then he lined the 3-and-1 pitch off the center-field fence for a double.

Clendenon, who was voted the outstanding player in the Series, fouled off two attempts to bunt. Then he lined a long fly into the right-field corner, just foul, then bounced out to Brooks Robinson, with Jones holding second base.

The next batter was Swoboda and, with first base open, the Orioles might have walked him intentionally. But they elected to challenge him and Swoboda drilled the second pitch down the left-field line, where Don Buford almost made a brilliant backhand catch off the grass. But the ball dropped in for a double as Jones streaked for home to put the Mets in front, 4-3, and tumult broke out across Flushing Meadow.

Ed Charles lifted a fly to Buford for the second out. But Grote followed with a low line drive toward John Powell and the 250-pound first baseman booted it for an error. He chased the ball, though, to his right and lobbed it to Watt, who was rushing over from the mound to cover first base.

By this time, Grote was flashing across the bag and, when Watt juggled the throw and dropped it, Swoboda was flashing across the plate with the second run of the inning.

That made it 5-3 and the Mets were three outs from fantasy. There was a brief delay when Frank Robinson opened the ninth with a walk. But then Powell forced him at second base, Brooks Robinson flied out to Swoboda in right and—at 3:17 P.M.—Johnson lifted a fly to Jones in left-center.

Jones made the catch with a flourish, then he and his old high-school mate from Mobile, Tommie Agee, turned and streaked across the outfield to the Mets' bull pen in right.

The beat the avalanche by a split second and, as they ducked into the safety of the stadium's caverns, the crowd let go. Children, housewives, mature men, all swarmed onto the field where the Mets had marched. They tore up home plate, captured the bases, ripped gaping holes from the turf, set off orange flares and firecrackers and chalked the wooden outfield fence with the signs of success.

The Mets were the champions of the world on Oct. 16, 1969.

"I never saw anything like it," said Joe DiMaggio, the old Yankee, who had thrown out the first ball.

October 17, 1969

Reserve Clause Breeds Bitterness

By LEONARD KOPPETT

BITTER feelings about baseball's reserve clause, and bitter feelings towards those who challenge it, are nothing new.

The whole subject, in fact, reached explosive proportions just 80 years ago, and the effects of what was known as the "Brotherhood War" linger on within the baseball community today. In many cases subliminal, in others an explicit view of history, the attitudes formed by that early baseball experience color the views of most baseball men.

About Baseball

More important even than what actually happened in 1890, when major league players formed a union, rebelled, started their own league and broke almost everyone concerned, is what baseball people believe happened. The stories of that time have been handed down from one generation of owners and players to another, and the assumptions have persisted among those who neither know nor care about the historical events.

A review of the Brotherhood War, therefore, sheds some light on the intensity of emotion in today's struggle, which centers on Curt Flood's antitrust suit. The hardest thing to understand, for most outsiders, is the apparent obtuseness of the baseball establishment in resisting any and all change. Even a few famous, high-priced players defend the status quo (although no minor-leaguer has yet leaped to its defense). After all, it sounds silly for supposedly responsible business men to hint at "total destruction" of their affairs if so much as a comma is changed.

●

But everything has origins, even unreason. It's easy enough for mid-Twentieth Century lawyers to say "devise a less restrictive substitute." Driven into the baseball consciousness, however, is the idea that the present system, which did evolve gradually, has worked profitably; that alternatives tried in the past—even if it was the dim past—did fail; and "alternatives" presented in theory can lead to numerous booby traps in reality.

In this light, the reluctance of the establishment to confront change is more comprehensible, if not necessarily more justified. Perhaps the real criticism of today's baseball brass should be on other grounds. Its rigid stance implies timidity, a self-confessed lack of confidence in its ability to act imaginatively, constructively and with goodwill, to devise improvements.

At any rate, this is what happened almost a century ago:

The first group that approximated a major league was formed in 1871. It was called the National Association of Professional Baseball Players, and it failed after five years because there was no way to keep players from jumping from team to team.

In 1876, the National League of Baseball Clubs was formed, putting all authority in the hands of club owners rather than players. This did provide stability—in financing, in team identity, in rooting interest. But players still could, and did, move around freely between seasons.

By 1879, the practice of putting several of a team's best players "on reserve" was adopted. This meant

that the other clubs in the league agreed not to sign the five players designated by any one club as "on reserve" for the following season. Quickly, the number on reserve grew to nine to 11 to

15. (Today, automatically, all players are "on reserve" with some club, with insignificant exceptions.)

But by 1882, there was a second "major" league in operation, the American Association, and in 1884 a third league took the field, the Union Association. Competition for experienced players was keen, and salaries were high. But the Union Association folded after one year, and the other two leagues arranged to observe each other's reserve lists, and a true reserve clause came into being in 1885.

Competitively, at the gate, and in public esteem, baseball thrived at that point. But the club owners also used the reserve clause to drive salaries down, and imposed a salary ceiling (at a level of about half what the top stars were already making).

Led by John Montgomery Ward, captain and star infielder of the New York Giants and a law school graduate, the players formed a union, called the Brotherhood of Professional Baseball Players. Through the union, they negotiated with the club owners to have the salary ceiling and some other restrictions removed. (It was Ward who first referred to the reserve clause as "slavery," at a time when men who had fought in the Civil War were still less than 50 years old.)

After the 1888 season, the owners agreed to Ward's proposals—and Ward went on a round-the-world baseball tour promoted by Albert Spalding. While he was out of the country, the owners reneged on their agreement. Ward returned to New York in March, 1889, on the eve of a new baseball season, and found his Brotherhood members ready to strike.

He persuaded them, instead, to play out 1889 under the oppressive contracts but to use the time to find investors so that they could form their own league.

They did. In 1890, the Players' League contained most of the established big leaguers from the National and the A.A.—Ward, Buck Ewing, King Kelly, Tim Keefe, Charles Comiskey and so forth. They purposely put teams into seven of the eight National League cities, and scheduled games at the same time, and they concentrated their fire on the New York franchise.

●

The total attendance for baseball reached a peak — but the burden for every individual club was intolerable. The National League owners persuaded the backers of the Players League that there was no future in such a competition. (Most of the Players League teams had their players as shareholders). Some backers quit, some bought into the National League—and in 1891, almost all the big leaguers were back in the National, burned by their excursion into free enterprise.

The National then proceeded to wipe out the A.A. and to operate as a 12-team monopoly—which failed badly. In 1901, the American League set itself up as a rival major league, raided the National for players, and won a peace treaty in 1902. The present system has been essentially unchanged since.

Was the Brotherhood War a valid test? Was it abandoned too quickly? Is it relevant to today? The probable answers are no, yes, no—but that's in the realm of opinion, and the men who built the present system (between 1900 and 1930) were men who had lived through that experience. Their ideas have been handed down to today's baseball leaders, and perhaps the time has come to re-examine them.

January 25, 1970

Pilots' Move to Milwaukee Is Cleared by Court Decision

REFEREE REJECTS DISMISSAL PLEA

Action in Bankruptcy Case Paves Way for Transfer of Seattle Franchise

SEATTLE, March 31 (UPI)—A Federal bankruptcy court referee granted owners of the financially-plagued Seattle Pilots permission tonight to sell their one-year-old American League baseball franchise to Milwaukee interests.

Sidney C. Volinn, the bankruptcy court referee to whom the Pilots turned for help, ruled a $10.8-million offer for the purchase of the club by the Milwaukee Brewers was in order.

Since the American League had voted approval for transfer of the club from Seattle to Milwaukee in a telephone conference call yesterday, the Pilots became the Milwaukee Brewers upon Volinn's consent. The Brewers had signed a purchase agreement for the Pilots on March 8 and the agreement was to expire tomorrow morning.

Thus, Milwaukee, without a big league club since the Braves moved to Atlanta four years ago, rejoined baseball's select group, only this time as a member of the American League.

Short-Lived Franchise

For Seattle, it marked one of the shortest-lived franchises in the history of baseball. One has to go all the way back to the turn of the century to find another city that held a big league franchise for so short a time. The Pilots reportedly lost $1-million in their one and only season in Seattle and stood to lose another $1.5-million if they remained there this year.

Milwaukee, a charter member of the American League in 1900 became the St. Louis Browns in 1902.

Volinn's ruling came after a last-ditch effort for dismissal of the case from bankruptcy court by William Dwyer, special Washington State Assistant Attorney General, was turned down.

Volinn listened to testimony in a steamy court room before calling a halt late in the afternoon.

He had set the next hearing for tomorrow morning but was reminded that he ran the risk of voiding the contract entered into by the Pilots and Brewers. It was then that he said he would reach a decision sooner.

Left standing is an antitrust suit filed by the City of Seattle and the State of Washington seeking $82-million in damages from the American League and the ire of Seattle baseball fans. Among them are two United States Senators Warren Magnuson and Henry Jackson. The two have said they would move for enactment of a bill that would do away with baseball's immunity from the antitrust laws, which the sport has enjoyed since a 1922 Supreme Court ruling.

The American League came out of the case with some embarrassment and William Daley and Dewey and Max Soriano, principal Pilot owners, with a $1-million profit for holding the franchise only one year.

Volinn said he pondered long and hard over his decision and came to the conclusion that he had only one way to go.

"This is a problem of major magnitude because of the time element," Volinn said. "It might be a burden on all parties under the circumstance, and because of the imminence of the baseball season, an emergency does exist.

"This matter presents a posture in which the debtor is without funds and the only alternative would be deficit financing by the American League, perhaps upwards of $10-million.

"It's obvious that the club cannot pay its debts and may well be insolvent.

"The unique character of a major league baseball team has been considered, and its importance to the community has been considered, but it's obvious the debtors (Pilots) are incapable of carrying on. That is beyond question."

Volin's concern, too, was the long line of creditors the Pilots have picked up. Under Chapter II of the Bankruptcy Act he is obliged to take their interests under consideration as well as the interests of those who came to him for help.

April 1, 1970

Seaver Strikes Out 19, Including Record 10 in a Row

GAME TOTAL TIES BIG-LEAGUE MARK

Victory Is His 13th in a Row —Padres Get Only 2 Hits, One a Homer by Ferrara

By JOSEPH DURSO

Tom Seaver pitched the New York Mets to a 2-1 victory over the San Diego Padres yesterday and pitched himself into the baseball records by striking out 19 batters—10 in a row.

Along the way, the cover boy of the Mets pitched a two-hitter, retired the last 16 men, scored his 13th straight victory in regular-season play and broke the club record of 15 strike-outs — which had been set only last Saturday by Nolan Ryan.

In fact, Seaver did everything but bat home the winning run and his roommate, Bud Harrelson, took care of that with a triple in the third inning. Otherwise, the 25-year-old Californian staged a one-man show for 14,197 fans on a clear and cool afternoon and these were the highlights:

¶He struck out 19, tying the major league record set by Steve Carlton of the St. Louis Cardinals last Sept. 15 against

the Mets. Carlton lost that game, 4-3, when Ron Swoboda reached him for a pair of two-run home runs.

¶Moreover, since Carlton pitched his strange game at night, Seaver broke the record for strike-outs in an old-fashioned daytime game. The previous high was 18, shared by Bob Feller of Cleveland, Sandy Koufax of Los Angeles and Don Wilson of Houston.

¶By knocking off the last 10 batters, he also broke the major league record of eight consecutive strike-outs. That was shared by four men in modern times, all National Leaguers — Max Surkont of Milwaukee, Johnny Podres of Los Angeles, Jim Maloney of Cincinnati and Wilson.

Seaver did all this on 136 pitches, 65 of which were fastball strikes. He threw another fastball strike, but Al Ferrara hit that one over the left-field fence in the second inning. The only other man who hit Seaver safely was Dave Campbell, who singled off Joe Foy's glove at third base in the fourth.

Ferrara Concerto No. 2

The only other man who reached base was Ferrara, who walked in the fourth — giving Ferrara his most memorable day since he played a piano solo in Carnegie Hall as a child.

Seaver showed a fine sense of history by his performance, too. Just before the game, he accepted the Cy Young Award as the outstanding pitcher in the National League in 1969— when he won 25 games, including a nearly perfect one-

hitter against the Chicago Cubs on July 9.

He started the business side of the afternoon a little slowly, though. The Mets scored in the first inning when Harrelson singled and Ken Boswell doubled. An inning later, Ferrara hit his home run for San Diego. But in the third, Tommie Agee singled, Harrelson tripled into the right-field corner and Seaver had a 2-1 lead with six innings to go.

"Actually, he wasn't that strong in the early innings," said Jerry Grote, his catcher. "He just kept building up as the game went on. The cool weather helped and by the end of the game he was stronger than ever."

With two out in the sixth, the game was still up for grabs and Seaver had struck out nine. Then he threw a third strike past Ferrara and began to run out his remarkable string of 10.

He struck out the side in the seventh and again in the eighth, when he broke Ryan's club record of 15. He broke it, moreover, by fanning Ivan Murell—who pinch-hit for Jose Arcia, the only man in the San Diego line-up who had not struck out.

"Everybody congratulated me when I got No. 16 in the eighth inning," Seaver said later, studying the day's pitching chart, which had been kept by Jerry Koosman. "I just told them, let's get some more runs. All I could think of was that Carlton had struck out 19 of us and still lost."

In the ninth, though, he threw three fastballs past Van

Kelly for No. 17 (and No. 8 in a row). Then he caught Clarence Gaston looking at a fastball over the plate for No. 18. And finally, he threw two sliders and two fastballs to Ferrara for No. 19 and No. 10 in a row.

Strikes While Iron's Hot

"I was still worried I'd make a mistake and Ferrara might hit it out," Seaver said. "But when I got two strikes on him, I thought I might never get this close again so I might as well go for it."

He went for it and got it and restored the Mets' poise after two weeks of indifferent play. He outpitched Mike Corkins, a rookie right-hander who allowed the Mets only four hits in seven innings. And Seaver did it with mainly hard stuff —81 fastballs, 34 sliders, 19 curves and two change-ups.

In fact, most of the time the man-child of the Mets seemed to be playing catch with Grote—who also set a record for catchers. Thanks to the strike-outs and one foul pop fly, Grote made 20 putouts, breaking the record of 19 that had been shared by John Roseboro of Los Angeles and Bill Freehan of Detroit.

April 23, 1970

The Box Score

SAN DIEGO (N.)					METS				
	ab.	r.	h.	bi		ab.	r.	h.	bi
Arcia, ss	4	0	0	0	Agee, cf	3	1	1	0
Roberts, p	0	0	0	0	Harrelson, ss	3	1	2	1
Kelly, 3b	4	0	0	0	Boswell, 2b	4	0	1	1
Gaston, cf	4	0	0	0	Jones, lf	4	0	0	0
Ferrara, lf	3	1	1	1	Shamsky, rf	2	0	0	0
Colbert, 1b	3	0	0	0	Swoboda, rf	1	0	0	0
Campbell, 2b	3	0	1	0	Foy, 3b	2	0	0	0
Morales, rf	3	0	0	0	Kranepool, 1b	2	0	0	0
Barton, c	2	0	0	0	Grote, c	3	0	0	0
Corkins, p	2	0	0	0	Seaver, p	3	0	0	0
Webster, ph	1	0	0	0					
Slocum, ss	0	0	0	0					
Total	29	1	2	1	Total	27	2	4	2

San Diego .... 010 000 000—1
Mets .... 101 000 00x—2
LOB—San Diego 3, Mets 6. 2B—Boswell.
3B—Harrelson. HR—Ferrara (1). SB—Agee.

	IP.	H.	R.	ER.	BB.	SO.
Corkins (L, 0-2)	7	4	2	2	5	5
Roberts	1	0	0	0	0	2
Seaver (W, 3-0)	9	2	1	1	2	19

T—2:14. A—14,197.

UMPIRES PICKET PITTSBURGH PARK

Substitutes, 6 From Minors, Work Playoff Game There and One in Minnesota

By MURRAY CHASS
Special to The New York Times

PITTSBURGH, Oct. 3—Major league umpires struck for the first time in baseball history

today. They picketed outside Three Rivers Stadium while four minor league umpires worked the opener of the National League playoff between Cincinnati and Pittsburgh.

At Bloomington, Minn., where the Twins faced the Baltimore Orioles in the American League playoff, there was no picketing, but an improvised umpire crew was on the job.

The strike developed over a dispute on the pay scale for the playoffs and World Series. The Major League Umpires Association asked an increase from $2,500 to $5,000 for the playoffs and $6,500 to $10,000

for the Series. The leagues offered $3,000 and $7,000.

Harry Wendelstedt, among the six umpires who had been scheduled to work the Reds-Pirates series, stood outside an entrance to the stadium carrying a sign that said, "Major League Umpires on Strike for Wages."

"We're not here to put on a demonstration," said Wendelstedt, wearing his blue umpire's uniform. "We came here to work. We're here in good faith. If they're ready to talk money with us, we're ready to go to work this minute.

"They've led people to believe we pulled this at the last minute, but we've been negotiating since July. All they've come up with in that time is $500.

"We don't want to do anything harmful to baseball. We love the game. We want people to see it. We just want fair compensation. All of us are sick that we're not working because we came here to work."

Standing next to him was Nick Colosi, another umpire originally assigned to the playoff. The four other members of the crew—Stan Landes, Bob Engel, Paul Pryor and Doug Harvey — picketed other stadium entrances.

Inside, meanwhile, four minor league recruits worked for $3,000-$2,500 in salary and $500 for "reporting"—plus $40 a day expenses. John Grimsley, 37 years old of Wilson, N. C., umpired behind the plate; Fred Blandford, 35, of Elmira, N.Y., was at first; Hank Morgenweck, 38, of Teaneck, N. J., at second and George Grygiel, 29, of South Bend, Ind., at third.

All worked in the Triple A level of the minors this season, Grimsley and Blandford in the American Association and Morgenweck and Grygiel in the International League.

On arriving at the stadium at 10:45 A.M., 45 minutes after the six National League umpires had removed their equipment from the umpires' locker room, the rookies talked briefly with newsmen, then toured the playing field before dressing for their major league debut.

They said they were asked last Tuesday about working and considered the situation. They also said there had been no discussion of special inducements, such as the promise of major league jobs in the future.

"I feel I had to come," said Grimsley, who has worked in the minors for 11 years, after the game. "I wanted to do what was good for baseball. Baseball is the primary object. I feel if they were going to put on this game, I was the best qualified to work it outside the major league umpires.

"Nobody in the union of 48 umpires has reached me to talk

this thing over. I think I'm one of the veteran umpires in baseball and they should go to myself or Mr. Blandford. We probably would like to be in a union—all minor league umpires—but no one has approached us.

"I'm an individual. I have to talk contract for myself. No one talks for me or for any of the minor league umpires. We all have to talk contract individually."

Besides Grimsley, who called balls and strikes, Blandford was the busiest of the rookies, getting several close plays at first. None of the calls resulted in an argument.

"I felt relaxed and confident," Blandford said. "I wouldn't have come here if I thought I would make a spectacle of myself. When I got the call, I figured it was a chance to prove to myself after 14 years in the minors that I could do the job at the major league level.

"I would like to think the regular umpires would accept what I did as something I had to do. It's strange, but last night I bumped into Paul Pryor on the street. I hadn't seen him in two years. I told him I believed I owed it to my family and myself to be here."

Blandford declined to say what Pryor had told him, saying it was Pryor's place to disclose his part of the conversation.

Grygiel, the youngest of the working umpires, guessed that their action would incur the wrath of the strikers.

"There probably will be a lot of umpires not happy with us for accepting this assignment," he said, "but we are victims of circumstances. We are controlled by the minor leagues, and if they ask us to work and we turn them down, we might as well forget about umpiring."

There were few instances where the Reds or Pirates questioned decisions. One instance was in the first inning when Roberto Clemente asked Grimsley about a called third strike.

"He asked me if the pitch was high enough, and I said yes," Grimsley related. "He's a real pro, and he was checking on my strike zone. The way I answered him probably convinced him I was right."

The major league umpires gained official recognition as a collective bargaining unit last year in a case stemming from the dismissal of two American League umpires, Bill Valentine and Al Salerno.

Wendelstedt said the association was 100 per cent behind the strike, and added he knew of several Triple A umpires who had rejected a request to work.

"In a way I feel rather sad about the umpires who agreed

to work," he said. "The minor leagues are not organized, so there's nothing we can do except appeal to their common sense. We feel whatever we gain will be to their benefit because they want to be major league umpires."

Neither the managers nor players seemed concerned about the game being handled by minor leaguers. But Marvin Miller, executive director of the Players Association, expressed doubt about the move.

"For a series this important," he said, "to have umpires less than major league caliber is disastrous. It's a mistake."

Miller believed the umpires had a point in seeking higher pay.

"For many, many years," he said, "they were unorganized and, like many unorganized people, they were vastly underpaid. I think a problem like this should've been resolved long ago. Owners don't realize a problem until it hits them in the face."

As for the substitute umpires, Miller declared, "Scabs are scabs."

Danny Murtaugh, the Pirate manager, didn't think of the situation in such labor terms.

"We're just going to play the game the way we've played it all year," he said.

The 20,000 empty seats did not appear to be an indication of the effect of the picketing. More likely, fans in the Pittsburgh area, not one of the most affluential in the country, had preferred to remain at home and watch on television.

At Bloomington, the American League umpires were: home plate, John Stevens; first, Bill Deegan; second, Donald Stachell, and third, Charlie Berry. There were no foul-line umpires.

Stevens and Berry were retired American League umpires, still working for the league in supervisory capacities. Stevens, as a swing man, worked about

65 games this season. He is 57 years old and was forced to retire two years ago because of a mandatory retirement rule.

Berry, who is 66, retired six or seven years ago, but has worked this season in the college world series and Mexican clinics. He scouts umpires for the league.

Deegan is 35 and has worked the last four years in the Southern League. Stachell, 34, has been in the International League the last two seasons and in the lower minors before that. Both have worked as instructors in the umpiring school supported by the Commissioner's office in Florida.

Neither Stevens nor Berry is a member of the Umpires Association, which was formed after their active careers. The newcomers do not belong to a union either.

Joe Cronin, American League president, said he wasn't sure yet whether they would shift positions for subsequent games, but they would remain throughout the playoff. The World Series is the Commissioner's problem.

Negotiations between both leagues and the regular umpires had been in progress for weeks. A key meeting was held in mid-September, which made the break obvious. However, the umpires did not take a strike vote until yesterday, and some baseball executives had expected them to vote against striking.

There are 12 umpires in the playoffs and six in the Series, so the pay issue comes to a difference of $24,000 plus $18,000 of a gross income of more than $4-million just from gate receipts, not counting radio and television.

Josh Gibson Was The Equal of Babe Ruth, But...

By ROBERT PETERSON

To give recognition to diamond greats who, in an earlier day, were barred from the big leagues, organized baseball's Hall of Fame now has a special niche for the likes of Satchel Paige and, eventually, Josh—"the other half of what was probably the greatest battery ever."

Satchel Paige, in the days when he was with the Kansas City Monarchs—the great symbol of Negro baseball, conceivably the finest pitcher who ever lived, and appropriately No. 1 in the Negro Hall of Fame.

SATCHEL PAIGE, pitcher, raconteur, hemispheric traveler and an authentic American legend, is in baseball's Hall of Fame. Approximately. When he is formally inducted Aug. 9 in ceremonies at the National Baseball Hall of Fame and Museum in Cooperstown, N. Y., his plaque will be hung in a special corner of the museum to be reserved for stars of Negro baseball. Those of seven old-time white major leaguers—none of whom made the impact on the sporting scene that Paige did—will be placed in the austere Hall of Fame gallery alongside Babe Ruth, Ty Cobb, Honus Wagner and Walter Johnson.

Baseball Commissioner Bowie Kuhn, in announcing Paige as the first of a one-a-year trickle into Cooperstown of black men who played behind baseball's color line during the first half of the century, noted that "technically" they would not be in the Hall of Fame because they had not played at least 10 years in the major leagues as required by the rules for election. In fact, nearly all of the players mentioned prominently as probable choices to follow Paige into the shrine (Negro baseball division) never played in the big leagues at all.

But Commissioner Kuhn described the Hall of Fame as "a state of mind," not merely a particular room in a particular place, and said that in his view Satchel and his successors will be Hall of Famers. Paige himself seemed bewildered by sportswriters' questions about his attitude toward the separate but presumably equal accommodations for black baseball's greats. "I'm proud to be in wherever they put me in the Hall of Fame," Satch said.

HE could hardly have been surprised by his niche apart from baseball's holy-of-holies. Satch had been there before. He spent nearly his whole career of 32 years pitching in the separate and very much unequal world of Negro baseball—2,500 games in metropolis and hamlet in every corner of the nation, in Puerto Rico, Mexico and other points.

It was another time and another place. When he started in baseball, the term "civil rights" rolled strangely off the tongue, black panther was lower case, and baseball's major leagues (and the organized minor

ROBERT PETERSON is the author of "Only the Ball Was White," a history of Negro baseball.

leagues) had been lily white for a generation.

Today, when more than a quarter of the major leaguers and a majority of the superstars are black, it takes an effort of the imagination to remember that only 25 years ago there was not a single Negro in organized baseball—and had not been since 1898. It was on April 18, 1946, that Jackie Robinson breached the color line with the Montreal Royals of the International League. A year later he moved to the old Brooklyn Dodgers as the first of a long line of black players who have dominated the big leagues now for nearly two decades. In 1962, Robinson achieved another first when he was selected for the authentic, nontechnical Hall of Fame in the annual election of the Baseball Writers' Association. A second black star, Dodger catcher Roy Campanella, joined him there in 1969.

Satchel Paige made it to the majors in 1948 as a venerable rookie of 42, give or take a couple of years. He helped the Cleveland Indians to win the American League pennant with six victories and one defeat, and in the process he established attendance records in Cleveland and Chicago. But in five years in the big leagues, Satch won only 28 and lost 31, hardly Hall of Fame performance.

NO, it is as the best-known symbol of the nether world of Negro baseball that Satchel Paige is joining his peers at Cooperstown, if only, once more, by the back door. His arrival will be the end of a long, meandering road that began in 1926. Satch was two years out of an Alabama reform school, in which he had spent five years for the theft of a handful of toy rings from a store, when he joined the Chattanooga Black Lookouts. He was about 20 years old, a 6-foot, 3½-inch, 140-pound scarecrow with a fastball that hissed as it passed the batter and exploded in the catcher's mitt. His salary was $50 a month.

The Black Lookouts were about as far from the Hall of Fame as it is possible to get. They were members of the Negro Southern League, a minor circuit in the loose configuration of Negro baseball. The parks were often rickety, rundown and rock-filled, the players sometimes came up empty-handed on payday because there was nothing in the till, and occasionally, after riding through the night to the next town, they slept in the bleachers at the ball park because there was no money for even a fifth-rate hotel.

But Satchel endured and even prospered, reaching the phenomenal salary level of $275 a month after serving five clubs during his first five years. Then in 1931 he joined the Pittsburgh Crawfords, a team he would later call the best in baseball history, black or white. The claim may be taken with several grains of salt, since there is by no means unanimity among old black ballplayers that it was even the best in Negro baseball history. Old-timers will cite the 1910 Leland Giants of Chicago, who won 123 and lost six, or the Lincoln Giants of New York in the pre-World War I era, the Chicago American Giants of 1921, the Kansas City Monarchs of the twenties and thirties, or the Homestead, Pa., Grays of 1939.

NEVERTHELESS, there is no denying that the Crawfords were a great team that could, and did, do better than hold its own against major leaguers. From 1932 to 1934, the roster listed, besides Paige, four men who are likely candidates for the Negro players' room at Cooperstown: catcher Josh Gibson, probably the pre-eminent power hitter in history, not excepting Babe Ruth; outfielder James (Cool Papa) Bell, said by Satchel Paige to be so fast that he could flip the light switch and jump into bed before the light went out; the manager, Oscar Charleston, a first baseman then but in his younger days an outfielder with whom, in the judgment of those who can remember, Willie Mays suffers by comparison; and third baseman Judy Johnson.

In addition, the Crawfords had such stars of only slightly lesser magnitude as pitchers Sam Streeter, a veteran lefthander, and a hard-throwing rookie named LeRoy Matlock; outfielders Jimmie Crutchfield and Ted Page, both defensive standouts and left-handed line-drive hitters; Chester Williams, a very quick, flashy infielder, and versatile W. G. Perkins, who could catch or play the outfield brilliantly. The word stars is used here in a qualitative sense; most of these men were unknown outside the ghettos of the Negro major-league cities and a few nearby small towns,

but they were the Willie Mayses, Henry Aarons, Bob Gibsons and Curt Floods of their time.

EXCEPT that the Crawfords were somewhat more solvent than most clubs, the story of their rise and decline is fairly representative of Negro baseball at the top level. Like most Negro clubs, the Crawfords were the brainchild and pet of one man. In this case he was W. A. (Gus) Greenlee, a tavern owner and the numbers king in Pittsburgh's black Hill District who, in 1935, also entered boxing as manager of John Henry Lewis, the light heavyweight champion. Greenlee took over a Pittsburgh semipro team called the Crawford Colored Giants in the summer of 1931 and began adding some certified pros. Among his early acquisitions were Paige and his catcher, W. G. Perkins, who came to Pittsburgh after their club, the Cleveland Cubs, disbanded—a casualty of the great Depression.

Other players, attracted by the promise of regular paydays with Greenlee, simply jumped their contracts with other teams (if they had contracts) to join the Crawfords. Outfielder Jimmie Crutchfield recalls that he was playing without a contract for the Indianapolis ABC's that year. "And we weren't being paid," Crutchfield said. "That would go on for maybe two months, till we had a good gate. Then perhaps you'd get some of your back pay." When the ABC's got to Pittsburgh for games in that area, Crutchfield said, he was recommended to Greenlee by Satchel, Perkins and Streeter, his teammates on the Birmingham Black Barons in 1930. "So Greenlee gave me $25 or $50 —more than I'd gotten all year—so I stayed," Crutchfield remembers. "They said they were going to have a good ball club, but just to be with Satchel was enough."

Crutchfield, who had gotten $90 a month from Birmingham, was signed by the Crawfords for $150, an average salary on a top black club in the early thirties and about one-fifth of what a young

white player of his talents commanded in the major leagues of that era. "If you asked the manager about a raise," he said, "you'd hear, 'Well, we're paying you more than we're paying so-and-so.' To be honest with you, I imagine they could have cut half the boys on the team and they still would have played baseball because, after all, in 1931 and '32, if you didn't play baseball, what were you going to do?"

AS befitted a man who was fast becoming Negro baseball's biggest drawing card, Satchel Paige was the highest paid member of the Crawfords at $250 a month, augmented by frequent bonuses of $100 to $500 for pitching for area semipro teams on loan from Greenlee.

With such windfalls coming his way, Paige would sometimes be away from the club for a week at a time. Crutchfield remembers: "Satchel would pitch for us on Sunday —he'd shut out some team in Yankee Stadium, and we wouldn't see him maybe until the following Sunday. Maybe we'd be playing in Cleveland or some other big city. We'd leave the hotel, go to the ball park—no Satchel. Fifteen minutes before game time, somebody would say, 'Hey, Satchel just came in the dressing room.' He was always full of life. You'd forgive him for anything because he was like a great big boy. He could walk in the room and have you in stitches in 10 minutes' time. He'd warm up by playing third base or clowning with somebody and then he'd go out and pitch a shutout. How could you get mad at a guy like that?"

Paige's talent for showmanship was not confined to pre-game antics. Sometimes, when a game was safely in hand, he would call in his outfielders and pitch with only his infielders behind him. Just the sight of him, tall and languorous and his face expressing the serene confidence that is the mark of the supreme artist, was enough to cow most batters.

If the look was not enough, Paige made them believers by

delivering Long Tom, his *fast* fastball, as distinguished from Little Tom, a pitch that merely hummed by the batter. Long Tom was once described by Biz Mackey, a Negro baseball veteran, in tones of awe. "Satchel's fastball," Mackey said, "tends to disappear. Yes, disappear. I've heard about Satchel throwing pitches that wasn't hit but that never showed up in the catcher's mitt nevertheless. They say the catcher, the umpire and the bat boys looked all over for the ball but it was gone. Now how do you account for that?"

THE question borders on the occult, and in 1931 Gus Greenlee realized that a man with such powers deserved his own showcase. So the following year, at a time when nearly all black clubs rented or leased parks, many of them from teams in white organized baseball, Greenlee built a ball park on Bedford Avenue in the Pittsburgh Hill District for Paige and Company.

It cost $75,000, a lavish sum to invest in Negro baseball during the Depression. Its brick grandstand and bleachers along the foul lines seated 7,000 for baseball and 10,000 for boxing. Greenlee Field was also the home field of the Crawfords' neighbors and arch rivals, the Homestead Grays, for several years until, with the growing popularity of Negro baseball in the late thirties, both clubs abandoned it in favor of the Pirates' Forbes Field.

Like most black teams, the Crawfords traveled by bus, a six-cylinder, 79-horsepower Mack which was, The Pittsburgh Courier, a Negro weekly, noted, "capable of 60 miles an hour"—presumably on the down grade. By midseason 1932, the new bus already had logged 17,000 miles for the Crawfords, who, like every other black club, were on the road a great deal of the time.

The bus became a second home for the players. "We'd come home to Pittsburgh once in a while and get clean clothes and ride right out," Judy Johnson remembers. Their destination might be New York, Chicago or Cleve-land, or it might be Steubenville, Canton or Warren in Ohio, Butler or Altoona in Pennsylvania, or a coal-mining town in West Virginia. Although during most of their years the Crawfords were members of the Negro National League, two-thirds of their 150 to 200 games a season were played against the white semipro teams that flourished all over the country until the early nineteen-fifties.

As a rule they played two or three league games a week. They might, for example, play the Philadelphia Stars a doubleheader in Philadelphia or New York on Sunday and go to Baltimore for a game with the Black Sox Tuesday night. During the rest of the week, they would play each evening against white semipro clubs within driving distance of those two cities. At home, they followed the same pattern, playing Negro league clubs two or three games in Pittsburgh and filling out the rest of the week's schedule with area semipro teams.

Until Negro baseball's boom period during and immediately after World War II, crowds for Negro league games were predominantly black, with only a speckling of white faces. For games with semipros, most of which were played in small towns, the crowds naturally were largely white.

Gate receipts for league games were split on a percentage basis, with the home club taking the lion's share, but for independent games, owners of black clubs had some latitude for shrewd negotiations. An old player explains their course: "When a white ball club wrote and asked us for a game, they might offer a $500 guarantee. Well, if they offered a guarantee, you won't accept that; you want a percentage. But if they say they will give you 60 per cent of the gate, *then* you ask for a guarantee. Simple as that! Because when they want to give you a big guarantee, they *know* they're going to make it. And when they're not sure they're going to make it, they want you to take a percentage, so you want a guarantee."

Because they played in a different town almost every day on the road — and sometimes in two or three towns on the same day — black teams were constantly on the move, some even more often and farther than the Crawfords. By common consent, the Homestead Grays were the most inveterate tourists, often riding 200 miles out of Pittsburgh, playing a ball game or two, and then riding 200 miles back home that night.

Bill Yancey, a shortstop who played for several black clubs from 1923 to 1936, recalls that when he reached the plateau of excellence demanded by Cumberland W. (Cum) Posey, who had built the Grays into a Negro baseball power, he rejected the idea of playing for them, "because those guys would play one of their 'home' games in New Orleans and the next night they were liable to be in Buffalo, man, ridin' over those mountains!" (Yancey signed instead with the Lincoln Giants, who rarely had to venture far from the New York metropolitan area to find a game.)

YANCEY exaggerates for effect, but not by much, for the memories of men who played on the Grays and nearly every other black club abound with tales of marathon trips. Negro baseball lived and died before the age of superhighways, and 35 to 40 miles an hour was a good average over the narrow, often tortuous roads that webbed the nation. The black barnstormers, packed nine men in a car or jouncing interminably in a bus as the Crawfords did, were itinerants because they had to be. In Negro baseball, barnstorming meant survival.

Judy Johnson, who, like Yancey, is now a scout for the Philadelphia Phillies, recalls a not-unusual, 800-mile endurance test the Crawfords had in 1935 after playing a night game in Chicago: "Right after the game we had a meal, and then we started out for Philadelphia. We had our bus all packed before the game. And we rode all the way to Philadelphia without sleeping, except for naps on the bus. The only thing we had to eat was sandwiches and pop. And when we got to Philadelphia, my ankles were swollen 10 inches wide. We got in Tuesday morning and played a doubleheader that afternoon."

The necessity for speed to make schedules was the main reason for such nonstop journeys, but it was not the only one. Another was the fact that black travelers could not be sure of getting restaurant service or lodging along the way except in cities with large black populations. Jack Marshall, an infielder for the Chicago American Giants during the thirties, remembers: "When we left Chicago to go to St. Louis and play, there was no place where we could stop and eat — not unless we stopped in a place where they had a colored settlement. From St. Louis to Kansas City, same thing. So many times we would ride all night and not have anything to eat because they wouldn't feed you. Going from Chicago to Cleveland, same thing. So the boys used to take sardines and a can of beans and pour them into a jar. They'd take some crackers, too, and that was their food. They'd eat out of that jar. That's the way we had to do it."

ENDURING as they did such traveling and living conditions, it is hard to believe that the top black clubs could play on even terms with major leaguers, but the evidence shows that they did. In 1932, for example, the Crawfords won five out of seven in a post-season series with a team of major leaguers headed by the Chicago Cubs' Hack Wilson, who still holds the National League home-run record of 56 for one season. In other years, Satchel and his mates won a majority of their tests against barnstorming major-leaguers, including such stars as Joe DiMaggio, Charlie Gehringer, Dizzy Dean (who called Paige the greatest pitcher he ever saw), Lefty Grove, Bill Dickey, Heinie Manush, Rogers Hornsby and Babe Herman.

Because statistics were kept casually, if at all, in Negro baseball — both for teams and individual players (and not much better for Negro league standings), it is impossible to measure objectively the quality of the Crawfords.

There is general agreement among black baseball veterans that the top clubs were not of major-league caliber day in and day out, chiefly because their rosters had little depth. Most teams carried from 14 to 18 players, and if a regular was injured, the lineup was considerably weakened. Only during the twilight years of Negro baseball in the middle forties did the rosters go up to 22 men, still three short of the major-league limit.

But, says Bill Yancey, "if we could have selected the best of the colored leagues and gone into the major leagues, I'd say we could have won the championship. We could have selected maybe five clubs out of all the colored teams that would have held their own in the major leagues."

Buck Leonard, a slugging first baseman for the Homestead Grays, who played Gehrig to Josh Gibson's Ruth from 1938 until Gibson's death in 1947, remembers, "We didn't have star men at every position. We didn't have — as the majors did — two good catchers and six or seven good pitchers and good infielders and outfielders. We had pitchers that we would pitch in league games and mediocre pitchers that we just used against white semipro teams. Sockamayocks, we used to call 'em."

When the sockamayocks were on the bench and the regular lineup was intact, however, the first-line black clubs were a match for anybody. And when black all-star teams were formed during the winter to barnstorm on the Pacific Coast or play in Latin American leagues, the available records indicate that Yancey is right in believing a Negro league all-star team could have been world's champions. In three winters during the middle thirties, for instance, the Paige Stars compiled a 128-23 record on the Coast, with at least 40 of their victories coming at the expense of major-league barnstormers.

BASEBALL in retrospect can exist on two levels: in the mind's eye and ear and in the cold numbers of the record book. An old fan easily can call up the vision of Babe Ruth trotting toward first with dainty, mincing steps and hear the deep-throated, rising roar from the crowd as the ball soars toward the fence. He can see again Joe DiMaggio, feet spread wide, bat cocked, waiting, waiting, and then the fluid swing and the crack of bat against ball. Or gangling Marty Marion moving to his left with balletlike grace, scooping up the hard grounder on the short hop and throwing almost disdainfully to nip the runner at first.

For these men, the fan can also consult the record book for Ruth's 60-home-run season, DiMaggio's 56-game hitting streak, and Marion's fielding averages. His intuitive certainty of their greatness is reinforced by the printed word.

But for Negro baseball's stars, no such reinforcement is possible. The old fan can bring to mind Josh Gibson standing loose and easy in the righthand batter's box at Yankee Stadium during a Negro league doubleheader in 1934 and almost effortlessly propelling the ball over the third tier next to the left field bull pen, the only fair ball ever hit out of the Stadium. He cannot go to a record book and find Gibson's career home-run total, which in his 17 years in black baseball probably surpassed Ruth's 714. He cannot even be certain about the top figure for a single year, which was reported to be 89.

And so the legends have grown, fed, in the absence of reliable statistics, by the stop-time visions of men who remember. Gibson's picture swing, the sharp retort of the bat, and the ball a white blur rising toward the distant horizon. Cool Papa Bell, his flying feet seeming barely to touch the ground as he goes from first to second in seven steps and a slide. Or centerfielder Oscar Charleston, sta-

tioning himself almost within spitting distance of second base, and then, just before bat meets ball, turning to race back to the distant reaches of the outfield, the ball appearing to hang overhead until he catches up with it.

There is truth in such visions, more truth perhaps than in statistics, but they can be shaky guides to team strength, too. For despite Satchel Paige's assertion that the Crawfords of the early thirties were the best team in history, the fact is that they won a clear-cut victory in the Negro National League pennant races only once in the four years they were in the league before they were wrecked by wholesale desertions in 1937.

GUS GREENLEE organized the second Negro National League in 1933 (the first had operated in the Midwest during the twenties) and entered his Crawfords. They finished one game behind the Chicago American Giants in the first half of the split-season schedule. The league broke up during the second half and, not unnaturally, the American Giants claimed the championship.

In the spring of 1934, Greenlee, as league president, awarded the 1933 pennant to his own club. The Chicago management protested, but without unseemly vigor, because the pennant carried with it no financial reward; the clubs merely split gate receipts for their games and there was no special incentive for placing high in the standings except the honor of it and the fact that for the following season the pennant winners could legitimately advertise themselves as "colored world's champions."

In 1934, the Crawfords finished second and third in the split-season schedule, despite Satchel Paige's record that season of 31-4. The following year, after Paige jumped the club in a salary dispute with Greenlee and went to Bismarck, N. D., to pitch for a white semipro team, the Crawfords finally won the N. N. L. pennant. In 1936, with an unrepentant Paige back in the fold, they won the second half, but no play-

off was held with the Washington Elite Giants, first-half winners.

Greenlee's dream of a baseball dynasty was souring that year, and toward the end of the season, Josh Gibson, the other half of what probably was the greatest battery ever, jumped the Crawfords to return to his first club, the Homestead Grays. Gibson was listed on the spring roster of the Crawfords in 1937 but was described as a holdout, and subsequently his contract was traded to the Grays for two journeymen players.

MEANWHILE, the foot-loose Paige was making ready to jump again. While at spring training with the Crawfords in New Orleans, he heard the rustle of money — $30,000 if he would recruit eight other Negro league stars and go to the Dominican Republic to play under the banner of President Rafael L. Trujillo Molina.

Unaccountably the dictator was being opposed for re-election, and his opponent had imported a ball club called Estrellas de Oriente that was capturing the attention of the volatile, baseball-mad Dominicans by drubbing every other club on the island. There was only one thing to do — assemble a club that could beat the Estrellas. Trujillo's lieutenants naturally went to the top — Satchel Paige.

Cool Papa Bell, a star for 30 years and now a guard at the St. Louis City Hall, recalls what happened:

"They got guys from Cuba, Panama and guys out of the Negro leagues — they had a lot of boys from the States—but they wanted Satchel. He was down in New Orleans training with the Crawfords, and he didn't want to go. So they trailed Satchel to a hotel in New Orleans. Someone told them Satchel was in there. So two of them went in to look for him, and Satchel slipped out the side door and jumped into his car and tried to get away from them, but they blocked the street and stopped him.

"Now Satchel was the type of guy that if you showed him money — or a car — you could lead him anywhere. He was that type of fella. He did a lot of wrong things in baseball, but he was easily led. So these fellas said they wanted him to go down to Santo Domingo, and he said, 'I don't wanna go.' He didn't really want to jump again, that's why he was ducking those people. But when they offered him a big salary, then he jumped and went down there.

"In that year, Gus Greenlee, who was in the numbers racket, had lost a lot of money. He had a little old boy working for him, sweeping around where they counted the numbers money, and he was tipping off the detectives whenever they was counting the money. Gus didn't know just why, but every time they would move, the detectives would be there.

"Gus Greenlee had lost so much money he was giving the ball players a tough way to go. So a lot of the boys on the Crawfords were ready to get out. Some of the boys got jobs in Pittsburgh in a mill where they had a team, and I had an application in there. I was going to quit as soon as I had a job. Some of the boys were jumping the league, too — it was going bad again.

"So then Satchel called from down in Santo Domingo and got in touch with LeRoy Matlock, Harry Williams and Sam Bankhead."

THAT phone call had an ominous ring for the Pittsburgh Crawfords because eight men from the club, including Bell, jumped to join

Satchel. Paige and his Trujillo Stars won the tournament in Santo Domingo under very close chaperonage. They lived under armed guard in a private club, and the games were played under the watchful eyes of a large part of Trujillo's army, with the sun glinting off long knives and bayonets. Satchel and his mates could not get out of Trujillo land fast enough after that series.

He and a few of the other refugees from Latin America returned to the Crawfords for 1938, paying a nominal fine of one week's salary for jumping, but the season had not begun before Satchel was on the run, this time to Mexico.

Paige never again appeared in a Crawfords uniform and their glory days were over for good. Greenlee Field was dismantled to make way for a housing development, and the Crawfords, bereft of both Paige and Gibson, the two top attractions in Negro baseball, moved on to other cities. In 1939 they played out of Toledo, and in 1940 they were in Indianapolis. For several years thereafter, they barnstormed in the Northwest, far from the pallid limelight of the Negro leagues.

In 1945, Greenlee, by now a pariah to Negro league owners, challenged them by forming the United States Baseball League, with franchises in several major cities, including one for his Pittsburgh Crawfords. The United States League did not become a threat to the two established Negro major leagues operat-

ing that year and barely managed to stumble through the season. But it qualified for a footnote in baseball history because the league included the Brooklyn Brown Dodgers, a club which Branch Rickey, president of the Brooklyn Dodgers, used as a screen to scout Negro players without upsetting his major-league brethren. That October, Rickey shocked the sports world and heralded the end of segregated baseball by signing Jackie Robinson to play for Montreal, the Dodgers' top farm club, in 1946.

THE Pittsburgh Crawfords, one of the brighter lights in the shadow world of Negro baseball, are only a vivid memory now in the minds of a dwindling band of men who once discerned greatness on a baseball field far from the magnificence of the big leagues. So, too, the Homestead Grays, Kansas City Monarchs, Hilldale Club of Darby, Pa., the Lincoln Giants, Baltimore Elite Giants, St. Louis Stars and Chicago American Giants — all once proud names in the black back streets of baseball. Their uniforms were worn with distinction by men named Rube Foster, John Henry Lloyd, Smoky Joe Williams, John Donaldson, Cannonball Dick Redding, Bullet Rogan, Bingo DeMoss, Willie Wells and Martin Dihigo, men who were lucky to make $1,000 a season at a time when apprentice major leaguers were earning three to four times as much. They played for love of the game on the only teams open to them.

Jimmie Crutchfield, now a postal worker in Chicago, thoughtfully closes his scrapbook of yellowing clippings about the Crawfords and says, "I have no ill feeling about never having had the opportunity to play in the big leagues. There have been times — you know, they used to call me the black Lloyd Waner. I used to think about that a lot. He was on the other side of town in Pittsburgh making $12,000 a year, and I didn't have enough money to come home on. I had to borrow money to come home.

"It seemed like there was something wrong there. But that was yesterday. There's no use in me having bitterness in my heart this late in life about what's gone by. That's just the way I feel about it. Once in a while I get a kick out of thinking that my name was mentioned as one of the stars of the East-West Game (the Negro all-star game) and little things like that. I don't know whether I'd feel better if I had a million dollars.

"I can say I contributed something." ∎

April 11, 1971

Baseball's Front Door Opens to Satchel Paige

Satchel Paige was given full membership yesterday in the Baseball Hall of Fame instead of being honored in a separate niche reserved for players of the old Negro leagues.

Earlier this year, it had been announced that a separate wing of the baseball museum was being set aside for players in the Negro leagues, which flourished before black

players were admitted to the major leagues, and Paige was chosen as the first player to be honored.

However, in response to severe criticism of this "separate-but-equal" treatment, Baseball Commissioner Bowie Kuhn and Paul Kirk, president of the Hall of Fame and museum at Cooperstown, N. Y., said Paige and future Negro league inductees would be given full membership.

July 8, 1971

Shifting of Senators to Texas Approved by American League

Vote Is 10 to 2 For Conditional Move in 1972

BOSTON, Sept. 21 (UPI) — American League owners voted tonight to shift the franchise of the financially ailing Washington Senators to Arlington, Tex., between Dallas and Fort Worth, for next season.

Joe Cronin, the league president, said the owners had approved the shift on a 10-2 vote with conditions relating to the number of seats and a lease for Turnpike Stadium in Arlington. The stadium now seats 21,000 and, it was said, could be expanded to 50,000.

The owner of the Senators, Robert Short, conceded that he had "failed in Washington to field a team successfully." He has said the Senators lost $3-million over the last three years.

Apologizes to Fans

"I was not able to do in Washington what I did my best to do," said Short. He thanked those who had "helped me try to find a solution," and apologized to Senator fans for shifting the club.

Short said he would continue as owner, indicating that he would not sell part of the franchise in making the move to Texas.

Baseball Commissioner Bowie Kuhn described the decison as "a sad day for Washington," but said the Texas area had "long deserved major league baseball."

Officials would not disclose the exact financial terms of the lease, but Short said they gave him "a more favorable position than any major league operator that I know of."

Mayor Thomas Vandergriff of Arlington said he was "most proud and pleased" to obtain the franchise and predicted it would be one of the most successful in baseball. He said Short would be charged a basic rental of $1 a year until at least a million in attendance had been reached.

Orioles, White Sox Dissent

Cronin said the league had received "a last offer" from a Washington food magnate, Joseph Danzansky, during the more than 12 hours of discussion. The Baltimore Orioles and the Chicago White Sox filed the two dissenting votes, he said.

Danzansky was both disappointed and puzzled. He said he and two other men originally offered $7-million for 80 per cent of the franchise stock months ago and later increased the offer to $7.5-million for 90 per cent of the stock.

Cronin said he had felt the Washington group was "thinly capitalized."

While there was discussion about President Nixon's suggestion of playing some Oriole games in Washington next season, he said, "we haven't had time to make a decision of any kind."

In Washington, the City Council chairman, Gilbert Hahn, expressed "bitter disappointment at the development. He said there was no chance any team would play in the capital next season.

"The baseball hierarchy discouraged any overtures to any other clubs while the Senators were here," Hahn said. But he insisted that the city would be interested in making offers to the San Diego Padres and San Francisco Giants.

Hahn also suggested that each major league club could play one game at Robert F. Kennedy Stadium next season.

"Considering the nature of Washington, which is made up of transients an dlarge numbers of people who are from other cities, it might be the best solution," he said.

President Nixon said earlier this week it would be disappointing to lose the Senators.

September 22, 1971

Baseball Strike Is Settled; Season to Open Tomorrow

By JOSEPH DURSO

The first general strike in baseball history ended in its 13th day yesterday when the players and owners agreed to start the season tomorrow without making up any of the 86 missed games.

The settlement was reached in Chicago, where the owners of the 24 major league teams gathered yesterday, and in New York, where the player representatives had been meeting for three days.

The original issue—an increase in the players' pensions, which are financed by television money—already had been solved by a compromise raise of $500,000. The final issue—whether to pay the players for games rescheduled because of the strike—was settled by the bobtailed season.

As a result, some teams like the Houston Astros and San Diego Padres will play nine games less than a full season of 162, all teams will miss at least six games and division championships will be decided on a straight percentage basis. They customarily are decided that way, but most clubs usually manage to complete full seasons, despite bad weather, by scheduling double-headers.

For the 600 players, whose salaries will begin tomorrow instead of a week ago yesterday, the cost will be nine days' pay. For those at the minimum level of $13,500, the loss will total $675; for those at the big league average of $32,500, it will be $1,600; for Henry Aaron of the Atlanta Braves, who is bearing down on Babe Ruth's home-run record at nearly $200,000 a season, just over $9,880.

Victory for Nobody

Despite the bitterness of the two-week strike, neither side made extravagant claims of victory after the settlement was announced at 4:15 P.M.

"Everybody recognizes that nobody won," said Donald Grant, chairman of the board of directors of the New York Mets.

"I think it's fair to say nobody ever wins in a strike situation," said Marvin Miller, the onetime steel-union economist who now directs the Players' Association. "This one is no exception. We're not going to claim victory even though our objectives were achieved."

"I really feel good that it's over," said Joe Torre of the St. Louis Cardinals, the ranking hitter in baseball last season, "but there will probably be some catcalls from the stands when we start to play ball."

"It's inevitable that there will be hard feelings," said Bowie Kuhn, the commissioner of baseball. "My job is to hold them to a minimum. Who won? Nobody. The players suffered. The clubs suffered. Baseball suffered."

In New York, the Yankees and Mets found their original timetables reversed by the strike. The Yankees, who had been scheduled to open the season at home April 6, now will open in Baltimore tomorrow after working out at Yankee Stadium this afternoon. The Mets, who would have started in Pittsburgh, now will open against the Pirates at home after working out in Shea Stadium this morning.

Some clubs, though, jumped the gun because the strike obviously was moving toward a close as the owners and players convened separately yesterday. In San Francisco, the Giants worked out for three hours in Candlestick Park before the settlement and Manager Charlie Fox said they were ready for the opener in Houston tomorrow. Across the Bay, the Oakland Athletics mustered about half their men and exercised, while Sal Bando, the team captain, observed:

"I don't know how we'll do at the start. When you lose two weeks at this time of year, you are almost in the position of having to go to spring training all over again."

Some early-birds, though, ruffled the feathers of their owner of the Kansas City Royals, said he would protest to the American League president any games his club had to play this weekend against the Chicago White Sox. His reason: the White Sox had "disregarded" a league stipulation that no players be allowed to work out in major league stadiums during the strike.

"I've talked on the telephone with most of our players and with all of our pitchers," said Ralph Houk, the manager of the New York Yankees and a career optimist. "And although we'll be more cautious for a time, I don't think there'll be any danger from the two-week layoff. The pitchers may be ahead of the hitters for a few days. We had three pitchers ready to go nine innings when we left Florida, and I don't think they lost anything."

As for the strike settlement, both sides went into the home stretch yesterday with a handshake agreement on the players' benefits fund, which had been financed by a $5.45-million allotment each year from national TV receipts from the World Series.

The players asked that their share this year be raised to cover the cost of living, and calculated the pension increase at 17 per cent, or $1-million. The owners eventually offered to add $490,000 to that part of the plan that covers medical benefits but insisted on no raise in pensions.

By last Tuesday, the 11th day of the strike, the players had lowered their demand to $600,-000 for pensions and the owners had raised their offer from zero to $400,000. By then, they were talking not about new money—but about the wisdom of diverting surplus money that had accumulated within the pension fund from investments.

They decided to split the difference at $500,000. But the question remained: Would the ball games that had been postponed be made up and, if so, would the players be paid for them? For the last 48 hours, that was the only issue left, but it delayed the season two more days.

The owners themselves were divided as they gathered in Chicago—the American League generally favoring a shorter season anyway, the National preferring the full 162 games. However, the National League did not make a fight of it and a formula was reached that was telephoned to New York, where Miller and the players were waiting.

The owners thereupon dispatched a task force to New York to translate the agreement into a memorandum, which must be signed by midnight tonight. They will be represented by Charles Feeney, president of the National League; Joe Cronin, president of the American, and John J. Gaherin, their labor-relations adviser, who bore the brunt of the negotiating with Miller.

By midnight, though, everybody expected players to be back with their clubs or en route from the West Coast and Caribbean, with 12 games scheduled tomorrow to pick up the pieces.

April 14, 1972

Baseball's Exempt Status Upheld by Supreme Court

By LEONARD KOPPETT
Special to The New York Times

United Press International

Curt Flood with his attorney, former Associate Justice Arthur J. Goldberg, during outfielder's trial in 1970.

WASHINGTON, June 19—Baseball, and only baseball, remains exempt from the antitrust laws, the Supreme Court ruled today by a 5-3 margin. But the Court again urged Congress to resolve the problem.

The decision ended the Curt Flood case in defeat for the player who challenged baseball's reserve system, a set of arrangements that ties a player to one club indefinitely.

Flood, then a 32-year-old outfielder earning $90,000 a year, objected to being traded from St. Louis to Philadelphia after the 1969 season. He sued for $3-million in damages, claiming that reserve rules had prevented him from playing for any other club. The Major League Players Association supported his suit financially and former Justice Arthur Goldberg represented him.

A trial in May, 1970, resulted in a lower court decision that the merits of the case need not be considered because baseball was made exempt from antitrust laws by Supreme Court decisions in 1922 and 1953.

Today's decision, delivered by Justice Harry A. Blackmun, also bypassed the merits of the reserve system and stressed the Court's refusal to overturn previous rulings. It acknowledged that baseball's special status was an "aberration" and an "anomaly," but re-affirmed the position taken in several prior cases that it was up to Congress to remedy the situation with legislation.

Voting with the majority were Chief Justice Warren E. Burger, who expressed "reservations," and Justices Byron R. White, Potter Stewart and William E. Rehnquist.

Justices William O. Douglas and Thurgood Marshall filed dissenting opinions, in which Justice William J. Brennan Jr. joined. Justice Lewis F. Powell Jr. did not participate.

The 1922 ruling, referred to as Federal Baseball, stated that baseball was not the sort of business that the antitrust laws were intended to cover.

In 1953, in a case called Toolson vs. New York, the Court ruled, 7-2, that the exemption should be continued, even though legal philosophy had changed, because the industry had been allowed to develop for 30 years on the assumption of its immunity.

Justice Blackmun stressed this point.

"We continue to loathe, 50 years after Federal Baseball and almost two decades after Toolson, to overturn those cases judicially when Congress, by its positive inaction, has allowed those decisions to stand for so long," he wrote.

During the last 20 years, many bills have been introduced to grant uniform antitrust exemptions to all major professional sports, but none has passed both houses of Congress in the same session.

Even as the Supreme Court was issuing today's ruling, a Senate hearing was in progress on a proposed Federal sports commission that would have jurisdiction over professional team sports, and the House Judiciary Committee was scheduling hearings starting July 24 on the general topic of sports and antitrust regulations.

Justice Douglas, in a footnote to his dissent, declared: "While I joined the Court's opinion in Toolson, I have lived to regret it, and I would now correct what I believe to be its fundamental error."

He argued that the inaction of Congress could be seen two ways.

"If Congressional inaction is our guide, we should rely upon the fact that Congress has refused to enact bills broadly exempting professional sports from antitrust regulation. . . . There can be no doubt that were we considering the question of baseball for the first time upon a clean slate, we would hold it to be subject to Federal antitrust regulation. The unbroken silence of Congress should not prevent us from correcting our own mistakes."

But Chief Justice Burger, in his brief concurring opinion, said:

"Like Mr. Justice Douglas, I have grave reservations as to the correctness of Toolson; as he notes in his dissent, he joined in that holding but has 'lived to regret it.' The error, if such it be, is one on which the affairs of a great many people have rested for a long time. Courts are not the forum in which this tangled web ought to be unsnarled.

"I agree with Mr. Justice Douglas that Congressional inaction is not a solid base, but the least undesirable course now is to let the matter rest with Congress: it is time the Congress acted to solve this problem."

Justice Marshall, in his dissent, stressed the importance of upholding antitrust laws in the general interest. "They are as important to baseball players as they are to football players, lawyers, doctors, or members of any other class of workers."

He pointed out, however, that overruling Federal Baseball and Toolson would not necessarily mean that Flood won. "I would remand this case to the District Court for consideration whether . . . there has been an antitrust violation."

The prevailing view, however, was Justice Blackmun's. He found that Federal laws took precedence over state antitrust suits, and that there was no need to consider the argument that the reserve system was a matter for labor negotiation and therefore exempt from antitrust.

"If there is any inconsistency of illogic in all this, it is an inconsistency and illogic of long standing that is to be remedied by the Congress and not by this Court," he wrote.

"Under these circumstances, there is merit in consistency even though some might claim that beneath that consistency is a layer of inconsistency."

June 20, 1972

Reds Take Flag on Wild Pitch

Pirates Are Beaten, 4-3; Bench's Clout Ties Score

By JOSEPH DURSO

Special to The New York Times

CINCINNATI, Oct. 11—The Cincinnati Reds won the National League pennant on a wild pitch today when they rallied for two runs in the last half of the ninth inning to defeat the Pittsburgh Pirates, 4-3.

It was a chaotic finish to a playoff that went the five-game limit and to a game that also went the limit, with the Pirates leading all the way in the defense of their world title—until the last inning.

Then Johnny Bench hammered a home run into the empty football seats beyond the right-field fence against Dave Giusti, and the Reds—the champions of the Western Division—were finally even. Two outs and two singles later, Bob Moose bounced his 1-and-1 pitch into the dirt past the pinch-hitting Hal McRae and the pennant bounced with it to Cincinnati.

13-10 Playoff Underdogs

For the Big Red Machine, the pitch that Moose uncorked into the dirt to the right of home plate marked the end of a long road back. Two years ago, the Reds won the West and swept the playoff against the Pirates. Last year, they subsided to fourth place while the Pirates won the pennant. And this year, they revived in the West while the Pirates dominated the East.

But in the playoff, which they entered as 13-10 underdogs, the Reds were always one day late. They dropped the opener, then tied the series the next day. Then they dropped behind again and were one defeat from extinction. But they survived with a 7-1 victory yesterday and then struggled today while Pittsburgh took leads of 2-0 in the second inning, 3-1 in the fourth and 3-2 in the fifth.

Going into their final turn at bat, they were still losing by 3-2 and had scrounged only four hits off Steve Blass, though one of the four was a homer by Cesar Geronimo that kept them within striking distance. And, with three outs to go, they struck.

For those final three outs, the Pirates switched to their longtime relief ace, Giusti, a 32-year-old right-hander who had pitched 54 times this summer with an earned-run average of only 1.92. But it was a calculated risk, because Giusti was replacing Ramon Hernandez, a 31-year-old left-hander who had pitched 53 times with an even better earned-run average, 1.67.

The risk was taken because Cincinnati's three hitters in the ninth were all right-handers. But it promptly backfired on Giusti's fourth pitch, which Bench pounded over the 375-foot marker in right field for his 41st homer of 1972.

Now the Reds were back in business, at 3-all, and business even picked up when Tony Perez hit the next pitch through the middle for a single. He was replaced by a pinch-runner, George Foster, who then raced to second when Denis Menke punched a single through the left side of the infield.

The crowd of 41,887 was up and howling just as it had been two hours earlier while the dramatic play-by-play from Detroit was being flashed on the electric scoreboard. And the noise grew louder when Giusti, trying to foil a bunt by Geronimo, threw two high pitches.

For Giusti, who had got nobody out, that was it. He was replaced by Moose, who had got nobody out in the first inning of the second game. But Moose was one of Pittsburgh's regular starters, a right-hander who had pitched 31 times this year, though only once in relief.

He did nobly, too, until the one disastrous pitch that cost the Pirates the pennant. But first he got Geronimo to foul off two pitches, one bunting and one swinging, and then Geronimo lifted a 370-foot fly to Roberto Clemente at the base of the right-field wall. Foster tagged up and flew to third.

When Darrel Chaney popped a high fly into short left field, Gene Alley ran back from shortstop and Rennie Stennett ran in from left, with Alley making the catch as they collided. But that made two outs, and now the Pirates stood one out from sending the game into extra innings.

They never got the out, though. With Foster leading off third and Menke off first, McRae pinch-hit for Clay Carroll. The count rose to one ball, one strike. Then, 159 games after the season had begun, Moose heaved the next pitch on the bounce past Manny Sanguillen.

And, as the ball skipped to the box-seat railing behind home plate, Foster scored the run that brought — and cost — the pennant.

It was a long time coming for the Reds, longer even than scheduled, because the game was delayed 1 hour 28 minutes by rain and didn't start until 4:30. The canvas covering the artificial turf was removed several times, and Don Gullett and Blass warmed up twice. Gullett, in fact, was ready to pitch from the mound when things were delayed the first time.

Pirates Score Twice

When he finally got his chance an hour and a half later, he looked off-target and Blass looked sharp, which is the way they looked in the opener last Saturday. Then, in the second inning, Sanguillen singled to left and Richie Hebner pulled a double down the right-field line. Sanguillen stopped at third, but when the relay got away from Chaney at second base he scored. And when Dave Cash singled to center, Hebner scored and it was 2-0, Pittsburgh.

One inning later, the Reds mounted their first comeback. Chaney singled to right and

Reds' Box Score

PITTSBURGH (N.)	ab	r	h	bi	CINCINNATI (N.)	ab	r	h	bi
Stennett, lf	4	0	1	0	Rose, lf	3	0	1	1
Oliver, cf	3	0	0	0	Morgan, 2b	4	0	0	0
Clemente, rf	3	1	0	0	Tolan, cf	4	0	0	0
Stargell, 1b	4	0	0	0	Bench, c	4	1	2	1
Robertson, 1b	0	0	0	0	Perez, 1b	4	0	1	0
Sanguillen, c	4	2	2	0	Foster, pr	0	1	0	0
Hebner, 3b	4	1	2	0	Menke, 3b	3	0	1	0
Cash, 2b	4	0	2	2	Geronimo, rf	4	1	1	1
Alley, ss	4	0	0	0	Chaney, ss	4	1	1	0
Blass, p	3	0	0	0	Gullett, p	0	0	0	0
R. Hernandez, p	0	0	0	0	Borbon, p	0	0	0	0
Giusti, p	0	0	0	0	Uhlaender, ph	1	0	0	0
Moose, p	0	0	0	0	Hall, p	0	0	0	0
					Hague, ph	0	0	0	0
					Concepcion, pr	0	0	0	0
					Carroll, p	0	0	0	0
					McRae, ph	0	0	0	0
Total	33	3	3	2	Total	31	4	7	3

Pittsburgh ... 0 2 0 1 0 0 0 0 0—3
Cincinnati ... 0 0 1 0 1 0 0 0 2—4

E—Chaney. DP—Cincinnati 1. LOB—Pittsburgh 5, Cincinnati 3. 2B—Hebner, Rose. HR—Geronimo (1), Bench (1). S—Gullett, Oliver, Rose.

	IP.	H.	R.	ER.	BB.	SO.
Blass	7⅓	4	2	2	2	4
R. Hernandez	0	1	0	0	0	0
Giusti (L, 0-1)	0	3	2	2	0	0
Moose	⅔	0	0	0	0	0
Gullett	3	6	3	3	0	2
Borbon	2	1	0	0	0	1
Hall	3	1	0	0	1	4
Carroll (W, 1-1)	1	0	0	0	0	0

*Two outs when winning run was scored.
Wild pitch—Gullett, Moose.
T—2:19. A—41,887.

Gullett bunted him to second. Pete Rose, who made nine hits in the five games, followed with a shot behind first base that took a high hop off Willie Stargell's glove for a double and a run.

But in the fourth, Sanguillen and Hebner led with singles and Gullett immediately was replaced by Pedro Borbón. That didn't work, either, because Cash singled again on Borbón's

second pitch and it was 3-1, Pirates.

The Reds narrowed the margin an inning after that when Gerónimo, who had only one hit in 17 times at bat in the playoff, pulled his homer over the fence in ight, making it 3-2. Then they bided their time while Borbón, Tom Hall and Carroll shut out the Pirates on one single over the last five innings.

Hall, the lithe left-hander who won the second game in long relief, did the fanciest work: three innings, one single by Stennett, one intentional walk, four strike-outs. His biggest strike-out was delivered against Stargell with two runners on base in the eighth. It was the 15th straight time the Reds had retired Stargell in the playoff, which proved to be one of the critical things that kept

them close to the hardest-hitting team in baseball.

That brought them to the ninth, with Pittsburgh's "dynasty" three outs from another pennant. But the Pirates saw it slip away as McRae leaned over the plate and Moose let fly his historic slider.

October 12, 1972

American League to Let Pitcher Have a Pinch-Hitter and Stay In

By JOSEPH DURSO

The owners of the 24 major league baseball teams took a radical step yesterday to put more punch into the game. They voted to allow the American League to use a "designated pinch-hitter," who may bat for the pitcher without forcing him from the game.

The plan will be tried experimentally for the next three seasons by the American League, which has been hurt financially in recent years and has been searching for ways to energize baseball. But it will not be used in the National League, which has resisted the change, or in the World Series, the All-Star Game between the two leagues or interleague exhibition games.

The action was voted at a joint meeting of the major leagues in Chicago yesterday, with Commissioner Bowie Kuhn breaking an impasse between the leagues. As a result, for the first time since the American League was organized in 1901, the two big leagues will play under differing rules.

Another proposal to dramatize baseball — regular games between teams from the rival leagues—was turned over to study committee, with expectations that it might be approved for 1974. And, in a further development, the owners got word of some easing of their labor-relations stalemate with the players.

The chief change in the bargaining talks reportedly was a proposal by the players that the crucial "reserve-clause" issue be separated from the oth-

ers. If so, the two sides would bypass the gravest danger of a strike when the season opens in April.

But the historic action of the seven-hour meeting of the owners concerned the "designated pinch-hitter," who would become the 10th man in the team's line-up but whose only function would be to bat for the pitcher.

By approving the experiment, which was tried in the high minor leagues three years ago, the club executives made the most basic change in the rules since 1903. That was when foul balls were ruled strikes. Since then, the spitball was banned in 1920, the "lively" ball was introduced in 1930, the strike zone was enlarged in 1962 and reduced again in 1969 and the pitcher's mound was lowered the same year.

But none of those changes revolutionized the rules that were essentially followed since the days of the old New York Knickerbockers baseball club a century and a quarter ago.

Pitcher Can Stay in Game

The rules called for nine men on a side with the stipulation that if a pinch-hitter went to bat for one of the nine, then that player had to leave the game. The most frequently replaced players were the pitchers because they were usually the weakest hitters.

Under the change forced yesterday by the American League, eight of whose 12 teams lost money last season, the manager would follow this procedure if he wished:

¶He would give the umpires a line-up card before the game with the nine regular players listed by position and the 10th player listed as the "designated pinch-hitter." His only job would be that. When it came

time for the pitcher to bat, the designated man would swing for him. The pitcher, though, would stay in the game and the pinch-hitter would go back to the bench until the next time round.

¶If the starting pitcher was replaced later by a relief pitcher, the designated pinch-hitter would bat for him.

¶If the manager decided to replace the designated pinch-hitter with another pinch-hitter, he could do that at any time. But the second man then could be used only for that purpose and could not play in the field, while the first pinch-hitter would be out of the game.

¶Except for the "designated" man, all the other players customarily used as pinch-hitters would follow the old rules. They could bat for a player, then stay in the game at any position the manager wished.

Games Are Shorter

When the experiment was tried in the International League in 1969, several things happened: Batting averages rose 10 per cent, the number of runs scored rose 6 per cent and games took six minutes less time to play on the average. The reason for that was no surprise to the fan or television viewer: Changing pitchers is the most time-consuming maneuver in baseball.

"I hope it works," Commissioner Kuhn said after casting the vote that broke the stalemate between the two leagues. "I would have preferred that both leagues did it. But if it's successful in one, then I hope the National follows suit."

"We are happy that the American League got the experimental ruling," said Charles S. Feeney, president of the National. "We can get a real test on it. If it does work out, we wouldn't be hesitant to adopt it."

"I don't think it will necessarily cause more scoring," observed Chuck Tanner, manager of the Chicago White Sox. "In fact, it may cut down scoring on one side if the other team

leaves a pitcher like Nolan Ryan in the game."

Tanner, though, foreshadowed the strategic stampede that is bound to follow. He said that he would immediately "put in a call to Orlando Cepeda"—the 35-year-old first baseman recently dropped by the Oakland A's. Cepeda, after knee surgery, can no longer run, but he can still hit home runs.

Another result was expected to be a cut in the number of pitchers carried on the 25-man squads. Most teams now carry 10 or 11 pitchers; they probably can get by with seven or eight now that the manager can use a pinch-hitter without losing his pitcher.

The National League's opposition to the change was bluntly expressed by Feeney: "We like the game the way it is."

But the American League, under heavy financial pressure, kept campaigning for innovations. Only three teams in the American League passed the million mark in attendance last season; only three teams in the National did not. The American League plays mostly in old stadiums, the National mostly in new ones with artificial turf.

At the baseball business meetings in Honolulu last month, the American League voted unanimously for the pinch-hit change. The National voted against it. The American League then forced a new vote yesterday, and it will be certified in the next week by the Playing Rules Committee of both leagues.

While the owners were mulling the impact of the change, they showed some signs of relief over a report by their labor-relations committee. The chief negotiator, John J. Gaherin, would not comment on the talks, but he said: "I like what happened here today."

He presumably was alluding to the players' offer to study the reserve clause for a year without forcing a decision now.

Ryan Exceeds Koufax

ANAHEIM, Calif., Sept. 28 (UPI) — Nolan Ryan of the California Angels broke Sandy Koufax's season strike-out record of 382 tonight by fanning Rich Reese of the Minnesota Twins in the 11th inning.

The Angels won the game for Ryan, 5-4, in the 11th. Ryan wound up with 16 strike-outs, 383 for the year and his 21st victory.

Ryan went into game needing 15 strike-outs to equal the record set by Koufax for the Los Angeles Dodgers in 1965. He tied the mark by getting Steve Brye in the eighth.

The 26-year-old right-hander from Alvin, Tex., also broke Koufax's two-season strike-out mark of 699 set in 1965-66 when he fanned Rod Carew in the second inning.

September 28, 1973

Mets Win East Title

By JOSEPH DURSO
Special to The New York Times

CHICAGO, Oct. 1 — The New York Mets completed their rousing dash from last place and finally won the most complicated race in baseball history today when they defeated the Chicago Cubs, 6-4, to capture the Eastern Division title in the National League.

They thereby eliminated the St. Louis Cardinals and Pittsburgh Pirates from the free-for-all one day after it was supposed to have ended and one day after the Montreal Expos and Cubs also had been eliminated.

The victory was the 23d in the last 32 games for the Mets, who spent two months in last place during waves of injuries this summer and were still last on Aug. 30.

But then they charged past the five other teams in the division, reached the top 10 days ago and clinched the title in a drizzle this afternoon before only 1,913 fans in Wrigley Field.

2d Game Called Off

The four umpires supervising the series, which had been twice delayed by rain, showed a neat regard for history by calling off the second game of today's doubleheader. The official reason was wet grounds. The practical reason was that the game had become moot and the net result was that the Mets were able to celebrate their dramatic comeback with full-flowing spirits.

Tug McGraw, who stopped the Cubs cold over the final three innings after Tom Seaver had been knocked out of the box, led the cheers in a victory scene reminiscent of the Met "miracle" of 1969. Only 11 players whooping it up in the vibrating little clubhouse were with the team four years ago, when it unexpectedly won the division title, the league pennant and the World Series.

The Mets still had a formidable course to follow before history could repeat, however. They will open the three-of-five-game playoff for the pennant Saturday in Cincinnati against the Reds, the best in the West. The winner will enter the World Series on Saturday, Oct. 13, against the Baltimore Orioles or the Oakland A's of the American League.

For a few hours this afternoon, the dangers of the future were drowned out by the noise of the present. While McGraw stood on an equipment trunk chanting, "You got to believe!" Manager Yogi Berra stood besieged in his tiny office, reflecting on a season that had almost cost him his job as successor to the late Gil Hodges.

"It's been a long year," Yogi said. "I was on 14 Yankee teams that won, but this has to be a big thrill because we had to jump over five clubs to do it. We were 12 games back and hurt.

"I told the guys here Friday, I'm proud of you whether you win or lose the next four. Just give me 100 per cent for the next few days."

The Mets responded by losing the first game of a double-header yesterday, 1-0. But they won the second, 9-2, assuring a tie for the top, although Pittsburgh and St. Louis still had mathematical shots.

Today, in a game that began at 11:20 A.M., after a short rain delay, they rushed to a 5-0 lead in 4½ innings.

The hitting heroes were Cleon Jones, who drove a home run into the bleachers in right-center field in the second, and Jerry Grote, who singled home two runs in the fourth.

Seaver, meanwhile, was struggling along, and for the third time in his last four starts, was unable to go the distance. He has been in a late-season slump, caused partly by a tender right shoulder.

Jones supplied his early margin, though, by hitting the 1-and-0 pitch from Burt Hooton above the ivy-covered brick wall. It was his 11th home run of the season, but his sixth in the final 10 games after he had suffered assorted injuries.

Two innings later the Mets loaded the bases with nobody out when Rusty Staub singled and John Milner and Jones walked. Then Grote lined his single to center and suddenly they led by three.

They wasted the chance for more runs then, but atoned in the next inning with two more. Wayne Garrett led that charge with a double down the right-field line, Felix Millan singled and, with Mike Paul now pitching, Staub singled to right to make it 4-0. And when Milner followed with a sacrifice fly to center, it became 5-0.

In the bottom of the inning the Cubs rattled Seaver with two runs, starting with a leadoff single by Ken Rudolph. Then, after a fly to center, they bunched singles by Rick Monday, Don Kessinger and Billy Williams.

Now the score was 5-2 and, with three innings to go in a bizarre season, the Mets managed a final run in the seventh off Jack Aker. It came on a single by Staub, his third in a row; a one-out walk to Jones and a two-out grounder that was booted by Ron Santo.

Cubs Narrow Gap

In the home half of the inning the Cubs narrowed the gap to 6-4 on a single by Dave Rosello and a home run by Monday, who had struck out five times yesterday. It was the 11th hit off Seaver and Berra promptly called for McGraw to hold off the Cubs.

McGraw responded by getting the final nine outs with only one ball hit out of the infield—a ground single by Rudolph in the ninth. The left-hander, pitching for the 60th time this year, struck out Rosello after Rudolph's hit, and when Glenn Beckert pinch-hit a looping fly behind first, Milner grabbed it and stepped on the bag to double off Rudolph and close out the Perils of Pauline.

For McGraw, the season's turnaround had been no less stunning than for the whole club. He didn't win a game until August, then won four and saved 12 during 17 appearances while the Mets rose implausibly through the ranks.

As they headed back to New York tonight, the Mets stood 1½ games ahead of St. Louis, 2½ in front of Pittsburgh, 3½ over Montreal and five over Chicago. They finished with the lowest winning percentage of any first-place team ever: 82 victories, 79 defeats for .509.

Since their melodramatic sweep in 1969, they had finished third three years in a row and had won 83 games in each of those years. This time, with one less victory, they took the big prize.

For the players, the aches and pains will be soothed by cash. For winning the division title each man is guaranteed $5,000. If they eventually win the World Series, the booty will total $20,000 apiece.

"I'm the eternal optimist," Seaver said while the locker room jumped and champagne flowed, "but this summer strained even my eternal optimism."

Mets' Box Score

METS (N.)	ab.r.h.bi	CHICAGO (N.)	ab.r.h.bi
Garrett, 3b	4 1 2 0	Monday, cf	4 2 3 2
Millan, 2b	5 1 2 0	Beckert, ph	1 0 0 0
Staub, rf	5 2 4 1	Kessinger, ss	4 0 1 1
Milner, 1b	3 1 0 1	Williams, lf	4 0 1 1
Jones, lf	3 1 1 1	Santo, 3b	4 0 0 0
Grote, c	4 0 2 2	Cardenal, rf	4 0 1 0
Hahn, cf	5 0 0 0	Marquez, 1b	3 0 2 0
Harrelson, ss	5 0 1 0	Fanzone, 1b	1 0 0 0
Seaver, p	3 0 1 0	Popovich, 2b	2 0 0 0
McGraw, p	0 0 0 0	Paul, b	0 0 0 0
		LaCoc , ph	1 0 0 0
		Aker, p	0 0 0 0
		Hickman, ph	1 0 0 0
		Locker, p	0 0 0 0
		Rudolph, c	4 1 3 2
		Hooton, p	1 0 0 0
		Rosello, 2b	3 1 1 0
Total	37 6 13 5	Total	37 4 12 4

```
Mets       010 220 100—6
Chicago    000 020 200—4
```

E—Santo. DP—Mets 2, Chicago 2. LOB—Mets 11, Chicago 6. 2B—Garrett, Harrelson. HRs—Jones (11), Monday (26). S—Garrett. SF—Milner.

	IP.	H.	R.	ER	BB.	SO.
Seaver (W. 19-10)	6	11	4	4	0	2
McGraw	3	1	0	0	0	4
Hooton (L. 14-17)	4	7	5	5	2	1
Paul	2	3	0	0	1	0
Aker	2	3	1	0	1	0
Locker	2	0	0	0	0	1

Save—McGraw (25). HBP—by Aker (McGraw). T—2:28. A—1,913.

October 2, 1973

Santo First to Veto Trade by His Club

By JOSEPH DURSO
Special to The New York Times

HOUSTON, Dec. 4—Baseball's winter trading market started to boom today when the Pittsburgh Pirates sent Nelson Briles to the Kansas City Royals and the Cincinnati Reds got Merv Rettenmund from the Baltimore Orioles for Ross Grimsley.

But the big news of the sport's business convention was made by a star player who refused to be traded: Ron Santo of the Chicago Cubs. He became the first major leaguer to invoke the new rule that allows a 10-year man to veto any deal, and he did it as the Cubs appeared on the verge of exchanging him for frontline pitching.

Santo, 34 years old, has been Chicago's third baseman for 14 seasons and has grown into a $110,000-a-year slugger with high value in the talent market. He hit 20 homers last season and was being hotly pursued by three or four clubs when he exercised his veto by telephone from his home in Chicago.

Santo conceded that he had been receiving vibrations that he was on the trading block, and he wasted no time refusing all offers. He acted under the "bill of rights" that the players won from the owners a year ago, specifically under a section that allows a man a choice if he has been in the majors 10 years, five with the same team.

"I got a call from John Holland today," Santo said in a telephone interview, referring to the Cubs' general manager. 'He didn't mention any clubs, but he did say that several were interested. I replied that I elected not to leave Chicago, for personal reasons."

It was learned that Holland also took the precaution of calling another senior slugger on the team, Billy Williams, the 36-year-old, $125,000 a-year left fielder.

He raised the same question: How would Williams react to a trade. And he got almost the same answer: Williams doubted that he would leave, but would think it over.

"He didn't say yes and he didn't say no," Holland acknowledged later.

The veto cast by Santo could be the first of many under the players' new privilege. In the National League, there are 16 men with enough service to qualify as "untouchables," ranging from Henry Aaron to Ed Kranepool. In the American, there are 11. But four veterans have recently acquiesced in trades: Willie McCovey, Jim Kaat, Jim Perry and Dick McAuliffe.

December 5, 1973

Aaron Hits 715th, Passes *Babe Ruth*

By JOSEPH DURSO
Special to The New York Times

ATLANTA, April 8—Henry Aaron ended the great chase tonight and passed Babe Ruth as the leading home-run hitter in baseball history when he hit No. 715 before a national television audience and 53,775 persons in Atlanta Stadium.

The 40-year-old outfielder for the Atlanta Braves broke the record on his second time at bat, but on his first swing of a clamorous evening. It was a soaring drive in the fourth inning off Al Downing of the Los Angeles Dodgers, and it cleared the fence in left-center field, 385 feet from home plate.

Skyrockets arched over the jammed stadium in the rain as the man from Mobile trotted around the bases for the 715th time in a career that began a quarter of a century ago with the Indianapolis Clowns in the old Negro leagues.

It was 9:07 o'clock, 39-years after Ruth had hit his 714th and four days after Aaron had hit his 714th on his first swing of the bat in the opening game of the season.

The history-making home run carried into the Atlanta bull pen, where a relief pitcher named Tom House made a dazzling one-handed catch against the auxiliary scoreboard. He clutched it against the boards, far below the grandstand seats, where the customers in "Home-Run Alley" were massed, waiting to retrieve a cowhide ball that in recent days had been valued as high as $25,000 on the auction market.

So Aaron not only ended the great home-run derby, but also ended the controversy that had surrounded it. His employers had wanted him to hit No. 715 in Atlanta, and had even benched him on alien soil in Cincinnati.

The commissioner of baseball, Bowie Kuhn, ordered the Braves to start their star yesterday or face "serious penalties." And tonight the dispute and the marathon finally came home to Atlanta in a razzle-dazzle setting.

The stadium was packed with its largest crowd since the Braves left Milwaukee and brought major league baseball to the Deep South nine years ago. Pearl Bailey sang the national anthem; the Jonesboro High School band marched; balloons and fireworks filled the overcast sky before the game; Aaron's life was dramatized on a huge color map of the United States painted across the outfield grass, and Bad Henry was serenaded by the Atlanta Boy Choir, which now includes girls.

The commissioner was missing, pleading that a "previous commitment" required his presence tomorrow in Cleveland, and his emissary was roundly booed when he mentioned Kuhn's name. But Gov. Jimmy Carter was there, along with Mayor Maynard Jackson, Sammy Davis Jr. and broadcasters and writers from as far away as Japan, South America and Britain.

To many Atlantans, it was like the city's festive premiere of "Gone With the Wind" during the 1930's when Babe Ruth was still the hero of the New York Yankees and the titan of professional sports. All that was needed to complete the evening was home run No. 715, and Aaron supplied that.

The first time he batted, leading off the second inning, Aaron never got the bat off his shoulder. Downing, a one-time pitcher for the Yankees, wearing No. 44, threw a ball and a called strike and then three more balls. Aaron, wearing his own No. 44, watched them all and then took first base while the crowd hooted and booed because their home town hero had been walked.

A few moments later, Henry scored on a double by Dusty Baker and an error in left field, and even made a little history doing that.

It was the 2,063d time he had crossed home plate in his 21-year career in the majors, breaking the National League record held by Willie Mays and placing Aaron behind Ty Cobb and Ruth, both American Leaguers.

Then came the fourth inning, with the Dodgers leading by 3-1 and the rain falling, with colored umbrellas raised in the stands and the crowd roaring every time Aaron appeared. Darrell Evans led off for Atlanta with a grounder behind second base that the shortstop, Bill Russell, juggled long enough for an error. And up came Henry for the eighth time this season and the second this evening.

Downing pitched ball one inside, and Aaron watched impassively. Then came the second pitch, and this time Henry took his first cut of the night. The ball rose high toward left-center as the

Braves' Box Score

LOS ANGELES (N.)	ab.	r.	h.	bi.	ATLANTA (N.)	ab.	r.	h.	bi.
Lopes, 2b	2	1	0	0	Garr, rf	3	0	0	1
Lacy, 2b	1	0	0	0	Lum, 1b	5	0	0	1
Buckner, lf	3	0	1	0	Evans...				
Wynn, cf	4	0	1	2	Evans, 3b	4	1	0	0
Ferguson, c	4	0	0	0	Aaron, lf	3	2	1	2
Crawford, rf	4	1	1	0	Office, cf	0	0	0	0
Cey, 3b	4	0	1	1	Baker, cf	2	1	1	0
Garvey, 1b	4	1	1	0	Johnson, 2b	3	1	1	0
Russell, ss	4	0	1	0	Foster, 2b	0	0	0	0
Downing, p	1	1	1	1	Correll, c	4	1	0	0
Marshall, p	1	0	0	0	Robinson, ss	0	0	0	0
Joshua, ph	1	0	0	0	Tepedino, ph	0	0	0	1
Hough, p	0	0	0	0	Perez, ss	2	1	1	0
Mota, ph	1	0	0	0	Reed, p	2	0	0	0
					Oates, ph	1	0	0	1
Total	34	4	7	4	Capra, p	0	0	0	0
					Total	29	7	4	6

Los Angeles .... 003 001 000—4
Atlanta .... 010 402 00x—7

E—Buckner, Cey, Russell 2, Lopes, Ferguson. LOB—Los Angeles 5, Atlanta 7. 2B—Baker, Russell, Wynn. HR—Aaron (2). S—Garr. SF—Garr.

	IP.	H.	R.	ER.	BB.	SO.
Downing, (L, 0-1)	3	2	5	2	4	2
Marshall	3	2	2	1	1	1
Hough	2	0	0	0	2	1
Reed (W, 1-0)	6	7	4	4	1	4
Capra	3	0	0	0	1	6

Save—Capra (1). Wild pitch—Reed. PB—Ferguson. T—2:27. A—53,775.

crowd came to its feet shouting, and as it dropped over the inside fence separating the outfield from the bull pen area, the skyrockets were fired and the scoreboard lights flashed in six-foot numerals: "715."

Aaron, head slightly bowed and elbows turned out, slowly circled the bases as the uproar grew. At second base he received a handshake from Dave Lopes of the Dodgers, and between second and third from Russell.

By now two young men from the seats had joined Aaron, but did not interfere with his 360-foot trip around the bases into the record books.

As he neared home plate, the rest of the Atlanta team had already massed beyond it as a welcoming delegation. But Aaron's 65-year-old father, Herbert Aaron Sr., had jumped out of the family's special field-level box and outraced everybody to the man who had broken Babe Ruth's record.

By then the entire Atlanta bull pen corps had started to race in to join the fun, with House leading them, the ball gripped tightly in his hand. He delivered it to Aaron, who was besieged on the grass about 20 feet in front of the field boxes near the Braves' dugout.

Besides the ball, Henry received a plaque from the owner of the team, Bill

Bartholomay; congratulations from Monte Irvin, the emissary from Commissioner Kuhn, and a howling, standing ovation from the crowd.

The game was interrupted for 11 minutes during all the commotion, after which the Braves got back to work and went on to win their second straight, this time by 7-4. The Dodgers, apparently shaken by history, made six errors and lost their first game after three straight victories.

"It was a fastball, right down the middle of the upper part of the plate," Downing said later. "I was trying to get it down to him, but I didn't and he hit it good—as he would."

"When he first hit it, I

didn't think it might be going. But like a great hitter, when he picks his pitch, chances are he's going to hit it pretty good."

Afterward the Braves locked their clubhouse for a time so that they could toast Aaron in champagne. Then the new home-run king reflected on his feat and on some intimations that he had not been "trying" to break the record in Cincinnati.

"I have never gone out on a ball field and given less than my level best," he said. "When I hit it tonight, all I thought about was that I wanted to touch all the bases."

April 9, 1974

Ryan Equals Record By Fanning 19 in Game

ANAHEIM, Calif., Aug. 12 (UPI)—Nolan Ryan, who came within two outs of a no-hitter in his last start, equaled the major league single-game strike-out mark by fanning 19 tonight while pitching the California Angels to a 4-2 triumph over the Boston Red Sox.

Ryan, who increased his major league leading strike-out total to 260, notched his 15th victory while tying the

major league record for most strikeouts in a single game established by Steve Carlton of the Philadelphia Phils in 1969 and Tom Seaver of the New York Mets in 1970. He broke Bob Feller's 36-year-old American League of 18 strikeouts.

Ryan also tied the major league record for most strikeouts in two consecutive games with 32. Luis Tiant of the Red Sox previously set the record.

August 13, 1974

Ryan's Fastball Clocked at 100.9 M.P.H.

ANAHEIM, Calif., Sept. 8 (AP)—Nolan Ryan almost matched his unpublicized record of 100.9 miles an hour for a pitched baseball last night and said he didn't care for the scientific scrutiny of his pitches. "I don't like to do it because it takes too much away from my concentration," the California Angel strike-out king said after beating the Chicago White Sox, 3-1. His fastest pitch recorded by infra-red radar was 100.8 m.p.h., a ninth-inning fastball to Bee Bee Richard, who wound up walking.

But it was disclosed before the game that Ryan actually broke Bob Feller's 28-year-old record of 98.6 m.p.h. last Aug. 20 when he struck out 19 Detroit Tigers in an 11-inning defeat. He threw 100.9 twice in that game, the first time against the Tigers' first batter, Ron LeFlore. The Angels said they did not reveal Ryan's Aug. 20 test because they had wanted to hold the contest last night where more than 6,000 fans guessed the speed. A crowd of 13,510 paid to see Ryan win his 18th game against 15 defeats. He gave up six hits, striking out nine and throwing 159 pitches.

September 9, 1974

Brock Breaks Record

ST. LOUIS, Sept. 10 (AP)—Lou Brock stole second base in the seventh inning of the Cardinals' game against the Philadelphia Phillies tonight and set a major league record of 105 stolen bases for one season.

Brock's theft, his second of the game, came during the Cards' 142d game and his 134th. It eclipsed the previous record of 104 set by the Los Angeles Dodgers' Maury Wills in 1962.

His first steal came in the opening inning following a single to left before an enthusiastic Busch Stadium crowd of 27,285.

Brock led off the seventh with a single to left. Following the steal, Brock's teammates and photographers poured onto the field and Brock was presented with the

historic base that he stole.

The game was stopped and Brock, who addressed the crowd, embraced the Cards' second baseman, Ted Sizemore, an injured player who usually bats behind him.

In a salute to his throng of admirers, the 35-year-old outfielder said, "The left-field fans probably knew I was going to steal 105 before I did. They were behind me all the way."

One of the dark moments for the crowd, however, was that the Cardinals lost, 8-2, and fell 3½ games behind Pittsburgh in the National League's Eastern Division. Mike Schmidt drove in four runs for the Phillies with a homer and two doubles, and Brock, trying for his 106th steal, was thrown out in the last inning.

PHILADELPHIA (N.)	ab.r.h.bi.	ST. LOUIS (N.)	ab.r.h.bi.
Cash, 2b	5 1 1 0	Brock, lf	5 1 2 0
Bowa, ss	4 3 2 0	Hunt, 2b	5 0 0 0
Schmidt, 3b	4 2 3 4	Smith, rf	4 1 2 1
Montanez, 1b	5 0 1 2	Simmons, c	4 0 1 1
Luzinski, lf	2 0 0 0	McBride, cf	3 0 1 0
Anderson, rf	0 0 0 0	Torre, 1b	4 0 0 0
Johnstone, lf	4 1 3 0	Reitz, 3b	4 0 1 0
Unser, cf	3 1 0 0	Tyson, ss	2 0 1 0
Boone, c	4 0 1 1	Hernandez, ph	0 0 0 0
Ruthven, p	4 0 1 1	Mumphrey, pr	0 0 0 0
		Siebert, p	0 0 0 0
		Cruz, ph	1 0 1 0
		Osteen, p	0 0 0 0
		Foster, p	2 0 0 0
		Folkers, p	0 0 0 0
		Dwyer, ph	1 0 0 0
		Heidemann, ss	1 0 0 0
Total	35 8 12 8	Total	36 2 9 2

Philadelphia   2 0 1 0 3 0 0 2 0—8
St. Louis   2 0 0 0 0 0 0 0 0—2

E—Boone, Ruthven, Bowa. DP—St. Louis 1. LOB—Philadelphia 5, St. Louis 10. 2B—Smith, Reitz, Johnstone, Schmidt 2. 3B—Bowa, Cash. HR—Schmidt (35). SB—Brock 2, Bowa, Johnstone, McBride.

	IP	H	R	ER	BB	SO
Ruthven (W, 9-11)	9	9	2	2	3	8
Foster (L, 7-10)	4	4	4	4	1	0
Folkers	2	2	1	1	2	3
Siebert	1	2	3	2	3	1
Osteen	1	0	0	0	0	0

T—2:43. A—27,285.

Brock, who had vowed to set the record before a home crowd, remained at first base for only one pitch before each steal.

He broke rapidly in the first inning as Philadelphia's

right-hander, Dick Ruthven, fired to the plate and reached second base well ahead of the throw.

In the seventh, Brock waited until the count was 0-1 and streaked to second, once again well ahead of the catcher's wide throw to the bag.

The thefts by Brock, who has been thrown out 29 times, also lifted him to 740 for his career, eclipsing the

previous record of 738 set by Max Carey of the Pittsburgh Pirates in 1929, his final season in the majors.

Only Ty Cobb, who has 892, and Eddie Collins, who had 743, stole more bases during their careers.

Brock, who has stolen 14 bases in 15 games this season against the Phillies, broke Carey's mark in the first inning after singling.

Ruthven, after yielding the

hit to Brock, threw a called strike to the Cardinals' Ron Hunt and tried one pickoff throw to first base before Brock took off on the second pitch.

His chase to the bag easily beat a throw into the dirt by the Philadelphia catcher, Bob Boone, and Brock continued on to third as the ball bounced into center field.

September 11, 1974

Baseball's Longest Night Ends 3½ Hours Before Sunrise

By JOSEPH DURSO

For all those anxious wives and mothers who telephoned Shea Stadium in the early morning hours yesterday, asking if there was a curfew on a baseball game, the answer—as they probably know by now—is no. At least, not for the team that Casey Stengel used to call "my amazing Mets."

If there were a curfew, then the Mets and St. Louis Cardinals would not have played 25 innings, starting shortly after 8 o'clock Wednesday night and ending at 3:13—a marathon that involved 50 players, 12 records, 15 dozen baseballs, five sweepings of the infield and many phone calls from worried relatives of the thousand or so diehard fans left from the original crowd of 13,460.

It was not the longest game in major league history, since it fell one inning short of the record of 26, played to a 1-1 tie in 1920 by the Brooklyn Dodgers and Boston Braves. Nor was it the longest in elapsed time: though it lasted 7 hours 4 minutes, it stopped 19 minutes shy of the record set by the Mets and San Francisco Giants on May 31, 1964. But it was the longest at night by any measure and even exceeded the previous longevity for the Mets, who went 24 innings in a night game at Houston in 1968.

But, apart from the fact that they lost all three of those never-ending games, the Mets did their bit to keep alive New York's reputation for late hours. And in that effort, they received support Wednesday night from the Yankees, who were playing, and also losing, in Baltimore in 17 innings and taking 4 hours 12 minutes to do it.

The Yankees started 2½ hours before the Mets because they were playing a double-header against the Orioles. But they still managed to go 17 innings in the first game and nine in the second before the American League's week-night curfew of 1 A.M. By then, the Mets were still grinding along back in Shea Stadium, wondering what would have happended if Ken Reitz of the Cardinals had not hit a two-run homer with two outs in the ninth and sent their game into five hours of extra innings.

Almanacs may someday note that the Mets finally lost the game, 4-3, and that the sun rose about three hours later at 6:34 A.M. Most of the players on both sides didn't get to bed until dawn, while a small army of 60 sweepers with brooms was cleaning out the debris until 9:30 in the morning when most of the city's commuters were already reaching their offices.

"I knew we were getting close to history," reflected Rusty Staub, the Mets' right-fielder. "I played all 24 innings in that game in Houston —against the Mets."

"Why does it always happen to me?" moaned Ed Sudol, the umpire at home plate, who called every pitch thrown to the record total of 202 batters.

It "always" happens to Sudol because he happens to be in the wrong place at the wrong time: around the Mets. He also was the umpire behind the plate when they went 23 innings in 1964 and when route to his personal record they went 24 in 1968. En of 25 innings this time, he got hit four times by baseballs and ejected Manager Yogi Berra from the game at 1:30 A.M. during a raging argument. So Yogi retreated to his office beneath the stands and watched glumly on his television set.

"I finally got home at 4:20," Berra reported when he arrived back at the stadium at 3:30 yesterday afternoon. "My wife and son Larry were with me, and one of the

neighbors who came to see the game.

"How does it feel? It feels bad. If you play 25 innings and win, you feel a lot better than when you play 25 and lose."

"I don't know," joked Joe Torre of the Cardinals, who saved the game with a diving catch in the 23d. "That was the fastest 25-inning game I ever played."

Nobody knows how much of the television audience

WEDNESDAY NIGHT

ST. LOUIS (N.)	ab.r.h.bi	METS (N.)	ab.r.h.bi
Brock	9 0 1 0	Harrelson, ss	7 0 0 0
Godby, lf	2 0 0 0	Boswell, 3b	4 0 0 0
Sizemore, 2b	10 1 1 0	Millan, 2b	10 1 4 0
Smith, rf	8 0 1 0	Jones, lf	9 2 3 2
Torre, 1b	*9 0 2 1	Webb, p	0 0 0 0
Simmons, c	3 0 1 0	Pemberton, ph	1 0 1 0
Herndon, pr	0 1 0 0	Milner, 1b	10 0 2 1
Hills, c	1 0 0 0	Garrett, ss	10 0 0 0
Scheinblm, ph	1 0 0 0	Schneck, cf	11 0 2 0
Billings, c	5 0 1 0	Ayala, rf	2 0 1 0
McBride, lf	10 1 4 0	Hahn, cf	6 0 0 0
Reitz, 3b	10 1 4 2	Gosger, lf	0 0 0 0
Tyson, ss	2 0 0 0	Dyer, c	9 0 2 0
Hernandez, ph	1 0 0 0	Boisclair, ph	1 0 0 0
Folkers, p	0 0 0 0	Hodges, c	0 0 0 0
Cruz, ph	1 0 0 0	Koosman, p	2 0 0 0
Bare, p	0 0 0 0	Martinez, ph	1 0 0 0
Osteen, p	4 0 0 0	Parker, p	0 0 0 0
Siebert, p	1 0 0 0	Kranepool, ph	1 0 0 0
Forsch, p	1 0 0 0	Miller, p	0 0 0 0
Melendez, ph	1 0 0 0	Theodore, ph	1 0 0 0
Garman, p	0 0 0 0	Apodaca, p	1 0 0 0
Hunt, ph	1 0 0 0	Cram, p	3 0 1 0
Hrabosky, p	0 0 0 0	Staub, rf	1 0 0 0
Dwyer, ph	0 0 0 0		
Heidemann, ss	6 0 3 0		
Total	**86 4 18 3**	**Total**	**89 3 16 3**

*Awarded first base on obstruction by catcher.

St. Louis .100 000 002 000 000 000 000 1—4
Mets .100 020 000 000 000 000 000 0—3

E—Tyson, Schneck, Dyer, Osteen, Webb, Hodges. DP—St. Louis 1, Mets 2. LOB—St. Louis 20, Mets 25. 2B—Milner, Schneck 2. HRs—Jones (13), Reitz (6). SB—McBride. S—Koosman, Forsch, Millan, McBride, Jones.

	IP.	H.	R.	ER.BB.SO.
Forsch	6	5	3	2 4 3
Garman	2	0	0	0 0 2
Hrabosky	3	2	0	0 0 3
Folkers	3	3	0	0 1 3
Bare	⅓	0	0	0 1 0
Osteen	9⅓	4	0	0 2 3
Siebert (W, 8-8)	2⅓	2	0	0 3 1
Koosman	9	5	3	3 4 5
Parker	3	2	0	0 0 1
Miller	1	1	0	0 0 1
Apodaca	3	2	0	0 1 1
Cram	8	7	0	0 2 4
Webb (L, 0-1)	1	1	1	1 0 0

HBP—by Koosman (Tyson), Parker (Dwyer). Wild pitch—Forsch, Koosman, Cram. PB—Simmons. T—7:04. A—13,460.

```
STL
24 LF
41 2B
7 RF
9 1B
12 C
21 CF
```

TONIGHT'S GAME FELL 1 INNING SHORT OF THE 26-INNING DODGERS-BRAVES LONGEST GAME IN HISTORY--MAY 1 1920   AND IS LONGEST IN TIME

stayed awake to the finish, but the Mets estimated that about a thousand hardy souls were still in the park when Bake McBride scored the deciding run on a wild pickoff throw by the pitcher, Hank Webb, and a fumbled throw home by the catcher, Ron Hodges.

The hot-dog venders had left the aisles in the ninth inning (around 10:20 P.M.), as they customarily do, but half the refreshment stands—and the Diamond Club upstairs—stayed in business to the bitter end.

"It was a good crowd," said James K. Thomson, vice president of the Mets, who has run stadiums for the Yankees, Dodgers and Mets. "One guy was even dancing in the aisles every inning in right field. It amazes me that the people stay that late. At 3 in the morning, you had a chant of 'Let's Go, Mets.' You didn't have it by many people, but you had it.

"It takes six to eight hours to sweep out the place after a game. They usually start at midnight because we don't sweep with people still in the seats. This time, they started at 3:30 in the morning and

kept going till 9:30. Everybody sort of worked a double day. We had 85 special guards on duty from 6 P.M. They usually work six hours. This time, they stayed until 4 in the morning.

"On electricity, it might cost us $1,700 to $2,000 alone. We pay a flat amount each month whether we turn the lights on or not, say $12,000. Then, when you do turn them on, there's what they call an energy charge, and that's where it cost us last night."

At 1:30 A.M., about the time Yogi Berra was getting the judicial heave-ho, a woman who had been listening to the game on the radio in Manhattan made a decision: She was so entranced that she drove out to the stadium in Flushing and bought two gift certificates for tickets to future games. She was able to buy them at that hour because the advanced-ticket window always stays open until the game ends—and this time it was open until 3:13 A.M.

The gift certificates were sold to her by Joe Millan, who was manning the office and who was impressed. But

he was distracted by a personal problem: He is also a student at Brooklyn College and he had an 8 A.M. class.

Emma Fuchs, chief telephone operator for the Mets, may have set a staff record during the marathon. She went to work at 9 o'clock Wednesday morning as usual, wondered why her relief operator didn't show up at 5:30 as usual, then ran the switchboard herself until 3:30 Thursday morning, completing an 18½-hour day.

Ralph Kiner, who never played 25 innings in one game as a home-run hitter, had his own endurance test as one of the Mets' broadcasters. He left the TV booth in the eighth to go below the stands to the studio where he conducts "Kiner's Corner" after the game. "I sat around for five hours working like mad," he said. "Every inning we had to change the film strips for the show. We kept getting new heroes."

Other endurance feats were performed by the nine players who went the full distance, three of the four umpires who never left the field; Commissioner Bowie Kuhn and his wife, who came out

to see Lou Brock and who wound up seeing seven hours of baseball; Brock, who got one hit in nine times at bat but who was thrown out trying to steal base No. 106 of the season; Claude Osteen, who pitched 9 1-3 scoreless innings for St. Louis without getting the victory; Duffy Dyer, who caught 23 innings for the Mets without setting a record (though a woman telephoned the Mets to complain that his uniform was dirty) and McBride, who sprinted from first base all the way home on the fateful pickoff throw.

The crowning irony of it all was that Bob Engel, the umpire at first base, called a balk on Webb's wild throw to first base in the 25th. Not many persons realized it and nothing was changed by it. But Engel said later, "before they revised the rule a few years ago, the runner would have been stopped at second base."

"Under that rule," he said, with a shudder, "McBride might not have scored and they could still be playing the game."

September 13, 1974

Ryan Pitches Third No-Hitter

By United Press International

ANAHEIM, Calif., Sept. 28 —Nolan Ryan pitched the third no-hitter of his career tonight, striking out 15 Minnesota batters and winning his 22d game of the season in a 4-0 victory for the California Angels over the Twins.

Ryan, traded by the New York Mets three seasons ago at age 24, became the sixth pitcher in major league history to throw three no-hitters. He joined Sandy Koufax, the only man to pitch four; Bob

Feller, Jim Maloney, Larry Corcoran and Cy Young.

The Angels' right-hander, who already this year has become the first pitcher to surpass 300 strikeouts for three seasons in a row, has 367 now to go with his major-league record 383 in 1973 and 329 in 1972.

He pitched no-hitters last season against the Kansas City Royals and Detroit Tigers and has thrown three one-hitters.

MINNESOTA (A.)	ab. r. h. bi.	CALIFORNIA (A.)	ab. r. h. bi.
Brye, cf	2 0 0 0	Nettles, rf	4 1 2 3
Carew, 2b	2 0 0 0	Doyle, 2b	4 0 1 0
Braun, 3b	3 0 0 0	Bochte, 1b	3 0 0 1
Darwin, rf	4 0 0 0	Lahoud, dh	4 0 1 0
Oliva, dh	4 0 0 0	Stanton, rf	4 0 1 0
Histle, lf	3 0 0 0	Chalk, 3b	2 1 0 0
Bourque, 1b	3 0 0 0	Balaz, lf	2 1 1 0
Killebrew, ph	0 0 0 0	Meoli, ss	2 1 1 0
Terrel, pr	0 0 0 0	Egan, c	2 0 0 0
Gomez, ss	2 0 0 0	Ryan, p	0 0 0 0
Soderholm, ss	2 0 0 0		
Borgman, c	3 0 0 0		
Decker, p	0 0 0 0		
Butler, p	0 0 0 0		
Total	27 0 0 0	Total	27 4 7 4

```
Minnesota .............. 000 000 000—0
California .............. 002 200 00x—4
E—Braun. LOB—Minnesota 8, California 4.
2B—Meoli, Balaz. SB—Nettles. S—Egan. SF—
Bochte.
```

	IP.	H.	R.	ER.	BB.	SO.
Decker (L. 16-14)	3⅔	4	2	1	0	1
Butler	5⅓	3	2	2	3	8
Ryan (W, 22-16)	9	0	0	0	8	15

T—2:22. A—10,872.

September 29, 1974

Frank Robinson Is First Black Manager

By DAVE ANDERSON
Special to The New York Times

CLEVELAND, Oct. 3—With the poise that has characterized his career as a slugger of 574 home runs and as a clubhouse leader, Frank Robinson was named today by the Cleveland Indians as major league baseball's first black manager. He received a one-year contract.

At a crowded news conference in Cleveland Stadium, a congratulatory telegram from President Ford was read by Phil Seghi, the Indians' general manager, who chose the 39-year-old Robinson to succeed Ken Aspromonte as the American League team's 28th manager and ninth player-manager, the most of any major league team.

President Ford described Robinson's selection as "welcome news for baseball fans across the nation" and a "tribute to you personally, to your athletic skills and to your unsurpassed leadership." Attending the news conference were Bowie Kuhn, the Commissioner of Baseball, and Lee MacPhail, the president of the American League.

"We got something done," Kuhn commented, "that we should have done before."

Wearing a black and white plaid suit with a vest, Robinson attempted to reduce his sociological burden.

"The only reason I'm the first black manager is that I was born black," he said calmly. "That's the color I am. I'm not a superman, I'm not a miracle worker. Your ballplayers determine how good a team you have. I might influence the ballplayers to some extent, but if we have a good team, they deserve the credit. If a ball club fails, I think the manager should be held responsible. I want to be judged by the play on the field."

Asked if he foresaw any additional pressure on him to succeed as a black manager, he replied:

"I don't see any pressure. I don't see any goals I have to achieve as the first black manager. The pressure from within is not there."

He was hired nearly three decades after the late Jackie Robinson was the major league's first black player in 1947.

"I thank the Lord that Jackie Robinson was the man he was in that position," the Indians' new manager said. "If he wasn't it would have set back the whole idea of signing more black players. The one wish I could have is that Jackie Robinson could be here today to see this happen."

Asked if he believed a similar reponsibility to succeed as a manager now was on him, Robinson replied:

"No, this is a different ball game altogether. Different society. I just hope baseball people don't say, 'All right, Frank Robinson is the first black manager, we have one, that's it.' In my heart, I don't think I was hired because I was black. I hope not. I think I've been hired because of my ability."

"Frank Robinson sits before you," Seghi said, "because I think he has the qualities that I was searching for in a manager, not because he was black or white. He has all the leadership qualities necessary to lead a major league ball club. You know what he did at Cincinnati, you know what he did in Baltimore; he's a true leader."

Robinson helped the Baltimore Orioles represent the American League in four World Series in his six seasons there. He had led the Reds to one National League pennant. He is the only major leaguer selected the most valuable player in both leagues. Through 19 seasons he has a career .295 average with 2,900 hits and 1,778 runs batted in.

Now a designated hitter, Robinson will be the major league's first playing manager since Solly Hemus of the St. Louis Cardinals in 1959. Eddie Joost, with the Philadelphia Athletics in 1954, was the American League's last playing manager.

His salary of $175,000 next season was agreed upon shortly after the Indians acquired him on Sept. 12 from the California Angels for the $20,000 waiver price. When the managerial position later developed, he sought a two-year contract through 1976, but accepted the one-year offer in return for the opportunity to fulfill his ambition to be a manager.

As a playing manager, Robinson will receive the same $175,000 plus the fringe benefits accorded managers such as a hotel suite on road trips and an expense account. Unlike other managers, he also will receive living expenses in Cleveland next year and the use of an automobile here. His contract was negotiated by Ed Keating of International Management, Inc.

In listing Robinson's credentials, Seghi also mentioned his five seasons managing Santurce in the Puerto Rican winter league.

In five seasons there, Robinson's teams finished first twice, third twice and fourth once. When he joined Santurce for the 1968-69 season, he was the first American black to manage an integrated team of white, black and Latin players.

During nearly two hours of questions and answers, Robinson spoke easily and articulately, more so than many major league managers. At the formal news conference in the stadium club, he was flanked by Seghi; Nick Mileti, the Indians' president, and Ted Bonda, the Indians' executive vice president. Later, in the press room, he sat with his wife, Barbara Ann, and Seghi while continuing to discuss his managerial philosophies:

¶On discipline: "I can't say I've never missed a curfew, but I've never been caught. I believe men are men. I'm not going to set a time limit on when they have to be in the hotel. I'm not going to be a baby-sitter. I'm not going to sit in the lobby to see who's late. I'll need my sleep because I'll be playing myself. But if I walk into a cocktail lounge and see a couple of players, I won't expect them to run out. I might even buy them a drink now that I've got an expense account."

¶On arguing with umpires: "I don't think I've had trouble with umpires. I've been thrown out of about 15 games in Puerto Rico in five seasons. But only twice last year. I select my words better now. Any manager that goes through a season without being thrown out isn't doing his job. You've got to show your players you're backing them up. And you've got to show the umpires that you're not going to let them run over you."

¶On his coaches: "I haven't had time to sit down and select my staff. I have a few people in mind, but I haven't talked to them yet. I'll say this, if I select two black coaches and one white coach, I don't want people reading anything into that. And if I select two white coaches and one black coach, I don't want people reading anything into that either. I'll pick my coaches on ability, people I think can do the job."

¶On himself as a player: "I'm counting on Frank Robinson the manager to talk to Frank Robinson the player. I'll be the first one not to write Frank Robinson's name in the line-up."

¶On the Indians, who finished fourth in the American League East with a 77-85 won-lost record: "In the years I was in Baltimore, we always figured we could win three out of four with the Indians and maybe all four. But this year the Indians became a team to be reckoned with. I think the strong part of the ball club is offense. Every team needs more pitching. But in my heart, I don't think there's a team in the American League with the youth and experience we have."

¶On the demand of Gaylord Perry, the Indians' ace pitcher, for $1 more in salary than Robinson's $175,000 contract: "I don't negotiate salaries. Mr. Seghi handles that. I don't think Gaylord and I are incompatible. Gaylord's a real competitor and a real professional. So am I, and if he's satisfied, I'm sure we'll get along."

With a one-year contract, the Indians' new manager obviously is on trial, but he commented:

"I hope that in September next year I will have justified the Indians' confidence in me and that I'll be rehired. If not, I don't foresee any problem in firing me or any black manager if he's not doing the job. If the Indians aren't satisfied with the job I'm doing, fire me. There won't be any repercussions.

"The public is pretty smart. That guy up in the stands knows if you're doing a good job or not."

October 4, 1974

A's Win World Series For Third Straight Time

By JOSEPH DURSO
Special to The New York Times

OAKLAND, Calif., Oct. 17 —The Oakland A's, fussing and feuding to the end, swept to their third straight baseball championship tonight when they defeated the Los Angeles Dodgers, 3-2, and won the 71st World Series.

Only one team in baseball history has won more World Series in consecutive years than the controversial and frequently rowdy American League champions—the New York Yankees. The Yankees won four straight starting in 1936 and five straight starting in 1949, but tonight the A's moved right behind them into the record book.

"Their record speaks for itself," conceded Manager Walter Alston of the Dodgers, whose team won 102 games this summer with the best performance in the major leagues. "They play the game the way it should be played. They don't make any mistakes."

They didn't make any tonight before 49,347 fans in the Oakland-Alameda County Stadium as they stopped the Dodgers for the third night in a row and took the Series four games to one.

At least, they didn't make any mistakes that could not be salvaged by late theatrics, and the theatrics were supplied chiefly by Joe Rudi in the seventh inning when he broke a 2-2 tie with a resounding home run off Mike Marshall, who was pitching in his 113th game of the year.

Rudi settled the issue just after the fans in the left-field seats had littered the grass with debris and at least one whisky bottle. The game was delayed briefly while the Dodgers considered taking shelter, but the outcome was not long delayed after the game was resumed and Rudi swung against Marshall.

In an era of workhorse relief pitching, Marshall was working for the fifth time in a five-game match. But Oakland produced an iron man of its own: Rollie Fingers, the man with the Svengali mustache who appeared 76

times during the six-month regular season and four times in the Series. The 29-year-old Ohioan worked the final two innings tonight, protected the lead provided by Rudi and then was voted the most valuable player on the scene.

So for the third October in a row, champagne flowed in the often tumultuous clubhouse of Charles O. Finley's ball team, including some that Reggie Jackson poured over the head of the commissioner of baseball, Bowie Kuhn, on national television.

Some of the best men on the Oakland team were still demanding to be traded from Finley's heavy-handed grip. The best pitcher, Jim (Catfish) Hunter, was still pursuing a grievance claim for half his $100,000 salary and his outright release. And there were reminders of the customary bickering in a season that was enlivened

by a fistfight or two and by the best record in recent times: four Western Division titles in a row, three American League pennants in a row and three world championships.

There was even the flashback to the rowdyism of recent years by fans in other cities. This time it broke out not long after the relief specialists had taken over for the starting pitchers — Vida Blue and Don Sutton, two of the heroes of the playoffs. But when it subsided, the A's charged ahead and won with their usual flourishes.

They also won by the usual score of 3-2, which proved the final score in four of the five games played since last Saturday — the first two in Los Angeles and the last three in Oakland in the first all-California World Series. And when Fingers retired the Dodgers in order in the ninth, the A's fans tumbled onto the grass and littered it with debris while Manager Alvin Dark surveyed the situation and said:

"I know a lot of people aren't going to understand this, but I say: Glory to God. I've leaned on him all through this season, and I'll continue to do so."

If the A's felt any nervousness about their date with history, because of their

strange behavior on such occasions in the past, they didn't betray it. Nor did Manager Dark, who took over the Oakland team this season after Dick Williams made an "abdication speech" on national television moments after the A's had defeated the Mets in last year's Series.

In fact, the A's seemed as unimpressed by events as ever, and they wasted no time treating Blue to a lead after he had retired the first three Dodger batters. Bert Campaneris led the charge as Oakland's first batter by lining a single to left field. Then Bill North twisted a double-play grounder to Bill Russell at shortstop, but the Dodgers didn't put enough zip into it and settled for the force-out at second base.

They lived to regret it when North promptly stole second and continued on to third after Steve Yeager's throw carried wide of the bag into right-center field. Then Sal Bando, with only one single in 13 times at bat in the Series. fetched the run home with a sacrifice fly to Bill Buckner in left field.

For a while it looked as though the A's were not only relaxed but also greedy. Reggie Jackson drew a base on balls; Rudi rammed a

Sal Bando leaping onto Ray Fosse, catcher, and other jubilant A's, as team celebrated its third straight World Series title by beating the Dodgers, 3-2.

Ray Fosse of the A's stroking a Don Sutton pitch for a home run in the second inning at Oakland last night.

Box Score of Fifth Series Game

LOS ANGELES [N.]	AB.	R.	H.	BI.	OAKLAND [A.]	AB.	R.	H.	BI.
Lopes, 2b	2	1	0	0	Campaneris, ss	4	0	2	0
Buckner, lf	3	0	1	0	North, cf	4	1	0	0
Wynn, cf	2	0	0	1	Bando, 3b	3	0	0	1
Garvey, 1b	4	0	1	1	Jackson, rf	2	0	0	0
Ferguson, rf	4	0	1	0	Rudi, 1b	3	1	2	1
Cey, 3b	3	0	1	0	C.Washington, lf	3	0	1	0
Russell, ss	3	0	0	0	Fingers, p	0	0	0	0
Crawford, ph	1	0	0	0	Fosse, c	3	1	1	1
Yeager, c	2	0	0	0	Green, 2b	3	0	0	0
Joshua, ph	1	0	0	0	Blue, p	2	0	0	0
Sutton, p	1	0	0	0	Odom, p	0	0	0	0
Paciorek, ph	1	1	1	0	Tenace, 1b	1	0	0	0
Marshall, p	0	0	0	0					
Total	**27**	**2**	**5**	**2**	**Total**	**28**	**3**	**6**	**3**

Los Angeles ......0 0 0 0 0 2 0 0 0—2
Oakland ....1 1 0 0 0 0 1 0 x—3

Errors—Yeager, North. Double plays—Oakland 1. Left on base—Los Angeles 6, Oakland 3. Two-base hits—Paciorek. Home runs Fosse (1), Rudi (1). Stolen bases—North, Campaneris. Sacrifice—Buckner. Sacrifice flies—Bando, Wynn.

	IP	H	R	ER	BB	SO
Sutton	5	4	2	2	1	3
Marshall (L, 0-1)	3	2	1	1	0	4
Blue	6⅔	4	2	2	5	4
Odom (W, 1-0)	⅓	0	0	0	0	0
Fingers	2	1	0	0	1	0

Save—Fingers (2). Time of game—2:23. Attendance—49,347.

single through the middle of the infield to center, and Sutton was surrounded by more trouble than he'd seen during his eight innings against Oakland last Sunday. But he survived it when Claudell Washington lifted a fly to right field for the final out.

In the second inning, Sutton pitched one strike to Ray Fosse, who had only one single in 11 times at bat. Then the 27-year-old catcher from Ohio drove a high home run into the seats in left field. That made it 2-0, Oakland, and it proved the final run allowed this year by Sutton, who won 12 straight games and 16 of his previous 17. It also guaranteed that Fosse would be remembered this season for something more than the neck injury he had suffered while breaking up a locker-room fight between Jackson and North.

After that, Sutton retired 11 of the next 12 batters—but they were the last 12 he faced because he was lifted for a pinch hitter in the top of the sixth with the A's still nursing their two-run lead.

They didn't nurse it for long, though. The pinch-hitter, Tom Paciorek, drilled the first pitch he saw into left-

center and it skipped to the wall for a double. Dave Lopes walked and Buckner, trying to get both runners into scoring position, duly bunted and did just that.

Now it was up to the fat part of the Los Angeles batting order—Wynn, the No. 3 hitter, and Steve Garvey, the No. 4. They produced, too, starting with a sacrifice fly to deep left field by Wynn for one run and ending with a single to left by Garvey for another. And for Garvey, the batting star of the Series, the hit was his eighth in 20 trips to the plate.

That's when the Dodgers got back in the game and that's when they turned over their game to Mike Marshall, who had pitched 106 times in their 162 regular-season games and who now was pitching for the fifth straight time in the World Series.

Marshall, a Ph.D. candidate at Michigan State, is a silent and often grim 31-year-old who gets votes as baseball's leading intellectual snob. He also gets votes as baseball's leading relief pitcher and, as he entered the game in the sixth inning, he had faced 21 batters so far in the Series and had produced 18 outs.

Marshall also won 15 games, "saved" 21 and threw just nine home-run pitches in 208 innings this season. He was a pitching fool—or, considering his academic attainments, a pitching genius. But after he had wiped out the side in the sixth inning, he went out to the mound for the seventh and immediately rediscovered why people associate the Oakland A's with bizarre things.

As Marshall warmed up, a fan in the left-field bleachers tossed an empty whisky bottle that landed in the vicinity of Buckner, the Los Angeles left fielder. Assorted other debris drifted down, somewhat in the manner of the garbage-flinging incident in the playoff game in Shea Stadium a year ago between the Mets and Cincinnati Reds.

Buckner decided that he wouldn't stay out there in the line of fire, so he came trotting in to complain to the umpires. Manager Alston joined him from the dugout, and Marshall joined him from the mound. It took a few minutes for the groundskeepers to clear off the **debris, then Marshall—without taking any more warmup pitches—turned to face Rudi leading off the bottom of the seventh.**

Rudi, who lost an arbitration hearing on his salary last February and had to set-

tle for $55,000, wasted no time making his point this time. He pulled the first pitch high into the second deck of the overhanging grandstand down the left-field line, and the amazing A's were back in front, 3-2.

They didn't seem too amazing in the top of the eighth, though, when Rollie Fingers took over Oakland's pitching and Buckner greeted him with a single to center that got past North in the outfield. By the time the ball was retrieved by Jackson, backing up the play, Buckner was circling second base and heading for third.

But the A's turned amazing again in the nick of time. As Buckner slid into the bag, the ball arrived in relays: Jackson, the rightfielder, to Dick Green, the secondbaseman, to Bando for a photo-finish out that sealed off potentially big trouble.

"It was something I did all year, and I'll do it again." Buckner said later, defending his unlucky dash to third base. "I can't stop taking a chance just because I got caught once."

"He did the only thing you could," Sutton said, joining Buckner's defense. "You've got to go for the run."

"They were just wild," Wynn complained, meaning the Oakland fans. "We got potatoes, balls, bottles and a little bit of everything thrown at us. I can see getting excited, but not throwing bottles and potatoes, you could get hurt."

"I got hit by an apple and was just missed by a whisky bottle," Buckner added. "The people that did those things were not good baseball fans.

Otherwise, they would have showed up during the year."

Marshall, who frequently refuses to discuss his performance after a game, refused this time to speculate on the throwing of the debris. Alston, Marshall's manager, said he doubted that the de-

lay had affected the pitcher. But Marshall skipped past that line of reasoning and tipped his hat to the champions.

"The A's played good baseball and won," he said. "It was good to see good fundamental baseball. The A's

played a tremendous Series. They did everything they had to, to score runs. What can you say when you do your best?"

October 18, 1974

Stennett Gets 7 Hits As Pirates Win, 22-0

CHICAGO, Sept. 16 (AP)— Rennie Stennett set a modern major league record with seven straight hits today as the Pittsburgh Pirates trounced the Chicago Cubs, 22-0, in the most lopsided shutout in modern major league history.

Stennett also tied a major league mark by twice collecting two hits in a single inning in one game. He had two doubles and four singles before tripling in the eighth, setting the record. He then was lifted for a pinch-runner.

The Pirates collected 24 hits at Wrigley Field and every player in the starting line-up had at least one hit and scored at least one run.

Their 22-run total was the highest in the majors this season and the most in the National League since Sept. 2, 1957, when the Milwaukee Braves routed the Cubs, 23-10.

Dave Parker hit his 24th home run and Richie Hebner his 15th. The onslaught included a 14-batter, nine-run first inning and an 11-batter, six run fifth inning.

John Candelaria, a rookie left-hander, raised his won-lost record to 8-5. He allowed three Chicago hits before he was lifted after the seventh inning.

Only three players before Stennett twice got two hits

in a single inning —three in the same game—Max Carey of Pittsburgh in 1925, John Hodapp of Cleveland in 1928 and Sherm Lollar of the Chicago White Sox in 1955.

Stennett's seven consecutive hits in a regulation game was achieved only once in major league history, by Wilbert Robinson of the Baltimore Orioles in 1892. Bill Madlock of the Cubs became this year the 22d player to get six hits in modern—after 1900—history.

The Pirates' 22-0 triumph surpassed the record of 21-0 set in 1901 by Detroit against Cleveland and matched in 1939 by the New York Yankees against the Philadelphia Athletics.

The victory also strengthened the Pirate's hold on first place in the National League East and moved them closer to their fifth title in the last six years.

Rick Reuschel, 10-16, start-

ed for the Cub but gave up six hits and two walks before being relieved with only one out in the first inning. Four Chicago relievers followed. Ken Brett worked two perfect innings in relief of Candelaria.

Stennett also scored five runs, high in the National League this year. Parker had five runs batted in, while Hebner, Willie Stargell and Frank Taveras each had three.

Stennett singled to open the game and later doubled in the first inning. His third-inning single preceded Hebner's home run. In the fifth, Stennett collected a double didn't allow his 24-year-old and a single. He got his sixth hit in the seventh inning and he tripled to short right in the eighth. His batting average rose from .278 to .287.

Manager Danny Murtagh of the Pirates said he almost second baseman get a chance at the record of seven hits. "I thought the record was six hits in a game and I kept wanting to take him out to rest him, but he kept getting hits," said Murtagh.

Rennie Stennett (6) returning to applause in Pirate dugout after his seventh hit in game at Chicago yesterday against the Cubs set major league record.

Associated Press

PITTSBURGH (N.)					CHICAGO (N.)				
	ab	r	h	bi		ab	r	h	bi
Stennett 2b	7	5	7	2	Kessinger 3b	3	0	0	0
Fang inb 2b	0	0	0	0	Dunn 3b	2	0	0	0
Hebner 3b	7	3	2	3	Tyrone lf	4	0	0	0
AOliver cf	4	2	1	1	JeMrales rf	3	0	0	0
D Jose cf	1	0	0	0	LaCock 1b	1	0	0	0
Stargel 1b	5	2	3	3	Cardenal rf	2	0	1	0
Robetsn 1b	3	1	1	0	Harris cf	1	0	0	0
DParker rf	5	1	2	5	Thornton 1b	3	0	1	0
Zisk lf	5	2	2	1	PRussl ss	0	0	0	0
Sanguil'n c	5	2	2	1	Trillo 2b	3	0	0	0
Brett p	1	0	0	0	Sperring 2b	1	0	0	0
Taveras ss	6	1	3	3	Mitterwald c	3	0	0	0
Candela p	5	1	2	2	Roselio ss	2	0	1	0
Ott ph	1	0	0	0	RRusl p	0	0	0	0
					Dettore p	0	0	0	0
					Zamora p	0	0	0	0
					Hosley ph	1	0	0	0
					Schultz p	0	0	0	0
					Summers rf	1	0	0	0
Total	53	22	24	21	Total	30	0	3	0

Pittsburgh............. 902 162 200—22
Chicago................ 000 000 000— 0

E—Dettore, Roselio, Dunn. LOB—Pittsburgh 12, Chicago 3. 2B—Stennett 2. 3B—Stennett. HR—Hebner (15), D. Parker (24). SF—D.Parker.

	IP	H	R	ER	BB	SO
Candelaria (W,8-5)	7	3	0	0	0	5
Brett	2	0	0	0	0	0
RRuscl (L,10-16)	1-3	6	8	2	0	0
Dettore	2 2-3	7	8	7	2	1
Zamora	4	4	2	2	0	2
Schultz	1	4	4	2	0	1
P.Reuschal	1	0	0	1	0	0

HBP—by Dettore (D.Parker). WP—Dettore. T—2:35. A—4,932.

September 17, 1975

Designated-Hitter Rule Restores Homer Parity

By LEONARD KOPPETT

Baseball offense in 1975 stayed at essentially the same level as the two preceding years, with the American League's designated hitter giving that league a discernible btu not very significant edge in power over the National, which doesn't allow the pitcher to escape coming to bat.

This was the third season that the leagues had different rules, and once again it was clear that the main contribution of the designated hitters was in home runs: They produced the same batting average as all the other players, but hit more home runs than other parts of the batting order (that is, more than one-ninth of the total), and far more than pitchers would hit.

Here is the three-year profile, with all the figures applying to both teams in one game:

	1973	1974	1975
Runs gm., A.L.	8.55	8.20	8.60
Runs gm., N.L.	8.30	8.30	8.25
Homers, A.L.	1.60	1.41	1.52
Homers, N.L.	1.60	1.32	1.27
Bat. Avg., A.L.	.257	.256	.258
Bat. Avg. N.L.	.254	.255	.257

These offensive levels are consistent with those of the late nineteen-fifties, before the majors expanded from 16 teams to 24 and before there was tampering with the rule-book definition of the strike zone.

Before adopting the designated-hitter rule, the American was falling far behind the National in run production. In 1972, the American hit nine points lower in batting average, scored 824 fewer runs and hit 184 fewer homers than the National. So the innovation did restore parity, and gave the American even a little more offense than the National.

Almost the entire difference is the home runs hit by the designated hitters. This year they hit 222, last year 167, the first year 227. Since the American League's total of homers exceeded the Nationals by 231 (1,464 to 1,-233), the effect is clear.

But the designated hitters have never compiled quite as high a batting average as all the others players in the league. In 1973 and 1974, their combined average was two points lower than the league average (which includes them); this year it was four points lower, at .254.

One other effect of the designated hitter has been to reduce the number of shut-outs in the American League —but it still has more score-less games pitched than the National. Here are the figures.

Year	A.L.	N.L.
1972	193	164
1973	150	143
1974	144	142
1975	137	129

In short, all the available measures indicate that the drastically different rules do not have a very great effect.

October 12, 1975

Red Sox Win to Tie Series

Fisk Homer Beats Reds, 7-6, in 12th, Forcing 7th Game

By JOSEPH DURSO
Special to The New York Times

BOSTON, Wednesday, Oct. 22—The Boston Red Sox rose to dramatic heights early this morning when they defeated the Cincinnati Reds, 7-6, on a 12th-inning home run by Carlton Fisk and stretched the World Series into a seventh and deciding game.

It was a tingling four-hour marathon that ended at 12:33 after the Red Sox had raised all sorts of rumpus before a roaring crowd of 35,205 in Fenway Park and a national television audience. They took a 3-0 lead the first time they batted, they lost it five innings later, they fell behind by 6-3 in the eighth and then four outs from losing the final honors of the baseball season, they struck back with theatrical flourishes.

Their first flourish was a three-run, pinch-hit homer in the bottom of the eighth by Bernie Carbo, who had pinch-hit a home run a week ago in Cincinnati. Then, while a record total of 12 pitchers tried to establish some sort of order on both sides, the Red Sox failed to score with the bases loaded and nobody out in the ninth; they survived a Cincinnati threat in the 11th on a circus catch by Dwight Evans in right field, and they won it on the second pitch to Fisk in the 12th.

As a result, the champions of the American League tied the champions of the National League at three games apiece in one of the most colorful matches in the 72-year history of the World Series. They will grapple for the title and the prize money of about $20,000 a man tonight at 8:30, with Bill Lee pitching for Boston and Don Gullett for Cincinnati. •

"The way I hurt all over," said Sparky Anderson, manager of the Reds, after they had missed a great chance for their first championship in 35 years, "it was probably as good a ball game as I've ever seen. A great game in a great series. And that catch by Evans in the 11th was as good a catch as you'll see."

"It was a fantastic game," agreed Fisk, a 27-year-old catcher from Vermont, who ended it against Pat Darcy in the 12th. "You're not exactly on top of the world when you're trailing a club like the Cincinnati Reds, 6-3, with four outs to go. Pete Rose came up to me in the 10th and said, 'This is some kind of game, isn't it?' And I said, 'Some kind of game.'"

"We had the championship within our grasp tonight," said Joe Morgan, the second baseman and leading base-stealer for the Reds, "and we'll have it within our grasp tomorrow night. We let it get away."

The big, bad "mean machine" of Cincinnati had the championship within its grasp, all right, especially after chasing 34-year-old Luis Tiant in the eighth inning. Tiant was trying to become the 13th pitcher to win three games in one World Series, but the Reds attacked him for six runs in the late middle innings and ended his advance on the record book.

But in the home half of the eighth, everything was reversed on one pitch from Rawly Eastwick, the sixth of eight pitchers thrown into the struggle by Cincinnati. The pitch was delivered to Carbo, an outfielder who once played for the Reds and who now frets on the Boston bench.

He drove the ball 400 feet into the center-field bleachers for his second home run in two times at bat a week apart, tying the game and the World Series record for pinch-hit homers set in 1959 by Chuck Essegian of the Los Angeles Dodgers.

"It was a fastball over the plate," said Carbo, who was born in Detroit 27 years ago and became National League "rookie of the yer" for Cincinnati in 1970 before he was traded to Boston from St. Louis.

"I was telling myself not to strike out. With four days off because of all the rain, I was just trying to put the ball in play someplace. It's funny, but my first hit in the big leagues was a home run for the Reds and, two years later, my first hit in a World Series was a home run for the Reds. And now this, against the Reds."

Carbo's three-run swing of the bat touched off waves of thunderous cheers from the Red Sox fans in the 63-year-old misshapen ballpark off Kenmore Square. More waves of noise followed when the Red Sox loaded the bases in the ninth with nobody out. But they were foiled when a fly ball on the left-field line was turned into a double play by the Reds, throwing the teams into extra innings.

Then Evans saved the game and the Series with a catch against the right-field seats in the 11th, starting an out-field double play for Boston. And finally, when everybody seemed to have no more tricks left, Fisk struck the haymaker.

The teams performed their unlikely feats on a pleasantly cool evening after the sixth game of their Series had been postponed three times by rain. They worked out in places like the Tufts University gymnasium and under the center-field stands in Fenway Park while an epidemic of virus infections spread through the Red Sox.

When they did take the field finally, the Red Sox faced the danger of being eliminated unless Tiant pitched some more of his magic. He was paunchy, he was at least 34 years old, he was declared "washed up" four years ago, he smoked big black Cuban cigars and he had a chest cold. But Luis Clemente Tiant was the man of the hour as the Red Sox fought for their lives.

They were chanting "Loo-ie, Loo-ie," even before he went to work against Gary Nolan with a strict mission: to keep the Reds from winning their 115th and final game of 1975.

The chanting subsided when "Loo-ie" fed a change-up pitch to the Cincinnati leadoff man, Pete Rose, who lined it to left field. But Carl Yastrzemski made a fine catch sliding on both knees along the grass, where five tons of a drying chemical had been sprinkled after the triple rain delay in Game No. 6. Then Ken Griffey walked, Joe Morgan fouled high to the catcher, Johnny Bench struck out and the Red Sox went to bat—swinging.

It took them two outs before they started swinging with effect, but the effect promptly proved devastating. On the 3-and-1 pitch, Yastrzemski pulled a solid single to right field. On the one-ball, no-strike pitch, Carlton Fisk bounced a single through the left side of the infield. Then came Freddie Lynn, the 23-year-old rookie center fielder from the Chicago area, who hit 21 home runs this summer while establishing himself as the leading candidate for most valuable player in the American

United Press International
Carlton Fisk after hitting home run in 12th inning to win game

League.

Nolan, who lasted only four innings a week ago in Cincinnati, threw ball one to Lynn before the rookie smashed a towering home run over the Boston bull pen in right-center, out where Ted Williams used to hit them, more than 400 feet away.

The battle plan of the Reds had been to start Nolan, bring in Jack Billingham quickly, if necessary, and hold back Don Gullett for a seventh game, if necessary. It was a plan that Manager Sparky Anderson was forced to follow a lot more closely than he wanted. After two innings, he pinch hit for Nolan and

Box Score of Sixth Game

CINCINNATI [N.]	AB.	R.	H.	BI.
Rose, 3b	5	1	2	0
Griffey, rf	5	2	2	2
Morgan, 2b	6	1	1	0
Bench, c	6	0	1	1
T. Perez, 1b	6	0	2	0
G. Foster, lf	6	0	2	2
Concepcion, ss	6	0	1	0
Geronimo, cf	6	1	2	1
Nolan, p	0	0	0	0
Chaney, ph	1	0	0	0
Norman, p	0	0	0	0
Billingham, p	0	0	0	0
Ambrister, ph	0	1	0	0
C. Carroll, p	0	0	0	0
Crowley, ph	1	0	1	0
Borbon, p	0	0	0	0
Eastwick, p	0	0	0	0
McEnany, p	0	0	0	0
Driessen, ph	1	0	0	0
Darcy, p	0	0	0	0
Total	50	6	14	6

BOSTON (A.)	AB.	R.	H.	BI.
Cooper, 1b	5	0	0	0
Drago, p	0	0	0	0
R. Miller, ph	1	0	0	0
Wise, p	0	0	0	0
Doyle, 2b	5	0	1	0
Yastrzemski, lf	6	1	3	0
Fisk, c	4	2	2	1
Lynn, cf	4	2	2	3
Petrocelli, 3b	4	1	0	0
Evans, rf	5	0	1	0
Burleson, ss	3	0	0	0
Tiant, p	2	0	0	0
Moret, p	0	0	0	0
Carbo, lf	2	1	1	3
Total	41	7	10	7

Cincinnati .... 0 0 0 0 3 0 2 1 0 0 0 0—6
Boston .... 3 0 0 0 0 0 0 3 0 0 0 1—7

Error—Burleson. Double plays—Cincinnati 1, Boston 1. Left base—Cincinnati 11, Boston 9. Two base hits—Doyle, Evans, G. Foster. Three base hit—Griffey. Home runs—Lynn (1), Geronimo (2), Carbo (2), Fisk 2. Stolen-base—Concepcion. Sacrifice—Tiant.

	IP	H	R	ER	BB	SO
Nolan	2	3	3	3	0	2
Norman	2/3	1	0	0	2	0
Billingham	1 1/3	1	0	0	1	1
C. Carroll	1	1	0	0	0	0
Borbon	2	1	2	2	2	1
Eastwick	1 1/3	2	1	1	1	2
McEnaney	2/3	0	0	0	1	0
Darcy (1, 0-1)	*2	1	1	1	0	1
Tiant	7	11	6	6	2	5
Moret	1	0	0	0	0	0
Drago	3	1	0	0	0	1
Wise (W,1-0)	1	2	0	0	0	1

*None out when winning run was scored.

Hit by pitch—Drago (Rose). T-4:01. A—Time of game—4:01. Attendance—35,205.

Associated Press

Fred Lynn of the Red Sox hitting his three-run homer in the first inning against the Reds. Johnny Bench is the catcher and Dave Davidson is the umpire.

Associated Press

Red Sox Dwight Evans overtaking drive by Joe Morgan for first half of double play in 11th inning.

called for the left-handed Fred Norman to face the Red Sox in the third.

The only element missing from the plan now was Billingham, but he was not missing very long. With one down, Denny Doyle doubled past first base; with two down, Norman gave Fisk an intentional walk. But he followed that by giving the precocious Lynn an unintentional walk, loading the bases and bringing Billingham into the "battle plan" to pitch to the right-handed Rico Petrocelli. It was a limited goal, but it worked when Petrocelli struck out half-swiping at an outside curve.

The Reds, meanwhile, were

not harassing Tiant terribly. They got their first hit when Rose singled to center with two down in the third. They got their second hit when Tony Perez singled to right field in the fourth. Then they got their first opportunity to regain some ground when George Foster followed Perez by hitting a grounder to the left of Rick Burleson, and the shortstop threw the ball low to second base for an error.

Two Reds on base now, still two out. But old Luis Tiant spun and twisted on the mound, and retired Dave Concepcion on a foul fly outside first base for the final out.

It didn't stay 3-0 very long, though. The Reds, who had the best record in baseball this summer, broke through Tiant's serve in the fifth after Ed Armbrister had pinch-hit for Billingham with one down. Armbrister was the player who had burted his way into the celebrated "interference" argument in Game No. 3, and he was appropriately booed by the Boston partisans. But he walked this time and raced to third when Rose lined Tiant's 3-2 pitch to center for a single.

The batter was Griffey, the Cincinnati right fielder, and for the first time in the Series the Great Wall played a

role in the plot. On the 2-2 pitch, Griffey laced a solid line drive to center field, where Lynn turned and sprinted to the 37-foot-high concrete fence. The ball and Lynn both struck the concrete at the same time, just alongside the white marker reading 379 feet, and both bounced off the wall at the same time.

Lynn, having lost the chase, slumped on the ground with a twisted foot while the ball caromed toward right field with Armbrister and Rose crossing the plate and Griffey dashing all the way to third. It took about five minutes for Lynn to get back to his feet, but he stayed in the game as Morgan popped up for the second out.

But then Bench, who had struck out twice, drilled Tiant's first pitch off the wall in left field—the first batter on either side to reach it— and Griffey crossed with the tying run while Yastrzemski played the rebound perfectly to hold Bench to a long single. And they were even at 3-3 with 4½ innings to go.

In the seventh, though, the Reds finally nailed their old antagonist without any help from the infield. Griffey started things with a single wide of first base and Morgan followed with a single to

left. The big guns were up — Bench and Perez, who knocked in 219 runs this summer — but Tiant responded nobly.

He got Bench on a lob to Yastrzemski in medium left field and he got Perez on a fly to Evans in medium right field, with Griffey making third after the catch. Now Tiant stood one out from surviving the Houdini act of the evening — but this time he did not escape.

With Morgan running on the one-strike pitch, Foster whacked a solid drive to straightaway center field, where the ball hit the concrete at the farthest point from home plate, 400 feet away.

Lynn gave it a good chase, but it banked off the wall for a double while Griffey and Morgan sped home and the Red Sox faithful suffered in silence. One inning after that, Geronimo led off with a high home run past the right-field foul pole, making it 6-3. And finally, old "Loo-ie" Tiant was excused from the 72d World Series to a standing ovation after he had almost dismantled the big, bad "Mean Machine" of Cincinnati.

October 22, 1975

181

Reds Win First Series in 35 Years

By JOSEPH DURSO

Special to The New York Times

BOSTON, Oct. 22—In the final inning of the final game, the Cincinnati Reds finally subdued the rambunctious Boston Red Sox, 4-3, tonight and won the 72d World Series in seven games.

There were two outs in the ninth, the 67th inning played by the teams over a 12-day span, when Joe Morgan singled to center field off the 50th pitcher used in the Series. The hit dropped about 10 feet in front of Fred Lynn while Ken Griffey scored the run that snapped a 3-3 tie. Half an inning later, the big bad "mean machine" of Cincinnati had captured the Reds' first championship in 35 years.

It was the end of a Series filled with new heroes, new geography and even new rivals, and the first ever played between Boston and Cincinnati since the American and National Leagues began grappling for baseball's first prize in 1903. It also was the third time in six years that the Reds had tried to win the Series, and, when they finally did it, they squeaked past an underdog Boston team that had been looking for its first championship since 1918.

"It was the greatest World Series ever played," said Sparky Anderson, the white-haired, 41-year-old manager of the Reds, who won 108 games in the National League this summer. "I think we're the best team in baseball—but not by much."

"Most ball clubs would have quit," said Pete Rose, referring to the fact that the Reds were trailing by 3-0 as late as the sixth inning. "But we didn't. I said last night's game was the best game ever played in baseball. Now I take it back. This one's got to be the greatest."

Emotionally, the difference for Rose probably lay in the fact that the Reds lost in 12 tumultuous innings last night and early this morning, when Boston deadlocked the Series at three games apiece, but won in nine tumultuous innings tonight. They won the hard way, too, after the Red Sox had scored three runs in the third inning and clung to the lead until the sixth.

Then, with a standing-room crowd of 35,205 thronging 63-year-old Fenway Park and filling the night air with noise, the Red Sox let the title slip away. Tony Perez put Cincinnati back in the game with a two-run home run, Rose singled home the tying run an inning later and they were still tied as they turned into the ninth.

But the Reds, with the best record in baseball, had managed to win 26 games in their final turn at bat this year and they were about to do their thing one more time.

A walk, a sacrifice bunt and an infield grounder nudged the critical run to third base and, finally, with two down, Morgan, a left-handed batter, lobbed his single to short center field —a hit that traveled perhaps 200 feet, but that was worth $20,000 a man for Cincinnati.

"A couple of years ago, I would have struck out on that pitch," Morgan said later, reflecting on the slider thrown to him by a left-handed rookie, Jim Burton. "It was down and away, and I hit it toward the end of my bat. But we get 27 outs allotted to us before we lose a ball game. We were down to outs tonight and were three runs behind, but we've won plenty of times after we had 26 outs."

"It was an even Series and we didn't disgrace ourselves," said Darrell Johnson, manager of the Red Sox, a man given to understatement. "he game was determined by a little flip here and a little flip there. That's how close it was."

The Series was the fourth in the last five years that went the full distance of seven games, and the first in four years that did not involve the Oakland A's, who were eliminated in three straight games in the American League playoff by the Red Sox. But whatever the arithmetic, it proved to be as close as a series can get. When is was over, Bill Lee added up the difference and said simply:

"They won by one run in seven games."

For two-thirds of the game tonight, Lee looked like Boston's newest hero as he pitched against Don Gullett of the Reds. They both had plenty of rest after the sixth game had been postponed three times by rain, but they were a study in contrasts: Gullett, a 24-year-old Kentuckian with old-fashioned manners and a old-fashioned

fastball; Lee, a 28-year-old Californian with a zest for words, distinct political views and free-thinking.

They struggled for the title on the grass field of the old ball park with its angles, high screens and forbiddingly close left-field wall, and Boston's loyalists reacted as though the Redcoats were coming again instead of the Redlegs.

When they went at it, the Red Sox struck first when their leadoff batter, Bernie Carbo, banked a double off the concrete wall in left-center field. It was Carbo's first start of the Series, but in four previous times at bat he had hit two home runs as a pinch-hitter.

Gullett, throwing mainly fastballs, stayed out of worse trouble by retiring the next three batters while Carbo got no farther than third base. Still, the 27-year-old pinch-hitter from Detroit continued to harass his former Cincinnati teammates from his newly won position in left field. When George Foster lined a hit off the wall with one down in the top of the second inning. Carbo handled the rebound like Carl Yastrzemski and whipped a per-

fect throw to nail Foster at second base.

The Reds made more menacing gestures in the third, when Ken Griffey led with a single. But this time, Denny Doyle handled Cesar Geronimo's bouncing ball near second base and started a double play that paid off a moment later when Gullett singled to right. That was all, though.

Then they went to the home half of the third, and the home side raised the rafters.

It began with one down when Carbo drew a walk and Doyle singled to right field, making the little second baseman the only player on either team to hit safely in all seven games. Then Yastrzemski, the 36-year-old hero of Boston's pennant-winner of 1967, pulled the next pitch on the ground into right field for a single and the Red Sox took a noisy 1-0 lead.

On the throw from the outfield to third base, Yastrzemski took second, so the Reds elected to fill the bases with an intentional walk to Carlton Fisk, whose home run won last night's marathon in the 12th inning this morning. Gullett stabilized things long enough to strike out Fred

Box Score of Seventh Game

CINCINNATI [N.]	AB.	R.	H.	RI.	BOSTON [A.]	AB.	R.	H.	BI.
Rose, 3b	4	0	2	1	Carbo, lf	3	1	1	0
Morgan, 2b	4	0	2	1	R. Miller, lf	0	0	0	0
Bench, c	4	1	0	0	Beniquez, ph	1	0	0	0
T. Perez, 1b	5	1	1	2	Doyle, 2b	4	1	1	0
G. Foster, lf	4	0	1	0	Montgomery, ph	1	0	0	0
Concepcion, ss	4	0	1	0	Yastrzemski, 1b	5	1	1	1
Griffey, rf	2	2	1	0	Fisk, c	3	0	0	0
Geronimo, cf	3	0	0	0	Lynn, cf	2	0	0	0
Gullett, p	1	0	1	0	Petrocelli, 3b	3	0	1	1
Rettenmund, ph	1	0	0	0	Evans, rf	2	0	0	1
Billingham, p	0	0	0	0	Burleson, ss	3	0	0	0
Ambrister, ph	0	0	0	0	B. Lee, p	3	0	1	0
C. Carroll, p	0	0	0	0	Moret, p	0	0	0	0
Driessen, ph	1	0	0	0	Willoughby, p	0	0	0	0
McEnany, p	0	0	0	0	Cooper, ph	1	0	0	0
					Burton, p	0	0	0	0
					Cleveland, p	0	0	0	0
Total	33	4	9	4	Total	31	3	5	3

```
Boston .........0 0 3   0 0 0   0 0 0—3
Cincinnati .....0 0 0   0 0 2   1 0 1—4
```

Errors—Doyle 2. Double plays—Cincinnati 1, Boston 2. Left on base—Cincinnati 9, Boston 9. Two-base hit—Carbo. Home run—T. Perez (3). Stolen bases—Morgan, Griffey. Sacrifice—Geronimo.

	IP	H	R	ER	BB	SO
Gullett	4	4	3	3	5	5
Billingham	2	1	0	0	2	1
C. Carroll (W, 1-0)	2	0	0	0	1	1
McEnany	1	0	0	0	0	0
B. Lee	6⅓	7	3	3	1	2
Moret	⅓	1	0	0	2	0
Willoughby	1⅓	0	0	0	0	0
Burton (L, 0-1)	⅔	1	1	1	2	0
Cleveland	⅓	0	0	0	1	0

Save—McEnaney (1). Wild pitch—Gullett. Time of game—2:52. Attendance—35,205.

Lynn on a disputed call, but then his control deserted him as his fastballs sailed high and wide.

He needed only one more out to survive the problem, but before he got it, he went to counts of three balls and no strikes on Rico Petrocelli and Dwight Evans. He did, manage to throw two strikes to Petrocelli before walking him to force in one run, but he threw four bad ones in a row to Evans and forced in another. By the time he fired strike three past Rick Burleson, the Red Sox had three runs and took the lead for the sixth time in the seven games.

"I was real concerned, down three runs," Anderson conceded later. "I wanted to stay with Gullett because he's my best, but he was too eager and was overthrowing the ball. I was ready to take him out right after he walked Evans and, if Burleson had gotten a hit, I probably would have second-guessed myself."

The Reds, who have won three National League pennants in the last six years, now were trailing by 3-0 and were finding themselves in a maddeningly familiar position: trying to salvage a World Series they had been favored to win.

They kept getting men on base against Lee, but they kept getting nothing for their trouble. Joe Morgan opened the fourth inning by beating out a drag bunt toward first base and Johnny Bench hammered a 400-foot drive to the dirt warning track in deep center field. But Lynn outran the ball and grabbed it. Then Tony Perez flied out to right and Foster fouled high to the catcher.

Reds' Threat Fails

In the fifth, Dave Concepcion led with an infield single wide of first base, beating Lee and Yastrzemski's throw to the bag. Then Griffey rammed a low line drive through Doyle into center field for an error on the second baseman, with Concepcion stopping at second.

Now the Reds had the ingredients for a possibly damaging inning, but again they wasted the chance. Geronimo, not bunting, took a third strike for the first out and Merv Rettenmund pinch-hit for Gullett and bounced straight to shortstop for a double play.

It was ironic that the Reds had played Gullett as their ace in the hole without winning the trick. He won 15 games this summer, although he missed two months with a broken thumb. He pitched dazzling ball in Cincinnati a week ago. And he waited in reserve since then as the rain fell and the Series took its strange bounces into the seventh-game showdown. But now he was gone after four innings and Jack Billingham was pitching for the Reds.

After all the flexing of muscle, though, the Reds finally punished Lee in the sixth. Rose opened the inning with a single to right, the sixth hit off Lee, and Morgan flied out to right field. Bench, who knocked in 110 runs this summer, rammed a grounder to the left of second base behind the bag and Burleson flipped the ball to Doyle.

It looked like another double play but Doyle, stepping around Rose's charge, threw high over Yastrzemski's head at first for his second error, and the Reds suddenly had another shot.

They made the most of it, too, when Perez powered Lee's second pitch high over everything in left-center: 37-foot-tall wall, 23-foot-high screen and out past Lansdowne Street beyond. It was the third home run for the 33-year-old Cuban since he had broken loose with a pair in the fifth game after suffering through an 0-for-15 slump, and it pulled the Reds close at 3-2 with three innings to go.

In the seventh, Lee got Concepcion on a grounder to shortstop, walked Griffey and suddenly was done. He was being troubled by a blister on the left thumb and he was replaced by Roger Moret, a left-hander, who had won 14 games and lost only three this summer.

They key man again was Geronimo, swinging for the third time with runners on base, but again he failed to deliver. He popped the 2-0 pitch high to shortstop, and the Red Sox needed only one more out to weather another storm.

But if the Red Sox were rambunctious in this series, the Reds were still resourceful. Ed Armbrister batted for Billingham and walked, putting runners on first and second with two down and the switch-hitting Rose at Bat. The 34-year-old "Charlie Hustle" of the Reds, who already had 2,547 hits in his career, drilled a single to center for his 10th hit of the Series, and the "mean machine" of Cincinnati finally was even at 3-3.

It was no time for tempting fate, but Moret did just that by walking Morgan to load the bases with two down and the dangerous Bench batting. The Red Sox decided it was no time for a wild left-hander, either, so they excused Moret and brought in the right-handed Jim Willoughby. And he rose to the occasion on two pitches by getting Bench to lift a twisting foul fly that Fisk grabbed leaning into the box seats behind home plate for the final out.

With two innings left, the pitchers were Clay Carroll for the Reds and Willoughby for the Red Sox in a park where one slip might prove fatal. Carroll almost made one by walking the leadoff batter in the bottom of the eighth, but escaped when Rose started a snappy double play on Burleson's grounder after the shortstop had twice failed to bunt.

Then the Red Sox pinch hit for Willoughby and, with one inning to go, placed the championship in the left hand of a rookie Jim Burton. He also walked the leadoff batter in the ninth, Griffey, who took second while Petrocelli was throwing out Geronimo from the seat of his pants after slipping while fielding a bunt.

Next Griffey took on a pinch-hit grounder by Dan Driessen and the energetic Rose walked on a 3-2 pitch, leaving things up to Morgan with two down.

And Little Joe lobbed a 1-2 pitch over the infield into short center field about 10 feet in front of Lynn for a single while Griffey crossed with the run that put the "mean machine" in front.

The Red Sox still had three outs remaining, but Will McEnaney made them quick ones in the final half-inning of 1975. He got two pinch-hitters and then the last hurrah was sounded for Boston by Yastrzemski, who lifted a fly ball to center field to end the suspense for good.

"It was like a poker game tonight," Morgan said after the teams had left the field to thousands of young fans who somehow wanted to stay. "But I feel like we had a full house going for us. Until we prove it on the field, we're nothing. Now I can go home and say, we're the best."

October 23, 1975

Lynn, Rookie, M.V.P.

By JOSEPH DURSO

Fred Lynn of the Boston Red Sox made history as a baseball prodigy yesterday when he became the first rookie to be voted the most valuable player in his league.

The 23-year-old outfielder from the University of Southern California began his sweep of honors three weeks ago when he was named rookie of the year in the American League. He completed it with flourishes yesterday when he was elected "most valuable," and he did it by the widest margin since the nation's baseball writers started bestowing such titles 44 years ago.

The only other baseball player who came close to winning the most valuable player award in his first season was Pete Reiser of the 1941 Brooklyn Dodgers, who finished second in the voting behind his older teammate, Dolph Camilli. And the only other professional athlete who scored a comparable sweep was Wes Unseld of the Baltimore Bullets basketball team five years ago: top rookie and top player in the National Basketball Association.

For most newcomers in the cut-throat world of sports these days, landing a job is challenge enough. But Frederic Michael Lynn of Chicago met his challenge in storybook style. After two seasons in the minor leagues, where he batted only .259 and .282, he landed the job as Boston's regular center fielder and hit .331 with 21 home runs and 105 runs batted in. He led the league with 103 runs scored and 47 doubles.

He and Jim Rice, another accomplished rookie, led the Red Sox to the pennant over the defending champion Oakland A's. Then, with Rice sidelined because of a broken hand, Lynn helped the Red Sox through a rousing World Series that they lost to the Cincinnati Reds in the Final inning of the final game. Even there the rookie supplied melodrama for a national television audience, colliding with the concrete wall in Fenway Park in the sixth game but returning to hit a three-run home run in the seventh.

When the post season honors were awarded, Lynn's performance proved just as spectacular. He received 23½ of 24 votes for Rookie of the Year, the other half-vote going to Rice. And for "most valuable," he got 22 of the first-place votes while the two others went to Rollie Fingers, the Oakland relief pitcher.

On the two ballots that named Fingers first Lynn was second and he finished with a total of 326 points. That put him 169 points ahead of the runner-up, John Mayberry of the Kansas City Royals, a record landslide that even surpassed the one last week that made Joe Morgan of Cincinnati the most valuable player in the National League.

After Lynn and Mayberry came Rice of the Red Sox, then Fingers, followed by Reggie Jackson of Oakland,

Jim Palmer of the Baltimore Orioles, Thurman Munson of the New York Yankees, George Scott of the Milwaukee Brewers, Rod Carew of the Minnesota Twins and Ken Singleton of the Orioles.

Of the 300 players in the American League, 31 received mention on the ballots cast by the baseball writers. Seven were members of the Red Sox: Lynn, Rice, Rick Burleson, Denny Doyle, Rick Wise, Bill Lee and Carl Yastrzemski. Three were Yankees: Munson in seventh place, Catfish Hunter in 12th and Bobby Bonds 30th.

Lynn, a quiet but articulate person who seems smaller than his listed dimensions of 6 feet 1 inch and 185 pounds, was on his way from Boston to his home in El Monte, Calif., when he got

word of his historic "double."

"To achieve this in my first season," he said, "is a very pleasant surprise and a big thrill.

"I have to thank a few persons who helped me get where I am today. First and foremost, my father, whose guidance and knowledge started me in the right direction. Secondly, my high school and college coaches, Dave Sadell and Rod Dedeaux, whose expert teaching in the field of baseball gave me a solid foundation on which to build. Also, I would like to thank my Red Sox teammates and my wife, Dee Dee, for their help and inspiration all season."

Asked how he had added 49 points to his batting average after graduating to the

big leagues, he reflected: "In a way it's easier to hit in the majors because the pitchers throw the ball over the plate."

"Fred would love to forget baseball in the winter," his wife reported. "I honestly believe he loves fishing more than baseball."

"I live two lives, a public and a private life," Lynn said, explaining his low profile. "But at all times I just try to be myself. I don't put on any facade. I'm not interested in a lot of publicity and having people all around me. I get my enjoyment between the foul lines and I get my enjoyment at home."

November 27, 1975

Arbitrator Frees 2 Baseball Stars

By JOSEPH DURSO

A labor arbitrator ruled yesterday that two pitchers, Andy Messersmith and Dave McNally, were free agents who were no longer bound by their baseball contracts and could sell their services to the highest bidder.

If upheld, the ruling could topple the major-league teams' legal right to "own" players indefinitely under their contracts. But it was expected to be challenged, and perhaps modified, either in court or in collective bargaining between the players and their clubs.

The decision by the arbitrator, Peter M. Seitz, was immediately cheered by the Players' Association as a major erosion of the controversial "reserve system" which binds an athlete to his team until he is traded or retires.

But it was denounced by the commissioner of baseball, Bowie Kuhn, who said: "If this interpretation prevails, baseball's reserve system will be eliminated by a stroke of the pen."

Both sides, though, agreed that the arbitrator had fired the first shot—but by no means the last—in a struggle that now would be waged in two places: in face-to-face bargaining between the 960 players in the big leagues and the 24 club owners, and ultimately in the courts.

Associated Press
Dave McNally

Associated Press
Andy Messersmith

The stakes and the emotions in the dispute were so high that the arbitrator barely survived his own blockbuster. As the ruling was announced, the owners handed Seitz a written notice "to terminate his role as chairman of the three-man panel that had heard the two cases. The reason was that "professional baseball no longer has confidence in the arbitrator's ability to understand the basic structure

of organized baseball."

At the heart of the controversy was the fact that baseball has long enjoyed stricter control over its players than the other professional sports. Twice in the last half-century, the Supreme Court has reviewed the game's "reserve system" and has allowed it to stand.

But in recent years, the contract system has been increasingly challenged in Con-

gress and in collective bargaining; and one year ago, Seitz declared Catfish Hunter free of his contract with the Oakland A's, after which Hunter auctioned himself to the New York Yankees for $3.75 million.

But that dispute involved a breach of contract by the Oakland team, which owed $50,000 to the pitcher. In the two cases yesterday, the issue was more basic: both Messersmith and McNally refused to sign contracts for 1975, pitched without contracts and then demanded their freedom in the open market.

Their appeal was heard by three officials: John Gaherin, who represents the teams' owners in labor matters; Marvin Miller, the economist who is executive Baseball Players Association, and Seitz, a professional arbitrator from New York who served as "impartial chairman." In a 70-page opinion, Seitz cast the deciding vote that ruled Messersmith free of the Los Angeles Dodgers and McNally free of the Montreal Expos.

"It was represented to me," Seitz said, "that any decision sustaining Messersmith and McNally would have dire results, wreak great harm to the reserve system and do serious damage to the sport of baseball [and] would encourage many other players to elect to become free agents.

"The panel's sole duty is to interpret and apply the agreements and understandings of the parties. If any of the expressed apprehensions and fears are soundly based, I am confident that the dislocations and damage to the reserve system can be avoided or minimized through good-faith collective bargaining between the parties."

The bargaining, in fact, has already been under way because the current "basic agreement" between the teams and players expires next Wednesday. It covers minimum pay, working conditions, the length of the season and the teams' legal hold on the players—that is, their right to "reserve" their services year after year.

In professional football, basketball and hockey, a team's control over its players is considerably less sweeping. A team generally may "own" an athlete for the length of his contract plus one year—the "option year." During the extra year, the player may take the option of working without a contract; after it, he is free to sign with another club. But the team that lost his services usually receives some compensation in return, a procedure (now under legal attack) known as the "Rozelle rule" because it was instituted by Pete Rozelle, commissioner of the National Football League.

In baseball, though, a team's control has been maintained through a paragraph in each player's contract. It permits the club to renew the contract the following year even if the player refuses to sign again. The players recently have argued that the renewal was good for only one year; the owners insisted it could be invoked indefinitely. Yesterday, Seitz sided with the players.

"I am not an Abraham Lincoln signing the Emancipation Proclamation," the arbitrator said at a news con-

---

"If this interpretation prevails, baseball's reserve system will be eliminated by a stroke of the pen."—Bowie Kuhn, commissioner of baseball.

---

ference in his home after the ruling had been announced. "Involuntary servitude has nothing to do with this case. I decided it as a lawyer and an arbitrator. This decision does not destroy baseball. But if the club owners think it will ruin baseball, they have it in their power to prevent the damage."

Even before the ruling was issued, though, the club owners took steps "to prevent the damage." They filed a that Seitz had no jurisdiction to decide such a fundamental matter. They were instructed by Judge John W. Oliver to go through the arbitration process and then return for a hearing.

Meanwhile, the Players' Association decided yesterday not to let its preliminary victory be diluted by the slow passage of legal time. Dick Moss, counsel to the association, filed a counterclaim asking the court to order the arbitrator's ruling enforced, and said: "I expect there will be hearings by Jan. 1, and we can then get a speedy resolution."

Miller, the "players' commissioner" in economic affairs, said:

"If you agree to accept binding arbitration and you don't get your way, you can't go running into court. You have to look at this decision in the proper perspective. The ruling itself covers only one facet of the reserve system. Now there's a safety valve for a dissatisfied player, and baseball has been raised toward the level of other team sports."

League Heads Upset

But Commissioner Kuhn, a lawyer, said:

"I am enormously disturbed by this arbitration decision. It is just inconceivable that after nearly 100 years of developing this system for the over-all good of the game, it should be obliterated in this way. It is certainly desirable that the decision should be given a thorough judicial review."

Lee MacPhail, president of the American League, and Charles Feeney, president of the National League, said in a joint statement that they were "deeply shocked and disturbed," too.

"The decision attacks a fundamental principle which has proved to be the keystone of competitive balance and integrity in professional baseball," they said. "For the arbitrator to assume the power to restructure the essential framework of the game, when the Supreme Court, the Congress and other suit last month in Federal Court in Kansas City, saying authorities have clearly placed the reserve system above narrow, individual disputes, is clearly an overreaching of authority.

"While this issue is being reviewed by the court, the clubs will continue to bargain in good faith with the Players' Association in an attempt to reach common agreement on provisions of the reserve structure. At this time, our clubs have not been advised by the league offices that Messersmith and McNally are free to negotiate

with other clubs."

Since December is usually the time when contracts are mailed to players for the next season, a quick settlement of the problem—either at the bargaining table or in court—was urgent. But whatever the final form of the "reserve clause," most baseball people felt that it would be modified or that more teams would offer more players long-term contracts.

Messersmith and McNally, like Catfish Hunter, are frontline pitchers with strong records. Messersmith is a 30-year-old right-hander, twice a 20-game winner, who pitched 19 victories for the Dodgers last summer after he had refused to sign his 1975 contract. The Dodgers said yesterday that he had "publicly stated he did not want to be traded." But MacPhail observed that "he certainly is in a better negotiating position [with the Dodgers] now."

McNally is a 33-year-old left-hander who pitched 12 seasons for the Baltimore Orioles and won 181 games, including four in World Series play. He was traded to Montreal a year ago, but left the Expos on June 9 with a sore arm and a record of three victories and six defeats and said he was retiring—his 1975 contract still not signed.

"The world of sports as we know it today," reflected Dave DeBusschere, commissioner of the American Basketball Association, after yesterday's flurry, "is in for major changes in the very near future. A compromise between the ownership and the players will be necessary for sports to maintain a competitive profile."

December 24, 1975

Deal Signed for Seattle Baseball Club

SEATTLE, Feb. 7 (AP)—An agreement to buy an American League expansion franchise has been signed, bringing major league baseball back to this city after a seven-year absence, Lester Smith and entertainer Danny Kaye said today. The two, speaking for a group of six, told a news conference that they would pay about $5.56 million for the franchise. A 20-year lease to the King County Domed Stadium will go along with the deal, though it has yet to be signed. A key feature of the lease will be a clause binding the franchise to stay in Seattle.

February 8, 1976

Toronto to A.L.

TAMPA, Fla., March 25 (UPI)—The American League will expand to 14 teams tomorrow with Toronto being awarded a franchise for the 1977 season, it has been learned. The action by the American League will mean it has beaten the National League to the Canadian city after both leagues announced their intention of establishing franchises in Toronto during a meeting last Saturday in New York. A Seattle team will also be added next season in the American League.

The National League will be left with 12 teams unless it decides to change its present position against expansion.

One of the reasons the American League was able to move into Toronto before the National League was that only nine of 12 votes are needed to admit a new franchise in the American League while the vote in the National League has to be unanimous.

Ten of 12 National League clubs voted for expansion to Toronto. Philadelphia and Cincinnati voted no.

Official certification of Toronto as a new franchise will be made here tomorrow when two Toronto groups make presentations before American League officials. Labatt's Brewery, which had offered $12 million for the San Francisco Giants last month, is expected to wind up with the franchise.

March 26, 1976

Schmidt: 4 Homers in Row

By The Associated Press

CHICAGO, April 17 — Mike Schmidt set a modern National League record with four consecutive home runs in one game today as he drove in eight runs and powered the Philadelphia Phillies to an 18-16 victory over the Chicago Cubs in 10 innings.

Only nine other players have hit four homers in a game, none in the last 15 years.

Schmidt, the Phillies' third baseman, also had a single in six times at bat in a game that saw nine homers and 43 hits.

Rick Monday hit two home runs and a pair of singles in the first four innings for Chicago as the Cubs ran up a 13-2 lead before Schmidt and the Phils began blasting away.

Schmidt hit a two-run homer in the fifth, a bases-empty shot in the seventh, capped a five-run eighth with a three-run homer and finally slugged his fourth straight and fifth this season in the 10th, a two-run belt that broke a 15-15 tie.

Schmidt became only the fourth player to hit four consecutive home runs in a ma-

jor league game and the first National Leaguer to do it since Bob Lowe of the Boston Braves on May 30, 1894.

The other two players to accomplish the feat were American Leaguers — Lou Gehrig of the New York Yankees on June 3, 1932, and Rocky Colavito of the Cleveland Indians on June 10, 1959.

Fourteen other players—including Mickey Mantle, Bobby Murcer and Ralph Kiner (twice)—have hit four successive homers, but they did it in more than one game. The only other players

to belt four homers in extra-inning games were another Phillie, Chuck Klein (10 innings), and Pat Seerey of the Chicago White Sox (11).

Schmidt's four-in-one-game feat puts him in a group with Ed Delehanty (1896), Gil Hodges (1950), Joe Adcock (1954) and Willie Mays (1961), in addition to Lowe, Gehrig, Klein, Seerey and Colavito.

The Phils tied the score 13-13 in the ninth with a leadoff homer by Bob Boone, then made it 15-13 on a single by Bobby Tolan, a triple by

Associated Press

Phillies' Mike Schmidt greeted by Billy DeMars, third-base coach, after hitting second of four home runs yesterday

PHILADELPHIA (N.)					CHICAGO (N.)				
	ab	r	h	bi		ab	r	h	bi
Cash, 2b	6	1	2	2	Monday, cf	6	3	4	4
Bowa, ss	6	3	3	1	Cardena, lf	5	1	1	0
Johnstone, rf	6	2	4	2	Mitterwald,ph	1	0	0	0
Luzinski, lf	4	0	1	1	Wallis, lf	1	0	0	0
Brown, 1b	1	0	0	0	Madlock, 3b	7	3	3	3
Allen, 1b	5	2	1	2	Morales, rf	5	2	1	0
Schmidt, 3b	6	4	5	8	Thornton, 1b	4	3	1	1
Maddox, cf	4	1	2	1	Trillo, 2b	4	0	3	3
McGraw, p	0	0	0	0	Swisher, c	5	3	2	1
McCarver, ph	1	1	1	0	Rosello, ss	4	1	2	1
Underwood, p	0	0	0	0	Kelleher, ss	0	0	0	0
Lonborg, p	0	0	0	0	Rreuschel, p	2	0	0	0
Boone, c	2	0	0	0	Garman, p	0	0	0	0
Carlton, p	1	0	0	0	Knowles, p	0	0	0	0
Schueler, p	0	0	0	0	Preuschel, p	0	0	0	0
Garber, p	0	0	0	0	Schultz, p	0	0	0	0
Hutton, ph	1	0	0	0	Adams, ph	1	1	1	0
Reed, p	0	0	0	0					
Martin, ph	1	0	0	0					
Twitchell, p	0	0	0	0					
Tolan, cf	2	2	2	0					
Total	50	18	24	18	**Total**	43	16	19	15

Philadelphia .... 0 1 0 : 2 8 : 3 5 3 —18
Chicago .... 0 2 5 : 0 0 0 0 2 1 —16

DP—Philadelphia 1, Chicago 12. LOB—Philadelphia 8, Chicago 12. 2B—Cardenal, Madlock, Thornton, Boone, Adams. 3B—Johnstone, Bowa. HRs—Maddox (1), Swisher (1), Monday 2 (3), Schmidt 4 (5), Boone (1). S—Rreuschel, Johnstone. SF—Luzinski, Cash.

	IP	H	R	ER	BB	SO
Carlton	1⅓	7	7	7	1	1
Schueler	2½	3	3	1	0	0
Garber	⅔	2	1	1	1	0
Reed		0	0	0	1	1
Twitchell		0	0	0	1	1
McGraw (W, 1-0)	1	0	0	0	0	0
Underwood	1	0	0	0	0	0
Lonborg	1	0	0	0	0	0
Rreuschel	1	4	5	5	1	1
Garman	1	4	5	3	1	0
Knowles (L, 1-1)	2	3	3	3	1	0
Preuschel	2	3	1	0	0	0
Schultz	2	0	0	0	0	0

Save—Lonborg (1). HBP—by Lonborg (Rreuschel), Garber (Thornton), Reed (Monday). T—3:42. A—28,287.

Larry Bowa and a squeeze bunt by Jay Johnstone.

But the Cubs came back to tie in the bottom of the ninth on a single by Jerry Morales, a double by Andy Thornton and a two-run single by Steve Swisher.

Monday slugged a three-run homer in a seven-run second inning when 12 Cubs batted. He singled and scored in a five-run third when 10 Cubs batted, and he opened the fourth inning with his second homer of the game and his third of the season.

Swisher also homered and had a run-scoring single, and Manny Trillo drove in three runs with singles for Chicago. Garry Maddox also homered for the Phillies.

With a 20 mile an hour wind blowing out, the Phillies made 24 hits and the Cubs 19. Schmidt, the major league home run leader the last two seasons, had hit two homers in a game 12 previous times.

"I was only trying to get a single to get Dick Allen in scoring position," Schmidt said of his fourth homer today. "No, I was not trying to get a home run because I wanted to win this game.

"I've been off to a very slow start, if you can call less than 20 times at bat a slow start. The team has been in somewhat of a slump and I have been trying to figure out what I've been doing wrong. After all, a .167 batting average in the first four games was not anything to write home about."

April 18, 1976

Kuhn Voids Player Sales; Finley Threatens to Sue

By JOSEPH DURSO

Commissioner Bowie Kuhn nullified the biggest sale of talent in baseball history yesterday when he ordered the New York Yankees and Boston Red Sox to return the three stars they had bought earlier in the week from the Oakland A's for $3.5 million.

He also may have provoked the biggest series of lawsuits in the sport, which is already embroiled in legal challenges and disputes over the "freedom" of the 600 players in the two major leagues.

His action stunned the baseball world and brought the prompt promise of a lawsuit by Charles O. Finley, owner of the Oakland team, who said the commissioner "sounds like the village idiot."

"We will be taking it to court on Monday," Finley said as soon as the commissioner had canceled the following sales: Vida Blue to the Yankees for $1.5 million and Joe Rudi and Rollie Fingers to the Red Sox for $1 million apiece.

The deals were made last Tuesday just hours before the midnight trading deadline in the big leagues. The next day the commissioner "froze" the sales because "they raise certain questions," and he called the teams' executives to a hearing. It was held Thursday in his office at Rockefeller Plaza, and then the players and their new and old owners waited for what they thought would be a routine decision.

Instead, the onetime Wall Street lawyer dropped a blockbuster. The deals, he ruled, broke no rules of procedure as such, but were "inconsistent with the best interests of baseball, the integrity of the game and the maintenance of public confidence in it."

"While I am, of course, aware that there have been cash sales of player contracts in the past," the commissioner said, "there has been no instance in my judgment which had the potential for harm to our game, particularly in the present unsettled circumstances of baseball's reserve system and in the highly competitive circumstance we find in today's sport and entertainment world.

"Nor can I persuade myself that the spectacle of the Yankees and Red Sox buying contracts of star players in the prime of their careers for cash sums totaling $3.5 million is anything but devastating to baseball's reputation for integrity and to public confidence in the game."

"Shorn of much of its finest talent in exchange for cash," Kuhn went on, "the Oakland club, which had been a divisional champion for the last five years, has little chance to compete effectively in its division."

Kuhn said his authority came from Article 1, Section 4, of the Major League Agreement, which was written in 1921 to define the relationships between the commissioner and the club owners who hire him. But many "rules" of professional sports have been challenged and even toppled in recent years in Congress and the courts, notably the "reserve system," which for years bound athletes to their teams indefinitely.

Both the Yankees and Red Sox were preparing replies last night to Kuhn's decision, though the Yankees said they would withhold comment until early next week. However, Manager Billy Martin roundly denounced the reversal of the sale just before the Yankees took the field in Chicago for a game against the White Sox that Blue had been scheduled to pitch.

Marvin Miller, executive director of the Players Association, said that Kuhn had "single-handedly plunged baseball into the biggest mess it has ever seen."

"I consider it sheer insanity," said the economist who has led the players' union through its series of legal victories. "It's raised the potential for litigation which would last for years. He is asserting a right to end all club owners' rights with respect to all transactions. Whenever there's a trade made, he can decide that one team did not get enough value and can veto that deal."

Support for Kuhn was expressed by several club owners not involved in the sale, including John Fetzer of the Detroit Tigers, Jim Baumer of the Milwaukee Brewers, Buzzy Bavasi of the San Diego Padres and Walter O'Malley of the Los Angeles Dodgers, who said: "The rich teams would have all the players and the poor teams would have none. These things escalate and you end up charging 15 or 20 bucks to go to a ball game."

But criticism was voiced by August A. Busch Jr. of the St. Louis Cardinals, who said:

"If I were Mr. Finley, I'd be up in arms, It's his money."

Finley has been dismantling his powerful team in recent weeks rather than lose his unsigned stars outright when they become free agents at the end of the season in October. He previously traded Reggie Jackson and Ken Holtzman to the Baltimore Orioles, who in turn traded Holtzman to the Yankees during the talent whirlwind Tuesday night.

At the hearing Thursday Finley made a ringing de-

Sec. 4. In the case of conduct by organizations not parties to this Agreement, or by individuals not connected with any of the parties hereto, which is deemed by the Commissioner not to be in the best interests of Baseball, the Commissioner may pursue appropriate legal remedies, advocate remedial legislation and take such other steps as he may deem necessary and proper in the interests of the morale of the players and the honor of the game.

fense of his transactions, insisting that the players were demanding "astronomical" salaries that would mean "bankruptcy."

"I don't even want them in uniform," he said last night,

referring to the three players the commissioner had ordered back to Oakland. "We're not going to use them. We're going to court Monday for an injunction."

But Kuhn stood fast on his

general powers to uphold "the best interests of baseball," an authority rarely invoked by any commissioner since Kenesaw Mountain Landis replaced the triumvirate known as the National

Commission after the "Black Sox scandal" in the 1919 World Series.

June 19, 1976

New Baseball Contract Limits Reserve System

By MURRAY CHASS
Special to The New York Times

PHILADELPHIA, July 12—Baseball's owners and players reached agreement today on a four-year pact that for the first time gives the players freedom of movement.

After 13 months of sometimes meandering, sometimes intensive negotiations, the executive board of the Major League Baseball Players Association and the Player Relations Committee, the owners' negotiating body, approved the intricate package that will enable a player to become a free agent after six years of major league service.

The agreement, on the eve of the All-Star Game here, replaces the so-called reserve system, which throughout baseball history has restricted a player to one club until that club traded, sold or released him.

The final ratification remains with all 24 club owners, who will meet here Wednesday, and the 600 major league players, who will vote in team meetings sometime in the next two weeks. Both groups are expected to approve the settlement although some owners, perhaps four, are likely to balk at the terms.

Asked if the dispute that delayed the start of spring training last March and threatened to disrupt the season was over, Marvin Miller, executive director of the Players Association, said, "I believe so."

Commissioner Bowie Kuhn, who remained on the sidelines during the negotiations, welcomed the agreement and said he would recommend its acceptance to the owners.

The agreement actually is

Associated Press
Marvin Miller

divided into two parts—a four-year basic agreement covering working conditions and economic terms other than players' salaries, and a four-year benefit plan. The eight-member player relations committee approved the terms unanimously. The players' executive board favored them 22-0 with one abstention.

Negotiators and other officials declined to disclose details of the settlement, saying they wanted to provide the owners and players with them first-hand. However, these key details were learned:

¶A player will have the right to demand a trade after having played in the majors for five years. He will have a veto right over six clubs. If he is not traded, he will become a free agent.

¶Players who become free agents, including those now governed by the Andy Messersmith decision, will be able to negotiate with a maximum of 12 teams, starting with the inverse order of the previous season standings. Each club will be limited in the number of free

agents it can sign, being permitted a maximum of one, for example, if the free-agent pool totals one to 14. However, a club will be able to sign as many free agents as it might lose in any one season.

¶The only compensation for a lost player will be draft choices. If one of the 12 lowest teams signs a player, it would lose its second choice in the next draft of college and high school players to the player's former team. If one of the top 12 teams signs a player, it would forfeit its No. 1 draft choice.

¶Players can take their salary differences to arbitration as they did before the 1974 season. However, if a player is eligible to become a free agent, his salary dispute can go to arbitration only by mutual consent of the player and the club.

¶The owners will increase their contribution to the benefit, or pension, plan, from $6.45 million to $8.3 million.

The minimum salary was raised, retroactive to the beginning of this season, from $16,000 to $19,000 this year, $19,000 next and $21,000 each in 1978 and 1979.

The players who will experience the first effects of the new agreement are the 39 who have not signed contracts this season. Under an arbitrator's interpretation of the renewal clause of the uniform players contract, the players can become free agents by playing one year without a new contract.

Players in this category now include Fred Lynn, Joe Rudi, Rollie Fingers, Reggie Jackson, Ken Holtzman, Graig Nettles and Bert Campaneris. However, the number of unsigned players has shrunk steadily all season and undoubtedly will shrink even more before the season ends Oct. 3.

It was a decision by Peter Seitz, a New York arbitrator, in the grievance filed by Messersmith and Dave McNally, that marked the beginning of the end of baseball's reserve system. Two Federal courts subsequently upheld that ruling and the owners finally—al-

though reluctantly — were convinced that they had to negotiate a new player control system.

If not, all players were eligible to become free agents by playing one year without a new contract.

Players who have signed contracts still will be able to exercise that right when their contracts eventually expire.

However, a new uniform players' contract without the controversial renewal clause will be drawn up and the 24 clubs will attempt to induce the already-signed players to sign those new documents as replacements. That would eliminate their opportunity to become free agents after an option year.

The new agreement will take effect as soon as it is ratified. The factor then governing a player's status would be the time he signed his contract. If he signed it before ratification of the agreement, he would be governed by the Messersmith decision. If he signs the contract after ratification, he will be covered by the six-year plan for free agency.

The members of the players' executive board were uncharacteristically close-mouthed about today's proceedings and the details of the agreement. However, it was learned that they were highly pleased with the terms. They realized there could never be an agreement if they didn't give in on their rights under the Messersmith ruling, but the owners were seen as giving considerably more ground than the players.

For example, in the owners' last previous proposals that were made public, in April, they offered free agency after eight years and the right to demand a trade after seven. For compensation, besides draft choices, they proposed a monetary formula that had a maximum of $270,000. The players, at the same time, were proposing free agency after six seasons, the right to demand a trade after five and no compensation.

Training Camps Closed

The negotiations actually began in June 1975, but nothing significant occurred until after Seitz's decision last December. Even then, talks dragged on until the owners decided last Feb. 23 that spring camps would not open until an agreement had been reached. However, Kuhn ordered camps opened March 18 and some people believed negotiations would speed up.

Others, however, foresaw the opposite and, indeed, the talks dragged so slowly that they came to a virtual halt. In recent weeks, however, the negotiators tried a new tactic. Instead of holding formal negotiating sessions in either Miller's office or that of John Gaherin, the owners' labor representative, they began meeting informally in seclusion at the Biltmore Hotel in New York.

This routine proved much more effective. The negotiators began making progress.

The movement last week was crucial. That was the final week before Miller would meet with his executive board for the last time this season. If no settlement were reached now, it was very likely the season would end without an agreement and players would become free agents in a conceivably chaotic situation.

Last Tuesday, the five negotiators met all day at the Biltmore. The group consisted of Miller and Richard Moss, the Players Association Counsel, and Gaherin and the two league presidents, Lee MacPhail and Charles (Chub) Feeney.

Traveling Talks

The following day, they held a brief session. Then the owners' trio flew to Chicago for a meeting of the player relations committee.

They returned to New York Thursday morning, leaving Chicago at 6:45 A.M., and again met with Miller and Moss at the Biltmore. Each day produced a little more movement.

On Friday, the tactics were altered somewhat. Miller, Moss and Gaherin discussed the differences in their positions during lunch at the Barclay Hotel. The Saturday negotiations took place strictly on the telephone, primarily between Miller and Gaherin. Then, yesterday, the five-man negotiating group gathered in Gaherin's office on 42d Street and added Barry Rona, Gaherin's counsel, and Jim Garner, the American League counsel. They met from 9:00 A.M. to 5:00 P.M. and when they were finished, they had their agreement.

The scene then shifted to

Philadelphia where Gaherin, MacPhail and Feeney met with the owners on the players' relation committee—Ted Bonda of Cleveland, Clark Griffith of Minnesota, Ed Fitzgerald of Milwaukee, Bob Howsam of Cincinnati, Dan Galbraith of Pittsburgh and John McHale of Montreal.

The committee unanimously approved the agreement and Gaherin informed Moss at 1 o'clock this morning. Miller, Moss, Gaherin and Rona then had breakfast together in the coffee shop of the Bellevue-Stratford Hotel and signed a memorandum of agreement. Finally, Miller and Moss reviewed the terms of the agreement with the executive board in a 2½-hour meeting and the long, tedious battle over player freedom was over.

July 13, 1976

Yankees Win, 7-6, on Homer in 9th, Capture First Pennant in 12 Years

By MURRAY CHASS

With a blow that rivaled Bobby Thomson's 1951 home run for stunning drama, Chris Chambliss hit a home run on the first pitch of the ninth inning last night and catapulted the New York Yankees to the American League pennant for the first time since 1964.

Chambliss's homer, off Mark Littell, gave the Yankees a 7-6 game victory and 3-2 playoff triumph over the plucky Kansas City Royals in the fifth game of the league's championship series. It sent New York into the World Series, where the Yankees will meet the Reds in Cincinnati beginning at 1 P.M. tomorrow.

The dramatic drive over the right-center field fence sent a torrent of fans from the sellout crowd of 56,821 onto the field at Yankee Stadium. They massed instantly on the infield and prevented Chambliss from touching home plate. However, the quiet first baseman returned to the field from the clubhouse and, escorted by two policemen, pushed and shoved his way back through the excited throng and touched the plate just to make sure.

Chambliss, whose homer broke championship series records for both hits (11) and runs batted in (8), was the 2-year-old son of a Navy chaplain 25 years ago when Thomson hit the homer that enabled the New York Giants to beat the Brooklyn Dodgers in the final inning of a three-game playoff for the National League pennant.

The home run last night gave the Yankees their 30th pennant and their first in the divisional setup that was created in 1969, the year the Royals were born as an expansion team.

"I'm sorry we couldn't win," said Whitey Herzog, the Royal manager "but I'm happy that the World Series is back in New York. And don't worry, you guys aren't going to be embarrassed."

The Royals, who staggered to the Western Division title despite losing nine of their last 11 games, almost embarrassed the Yankees, who didn't win the pennant playoff as easily as they won the Eastern Division crown.

With Mickey Rivers getting four hits, Thurman Munson rapping three hits and driving in two runs, and Chambliss contributing two of each, the Yankees built a 6-3 lead in the sixth inning after the Royals had grabbed a 2-0 lead on John Mayberry's two-run homer in the first inning.

But George Brett, the league's No. 1 hitter, who had doubled off Ed Figueroa ahead of Mayberry's homer, brought the Royals back with stunning suddenness in the eighth inning. Al Cowens started the eighth with a single and, after Grant Jackson, a left-hander, replaced Figueroa, Jim Wohlford singled.

Brett's double in the first had raised his career record against Figueroa to 19 hits in 28 times at bat, and when he came to the plate in the eighth, he must have thought the Puerto Rican right-hander was still in the game because he hit a home run into the right-field stands off Jackson, tying the game at 6-6.

Clearing the Way

"We weren't down," insisted Chambliss, an unlikely candidate for the kind of champagne celebration that raged in the Yankee clubhouse afterward. "It just tied the game. We knew we had to score some more runs."

The Yankees didn't score any runs in the last half of the eighth inning and Dick Tidrow held the Royals scoreless in their half of the ninth.

Before the Yankee half of the ninth could start, the game was delayed for about five minutes while members of the ground crew cleared the outfield of bottles that had been tossed from the stands.

"It was unfortunate that people were throwing bottles," Chambliss said. "You know these people; they're crazy."

A Fan Steals Second

When the bottles finally had been toted off the field, Chambliss stepped into the left-handed side of the batter's box and Littell took the sign from Buck Martinez, the catcher. The 23-year-old right-handed relief pitcher threw his first pitch, a high fastball, and Chambliss swung.

"I just wanted to be aggressive," said the 6-foot-1-inch, 209-pounder the Yankees acquired from Cleveland in a controversial trade in 1974. "I didn't want to be taking."

As Chambliss started running toward first base, he saw the ball disappear behind the padded blue fence and thrust his arms into the air. He reached first base and touched it easily enough, but by the time he headed for second, the overzealous fans were pouring onto the field. As he reached second base, a fan already had taken the bag out of the ground and Chambliss was forced to touch it with his right hand.

When he neared the spot that a shortstop normally plays, Chambliss ran into a fan and fell. After getting back to his feet, he zigged and zagged his way through human roadblocks

Yankees Box Score

KANSAS CITY (A.)	ab.r.h.bi.		YANKEES (A.)	ab.r.h.bi.
Cowens, cf	4 1 1 0		Rivers, cf	5 3 4 0
Poquette, lf	3 0 0 0		White, lf	5 2 1 1
Wohlford, lf	2 1 1 0		Munson, c	5 0 3 2
Brett, 3b	4 2 2 3		Chambliss, 1b	4 2 3 5
Mayberry, 1b	4 1 2 2		May, dh	4 0 0 0
McRae, rf	4 0 0 0		Alomar, pr	0 0 0 0
Quirk, dh	4 0 0 0		Nettles, 3b	3 0 0 0
Rojas, 2b	4 1 1 0		Gamble, rf	3 0 0 0
Patek, ss	4 0 1 0		Randolph, 2b	3 0 0 0
Martinez, c	3 0 3 1		Stanley, ss	3 0 0 0
Leonard, p	0 0 0 0		Figueroa, p	0 0 0 0
Splittorff, p	0 0 0 0		Jackson, p	0 0 0 0
Pattin, p	0 0 0 0		Tidrow, p	0 0 0 0
Hassler, p	0 0 0 0			
Littell, p	0 0 0 0			
Total	**37 4 11 6**		**Total**	**38 7 11 6**

No one out when winning run was scored.
Kansas City ..... 2 1 0 000 030—6
Yankees .... 2 0 2 002 001—7
E—Gamble, Brett. DP—Yankees 1. LOB—Kansas City 5, Yankees 9. 2B—Brett, Chambliss. 3B—Rivers. HR—Mayberry (1), Brett (1), Chambliss (2). 3B—Rojas, White, Chambliss. S—White, Gamble. SF—Chambliss.

	IP.	H.	R.	ER.	BB.	SO.
Leonard	0	2	2	2	0	0
Splittorff	3⅔	3	2	2	2	1
Pattin	⅓	0	0	0	1	0
Hassler	2⅔	5	2	2	1	1
Littell (L,0-1)	1⅓	1	1	1	0	1
Figueroa	7	8	6	4	2	0
Jackson	2	2	2	2	0	1
Tidrow (W, 1-0)	0	1	0	0	0	0

T—3:13. A—56,821.

Chris Chambliss connecting for the winning home run in ninth inning

and reached his next objective, third base.

Home plate was another matter. He turned wide around third and took a circuitous route that carried him well wide of the plate and into the Yankee dugout. To manage that final stretch, he pushed people out of the way and once spun completely around, like a fullback trying to get through a small hole in the line.

"Home plate was completely covered with people," Chambliss related, taking an occasional sip from a magnum of champagne. "I wasn't sure if I tagged it or not. I came in the clubhouse and all the players were talking about whether I got it. I wasn't sure, so I went back out."

Graig Nettles who touched home plate 32 times this year as the league's home run champion, was one of the players who urged Chambliss to go back out and touch the plate.

"I wanted to make sure there was no way we were going to lose it," Nettles said.

Rivers Takes Charge

Rivers wanted to make sure the Yankees wouldn't lose it, too. The center fielder, who played such an important role in the Yankees' season, was having a rough series four hits in 18 times at bat—and George Steinbrenner, the team's chief owner, had called him to his office for a private chat after Wednesday's fourth-game defeat.

"Without the Mickey Rivers we had during the season, we aren't going to win this thing," Steinbrenner told him. "You're the team leader. You make the team go."

Rivers apparently had some problems that he discussed with the owner. When he left the meeting, Rivers was determined that this would be his best game of the season.

"This game meant a lot to me," said Rivers, who batted .312 as one of 11 Yankees who played for the team for the first time this season. "I told myself I had to go out and do the best

job I could. I was looking bad, I was sick, my shoulder was hurting, but I knew I had to play, so I went out and I put forth every effort to my game."

Rivers's game consisted of a leadoff triple in the first inning (he scored on Roy White's single), a leadoff single in the third (he scored on Munson's single), a single in the fourth and a leadoff bunt single in the sixth (he scored on Munson's single).

Chambliss Does It All

Before his home run, Chambliss had tied the game at 2-2 with a sacrifice fly in the first; had driven in a run with a force-play grounder in the third that put the Yankees ahead, 4-3; had doubled in the fifth and had singled, stolen second base and scored on Brett's wild throw in the sixth.

Dennis Leonard, the Kansas City starter, lasted only nine pitches. Herzog removed him after Rivers tripled and White and Munson singled.

Figueroa, the Yankee starter, fared much better, despite allowing three runs in the first two innings. He settled

down and didn't allow more than one runner an inning in the next five.

But when Cowens led off the eighth with a single, Manager Billy Martin brought in Jackson. He might have regretted that move when Brett planted a home run just a few rows into the right-field stands and a few feet on the fair side of the foul pole, but Chambliss erased whatever negative thoughts the manager might have had.

"I was never so excited," said Martin, who won his first pennant as a manager in three playoff attempts with three teams. "Even as a player, when I got the big hit in the '53 Series, I didn't jump as high as I did tonight."

Martin and the rest of the Yankees have until 1 P.M. tomorrow to come down.

October 15, 1976

Sadaharu Oh of the Yomiuri [Japan] Giants hitting the 756th home run of his career during game in Tokyo yesterday.

Oh Surpasses Aaron With 756th Home Run

By ANDREW MALCOLM
Special to The New York Times

TOKYO, Sept. 3—Sadaharu Oh hit the 756th homer of his Japanese baseball career here tonight, making him the most prolific home-run hitter in professional history.

The 37-year-old first baseman for the Yomiuri Giants hit his 755th home run last Wednesday night, tying the number that the retired Henry Aaron achieved in setting a major league mark in the United States. Oh's homer tonight, an arching 328-foot shot into the right-field stands of Tokyo's Korakuen Stadium, ignited nationwide celebrations by millions of cheering fans, who have adopted Oh as a Japanese national hero—even though he is actually Chinese and cannot vote in Japan.

Oh has said, "I don't think I would do as well in American baseball," but comparisons are difficult to draw. Japanese parks are slightly smaller than those in the United States, and coast-to-coast travel takes a more severe toll on American ballplayers. On the other hand, Oh has had to achieve his feat in considerably shorter seasons played in Japan.

Joe DiMaggio, a frequent visitor to Japan, had rated Japanese baseball quality as somewhere between the American triple-A minors and the major leagues. Other American observers also believe that Oh faced pitchers less effective than those who threw to Aaron.

Tomorrow Oh, the shy, modest son of an immigrant Chinese noodle vender, will meet Prime Minister Takeo Fukuda to receive a special Japan medal of honor. Then he will proceed to the ballpark to resume his left-handed assault on the 800 home-run goal.

But tonight, even as chanting fans bearing banners converged on his modest Tokyo home, Oh, bathed in spotlights, stood hatless in the middle of the field and told a hushed, hoarse crowd: "As long as my body can stand it, I will swing a bat and hit more home runs, with everybody's help."

To make matters even better, the historic home run helped Oh's Giants, the perennial pennant-winners in Japan's two-league, 12-team professional baseball system, to top the second-place Yakult Swallows, 8-1, and keep a 14-game hold on first place.

The 'Oh Shift'

The homer came in the bottom of the third inning, with none on and one out. Oh, who has been hitting .321, had walked his previous time at bat, a tactic opposing pitchers have taken 2,180 times during his 19-year career. The Swallows also had gone into the "Oh shift," in which players move to the batter's right.

The count was 3 and 2. Oh, who admits he still gets tense before every game, nervously tapped his shoes with his bat, spit into his ungloved hands and faced the Swallows pitcher, a 28-year-old, five-year veteran named Yasumiro Suzuki.

As the ball left Suzuki's hand, Oh lifted his right leg in his distinctive one-legged "flamingo" batting style. The pitch was supposed to be a sinker. But Oh slammed his right foot down hard and swung the bat around waist-high. The ball rose into the muggy air, along with 55,000 screaming fans.

Four seconds later Saneyoshi Furuya, a 25-year-old office worker who was at his fifth game in five days hoping to see the big homer, caught the ball. In return for it, the Giants gave him a new autographed ball, bat and a trip to a hot springs spa.

"I knew instantly that it was gone," said a smiling Oh, who held his arms up high and circled the bases slowly, as his coach had instructed, so he could savor the achievement. Oh jumped on home plate with both feet and was mobbed by teammates. "Now I can sleep well tonight," he told them.

Pitcher Declines 'Honor'

Confetti, streamers and fireworks flew while Suzuki, the pitcher, watched quietly. Continental Air Micronesia, a United States airline, had offered the pitcher of home run No. 756 a trip to Saipan. But a disappointed Suzuki declined tonight.

Absent from the crowd were Oh's wife, Kyoko, and their three daughters. Oh, who is protective of their privacy from his fame, had them watch on TV at home. But his aging father, Shufuku, 76, and his mother, Tomi, were in their reserved seats as usual. And Oh presented them with his prize bouquet. "At last," said the elder Oh, "the pressure is off."

Oh will get a substantial bonus on top of his $240,000 salary for a 130-game season. He will also receive an oil painting, a new car, an electric organ, a spa trip and 756 bath towels.

"I've been wearing the uniform of the Yomiuri Giants for 19 years," Oh told the crowd. "I've had my difficulties and disappointments. But thanks to your strong support, my dream has been realized. I am a fortunate man."

Oh, who like Babe Ruth began his career as a pitcher, has been the premier Japanese player almost from the day he graduated from high school and signed with the Giants. He has hit four home runs in one game, seven in seven consecutive games and 13 with the bases loaded, including one in the opening game this year.

September 4, 1977

YANKEES TAKE SERIES; JACKSON EQUALS MARK OF 3 HOMERS IN GAME

By JOSEPH DURSO

With Reggie Jackson hitting three home runs in three straight times at bat, the New York Yankees swept all those family feuds under the rug last night and overpowered the Los Angeles Dodgers, 8-4, to win their first World Series in 15 years.

They won it in the sixth game of a match that had enlivened both coasts for the last week, and that rocked Yankee Stadium last night as hundreds of fans poured through a reinforced army of 350 security guards and stormed onto the field after the final out.

For a team that already had made financial history by spending millions for players in the open market, the victory in the 74th World Series also brought new baseball history to the Yankees: It was the 21st time that they had won the title, but the first time since they defeated the San Francisco Giants in 1962 toward the end of their long postwar reign. And it marked a dramatic comeback from the four-game sweep they suffered last October at the hands of the Cincinnati Reds.

But for Jackson, the $3 million free agent who led the team in power hitting and power rhetoric, this was a game that perhaps had no equal since the World Series was inaugurated in 1903. He hit his three home runs on the first pitches off three pitchers, and he became the only man in history to hit three in a Series game since Babe Ruth did it for the Yankees twice, in 1926 and again in 1928.

But nobody had ever before hit five in a World Series—let alone five in his last nine official times at bat—a feat that the 31-year-old Pennsylvanian accomplished during the last three games in California and New York.

"Perhaps for one night," Jackson reflected later inside the Yankees' tumultuous locker room, "I reached back and achieved that level of the overrated superstar. I'm also happy for George Steinbrenner, whose neck was stuck out farther than mine."

Steinbrenner's neck was stuck out, and his bankroll extended, because he and his 15 partners had spent a fortune during the last three years to sign Jackson, Catfish Hunter, Don Gullett and other stars of baseball's changing world. And Jackson also stood in the center of the feuding that had embroiled the team and its manager, Billy Martin, who received a bonus and a vote of confidence during the uncertain hours before the Yankees turned their trick.

The Yankees' return to the front rank of the major leagues also was marked by the pitching of Mike Torrez, the 31-year-old right-hander from Kansas, who had unwittingly touched off another family fuss by superseding Ed Figueroa on the mound. Torrez pitched a seven-hitter last Friday night in Los Angeles, where he won Game 3, and a nine-hitter last evening in the Bronx, where he outlasted four Dodger pitchers starting with Burt Hooton.

But this was mainly a night for hitting by both the Yankees and the Dodgers, late of Brooklyn—the teams that once produced the perfect game, the dropped third strike and the Subway Series. And this time they produced

The Yankee's controversial Reggie Jackson connects for the second of three home runs he hit in the final game of the 1977 World Series.

another extravaganza before a throng of 56,407 that tossed balloons, paper streamers and firecrackers onto the field and even forced Jackson to leave right field in the ninth inning for a batting helmet to protect his head.

"This is very rewarding," Manager Billy Martin said later, referring to the quarrels his team had surmounted while beating the Kansas City Royals for the American League pennant and then the Dodgers for the World Series. "We had to beat two great teams. I'm proud of our players and what they accomplished this year. What made them overcome all those obstacles? We had five or six guys help patch things up during the season. Reggie? He was sensational."

Martin's Day to Remember

For Martin, who lived in the center of the storm surrounding the Yankees this summer, the occasion was rewarding in more ways than one. In a belated bid to bring unity out of chaos, the owners announced during the afternoon that they were rewarding the manager "for a fine job." He received a bonus of perhaps $35,000, a gift of a Lincoln Continental, a subsidy toward his rent and a new assurance that he would stay on the job despite rumors that he would go.

The Yankees also shook down some of the old traditions that had brought them 31 pennants as the monopoly team of baseball for much of the last half-century. The first ball last night was thrown out by Joe DiMaggio, who strode to the pitcher's mound in a blue suit and tossed one to Thurman Munson, one week after he had boycotted the Stadium during a mixup over tickets. And Robert Merrill, a familiar voice in the ball park, sang the national anthem from the grass behind home plate.

But the Dodgers, the champions of the National League twice in the last four seasons, were flanked by celebrities, too. Lillian Carter, the mother of President Carter, attended her third straight game as a self-proclaimed "loyal Dodger fan." And Mayor Tom Bradley of Los Angeles watched from a box alongside the visitors' dugout.

Dodgers Begin Crisply

When the players got around to the main event, the Dodgers knew full well that only three teams in baseball history had lost three of the first four games in a World Series and then won three straight for the title. Inside one inning, they rattled Torrez for two runs as they fought to force this Series into a winner-take-all finale.

But inside of two innings, the Yankees retaliated on a home run by Chris Chambliss. Then, after Reggie Smith hit one for the Dodgers in the third inning, Reginald Martinez Jackson took charge on three swings of the bat: a home run off Hooton in the fourth inning, another off Elias Sosa in the fifth and another off Charlie Hough in the eighth.

He also knocked in five runs, and later suggested: "Babe Ruth was great. I'm just lucky."

At the start, though, it was the Dodgers who came out swinging as they tried to recoil from the point of no return. With two down in the first inning, Smith rammed a grounder off Bucky Dent's glove at shortstop for an error. Then a pitch got past Munson for a passed ball, and Smith moved to second base. Then came big trouble: Ron Cey walked and Steve Garvey lined one past first base for three bases and two runs.

The New York Times/Larry Morris

Reggie Jackson acknowledges standing ovation after his third home run.

Chambliss Belts One

Hooton protected that bonanza only until the second inning, when he walked Jackson and threw a pitch that Chambliss described as "a fastball, low and out over the plate." The big first baseman pounded the ball 400 feet into the bleacher seats in right-center field, and just like that, the old rivals were tied.

They came untied again when the Dodgers batted in the top of the third and, with two down, Smith hit the 1-and-1 pitch from Torrez even deeper to right-center. It was the third home run of the Series for the Dodger outfielder, equaling the six-game record for a National League player, and again the Dodgers moved in front. And again, only briefly.

They went to the fourth inning still leading but then, before Hooton got anybody out, the Yankees fired the fatal shots. Munson led off with a single past third base and, on the next pitch, Jackson hammered one into the right-field grandstand.

Now the Yankees were back in front, 4-3, and Hooton was replaced by Sosa, who was victimized when Chambliss lifted a towering pop fly that came down within reach of two Dodgers armed with gloves. They were Dusty Baker, the left fielder, and Bill Russell, the shortstop.

Both went for the ball, both could have caught it, both shied away at the last moment and it dropped untouched for a double. Then Chambliss took third on an infield grounder and scored on a sacrifice fly by Lou Piniella, making it 5-3, and time was growing short for the 1977 Dodgers.

Wait 'Til Next Year

One inning later, it was growing even shorter when Mickey Rivers singled and Jackson drilled the first pitch beyond the right-field railing past the $15 box seats for his second home run. And now the Yankees were in control, 7-3.

As memorable as that was, Jackson went even farther in the eighth inning when he went to bat for the last time in an unlikely season. For the third straight time, he pounced on the first pitch and bombed it 450 feet into the center-field bleachers for his third consecutive home run, his fourth in his last four swings and his record-breaking fifth in the 74th World Series.

"It's very tough to lose a World Series," conceded Tommy Lasorda, the manager of the Dodgers, who lost this one 3,000 miles from their movieland cheerleaders. "We didn't hit like we were capable of hitting, but I don't want to alibi and take anything away from a great Yankee victory."

Will next year be calmer for the rebellious Yankees?

"I really doubt it," Chambliss said. "We did it this year amidst controversy all season long. We'll just have to wait and see."

October 19, 1977

Sixth Series Box Score

LOS ANGELES (N)	AB.	R.	H.	BI.
Lopes, 2b	4	0	1	0
Russell, ss	3	0	0	0
Smith, rf	4	2	1	1
Cey, 3b	3	1	1	0
Garvey, 1b	4	1	2	2
Baker, lf	4	0	1	0
Monday, cf	4	0	1	0
Yeager, c	3	0	0	0
Davalillo, ph	1	0	1	1
Hooton, p	2	0	0	0
Sosa, p	0	0	0	0
Rau, p	0	0	0	0
Goodson, ph	1	0	0	0
Hough, p	0	0	0	0
Lacy, ph	1	0	0	0
Total	34	4	9	4

YANKEES (A)	AB.	R.	H.	BI.
Rivers, cf	4	0	2	0
Randolph, 2b	4	1	0	0
Munson, c	4	1	1	0
Jackson, rf	3	4	3	5
Chambliss, 1b	4	2	2	2
Nettles, 3b	4	0	0	0
Piniella, lf	3	0	0	1
Dent, ss	2	0	0	0
Torrez, p	3	0	0	0
Total	31	8	8	8

	1	2	3	4	5	6	7	8	9	
Los Angeles	0	0	1	0	0	0	0	0	1	—4
Yankees	0	2	0	3	2	0	1	x		—8

Error—Dent. Double plays—Yankees 2. Left on base—Los Angeles 5, Yankees 2. Two base hit—Chambliss. Three base hit—Garvey. Home runs—Chambliss (1), Smith (3), Jackson 3, (5). Sacrifice fly. Piniella.

	IP.	H.	R.	ER	BB	SO
Hooton (L, 1-1)	3	3	4	4	1	1
Sosa	1⅔	3	3	3	1	0
Rau	1⅓	0	0	0	0	1
Hough	2	2	1	1	0	2
Torrez (W, 2-0)	9	9	4	2	2	6

Passed ball—Munson. Time of game—2:19. Attendance—56,407.

Scrappy, Controversial Yankee Manager
Alfred Manuel (Billy) Martin

By LEONARD KOPPETT

He used to be called The Kid, as in Billy the Kid, a symbol of American Western banditry. When he was in his 20's, Billy Martin played three infield positions for Yankee teams that were winning championships every year. He was also described as "scrappy" and "street smart." His ability to play winning ball and occasionally star in a World Series was regarded as an admirable example of a type his manager, Casey Stengel, liked best: a player of limited physique who could beat more-talented men by using his nerve, wits, concentration and determination.

Now 49 years old, he reached the pinnacle of his eight years as a major league manager by leading the Yankees to their Series conquest last night. They were the fourth team he had managed in the majors.

Martin is rarely referred to as The Kid now. He remains scrappy and controversial and retains the knack of winning. Every team he has taken over has made dramatic improvement within two years: Minnesota, Detroit and the Yankees rose to first place. The Texas Rangers went from sixth to second, finishing behind the champion Oakland A's of 1974.

Everywhere he has worked he has been embroiled in controversy with top management and players. In Los Angeles during this Series he was relaxing with a beer in the manager's office at the ball park. The latest battle in his war of words with Reggie

Jackson had just reached a climax and someone was explaining to him that Jackson's remarks had often stemmed from the star's feeling of insecurity.

'I'm Insecure, Too'

"I'm insecure too," said Martin, "but I'm insecure because I don't have a lot of money, and that's natural, isn't it." Then he smiled and said: "How about that? One beer and I'm philosophizing."

Someone suggested Martin get a foundation to back a psychological experiment: A million dollars would be deposited to his account, and a psychiatrist could study how such an event would change his character.

Martin grinned and said, "I'll never change and I never have changed."

Alfred Manuel Martin was born on May 16, 1928, in Berkeley, Calif., just north of Oakland, an area that was then producing some of baseball's greatest figures. His father left the family before he was born, and with his mother working, he was brought up by his grandparents, who lived a few blocks away. It was a warm, enduring relationship and gave Martin pride in his Italian ancestry. But most of his growing up was done in the streets.

His grandmother called him "Bellissimos "Most Beautiful," which was shortened to "Bcelli." Other kids, hearing him called that, naturally made it "Billy." When he started school and the teacher asked for "Alfred Martin," he didn't answer; he didn't know who

Alfred was. He remained Billy ever since.

In 1946, at 18, he was graduated from Berkeley High and signed a professional contract with the Oakland team of the Pacific Coast League, the top minor league then. He spent the rest of the summer playing at Idaho Falls, in the low minors, and most of 1947 in Phoenix, a modest step up the baseball ladder.

For the last few days of that season he was brought up to Oakland, where the manager was Stengel. In 1948 he played fulltime for Casey at three infield positions and the Oaks won the pennant. The next year he played virtually every game at second or short as the team finished second under a new manager (Charley Dressen) because Stengel had been given the unexpected opportunity to manage the Yankees.

But Stengel remembered. In 1949 he won the first of his 10 pennants in 12 years with the Yankees. The team was loaded with established stars and important younger players like Gene Woodling, Hank Bauer and Yogi Berra. It had spectacular, still-younger players on the way up: Mickey Mantle, Whitey Ford, Gil McDougald. All their ratings exceeded Martin's, but Stengel had seen Martin's competitiveness first hand. Second base was one position with an opening, and Stengel had the Yankees buy Martin as a utility man.

He started the 1950 season in Kansas City, the top Yankee farm club then, but was in the Bronx by midseason. The next year, when Mantle joined the club, a strong friendship developed between the street-smart utility infielder and the fantastically publicized but naive star from Oklahoma.

In 1952 Martin became the regular second baseman. He spent 1954 and most of 1955 in the Army, and was back at work in 1956.

Although brash and irreverent, Martin worshiped Stengel like a father, which didn't prevent him from arguing with "the old man" while he was learning. Stengel, who had no children, loved Martin like a favorite son, seeing his own pugnacious and "slick" character reflected in Billy.

But in May 1957, a coincidence of birthdays had strange consequences. Berra's was May 12, Martin's May 16; the 16th was to be an open date, so a party was arranged for the night of the 15th by half a dozen players to celebrate the two birthdays at the Copacabana night club. All would bring their wives except Martin, who was divorced.

There was a confrontation in the night club between Bauer and an annoying drunk, which ended in Bauer's arrest, enormous headlines, little sleep, $1,000 fines (although Bauer was eventually cleared of all charges) and a cause célèbre.

George Weiss, the Yankee general manager, had never appreciated Martin and resented his nonconformity to the image he thought the team should have. He seized the opportunity to trade him to Kansas City, saying Martin was a "bad influence" on Mantle.

Martin would not forgive Stengel for not having prevented his exile, and didn't speak to him for several years. But later they made up.

Away from the Yankees, Martin drifted. He played for six more teams, winding up in Minnesota in 1961, as 33. In 1959 he had remarried. He worked for the Twins as a scout, then became a coach for them in 1965 (when they won a pennant). In 1968 he was offered a minor league managing job in Denver but was afraid to take it

"I'll never change and I never have changed."
A victorious Billy Martin toasts the Yankees' world championship.

because he might not get back to the majors. But he did take it, in midseason, and at the end of the year was promoted to manager of the Twins, succeeding Paul Ermer.

His Twins Win the Pennant

He brought the Twins home first in 1969, but was dismissed after conflicts with Calvin Griffith, the owner, and other club officials. In 1971 he became manager of the Detroit Tigers, who had an aging team. They finished second, then first in 1972, and when they were running third with a month to go in the 1973 season, he was dismissed again.

Within a week, he was managing again at Texas. The Rangers were finishing last for the third straight year, and had never finished in the top half of the league. In 1974 he made them a contender, finishing a close second to an Oakland team about to win its third straight Series.

But on July 20, 1975, frictions with the owner, Brad Corbett, ended in Martin's dismissal. Twelve days later the Yankees hired him and he was in the chair once occupied by Stengel and only a few weeks before Stengel's death.

Had he changed? Yes, in some ways.

His 12-year-old son, Billy Joe, is around the clubhouse as often as having a permanent home in Texas and school obligations permit. And Martin glows in his presence. For all his outbursts and occasional shows of temper, he holds in his emotions much more now than two decades ago, or even a few years ago. His face, when he doesn't wear a mustache, remains youthful, but the emotional toll of this season has put more lines on it.

Those who dislike him, and there are many, call him egotistical, unreasonable, uncontrollable, uncommunicative and untruthful. In his eyes, he is the victim of constant attack on the one thing he will not compromise—his decision-making power as manager, which he considers his deepest integrity.

But he has retained his sense of humor, his competitive urge, his stubborn belief in "my own way" and an astonishing amount of sentimentalism about the Yankee uniform. And few of the Western gunfighters of the Billy the Kid image were still in action at 49.

October 19, 1977

Pirates Capture Series With 4-1 Triumph

Stargell Hits 2-Run Clout in 6th — Tekulve Ends Oriole Threat

By MURRAY CHASS
Special to The New York Times

BALTIMORE, Oct. 17 — Willie Stargell, who is Pops to Pittsburgh's most-famous family, helped the Pirates win their fifth World Series championship tonight.

The Pirates, trailing Baltimore by three games to one four days ago, never lost again as they snatched the Series from the expectant but wilting hands of the Orioles by winning the seventh game, 4-1. Only three other teams have achieved such a seven-game comeback in the 76-year history of the

Series — the 1925 Pirates, 1958 New York Yankees and 1968 Detroit Tigers.

Stargell, who scored the winning run in the seventh game of the Pirates' 1971 Series triumph over the Orioles, lashed four hits tonight, including a two-run homer off Scott McGregor in the sixth inning that wiped out Baltimore's 1-0 lead.

In hitting his third homer of the Series, the 38-year-old Stargell duplicated his 1971 feat by scoring what

stood up as the winning run. The patriarch of the close-knit group the Pirates call their family also walked away with the most-valuable-player award for his 12 Series hits and .400 batting average.

In the end, though, it wasn't only Stargell's hitting or the team's collective .323 average, second highest in Series history, that made the Pirates champions. It also was the pitching that shut down the Orioles, who had hit 181 home runs during the romp to their fourth American League pennant in

Earl Weaver's 11-year managerial reign.

Jim Bibby, Don Robinson, Grant Jackson and Kent Tekulve limited the Orioles to four hits tonight, which meant that the losers had staggered through the last three games with only two runs and 17 hits.

The most surprising hole in the Oriole attack was the bat swung by Eddie Murray, their young first baseman who had hit .295 and driven in 99 runs during the season. Murray finished the Series with no hits in his last 21 times at bat covering the final five games; he also wiped out two runners by hitting into double plays and stranded 13 others. The final three were left hanging in the eighth inning, when the Orioles, trailing by 2-1, had one of their best scoring opportunities of the last three games. With the bases loaded and two out, Tekulve, the spindly relief pitcher, retired Murray on a long fly to right field.

President at Game

President Carter, the first President to see a Series game since President Eisenhower visited Ebbets Field in Brooklyn in 1956, was on hand. From a first-row box seat just to the third-base side of home plate, the President watched and smiled, then stood and applauded Rich Dauer's home run off Bibby in the third inning and Stargell's first-pitch shot over the right-field fence in the sixth. He also presented the championship trophy to Chuck Tanner, the Pirate manager, in the wild Pirate clubhouse.

Stargell did not rattle any fences with his first two hits tonight. With McGregor keeping him off stride on breaking pitches, the first baseman sliced a single to left in the second inning, then blooped a double to left in the fourth.

When he came up in the sixth, Bill Robinson was on first with a one-out ground single that deflected off Kiko Garcia's glove at short and continued into left. McGregor, who had pitched a shutout in the pennant-clinching game against California and had won the third game of the Series, threw a slider on his first pitch to Stargell and it caught too much of the plate. Unable to pull McGregor's previous pitches, the left-handed Stargell swung and sent this one over the right-field fence, giving the Pirates a 2-1 lead.

It was the Pirates' third homer of the Series and the likable first baseman had hit them all. Dauer's homer in the third was the Orioles' fourth.

The Orioles, who had been slight favorites to win their third Series, threatened to score again in the fifth after Don Robinson took over from Bibby, who had been removed for a pinch-hitter. But with runners at first and second, Jackson replaced Robinson and retired Al Bumbry on a foul out.

Jackson, a 37-year-old left-hander who pitched for Baltimore in the 1971 Series, set the Orioles down in order in the sixth and seventh, but encountered control trouble with one out in the eighth. First he walked Lee May, a pinch-hitter, and then he walked Bumbry after Bumbry had fouled off three 3-2 pitches.

Tanner, who replaces pitchers more

Pirates' Willie Stargell, top, rushing to join teammates.

often than a parent changes a baby's diapers, decided it was time for Tekulve, who had lost the fourth game but saved the second and sixth.

The 6-foot-4-inch, 160-pound right-hander induced Terry Crowley, a pinch-hitter, to ground out, moving the runners to third and second. Then Tanner ordered an intentional walk to Ken Singleton, the Orioles' most dangerous hitter, with Murray, their biggest enigma, batting next.

"I had my choice of pitching to Singleton or Murray," explained Tanner. "With Tekulve throwing the ball the way he was throwing it, I had to go for a force at any base. If I had pitched to Singleton and he had gotten a hit, I would've kicked myself. Besides, Murray wasn't hitting well."

A Matter of Adjustment

Murray, trying desperately to snap out of his slump, stepped to the plate. Before the game, Frank Robinson, the Oriole coach, said that the Pirates had adjusted their way of pitching to Murray after he had stroked three hits in the second game, but that Murray had not adjusted to their adjustment. The Pirates, Robinson said, were throwing him breaking balls in tight.

Murray fouled off Tekulve's first two pitches, then watched as the next two sailed outside.

"I wanted to get the ball far enough away from him," the Pirates' No. 1 reliever explained, "where he couldn't

take the ball out. Or if he did hit it, he might take it the other way."

Tekulve fired his fifth pitch, a side-arm fastball that tailed away, and Murray pulled it to right field. Dave Parker, the 6-foot-5-inch right fielder, turned to his right and staggered backward several steps before grabbing it a couple of steps in front of the warning track.

Minutes later, the Pirates scored a pair of anticlimactic runs. Those came off five pitchers in one inning, a Series record. Tim Stoddard pitched to two batters, Mike Flanagan, Don Stanhouse and Tippy Martinez one each and Dennis Martinez two. Omar Moreno drove in one run with his third single and sixth in the last two games, and Dennis Martinez forced home the other when he hit Bill Robinson with a bases-loaded pitch.

The next batter was Stargell, who had added an eighth-inning double to his onslaught and set a Series mark with seven extra-base hits. This time, though, he grounded into an inning-ending double play, bringing the Orioles to bat for the last time.

The man who operates the Memorial Stadium phonograph marked the occasion by playing a record of Elvis Presley's singing, "It's Now or Never."

Tekulve struck out Gary Roenicke and "never" was a little closer. He struck out Doug DeCinces and never was only one out away. Then Pat Kelly lofted a fly to Moreno in center, and it was never for the Orioles and "now" for the Pirates.

Pirates 4, Orioles 1

GAME SEVEN

PITTSBURGH					BALTIMORE				
	ab	r	h	bi		ab	r	h	bi
Moreno cf	5	1	3	1	Bumbry cf	3	0	0	0
Foli ss	4	0	1	0	Garcia ss	3	0	1	0
Parker rf	4	0	0	0	Ayala ph	0	0	0	0
B Robinson lf	4	1	1	1	Crowley ph	1	0	0	0
Stargell 1b	5	1	4	2	Stoddard p	0	0	0	0
Madlock 3b	3	0	0	0	Flanagan p	0	0	0	0
Nicosia c	4	0	0	0	Stanhouse p	0	0	0	0
Garner 2b	3	1	1	0	T Martinez p	0	0	0	0
Bibby p	1	0	0	0	D Martinez p	0	0	0	0
Sanguillen ph	1	0	0	0	Singleton rf	3	0	0	0
D Robinson p	0	0	0	0	Murray 1b	4	0	0	0
Jackson p	1	0	0	0	Lowenstein lf	2	0	0	0
Tekulve p	1	0	0	0	Roenicke lf	2	0	0	0
					DeCinces 3b	4	0	2	0
					Dempsey c	3	0	0	0
					Kelly ph	1	0	0	0
					Dauer 2b	3	1	1	1
					McGregor p	1	0	0	0
					May ph	0	0	0	0
					Belanger ss	0	0	0	0
Total	36	4	10	4	**Total**	30	1	4	1

```
Pittsburgh   000 002 002— 4
Baltimore    001 000 000— 1
```

E—Lowenstein, Garcia. DP—Baltimore 1. LOB—Pittsburgh 10, Baltimore 6. 2B—Stargell 2, Garner. HR—Dauer (1), Stargell (3). S—Foli.

	IP	H	R	ER	BB	SO
Pittsburgh						
Bibby	4	3	1	1	0	3
D. Robinson	2/3	1	0	0	1	0
Jackson (W)	2 2/3	0	0	0	2	1
Tekulve	1 2/3	0	0	0	1	2
Baltimore						
McGregor (L)	8	7	2	2	2	2
Stoddard	1/3	1	1	1	0	0
Flanagan	0	1	1	1	0	0
Stanhouse	0	1	0	0	0	0
T. Martinez	0	0	0	0	0	0
D. Martinez	2/3	0	0	0	0	0

Flanagan pitched to 1 batter in 9th; Stanhouse pitched to 1 batter in 9th; T. Martinez pitched to 1 batter in 9th.

HBP—by T. Martinez (Parker); by D. Martinez (B. Robinson). T—2:54. A—53,733.

BASEBALL, bas'bôl, is a game between two teams of nine players each, played on a field with bat and ball, and refereed by one or more umpires. Beloved by millions of Americans, it is generally regarded as their national game. Though a growing minority now questions its claim to that distinction, it is hard to dispute baseball's preeminent position among American sports when one considers its deep roots in American life, its great appeal to the young, and the tremendous popular interest that develops each year in the major league pennant races and the world series.

Unlike certain other sports (soccer, basketball, track), baseball does not have a worldwide following. Outside the United States it is played chiefly in Latin America, Canada, and Japan. The game became very popular in Japan during the American occupation after World War II.

The following section describes the rules of baseball as it is played professionally in the United States:

HOW BASEBALL IS PLAYED

The Players. The nine-man team is made up of a pitcher and catcher (together called the battery); a first, second, and third baseman, and a shortstop (infielders); and a left, center, and right fielder (outfielders). A professional baseball squad also includes substitutes, coaches, and a manager, who directs the team. Players may be shifted from one position to another during the game. Managers are permitted to substitute players freely, but a player yielding to a substitute is not permitted to reenter the game. Major league squads are limited (from a period 30 days after the start of the season to September 1) to 25 active players.

Equipment and Uniforms. All players on a team wear uniforms identical in color, trim, and style. The uniform usually consists of knee stockings, knickers, and a half-sleeved flannel shirt, under which a long-sleeved jersey is worn. The shirt usually displays the name of the team and a number to identify the player. A visored cap, often with team initials, completes the uniform. Players wear spiked oxford-style shoes.

The regulation baseball is a sphere formed by winding yarn around a core of cork and rubber; its cover consists of two stripes of tightly stitched white horsehide. The ball must weigh not less than 5 or more than 5¼ ounces and must measure not less than 9 or more than 9¼ inches in circumference. The bat, a smooth round stick generally made of ash, can be no more than 2¾ inches in diameter at its thickest point and no more than 42 inches in length.

Each of the infielders (excepting the first baseman), each outfielder, and the pitcher wears on one hand a flexible leather finger glove with some padding. The catcher uses a heavily padded glove with a cleft between the thumb and index finger, and wears a chest protector, shin guards, and a wire mask to protect his face. The first baseman uses a glove which is smaller and more flexible than that used by the catcher. When at bat, the player usually wears a plastic helmet as a skull protector.

The Playing Field. Much of the play of the game takes place within a square called the infield or diamond. The sides of this square measure 90 feet and its four corners constitute four bases, the most important of which is the home base, called home plate. First base is diagonally to the right and third base diagonally to the left of home plate. The distance between home plate and second base, and between first base and third base is 127 feet, 3⅜ inches. White lines (called the foul lines) run from home plate past first and third base to the grandstands or outfield fences. All of the territory within the 90° angle formed by the foul lines is called fair territory; that outside is considered foul territory.

Home plate, 17 inches long and 17 inches wide, is marked by a five-sided slab of whitened rubber at ground level. At each of the other three bases are white canvas bags, 15 inches square and not less than 3 inches nor more than 4 inches thick. The bags are tied down by straps, and are located entirely within fair territory. The pitcher's rubber is a slab 2 feet long and 6 inches wide, situated 60 feet 6 inches from home plate in the direction of second base. It is located on the pitcher's mound, also called the "hill"; this is a circular mound with gradual slopes, which rises to a height of 10 inches above the base lines and home plate at the point of its greatest elevation.

Beyond the infield are the wide ranges of the outfield, which vary in area in different ball parks (although there has been a recent tendency to standardize playing fields). Under present rules, the minimum distance from home plate to an outfield grandstand or fence at the foul lines is 250 feet. However, since 1958 no professional club has been permitted to build a new field that does not have a minimum distance of 325 feet at the foul lines and 400 feet in center field.

General Principles of the Game. The object of baseball is the scoring of more runs than the opposition, and the zest of the game and all of its strategy hinges on the continuous struggle between the offense (the team at bat), which attempts to score, and the defense (the team in the field), which attempts to prevent such scoring. Initially, and throughout much of the game, the struggle is centered in the contest between the pitcher and the batter. As the pitcher throws (pitches) the ball to the catcher behind the plate, the batter attempts to judge whether the pitch is in the strike zone and, if it is, to hit it out of reach of the defensive players in the field. Members of the offensive team come to bat one at a time, each attempting to reach base safely, that is, without being put out. When a batter reaches base, he becomes a runner, and it becomes the task of the succeeding batter to advance him to the next base. Only one runner may occupy a base at any one time. A run is scored when a member of the team at bat, having advanced around the diamond counterclockwise, touching first, second, and third base in succession, completes the circuit and touches home plate. Three put-outs (that is, the retirement of three players) retires the side, whereupon the team which has been defending comes to bat and its opponents take the field.

Each team's time at bat constitutes a half-inning, an inning being that portion of the game in which both teams take one turn at bat. The standard game consists of 9 innings. The visiting team bats first, and if the home team is ahead after 8½ innings, the game ends. In the event that the score is tied after 9 innings, the game continues until the tie is broken, unless darkness or other conditions prevent further play. When a game is terminated by rain, failure of lighting, or some other factor which in the judgment of the umpire interferes with the play, 5 innings constitute a legal game (4½ innings if the home team is ahead).

The Start of the Game. Before the game begins, each team presents to the umpire in chief its starting lineup or batting order, the order in which the players will bat. As play is about to start, the home team players take their positions on the playing field. The pitcher takes his place on the mound; the catcher stands in a prescribed catcher's box (a rectangular area marked out behind home plate); and the other players move to the best strategic positions to cope with a ball hit in fair territory by the batter. Infielders rarely "hug" their bases, standing 5 to 20 feet from the bags, and the shortstop generally plays far back ("deep") in the infield between second and third base. The game begins when the umpire calls "Play ball."

Balls and Strikes. The batsman or batter stands in either of two 4-foot by 6-foot batter's boxes marked out on either side of home plate (for the convenience of right-handed or left-handed hitters). The pitcher directly faces the batter in one of two legal pitching positions—the windup or the set. His purpose is to throw the ball in the strike zone, the space directly over the plate and between the batter's armpits and the top of his knees as he takes a natural stance. A pitch in this area, if not hit by the batter, is called a strike. A strike is also a legal pitch that is struck at by the batter and missed; or which is hit into foul territory, when the batter has less than two strikes against him; or which is nicked (or tipped) by the bat and is held by the catcher; or which touches a batter while he swings at the ball. Three strikes constitute a put-out (in this instance called a strike-out), and the man thus retired is succeeded at the plate by the next player in the batting order.

Any pitch outside of the strike zone is called a ball if not struck at by the batter. Four balls, called a base on balls (also called a walk or a pass), permit the batter to go to first base. The batter also reaches first base if hit by a pitched ball which he has tried to avoid, or if the catcher or any other fielder interferes with his batting swing.

Base Hits and Errors. The primary aim of the batter is to get a base hit, that is, to hit the ball anywhere in fair territory and reach as many bases as he possibly can without being put out. A hit is called a single, when the batter stops at first base; a double, when the batter safely reaches second base; a triple, when he reaches third base; and a home run (or homer), when he makes a complete circuit of the bases and touches home plate. The great majority of home runs occur when the ball is hit on the fly (in the air without touching the ground) over an outfield barrier in fair territory. When a ball bounces over the barrier the batter is usually required to stop at second base (a "ground rules" double).

A batter may also reach base safely on an error. An error occurs when, in the opinion of the official scorer a fielder mishandles the ball.

Bunts. In some situations, the batter may attempt to

bunt, that is, instead of swinging at the ball he may attempt to block it with his bat and thus tap it onto the infield. While this usually results in the retirement of the batter, it also usually serves to advance a runner; when both of these circumstances obtain, the play is called a sacrifice. Some fleet-footed batters occasionally bunt to reach first base safely, especially when the infielders are playing deep.

Put-outs. The aim of the team in the field is to make three put-outs (or outs) and thus to retire the team at bat. The defensive players may make put-outs in a number of ways: by catching a ball hit by the batter in either fair or foul territory before it touches the ground (called a fly ball or a fly); fielding a grounder (that is, catching a ball bouncing on the ground in fair territory) and relaying the ball to a defensive player at first base before the batter reaches that base; by tagging a runner between bases; or, in certain circumstances, when there is a runner on base, by throwing the ball to the succeeding base before the runner reaches it. This last is called a force-out and is possible only when a runner is forced to advance by one base to prevent a put-out from being made, as when the runner is on first base and the batter hits a grounder.

Three strikes also constitute an out, provided the catcher does not drop the third strike. In the event that a third strike is dropped, the out can be secured only if the batter is tagged before he can run to first base or the ball is thrown to first base before he can reach the bag.

Outs are also made: when a batter against whom there are two strikes bunts foul; when, with two or three runners on base and less than two outs, the batter hits an infield fly; when the batter attempts to hit a third strike and the ball touches him; when, in the umpire's judgment, a spectator's interference clearly prevents a fielder from catching a fly ball; or when a runner is hit by a batted ball.

Double and Triple Plays. It is often possible to retire two men on one play, as when, with a runner on first base, the batter hits a grounder to the second baseman. The latter may step on second base, "forcing" the runner (putting him out on a force play, see above), and then relay the ball to the first baseman, who may touch first base, retiring the batter before he can reach the bag. This is called a double play and can occur only if less than two men are out before the play begins. Another type of double play may result when, for instance, an infielder catches a hard-hit ball (a line drive) before it touches the ground, automatically retiring the batter, and steps on the base behind a runner, "doubling off" the runner. This possibility arises from a rule which forbids a runner to advance to the next base before a fly ball is caught and which therefore makes it mandatory for him to "tag up," that is, to touch his base after the catch is made. Since runners normally take a "lead" (move several steps toward the next base befor9 the pitch is thrown) in order to take full advantage of a hit, or to be in a position to steal, or to protect themselves against a force play, they are occasionally unable to return to their base and are doubled off.

Triple plays, or three outs on one play, are rare, but, through various combinations of the circumstances described above, they can and do occur. A triple play is possible only when there are no outs and two or more runners are on base.

Baseball Strategy. The strategy followed by each team during the course of a game is determined by the manager, aided by the coaches. The manager decides which players are to play, when substitutions are to be made, where the players should play, how batters should be pitched to, and, often, whether a batter should swing or not swing at a particular pitch. The catcher is expected to know the weaknesses of opposition hitters and, before each pitch, to "call" for a certain kind of pitch by means of a hidden signal to the pitcher, and the pitcher is permitted to request a different call from the catcher by shaking his head negatively, but both men often operate under strict instructions from the manager.

When there is a runner on second or third base and first base is unoccupied, the manager may order his pitcher to deliver an intentional base on balls to a dangerous hitter to set up the possibility of a double play, or in order to have his pitcher face a weaker hitter; such a decision may often hinge on a consideration of the right-handed pitcher's slight advantage over a right-handed batter as against a left-handed batter, a fact borne out by voluminous statistics.

Much of baseball's strategy has to do with the running game, that is, the tactics resorted to by men on base in their efforts to advance and score. The team at bat stations coaches in foul territory behind first and third bases to coach the runners. The third base coach has the responsibility of deciding whether a runner speeding toward third base can reasonably be expected to score before the ball is relayed to home plate, and he must signal the runner accordingly.

The stolen base is an important part of the running game. A runner is permitted to attempt to steal a base, that is, advance to the next base, while the pitcher is in the process of delivering a pitch to the batter. (If the batter hits a foul ball, the runner is not allowed to advance, and if he hits a fly or line drive which is caught in either foul or fair territory, the runner must tag up, as described in the section above.) Chances of success in the base-stealing maneuver depend on several variables, including among others, the element of surprise, the runner's speed, and the catcher's ability to throw accurately to the fielder who moves over to defend the base (and who, in order to retire the runner, must actually tag him with the ball before he reaches the bag). The manager often reserves to himself the decision as to whether the steal attempt is to be made, especially when a double steal is involved (that is, when two runners simultaneously attempt to advance by means of stolen bases).

The hit-and-run play is almost invariably undertaken only on the manager's initiative and requires prearrangement with the batter and the runner, who are usually informed that they are to attempt the play, by means of secret signals relayed to them by one of the coaches. In the typical hit-and-run play, a runner at first base begins to steal as the ball is pitched, drawing the second baseman toward second base to defend against the steal. The batter, knowing that this will happen, attempts to hit the ball through the wide gap created in the right side of the infield when the second baseman leaves his normal fielding position. The success of the play usually results in advancing the runner to third base and putting another runner on firsj base.

The art of moving runners around the bases by means of the stolen base, the sacrifice bunt, and the hit-and-run play, has been called "inside baseball." Such great teams as the Baltimore Orioles (1894–1896) and the Chicago Cubs (1906–1910) were most adept exponents of inside baseball, and John McGraw (q.v.), who managed the New York Giants from 1902, was extremely successful with this strategy for over a quarter of a century. However, with the steady advance of home run hitting since the early 1920's, inside baseball has largely given way to what has been facetiously termed "outside baseball." While there were 358 home runs hit in the major leagues in 1910, there were 2,688 in 1965. This development has been variously ascribed to a "livelier" ball, to changes in the design of the bat, or to the increasing average size and strength of ballplayers, but whatever the reason, most managers today prefer to play for a block of runs from a home run, rather than for the single run. Such teams as the Los Angeles Dodgers, however, continued to play the old style of baseball in the 1960's.

Hitting and Pitching. Willie Keeler is credited with developing hitting into a science. He described his technique as follows: "I hit 'em where they ain't." The earmarks of the great hitters have included keen eyesight, good physical development, powerful wrists, and an intuitive knowledge of the pitcher's strong and weak points.

If there is a science of hitting, as demonstrated by such outstanding practitioners as Keeler, Ty Cobb, Rogers Hornsby, Ted Williams, and Stan Musial, there is also a science of pitching. A strong, wiry, durable arm which enables a pitcher to throw the ball with exceptional speed is a great advantage,

and such Hall of Fame pitchers as Rube Waddell and Walter Johnson have won baseball immortality largely on their ability to "throw the ball past the hitters." But pitchers without such natural gifts must resort to every wile of their craft, and even fast-ball pitchers find that a variety of deliveries increases their effectiveness. Since a pitcher often loses his speed as he ages, many pitchers noted initially for their fast balls (Bob Feller, Warren Spahn, Robin Roberts) have extended their careers to the two-decade mark and beyond by mastering the subtler aspects of the science, most importantly, the ability to control sharply breaking pitches.

In addition to the standard deliveries—the fast ball, curve, and change of pace (slow ball)—modern pitchers have developed such pitches as the knuckler (pitched off the knuckles), screw ball, fork ball, slider, palm ball, and a so-called "junk ball" (a slowly revolving ball thrown at various speeds). Many of these present-day pitches were termed drops, outcurves, incurves, and slow balls by earlier generations. The famed "fadeaway" of Christy Mathewson, who pitched between 1900 and 1916, is the present-day screw ball, a ball which, when thrown by a right-handed pitcher, breaks in toward a right-handed batsman instead of curving away from him as does the standard curve ball.

Yet pitchers must also live with the human frailty of the men that support them in the field. A perfectly executed pitch may be negated when an infielder fumbles a simple grounder, or when a pair of outfielders, each expecting the other to catch a high fly ball, let the ball drop between them. Errors of commission and omission are important factors in baseball, and crucial errors and mental lapses have lost league championships and world series.

Umpires. The game is supervised by umpires, who are in full charge of the game and are responsible for its conduct according to the rules. The umpire's decisions on all matters requiring judgment are final. Only reasonable doubt as to his interpretation of the rules can be appealed. Some decisions are made by the umpire only after direct protest by the offended team. For example, a runner is declared out for failing to touch a bag, and a batter is declared out for batting out of turn, only after the defending team has appealed to the umpire by means of an "appeal play."

In the major and minor leagues, umpires are appointed by the league presidents; for world series and all-star games, they are appointed by the commissioner of baseball. The number of umpires assigned to a game varies. In the major leagues, there are four, with the umpire behind the plate designated as the umpire in chief. The latter is also the sole judge of whether a pitch not struck at by the batter is a ball or a strike, and must make each "call" without a moment's hesitation. For the World Series and the All-Star games, there are six umpires. In minor league play, there are usually two umpires, one behind the plate and one on the bases.

Umpires are dressed in dark blue uniforms, of which they sometimes remove the coat. They wear shin guards and steel protectors for their shoes. The plate umpire wears, in addition, a chest protector and face mask.

GLOSSARY OF BASEBALL TERMS

The following are terms used in baseball that have not been defined in the text:

Assist. A throw or deflection by a fielder that aids in making a put-out.

Bag. First, second, or third base. Also called sack or cushion. The terms two-bagger, three-bagger, and four-bagger refer, respectively, to a double, triple, and home run (also called a four-sacker).

Balk. An illegal act by a pitcher with one or more runners on base, permitting each to advance one base.

Bases loaded. A runner at each base.

Batting average. Though often called a percentage, it is actually a fraction carried to the third decimal point and represents the number of hits produced by a batter divided by his number of "official at bats"; the latter excludes walks, sacrifices, hit batsmen, and catcher's interferences, but includes the times that the batter reached base on errors.

Bean ball. A ball pitched at a batter's head in order to drive him back from the plate; the pitch is illegal, but premeditation is difficult to prove.

Blank. To pitch any number of innings or a full game without permitting a run.

Bleachers. The cheapest seats, usually beyond the outfield's boundaries, in the sun, but now covered in some ball parks.

Blooper. A softly hit ball that drops or dribbles safely for a hit.

Bobble. To fail to hold on to a fielded ball. Also called fumble or muff.

Bonus player. An amateur player who is given more than the minimum established by the commissioner's office for signing a professional contract.

Book. (1) The records of baseball; hence, any unusual play is "one for the book." (2) The store of knowledge about a player's weaknesses and strengths. (3) The standard unwritten rules of strategy that are ordinarily followed in any given situation.

Bullpen. A special area where relief pitchers warm up during the game.

Bush league or bush. (1) A minor or semipro league. (2) By extension, conduct below major league standards of dignity or quality.

Called game. A game in which, for any reason, the umpire terminates play.

Cellar. Last place in the league standing.

Cheap or Chinese homer. A pop fly that just falls into the grandstands near a short foul line for a home run.

Choke. (1) To hold the bat well up on the handle. (2) To be too nervous or frightened to cope with a difficult situation.

Circuit clout. A home run.

Cleanup hitter. The fourth man in the batting order.

Clothesline. A line drive to the outfield, usually a single, which travels "straight as a clothesline," no more than 10 to 15 feet above the ground.

Clutch hitter. A batter with a reputation for delivering a hit with runners on base, or at a crucial point of the game.

Crowding the plate. Standing in a crouch position as close to home plate as the boundaries of the batter's box permit.

Dead ball. A ball that is out of play because of a legally created suspension of play.

Designated hitter. A player who bats for the pitcher throughout the game but does not play a position; in effect in the American League since 1973.

Double header. Two ball games, played consecutively on a single day, for only one admission charge.

DP. A double play.

Drag bunt. A ball bunted by a batter who has started to run while in the act of reaching for the ball with the bat.

Dugout. The seating facilities (usually below the level of the playing field) reserved for players, substitutes, manager, and coaches. Only men in uniform may sit in the dugout. Also called the bench.

Duster. An inside pitch thrown at the batter, forcing him to throw himself on the ground (in the dust) to prevent being hit.

Earned run average. An earned run is a run scored without the aid of an error or passed ball. A pitcher's earned run average represents the average number of runs legitimately scored off his deliveries per full nine-inning game (27 outs); the figure is usually carried to two decimal points.

Fan. (1) A spectator at a ball game. (2) An intense devotee of the sport. (3) To strike out.

Fielder's choice. The decision of a fielder, when a ball is hit, to retire a runner instead of throwing to first base to retire the batter.

First division. The top half of the league standing.

Flag. The pennant, symbol of league championship.

Forfeited game. A game declared ended by the umpire for illegal acts on the part of one team, such as the obvious employment of stalling tactics, or failure to remove an ejected player. The game is officially scored 9 to 0. A game may also be forfeited to a visiting team because of unruly behavior by hometown fans.

Full count. Three balls and two strikes on the batter.

Fungo. A fly ball hit to a fielder during fielding practice with a light bat called a fungo stick.

Gopher ball. Any pitch which is hit for a homer.

Grand slam. A home run with bases loaded.

Grandstander. A player who is conscious of impressing the fans; one who makes easy chances look difficult.

Grapefruit league. Informal league of major league teams in spring training in Florida. Teams training in Arizona belong to the Cactus league.

Hitting the dirt. (1) Quick action by the batter in throwing himself on the ground to avoid being hit by a close pitch, or duster. (2) Sliding into a base.

Hot corner. Third base.

Keystone. Second base.

Knocked out of the box. Said of a pitcher forced to retire from the game under a barrage of hits.

Leadoff man (1) First man in the batting order. (2) First hitter in any half-inning.

Liner. A line drive.

Live ball. A ball which is in play.

No-hitter. A game in which the pitcher does not yield a single hit.

On deck. Said of the player who follows the man at bat; he normaly waits in a large, white circle near the batter's box.

Passed ball. A pitch that goes past the catcher, allowing a runner to advance; it differs from a wild pitch in that the official scorer rules that the catcher should have stopped it.

Perfect game. A no-hitter in which no opponent reaches base, 27 men being retired in order.

Pick-off. A throw by a pitcher or a catcher to a fielder, catching a runner off base.

Pinch hitter. A substitute sent in to bat for the scheduled batter. A pinch runner is a substitute sent in to run for a batter who has reached base.

Pitchout. A pitch deliberately thrown wide of the plate, so that the catcher is in a better position for a pick-off throw.

Pop fly or pop-up. A short, high, easily handled fly ball, usually over the infield.

Pull hitter. A hitter who normally hits "ahead" of the ball; that is, a left-handed batter who usually hits the ball to right field, or a right-handed batter who usually hits the ball to left field.

Quick return. An illegal pitch, hurried, with the obvious intent to catch the batter off balance.

Rabbit ball. Extremely lively ball, which, it is said, jumps like a rabbit.

Rally. Combination of hits, bases on balls, or opponents' errors which produces several runs.

RBI. Run batted in. A batter is credited with an RBI when he bats in a run with a hit (including himself on a home run), an infield out, a sacrifice fly, a bunt, or when he gets a base on balls with the bases loaded.

Relief pitcher. A pitcher who has been substituted for another pitcher in a game, or one who is normally used to relieve other pitchers rather than to start ball games.

Rhubarb. Noisy, turbulent argument between players, or between players and umpires.

Riding the bench. (1) The yelling of taunting, derisive remarks at rival players or at the umpires from a seat in the dugout; also called bench jockeying. (2) Said of a player who has not played for a long time.

Rookie. (1) Young player trying for a big league berth. (2) Any player playing his first year in the major leagues.

Round tripper. A home run.

Rundown. The act of running down and tagging out a runner who has been trapped between bases.

Sacrifice fly. A long fly ball, fair or foul, permitting a runner on third to score after the catch.

Second division. The lower half of the league standing.

Seventh inning stretch. A tradition which dictates that the fans rise to their feet in the seventh inning when their favorite team comes to bat, supposedly to bring it luck.

Shake off. Negative motion of the pitcher's head, indicating to the catcher that the pitcher prefers to throw a different pitch than that signaled for by the catcher.

Shoestring catch. A ball caught at the height of the outfielder's shoe tops, often made possible by a lunge or dive at the last moment.

Shutout. A game in which the losing team does not score a single run. Also called a whitewash.

Slide. The forward thrust of a runner who throws himself to the ground either feet first or head first to reach base ahead of a throw.

Slugger. A heavy hitter, one that produces home runs and extra-base hits.

Southpaw. A left-handed pitcher.

Spitball or spitter. The pitching of a ball which has been moistened with saliva so that it will curve or break more sharply; such a pitch is now illegal.

Spray hitter. A player who can hit the ball to any part of the field.

Squeeze play. An attempt to score a runner from third by means of a bunt. In the suicide squeeze, the runner starts for home on the pitch; is a safety squeeze, he waits until the batter has bunted.

Streak. A succession of victories, hits, brilliant catches, or whatever. A losing streak (for a team or a player) is often called a slump.

Stuff. Amount of spin, curve, and break a pitcher can apply to the ball.

Switch hitter. A batter who can bat from either side of the plate.

Taking a pitch. Not swinging at a pitch, even if it is in the strike zone.

Texas leaguer A short fly ball that falls between the infield and the outfield for a hit.

Tie game. A game that ends without either team winning. Such a game must be replayed.

Trapped ball. A batted ball that the defensive player takes on a short, first hop, often pretending that he has caught the ball before it touched the ground.

Triple Crown. Distinction won by a batter who, at the end of the year, leads his league in batting average, RBI's, and home runs.

Waivers. Except for certain optionable players, a major league club must obtain waivers from the clubs in its league, and then from the clubs in the other major league, before it can send a player to the minor leagues or give him an unconditional release. A club refusing to waive claim may obtain the player at a fixed price.

Warm-up. Physical activity readying a player for service in a game, applied especially to a pitcher, who normally executes several warm-up pitches to loosen his arm muscles.

Waste pitch. A pitch deliberately thrown outside of the strike zone to a batter against whom there are two strikes and no balls, in the hope that he will misjudge it and strike out.

Wild pitch. A pitch that is too high, or low, or wide for the catcher to handle, thus allowing a runner to advance.

Windup. Movements of a pitcher before he releases the ball, whereby he attempts to get the maximum speed, stuff, and body follow-through behind his pitch. Used when it is not necessary to hold a runner on base.

Official Scorers. Baseball is a game whose avid followers demand accurate and detailed statistics. The man appointed by the league president to tabulate every play made in a game is called the official scorer. Picked from among the newspaper reporters, the official scorer has the sole authority to make "scoring" decisions requiring judgment, such as a decision as to whether a fielder who fails to hold a sharply hit ball and complete the put-out is to be charged with an error. Many fans enjoy keeping an "official" score.

Bibliography

Allen, Ethan N., *Baseball Play and Strategy,* 2d ed. (Ronald 1969).

Allen, Lee, *The American League Story* (Hill & Wang 1962).

Allen, Lee, *The National League Story* (Hill & Wang 1961).

Anderson, Clary, *The Young Sportsman's Guide to Baseball* (Nelson 1963).

Baseball Register (Spink, C.C. annually).

Crosetti, Frank, *Secrets of Baserunning and Infield Play* (Putnam 1966).

Danzig, Allison, and Reichler, Joe, *The History of Baseball, Its Great Players, Teams and Managers* (Prentice-Hall 1959).

Hollander, Zander, *The Complete Handbook of Baseball* (NAL 1977).

Koppett, Leonard, *All About Baseball,* rev. ed. (Quadrangle 1974).

Lieb, Frederick G., *Baseball As I Have Known It* (Coward 1977).

Macmillan, *The Baseball Encyclopedia* (Macmillan 1976).

Official Baseball Guide (Spink, C.C. annually).

Olan, Ben, *Big-time Baseball* (Hart 1965).

Reichler, Joe, ed., *Ronald Encyclopedia of Baseball,* 2d ed. (Ronald, 1964).

Rickey, Branch, and Riger, Robert, *The American Diamond* (Simon & Schuster 1965).

Turkin, Hy, and Thompson, S.C., *Official Encyclopedia of Baseball,* 9th ed. (Barnes, A.S. 1977).

Wolfe, Harold H., *The Complete Book of Baseball Strategy* (Cornerstone 1977).

BASEBALL

MAJOR LEAGUE CHAMPIONS

(For year 1969 and later: E = Eastern Division; W = Western Division)

	National League	Won	Lost	Percentage
1901	Pittsburgh Pirates	90	49	.647
1902	Pittsburgh Pirates	103	36	.741
1903	Pittsburgh Pirates	91	49	.650
1904	New York Giants	106	47	.693
1905	New York Giants*	105	48	.686
1906	Chicago Cubs	116	36	.763
1907	Chicago Cubs*	107	45	.704
1908	Chicago Cubs†*	99	55	.643
1909	Pittsburgh Pirates*	110	42	.724
1910	Chicago Cubs	104	50	.675
1911	New York Giants	99	54	.647
1912	New York Giants	103	48	.682
1913	New York Giants	101	51	.664
1914	Boston Braves*	94	59	.614
1915	Philadelphia Phillies	90	62	.592

Year	Team	Won	Lost	Pct.
1916	Brooklyn Dodgers	94	60	.610
1917	New York Giants	98	56	.636
1918	Chicago Cubs	84	45	.651
1919	Cincinnati Reds*	96	44	.686
1920	Brooklyn Dodgers	93	61	.604
1921	New York Giants*	94	59	.614
1922	New York Giants*	93	61	.604
1923	New York Giants	95	58	.621
1924	New York Giants	93	60	.608
1925	Pittsburgh Pirates*	95	58	.621
1926	St. Louis Cardinals*	89	65	.578
1927	Pittsburgh Pirates	94	60	.610
1928	St. Louis Cardinals	95	59	.617
1929	Chicago Cubs	98	54	.645
1930	St. Louis Cardinals	92	62	.597
1931	St. Louis Cardinals*	101	53	.656
1932	Chicago Cubs	90	64	.584
1933	New York Giants*	91	61	.599
1934	St. Louis Cardinals*	95	58	.621
1935	Chicago Cubs	100	54	.649
1936	New York Giants	92	62	.597
1937	New York Giants	95	57	.625
1938	Chicago Cubs	89	63	.586
1939	Cincinnati Reds	97	57	.630
1940	Cincinnati Reds*	100	53	.654
1941	Brooklyn Dodgers	100	54	.649
1942	St. Louis Cardinals*	106	48	.688
1943	St. Louis Cardinals	105	49	.682
1944	St. Louis Cardinals*	105	49	.682
1945	Chicago Cubs	98	56	.636
1946	St. Louis Cardinals†*	98	58	.628
1947	Brooklyn Dodgers	94	60	.610
1948	Boston Braves	91	62	.595
1949	Brooklyn Dodgers	97	57	.630
1950	Philadelphia Phillies	91	63	.591
1951	New York Giants†	98	59	.624
1952	Brooklyn Dodgers	96	57	.627
1953	Brooklyn Dodgers	105	49	.682
1954	New York Giants*	97	57	.630
1955	Brooklyn Dodgers*	98	55	.641
1956	Brooklyn Dodgers	93	61	.604
1957	Milwaukee Braves*	95	59	.617
1958	Milwaukee Braves	92	62	.597
1959	Los Angeles Dodgers†*	88	68	.564
1960	Pittsburgh Pirates*	93	61	.604
1961	Cincinnati Reds	95	59	.617
1962	San Francisco Giants†	103	62	.624
1963	Los Angeles Dodgers*	99	63	.611
1964	St. Louis Cardinals*	93	69	.574
1965	Los Angeles Dodgers*	97	65	.599
1966	Los Angeles Dodgers	95	67	.586
1967	St. Louis Cardinals*	101	60	.627
1968	St. Louis Cardinals	97	65	.599
1969	New York Mets*† (E)	100	62	.617
	Atlanta Braves (W)	93	69	.574
1970	Cincinnati Reds† (W)	102	60	.630
	Pittsburgh Pirates (E)	89	73	.549
1971	Pittsburgh Pirates*† (E)	97	65	.599
	San Francisco Giants (W)	90	72	.556
1972	Cincinnati Reds† (W)	95	59	.617
	Pittsburgh Pirates (E)	96	59	.619
1973	New York Mets† (E)	82	79	.509
	Cincinnati Reds (W)	99	63	.611
1974	L.A. Dodgers† (W)	102	60	.630
	Pittsburgh Pirates (E)	88	74	.543
1975	Cincinnati Reds*† (W)	108	54	.667
	Pittsburgh Pirates (E)	92	69	.571
1976	Cincinnati Reds*† (W)	102	60	.630
	Philadelphia Phillies (E)	101	61	.623
1977	L.A. Dodgers† (W)	98	64	.605
	Philadelphia Phillies (E)	100	61	.623
1978	L.A. Dodgers† (W)	95	67	
	Philadelphia Phillies (E)	90	72	

*Won World Series. †Won pennant in postseason playoffs.

MAJOR LEAGUE CHAMPIONS

(For year 1969 and later: E = Eastern Division; W = Western Division)

Year	American League	Won	Lost	Percentage
1901	Chicago White Sox	83	53	.610
1902	Philadelphia Athletics	83	53	.610
1903	Boston Red Sox*	91	47	.659
1904	Boston Red Sox	95	59	.617
1905	Philadelphia Athletics	92	56	.622
1906	Chicago White Sox*	93	58	.616
1907	Detroit Tigers	92	58	.613
1908	Detroit Tigers	90	63	.588
1909	Detroit Tigers	98	54	.645
1910	Philadelphia Athletics*	102	48	.680
1911	Philadelphia Athletics*	101	50	.669
1912	Boston Red Sox*	105	47	.691
1913	Philadelphia Athletics*	96	57	.627
1914	Philadelphia Athletics	99	53	.651
1915	Boston Red Sox*	101	50	.669
1916	Boston Red Sox*	91	63	.591
1917	Chicago White Sox*	100	54	.649
1918	Boston Red Sox*	75	51	.595
1919	Chicago White Sox	88	52	.629
1920	Cleveland Indians*	98	56	.636
1921	New York Yankees	98	55	.641
1922	New York Yankees	94	60	.610
1923	New York Yankees*	98	54	.645
1924	Washington Senators*	92	62	.597
1925	Washington Seantors	96	55	.636
1926	New York Yankees	91	63	.591
1927	New York Yankees*	110	44	.714
1928	New York Yankees*	101	53	.656
1929	Philadelphia Athletics*	104	46	.693
1930	Philadelphia Athletics*	102	52	.662
1931	Philadelphia Athletics	107	45	.704
1932	New York Yankees*	107	47	.695
1933	Washington Senators	99	53	.651
1934	Detroit Tigers	101	53	.656
1935	Detroit Tigers*	93	58	.616
1936	New York Yankees*	102	51	.667
1937	New York Yankees*	102	52	.662
1938	New York Yankees*	99	53	.651
1939	New York Yankees*	106	45	.702
1940	Detroit Tigers	90	64	.584
1941	New York Yankees*	101	53	.656
1942	New York Yankees	103	51	.669
1943	New York Yankees*	98	56	.636
1946	Boston Red Sox	104	50	.675
1947	New York Yankees*	97	57	.630
1948	Cleveland Indians†*	97	58	.626
1949	New York Yankees*	97	57	.630
1950	New York Yankees*	98	56	.636
1951	New York Yankees*	98	56	.636
1952	New York Yankees*	95	59	.617
1953	New York Yankees*	99	52	.656
1954	Cleveland Indians	111	43	.721
1955	New York Yankees	96	58	.623
1956	New York Yankees*	97	57	.630
1957	New York Yankees	98	56	.636
1958	New York Yankees*	92	62	.597
1959	Chicago White Sox	94	60	.610
1960	New York Yankees	97	57	.630
1961	New York Yankees*	109	53	.673
1962	New York Yankees*	96	66	.593
1963	New York Yankees	104	57	.646
1964	New York Yankees	99	63	.611
1965	Minnesota Twins	102	60	.630
1966	Baltimore Orioles*	97	63	.606
1967	Boston Red Sox	92	70	.568
1968	Detroit Tigers*	103	59	.636
1969	Baltimore Orioles† (E)	109	53	.673
	Minnesota Twins (W)	97	65	.599
1970	Baltimore Orioles*† (E)	108	54	.667
	Minnesota Twins (W)	98	64	.605
1971	Baltimore Orioles† (E)	101	57	.639
	Oakland A's (W)	101	60	.627
1972	Oakland A's*† (W)	93	62	.600
	Detroit Tigers (E)	86	70	.551
1973	Oakland A's*† (W)	94	68	.580
	Baltimore Orioles (E)	97	65	.599
1974	Oakland A's*† (W)	90	72	.556
	Baltimore Orioles (E)	91	71	.562
1975	Boston Red Sox† (E)	95	65	.594
	Oakland A's (W)	98	64	.605
1976	New York Yankees† (E)	97	62	.610
	Kansas City Royals (W)	90	72	.556
1977	New York Yankees*† (E)	100	62	.617
	Kansas City Royals (W)	102	60	.630
1978	New York Yankees*† (E)	100	63	
	Kansas City Royals (W)	92	70	

BATTING CHAMPIONS

National League

Year	Player	Team	AVG		Year	Player	Team	AVG
1901	Jesse C. Burkett	St. Louis	.382		1940	Debs Garms	Pittsburgh	.355
1902	Clarence H. Beaumont	Pittsburgh	.357		1941	Pete Reiser	Brooklyn	.343
1903	John P. Wagner	Pittsburgh	.355		1942	Ernie Lombardi	Boston	.330
1904	John P. Wagner	Pittsburgh	.349		1943	Stan Musial	St. Louis	.357
1905	John B. Seymour	Cincinnati	.377		1944	Dixie Walker	Brooklyn	.357
1906	John P. Wagner	Pittsburgh	.339		1945	Phil Cavarretta	Chicago	.355
1907	John P. Wagner	Pittsburgh	.350		1946	Stan Musial	St. Louis	.365
1908	John P. Wagner	Pittsburgh	.354		1947	Harry Walker	Philadelphia	.363
1909	John P. Wagner	Pittsburgh	.339		1948	Stan Musial	St. Louis	.376
1910	Sherwood R. Magee	Philadelphia	.331		1949	Jackie Robinson	Brooklyn	.342
1911	John P. Wagner	Pittsburgh	.334		1950	Stan Musial	St. Louis	.346
1912	Henry Zimmerman	Chicago	.372		1951	Stan Musial	St. Louis	.355
1913	Jacob E. Daubert	Brooklyn	.350		1952	Stan Musial	St. Louis	.336
1914	Jacob E. Daubert	Brooklyn	.329		1953	Carl Furillo	Brooklyn	.344
1915	Larry Doyle	New York	.320		1954	Willie Mays	New York	.345
1916	Hal Chase	Cincinnati	.339		1955	Richie Ashburn	Philadelphia	.338
1917	Edd Rousch	Cincinnati	.341		1956	Hank Aaron	Milwaukee	.328
1918	Zack Wheat	Brooklyn	.335		1957	Stan Musial	St. Louis	.351
1919	Edd Roush	Cincinnati	.321		1958	Richie Ashburn	Philadelphia	.350
1920	Rogers Hornsby	St. Louis	.370		1959	Hank Aaron	Milwaukee	.355
1921	Rogers Hornsby	St. Louis	.397		1960	Dick Groat	Pittsburgh	.325
1922	Rogers Hornsby	St. Louis	.401		1961	Roberto Clemente	Pittsburgh	.351
1923	Rogers Hornsby	St. Louis	.384		1962	Tommy Davis	Los Angeles	.346
1924	Rogers Hornsby	St. Louis	.424		1963	Tommy Davis	Los Angeles	.326
1925	Rogers Hornsby	St. Louis	.403		1964	Roberto Clemente	Pittsburgh	.339
1926	Eugene Hargrave	Cincinnati	.353		1965	Roberto Clemente	Pittsburgh	.329
1927	Paul Waner	Pittsburgh	.380		1966	Matty Alou	Pittsburgh	.342
1928	Rogers Hornsby	Boston	.387		1967	Roberto Clemente	Pittsburgh	.357
1929	Lefty O'Doul	Philadelphia	.398		1968	Pete Rose	Cincinnati	.335
1930	Bill Terry	New York	.401		1969	Pete Rose	Cincinnati	.348
1931	Chick Hafey	St. Louis	.349		1970	Rico Carty	Atlanta	.366
1932	Lefty O'Doul	Brooklyn	.368		1971	Joe Torre	St. Louis	.363
1933	Charles Klein	Philadelphia	.368		1972	Billy Williams	Chicago	.333
1934	Paul Waner	Pittsburgh	.362		1973	Pete Rose	Cincinnati	.338
1935	Arky Vaughan	Pittsburgh	.385		1974	Ralph Garr	Atlanta	.353
1936	Paul Waner	Pittsburgh	.373		1975	Bill Madlock	Chicago	.354
1937	Joe Medwick	St. Louis	.374		1976	Bill Madlock	Chicago	.339
1938	Ernie Lombardi	Cincinnati	.342		1977	Dave Parker	Pittsburgh	.338
1939	John Mize	St. Louis	.349		1978	Dave Parker	Pittsburgh	.334

BATTING CHAMPIONS

American League

Year	Player	Team	AVG		Year	Player	Team	AVG
1901	Napoleon Lajoie	Philadelphia	.405		1940	Joe DiMaggio	New York	.352
1902	Edward J. Delahanty	Washington	.376		1941	Ted Williams	Boston	.406
1903	Napoleon Lajoie	Cleveland	.355		1942	Ted Williams	Boston	.356
1904	Napoleon Lajoie	Cleveland	.381		1943	Luke Appling	Chicago	.328
1905	Elmer H. Flick	Cleveland	.306		1944	Lou Boudreau	Cleveland	.327
1906	George R. Stone	St. Louis	.358		1945	George Stirnweiss	New York	.309
1907	Ty Cobb	Detroit	.350		1946	Mickey Vernon	Washington	.353
1908	Ty Cobb	Detroit	.324		1947	Ted Williams	Boston	.343
1909	Ty Cobb	Detroit	.377		1948	Ted Williams	Boston	.369
1910	Ty Cobb	Detroit	.385		1949	George Kell	Detroit	.343
1911	Ty Cobb	Detroit	.420		1950	Billy Goodman	Boston	.354
1912	Ty Cobb	Detroit	.410		1951	Ferris Fain	Philadelphia	.344
1913	Ty Cobb	Detroit	.390		1952	Ferris Fain	Philadelphia	.327
1914	Ty Cobb	Detroit	.368		1953	Mickey Vernon	Washington	.337
1915	Ty Cobb	Detroit	.369		1954	Roberto Avila	Cleveland	.341
1916	Tris Speaker	Cleveland	.386		1955	Al Kaline	Detroit	.340
1917	Ty Cobb	Detroit	.383		1956	Mickey Mantle	New York	.353
1918	Ty Cobb	Detroit	.382		1957	Ted Williams	Boston	.388
1919	Ty Cobb	Detroit	.384		1958	Ted Williams	Boston	.328
1920	George Sisler	St. Louis	.407		1959	Harvey Kuenn	Detroit	.353
1921	Harry Heilmann	Detroit	.394		1960	Pete Runnels	Boston	.320
1922	George Sisler	St. Louis	.420		1961	Norm Cash	Detroit	.361
1923	Harry Heilmann	Detroit	.403		1962	Pete Runnels	Boston	.326
1924	Babe Ruth	New York	.378		1963	Carl Yastrzemski	Boston	.321
1925	Harry Heilmann	Detroit	.393		1964	Tony Oliva	Minnesota	.323
1926	Henry Manush	Detroit	.378		1965	Tony Oliva	Minnesota	.321
1927	Harry Heilmann	Detroit	.398		1966	Frank Robinson	Baltimore	.316
1928	Goose Goslin	Washington	.379		1967	Carl Yastrzemski	Boston	.326
1929	Lew Fonseca	Cleveland	.369		1968	Carl Yastrzemski	Boston	.301
1930	Al Simmons	Philadelphia	.381		1969	Rod Carew	Minnesota	.332
1931	Al Simmons	Philadelphia	.390		1970	Alex Johnson	California	.328
1932	Dale Alexander	Detroit-Boston	.367		1971	Tony Oliva	Minnesota	.337
1933	Jimmy Foxx	Philadelphia	.356		1972	Rod Carew	Minnesota	.318
1934	Lou Gehrig	New York	.363		1973	Rod Carew	Minnesota	.350
1935	Buddy Myer	Washington	.349		1974	Rod Carew	Minnesota	.364
1936	Luke Appling	Chicago	.388		1975	Rod Carew	Minnesota	.359
1937	Charlie Gehringer	Detroit	.371		1976	George Brett	Kansas City	.333
1938	Jimmy Foxx	Boston	.349		1977	Rod Carew	Minnesota	.388
1939	Joe DiMaggio	New York	.381		1978	Rod Carew	Minnesota	.333

HOME RUN LEADERS

National League

1901	Samuel E. Crawford	Cincinnati	16
1902	Thomas W. Leach	Pittsburgh	6
1903	S. James Sheckard	Brooklyn	9
1904	Harry G. Lumley	Brooklyn	9
1905	Fred W. Odwell	Cincinnati	9
1906	Timothy J. Jordan	Brooklyn	12
1907	David L. Brain	Boston	10
1908	Timothy J. Jordan	Brooklyn	12
1909	John J. Murray	New York	7
1910	Fred T. Beck	Boston	10
	Frank Schulte	Chicago	10
1911	Frank Schulte	Chicago	21
1912	Henry Zimmerman	Chicago	14
1913	Clifford C. Cravath	Philadelphia	19
1914	Clifford C. Cravath	Philadelphia	19
1915	Clifford C. Cravath	Philadelphia	24
1916	Davis A. Robertson	New York	12
	Frederick Williams	Chicago	12
1917	Davis A. Robertson	New York	12
	Clifford C. Cravath	Philadelphia	12
1918	Clifford C. Cravath	Philadelphia	8
1919	Clifford C. Cravath	Philadelphia	12
1920	Frederick Williams	Philadelphia	15
1921	George Kelly	New York	23
1922	Rogers Hornsby	St. Louis	42
1923	Cy Williams	Philadelphia	41
1924	Jacques Fournier	Brooklyn	27
1925	Rogers Hornsby	St. Louis	39
1926	Hack Wilson	Chicago	21
1927	Hack Wilson	Chicago	30
	Cy Williams	Philadelphia	30
1928	Hack Wilson	Chicago	31
	Jim Bottomley	St. Louis	31
1929	Charles Klein	Philadelphia	43
1930	Hack Wilson	Chicago	56
1931	Charles Klein	Philadelphia	31
1932	Charles Klein	Philadelphia	38
	Mel Ott	New York	38
1933	Charles Klein	Philadelphia	28
1934	Collins	St. Louis	35
	Mel Ott	New York	35
1935	Walter Berger	Boston	34
1936	Mel Ott	New York	33
1937	Mel Ott	New York	31
	Joe Medwick	St. Louis	31
1938	Mel Ott	New York	36
1939	John Mize	St. Louis	28
1940	John Mize	St. Louis	43
1941	Dolph Camilli	Brooklyn	34
1942	Mel Ott	New York	30
1943	Bill Nicholson	Chicago	29
1944	Bill Nicholson	Chicago	33
1945	Tommy Holmes	Boston	28
1946	Ralph Kiner	Pittsburgh	23
1947	Ralph Kiner	Pittsburgh	51
	John Mize	New York	51
1948	Ralph Kiner	Pittsburgh	40
	John Mize	New York	40
1949	Ralph Kiner	Pittsburgh	54
1950	Ralph Kiner	Pittsburgh	47
1951	Ralph Kiner	Pittsburgh	42
1952	Ralph Kiner	Pittsburgh	37
	Hank Sauer	Chicago	37
1953	Ed Mathews	Milwaukee	47
1954	Ted Kluszewski	Cincinnati	49
1955	Willie Mays	New York	51
1956	Duke Snider	Brooklyn	43
1957	Hank Aaron	Milwaukee	44
1958	Ernie Banks	Chicago	47
1959	Ed Mathews	Milwaukee	46
1960	Ernie Banks	Chicago	41
1961	Orlando Cepeda	San Francisco	46
1962	Willie Mays	San Francisco	49
1963	Hank Aaron	Milwaukee	44
	Willie McCovey	San Francisco	44
1964	Willie Mays	San Francisco	47
1965	Willie Mays	San Francisco	52
1966	Hank Aaron	Atlanta	44
	Willie McCovey	San Francisco	44
1967	Hank Aaron	Atlanta	39
1968	Willie McCovey	San Francisco	36
1969	Willie McCovey	San Francisco	45
1970	Johnny Bench	Cincinnati	45
1971	Willie Stargell	Pittsburgh	48
1972	Johnny Bench	Cincinnati	40
1973	Willie Stargell	Pittsburgh	44
1974	Mike Schmidt	Philadelphia	36
1975	Mike Schmidt	Philadelphia	38
1976	Mike Schmidt	Philadelphia	38
1977	George Foster	Cincinnati	52
1978	George Foster	Cincinnati	40

HOME RUN LEADERS

American League

1901	Napoleon Lajoie	Philadelphia	13
1902	Ralph O. Seybold	Philadelphia	16
1903	John F. Freeman	Boston	13
1904	Harry H. Davis	Philadelphia	10
1905	Harry H. Davis	Philadelphia	8
1906	Harry H. Davis	Philadelphia	12
1907	Harry H. Davis	Philadelphia	8
1908	Samuel E. Crawford	Detroit	7
1909	Tyrus R. Cobb	Detroit	9
1910	J. Garland Stahl	Boston	10
1911	J. Franklin Baker	Philadelphia	9
1912	J. Franklin Baker	Philadelphia	10
1913	J. Franklin Baker	Philadelphia	12
1914	J. Franklin Baker	Philadelphia	8
	Samuel E. Crawford	Detroit	8
1915	Robert F. Roth	Chicago-Cleveland	7
1916	Walter C. Pipp	New York	12
1917	Walter C. Pipp	New York	9
1918	Babe Ruth	Boston	11
	Clarence W. Walker	Philadelphia	11
1919	Babe Ruth	Boston	29
1920	Babe Ruth	New York	54
1921	Babe Ruth	New York	59
1922	Ken Williams	St. Louis	39
1923	Babe Ruth	New York	41
1924	Babe Ruth	New York	46
1925	Bob Meusel	New York	33
1926	Babe Ruth	New York	47
1927	Babe Ruth	New York	60
1928	Babe Ruth	New York	54
1929	Babe Ruth	New York	46
1930	Babe Ruth	New York	49
1931	Babe Ruth	New York	46
	Lou Gehrig	New York	46
1932	Jimmy Foxx	Philadelphia	58
1933	Jimmy Foxx	Philadelphia	48
1934	Lou Gehrig	New York	49
1935	Jimmy Foxx	Philadelphia	36
	Hank Greenberg	Detroit	36
1936	Lou Gehrig	New York	49
1937	Joe DiMaggio	New York	46
1938	Hank Greenberg	Detroit	58
1939	Jimmy Foxx	Boston	35
1940	Hank Greenberg	Detroit	41
1941	Ted Williams	Boston	37
1942	Ted Williams	Boston	36
1943	Rudy York	Detroit	34
1944	Nick Etten	New York	22
1945	Vern Stephens	St. Louis	24
1946	Hank Greenberg	Detroit	44
1947	Ted Williams	Boston	32
1948	Joe DiMaggio	New York	39
1949	Ted Williams	Boston	43
1950	Al Rosen	Cleveland	37
1951	Gus Zernial	Chicago-Philadelphia	33
1952	Larry Doby	Cleveland	32
1953	Al Rosen	Cleveland	43
1954	Larry Doby	Cleveland	32
1955	Mickey Mantle	New York	37
1956	Mickey Mantle	New York	52
1957	Roy Sievers	Washington	42
1958	Mickey Mantle	New York	42

Year	Player	Team	HR		Year	Player	Team	HR
1959	Rocky Colavito	Cleveland	42		1969	Harmon Killebrew	Minnesota	49
	Harmon Killebrew	Washington	42		1970	Frank Howard	Washington	44
1960	Mickey Mantle	New York	40		1971	Bill Melton	Chicago	33
1961	Roger Maris	New York	61		1972	Dick Allen	Chicago	37
1962	Harmon Killebrew	Minnesota	48		1973	Reggie Jackson	Oakland	32
1963	Harmon Killebrew	Minnesota	45		1974	Dick Allen	Chicago	32
1964	Harmon Killebrew	Minnesota	49					
1965	Tony Conigliaro	Boston	32		1975	George Scott	Milwaukee	36
1966	Frank Robinson	Baltimore	49			Reggie Jackson	Oakland	36
1967	Carl Yastrzemski	Boston	44					
	Harmon Killebrew	Minnesota	44		1976	Graig Nettles	New York	32
1968	Frank Howard	Washington	44		1977	Jim Rice	Boston	39
					1978	Jim Rice	Boston	46

RBI LEADERS

National League

Year	Player	Team	RBI		Year	Player	Team	RBI
1914	Sherwood Magee	Philadelphia	101		1946	Enos Slaughter	St. Louis	130
1915	Cliff Cravath	Philadelphia	118		1947	Johnny Mize	New York	138
1916	Hal Chase	Cincinnati	84		1948	Stan Musial	St. Louis	131
1917	Heinie Zimmerman	New York	100		1949	Ralph Kiner	Pittsburgh	127
1918	Fred Merkle	Chicago	71		1950	Del Ennis	Philadelphia	126
1919	Henry (Hi) Myers	Brooklyn	72		1951	Monte Irvin	New York	121
1920	George Kelly	New York	94		1952	Hank Sauer	Chicago	121
	Rogers Hornsby	St. Louis	94		1953	Roy Campanella	Brooklyn	142
1921	Rogers Hornsby	St. Louis	126		1954	Ted Kluszewski	Cincinnati	141
1922	Rogers Hornsby	St. Louis	152		1955	Duke Snider	Brooklyn	136
1923	Irish Meusel	New York	125		1956	Stan Musial	St. Louis	109
1924	George Kelly	New York	136		1957	Hank Aaron	Milwaukee	132
1925	Rogers Hornsby	St. Louis	143		1958	Ernie Banks	Chicago	129
1926	Jim Bottomley	St. Louis	120		1959	Ernie Banks	Chicago	143
1927	Paul Waner	Pittsburgh	131		1960	Hank Aaron	Milwaukee	126
1928	Jim Bottomley	St. Louis	136		1961	Orlando Cepeda	San Francisco	142
1929	Hack Wilson	Chicago	159		1962	Tommy Davis	Los Angeles	153
1930	Hack Wilson	Chicago	190		1963	Hank Aaron	Milwaukee	130
1931	Chuck Klein	Philadelphia	121		1964	Ken Boyer	St. Louis	119
1932	Frank Hurst	Philadelphia	143		1965	Deron Johnson	Cincinnati	130
1933	Chuck Klein	Philadelphia	120		1966	Hank Aaron	Atlanta	121
1934	Mel Ott	New York	135		1967	Orlando Cepeda	St. Louis	111
1935	Wally Berger	Boston	130		1968	Willie McCovey	San Francisco	105
1936	Joe Medwick	St. Louis	138		1969	Willie McCovey	San Francisco	126
1937	Joe Medwick	St. Louis	154		1970	Johnny Bench	Cincinnati	148
1938	Joe Medwick	St. Louis	122		1971	Joe Torre	St. Louis	137
1939	Frank McCormick	Cincinnati	128		1972	Johnny Bench	Cincinnati	125
1940	Johnny Mize	St. Louis	137		1973	Willie Stargell	Pittsburgh	119
1941	Dolph Camilli	Brooklyn	120		1974	Johnny Bench	Cincinnati	129
1942	Johnny Mize	New York	110		1975	Greg Luzinski	Philadelphia	120
1943	Bill Nicholson	Chicago	128		1976	George Foster	Cincinnati	121
1944	Bill Nicholson	Chicago	122		1977	George Foster	Cincinnati	149
1945	Dixie Walker	Brooklyn	124		1978	George Foster	Cincinnati	120

RBI LEADERS

American League

Year	Player	Team	RBI		Year	Player	Team	RBI
1914	Sam Crawford	Detroit	112		1947	Ted Williams	Boston	114
1915	Sam Crawford	Detroit	116		1948	Joe DiMaggio	New York	155
1916	Wally Pipp	New York	99		1949	Ted Williams	Boston	159
1917	Robert Veach	Detroit	115			Vern Stephens	Boston	159
1918	George Burns	Philadelphia	74		1950	Vern Stephens	Boston	144
	Robert Veach	Detroit	74			Walt Dropo	Boston	144
1919	Babe Ruth	Boston	112		1951	Gus Zernial	Chicago-Philadelphia	129
1920	Babe Ruth	New York	137		1952	Al Rosen	Cleveland	105
1921	Babe Ruth	New York	170		1953	Al Rosen	Cleveland	145
1922	Ken Williams	St. Louis	155		1954	Larry Doby	Cleveland	126
1923	Tris Speaker	Cleveland	130		1955	Ray Boone	Detroit	116
	Babe Ruth	New York	130			Jackie Jensen	Boston	116
1924	Goose Goslin	Washington	129		1956	Mickey Mantle	New York	130
1925	Bob Meusel	New York	138		1957	Roy Sievers	Washington	114
1926	Babe Ruth	New York	145		1958	Jackie Jensen	Boston	122
1927	Lou Gehrig	New York	175		1959	Jackie Jensen	Boston	112
1928	Babe Ruth	New York	142		1960	Roger Maris	New York	112
	Lou Gehrig	New York	142		1961	Roger Maris	New York	142
1929	Al Simmons	Philadelphia	157		1962	Harmon Killebrew	Minnesota	126
1930	Lou Gehrig	New York	174		1963	Dick Stuart	Boston	118
1931	Lou Gehrig	New York	184		1964	Brooks Robinson	Baltimore	118
1932	Jimmy Foxx	Philadelphia	169		1965	Rocky Colavito	Cleveland	108
1933	Jimmy Foxx	Philadelphia	163		1966	Frank Robinson	Baltimore	122
1934	Lou Gehrig	New York	165		1967	Carl Yastrzemski	Boston	121
1935	Hank Greenberg	Detroit	170		1968	Ken Harrelson	Boston	109
1936	Hal Trosky	Cleveland	162		1969	Harmon Killebrew	Minnesota	140
1937	Hank Greenberg	Detroit	183		1970	Frank Howard	Washington	126
1938	Jimmy Foxx	Boston	175		1971	Harmon Killebrew	Minnesota	119
1939	Ted Williams	Boston	145		1972	Dick Allen	Chicago	113
1940	Hank Greenberg	Detroit	150		1973	Reggie Jackson	Oakland	117
1941	Joe DiMaggio	New York	125		1974	Jeff Burroughs	Texas	118
1942	Ted Williams	Boston	137		1975	George Scott	Milwaukee	109
1943	Rudy York	Detroit	118		1976	Lee May	Baltimore	109
1944	Vern Stephens	St. Louis	109		1977	Larry Hisle	Minnesota	119
1945	Nick Etten	New York	111		1978	Jim Rice	Boston	139
1946	Hank Greenberg	Detroit	127					

EARNED RUN LEADERS

National League

Year	Pitcher	Team	Inn. pitched	E.R. avg.	Year	Pitcher	Team	Inn. pitched	E.R. avg.
1913	C. Mathewson	New York	306	2.06	1946	H.J. Pollet	St. Louis	266	2.10
1914	W.L. Doak	St. Louis	256	1.72	1947	W.E. Spahn	Boston	290	2.33
1915	G.C. Alexander	Philadelphia	376	1.22	1948	H.D. Brecheen	St. Louis	233	2.24
1916	G.C. Alexander	Philadelphia	389	1.55	1949	G.B. Koslo	New York	212	2.50
1917	G.C. Alexander	Philadelphia	388	1.85	1950	J.T. Hearn	St. Louis-New York	134	2.49
1918	J.L. Vaughn	Chicago	290	1.74	1951	C. Nichols	Boston	156	2.88
1919	G.C. Alexander	Chicago	235	1.72	1952	J.H. Wilhelm	New York	159	2.43
1920	G.C. Alexander	Chicago	363	1.91	1953	W.E. Spahn	Milwaukee	266	2.10
1921	W.L. Doak	St. Louis	209	2.58	1954	J.A. Antonelli	New York	259	2.29
1922	W.D. Ryan	New York	192	3.00	1955	R.B. Friend	Pittsburgh	200	2.84
1923	A. Luque	Cincinnati	322	1.93	1956	L. Burdette	Milwaukee	256	2.71
1924	A.C. Vance	Brooklyn	309	2.16	1957	J. Podres	Brooklyn	196	2.66
1925	A. Luque	Cincinnati	291	2.63	1958	S. Miller	San Francisco	182	2.47
1926	Ray Kremer	Pittsburgh	231	2.61	1959	S. Jones	San Francisco	271	2.82
1927	Ray Kremer	Pittsburgh	226	2.47	1960	M. McCormick	San Francisco	253	2.70
1928	A.C. Vance	Brooklyn	280	2.09	1961	W. Spahn	Milwaukee	263	3.01
1929	Wm. Walker	New York	178	3.08	1962	S. Koufax	Los Angeles	184	2.54
1930	A.C. Vance	Brooklyn	259	2.61	1963	S. Koufax	Los Angeles	311	1.88
1931	Wm. Walker	New York	239	2.26	1964	S. Koufax	Los Angeles	223	1.74
1932	L. Warneke	Chicago	277	2.37	1965	S. Koufax	Los Angeles	336	2.04
1933	C.O. Hubbell	New York	309	1.66	1966	S. Koufax	Los Angeles	323	1.73
1934	C.O. Hubbell	New York	313	2.30	1967	P. Niekro	Atlanta	207	1.87
1935	D.E. Blanton	Pittsburgh	254	2.59	1968	B. Gibson	St. Louis	305	1.12
1936	C.O. Hubbell	New York	303	2.31	1969	J. Marichal	San Francisco	300	2.10
1937	J.R. Turner	Boston	257	2.38	1970	T. Seaver	New York	291	2.81
1938	W.C. Lee	Chicago	291	2.66	1971	T. Seaver	New York	286	1.76
1939	W.H. Walters	Cincinnati	319	2.29	1972	S. Carlton	Philadelphia	346	1.98
1940	W.H. Walters	Cincinnati	305	2.48	1973	T. Seaver	New York	290	2.07
1941	E.R. Riddle	Cincinnati	217	2.24	1974	B. Capra	Atlanta	217	2.28
1942	M.C. Cooper	St. Louis	279	1.77	1975	R. Jones	San Diego	285	2.24
1943	H.J. Pollet	St. Louis	118	1.75	1976	J. Denny	St. Louis	207	2.52
1944	E.B. Heusser	Cincinnati	193	2.38	1977	J. Candelaria	Pittsburgh	231	2.34
1945	H.L. Borowy	Chicago	122	2.14	1978	C. Swan	New York	207	2.43

EARNED RUN LEADERS

American League

Year	Pitcher	Team	Inn. pitched	E.R. avg.	Year	Pitcher	Team	Inn. pitched	E.R. avg.
1913	W.P. Johnson	Washington	346	1.09	1946	H. Newhouser	Detroit	293	1.94
1914	H.B. Leonard	Boston	222	1.01	1947	S.F. Chandler	New York	128	2.46
1915	W.P. Johnson	Washington	337	1.55	1948	H.E. Bearden	Cleveland	230	2.43
1916	G.H. Ruth	Boston	324	1.75	1949	M.L. Parnell	Boston	295	2.78
1917	E.V. Cicotte	Chicago	346	1.53	1950	E. Wynn	Cleveland	214	3.20
1918	W.P. Johnson	Washington	325	1.28	1951	S. Rogovin	Detroit-Chicago	217	2.78
1919	W.P. Johnson	Washington	290	1.49	1952	A.P. Reynolds	New York	244	2.07
1920	J.R. Shawkey	New York	267	2.46	1953	E.W. Lopat	New York	178	2.43
1921	U.C. Faber	Chicago	331	2.48	1954	E.M. Garcia	Cleveland	259	2.64
1922	U.C. Faber	Chicago	353	2.81	1955	W.W. Pierce	Chicago	206	1.57
1923	S. Coveleskie	Cleveland	228	2.76	1956	E. Ford	New York	226	2.47
1924	W.P. Johnson	Washington	278	2.72	1957	R. Shantz	New York	173	2.45
1925	S. Coveleskie	Washington	241	2.84	1958	E. Ford	New York	219	2.01
1926	R.M. Grove	Philadelphia	258	2.51	1959	H. Wilhelm	Baltimore	226	2.19
1927	W. Wiley Moore	New York	213	2.28	1960	Frank Bauman	Chicago	185	2.68
1928	E.G. Braxton	Washington	218	2.52	1961	D. Donovan	Washington	169	2.40
1929	R.M. Grove	Philadelphia	275	2.82	1962	H. Aquirre	Detroit	216	2.21
1930	R.M. Grove	Philadelphia	291	3.00	1963	G. Peters	Chicago	243	2.33
1931	R.M. Grove	Philadelphia	289	2.05	1964	D. Chance	Los Angeles	278	1.56
1932	R.M. Grove	Philadelphia	292	2.84	1965	S. McDowell	Cleveland	274	2.17
1933	M.L. Harder	Cleveland	253	2.95	1966	G. Peters	Chicago	204	2.03
1934	V. Gomez	New York	282	2.33	1967	J. Horlen	Chicago	258	2.06
1935	R.M. Grove	Boston	273	2.70	1968	L. Tiant	Cleveland	258	1.60
1936	R.M. Grove	Boston	253	2.81	1969	D. Bosman	Washington	193	2.19
1937	V. Gomez	New York	278	2.33	1970	D. Segui	Oakland	162	2.56
1938	R.M. Grove	Boston	164	3.07	1971	V. Blue	Oakland	312	1.82
1939	R.M. Grove	Boston	191	2.54	1972	L. Tiant	Boston	179	1.91
1940	R.W. Feller	Cleveland	320	2.62	1973	J. Palmer	Baltimore	296	2.40
1941	T.S. Lee	Chicago	300	2.37	1974	C. Hunter	Oakland	318	2.49
1942	T.A. Lyons	Chicago	180	2.10	1975	J. Palmer	Baltimore	323	2.09
1943	S.F. Chandler	New York	253	1.64	1976	M. Fidrych	Detroit	250	2.34
1944	P.H. Trout	Detroit	352	2.12	1977	F. Tanana	California	241	2.54
1945	H. Newhouser	Detroit	313	1.81	1978	R. Guidry	New York	274	1.74